THE ENCYCLOPAEDIA OF ISLAM

GLOSSARY AND INDEX OF TERMS

THE ENCYCLOPAEDIA OF ISLAM

NEW EDITION

UNDER THE EDITORSHIP OF

P. J. BEARMAN, TH. BIANQUIS, C. E. BOSWORTH,
E. VAN DONZEL AND W. P. HEINRICHS

GLOSSARY AND INDEX OF TERMS

to Volumes I-IX

and to the Supplement, Fascicules 1-6

BRILL
LEIDEN · BOSTON · KÖLN
2000

This book is printed on acid-free paper.

ISBN 90 04 11635 4

PRINTED IN THE NETHERLANDS

PREFACE TO THE THIRD EDITION

This edition of the *Glossary and Index of Terms* to *The Encyclopaedia of Islam* incorporates Volume IX, which was published in December 1997. A change in title, omitting the adjective 'technical' to describe the terms, is meant to more accurately define the contents of this volume. The basis of this index was laid by Dr Hakeem Uddeen Qureshi (Vols. I to III) and Jos van Lent (Vols. IV to VIII), whose work was then collated, augmented and edited by Peri Bearman (Supplement, Vol. IX), who also has begun the process of adding terms and entries missing in the first two editions.

The entries in the index are listed alphabetically following the Roman alphabet; the root system common to Semitic languages is therefore ignored. Those marked in bold refer to articles in the *Encyclopaedia*. The entry appears where possible under the singular form of the word, with the *pluralis* following in parentheses, unless the plural form has a separate meaning altogether, or the singular was not specified in the *Encyclopaedia*. All cross-references to entries within the glossary are given in small capitals. A term made up of more than one component, as e.g. *ahl al-ʿahd*, is generally listed in the entry of the first element; thus *ahl al-ʿahd* is found under *ahl*. The same is true for adjectives, plurals, etc. of a word, e.g. *ʿaskarī* (under *ʿaskar*), *ʿaḳliyyāt* (under *ʿaḳl*). When an exception is made, a cross-reference is included.

The transcription in the glossary follows for the most part that of the *Encyclopaedia*. Certain words such as Baghdad and sultan, which are now part and parcel of the English language, have not been transcribed; for easy recognition, Qurʾān is written thus and not as Ḳurʾān. In words of Berber or North African origin, a schwa has been used to reproduce a neutral vowel.

August 1999 The Editors of the *Encyclopaedia*

LIST OF ABBREVIATIONS

A	Arabic
Akk	Akkadian
Alg	Algerian Arabic
Alt	Altaic languages
Ar	Aramaic
Ass	Assyrian
B	Berber
Bed	Bedouin
C	Coptic
Cau	Caucasian
Ch	Chinese
Dem	Demotic
Egy	Egyptian Arabic
Eng	English
Eth	Ethiopic
Fr	French
Ger	German
Gk	Greek
Goth	Gothic
H	Hindi
Hau	Hausa
Heb	Hebrew
Hun	Hungarian
Ind	Indonesian
Ind.P	Indo-Persian
Ir	Iraqi Arabic
It	Italian
J	Javanese
K	Kurdish
Kash	Kashmiri
L	Latin
Leb	Lebanese Arabic
Mal	Malay
Mid.P	Middle Persian
Mon	Mongolian
Mor	Moroccan Arabic
N.Afr	North African
O.Fr	Old French
Ott	Ottoman
P	Persian
Pah	Pahlavi
Pash	Pashto
Ph	Phoenician
Por	Portuguese
Pu	Punjabi
Rus	Russian
San	Sanskrit
Sem	Semitic languages
Serb	Serbo-Croatian
Sic	Sicilian Arabic
Sin	Sindhi
Sl	Slavic
Sp	Spanish
SpA	Spanish Arabic
Sun	Sundalese
Sw	Swahili
Syr	Syriac
T	Turkish
Tun	Tunisian Arabic
U	Urdu
Yem	Yemeni Arabic

dim.	diminutive
fem.	feminine
f. / ff.	and following column(s)
g	gram
lit.	literally
pl.	plural
pop.	popular
s.	singular
syn.	synonym
ult.	ultimately
var.	variant
→	see

A

a'aban (Mor) : a large outer wrap for Berber men. V 745b

'abā' (A), or *'abā'a* : a coat, shoulder mantle, worn by both sexes in the Arab East. V 740a

'abā'a → 'ABĀ'

abad (A) : time in an absolute sense. I 2a

In philosophy, ~ or *abadiyya* is a technical term corresponding to ἀφθαρτός, meaning incorruptible, eternal *a parte post*, in opposition to AZAL or *azaliyya*. I 2a; V 95a

♦ abadī : 'having no end'. I 333a

♦ abadiyya → ABAD

ab'ādiyya (A, pl. *abā'id*), or **ib'ādiyya** : uncultivated or uncultivable land in Egypt under Muḥammad 'Alī; estates reclaimed from lands uncultivated at the time of the 1813-14 cadaster and granted on favourable terms. II 149a; S 379a

abadjad → ABDJĀD

abanūs (A, P, T, < Gk) : ebony wood. I 3a

abardī → BARDĪ

'abāya (Alg) : a sleeveless, long overblouse for men; a sleeveless, flowing dress for women. V 745b

abayān (A) : in zoology, the prawn and the shrimp. IX 40a, where many more synonyms are given

'abaytharān (A) : in botany, a type of artemisia, also called *rayḥān al-tha'ālib* 'the foxes' basilicum'. IX 435a

abbāla : camel nomads in the central Sudan belt of Africa. IX 516a

'abbas (Alg) : a verb signifying in Algeria 'to go among the peasants to levy contributions of grain, butter, dried fruits, etc.' in the name of Abu 'l-'Abbās al-Sabtī, a renowned Moroccan saint of the 12th century. VIII 692a

'abbāsī (P) : a Ṣafawid coin introduced by Shāh 'Abbās I, the value of which was 4 SHĀHĪ, 200 dīnārs, 50 per TŪMĀN. It remained the normal Persian denomination for most of the remainder of the dynasty. VIII 790a; IX 203b

♦ 'abbāsiyya (A) : in Morocco, charitable gifts of grain, fritters, fruit, meat or fish, made to the poor in the name of Abu 'l-'Abbās al-Sabtī, a renowned Moroccan saint of the 12th century. VIII 692a

'abd (A, pl. *'abīd*) : a slave, in particular a male slave, a female slave being termed *ama* (pl. *imā'*). I 24b

In theology, ~ means 'the creature'. In the Qur'ān, the angels are also called ~ . IV 82b

♦ ʿabd ḳinn : a slave born in his master's house; later applied to the slave over whom one has full and complete rights of ownership. I 25a

♦ ʿabd mamlūka : a purchased slave. I 25a

♦ ʿabīd al-bukhārī : descendants of the black slaves who had been imported in large numbers by the Saʿdids into Morocco. I 34b; I 47a; I 356a

♦ ʿabīd al-shirāʾ : black Sudanese slaves bought for the army under the Fāṭimids. II 858b

abdaʾa → ITHTHAGHARA

abdāl (A, s. BADAL) : in mysticism, the highest rank in the ṣūfī hierarchical order of saints (syn. GHAWTH). I 69b; generally accepted as the fifth place descending from the ḲUṬB. I 94b; ascetic or pietistic persons who are regarded as intercessors and dispensers of BARAKA. VIII 498a

In the Ottoman empire, ~ was used for the dervishes in various dervish orders. I 95a; later, when the esteem enjoyed by the dervishes declined, ~ (and *budalāʾ*, s. *badīl,* both used as a singular) came to mean 'fool' in Turkish. I 95a

abdjād (A), or *abadjad*, *abū djād* : the first of the mnemotechnical terms into which the twenty-eight consonants of the Arabic alphabet are divided. I 97a

ābiḳ (A) : a runaway slave. I 26b

ʿabḳarī (A) : a genie of great intelligence. IX 406b

abnāʾ (A, s. IBN) : sons.

As a denomination, it is applied to two tribes, viz. the descendants of Saʿd b. Zayd Manāt b. Tamīm, and the descendants born in Yaman of Persian immigrants. I 102a; S 115b

♦ abnāʾ al-atrāk : a term sometimes used in the Mamlūk sultanate to designate the Egyptian or Syrian-born descendants of the Mamlūks. I 102a; and → AWLAD AL-NĀS

♦ abnāʾ al-daraza : lit. sons of sewing, a proverbial expression current in the ʿAbbāsid period to refer to the tailors of Kūfa, who had taken part in the revolt of Zayd b. ʿAlī against the Umayyads (120-2/738-40). IV 1161a

♦ abnāʾ al-dawla : a term applied in the early centuries of the ʿAbbāsid caliphate to the members of the ʿAbbāsid house, and by extension to patrons (*mawālī*, s. MAWLA) who entered its service and became adoptive members. I 102a; Khurāsānian guards and officials in the ʿAbbāsid caliphate. V 57b

♦ abnā-yi sipāhīyān (T) : a term sometimes used in formal Ottoman usage, in place of the more common *sipāhī oghlanlarï* (→ DÖRT BÖLÜK), to denote the first of the six regiments of cavalry of the standing army. I 102a

abraḳ → BARḲĀʾ

abrāmīs (A) : in zoology, the bream. VIII 1023a

ābshār (P) : in Muslim India, large water chutes, made of inclined and carved marble slabs, which intercepted the flow of water in the long channels that ran the entire length of gardens, providing the transition from one level to another. IX 175a abū (A) : father.

♦ **abū barāḳish** : a name, no longer in use, given to two birds with brilliant plumage: the Franciscan or Grenadier weaver-bird, or Durra-bird (*Euplectes oryx franciscana*), and the Porphyrion or Blue Taleva/Purple Gallinule (*Porphyrio porphyrio*), better known as the Sultan-fowl. In the Ḥidjāz, ~ was used in place of *birḳish* to denote the chaffinch (*Fringilla coelebs*), also called *shurshur*. S 19a; and → ḤIRBĀʾ

♦ abū būz : 'having a snout', a simple but functional transport vessel, driven by a motor, with a prow which resembles that of a schooner and with a square stern, built in Oman. VII 53b

♦ abū dhaḳan : the goat fish or mullet (*Mullus barbatus*). VIII 1021a

♦ abū djād → ABDJĀD

♦ **abu 'l-hawl** : lit. father of terror; Arabic name for the sfinx of Giza. I 125b

♦ abū isḥāḳī → FĪRŪZADJ

♦ **abū ḳalamūn** : originally, a certain textile of a peculiar sheen, then a precious stone, a bird, and a mollusc. In Persian, ~ is said to have the meaning of chameleon. I 131a

♦ abū ḳarn : the unicorn fish (*Naseus unicornis*). VIII 1021a; and → KARKADDAN

♦ abū marīna : the monk seal. VIII 1022b

♦ abū mihmāz : the ray or skate. VIII 1022b

♦ abū minḳar : the half-beak (*Hemiramphus*). VIII 1021a

♦ abū minshar : the sawfish (*Pristis pristis*). VIII 1021a

♦ abū miṭraḳa : the hammer-head shark (*Sphyrna zygaena*). Other designations are *baḳra*, *miṭrāḳ al-baḥr*, and *samakat al-Iskandar*. VIII 1021a; VIII 1022b

♦ (a)bū mnīr : the seal. VIII 1022b

♦ (a)bū nawwāra : lit. the one with the flower; a Saharan name which is used for the hare as well as for the fox. S 85b

♦ abu 'l-rakhwa → SALWĀ

♦ abū ṣanṣūn : the sansun kingfish. VIII 1021b

♦ abū sayf : the swordfish (*Xiphias gladius*). VIII 1021a

♦ abū shinthiyā → SHĪḤ

♦ abū ṣundūḳ : the coffer fish (*Ostracion nasus*). VIII 1021a

abyaḍ → ZAHR

ʿād (A) : from the expression *min al-ʿād*, it has been suggested that ~ means 'the ancient time' and that the tribe ʿĀd arose from a misinterpretation of this. I 169b

♦ ʿādī : very ancient. I 169b

ʿāda (A), or *ʿurf* : a (pre-Islamic) custom; customary law. I 170a; I 744b; I 1179a; IV 155a ff.; VIII 486a

adāʾ (A) : lit. payment, accomplishment.

In law, ~ is a technical term to designate the accomplishment of a religious duty

in the time prescribed by the law, a distinction being drawn between the perfect accomplishment, *al-adāʾ al-kāmil*, and the imperfect, *al-adāʾ al-nāḳis*. I 169b
In the reading of the Qurʾān, ~ means the traditional pronunciation of the letters (syn. ḲIRĀʾA). I 169b

adab (A, pl. *ādāb*) : originally, a habit, a practical norm of conduct, equivalent to SUNNA; during the evolution of its sense, ~ came to mean an ethical 'high quality of soul, good upbringing, urbanity and courtesy', in contrast to Bedouin uncouthness. From the first century of the HIDJRA, it came to imply the sum of intellectual knowledge which makes a man courteous and 'urbane', based in the first place on poetry, the art of oratory, the historical and tribal traditions of the ancient Arabs, and also on the corresponding sciences: rhetoric, grammar, lexicography, metrics. As a result of contact with foreign cultures, this national concept of ~ gradually came to include a knowledge of those sections of non-Arab literature with which Arab Muslim civilisation became familiar from the early ʿAbbāsid period; it widened its Arab content into *humanitas* without qualification. In the modern age ~ and its plural *ādāb* are synonyms of literature. I 175b
In mysticism, the norms of conduct which govern relations between master and disciples, and those between the disciples themselves. IV 94b
In military science, the plural form *ādāb* is a synonym of ḤIYAL, strategems in war. III 510b
♦ adab al-djadal : in theology and law, a method of debating in which were discussed questions that were controversial. It was not a matter of finding the truth, but of convincing the opponent of the greatest possible probability which one believes to have found. VII 566a

ʿadāla (A) : the quality of ʿADL; the state of a person who in general obeys the moral and religious law. I 209b
In public law, ~ is one of the principal conditions for carrying out public functions, while in private law, ~ belongs to the theory of evidence. I 209b

ʿadam (A) : the absence of existence or being, used by the Muslim philosophers as the equivalent of Aristotle's στέρησις. I 178b; V 578b

adan (J, Sun) : the Javanese and Sundanese form of ADHĀN. VI 675b

adat (Mal, < A ʿĀDA) : a custom, usage, practice; customary law, the juridical customs of Indonesia. I 173a; for taxes and tolls having to do with *adat*, e.g. *adat cap*, *adat ḥakk al-ḳalam*, *adat hariya*, *adat kain*, etc., S 200b

aḍāt (A, N.Afr *ḍāya*) : in the Sahara of southern Morocco and Algeria, small basins where the limestone of the ḤAMMĀDAS has dissolved. III 136b

aḍdād (A, s. ḌIDD) : lit. opposites; in linguistics, words which have two meanings that are opposite to each other. I 184b

ʿaddān (A) : in Syria, a conventional rotation, according to which the distribution of the separate sections of water in the irrigation of the GHŪṬA is carried out. II 1105b

ʿādet-i aghnām → ḲOYUN RESMI

ʿadhāb (A) : 'torment, suffering, affliction', inflicted by God or a human ruler. I 186b

♦ ʿ**adhāb al-ḳabr** : in eschatology, the punishment in the tomb. I 186b; V 236b

adhān (A, T *ezan*) : 'announcement'; as technical term, ~ indicates the call to the divine service of Friday and to the five daily prayers. I 187b; II 593b; VI 361b; VIII 927b

♦ ezan adi̊ (T) : the regular name of a child, chosen at leisure by the family and bestowed, with a recitation of the ADHĀN, a few days after birth. IV 181a

adhargūn (P, A *adharyūn*) : lit. flame-coloured; a plant about 2-3 feet high with finger-long elongated leaves, of a red-yellow colour, and malodorous blossoms with a black kernel, thought to be either the *Buphthalmos* or the *Calendula officinalis* 'marigold'. I 191b

ʿadhrāʾ → SUNBULA

ʿādj (A) : ivory, exported in the Islamic period in all probability solely from East Africa. I 200a

ʿadjāʾib (A) : 'marvels', especially the marvels of Antiquity, e.g. the Pharos of Alexandria. I 203b

In the Qurʾān, the ~ denote the marvels of God's creation. I 203b; II 583b

In geographical literature, the ~ form a peculiar literary genre, reaching its full development in the cosmographies of the 8th/14th century. I 203b

adjal (A) : the appointed term of a man's life or the date of his death; the duration of existence. I 204a

ʿadjala (A) : the generic term for wheeled vehicles drawn by animals; carriage. In Mamlūk Egypt, ~ was supplanted by ʿARABA as a generic term. In modern Egypt, ~ is now the word for bicycle. I 205a

ʿadjam (A) : people qualified by *ʿudjma*, a confused and obscure way of speaking, as regards pronunciation and language, i.e. non-Arabs, primarily the Persians. I 206a

♦ ʿ**adjami oghlān** (T) : 'foreign boy', the term applied to Christian youths enrolled for service in the Ottoman sultan's palace troops. I 206b; II 1087a; IV 242b

♦ ʿ**adjamiyya** : the term used for the writing of non-Arabic languages in Arabic characters. I 207a; I 404b; and → ALJAMÍA

adjīr (A) : in the hierarchy of guilds, an apprentice (syn. *mubtadiʾ*). Other levels were worker, *ṣāniʿ*, and master, MUʿALLIM or *usṭā*. IX 644b; IX 794a

adjlāf → AṬRĀF

adjnād → DJUND

adjr (A, < Akk) : reward, wages, rent.

In theology, ~ denotes the reward, in the world to come, for pious deeds. I 209a

In law, ~ denoted in Mecca, in the time of the Prophet, any payment for services rendered. Later, the term was restricted to wages or rent payable under a contract of hire, IDJĀRA. I 209a

♦ adjr al-mithl : in law, the remuneration in a contract to hire that is determined by the judge. III 1017a

♦ adjr musamma^{n} : in law, the remuneration in a contract to hire that is fixed in the contract. III 1017a

ādjurr (A) : baked brick, used notably in public baths; of varying dimensions, and sometimes cut on an angle or partly rounded off, ~ is used in parts of buildings where accuracy of line is important (pillars, pedestals, stairways, etc.) and functions as horizontal tying material alternating with courses of rubble to maintain regularity of construction. I 1226b; V 585b

ʿadjuz (A) : in prosody, the name for the second hemistich of an Arabic poem. I 668b; VIII 747b; the name of the last foot of a verse. VIII 747b; another meaning of ~ in prosody occurs in the context of MUʿĀḲABA, to describe the case of e.g. in the RAMAL metre, the foot *fāʿilātun* having its last cord *-tun* shortened, thus *fāʿilātu*, when the first cord *fā-* of the following foot is not shortened. VIII 747b

ʿadjwa → TAMR

ʿadl (A) : justice; rectilinear, just.

In Muʿtazilite doctrine, ~ means the justice of God and constitutes one of the five fundamental dogmas. I 209a; I 334b; I 410a; III 1143b

In law, ~ (pl. *ʿudūl*) is a person of good morals, the *ʿudūl* being the scriveners or notaries in the judiciary administration. In public law, ~ is one of the principal conditions for carrying out public functions, and in private law, it is a principal condition of a witness for the bringing of evidence. I 209a ff.; IX 207a; professional witness in the law courts. VIII 126a; IX 208a

In numismatics, ~ means ‘of full weight’. I 210a

adrama (al-ṣabiyy) → ITHTHAGHARA

adrar (B) : ‘mountain’, Berber geographical term applied to a number of mountainous regions of the Sahara. I 210b

adwiya → DAWĀʾ

afʿā (A) : the viper; also other similar kinds of snakes. Most sources state that ~ denotes the female, with the male being called *ufʿuwān*, but ~ is always employed in a generic sense. I 214b

afādhān → KŪNIYA

afāriḳa : the descendants of the Graeco-Romans and the latinised Berbers, mostly Christians, living in Gabès in Tunisia in the 3rd/9th century. They were no longer mentioned as a separate ethnic group by the 7th/13th century. IV 338b ff.

afāwīh (A, pl. of *afwāh*, s. *fūh*) : spices, aromatic substances added to food and beverages to increase pleasant flavour and promote digestion (syn. *maṣāliḥ*). The meaning of ~ is not sharply marked off from *ʿiṭr*, *ṭīb* ‘scents’ and *ʿaḳḳār* ‘drugs’. S 42a, where many spices are listed

afghānī : a coin introduced in Afghanistan by Shīr ʿAlī in place of the rupee. IX 446b

ʿafiṣ (A) : the quality of food being pungent. II 1071b

āfrāg (B 'enclosure') : in Morocco, an enclosure of cloth, which isolates the encampment of the sovereign and his suite from the rest of the camp. ~ corresponds to the Persian *sarāča* or SARĀPARDA. I 236a; V 1206a

ʿafṣ (A) : the gall, an excrescence which forms on certain kinds of trees and shrubs as the result of the sting of various insects. The Arabic term was probably applied to the oak-gall in particular, but also denotes the fruit of the oak or a similar tree and the tree itself. I 239a

afsantīn (A, < Gk), or *afsintīn*, *ifsintīn* : in botany, the common wormwood (*Artemisia absinthium*); other similar kinds of plants. In medicine, ~ is often called *kashūth rūmī*. I 239b; IX 434b; and → SHĪḤ

afshīn : a pre-Islamic title borne by princes in Central Asia. I 241a

afsūn (P) : charm, incantation; now used in Iran to designate especially a charm against the biting of poisonous animals. I 241b

ʿāfūr (A) : a sand devil; the word has an echo of ʿIFRĪT in it. III 1038a

ʿafw → GHUFRĀN

afwāh → AFĀWĪH

afyūn (A, < Gk) : opium; in Iran and Turkey often called TIRYĀḲ 'antidote'. I 243a

agadir (B, < Ph *gadir*) : in North Africa, one of the names of a fortified enclosure among the Berbers, also called *ḳaṣr* (*gasr*), *temidelt*, *ghurfa*, *ḳalʿa* (*gelāa*), and *igherm*. I 244b

āgdāl (A, < B) : pasturage reserved for the exclusive use of the landowner. I 245b
In Morocco, ~ has acquired the sense of a wide expanse of pasture lands, surrounded by high walls and adjoining the sultan's palace, reserved for the exclusive use of his cavalry and livestock. I 245b; I 1346b; V 1206a

agha (T, P *āḳā*) : in Eastern Turkish, 'elder brother', 'grandfather', 'uncle', 'elder sister'. I 245b; in Persian, ~ sometimes signifies eunuch. I 246a
In Ottoman times, ~ meant 'chief', 'master', and sometimes 'landowner'. As a title ~ was given to many persons of varying importance employed in government service, usually of a military or non-secretarial character, and came to be also used for eunuchs in the harems of the sultans of Constantinople. I 245b; V 472b

aghač (T) : in Ottoman Turkish, a 'tree', 'wood'. In Eastern Turkish, ~ means both 'the male member' and a measure of distance, a parasang, three times the distance at which a man standing between two others can make himself heard by them. I 247a

aghānī → MAGHĀNĪ

aghi̊t (T) : in Turkish folklore, lyrical compositions expressive of grief. They commemorate the deceased and treat of general aspects of death or express sorrow over collective calamities. VI 610a

aghriba (A), or *aghribat al-ʿarab* : lit. the crows [of the Bedouin]; a designation in early Islam for poets of negroid maternal ancestry. IX 864a

aghtham → SHAYB
agurram (B) : among the Berbers of Morocco, the name for a saint. V 1201a
aḥābīsh (A) : Abyssinians (→ ḤABASH); companies or bodies of men, not all of one tribe. III 7b; possibly the Meccan militia of slaves of Ethiopian origin in the period immediately before the HIDJRA. I 24b, but see III 8a
The word is also applied to men who formed a confederacy either at a mountain called al-Ḥubshī or at a WĀDĪ called Aḥbash. III 7b
āḥād (A, s. *aḥad*) : in the science of Tradition, ~ are Traditions from a relatively small number of transmitters, not enough to make them MUTAWĀTIR. III 25b; and → FARD
ʿahd (A, pl. *ʿuhūd*) : 'joining together'; a contract. I 255a; a written designation of succession left by a caliph from the time of the Umayyad caliph ʿAbd al-Malik onwards. I 255b; IV 938b; and → AHL AL-ʿAHD
As a Qurʾānic term, ~ denotes God's covenant with men and His commands, the religious engagement into which the believers have entered, political agreements and undertakings of believers and unbelievers towards the Prophet and amongst each other, and ordinary civil agreements and contracts. I 255a
In law, ~ is generally restricted to political enactments and treaties. I 255a; land which had capitulated before conquest was known as ~ land. IV 14b
In mysticism, ~ is the covenant, consisting of religious professions and vows which vary in the different orders, with which the dervish is introduced into the fraternity. II 164b
In the science of diplomatic, ~ was a supreme grade of appointment, which concerned only the highest officials. It has fallen into disuse since the time of the Fāṭimids. II 302b
In Christian Arabic, *al-ʿahd al-ʿatīḳ* is the term for the Old Testament, and *al-ʿahd al-djadīd* the term for the New Testament. I 255a
♦ ʿahdnāme (T) : in the Ottoman empire, the document drawn up to embody the covenant, *ʿahd*, made with a ḤARBĪ. The items in an ~ are called *ʿuhūd*, or *shurūṭ* (s. SHARṬ). III 1179b; treaty of dependence. IX 483b
aḥdab (A) : hunchback. I 161a
aḥdāth (A) : lit. young men; a kind of urban militia, whose function was that of a police, which played a considerable role in the cities of Syria and Upper Mesopotamia from the 4th/10th to the 6th/12th centuries. I 256a; I 1332b; II 963a; VIII 402a; arbitrary actions at odds with the divine Law. I 384a
In Ṣafawid Persia, the ~ were the night patrols in the cities, also called *gezme* and ʿASAS. I 687a
aḥfara → ITHTHAGHARA
ʿāhira (pl. *ʿawāhir*) → BAGHIYY
aḥḳāf (A) : the title of SŪRA xlvi of the Qurʾān; in geography, a term variously translated as 'curved sand dunes', the name of a sand desert in Southern Arabia, and the whole of al-Ramla or just its western half. I 257a

aḥkām (A, s. ḤUKM) : judicial decisions. I 257a; juridical and moral rules. IV 151b; astrological signs. VII 558a

♦ al-aḥkām al-khamsa : in law, the 'five qualifications' (obligatory, recommended, indifferent, reprehensible, forbidden), by one or the other of which every act of man is qualified. I 257b; IX 324b

♦ aḥkām al-nudjūm : astrology. VII 558a

♦ aḥkāmī, or *munadjdjim* : an astrologer who interprets the astrological signs. VII 558a

ahl (A) : family, inmates, people, meaning those dwelling in a defined area but not specifically a nation. I 257b; IV 785b; in the tribal structure of the Bedouin, ~ (syn. ĀL) denotes offspring up to the fifth degree. I 700b; in combinations, ~ often means 'sharing in a thing, belonging to it' or 'owner of the same'. I 257b

♦ ahl al-ʿabāʾ → AHL AL-BAYT

♦ ahl al-ʿahd : non-Muslims living outside the Islamic state. The term was extended occasionally to both the MUSTAʾMIN, the foreigner granted the right of living in Islamic territory for a limited period of time, and the DHIMMĪ. I 255b

♦ **ahl al-ahwāʾ** : term applied by orthodox theologians to those followers of Islam whose religious tenets in certain details deviate from the general ordinances of the sunnī confession. I 257b

♦ **ahl al-**(baḥth wa 'l-)**naẓar** : 'those who apply reasoning', a term probably coined by the Muʿtazila to denote themselves; later, it came to mean careful scholars who held a sound, well-reasoned opinion on any particular question. I 266a

♦ **ahl al-bayt** : lit. the people of the house, viz. the family of the Prophet. The term has been interpreted variously; the current orthodox view is based on a harmonising opinion, according to which the term includes the *ahl al-ʿabāʾ* (the Prophet, ʿAlī, Fāṭima, al-Ḥasan and al-Ḥusayn) together with the wives of the Prophet. I 257b; II 843b; IX 331a; among the shīʿa, the ~ (which they call by preference *ʿitra*) is limited to the AHL AL-KISĀʾ and their descendants. I 258a; IX 331a

♦ **ahl al-buyūtāt** : those who belong to Persian families of the highest nobility; later, the nobles in general. I 258b

♦ **ahl al-dār** : lit. the people of the house; the sixth order in the Almohad hierarchy. I 258b

♦ ahl al-daʿwa → MADHHAB

♦ ahl al-dhikr : 'possessors of edification', a Qurʾānic term signifying witnesses of previous revelations. I 264a

♦ ahl al-dhimma → DHIMMA

♦ ahl al-djamāʿa : lit. the people of the community, an alternative of the appellative *ahl al-sunna wa 'l-djamāʿa*, an early designation of one of the warring parties at Ṣiffīn, and one of the 73 factions into which the Islamic community will be divided and the only one which will eventually attain salvation. IX 880b

♦ ahl al-faḍl : aristocrats, in contrast to the rude and untutored masses (*arāḏhil*, *sufahā'*, *akhissā'*). IX 330a
♦ **ahl al-ḥadīth**, and *aṣḥāb al-ḥadīth* : the partisans of Traditions, ḤADĪTH; traditionists, as opposed to the AHL AL-RA'Y. I 258b
♦ **ahl al-ḥall wa 'l-ʿaḳd** : 'those who are qualified to unbind and to bind'; term for the representatives of the Muslim community who act on its behalf in appointing and deposing a caliph or another ruler. I 263b
♦ ahl al-ḥarb → ḤARBĪ
♦ ahl al-ikhtiyār → IKHTIYĀR
♦ ahl al-ithbāt : 'people of the firm proof'; an appellation for Ḍirār b. ʿAmr and his school by al-Ashʿarī. III 1037a; III 1144a
♦ **ahl al-ḳibla** : the people of the ḲIBLA, viz. the Muslims. I 264a
♦ **ahl al-kisā'** : the people of the cloak, viz. the Prophet and his daughter Fāṭima, his son-in-law ʿAlī, and his grandsons al-Ḥasan and al-Ḥusayn, whom the Prophet sheltered under his cloak. I 264a; IX 331a
♦ **ahl al-kitāb** : lit. the people of the Book, viz. Jews and Christians, and later also extended to Sabeans, Zoroastrians and, in India, even idolaters. I 264b; IV 408b
♦ ahl al-ḳiyās : the name given to the Muʿtazila by their adversaries. II 102b
♦ ahl al-madar : people who lived in mud-brick houses in Arabia at the rise of Islam. I 608b; V 585a
♦ ahl al-madhhab → MADHHAB
♦ ahl al-milla → MILLA
♦ ahl al-naṣṣ → IKHTIYĀR
♦ ahl al-naẓar → AHL AL-(BAḤTH WA 'L-)NAẒAR
♦ ahl al-ra'y, and *aṣḥāb al-ra'y* : partisans of personal opinion, as opposed to the traditionists, AHL AL-ḤADĪTH. I 692a
♦ **ahl al-ṣuffa** : a group of the Prophet's Companions who typify the ideal of poverty and piety. I 266a
♦ **ahl al-sunna** : the sunnīs, i.e. the orthodox Muslims. I 267a; III 846a; IV 142a; party of the orthodox traditionists. I 694a; I 1039b; and → AHL AL-DJAMĀʿA
♦ ahl al-taswiya : in early Islam, advocates of equality between non-Arabs and Arabs. IX 514a
♦ ahl al-wabar : Bedouin living in tents of camel's-hair cloth in Arabia at the rise of Islam. I 608b; V 585a
♦ **ahl-i ḥadīth** : a designation used in India and Pakistan for the members of a Muslim sect, who profess to hold the same views as the early AHL AL-ḤADĪTH and not be bound by any of the four sunnī legal schools. I 259a
♦ **ahl-i ḥaḳḳ** : 'men of God', a secret religion prevalent mainly in western Persia. They are also called ʿAlī Ilāhī, but this is an unsuitable title. The central point in their dogma is the belief in the successive manifestations of God, the number of these being seven. I 260a

♦ **ahl-i wāris** (Mal, < P, < A) : inheritors, used among the Muslims of Indonesia. I 267a

♦ ahliyya (A) : a diploma from al-Azhar after a minimum of 8 years of study. I 818a

In law, the legal capacity of an individual to be a subject of the law, either a right-acquiring capacity, *ahliyyat wudjūb*, or an execution capacity, *ahliyyat idāʾ*. IX 248a; in Persian modern legal language, *ahliyyat* is used to mean nationality. IV 785b

ahlīladj → HALĪLADJ

ahliyya(t) → AHL

aḥmar → ZAHR

aḥmas, aḥmasī, aḥmasiyya → ḤUMS

aḥnāf (A) : the characteristic of having misshapen feet. I 303b

āhū : gazelles, or deer, on the island of Samos. IX 679b

ʿāʾila (A) : family, given way today mostly to *usra*. I 305b

āʾīn (P) : 'law, rite, institution', found in a title translated from Pahlawī into Arabic by Ibn Muḳaffaʿ in the middle of the 2nd/8th century, and in later titles on Persian Islamic history. I 306b

āḳ birčak → ĀḲ SĀḲĀL

aḳ daryā → AḲ ṢU

āḳ sāḳāl (P) : 'grey-beard', the elder of a Shāhsewan group. Women elders were known as *āḳ birčak* 'grey hairs'. IX 224a

aḳ ṣu (T) : white water.

As a technical term, ~ denotes the original bed of a river (syn. *aḳ daryā*). I 313b

āḳā → AGHA

ʿaḳaba (A, pl. *ʿiḳāb*) : a mountain road, or a place difficult of ascent on a hill or acclivity. The best-known place of this name is *al-ʿaḳaba*, between Minā and Mecca, where the ritual stone-throwing of the pilgrimage takes place. I 314b

ʿaḳāl (A), or *brīm* : ringed cord or rope to go over the headscarf worn by men. V 740b

ʿaḳār (A) : in law, ~ denotes immovable property, such as houses, shops and land, and as such is identical with 'realty' or 'real property'. The opposite is *māl manḳūl*. The owner of ~ is also deemed to be the owner of anything on it, over it or under it, to any height or depth. S 55a

ʿakawwak (A) : thick-set. I 315b

aḳče (T) : 'small white', the name for the Ottoman silver coin referred to by European authors as *aspre* or *asper*. I 317b; II 119a; V 974a; VIII 978a; those taxes and dues (*rüsūm*, → RASM) which were paid in cash were often called ~ . VIII 486a

ʿaḳd (A) : the legal act, especially that which involves a bi-lateral declaration, viz. the offer and the acceptance. I 318a

In the science of diplomatic, ~ is used for contract (syn. ʿAHD, **mīthāḳ**), in particular a civil contract, often more clearly defined by an additional genitive, such as *ʿaḳd al-nikāḥ*, *ʿaḳd al-ṣulḥ*, etc. II 303a

In rhetoric, ~ 'binding' denotes the IḲTIBĀS when it is put into verse and its source is indicated. III 1091b

In archery, ~ , or *ḳafla*, denotes the lock, locking, sc. the position on the bowstring of the fingers of the right hand, and especially that of the thumb in the 'Mongolian' technique of locking. IV 800b

In grammar, ~ is the nexus linking the two terms of the nominal and verbal phrases. IV 895b

In astronomy, ~ means node, and it is often used, in combination with *raʾs* and *dhanab*, instead of DJAWZAHAR to indicate the two opposite points in which the apparent path of the moon, or all planets, cuts the ecliptic. V 536a

akdar (A) : troubled, obscure; for some Muslim scholars, the origin of the name AKDARIYYA for a difficult question of law. I 320b

♦ **akdariyya** (A) : in law, the name of a well-known difficult question about inheritance, viz. whether a grandfather can exclude a sister from her inheritance in the case of a woman leaving behind as her heirs her husband, her mother, her grandfather, and her sister. I 320a

ʿakf (A) : a word used in the Qurʾān to designate the ceremonial worship of the cult and also the ritual stay in the sanctuary, which was done, for example, in the Meccan temple. VI 658a

akhawi (Touareg) : a woman's camel saddle, provided with semi-circular hoops attached to the side, used by the Touareg of the Sahara. III 667a

akhbār → KHABAR

♦ **akhbāriyya** : in Twelver shīʿism, those who rely primarily on the Traditions, *akhbār*, of the IMĀMS as a source of religious knowledge, in contrast to the *uṣūliyya*, who admit a larger share of speculative reason in the principles of theology and religious law. S 56b

akhḍar → ZAHR

akhfash (A) : nyctalope, or devoid of eyelashes. I 321a

akhī (T < *aḳi̊* 'generous') : a designation of the leaders of associations of young men organised as guilds in Anatolia in the 7th-8th/13th-14th centuries, who adopted the ideals of the FUTUWWA. I 321a; II 966b ff.; a Turkish trade guild. IX 646a; one of three grades in the ~ organisation, denoting the president of a corporation of *fityān* (s. FATĀ) and owner of a meeting-house, ZĀWIYA. I 322b; II 967b; one of nine categories in the trade guild, itself divided into six divisions: the first three divisions were *aṣḥāb-tark*, the experienced, and the last three, *naḳībler*, the inexperienced. IX 646a

ākhira (A) : the life to come, the condition of bliss or misery in the hereafter. I 325a

akhissāʾ → AHL AL-FAḌL

akhlafa (A) : a verb conveying the notion 'he [the child] passed the time when he had nearly attained to puberty'. VIII 822a

aḵẖlāḳ (A, s. *ḵẖulūḳ* ‘innate disposition’) : in philosophy, ethics. I 325b
aḵẖnif (A), or *ḵẖnīf* : a short Berber cape of black wool, woven in one piece, with a large red or orange medallion on the back, hooded for men, unhooded for women. II 1116a; V 745b
aḵẖras (A) : mute. I 330b
āḵẖtabēgī → ĀḴẖŪRBEG
aḵẖṭal (A) : loquacious. I 331a
āḵẖūnd (T, P) : a title given to scholars; in Persian it is current since Tīmūrid times in the sense of ‘schoolmaster, tutor’. I 331b
āḵẖūr-sālār → SĀLĀR
āḵẖūrbeg (Ind.P) : under the Dihlī sultanate, the superintendent of the royal horses, there being one for each wing of the army. Under the Muḡẖals, this officer was known as the *ātbēgī* or *āḵẖtabēgī*. V 689b
ʿaḳīd (A) : a leader of a Bedouin raid. II 1055a; among the Jordanian tribes, in early modern times, a specific leader of raids at the side of the chief, known in full as ~ *al-ḡẖazw*. IX 115b
ʿaḳīda (A, pl. *ʿaḳāʾid*) : creed; doctrine, dogma or article of faith. I 332b; IV 279b
ʿaḳīḳ (A) : cornelian; the name has been transferred to any kind of necklace which is of a red colour. I 336a; VIII 269a
ʿaḳīḳa (A) : the name of the sacrifice on the seventh day after the birth of a child; also, the shorn hair of the child, which is part of the seventh-day ritual. I 337a; IV 488a; VIII 824b
ʿāḳil (A, pl. *ʿuḳḳāl*) : ‘sage’; in law, *compos mentis*. IX 63a
Among the Druze, a member initiated into the truths of the faith; those not yet initiated, yet members of the community, are called *ḏjuhhāl* (→ ḎJĀHIL). II 633a
ʿāḳila (A, pl. *ʿawāḳil*) : in penal law, the group of persons upon whom devolves, as the result of a natural joint liability with the person who has committed homicide or inflicted bodily harm, the payment of compensation in cash or in kind, the DIYA. I 29a; I 337b
aḳi̊nḏji̊ (T) : irregular cavalry during the first centuries of the Ottoman empire, based on and primarily for service in Europe. I 340a
aḳiṭ (A) : sour-milk cheese, made by pre-Islamic Arabs. II 1057b
akkār (A, < Ar; pl. *akara*) : lit. tiller, cultivator of the ground; term applied to the peasantry of Aramaean stock in Syria and Iraq with a pejorative sense. S 58b
ʿaḳḳār → AFĀWĪH
ʿaḳl (A) : reason; intellect or intelligence. I 341b; IV 157a
In neoplatonic speculation, ~ is the first, sometimes the second, entity which emanates from the divinity as the first cause, or proceeds from it by means of intellectual creation. I 341b
In scholastic theology, ~ is a natural way of knowing, independently of the authority of the revelation, what is right and wrong. I 341b
To the philosophers of Islam, who followed Aristotle and his Greek commenta-

tors, more especially Alexander of Aphrodisias, ~ is that part of the soul by which it 'thinks' or 'knows' and as such is the antithesis of perception. The Muslim philosophers recognised a hierarchy of separate intelligences (*ʿuḳūl mufāriḳa*), usually ten in number, each lower one emanating from the higher. I 341b

In penal law, ~ (pl. *ʿuḳūl*) is the compensation in cash or in kind required by the ʿĀḲILA in cases of homicide or instances of bodily harm. I 338a; and → DIYA

In prosody, a deviation from the proper metre, in particular a missing *la* in the foot *mufāʿa[la]tun*. I 672a

In Druze hierarchy, the highest of the five cosmic ranks in the organisation. II 632a

♦ al-ʿaḳl al-awwal : in ʿAbd al-Razzāḳ al-Ḳāshānī's mystical thought, the Universal Reason, which proceeds by a dynamic emanation from God. This is a spiritual substance and the first of the properties which the divine essence implies. I 89b

♦ **ʿaḳliyyāt** : a technical term in scholastic theology, signifying the rational (and natural) knowledge which the reason can acquire by itself. According to the Muʿtazilī tradition and Saʿadya al-Fayyūmī, ~ denotes that which is accessible to the reason and especially, on the ethical level, the natural values of law and morals. The term also denotes a genus of theological dissertations, going back to the 6th/12th century. I 342b

aklat al-maḥabba (A) : a feast-day meal among the Ṣārliyya in northern Iraq, once every lunar year, to which everyone contributed a cock boiled with rice or wheat. IX 64a

aḳligh → MUṢAFFAḤĀT

aḳraʿ (A) : bald. I 343a

ʿaḳrab (A, pl. *ʿaḳārib*) : in zoology, the scorpion. I 343b

In astronomy, *al-~* is the term for Scorpius, one of the twelve zodiacal constellations. I 343b; VII 83b

aḳrābādhīn (A, < Syr) : a title of treatises on the composition of drugs; pharmacopoeias. I 344a

aḳsaḳal : in traditional Özbeg society, the respected older headman of a village, who mediated disputes. VIII 233b

aḳsimā : a term usually translated as 'liquid, syrup', but, since one of the recipes mentions the presence of yeast among the ingredients of this drink, it must presumably be a variety of sweetened beer such as FUḲḲĀʿ. VI 721b; IX 225a

aḳūniṭun (A, < Gk) : in medicine, a particularly deadly poison originating from a plant root. Synonyms are *khāniḳ al-nimr*, *khāniḳ al-dhiʾb*, *ḳātil al-nimr*, *nabbāl*, and *bīsh*. S 59b

āl (A) : a clan, a genealogical group between the family and the tribe. Later, ~ came to mean the dynasty of a ruler. I 345b; a demon who attacks women in childbed, a personification of puerperal fever. I 345b; and → AHL; SARĀB

āla (A, pl. *ālāt*) : an instrument, utensil.
In grammar, ~ is found in expressions as *ālat al-taʿrīf*, instrument of determination, and *ālat al-ta<u>sh</u>bīh*, instrument of comparison. I 345b
In the classsification of sciences, *ālāt* is the name of such attainments as are acquired not for their own sake, but 'as a means to something else'. I 345b
In philosophy, ~ is another term for logic, following the peripatetic view that it is an instrument, not a part, of philosophy. I 345a
For ~ in Moroccan music, → <u>GH</u>INĀʾ

aʿlā (A) : higher; *al-aʿlā* is used as an epithet to differentiate between the patron and the client, when both are referred to as MAWLĀ. I 30b

alaaqad (Somali) : in Somali society, a woman specialist who relieves people of spirits through the performance of a ritual. IX 723b

ālaba (A) : a geographical term used to denote the northern part of the Iberian peninsula beyond the left bank of the upper valley of the Ebro. I 348b
♦ **ālaba wa 'l-ḳilāʿ** : a geographical expression used in the 2nd-3rd/8th-9th centuries to denote that part of Christian Spain which was most exposed to the attacks of summer expeditions sent from Cordova by the Umayyad AMĪRs. I 348b

alābāl<u>gh</u>ā (A) : the trout. VIII 1021a

ālāčig<u>h</u> (P) : the dwelling of the <u>Sh</u>āhsewan in Persia, which is hemispherical and felt-covered; within each one lives a household of on average seven or eight people. IX 223b

ala<u>dj</u>a (T) : chintz with coloured stripes; used in many geographical names. I 348b

ʿalam (A, pl. *aʿlām*) : signpost, flag (syn. LIWĀʾ, RĀYA). I 349a
♦ ʿalamdār → SAN<u>DJ</u>AḲDĀR
♦ ʿalem-i nebewī → SAN<u>DJ</u>AḲ-I <u>SH</u>ERĪF

ʿālam (A, pl. *ʿālamūn*, *ʿawālim*) : world. I 349b
♦ ʿālam al-<u>dj</u>abarūt : 'the world of (divine) omnipotence', BARZA<u>KH</u>, to which belong, according to al-<u>Gh</u>azālī, the impressionable and imaginative faculties of the human soul. I 351a
♦ ʿālam al-malakūt : a Qurʾānic term for 'the world of Kingdom, of Sovereignty', the world of immutable spiritual truths, and hence of the angelic beings, to which are added all of Islamic tradition, the Preserved Table, the Pen, the Scales, and often the Qurʾān. I 351a
♦ ʿālam al-mulk : a Qurʾānic term meaning 'the world of kingship', i.e. the world of becoming, the world here below. I 351a

ʿalāma (A, T *ʿalāmet*) : emblem, presented by early Islamic rulers to their close pages as a sign of honour. VIII 432b
In the science of diplomatic, the signature of the person drawing up the document, part of the concluding protocol in the classical period. II 302a
In the Muslim West, a mark of ratification or initialling, on all official chancery documents. I 352a; the formula of authorisation (*wa 'l-ḥamdu li-llāhi waḥdah*), written in large lettering at the head of despatches and commissions. II 331b

ālāp (H) : the introductory improvisation, the first part in a performance of classical or art music of India. III 454a

ʿalas (A) : in agriculture, a variety of wheat. II 1060b

ālāt → ĀLA

ʿalat͟h (A) : in botany, the wild endive (*hindibāʾ barrī*), known under a variety of names: *g͟halat͟h, yaʿḍīd, bak͟la murra*, ṬARK͟HASH͟ḲŪḲ and variants. S 370b

alay (T, prob. < Gk *allagion*) : in Ottoman usage, a troop, a parade, and hence a crowd, a large quantity. It was used from the time of the 19th-century military reforms to denote a regiment. I 358a

albasti : in Özbeg folk tradition, a witch-like D͟JINN. VIII 234b

ʿalem → ʿALAM

ʿālim → FAḲĪH

♦ **ʿālima** (A, pl. *ʿawālim*) : lit. a learned, expert woman, ~ is the name of a class of Egyptian female singers forming a sort of guild, according to sources of the 18th and 19th centuries. I 403b

ʿāliya (A, pl. *ʿawālī*) : grand master, the highest rank in the game of chess. IX 367a

aljamía (Sp, < A *al-ʿad͟jamiyya* 'non-Arabic') : the name used by the Muslims of Muslim Spain to denote the Romance dialects of their neighbours in the north of the Iberian peninsula. In the later Middle Ages, ~ acquired the particular meaning which is attributed to it today: a Hispanic Romance language written in Arabic characters. The literature in ~ is termed *aljamiada*. I 404b

allāh (A) : God, the Unique One, the Creator; already to the pre-Islamic Arabs, ~ was one of the Meccan deities, possibly the supreme deity. I 406a

♦ **allāhumma** (A) : an old formula of invocation, used in praying, offering, concluding a treaty and blessing or cursing. I 418a

ʿalma → G͟HĀZIYA

almās (A, < Gk) : in mineralogy, the diamond. I 419a

almogávares (Sp, < A *al-mug͟hāwir*) : the name given at the end of the Middle Ages to certain contingents of mercenaries levied from among the mountaineers of Aragon. I 419b

alp (T) : 'hero', a figure which played a great role in the warlike ancient Turkish society (syn. *batur* (→ BAHĀDUR), *sökmen, čapar*); used also as an element in compound proper names or as a title by Sald͟jūḳ and subsequent rulers. I 419b

altïn (T), or *altun* : in mineralogy, gold, also used of gold coins. I 423b

aluka → MAʾLUKA

āluwī (A, < Gk) : the aloe drug, i.e. the juice pressed from the leaves of the aloe. VIII 687b

alwān (A) : in music, a lute with a long neck and plucked strings. VI 215b

alya (A) : the fat tail of a sheep. II 1057b; S 318a

ama → ʿABD

ʿamā (A) : in the mystical thought of ʿAbd al-Karīm al-D͟jīlī, the simple hidden pure Essence before its manifestation, one of the important scales or 'descents' in which Absolute Being develops. I 71a

āmad (U) : in Urdu poetry, the part of the elegy, MARTHIYA, where the army's preparation for battle is described, sometimes including a detailed description of the hero's horse. VI 611b

ʿamal (A) : performance, action. I 427a; II 898a; 'that which is practised', the moral action in its practical context and, secondarily, the practical domain of 'acting'. I 427b

In law, ~ is judicial practice. I 427b

As a legal and economic term, ~ denotes labour, as opposed to capital. I 428a

In later Muslim administration, ~ means 'fief'. IX 153b; region. IX 739a

♦ ʿamal bi 'l-yad (*ʿamal al-yad*) : in medicine, the early expression for surgery, later replaced by *djirāḥa*. II 481b

♦ ʿilm ʿamalī → ʿILM

♦ ʿamaliyya : the practical sciences, viz. ethics, economics and politics, as determined by the philosophers. I 427b

ʿamāla (A) : an administrative allowance, e.g. that given to an AMĪR. I 439a

amān (A) : safety, protection.

In law, a safe conduct or pledge of security by which a non-Muslim not living in Muslim territory becomes protected by the sanctions of the law in his life and property for a limited period. I 429a; II 303b; III 1181b; and → IDHN

ʿamārī → HAWDA

amazzal (B), and *amzyad*, *amḥaz*, *amḥars*, *awrith* : an institution concerning an individual, occurring in the case of a stranger to the group who, usually after committing some offence in his own clan, has imposed the ʿĀR, 'transfer of responsibility', and obtained the protection of another group which he makes henceforward the beneficiary of his work. The stranger becomes ~ when his protector has given to him in marriage his own daughter or another woman over whom he holds the right of DJABR. S 79b

ʿamd (A) : in law, an intentional act; one that is quasi-deliberate is called *shibh* (→ SHUBHA) *ʿamd*. II 341a; IV 768b; IV 1101b

āmeddji (T, < P *āmad*) : an official of the central administration of the Ottoman empire, who headed the personal staff of the REʾĪS ÜL-KÜTTĀB 'chief Secretary'. The office seems to have come into being later than the 17th century and increased in importance after the reforms. I 433a; II 339a; referendar or reporter of the Imperial Dīwān. VIII 481b

aménokal (B) : any political leader not subordinate to anyone else. The title is applied to foreign rulers, to high-ranking European leaders, and to the male members of certain noble families; in some regions of the Sahara, ~ is also given to the chiefs of small tribal groups. I 433b

amghar (B) : an elder (by virtue of age or authority); ~ is used for different functions among the various Berber tribes. I 433b

amḥars → AMAZZAL

amḥaz → AMAZZAL

ʿamīd (A) : lit. pillar, support; a title of high officials of the Sāmānid-G͟haznawid administration, denoting the rank of the class of officials from whom the civil governors were recruited. I 434a; under the Sald͟jūḳs, an official in charge of civil and financial matters. VI 275a; a designation for the tribal chief (syn. *ʿimād*). IX 115b

ʿāmil (A, pl. *ʿummāl*, *ʿawāmil*) : a Muslim who performs the works demanded by his faith; as technical term, it came to denote tax-collector, government agent; (provincial) governor [in North Africa and Spain] in charge of the general administration and finance. I 435a; financial administrator. I 19b

In law, the active partner in a MUḌĀRABA partnership. I 435a

Among the Bohorās sect in India, ~ denotes a local officiant appointed by the head of the sect to serve the community in respect of marriage and death ceremonies, and ritual prayer. I 1255a

In grammar, ~ signifies a *regens*, a word which, by the syntactical influence which it exercises on a word that follows, causes a grammatical alteration of the last syllable of the latter. I 436a; IX 360a; IX 527b

♦ ʿawāmil al-asmāʾ : in grammar, the particles governing nouns. III 550a

amīn (A) : safe, secure; with the more frequent form *āmīn*, a confirmation or corroboration of prayers, Amen. I 436b; (pl. *umanāʾ*) trustworthy; an overseer, administrator. I 437a; VIII 270b

As a technical term, ~ denotes the holders of various positions ‘of trust’, particularly those whose functions entail economic or financial responsibility. I 437a; and → EMĪN

In law, ~ denotes legal representatives. I 437a

In the Muslim West, ~ carried the technical meaning of head of a trade guild, which in the East was called ʿARĪF. I 437a

♦ amīn al-ʿāṣima : the chairmen of the municipalities of Damascus, Beirut, Baghdad and Amman, thus called in order to emphasise their particular importance in relation to the seat of the government; elsewhere in the Arab East, the original designation, *raʾīs al-baladiyya*, is retained. I 975b

♦ amīn al-ḥukm : the officer in charge of the administration of the effects of orphan minors (under the early ʿAbbāsids). I 437a

amīr (A, pl. *umarāʾ*; T *emīr*) : commander, governor, prince. I 438b; a person invested with command (AMR), and more especially military command. I 445a; III 45b; IV 941 ff.

♦ **amīr āk͟hūr** : the supervisor of the royal stables. I 442b; IV 217b; and → MĪR-ĀK͟HŪR

♦ **amīr dād** : the minister of justice under the Sald͟jūḳs. I 443b

♦ amīr d͟jāndār : in Mamlūk Egypt, ‘Marshal of the Court’, under whose command the RIKĀBDĀR ‘groom’ was. VIII 530a

♦ **amīr al-ḥād͟jd͟j** : the leader of the caravan of pilgrims to Mecca. I 443b

♦ **al-amīr al-kabīr**, or amīr kabīr → ATABAK

♦ **amīr madjlis** : the master of audiences or ceremonies. Under the Saldjūḳs of Asia Minor, the ~ was one of the highest dignitaries. Under the Mamlūks, the ~ had charge of the physicians, oculists and the like. I 445a

♦ **amīr al-muʾminīn** : lit. the commander of the believers; adopted by ʿUmar b. al-Khaṭṭāb on his election as caliph, the title ~ was employed exclusively as the protocollary title of a caliph until the end of the caliphate as an institution. I 445a

♦ **amīr al-muslimīn** : lit. commander of the Muslims; title which the Almoravids first assumed. I 445b

♦ amīr shikār : an institution, first known as *amīr al-ṣayd* 'master of the chases', established by the Umayyads. I 1152a

♦ **amīr silāḥ** : the grand master of the armour. Under the Mamlūks, the ~ was in charge of the armour-bearers and supervised the arsenal. I 445b

♦ **amīr al-umarāʾ** : the commander-in-chief of the army. I 446a; II 507b

♦ al-umarāʾ al-muṭawwaḳūn → ṢĀḤIB AL-BĀB

amladj (A) : the fruit of the *Phyllanthus emblica*, which was useful against haemorrhoids. The Arabs and Europeans in the Middle Ages mistook it for a myrobalanus. S 349b

ʿamlūḳ (A) : the offspring of a DJINN and a woman. III 454b

ʿamm (A, pl. *aʿmām*) : paternal uncle. IV 916b

♦ ʿamm waḍḍāḥ : a child's game described as searching (in the dark) for a very white bone tossed far away, with the finder being allowed to ride upon his playmates. The Prophet is said to have engaged in this as a child. V 615b

āmma (A), or *maʾmūma* : a wound penetrating the brain; a determining factor in the prescription of compensation following upon physical injury, DIYA. II 341b

ʿāmma (A, pl. *ʿawāmm*) : the plebs, common people. I 491a; I 900a ff.; IV 1098a; V 605b; and → KHĀṢṢ

♦ ʿāmmī : one who is secular in religious matters. IX 185b; among the Uṣūliyya, a lay believer. VIII 777b; one not trained in the law. IX 324b

♦ ʿāmmiyya : a revolt among the common people. IX 270b

amr (A) : as Qurʾānic and religious term, divine command. I 449a

For ~ in Ottoman Turkish, → EMR

ʿamūd (A) : a tent pole; a monolithic column and capital; a constructed pillar. I 457b; the main stream of a river, in particular the Nile, as distinguished from the minor branches and the canals. VIII 38a

♦ ʿamūd al-ḳaṣīda → MUSAMMAṬ

amzwār → MIZWĀR

amzyad → AMAZZAL

ānā : originally, an Indian money of account, a sixteenth share, one rupee being 16 ~ . Later, the name was given to an actual coin. VI 121b

ʿāna → ISTIḤDĀD

ʿanāʾ → DJALSA

ʿanāḳ (A) : in zoology, ~ or *ʿanāḳ al-arḍ* denotes a kind of lynx, the caracal (< T *ḳaraḳulaḳ*). I 481a; II 739b; IX 98b; and → SAKHLA

In astronomy, *ʿanāḳ al-arḍ* is γ Andromedae and *ʿanāḳ al-banāt* is the ζ of the Great Bear. I 481a

anayasa → ḲĀNŪN-I ESĀSĪ

ʿanaza (A) : a short spear or staff, syn. *ḥarba*. I 482a; and → KARKADDAN

In North Africa, ~ survives as an architectural term signifying an external MIḤRĀB for those praying in the court of the mosque. I 482a

ʿanbar (A) : ambergris (*ambra grisea*), a substance of sweet musk-like smell, easily fusible and burning with a bright flame, highly valued in the East as a perfume and medicine. I 484a; a large fish, also called *bāl*, which swallows a form of ambergris called *al-mablūʿ* 'swallowed ambergris' or 'fish-ambergris', which floats on the sea; the sperm-whale. I 484a; VIII 1022b

♦ ʿanbar shiḥrī : ambergris. IX 439a

anbata (A) : a verb which conveys the meaning 'his [a boy's] hair of the pubes grew forth, he having nearly attained the age of puberty'. VIII 822a

anbīḳ (A, < Gk) : in alchemy, the part known as the 'head' or 'cap' of the distilling apparatus (syn. *raʾs*); also, the additional faucet-pipe which fits onto the 'cap'. I 486a

ʿandam → BAḲḲAM

andargāh (P, A *mustaraḳa*) : epagomenae, the five odd days added at the end of the Persian year as intercalary days. II 398a

andjudhān → ḤILTĪT

andjuman (P, T *endjümen*) : meeting, assembly, army. I 505a; for its modern use → DJAMʿIYYA

anflūs → MIZWĀR

anghām (A, s. *naghm*) : in music, musical modes. IX 101a

angusht (P) : fingerbreadth; a unit of measurement under the Mughals which was standardised at 2.032 cm by the emperor Akbar at the end of the 10th/16th century. II 232a

angusṭ : in zoology, the crawfish, spiny lobster (*Palinarus vulgaris*), also known as *ankūsh*. IX 40a, where many more synonyms are given

angūza (Pash), or *hing* : in botany, term for the *Ferula assafoetida*, very abundant in Afghanistan. I 223a

ʿanḳāʾ (A) : a fabulous bird approximating the phoenix, in all likelihood a type of heron. I 509a

In music, an ancient instrument described as having open strings of different lengths but identically situated bridges. The name suggests a long-necked instrument, probably a trapezoidal psaltery, one species of which was known later as the ḲĀNŪN. VII 191a

ʿankabūt (A) : spider. I 509a; and → SAMAK ʿANKABŪT

In astronomy, a movable part on the front of the astrolabe. I 723a
anḳad (A) : a generic name for the tortoise and the hedgehog. V 389b
anḳalīs (A, L *Anquilla*) : the eel. VIII 1021a
ankū<u>sh</u> → ANGUSṬ
anniyya (A) : an abstract term formed to translate the Aristotelian term τὸ ὅτι, 'thatness' of a thing (syn. *al-anna*); ~ is also used for non-existential being. I 513b
anṣāb → NUṢUB
anṣār (A) : 'helpers'; those men of Medina who supported Muḥammad. I 514a
ʿansāra (A) : the name of a festival. Among the Copts, ~ is the name for Pentecost, while in North Africa, ~ denotes the festival of the summer solstice. I 515a
an<u>sh</u>ūyah (A, < Sp *anchoa*), or *an<u>dj</u>ūyah* : the anchovy (*Engraulis boelema*). VIII 1021a, where many synonyms are found
ʿantarī (A) : in Egypt, a story-teller who narrates the Romance of ʿAntar. I 522a; (< T) a short garment worn under the ḲAFṬĀN; a lined vest ranging from short to knee length, worn by women. I 522a; V 740b
anwāʾ (A, s. *nawʾ*) : a system of computation based on the acronychal setting and helical rising of a series of stars or constellations. I 523a; VIII 98a; VIII 734a
ʿanz (A), or *ṣafiyya* : a one-year old female goat, called thereafter, progressively, *<u>th</u>anī*, *rabāʿī*, *sadīs* and, after seven years, *sāli<u>gh</u>*. S 319a
anzarūt (A) : a gum-resin from a thorn-bush which cannot be identified with certainty. It was used for medical purposes. S 77b, where synonyms are found
āpa : 'older sister', an important term in Özbeg kinship terminologies. VIII 234a
apadāna (Mid.P) : in architecture, a hypostile audience-hall of the Persian kings. I 609b f.
ʿār (A) : shame, opprobrium, dishonour. S 78a
In North Africa, ~ presupposes a transfer of responsibility and of obligation, arriving at a sense of 'protection' for the suppliant, in default of which dishonour falls on the supplicatee, who is obliged to give satisfaction to the suppliant. The most simple transfer is by saying *ʿār ʿalīk* 'the ~ on you', and making a material contact with the person to whom the appeal is made, for example touching the edge of his turban or laying one's hand on him or his mount. ~ is also used towards saints, to whom sacrifices are offered to obtain their intercession. III 396a; S 78a
ʿaraba (T, < A ʿARRĀDA), or *ʿarabiyya* : a cart, introduced into Mamlūk Egypt. Its name supplanted ʿA<u>DJ</u>ALA in popular use as a generic term for carriage. I 205b; I 556b
♦ ʿaraba pāzārï (T) : in certain Rumelian towns under the Ottomans, a market presumably located on the outskirts of the town or along a major road. IX 797a
♦ ʿarabiyyat ḥanṭūr (Egy, < Hun *hintó*), and *ʿarabiyyat kārrō* (< It *carro*) : a cab. I 206a
ʿarabī → ḲAṬĀ; for ~ (ḥaḍramī), → SUḲUṬRĪ

♦ **ʿarabiyya** (A) : the Arabic language. I 561b; and → ʿARABA

ʿaraḍ (A, pl. *aʿrāḍ*) : the translation of the Aristotelian term συμβεβηκός 'accident', denoting 1) that which cannot subsist by itself but only in a substance of which it is both the opposite and the complement, and 2) an attribute which is not a constituent element of an essence. I 128b; I 603b

arā<u>dh</u>il → AHL AL-FAḌL

aʿra<u>dj</u> → ʿAR<u>DJ</u>Ā

aʿrāf (A, s. *ʿurf*) : 'elevated places'; a term used in the Qurʾān, in an eschatological judgement scene, and interpreted as 'Limbo'. I 603b

ʿarāʾi<u>sh</u> (A) : brushwood huts, in Western Arabia. I 106b; trellises of grape vines. I 604b

arāk → KABĀ<u>TH</u>

ʿaraḳčīn → ʿARAḲIYYA

ʿaraḳiyya (A) : a skull cap, often embroidered, worn by both sexes by itself or under the head-dress in the Arab East; called *ʿaraḳčīn* in ʿIrāḳ. A synonym in the Arabian peninsula is *maʿraḳa*. V 740b ff.; in the Turkish Ḳādirī dervish order, a small felt cap which the candidate for admission to the order brought after a year and to which the <u>SH</u>AY<u>KH</u> attached a rose of 18 sections; the cap is then called *tā<u>dj</u>*. IV 382b

ʿaraṣa (A) : in Mamlūk times, an open unroofed space used e.g. for storing cereals. IX 793b

ārāsta → PASA<u>ZH</u>

arbaʿīniyya → ČILLA

arbaʿūn (A) : forty.

arbaʿūn ḥadī<u>th</u>an (A, T *ḳi̊rḳ ḥadī<u>th</u>*, P *čihil ḥadī<u>th</u>*) : a genre of literary and religious works centred around 40 Traditions of the Prophet. S 82b

arḍ (A) : earth, land.

♦ arḍ amīriyya : in law, land to which the original title belongs to the State, while its exploitation can be conceded to individuals. II 900b

♦ arḍ madhūna : an expression occasionally heard in Saudi Arabia which is used to distinguish the sands of al-Dahnāʾ from those of al-Nafūd, the colour of which is said to be a lighter shade of red; ~ is also equated with *arḍ mundahina* 'land only lightly or superficially moistened by rain'. II 93a

♦ arḍ mamlūka : in law, land to which there is a right of ownership. II 900b

♦ arḍ matrūka : in law, land placed at the disposal of corporate bodies. II 900b

♦ arḍ mawāt : in law, waste land, defined as free land, situated away from inhabited areas and out of ear-shot of houses. II 900b

♦ arḍ mawḳūfa : in law, land set aside for the benefit of a religious endowment. II 900b

♦ arḍ mundahina → ARḌ MADHŪNA

ʿarḍ (A) : review of an army or troops. I 24a; petition. IX 209a; and → ISTIʿRĀḌ

♦ **ʿarḍ ḥāl** : petition, used in the Ottoman empire. I 625a

♦ ʿarḍ odasi̊ : in Ottoman palace architecture, the audience hall. IX 46b

ʿar<u>dj</u>ā (A) : lame.

In poetry, ~ is used to designate the unrhymed line inserted between the third line and the last line of a monorhyme quatrain, RUBĀʿĪ. The composition is then called *aʿra<u>dj</u>*. VI 868a

arəḳḳas (Kabyle, < A RAḲḲĀṢ) : a simple contrivance of a water-mill made from a pin fixed on a small stick floating above the moving mill-stone; this pin, fixed to the trough containing grain, transmits a vibration to it which ensures the regular feeding of the grain into the mouth of the mill. VIII 415b

argan (B) : in botany, the argan-tree (*argania spinosa* or *argania sideroxylon*), growing on the southern coast of Morocco. I 627b

ar<u>gh</u>ūl (A) : a type of double reed-pipe which has only one pipe pierced with finger-holes, while the other serves as a drone. The drone pipe is normally longer than the chanter pipe. When the two pipes are of equal length, it is known as the ZUMMĀRA. The ~ is played with single beating reeds. The drone pipe is furnished with additional tubes which are fixed to lower the pitch. In Syria, the smaller type of ~ is called the *masḥūra*. VII 208a

ʿāriḍ (A, pl. *ʿurrāḍ*) : the official charged with the mustering, passing in review and inspection of troops. III 196a; IV 265a ff.

♦ ʿāriḍ-i mamālik : the head of the military administration in Muslim India. He was also known as *ṣāḥib-i dīwān-i ʿarḍ*. The Mu<u>gh</u>al name was *mīr ba<u>kh</u><u>sh</u>ī*. As a minister, he was second only to the WAZĪR. He was the principal recruiting officer for the Sulṭān's standing army; he inspected the armaments and horses of the cavalry at least once a year, kept their descriptive rolls, and recommended promotions or punishments accordingly. The ~ was also responsible for the internal organisation and the discipline of the standing army and the commissariat. V 685b

ʿarīḍ → ʿATŪD

♦ ʿarīḍa (A) : a subtraction register, for those categories where the difference between two figures needs to be shown. It is arranged in three columns, with the result in the third. II 78b

ʿarīf (A, pl. *ʿurafāʾ*) : lit. one who knows; a gnostic. IV 326a; as a technical term, applied to holders of certain military or civil offices in the early and mediaeval periods, based on competence in customary matters, *ʿurf*. I 629a

In the Muslim East, ~ was used for the head of the guild. I 629b

In Oman and trucial Oman, ~ is the official in charge of the water distribution. IV 532a

Among the Ibāḍiyya, the plural form *ʿurafāʾ* are experts (inspectors, ushers) appointed by the assistant of the <u>SH</u>AY<u>KH</u>, *<u>kh</u>alīfa*. One of them supervised the collective recitation of the Qurʾān, another took charge of the communal meals, and others were responsible for the students' education, etc. III 96a

ʿariyya (A, pl. *ʿarāyā*) : in law, fresh dates on trees intended to be eaten, which it is permitted to exchange in small quantities for dried dates. VIII 492a

ʿāriyya (A) : in law, the loan of non-fungible objects, distinguished as a separate contract from the loan of money or other fungible objects. ~ is defined as putting someone temporarily and gratuitously in possession of the use of a thing, the substance of which is not consumed by its use. I 633a; VIII 900a

arkān → RUKN

arnab (A, pl. *arānib*) : in zoology, the hare. S 85b

In astronomy, ~ is the Hare constellation found beneath the left foot of Orion, the legendary hunter. S 85b

♦ arnab baḥrī : in zoology, the term for *aplysia depilans*, a nudibranch mollusc of the order of *isthobranchia*, found widely in the sea. S 85b

♦ arnaba, or *rabāb turkī* : a pear-shaped viol with three strings, which in Turkey appears to have been adopted from the Greeks, possibly in the 17th century, and which plays a prominent part in concert music today. VIII 348a

arpa (T) : barley. I 658a

♦ arpa tanesi : a barley grain, used under the Ottomans to denote both a weight (approximately 35.3 milligrams) and a measure (less than a quarter of an inch). I 658a

♦ **arpalik̊** : barley money, used under the Ottomans up to the beginning of the19th century to denote an allowance made to the principal civil, military and religious officers of state, either in addition to their salary when in office, or as a pension on retirement, or as an indemnity for unemployment. In the beginning it corresponded to an indemnity for fodder of animals, paid to those who maintained forces of cavalry or had to look after the horses. I 658a

ʿarrāda (A) : a light mediaeval artillery siege engine, from which the projectile was discharged by the impact of a shaft forcibly impelled by the release of a rope. I 556b; I 658b; III 469b ff.; and → MAND̲J̲ANĪḲ

ʿarrāf (A) : eminent in knowledge, a professional knower; a diviner, generally occupying a lower rank than the KĀHIN in the hierarchy of seers. I 659b; IV 421b

arrang (A, < Sp *arenque*), or *ranga*, *ranka* : the herring. VIII 1021a

ars̲h̲ (A) : in law, the compensation payable in the case of offences against the body; compensation in cases of homicide is termed DIYA. II 340b

ʿars̲h̲ (A) : throne. V 509a; in North African dialects, ‘tribe’, ‘agnatic group’, ‘federation’. I 661a; IV 362a

In Algerian law, the term given, during about the last hundred years, to some of the lands under collective ownership. I 661a

ʿarsī (A) : in mediaeval ʿIrāḳ, a beggar who stops the circulation of blood in an arm or leg so that people think the limb is gangrenous. VII 494a

aru (B, pl. *irwan*) : the Berber equivalent of *ṭālib*, student, from whom the Ibāḍiyya of the Mzāb recruit their ʿAZZĀBA for the religious council. III 98b

ʿarūḍ (A) : in prosody, the last foot of the first hemistich, as opposed to the last foot of the second hemistich, the ḌARB. I 667b; IV 714b; VIII 747b

♦ ʿilm al-ʿarūḍ : the science of metrics, said to have been developed by al-Khalīl of Mecca. I 667b; IV 57a; VIII 894a

ʿarūs resmi (T) : an Ottoman tax on brides. The rate varied depending on whether the bride was a girl, widow, divorcee, non-Muslim, Muslim, rich or poor. In some areas, it was assessed in kind. The tax, which seems to be of feudal origin, is already established in the ḲĀNŪNs of the 15th century in Anatolia and Rumelia, and was introduced into Egypt, Syria and ʿIrāḳ after the Ottoman conquest. It was abolished in the 19th century and replaced by a fee for permission to marry. I 679a

aruzz → RUZZ

♦ aruzz mufalfal : a very popular mediaeval dish which resembled a type of Turkish *pilaw*. Made with spiced meat and/or chickpeas or pistachio nuts, the dish may contain rice coloured with saffron, white rice alone, or a combination of both. A variation of this dish, made from lentils and plain rice, was called *al-mudjaddara* and is similar to the modern preparation of the same name. VIII 653a

♦ al-aruzziyya : a mediaeval dish containing meat and seasonings (pepper, dried coriander and dill), into which a small amount of powdered rice was added during cooking, and washed (whole) rice towards the end of the preparation. VIII 653a

arzal → AṬRĀF

ās (A, < Akk) : in botany, the myrtle (*Myrtus communis*). IX 653a; S 87a

ʿaṣā (A) : a rod, stick, staff (syn. ḲAḌĪB). Among the ancients Arabs, ~ was in common use for the camel herdsman's staff. In the Qurʾān, it is used a number of times, in particular for Moses' stick. I 680b

♦ shāḳḳ al-ʿaṣā : 'splitter of the ranks of the faithful'; under the Umayyads, a term used to characterise one who deserted the community of the faithful and rebelled against the legitimate caliphs. VII 546a

ʿaṣaba (A) : male relations in the male line, corresponding to the agnates. I 681a; IV 595b; VII 106b

♦ **ʿaṣabiyya** (A) : spirit of kinship in the family or tribe. Ibn Khaldūn used the concept of this term as the basis of his interpretation of history and his doctrine of the state; for him it is the fundamental bond of human society and the basic motive force of history. I 681a; II 962b; III 830b

asad (A, pl. *usūd*, *usud*, *usd*) : in zoology, the lion; in astronomy, *al-~* is the term for Leo, one of the twelve zodiacal constellations. I 681a; VII 83a

ʿaṣāʾib (A) : the 'troops', 500 in number, the eighth degree in the ṣūfī hierarchical order of saints. I 95a

asaliyya → DHAWLAḲIYYA

aṣamm (A) : deaf.

In mathematics, ~ is the term used for the fractions, such as 1/11 or 1/13, which cannot be reduced to fractions called by words derived from names of their denominators, such as 1/12, which is half one sixth, 'sixth' being derived from six. III 1140b

ʿ**asas** (A) : the night patrol or watch in Muslim cities. Under the Ottomans, the ~ was in charge of the public prisons, exercised a kind of supervision over public executions, and played an important role in public processions. He received one tenth of the fines imposed for minor crimes committed at night. I 687a; IV 103b

In North Africa, the ~ assured not only public security but also possessed a secret and almost absolute authority in the important affairs of the community. He kept guard at night in the central market, at warehouses and on the ramparts till the advent of the French. I 687b

asāṭīr → USṬŪRA

ʿaṣb (A) : in early Islam, a Yemenite fabric with threads dyed prior to weaving. V 735b

In prosody, a deviation from the proper metre, in particular a missing FATḤA in the foot *mufāʿal[a]tun*. I 672a

♦ ʿaṣba (A) : a folded scarf worn by women in the Arab East. V 740b

aṣbaʿ → IṢBAʿ

asbāb → SABAB

asfal (A) : lower; *al-asfal* is used as an epithet to differentiate between the patron and the client, when both are referred to as MAWLĀ. I 30b

aṣfar (A) : yellow; also, in distinction from black, simply light-coloured. I 687b

♦ banu 'l-aṣfar : the Greeks; later, applied to Europeans in general, especially in Spain. I 687b ff.

as<u>h</u> → TOY

aṣḥāb (A, s. **ṣāḥib**) : followed by the name of a locality in the genitive, ~ serves to refer to people who are companions in that particular place. Followed by a personal name in the genitive, ~ is, alongside the NISBA formation, the normal way of expressing the 'adherents of so-and-so' or the 'members of his school'. When followed by an abstract noun in the genitive, ~ denotes adherents of a specific concept. VIII 830b; and → ṢAḤABA; ṢĀḤIB

♦ aṣḥāb al-arbāʿ : in Mamlūk times, night patrols coming under the authority of the chief of police, *wālī*. I 687a

♦ aṣḥāb al-a<u>sh</u>āʾir : the four orders of the Burhāmiyya, Rifāʿiyya, Ḳādiriyya and Aḥmadiyya, according to <u>D</u>jabartī. II 167a

♦ aṣḥāb al-ḥadī<u>th</u> → AHL AL-ḤADĪ<u>TH</u>

♦ **aṣḥāb al-kahf** : 'those of the cave', the name given in the Qurʾān for the youths who in the Christian West are usually called the 'Seven Sleepers of Ephesus'. I 691a; IV 724a

♦ aṣḥāb al-naḳb → NAḲB

♦ **aṣḥāb al-rass** : 'the people of the ditch' or 'of the well'; a Qurʾānic term, possibly alluding to unbelievers. I 692a; III 169a

♦ **aṣḥāb al-raʾy** → AHL AL-RAʾY

♦ aṣḥāb al-saṭḥ, or *suṭūḥiyya* : 'the roof men', designation for the followers and disciples of the 7th/13th-century Egyptian saint Aḥmad al-Badawī. I 280b

♦ aṣḥāb al-s̲h̲ad̲j̲ara : 'the men of the tree'; those who took the oath of allegiance to the Prophet under the tree in the oasis of al-Ḥudaybiya, as mentioned in Q 48:18. VIII 828a; S 131a

♦ **aṣḥāb al-uk̲h̲dūd** : 'those of the trench'; a Qurʾānic term, possibly alluding to unbelievers. I 692b

♦ aṣḥāb-tark → AK̲H̲Ī

ashām → ESHĀM

aṣḥar → ṢAḤRĀʾ

ʿas̲h̲ara (A) : ten.

♦ **al-ʿas̲h̲ara al-mubas̲h̲s̲h̲ara** : the ten to whom Paradise is promised. The term does not occur in canonical Traditions and the list of names differs, Muḥammad appearing in only some. I 693a

ās̲h̲d̲j̲i̊ (T) : lit. cook; an officer's rank in an ORTA, subordinate to that of the ČORBAD̲J̲I̊, or 'soup purveyor'. VIII 178b

as̲h̲hada (A) : a technical term of childhood, said of a boy (or girl: *as̲h̲hadat*) who has attained to puberty. VIII 822a

ʿās̲h̲iḳ (A) : lover; a term originally applied to popular mystic poets of dervish orders. It was later taken over by wandering poet-minstrels. Their presence at public gatherings, where they entertained the audience with their religious and erotic songs, elegies and heroic narratives, can be traced back to the late 9th/15th century. I 697b; III 374a; IV 599a; V 275a ff.

ʿās̲h̲ik̲h̲ (Azerī Turkish, < ʿĀS̲H̲IḲ) : in Azerī literature, a genre of folk-literature comprising romantic poems, which made great advances in Ād̲h̲arbayd̲j̲ān in the 17th and 18th centuries and formed a bridge between the classical literary language and the local dialects. I 193b

ʿas̲h̲īra (A) : usually a synonym of ḲABĪLA 'tribe', ~ can also denote a subdivision of the latter. I 700a; IV 334a

ʿas̲h̲iyya (A), and variants : a word loosely taken in the sense of evening, although it used to designate more precisely the end of the day, NAHĀR. In this sense it was the opposite of ḌUḤĀ. V 709b

as̲h̲l (A, P *ṭanāb*) : rope; a unit of measurement equalling 39.9 metres. II 232b

as̲h̲rāf (A, s. S̲H̲ARĪF) : in India, ~ denoted Muslims of foreign ancestry. They were further divided into *sayyid* (those reckoning descent from the Prophet through his daughter Fāṭima), *s̲h̲ayk̲h̲* (descendants of the early Muslims of Mecca and Medina), *mug̲h̲al* (those who entered the sub-continent in the armies of the Mug̲h̲al dynasty), and *paṭhān* (members of Pas̲h̲tō-speaking tribes in north-west Pakistan and Afghanistan). III 411a; IX 330b; and → S̲H̲ARĪF

as̲h̲rafī (A) : in numismatics, a Burd̲j̲ī Mamlūk gold coin, the coinage of which was continued by the Ottomans after their conquest of Egypt and Syria. VIII

228b; an Ottoman gold coinage, introduced under Muṣṭafā II to replace the discredited SULṬĀNĪ. VIII 229b; an Aḳ Ḳoyunlu gold coin, copied exactly on the Burdjī Mamlūk ~ . Its weight was ca. 3.45 g. VIII 790a; in Ṣafawid Persia, all the gold coins were popularly called ~ , but there were actually several different varieties to which the name was given, which were distinguished from one another by their weights rather than by their designs or legends. The true ~ , used by Ismāʿīl as a standard for his gold coinage, weighed 18 *nukhūd*s (approximately 3.45 g), and had its origin in the weight of the Venetian gold ducat. VIII 790b

ʿashshāb (A) : from *ʿushb*, a fresh annual herb which is afterwards dried and, in medical literature, denotes simples, ~ means a gatherer or vendor of herbs; a vendor or authority on medicinal herbs. I 704a

ʿāshūrāʾ (A, < Heb) : the name of a voluntary fast-day, observed on the 10th of Muḥarram. I 265a; I 705a; S 190a; in South Africa, a festival commemorating the martyrdom of al-Ḥusayn, the grandson of the Prophet. IX 731a

aṣīl (A) : a term used in reference to the time which elapses between the afternoon, ʿAṢR, and sunset; in the contemporary language this word tends to be employed for the evening twilight. V 709b; and → KAFĀLA

ʿasīr (A) : lit. captive, term also sometimes used for slave. I 24b

ʿaskar (A) : army, in particular one possessing seige artillery. II 507a; 'garrison settlements' (syn. *muʿaskar*, *maʿaskar*) founded in the Arab East during the caliphate period. IV 1144a

♦ **ʿaskarī** (A, < ʿASKAR; T *ʿaskerī*) : in Ottoman technical usage a member of the ruling military caste, as distinct from the peasants and townspeople; ~ denoted caste rather than function, and included the retired or unemployed ~ , his wives and children, manumitted slaves of the sultan and of the ~ , and also the families of the holders of religious public offices in attendance on the sultan. I 712a; IV 242a; IV 563a; IX 540a

ʿaskerī → ʿASKARĪ

askiya (Songhay) : a dynastic title of the Songhay empire of West Africa, first adopted in 898/1493 by Muḥammad b. Abī Bakr. IX 729b

aṣl (A, pl. *uṣūl*) : root, base. III 550a

In classical Muslim administration, ~ is the estimated figure, as opposed to the amount actually received, ISTIKHRĀDJ. II 78b

In military science, *uṣūl* were the theoretical divisions of the army into five elements: the centre, the right wing, the left wing, the vanguard, and the rear guard. III 182a

In music, the *uṣūl* are the basic notes which, with the pause, make up the cycles of an ĪḲĀʿ. S 408b; metres. IX 418a

For *uṣūl* in prosody, → FARʿ

♦ uṣūl al-fiḳh : the 'roots' or sources of legal knowledge, viz. the Qurʾān, *sunna*, consensus and analogy. II 887b; legal theory. II 182b; IX 323b

♦ uṣūliyya → AKHBĀRIYYA

aṣlaḥ (A) : most suitable or fitting.

In theology, the 'upholders of the *aṣlaḥ*' were a group of the Muʿtazila who held that God did what was best for mankind. I 713b

aslamī (A) : a term used to designate first-generation Spanish converts, who were formerly Christians, whereas the term *islāmī* was reserved for the former Jews. VII 807b

asmāʾ → ISM

asp-i dāghī (Ind.P) : under the Mughals, a payment in accordance with the actual number of horsemen and horses presented at muster, unlike the BAR-ĀWARDĪ, a payment based on an estimate. IX 909a

ʿaṣr (A) : time, age; the (early part of the) afternoon. This period of day follows that of the midday prayer, ẒUHR, and extends between limits determined by the length of the shadow, but is variable, according to the jurists. I 719a; V 709b

♦ ṣalāt al-ʿaṣr : the afternoon prayer which is to be performed, according to the books of religious law, in between the last time allowed for the midday prayer, ẒUHR, and before sunset, or the time when the light of the sun turns yellow. According to Mālik, the first term begins somewhat later. I 719a; VII 27b; VIII 928b

ʿassās (A) : night-watchman. This term is used particularly in North Africa; at Fez at the beginning of the 20th century, ~ also was used for policemen in general. I 687b

In the Mzāb, ~ is used for the minaret of the Abāḍī mosques. I 687a

astān (P) : in mediaeval administration, a province. I 2b; a district. I 3a

asṭurlāb (A, < Gk), or *aṣṭurlāb* : astrolabe. The name of several astronomical instruments serving various theoretical and practical purposes, such as demonstration and graphical solution of many problems of spherical astronomy, the measuring of altitudes, the determination of the hour of the day and the night, and the casting of horoscopes. When used alone ~ always means the flat or planispheric astrolabe based on the principle of stereographic projection; it is the most important instrument of mediaeval, Islamic and Western, astronomy. I 722b

aṣṭūrū (A, < Gr) : the oyster. VIII 707a

ata (T) : father, ancestor; among the Oghuz, ~ was appended to the names of people who had acquired great prestige. ~ can also mean 'wise', or even 'holy', 'venerated'. I 729a

ʿaṭāʾ (A) : lit. gift; the term most commonly employed to denote, in the early days of Islam, the pension of Muslims, and, later, the pay of the troops. I 729a

ʿataba (A, pl. **ʿatabāt**) : doorstep.

In (folk) poetry, ~ (or *farsha* 'spread, mat') is used to designate the first three lines of a monorhyme quatrain (*a a a a*), or each of the three lines, when insertions have been made between the third line and the last, e.g. as in *a a a x a*. The last line is then called the *ghaṭā* 'cover' or, in longer compositions, the *ṭāḳiyya* 'skull-cap'. VI 868a

In its plural form, more fully *ʿatabāt-i ʿāliya* or *ʿatabāt-i muḳaddasa*, *ʿatabāt* designates the shīʿī shrine cities of ʿIrāḳ (Nadjaf, Karbalāʾ, Kāẓimayn and Sāmarrā) comprising the tombs of six of the IMĀMs as well as a number of secondary shrines and places of visitation. S 94a

ʿatāba (A) : a modern Arabic four line verse, common in Syria, Palestine, Mesopotamia and ʿIrāḳ, in a sort of WĀFIR metre. The first three lines not only rhyme, but generally repeat the same rhyming word with a different meaning. The last line rhymes with the paradigm ~ 'lovers' reproach', the last syllable of which is often supplied without making sense. I 730b

atabak (T *atabeg*) : the title of a high dignitary under the Saldjūḳs and their successors; under the Turks, a military chief. I 731a; commander-in-chief of an army (syn. *amīr kabīr*). I 138a; I 444a

♦ **atābak al-ʿasākir** : commander-in-chief of the Mamlūk army, who after the decline of the office of the viceroy, *nāʾib al-salṭana*, became the most important AMĪR in the Sultanate. I 732b

atalik̊ (T) : a title which existed in Central Asia in the post-Mongol period meaning in the first place a guardian and tutor of a young prince, then a close counsellor and confidant of the sovereign. It was synonymous with *atabeg* (→ ATABAK). I 733b; S 96b

atalikat (Cau) : a custom among the Čerkes tribes of the Caucasus, which consisted of having children raised from birth (boys until 17-18 years) in the families of strangers, often vassals. This created a sort of foster brotherhood which served to tighten the feudal bonds and unite the various tribes. II 23a

aṭam (A) : a fabulous marine creature mentioned by mediaeval Arab authors. It lurks in the Sea of China, has the head of a pig, is covered with a hairy fleece instead of scales, and shows female sexual organs. VIII 1023a

ʿatama (A) : the first third of the night from the time of waning of the red colour of the sky after sunset, SHAFAḲ. I 733b; a variant name given to the *ṣalāt al-ʿishāʾ* (→ ʿISHĀʾ). VII 27a

atān → ḤIMĀR

ātāy → ČAY

ātbēgī → ĀKHŪRBEG

ʿaṭf (A) : connection.

In grammar, ~ denotes a connection with the preceding word. There are two kinds of ~ : the simple co-ordinative connection, *ʿaṭf al-nasaḳ*, and the explicative connection, *ʿaṭf al-bayān*. In both kinds, the second word is called *al-maʿṭūf*, and the preceding *al-maʿṭūf ʿalayhi*. I 735b

♦ ʿaṭfa → SHĀRIʿ

athar (A) : trace; as a technical term, it denotes a relic of the Prophet, e.g. his hair, teeth, autograph, utensils alleged to have belonged to him, and especially impressions of his footprints, *ḳadam*. I 736a

In the science of Tradition, ~ usually refers to a Tradition from Companions or Successors, but is sometimes used of Traditions from the Prophet. I 1199a; III 23a

In astrology, ~ is also used as a technical term in the theory of causality, with reference to the influence of the stars (considered as higher beings possessing a soul) on the terrestrial world and on men. I 736b

athāth (A) : lit. belongings, ~ means various household objects and, especially in modern Arabic, furniture. S 99a

ʿaththarī (A, < the name of the deity ʿAthtar) : a term equivalent to *baʿl* 'unwatered cultivated land'. I 969a

ʿāṭif → MUSALLĪ

ʿatīḳ → ʿITḲ

ʿātiḳa (A) : in archery, an old bow of which the wood has become red. IV 798a

ʿātikī (A, < *Ḳabr ʿĀtika*, a concentration of textile workshops in Damascus) : in the 11th/17th century, a Syrian fabric, sufficiently renowned to be exhibited in the markets of Cairo. IX 793b

ʿatīra (A) : among the Arabs of the DJĀHILIYYA, a ewe offered as a sacrifice to a pagan divinity, as a thanksgiving following the fulfillment of a prayer concerning in particular the increase of flocks. Also called *radjabiyya*, since these sacrifices took place in the month of Radjab. I 739b; S 317a

ātishak : in medicine, syphilis. VIII 783a

atmadja → ČAKÏR

aṭrāf (Ind.P, < A) : a term used to designate the higher stratum of the non-ASHRĀF population of India, which consists for the most part of converts from Hinduism, embracing people of many statuses and occupations. The terms *adjlāf* and *arzal* (or *ardhāl*) are used to designate the lower stratum. III 411a; IX 330b

In the science of Tradition, a so-called ~ compilation is an alphabetically-arranged collection of the Companions' MUSNADs, with every Tradition ascribed to each of them shortened to its salient feature (→ ṬARAF), accompanied by all the ISNAD strands supporting it which occur in the Six Books and a few other revered collections. VIII 518b

ʿattābī (A) : a kind of silk-cotton cloth, woven around 580/1184 in ʿAttābiyya, one of the quarters of Baghdad. I 901b

ʿaṭṭār (A) : a perfume merchant or druggist; later, as most scents and drugs were credited with some healing properties, ~ came to mean chemist and homeopath; sometimes dyers and dye merchants are also known by this term. I 751b

In India, ~ denotes an alcohol-free perfume-oil produced by the distillation of sandalwood-oil through flowers. I 752b

attūn (A) : a kiln used for firing bricks, similar to that of the potters, consisting of a furnace with a firing-room on top. V 585b

ʿatūd (A), or *ʿarīḍ* : a one-year old male goat, called, progressively, *djadhaʿ* or *tays* when two years old, then thanī, *rabāʿī*, *sadīs* and, after seven years, *sāligh*. S 319a

aṭūm (A) : in zoology, the dugong, one of the sirenian mammals or 'sea cows'. Other designations are *maliṣa*, *nāḳa al-baḥr*, *zālikha*, and *ḥanfāʾ*. VIII 1022b; the caret or caouane turtle (*Caretta caretta*) (syn. *ḥanfāʾ*). IX 811a

awāʾil (A, s. AWWAL 'first') : a term used to denote e.g. the 'primary data' of philosophical or physical phenomena; the 'ancients' of either pre-Islamic or early Islamic times; and the 'first inventors' of things (or the things invented or done first), thus giving its name to a minor branch of Muslim literature with affinities to ADAB, historical, and theological literature. I 758a

♦ awāʾil al-suwar → FAWĀTIḤ AL-SUWAR

awāradj (A) : in classical Muslim administration, a register showing the debts owed by individual persons and the instalments paid until they are settled. II 78b; VIII 652a

ʿawāriḍ (A) : a term used under the Ottomans down to the second quarter of the 19th century to denote contributions of various types exacted by the central government in the sultan's name. The Ottoman fief-system and the institution of the WAḲF deprived the government to a great extent of the vast revenues. Therefore it resorted, at first in emergencies and later annually, to the imposition of the ~ , either in cash or in kind. I 760a; IV 234b; VIII 486b

awārik (A) : 'eaters of *arāk* leaves', the name of a famous breed of white camels raised by the Bedouin living near the oasis of Bīsha, in western Arabia. I 541a; I 1239b

ʿawāṣim (A, s. *ʿāṣima*) : lit. protectresses; strongholds in the frontier zone extended between the Byzantine empire and the empire of the caliphs in the north and north-east of Syria. Those situated more to the front were called *al-thughūr*. I 465b; I 761a; a separate government founded by Hārūn al-Rashīd in 170/786-87, made up of the frontier strongholds which he detached from the Djazīra and DJUND of Ḳinnasrīn. I 761a; II 36a

āwāz → BAḤR

ʿawbar (A), or *hawbar* : in zoology, the whelp of the cheetah. II 740b

awbāsh (A) : 'riff-raff', the name given to groups of young men who were considered elements of disorder in mediaeval Baghdad. II 961b

awdj (A, < San *ucča*) : in astronomy, the apogee, the farthest point in a planet's orbit. The lowest point, the perigee, is called *ḥaḍīḍ*. VIII 101b; IX 292a

awḳā → WUḲĀ

awḳaʿa → WAḲĀʿA

ʿawl (A) : lit. deviation by excess; in law, the method of increasing the common denominator of the fractional shares in an inheritance, if their sum would amount to more than one unit. I 764b

awlād (A, s. *walad* 'child') : sons, children; for the many other designations for childhood and its subdivisions, VIII 821b ff.

♦ **awlād al-balad** : the term used during the Sudanese Mahdi period (1881-98) to designate persons originating from the northern riverain tribes. Under the Mahdi Muḥammad Aḥmad, they became the ruling class but gradually lost their status under his successors. I 765a; V 1250a

♦ **awlād al-nās** : lit. children of the people; the term used among the Mamlūks for the sons of mamlūks who could not join the exclusive society of the Mamlūk upper class. Only those who were born an infidel and brought as a child-slave from abroad, were converted to Islam and set free after completing military training, and bore a non-Arab name, could belong to that society. The ~ were joined to a unit of non-mamlūks called the ḤALḲA, which was socially inferior to the pure mamlūk units, and formed there the upper stratum. The term ABNĀʾ AL-ATRĀK was sometimes used as an alternative. I 102a; I 765a; III 99b

awri<u>th</u> → AMAZZAL

awtād (A, s. *watid* 'tent peg') : in prosody, one of two pairs of metrical components distinguished by al-<u>Kh</u>alīl. The ~ consist of three consonants each and are called *watid ma<u>dj</u>mūʿ* (when the first two consonants are 'moving', i.e. have a short vowel, and the last 'quiescent') and *watid mafrūḳ* (when the first and the third consonants are 'moving' and the middle one 'quiescent'). I 670b

In mysticism, ~ (s. *watad*; syn. *ʿumud*) 'stakes' is the third category of the hierarchy of the RIDJĀL AL-<u>GH</u>AYB, comprising four holy persons. I 95a; I 772a

ʿawwāʾ (A) : in mediaeval ʿIrāḳ, a vagabond who begs between sunset and the evening worship, at times singing. VII 494a

awwal (A, pl. AWĀʾIL) : first.

In philosophy, ~ was brought into Muslim thought by the Arab translators of Aristotle and Plotinus to indicate either the First Being or the First Created. I 772a

♦ awwaliyya : an abstract noun derived from *awwal* indicating the essence of 'that which is first'. Its plural *awwaliyyāt* means the First Principles in the order of knowledge, i.e. the propositions and judgements immediately evident by themselves. I 772b

awzān (A, s. WAZN) :

♦ awzān al-<u>sh</u>iʿr : in prosody, deviations in the metrical forms, e.g. shortening of the metre. I 671a; VIII 667b

āya (A) : sign, token; miracle; a verse of the Qurʾān. I 773b; V 422a

♦ **āyatullāh** (< *āyat Allāh*) : lit. miraculous sign of God; a title with a hierarchical significance used by the Twelver <u>sh</u>īʿīs, indicating one at the top of the hierarchy, amongst the elite of the great MU<u>DJ</u>TAHIDs. S 103b

aʿyān (A, s. ʿAYN) : notables, the eminent under the caliphate and subsequent Muslim regimes. I 778a; II 640b

Under the Ottomans in the eighteenth century, ~ acquired a more precise significance and came to be applied to those accorded official recognition as the chosen representatives of the people vis-à-vis the government, later to become local magnates and despots. I 778a ff.; II 724a; III 1187b

In philosophy, ~ is used for the particular things that are perceived in the exterior world, as opposed to those things that exist in the mind. I 784a

♦ aʿyāniyye (T) : in the Ottoman period, a fee paid by the Aʿyān to obtain documents from the provincial governors according them official recognition as the chosen representatives of the people vis-à-vis the government. I 778b

ayfd → s̲h̲awka

ayhuḳān (A) : in botany, wild rocket. VII 831a

ayḳas̲h̲ (A) : a system according to which the *ṭālib*s 'students' of North Africa use the numerical value of letters for certain magical operations; a specialist in this technique is called in the vernacular *yaḳḳās̲h̲*. I 97b

aym (A) : in zoology, a large snake, called *yaym* on the Arabian Peninsula. I 541b

ʿayn (A) : eye; evil eye; the thing viewed; source. I 784b; a flowing spring. I 538b; observer, spy. II 486b

In Algeria, in the region of Oued Righ, and in Libya, in the eastern parts of the S̲h̲āti, ~ is an artesian well, formerly dug by specialists and very fragile, but now drilled and harnessed according to modern techniques. I 1232a

In the mediaeval kitchen, ~ is the top of an oven which could be opened or closed to adjust the oven's temperature. A synonym is *fam*. VI 808a

In mysticism, ~ is used to indicate the super-existence of God's deepest essence. I 785a

♦ ʿayn al-ḳiṭṭ : 'cat's eye', in botany, applied to five plants: the Corn camomile (*Anthemis arvensis*), Camomile (*A. nobilis*), Wild camomile (*Matricaria chamomilla*), Water speedwell (*Veronica anagallis aquatica*), and Minor phalaris (*Phalaris minor*). IX 653a

♦ ʿayn al-yaḳīn : 'the contemplation of the evident'; a mystical term which can be used in the double sense of intuition, i.e. the pre-rational sense of intuitive understanding of the philosophical first principles, and the post-rational sense of the intuitive understanding of super-rational mystical truth. I 785a

ʿays̲h̲ → kuskusū

ayt (B) : 'sons of', used either in compounds, or before a proper noun to indicate a tribe. I 792a

aywaz (T, < A *ʿiwaḍ*) : a term applied to the footmen employed in great households in the later Ottoman empire. They were generally Armenians of Van, sometimes Kurds; Greeks are also said to have been among them. Their duties included waiting at table, filling and cleaning the lamps and doing the shopping for the household. I 792a

ayyām → yawm

ʿayyār (A) : lit. rascal, tramp, vagabond; a term applied to certain warriors who were grouped together under the futuwwa in ʿIrāḳ and Persia from the 9th to the 12th centuries, on occasions appearing as fighters for the faith in the inner Asian border regions, on others forming the opposition party in towns and coming into power, indulging in a rule of terror against the wealthy part of the population. I 794a; I 900b ff.; II 961b; VIII 402a; VIII 795b; VIII 956a

ayyil (A) : in zoology, the mountain goat. The descriptions given by the zoologists, however, apply rather more to the deer, but in pre-Islamic and early Islamic poetry, ~ may actually mean the mountain-goat, since the deer probably never existed in the Arabian peninsula. I 795a

ʿazab (A, T *ʿazeb*) : lit. an unmarried man or woman, a virgin; the term applied to several types of fighting men under the Ottoman and other Turkish regimes between the 13th and the 19th centuries, who were forbidden to marry before retirement. I 807a; Ottoman light infantry. IX 128b

azal (A) : eternity.

In philosophy, ~ or *azaliyya* is a technical term corresponding to ἀγενητός, meaning ungenerated, eternal *a parte ante*; Ibn Rus̲h̲d used *azaliyya* for ‘incorruptible’. I 2a; V 95a; and → DAHRIYYA

azala (A) : a special unit of 100 cubic cubits ‘of balance’, used in mediaeval ʿIrāḳ to count the volume of earth, reeds and brushwood which had to be transported when constructing and upkeeping raised canal banks. V 865a

azalay (B) : a term for the great caravans made up of several thousand dromedaries which carry the salt from the salt deposits of the Southern Sahara to the tropical regions of the Sahel in spring and autumn. I 808b; I 1222a

azaliyya → AZAL

azharī → FĪRŪZAD̲J̲

ʿazīb (A), or *ʿazl*, *hans̲h̲īr* : ‘latifundium’, a form of land tenure in ancient North Africa. I 661a; lands owned by a ZĀWIYA which are let out and whose profits are shared with the tenants (*ʿazzāb*). V 1201b

ʿazīma (A) : determination, resolution, fixed purpose.

In religious law, ~ is an ordinance as interpreted strictly, the opposite of RUK̲H̲ṢA, an exemption or dispensation. I 823a

In magic, ~ is an adjuration, or the application of a formula of which magical effects are expected. I 823a

ʿazīz (A) : powerful, respected.

In the science of Tradition, a Tradition coming from one man of sufficient authority to have his Traditions collected when two or three people share in transmitting them. III 25b

ʿazl (A) : *coitus interruptus*. I 826a; and → ʿAZĪB

azr → IZĀR

azyab (A) : in Yemen, the southeast wind. I 180b

ʿazzāba (A, s. *ʿazzābī*) : ‘recluses’, ‘clerks’.

Among the Ibāḍiyya, members of a special council, ḤALḲA, presided over by a S̲H̲AYK̲H̲, who were distinguished from the laity by their tonsure (they had to shave their heads completely) and by their simple white habits. Their lives were subject to a severe discipline; they were governed by a strict moral code and any misdemeanour was punished immediately. III 95a

B

bā (A) : a genealogical term used in South Arabia to form individual and (second-arily) collective proper names. I 828a

♦ bā-s̲h̲arʿ (P) : lit. with law, i.e. following the law of Islam; one of the two categories into which dervishes in Persia are divided. The other is BĪ-S̲H̲ARʿ. II 164b

bāʿ (A), or *k̲āma* : a basic measure of length consisting of the width of the two arms outstretched, i.e. a fathom, canonically equal to four DHIRĀ's (199.5 cm) or approximately 2 metres, and thus the thousandth part of a mile. In Egypt, the ~ is four 'carpenter's' cubits, or 3 metres. I 535b; II 232b; VII 137b

baʿʿādjūn (A) : 'cleavers', according to e.g. Ibn K̲h̲aldūn, magicians who had only to point their finger at a piece of clothing or a skin, while mumbling certain words, for that object to fall into shreds; with the same gestures, fixing upon sheep, they could instantaneously cleave them. VIII 52b

bāb (A) : gate. I 830a

In early s̲h̲īʿism, ~ denotes the senior authorised disciple of the IMĀM, and among the Ismāʿīliyya, ~ is a rank in the hierarchy, denoting the head of the DAʿWA and thus the equivalent in Ismāʿīlī terminology of the *dāʿī al-duʿāt*. I 832b; and → SAFĪR

Among the Bābīs, ~ is the appellation of the founder, Sayyid ʿAlī Muḥammad of S̲h̲īrāz. I 833a

♦ bāb marzūk̲ : 'lucky door', the term used for the hyena by the Arab nomads of the Sahara regions. S 173b

♦ **bāb-i ʿālī** (T) : the (Ottoman) Sublime Porte, the name for the Ottoman government. I 836a

♦ **bāb-i humāyūn** (T) : lit. Imperial Gate, the principal entrance in the outer wall of the sultan's New Serail. I 836b

♦ **bāb-i mas̲h̲īk̲h̲at** (T) : the name for the office or department of the S̲H̲AYK̲H̲ AL-ISLĀM under the Ottomans in the 19th century. I 837b

♦ bāb al-saʿādet (T) : lit. the Gate of Felicity, the gate leading from the second into the third court, proceeding inward, of the imperial palace of the Ottomans. II 697b

♦ **bāb-i serʿaskeri** (T) : the name for the War Department in the Ottoman empire during the 19th century. I 838a

baba → MURS̲H̲ID

babbag̲h̲āʾ (A), or *babg̲h̲āʾ* : in zoology, both parakeet and parrot. The term represents both female and male, singular and collective. I 845b

babg̲h̲āʾ → BABBAG̲H̲Āʾ

babr (A, pl. *bubūr*) : in zoology, the tiger. II 739a

bābūnadj (A, < P *bābūna*) : in botany, the common camomile, primarily

Anthemis nobilis, also called Roman camomile, but also *Matricaria chamomilla* and other varieties. S 114b

bād-i hawā (T), or *ṭayyārāt* : lit. wind of the air; a general term in Ottoman fiscal usage for irregular and occasional revenues from fines, fees, registration, charges, and other casual sources of income which appeared for the first time in the first quarter of the 10th/16th century and continued through the 18th century. I 850a; II 147a; VIII 487b; IX 474a

badāʾ (A) : appearance, emergence.

In theology, the alteration of God's purpose. I 265b; the emergence of new circumstances which cause a change in an earlier ruling. I 850a

bādahandj → BĀDGĪR; MALḲAF

badal (A, T *bedel*) : substitute; and → ABDĀL; ʿIWAḌ

In the Ottoman empire, a term used to denote a contribution made by a taxpayer in lieu of his performing some service for the government or furnishing it with some commodity. These special 'substitute' cash contributions were exacted when either the subjects failed to fulfil their obligations or the government forwent its rights in this regard. I 760b; I 855a; II 147a

In Afghanistan, ~ means revenge by retaliation, vendetta, and is one of the three main pillars of the special social code of the Afghans. I 217a

♦ bedel-i ʿaskerī (T) : an exemption tax in the place of enrollment in the national service. VIII 201a

badan (A) : body, in particular the human body, often only the torso. II 555a; in mediaeval Islam, a short, sleeveless tunic from cotton or silk, worn by both sexes and usually associated with the Arabian peninsula, but it has been shown to have also been a fairly common article of feminine attire in mediaeval Egypt. V 739a

In seafaring, ~ is used to designate a kind of boat typical of Northern Oman which is constructed according to two models: one for fishing, the other for the transportation of goods and for cabotage. This is the typical boat with an entirely sewn hull in order to avoid damage in case of a collision with reefs at water level. VII 53b

As zoological term, → WAʿL

bādandj → BĀDGĪR

baddāʿ (Bed) : among the Sinai Bedouin, a composer adept at spontaneous improvisation. IX 234b

bādgīr (P) : lit. wind-catcher; an architectural term used in Persia for the towers containing ventilation shafts and projecting high above the roofs of domestic houses. In mediaeval Arabic, the device was known as *bādahandj* or *bādandj*. IX 49b; S 115a

badhadj → SAKHLA

bādhāward → SHAWKA

badhr al-kattān (A) : in botany, linseed. IX 615a

badīʿ (A) : innovator, creator, thus, one of the attributes of God. I 857b; III 663b
In literature, ~ is the name for the innovations of the ʿAbbāsid poets in literary figures, and later for trope in general. I 857b; IV 248b; V 900a
♦ badīʿiyya : in literature, a poem in which the poet uses all kinds of figures of speech. I 858a; I 982b
♦ ʿilm al-badīʿ : the branch of rhetorical science which deals with the beautification of literary style, the artifices of the ornamentation and embellishment of speech. I 857b; I 982b

badīha → IRTIDJĀL

bādiya (A) : in the Umayyad period, a residence in the countryside, an estate in the environs of a settlement or a rural landed property in the Syro-Jordanian steppeland. S 116b

baʿdiyya → IFTITĀḤ

bādj (A, < P *bāzh*) : a fiscal technical term among the Turks, ~ was applied to various forms of tax as well as being used for 'tax' in general. I 860b; II 147a
♦ bādj-i buzurg : in the Īlkhānid and Djalāʾirid periods, the customs-duty levied on goods in transit through or imported into the country. I 861b
♦ bādj-i tamgha : in the Īlkhānid and Djalāʾirid periods, the tax levied on all kinds of goods bought and sold in cities, on woven stuffs and slaughtered animals; it is normally referred to as *tamgha-i siyāh* 'black tamgha'. I 861b
♦ bādjdār : in the Īlkhānid and Djalāʾirid periods, a tax collector, who collected tolls at certain places according to a tariff fixed by the central government. I 861a

badjdja → SUDJDJA

badjrā : the common Indian river-boat, a sort of barge without a keel, propelled by poles or by oars, on the deck of which cabins might be mounted. VII 933a

badr → ḲAMAR

badw (A) : pastoral nomads of Arabian blood, speech and culture, the Bedouin. I 872a

bāgh (P) : term for a suburban palace in Tīmūrid times, meaning a park or estate with building and gardens. IX 46a

baghbūr → FAGHFŪR

baghdādī → SABʿĀNĪ

bāghī → BUGHĀT; MULḤID

baghiyy (A, pl. *baghāyā*), and *mūmis*, *ʿāhira*, *zāniya* : prostitute. A more vulgar word was *ḳaḥba*, from the verb 'to cough', because professional prostitutes used to cough to attract clients. S 133a

baghl (A, fem. *baghla*) : mule; hinny (offspring of a stallion and she-ass). I 909a
In Egypt, the feminine form *baghla* (pl. *baghalāt*) also denoted a female slave born of unions between ṢAḲĀLIBA and another race. I 909a
♦ baghl al-sammān → SALWĀ
♦ baghla (< Sp/Por *bajel/baxel*) : in the Gulf area, a large sailing ship used in the Gulf of Oman and the Indian waters. VIII 811b; and → BAGHL

♦ baghlī : the earliest Arab DIRHAMS which were imitations of the late Sasanian *drahm*s of Yezdigird III, Hormuzd IV and (chiefly) Khusraw II; ʿAbd al-Malik's monetary reforms in 79/698-9 drastically altered the style. II 319a

bağlama → SĀZ

bagsı → OZAN

bagtal : a word used in Laḳ society to designate the KHĀN's family and the nobility. V 618a

bāh (A), and *waṭʾ* : coitus. I 910b

bahādur (Alt) : courageous, brave; hero. Borrowed into many languages, ~ also frequently appears as a surname and an honorific title. I 913a; and → SARDĀR

bahaḳ → DJUDHĀM

bahār → NARDJIS

baḥīra (A) : the name in the pre-Islamic period for a she-camel or ewe with slit ears. I 922a

bahlawān → PAHLAWĀN

bahma → SAKHLA

baḥr (A, pl. *buḥūr*) : a place where a great amount of water is found. Accordingly, ~ is not only applied to the seas and oceans but also, uniquely, because of its outstanding size, to the Nile. I 926b; VII 909b; VIII 38a

The plural *buḥūr* means, in prosody, the ideal metric forms as given in the circles devised by al-Khalīl. I 671a; VIII 667b; in music, secondary modes, alongside main modes (*anghām*) and *āwāz* modes. IX 101a

♦ **al-baḥrayn** : lit. the two seas; a cosmographical and cosmological concept appearing five times in the Qurʾān. I 940b

♦ **baḥriyya** : the navy. I 945b; S 119b

baḥth (A) : study, examination, inquiry. I 949a; and → AHL AL-(BAḤTH WA 'L-) NAẒAR

bahw (A) : an empty and spacious place extending between two objects which confine it; the axial nave in a mosque, ~ is a term primarily belonging to the vocabulary of Western Muslim architecture. It also is defined as a tent or pavilion chamber situated beyond the rest. I 949b

bāʿidj → KHANNĀḲ

bāʾika → ḤĀṢIL

bāʾin (A) : in law, an irrevocably divorced woman. III 1011b

baʾīn → BĀʾOLĪ

baʿīr (A) : the individual camel, regardless of sex, as opposed to *ibil*, the species and the group. III 666a

baḳʿa (A) : a term applied especially to a place where water remains stagnant. I 1292b; and → BUḲʿA

baḳāʾ wa-fanāʾ (A) : 'subsistence' and 'effacement', ṣūfī terms referring to the stages of the development of the mystic in the path of gnosis. I 951a; IV 1083b; VIII 306b; VIII 416a

bāḳālāw (A, < Sp *bacallao*), with var. *bāḳālyū*, *baḳala*, *baḳlāwa* : the stockfish. VIII 1022b

baḳar (A) : cattle; mediaeval Arab authors distinguished between the domestic ~ *ahlī* and the wild ~ *waḥshī*, meaning either the *mahā* (*Oryx beatrix*) or the AYYIL, or even the *yaḥmūr* 'roedeer' and the *thaytal* 'bubale antelope'. I 951b

bakhīl → BUKHL

bakhnūḳ (Tun) : an embroidered head shawl for women, worn in Tunisia. V 745b

bakhshī (< Ch *po-che* ?) : a Buddhist priest, monk; later 'writer, secretary', a term stemming from Mongol administrative usage. In the 15th and 16th centuries, it came to mean a wandering minstrel among the Turkomans and the Anatolian Turks. I 953a; bard. I 422a

In Persia, a subdistrict or county. VIII 154a; VIII 586a

♦ bakhshī al-mamālik or MĪR-BAKHSHĪ : in Mughal India, more or less the equivalent of the classical ʿĀRIḌ, the official charged with the mustering, passing in review and inspection of troops. IV 268b; V 686a; IX 738b

bākhshī : in traditional Özbeg society, a practitioner of shamanistic healing, especially the removal of spirits. He often was a MOLLĀ learned in the Qurʾān. Synonyms are *parīkhʷān* or *duʿākhʷān*. VIII 234b

bakhshīsh (P) : a gratuity bestowed by a superior on an inferior, a tip or 'consideration' thrown into a bargain, and a bribe, particularly one offered to judges or officials. Under the Ottomans, ~ came to mean the gratuity bestowed by a sultan upon his accession on the chief personages of state, the Janissaries and other troops of the standing army. I 953a

baḳḳ (A) : in zoology, a bug. II 248a; IV 522a

bakkāʾ (A) : lit. weepers; in early Islam, ascetics who during their devotional exercises shed many tears. I 959a

baḳḳāl (A) : retailer of vegetables; grocer (syn. *khaḍḍār*). I 961a, where many synonyms used regionally are listed

baḳḳam (A, < San) : sappan wood, an Indian dye wood obtained from the *Caesalpinia Sappan L.* The Arabic equivalent frequently given by Arab philologists is *ʿandam*, which, however, denotes the dragon's blood, a red gum exuding from certain trees. I 961b

baḳḳāra : cattle nomads in the central Sudan belt of Africa. IX 516a

baḳla → ʿALATH

baḳṭ (A, < Lat *pactum*, Gk) : an annual tribute yielded by Christian Nubia to the Muslims. I 32a; I 966a

bāl → ʿANBAR

baʿl (A) : master, owner, husband.

In law, ~ denotes unwatered tillage and unwatered cultivated land. I 968a

♦ baʿlī : as an adjective, frequently attached to the name of a vegetable or fruit; in such cases, it stresses the good quality. At Fez, ~ describes a man, avaricious, dry and hard, while the feminine *baʿliyya* is applied to a succulent fig. I 969b bāla (Yem) : a folk poetry genre for men in northern Yemen tribal areas, usually improvised and sung at weddings and other celebrations. IX 234a f.

bālā (P) : height, high; since 1262/1846 the term for a grade in the former Ottoman Civil Service, to which the Secretary of State and other senior officials belonged. I 969b

balad → SHAYKH

♦ **baladiyya** (A) : municipality; the term used to denote modern municipal institutions of European type, as against earlier Islamic forms of urban organisation. I 972b

balāgha (A) : eloquence. I 858a; I 981b; I 1114a; II 824a; to Ḳazwīnī (d. 1338), ~ was the term for the science of rhetoric as a whole. I 1116a

balam (A) : a typically ʿIrāḳī term for a barque which has both bows and stern pointed in shape, with a flat deck and a capacity of transporting from 5 to 10 tons, and is used on the Euphrates river. VII 53b

In zoology, a term for anchovy, found again in the Latinised term to specify a sub-species limited to a particular region (*Engraulis boelema*), and for the sand-smelt, both small fish. VIII 1021b; VIII 1023a

balamīda (A, < *Pelamys*) : in zoology, the pelamid, also called *būnīt*, the bonito. VIII 1021a

balāṭ (A, < L or Gk *palatium*) : a paved way; flagging; the term most usually applied to the naves of a mosque. I 950a; I 987b; I 988a; palace. IX 44a

♦ balāṭa : a 'flag-stone' of any kind of material serving to pave the ground or to bear a monumental or memorial inscription. I 987b

balgham (A, < Gk) : phlegm, one of the four cardinal humours. S 188b

bāligh (A) : in law, major, of full age. I 993a

balīladj (P) : in botany, a variety of myrobalanus (*Terminalia bellerica*). S 349b

bālish (P 'cushion') : a 13th-century Mongolian monetary unit, coined both in gold and silver. It was in use particularly in the eastern part of the empire. Its value was assessed at 6,192 gold marks. I 996b

baliyya (A, pl. *balāyā*) : a name given, in pre-Islamic times, to a camel (more rarely a mare) tethered at the grave of his master and allowed to die of starvation, or sometimes burnt alive. Muslim tradition sees in this practice proof of the pre-Islamic Arabs' belief in resurrection, because the animal thus sacrificed was thought to serve as a mount for its master at the resurrection. I 997a

baʿliyya → BAʿL

ballūṭ (A, pl. *balāliṭa*) : in botany, acorn, fruit of the oaktree. II 744a

balshūn (A) : in zoology, the heron. I 1152b

balṭadji (T) : a name given to men composing various companies of palace guards under the Ottomans down to the beginning of the nineteenth century. The ~ was originally employed in connection with the army in the felling of trees, the levelling of roads and the filling of swamps. The term was used alternatively with the Persian equivalent, *tabardār*, both meaning 'axe-man', and hence 'woodcutter', 'pioneer', 'halberdier'. I 1003b

balyemez (T, < Ger *Faule Metze*) : lit. that eats no honey; a large caliber gun, which name (probably a jesting and popular transformation of the famous German cannon "Faule Metze" of the year 1411) came to the Ottomans through the numerous German gun-founders in the Turkish services; the ~ was first introduced into the Ottoman army in the time of sultan Murād II. I 1007b; I 1062b

bālyōs (T, < It *bailo*) : the Turkish name for the Venetian ambassador to the Sublime Porte. With the generalised meaning of European diplomatic or consular agent, the word is also encountered in some Arabic dialects and Swahili. I 1008a; II 60b

bān (A, P) : the ben-nut tree (*Moringa aptera Gaertn.*), the wood of which was used for tent-poles. Its fruit, called s͟hū‘, was a commodity and greatly in demand. The ~ was used as a simile by poets for a tender woman of tall stature. I 1010b

bāna → ĪLĪDJA

band (P) : anything which is used to bind, attach, close or limit; a dam built for irrigation purposes. I 1012a

bandar (P) : a seaport or port on a large river. The word ~ passed into the Arabic of Syria and Egypt where it is used in the sense of market-place, place of commerce, banking exchange and even workshop. I 1013a

bandayr (Alg, < Goth *pandero*), or *bandīr* : in Algeria, a round tambourine with snares stretched across the inside of the head, probably called GHIRBĀL in the early days of Islam. II 620b

bandis͟h : the composition, the second part in a performance of classical or art music of India, which in vocal music may be KHAYĀL, *dhrupad,* TARĀNA or one of several more modern forms; in instrumental music, as played on the stringed instruments, *sitār* and *sarod*, it is generally called *gat*. III 454a

bandj (A, P *bang*, < San) : henbane, a narcotic drug. In the popular dialect of Egypt, ~ is used for every kind of narcotic. I 1014b; III 266b

bandjārā : a term used in India to designate dealers rather than mere commissariat carriers, who travelled all over the country with large droves of laden cattle and regularly supplied the Indian armies and hunting camps. VII 932b

bang → BANDJ

banīḳa (A, pl. *banāʾiḳ*) : originally, in early Arabic, any piece inserted to widen a tunic or a leather bucket; in the Arab West, ~ was used for a kind of man's tunic and, more frequently, for an element of women's hair-covering. In Algiers, ~ is still used for a kind of square headdress, provided with a back flap, which women use to cover their heads to protect themselves against the cold when leaving the baths. I 1016a

In Morocco, ~ means a dark padded cell; a closet serving as an office for a 'minister'. I 1016b

banis͟h (A), or *banīs͟h* : a wide-sleeved man's coat, worn in the Arab East. V 740b bānuwānī : in mediaeval ʿIrāḳ, a vagrant who stands before a door, rattles the bolt and cries "O Master", in order to get alms. VII 494a

bāʾolī (U, H), and *baʾīn* : a step-well in Muslim India, usually found at the principal shrines associated with Čis̲h̲tī *pīr*s (→ MURS̲H̲ID). They are meant for the use of men and animals. I 1024a; V 884b; V 888b

bar-āwardī (Ind.P) : lit. by estimate; under the Mug̲h̲al emperor Akbar, the payment at a rather low rate made in advance for a contingent of a size less than the titular rank, ultimately coming to define the number of the second or *sawār* (→ SUWĀR) rank. IX 909a

bārā wafāt (U) : a term used in the subcontinent of India for the twelfth day of Rabīʿ I, observed as a holy day to commemorate the death of the Prophet Muḥammad. I 1026a

barāʾa (A) : release, exemption; freedom from disease, cure.

As a Qurʾānic term, ~ also means the breaking of ties, a kind of dissociation or excommunication, which theme was developed by the K̲h̲ārid̲j̲ites as being the duty to repudiate all those who did not deserve the title of Muslim. I 207a; I 811a; I 1027b

In law, ~ is the absence of obligation; *barāʾat (al-d̲h̲imma)* means freedom from obligation. I 1026b

In classical Muslim administration, ~ is a receipt given by the D̲J̲AHBAD̲H̲ or K̲H̲ĀZIN to taxpayers. II 78b; ~ has been increasingly employed in a concrete sense to denote written documents of various kinds: licence, certificate, diploma, demand for payment, passport, a label to be attached to a piece of merchandise, a request or petition to the sovereign. I 1027a

In the science of diplomatic, ~ (syn. *risāla*) in Morocco was a letter addressed to a community, in order to announce an important event, or in order to exhort or to admonish. It was generally read from the MINBAR in the mosque on Friday. II 308a

♦ barāʾat al-d̲h̲imma → BARĀʾA

♦ barāʾat al-tanfīd̲h̲ : the consular *exequatur*. I 1027b

♦ barāʾat al-t̲h̲iḳa : diplomatic 'credentials'. I 1027b

barāʿa (A) :

♦ barāʿat al-istihlāl : in rhetoric, the 'skilful opening', an introduction that contains an allusion to the main theme of the work. III 1006a

bāradarī (H) : a term, also applied to Muslim buildings in India, for a hall with twelve adjacent bays or doors, three on each side; ~ was figuratively used to designate 'summer house' as well. V 1214b

baraka (A) : (divine) blessing; in practice, ~ has the meaning of 'very adequate quantity'. I 1032a

In the vocabulary of the Almohads, ~ was used in the sense of 'gratuity which is added to a soldier's pay'. I 1032a

baramis (A, < L *Abramis brama*) : the bream. VIII 1021a

baranta (T) : an Eastern Turkish term, though now regarded as old-fashioned, for ‘foray, robbery, plunder’, ‘cattle-lifting’. I 1037b
Among the nomad Turkish peoples, ~ once represented a specific legal concept involving a notion of ‘pledge, surety’, e.g. the appropriation of a quantity of his adversary’s property by a man who has been wronged, in order to recover his due. I 1037b

baraṣ (A, pl. *abraṣ*) : in medicine, a term used for leprosy, but could be applied to other skin diseases as well. S 271a; and → D̲J̲UD̲H̲ĀM

barastūk → BARASŪD̲J̲

barasūd̲j̲ (A, < P *parastūg*) : the mullet. Variants are *barastūk* and *ṭarastud̲j̲*. VIII 1021a

barata (T) : a special type of headdress, KÜLĀH, of woollen cloth in the shape of a sleeve whose rear part fell on the back, worn by palace domestics in Ottoman Turkey. V 751b

barbā (A, < C *p’erpé* ‘temple’) : name given by the Egyptians to solidly constructed ancient buildings of pagan times. I 1038b

barbūs̲h̲a (B) : a variety of couscous, made with barley semolina. This is called *ṣīkūk* in Morocco. V 528a

barda (A) : in zoology, the pink sea-bream, whose Arabic term is found again in the Latinised nomenclature to specify a sub-species limited to a particular region (*Chrysophrys berda*). VIII 1021a

bardī (A), *warak al-~* and *abardī* : the term for papyrus. VIII 261b; VIII 407b

bard̲j̲īs → MUS̲H̲TARĪ

bārgāh : guy ropes, used to support the Mongol ruler’s large tent. IX 45b

bārgīr-suwār → SUWĀR

barīd (Ass, < L *veredus* / Gk *beredos*) : postal service; post horse, courier, and post ‘stage’. I 1045a; II 487a; III 109b

bāriḥ (A) : a term applied to a wild animal or bird which passes from right to left before a traveller or hunter; it is generally interpreted as a bad omen. I 1048a; ‘that which travels from left to right’, one of the technical terms designating the directions of a bird’s flight, or an animal’s steps, which play an important part in the application of divination known as FAʾL, ṬĪRA and ZAD̲J̲R. II 760a

barḳ (A) : lightning; telegraph. I 573a

barḳāʾ (A), and *abraḳ* : a Bedouin term from the Arabian peninsula denoting a hill whose sides are mottled with patches of sand. I 536b

barmāʾiyyūn (A), or *ḳawāzib* : the amphibian mammals, such as the seal, the walrus, the sea lion etc. VIII 1022b

barnāmad̲j̲ → FAHRASA

barnī (A) : a variety of dates. S 366b

baro (Oromo) : a hymn with alternate verses. IX 399a

barrakān (N.Afr) : a heavy wrap worn by men in Tunisia in mediaeval times. V 745a; a large enveloping outer wrap for both sexes in present-day Libya. V 745b barrānī (A), or *muḍāf* : one of the three main sources of revenue for the Egyptian government in the years immediately preceding the Napoleonic invasion of 1798, ~ were extraordinary taxes, the payment of which was demanded by the *multazim*s (→ MÜLTEZIM) to increase their profits; they were collected regularly despite their illegality. II 148a

barrāz → MUBĀRIZ

bar<u>sh</u>a (A) : a term, used round the South Arabian coasts, for a long, covered boat; also applied to large warships (cf. Ott *barča*, < It *bargia, barza*). VIII 811b

barsīm → ḲATT

bārūd (A, < Ar ?) : saltpetre; gunpowder. I 1055b

barza<u>kh</u> (A, P) : obstacle, hindrance, separation.

In eschatology, the boundary of the world of human beings, which consists of the heavens, the earth and the nether regions, and its separation from the world of pure spirits and God; Limbo. I 1072a

basbās (A), or *rāziyāna<u>dj</u>* : in botany, the fennel (*Foeniculum vulgare*), in North Africa termed *bisbās*, which in the Eastern countries means the red seed-shell of the nutmeg (*Myristica frangrans*). I 214b; S 128b

♦ basbāsa : nutmeg. S 128b

ba<u>sh</u> (T) : head, chief.

♦ ba<u>sh</u> ḳara ḳulluḳ<u>dj</u>u : lit. head scullion; in Ottoman times, an officer's rank in an ORTA, subordinate to that of the ČORBA<u>DJ</u>Ï, or 'soup purveyor'. VIII 178b

♦ **ba<u>sh</u>ï-bozuḳ** : lit. leaderless, unattached; in the Ottoman period, ~ was applied to both homeless vagabonds from the province seeking a livelihood in Istanbul and male Muslim subjects of the sultan not affiliated to any military corps; from this last usage, ~ came to signify 'civilian'. I 1077b; IX 406b

ba<u>sh</u>a (T) : a Turkish title, not to be confused with PA<u>SH</u>A, nor with the Arabic or old eastern pronunciation of it. Put after the proper name, it was applied to soldiers and the lower grades of officers (especially Janissaries), and, it seems, also to notables in the provinces. VIII 281b

ba<u>sh</u>arū<u>sh</u> → NUḤĀM

ba<u>sh</u>ï-bozuḳ → BA<u>SH</u>

ba<u>sh</u>īr (A) : in zoology, the polypterus Bichir. VIII 1021a; and → NA<u>DH</u>ĪR

ba<u>sh</u>maḳlïḳ (T) : a term applied in 16th and 17th-century Ottoman Turkey to fief revenues assigned to certain ranks of ladies of the sultan's harem for the purchase of their personal requirements, particularly clothes and slippers. I 1079b

ba<u>sh</u>tarda (T, < It *bastarda*) : the term for the great galley of the commander-in-chief of the Ottoman navy. The principal types of Ottoman ships in the period of the oared vessels were the *ḳādïr<u>gh</u>a* (< Gk *katergon*) 'galley', the *ḳālīte* 'galliot', and the *firḳate* 'frigate'. Although the ~ was not the largest unit of the fleet, it was a galley larger than the *galea sensile* (T *ḳādïr<u>gh</u>a* or *čektiri*), but smaller than the galeazza or galiass (T *mawna*). I 948a ff.; VIII 565a; VIII 810b

ba<u>sh</u>tina → ČIFTLIK
ba<u>sh</u>wekīl → ṢADR-I AʿẒAM
basīṭ (wa murakkab) (A) : simple (and composite), the translation of Gk απλους and συνθετος. Used as such in pharmacology, in grammar, philosophy and medicine, MUFRAD is found for *basīṭ*, and in logic, mathematics and music, *muʾallaf* is more commonly used for *murakkab*. I 1083b; and → MURAKKAB
In prosody, the name of the second Arabic metre, formed by the two feet *mustafʿilun fāʿilun*. I 670a; I 675a
♦ basīṭa → MIZWALA
basḳaḳ (T) : governor, chief of police. VIII 281a
Among the Mongols, an official whose main duty was to collect taxes and tribute; the commissioners and high commissioners sent to the conquered provinces (or the West only?), notably in Russia. Its Mongol equivalent was DĀRŪ<u>GH</u>A or *daro<u>gh</u>a*. VIII 281a; IX 438a
basmala (A) : the formula *biʾsmⁱ llāhⁱ l-raḥmānⁱ l-raḥīmⁱ*, also called *tasmiya*. I 1084a; III 122b; V 411b
bast (P) : sanctuary, asylum; a term applied to certain places (mosques and other sacred buildings, especially the tombs of saints; the royal stables and horses; the neighborhood of artillery) which were regarded as affording inviolable sanctuary to any malefactor, however grave his crime; once within the protection of the ~ , the malefactor could negotiate with his pursuers, and settle the ransom which would purchase his immunity when he left it. I 1088a
basṭ (A) : in mysticism, a term explained as applying to a spiritual state corresponding with the station of hope, 'expansion'. I 1088b; III 361a; IV 326a
In mathematics, ~ is the part or the numerator of a fraction. IV 725b
baṭāna → <u>DJ</u>ARF
baʿ<u>th</u> (A) : lit. to send, set in motion; in theology, ~ denotes either the sending of prophets or the resurrection. I 1092b
ba<u>th</u>n (A) : on the Arabian Peninsula, a small, deadly but innocent-appearing snake living in the sands. I 541b
baṭīḥa (A, pl. *baṭāʾiḥ*) : marshland, the name applied to a meadowlike depression which is exposed to more or less regular inundation and is therefore swampy. In particular, it was applied in the ʿAbbāsid period to the very extensive swampy area on the lower course of the Euphrates and Tigris, also called *al-baṭāʾiḥ*. I 1093b
bāṭil → FĀSID
bāṭin (A) : in Ismāʿīlī theology, the inner meaning of sacred texts, as contrasted with the literal meaning, *ẓāhir*. I 1099a
♦ **bāṭiniyya** : the name given to the Ismāʿīlīs in mediaeval times, referring to their stress on the BĀṬIN, and to anyone accused of rejecting the literal meaning of such texts in favour of the *bāṭin*. I 1098b
batman (P) : a measure of capacity introduced in Persia in the 15th century, equal

to 5.76 kg. This was apparently the standard weight in most Persian provinces under the rule of the Ṣafawids. VI 120a

baṭn (A, < Sem 'stomach', cf. Heb 'uterus') : in Arabic 'a fraction of a tribe', designating a uterine relationship; in geography, ~ is used in geographical names with the meaning of 'depression, basin'. I 1102a

batr → BAṬṬ

batrāʾ (A) : in early Islam, a term for a Friday sermon, *khuṭba*, lacking the ḤAMDALA. III 123a

baṭrakh : botargo, a fish delicacy like caviar, *khibyāra*, not widely consumed in Arab countries. VIII 1023a

baṭṭ (A), or *batr* : in medicine, an incision (for the removal of morbid matter). II 481b In zoology, a duck. IX 98b

batur → ALP

baʿūḍ (A) : in zoology, the gnat. II 248a; mosquitos. IV 522a

bavik (K), or *mal* : a Kurdish extended family, consisting of a group of houses or household or family in the strict sense of father, mother and children. The union of many *baviks* constitutes the clan, or *ber*. V 472a

bawārid (A) : cooked green vegetables preserved in vinegar or other acid liquids. II 1064a

♦ bawāridiyyūn : makers and sellers of *bawārid*. II 1064a

bawraḳ (A, < P *būra*), and *būraḳ* : natron, sesqui-carbonate of soda. It was found either as a liquid in water or as a solid on the surface of the soil. S 130b; borax. VIII 111b

bay (A, T *beg*) : name applied to the ruler of Tunisia until 26 July 1957, when a Republic was proclaimed in Tunisia. I 1110b; and → BEY

♦ bay al-amḥāl : in Tunisia, the heir apparent to the Bey and head of the army until the advent of the Protectorate. I 1111a

bayʿ (A) : in law, a contract of sale, which is concluded by an offer, **idjāb**, and acceptance, *ḳabūl*, which must correspond to each other exactly and must take place in the same meeting. I 1111a

♦ bayʿ al-barāʾa : in law, a sale without guarantee wherein the seller is freed from any obligation in the event of the existence, in the sale-object, of such a defect as would normally allow the sale to be rescinded. I 1026b

♦ bayʿ al-ʿīna, or *ʿīna* : in law, a 'sale on credit', also known as MUKHĀṬARA. VII 518b; VIII 493a

♦ bayʿ bi'l-istighlāl → GHĀRŪḲA

♦ al-bayʿ bi'l-wafāʾ : in law, a 'conditional sale' of part of the plot of a debtor to the lender, to be nullified as soon as the debt is redeemed. S 322b

♦ bayʿatān fī bayʿa : in law, a double sale, which is a legal device to get around the prohibition of interest. An example is the transaction called MUKHĀṬARA, where e.g. the (prospective) debtor sells to the (prospective) creditor a slave for cash, and immediately buys the slave back from him for a greater amount payable at a future date; this amounts to a loan with the slave as security, and the difference between the two prices represents the interest. III 511b; VII 518b

bayʿa (A) : a term denoting, in a very broad sense, the act by which a certain number of persons, acting individually or collectively, recognise the authority of another person. I 1113a; II 302b; VI 205b

♦ bayʿat al-ḥarb : 'the pledge of war', the name of a promise given to the Prophet at 'the second ʿAḳaba' in 622 by seventy-three men and two women who promised to defend Muḥammad, if necessary, by arms. I 314b; V 995b

♦ bayʿat al-nisāʾ : 'the pledge of the women', the name of a meeting between the Prophet and twelve men from Medina at 'the first ʿAḳaba' in 621 where the latter formally accepted Islam and made certain promises. I 314b; V 995b

♦ **bayʿat al-riḍwān** : the name given to an oath of allegiance exacted by the Prophet from some of his followers during the Medinan period. S 131a

bayāḍ (A) : 'blank book', a technical term in literature referring to a sort of anthology in the form of an informal notebook with poetical fragments. VII 529a

bayaḍ (A), or *bayyāḍ* : a silurus of the Nile, whose Arabic term is found again in the Latinised nomenclature to specify a sub-species limited to a particular region (*Bagrus bajad*). VIII 1021a

bayān (A) : lucidity, distinctness, clarity.

In rhetoric, a near syn. of BALĀGHA 'eloquence'; *ḥusn al-bayān* means distinctiveness (of expression). I 1114a; VIII 614b; and → AL-MAʿĀNĪ WA 'L-BAYĀN

bayāt (A) : a night-attack (of a raiding group of Bedouin). II 1055b

bayḍ al-ḳiṭṭ (A) : 'cat's testicles', in botany, the variety *Astralagus sieberi* of the genus Milk vetch. IX 653b

bayḍa → MIGHFAR

baydaḳ → SHAṬRANDJ

bāyina (A) : a bow which uses too long an arrow, this being considered a fault because it reduces the draw and consequently makes the shot less powerful. IV 798a

bayn (U) : in Urdu poetry, the part of the elegy, *marthiya*, where the martyr's family, the poet himself and all believers are lamented. VI 611b

♦ bayniyya (A) : 'intermediary'; in grammar, a division of consonants in between the occlusive and the constrictive, designating the letters ʿ, *l*, *m*, *n*, *r*, *w*, *y*, *alif*. The term ~ is recent, from 1305/1887; the ancient practice was to say e.g. 'those which are between the SHADĪDA 'occlusive' and the RIKHWA 'constrictive''. III 599a

bayraḳdār (T *bayraḳ*, P *dār*) : 'standard-bearer', under the Ottomans, applied to various officers of both the 'feudal' and the 'standing' army and to certain hereditary chieftains of Albania. I 1134b

bayt (A, pl. *buyūt*) : dwelling; covered shelter where one may spend the night. In pre-Islamic Arabia, the ~ , or *bayt shaʿar*, was a tent of goat's hair and of average size. It served as a dwelling for breeders of small livestock (that is to say, of numerous Bedouin). I 1139b; II 113b; IV 1147a; and → DĀR; ~ may sometimes designate a 'sanctuary'; thus, when used with the definite article, *al-bayt*, or *al-bayt al-ḥarām*, *al-bayt al-ʿatīḳ*, it signifies the holy place at Mecca. I 1139b

In prosody, ~ (pl. *abyāt)* is a line of poetry consisting of two clearly distinct halves called MIṢRĀʿ. I 668a; two hemistichs with between 16 and 30 syllables and a caesura. VIII 583a

In the game of chess, the term for a field on which a chesspiece stands. IX 366b

♦ bayt al-ibra → IBRA

♦ **bayt al-māl** : the 'fiscus' or treasury of the Muslim state. The notion of public as distinct from private ownership and the idea of properties and monies designed to serve the interests of the communities is said to have been introduced first by ʿUmar b. al-Khaṭṭāb; coupled with the institution of the DĪWĀN, it marks the starting point of the ~ as the state treasury. Previously the term designated the depository where money and goods were temporarily lodged pending distribution to their individual owners. In the administration of the later caliphate, the term MAKHZAN seems to have almost replaced the ~ , which reflects the proportionate increase of presentations in kind and the diminution of fiscal receipts in hard cash. I 1141b

♦ bayt al-māldjī (Alg) : the trustee of vacant estates, a member of the council governed by the DEY. I 368a

♦ bayt al-sadjdjāda : in modern Egyptian usage, the central office of a ṣūfī order, serving as the residence and the office of the order's SHAYKH or his senior aide, *wakīl*. VIII 744a

♦ bayt al-ṭāʿa : in Egypt and Sudan, the institution of police-executed enforced obedience of rebellious wives, abolished since the late 1960s. VIII 32a

♦ al-abyāt al-mushadjdjara : in prosody, verses which can be read from beginning to end and from end to beginning. IX 461a

bayṭār (A, < Gk) : veterinary surgeon. I 1149b

bayyāz (A), and *bayyāzī*, *biyāz*, *bāziyy*, *bayzārī* : Spanish-Maghribī terms for hawker, which frequently gave way to *ṭayyār*, or *ṣaḳḳār* 'falconer'. I 1152b

bayyina (A, pl. *bayyināt*) : clear, evident.

In the Qurʾān, ~ appears as a substantive, meaning 'manifest proof'. I 1150b

In law, ~ denotes the proof *per excellentiam*—that established by oral testimony—, although from the classical era the term came to be applied not only to the fact of giving testimony at law but also to the witnesses themselves. I 1150b

bayzara (A, < P *bāzyār* 'ostringer') : the art of the flying-hunt; falconry. I 1152a

bāz (P) : in zoology, goshawk. I 1152a

bāzahr (A, < P *pā(d)-zahr* 'against poison') : bezoar, a remedy against all kinds of poisons, highly esteemed and paid for up to the 18th century. The bezoar-stone, a gall stone, is obtained from the bezoar-goat (*Capra aegagrus Gm.*). I 1155b

bāzār (P, T *pāzār*) : syn. of SŪḲ, in some villages in Afghanistan, ~ is used for the town itself, in its entirety. IX 789a

♦ bāzār-i khāṣṣ : in Muslim India, the market on the principal streets of the city. IX 800b

♦ mīnā bāzār : in Muslim India during the Mughal period, a market in the nature of a fête, arranged in the palace, in which the ladies of the nobles set up shops and the Emperor, along with his queens, made purchases. IX 801a

bāzinḳir (T or P) : slave-troops equipped with fire-arms; a term current during the late Khedivial and Mahdist periods in the Sudan. I 1156b

bazirgan (T, < P 'merchant') : under the Ottomans, ~ was applied to Christian and especially Jewish merchants, some of whom held official appointments in the Ottoman palace or armed forces. I 1157a

♦ bazirgan-bashi : under the Ottomans, the chief purveyor of textiles to the Imperial household. I 1155b

bazr (A) : clitoris. IV 913a

♦ bazrāʾ : a woman who is affected by clitorism, or is believed to be so. An uncircumcised woman is called *lakhnāʾ*. IV 913a

bazz → ḲUMĀSH

bedestān (T), or *bezzāzistān* : the centre of a city's economic life as the place of business of the leading merchants, and the centre for financial transactions, where valuable imported wares were sold. IV 227a

bədʿiyya (B) : in North Africa, a sleeveless vest for men; in Morocco, a sleeveless KHAFṬĀN for women. V 745b

beg (T) : a title, 'lord', used in a number of different ways. Under the Īlkhāns, ~ was sometimes used for women, and under the Mughals the feminine form, *begam* (→ BEGUM), was common. Under the Ottomans, ~ was in wide use for tribal leaders, high civil and military functionaries, and the sons of the great, particularly PASHAS. I 1159a; and → BEY; ULU BEG

♦ **begum** (Ind.P), and *begam* : feminine of BEG, and an honorific title of the royal princesses under the Mughals. I 1161a

♦ **beglerbegi** (T), or *beylerbeyi* : a title, 'beg of the begs', 'commander of the commanders'. Originally designating 'commander-in-chief of the army', ~ came to mean provincial governor and finally was no more than an honorary rank. I 1159b; II 722a ff.

♦ beglerbegilik : a term used for an administrative division in the Ottoman empire until it was replaced by EYĀLET. Thereafter, ~ continued to be used for the office of a BEGLERBEGI. II 722a

bekči (T) : a watchman who, by a decree of 1107/1695, patrolled the quarters, *maḥalle* (→ MAḤALLA), in Ottoman Istanbul with a lantern in his hands and arrested any strangers found there after the bed-time prayer. The ~ became a characteristic figure in the folklore of Istanbul. IV 234b

beledī → ḲASSĀM

bəlgha (B) : flat slippers, usually pointed at the toe, but sometimes rounded, worn by both sexes in North Africa. V 745b belŭk : a vocal art in West Java which marks religious, family and agrarian rites, and which is in the course of disappearing. VIII 153b

belwo (Somali) : in Somali literature, a genre of poetry dealing specifically with the theme of love, developed during the late 1940s and 1950s, which grew into an important vehicle for the expression of nationalist, anti-colonial feeling. A similar genre is *heello*. IX 726a

ben-ʿamma (A) : among the Arabs of Transjordania, a form of agreement, the object of which is to establish a state of peace between tribes. III 389a

bendahara (Mal) : the Chief Minister in Malay sultanates, the highest dignitary after the sultan. He is followed by the PENGHULU *bendahari*, who is responsible for maintaining the sacred traditions, the *temenggung*, responsible for security, and the *laksamana*, the supervisor of the fleet. IX 852a

bender (A) : in music, a sort of big tambourine without bells. IV 382b

benlāk → BENNĀK

bennāk (T, < A *banaka* ?), or *benlāk* : an Ottoman poll tax paid by married peasants possessing a piece of land less than half a *čift* (→ ČIFTLIK) or no land. The former were also called simply ~ , or in full *ekinlü bennāk*. I 1169b; II 32b; and → DJABĀ

ber (K) : the Kurdish clan, formed by the union of many extended families, BAVIK. A collection of ~ constitutes the tribe. V 472a

berāt (T, < A BARĀʾA) : a term in Ottoman Turkish denoting a type of order issued by the sultan. In its more limited sense, ~ meant also 'a deed of grant', 'a writ for the appointment to hold an office'. All appointments throughout the empire, whether that of a high-ranking pasha, even that of the Syrian Church bishops, or that of a low-ranking employee of a mosque, were effected by a ~ . Its constant attribute was *sherif* or *humāyūn* 'imperial'. I 1170a

♦ **berātli** (T) : holder of a BERĀT; a term applied in the late 18th and early 19th centuries to certain non-Muslim subjects of the Ottoman empire, who held *berāt*s conferring upon them important commercial and fiscal privileges. These *berāt*s were distributed by the European diplomatic missions in abusive extension of their rights under capitulation. I 1171b

bərbūkh (Alg) : a variety of couscous, with fine grain, eaten cold, without butter, and moistened with a little milk. V 528a

beshlik → ČEYREK

beste (T) : a vocal composition in four verses each followed by the same melodic passage. IX 876a

bey (T) : var. of BEG, title given to the sons of pashas, and of a few of the highest civil functionaries, to military and naval officers of the rank of colonel or lieutenant colonel, and popularly, to any persons of wealth, or supposed distinction. I 1159a; II 507b; V 631a; the name applied to the ruler of Tunisia until 26 July 1957 when Bey Lamine was deposed and the Republic was proclaimed. I 1110b

♦ beylerbeyi → BEGLERBEGI

♦ **beylik** : a term denoting both the title and post (or function) of a BEY, and the territory (or domain) under his rule. Later, by extension, it came to mean also 'state, government', and, at the same time, a political and administrative entity sometimes enjoying a certain autonomy. In North Africa, the term is used in the former Ottoman possessions, but not in Morocco or in the Sahara, and refers to government and administrative authority at every stage. I 1191a; II 338b
In Ottoman administration, the most important of three offices into which the Ottoman chancellery was divided, the ~ saw to the despatch of imperial rescripts, orders of the viziers, and in general all ordinances other than those of the department of finance. VIII 482a

beza : a type of salt in the salt works near Bilma, in Niger, ~ is in the form of crystals and, not treated in any way, is used for human consumption. I 1221b

bezzāzistān → BEDESTĀN

bhakti (H) : a north Indian movement, sometimes seen incorrectly as a Hindu reaction seeking to strengthen Hinduism against the advancing pressure of conversions to Islam. III 456b

bi-lā kayf (A) : lit. without how, i.e. without specifying manner or modality; in theology, a doctrine taking a central position between those who interpreted the anthropomorphic expressions in the Qurʾān literally and those who interpreted them metaphorically. I 333b

bī-sharʿ (**bīsharʿ**) (P) : lit. without law, i.e. rejecting not only the ritual but also the moral law of Islam; one of the two categories into which dervishes in Persia are divided. The other is BĀ-SHARʿ. The term seems primarily to denote the adepts of the Malāmatiyya ṣūfī sect. I 1239b; II 164b

bīʿa → KANĪSA

bībī (T) : originally, 'little old mother', 'grandmother', 'woman of high rank', ~ was used in Ottoman Turkish in the sense of 'woman of consequence', 'lady', and in 13th-century Khurāsān as a title for women of distinction. I 1197b

bidʿa (A) : innovation, a belief or practice for which there is no precedent in the time of the Prophet. I 1199a; IV 141b

♦ bidʿat (T) : dues in contradiction to the sharīʿa or to Ottoman administrative principles, which nevertheless continued to be levied either by the State or *tīmār*-holders (→ SERBEST), e.g. the *bidʿat-i khinzīr* 'pig-tax' which provided the treasury with a large revenue. II 147a; VIII 486b

♦ bidʿat marfūʿe : in Ottoman administration, pre-conquest taxes and dues that were abolished by the sultan's specific order. VIII 486b

♦ bidʿat maʿrūfe : in Ottoman administration, pre-conquest taxes and dues that were customarily recognized. VIII 486b

bīdār (A) : in Oman and Trucial Oman the official subordinate to the ʿARĪF, the latter being in charge of the water distribution. IV 532a

bīghā : a standard measure of area in Muslim India, divided into twenty BĪSWĀ. The ~ varied considerably by region, with a distinction between a larger

(*pakkā*) and a smaller (*kaččā*) measure. VII 140a
bighā᾿ (A) : the Qur᾿ānic term for prostitution. S 133a
bikāsīn → SHUNḲUB
bikr (A) : a virgin girl. III 17a
billawr (A, < Gk ?) : in mineralogy, rock-crystal. I 1220b
bilmedje (T) : the name given to popular riddles among the Ottoman Turks. I 1222a
bilyūn (Mor), or *gersh* : a coin with the value of a twentieth of a douro or RIYĀL. III 256a
bīmāristān (P) : a hospital; in modern usage, a lunatic asylum. I 1222b
binā᾿ (A) : building, the art of the builder or mason. I 1226a
In grammar, the state of a word that is fixed to one final short vowel or to none at all, and thus the opposite of IʿRĀB. III 1249b
biñbashi̊ (T) : 'head of a thousand'; a Turkish military rank. It appears as early as 729/1328-29 among the Western Turks. Although it was not much used in the regular Ottoman forces of the classical period, it reappeared in the 18th century when it designated the officers of the newly raised treasury-paid force of infantry and cavalry. From the end of the 18th century, it became a regular rank in the new European-style armies. I 1229a; VIII 370b
binish (T) : a kind of very full caftan with wide sleeves, worn most frequently as a travelling or riding garment in the Ottoman period. V 752a; all public appearances of the sultan, whether on horseback or in a boat. VIII 529a
binn : a Druze term denoting one of a number of earlier races or sects, said to have been a group of inhabitants of Hadjar in the Yemen who believed in the message of Shaṭnīl, the incarnation of Ḥamza in the Age of Adam. S 135b
bi᾿r (A, pl. *abyār*) : well; cistern, reservoir; even any hole or cavity dug in the ground, whether containing water or not. I 538b; I 1230a
birdhawn (A) : 'of common parentage', one of four classifications of a horse, usually used for the draught-horse or pack-horse. II 785b
birdjāṣ (A) : during the early ʿAbbāsid period, a kind of equestrian game, in which the contestant had to get his lance-point through a metal ring fixed to the top of a wooden column, thus revealing his skill or otherwise in controlling his horse and aiming his weapon. IV 265b
birindjāsaf → SHĪḤ
birka (A) : an external cistern; fish pond. VIII 816a; VIII 1022a
At Fez and Rabat and in Tunisia, a special (slave) market, existing until well into the 20th century. I 35a
birḳish → ABŪ BARĀḲISH
birr (A) : a Qur᾿ānic term meaning 'pious goodness'. I 1235b; charitable gift. VIII 712a
birsām : in medicine, pleurisy. IX 9b
bīrūn (P) : outside.

In Ottoman Turkish, the name given to the outer departments and services of the Ottoman imperial household, in contrast to the inner departments, known as ENDERŪN. The ~ was thus the meeting-point of the court and the state and, besides palace functionaries, included a number of high officers and dignitaries concerned with the administrative, military, and religious affairs of the empire. I 1236a; II 1089a

bisāṭ (A, pl. *busṭ*, *busuṭ*, *absiṭa*) : a generic term for carpet. S 136a

bisbās → BASBĀS

bīsh → AḲŪNĪṬUN

bīshar' → BĪ-SHAR'

bishṭ (A) : a mantle, jacket, worn by both sexes in Syria and Palestine. V 740b

biṣṣasfalṭus → MŪMIYĀ'

bīswā : a standard measure of area used in Muslim India, divided into twenty *bīswānsā*. In turn, twenty ~ was one BĪGHĀ. The ~ varied considerably by region. VII 140a

bit' (A) : an alcoholic drink consisting of a mixture of honey and wine. The Egyptians used to be very fond of it in mediaeval times. VII 907b

biti (T) : an Ottoman sultan's order, more or less obsolete after 1500. I 1170a

bitikči (T) : secretaries in Mongolian Persia, especially in the military administration, who were especially knowledgeable in Turkish or Mongolian. It was their task to translate into these two languages original documents probably written in Persian, and in 'Irāḳ also in Arabic. I 1248b; IV 757a

biṭrīḳ (A, < L *Patricius*) : patriciate; an honorary dignity, not connected with any office, and conferred for exceptional services to the state. In the history of the Arabs before Islam, only two Ghassānid dynasts, viz. al-Ḥārith b. Djabala and his son al-Mundhir, are known to have received this much coveted Roman honour. The term found its way into Muslim literature, and in the military annals of Arab-Byzantine relations, it became the regular term for a Byzantine commander. I 1249b; V 620a

biṭṭīkh ('ayn) al-nims → NIMS

bīwe resmī (T) : under the Ottomans, the ISPENDJE tax paid by widows at the rate of 6 AḲČEs per person. II 146b

bölük (T) : in Eastern Turkish and in Persian, ~ designated a province or region. I 1256a

In Ottoman Turkey, from the time of the reforms on, ~ designated units of infantry or cavalry of the standing army. I 102a; I 1256a; II 1097b; II 1121a; and → DÖRT BÖLÜK

♦ **bölük-bashi̊** : the title given to the commanders of the BÖLÜKs of the AGHA. The ~ was mounted and had an iron mace and a shield tied to his saddle; when the sultan left the Palace for the mosque, the ~ was present wearing ornate clothes and holding in his hand a reed instead of a spear. I 1256b

börk (T) : the most widespread Turkish head-gear in Ottoman Turkey, the ~ was in a cone or helmet shape, raised in front and decorated at the base with gold braid; officers wore it decorated in addition with a plume. V 751b

boru (T), and NEFĪR : a trumpet without holes which could produce five notes within an ambitus of one and a half octaves. Older *boru*s were apparently made of bronze, but by the 10th/16th century brass was in use. VI 1007b

bostāndji̊ (T, < P **būstān** 'garden') : a term applied in the old Ottoman state organisation to people employed in the flower and vegetable gardens, as well as in the boathouses and rowing-boats of the sultan's palaces. The ~s formed two ODJAḲS 'army units'. I 1277b; IV 1100b

♦ **bostāndji-bashi̊** : the senior officer of the ODJAḲ of the BOSTĀNDJI̊s. As the person responsible for the maintenance of law and order on the shores of the Golden Horn, the Sea of Marmora and the Bosphorus, he used to patrol the shores in a boat with a retinue of 30 men, as well as inspect the countryside and forests around Istanbul. He was very close to the sultan. I 1278b

brīm → ʿAḲĀL; ḤAKW

budalāʾ → ABDĀL

budd (A, P *but*; pl. *bidada*) : a temple, pagoda; Buddha; an idol. I 1283b

būdjādī (A, < *abdjād*) : in North Africa, used for 'beginner', literally, 'one still at the abecedarian stage'. I 98a

budna → SINĀM

budūḥ (A) : an artificial talismanic word formed from the elements of the simple three-fold magic square. The uses of the word are most various, to invoke both good and bad fortune, but by far the most common use is to ensure the arrival of letters and packages. II 370a; S 153a

bughāt (A, s. *bāghī*) : 'rebels', considered by the Zaydīs and Imāmīs as unbelievers, for they rose against a legitimate ruler, but by the Sunnīs as erring Muslims. IX 205a

bughtāḳ : a bonnet worn by Īlkhānid princesses. It consisted of a light wood frame covered with silk, from the top of which protruded a long feather. The ~ could be ornamented with gold and precious stones and sometimes had a long train which hung down behind. V 748b

buhār (A) : in zoology, the diacope, whose Arabic term is found again in the Latinised nomenclature to specify a sub-species limited to a particular region (*Diacope bohar*). VIII 1021a

buḥayra (A, dim. of *baḥra*) : lake. In North Africa, ~ (*bḥēra*) denotes a low-lying plain; its most common meaning, however, is 'vegetable garden, field for market gardening'. I 1288a

In Almohad times, ~ meant an irrigated garden. I 1288a

buḥūr → BAḤR

būḳ (A) : the generic name for any instrument of the horn or trumpet family. I 1290b; a kind of reed-pipe that became quite famous in Western Europe. The original ~ was a horn or clarion, and was made of horn or metal. Pierced with holes for fingering, and played with a reed, the ~ evolved into a new type of instrument, somewhat similar to the modern saxophone. VII 207b

buḳʿa (A), or *baḳʿa* : a region which is distinguishable from its surroundings, more particularly a depression between mountains. I 1292b; a patch of ground marked out from adjoining land by a difference in colour, etc. or a low-lying region with stagnant water. S 154a

In the central and eastern parts of the Islamic world, ~ acquired the sense of 'dervish convent', 'mausoleum' or in general 'a building for pious, educational or charitable purposes'. IX 474b; S 154a

būḳalā (Alg) : a two-handled pottery vase used by women in the course of the divinatory practices to which it gave its name. I 1292b; III 290a

bukhl (A) : avarice, the person who practices it being called *bakhīl* or, less often, *bākhil*. I 1297b

bukht (A, s. *bukhtī*, pl. *bakhātī*) : the species produced as a result of the crossing of two-humped stallions with Arab female camels; it did not breed and was mainly used as a beast of burden. III 665b

būḳīr (A) : in zoology, a kind of bird. I 168b

bukra → GHUDWA

bulbīs (A) : in zoology, the barbel. VIII 1021a

bulbul (A) : in zoology, the Syrian nightingale. I 541b; I 1301a

♦ bulbula → IBRĪḲ

bunbuk → KHINZĪR AL-BAḤR

bunduḳ (A) : the crossbow; in Mamlūk terminology, one of the branches of horse-riding. II 955a

bunīča (P) : in Persia, a group assessment, on the basis of which taxes were levied on the craft guilds. The tax based on this assessment was subsequently allocated among the individual members of the guild. This form of tax was abolished in 1926. II 151b; the right to exercise a trade, given to some guilds, was called *ḥaḳḳ al-~* . IX 645b

būnīt → BALAMĪDA

bunn (A) : in zoology, the carp. VIII 1023a; and → ḲAHWA

♦ bunnī al-Nīl (A) : in zoology, the Nile barbel, whose Arabic term is found again in the Latinised nomenclature to specify a sub-species limited to a particular region (*Barbus bynni*). VIII 1021b

būraḳ → BAWRAḲ

burd → BURDA

burda (A), or *burd* : a wrap of striped woollen cloth produced in the Yemen, before and during the Prophet's time, usually worn by men. I 1314b; III 316a; V 734a

burdj (A, pl. *burūdj*) : a square or round tower, whether adjacent to a rampart or isolated and serving as a bastion or dungeon; masonry pier of a bridge. I 1315a; a moveable tower, used as a siege instrument. III 473a; a pigeon-house. III 109a In astronomy, each of the twelve signs of the zodiac. I 1315a; and → MINṬAḲAT AL-BURŪDJ

In music, ~ denotes a mode. I 1315a
burdjās (A) : a chivalrous duel with lances, an equestrian sport regularly practised in the 6th-7th/12th-13th centuries. II 954a
burghul (A, T *bulgur*) : crushed wheat, considered a dish of the poor. II 1067a
burghūth (A) : in zoology, fleas, diptera of the *pulex* family. IV 522a
♦ burghūth al-māʾ (A) : the water-beetle (*Daphnia pulex*). VIII 1022a
burhān (A) : decisive proof, clear demonstration; a Qurʾānic term signifying a brilliant manifestation, a shining light from God. In correlation, ~ is also the decisive proof which the infidels are called upon to furnish as justification of their false beliefs. I 1326b
In law, ~ refers to the quality of certitude (based upon an argument of authority, which can be either a scriptual text or the eye-witnessing of an obvious fact) which is proper to reasoning 'in two terms', in order to prove the radical distinction between or the identity of two comparable 'things'; it is found especially in al-Shāfiʿī, Ibn Ḥanbal and Dāwūd. I 1326b
In logic, ~ came to designate syllogistic demonstration. I 1327a
būrī (A) : in zoology, the grey mullet. I 168b; VIII 1023a
burḳuʿ (A) : in early Islam, a woman's face veil consisting of a fabric suspended from the centre front of the headband by a string creating a mask-like effect. It is still worn by married women among the Sinai Bedouin. V 735a
burnus (A) : a sort of high cap or bonnet, worn in the Prophet's time. Already this early, the ~ must also have designated by extension a woollen hooded cloak. V 734b
burt (A, < L *portus*) : 'gate', the northeastern border of Muslim Spain, called as such by the geographers, although they differed as to where it lay. I 1337a
būsh (A) : a variety of ʿABĀʾ made in North Syria. V 740b
♦ būshī (A), or *pūshī* : a black face veil worn by women in Iraq. V 740b
būsḥāḳī → FĪRŪZADJ
busht (A) : woollen wraps. IX 765a
busr → TAMR
bussadh (P) : a synonym of *mardjān* 'coral', ~ is strictly speaking the root of the coral as well as the subsoil to which it is stuck. VI 556a
būstān → BOSTĀNDJİ
buṭṭa (A) : a measure used in Egypt for weighing flour. The ~ was equal to 50 Egyptian RAṬLs, i.e. 22.245 kg. VI 119a
buyuruldu (T) : an order of an Ottoman grand vizier, vizier, BEGLERBEGI, *defterdār* (→ DAFTARDĀR), or other high official to a subordinate. A ~ is of two main types: a decision written in the margin of an incoming petition or report, or an order issued independently. It deals with various administrative matters, especially appointments, grants of fiefs, economic regulations, safe-passage, etc. I 1357b
buyūtāt (P) : under the Ṣafawids, the Royal Household, which was divided into a number of offices and workshops. II 335a

būz (A) : snout.

♦ abū būz → ABŪ BŪZ

buzurg → BĀDJ-I BUZURG; SHASHMAḲOM

C

čadirkhäyal (T) : one of two varieties of puppet theatre in Central Asia, a marionette show with full-bodied miniature marionettes suspended and activated from above on strings. VI 765a

čādur → RŪ BAND; SHAWDAR

čahār (P) : four

♦ čahār sūḳ → SŪḲ

♦ čahār tāḳ : the mostly diminutive Sasanian fire temple with four axial arched openings. Set in the midst of a large open space, it served to house the sacred fire. This layout obviously lent itself to Muslim prayer, and literary sources recount how such fire temples were taken over and converted into mosques. The domed chamber, characteristic of Iranian mosques, derives from the ~ . VI 684a

čakȉr (T) : a merlin and falcon, one of the birds of prey making up the traditional sport of hawking at the Ottoman court. The others were the *shāhīn* 'peregrine falcon' and the *atmadja* 'sparrow-hawk'. II 614b

♦ **čakȉrdjȉ-bashȉ** (T) : chief falconer, a high official of the Ottoman court and head of the whole organisation of hawking. II 6a; II 614b

čaḳshīr (T, A *shaḳshīr*) : Turkish-style pantaloons, underdrawers, worn by both sexes in Egypt, Syria and Palestine. V 740b

čālpāra → MUṢAFFAḤĀT

čańdi : a temple of either Hindu or Buddhist intention, ultimately of Indian origin but modified by Indonesian religious concepts. The ~ has been proposed as one of the origins of the basic Indonesian mosque. VI 701b

canḳri : a word used in Laḳ society to designate children of marriages between BAGTALS and women of lower social orders. V 618a

čao (P, < Ch *ṭṣʿau*) : the name given to paper currency in circulation in Iran for about two months in 693/1294. It was made of the bark of the mulberry tree, was oblong in shape, and bore the SHAHĀDA. II 14a

čapar → ALP

čarkhadjȉ → ḲARĀGHUL

čarpāra → MUṢAFFAḤĀT

čarshȉ (T) : in Ottoman times, common term for both individual business locales and covered markets, which may encompass over a hundred shops, contrasting with *pāzār*, an open-air market held once or several times a week. IX 796b

čāshna-gīr (P, A *dhawwāḳ*) : 'taster', the title of an official, generally an AMĪR, at the court of the Muslim sovereigns from the time of the Saldjūḳs. The title does not appear to be found under previous dynasties, although caliphs and princes did undoubtedly have overseers for their food. The term ~ is also found as the name of a kind of crystal decanter. II 15a

♦ **čāshnagīr-bāshī** (T) : 'chief taster', a high official at the Ottoman court. A document dated 883/1478-9 lists 12 tasters as subordinate to the ~ . Later, the number employed rose considerably, reaching as high as 117. By the 18th century, the ~ had clearly fallen in status and had responsibilities more related to the preparation of food. II 15a; an Ottoman court dignitary, whose duty it was to assist the sultan in mounting his horse by holding him under the arm or under the armpit. VIII 529b

čatr (P), or *čitr* : a term used in the Iranian cultural sphere to designate a parasol held over the sovereign and considered as one of the insignia of rank. In this, it is the synonym of the Arabic MIẒALLA. VII 192b; the variant *čitr* gave rise to the Arabicised forms *djitr* and *shitr* which were used in the Mamlūk sultanate. VII 192a

čā'ūsh (T) : officials staffing the various Ottoman Palace departments; low-ranking military personnel. In Uygur, ~ refers to a Tou-kiu ambassador. In North Africa, it is still seen in its Arabic form of *shā'ūsh*, where it means a court usher or mace-bearer. II 16a

Under the ancient Turks, the Saldjūḳs, the Ayyūbids and the Mamlūks, the ~ formed a privileged body under the direct command of the ruler; under the Ottomans, they were part of the official ceremonial escort of the sultan on his departure from the palace or when he had an audience with foreign dignitaries. Their services were also used as ambassadors or envoys by the sultan or his grand vizier. The ranks of ~ and *čā'ūsh wekīlī* were used in the cavalry and the navy at the beginning of the 19th century. After the army reorganisation in 1241/1826, a ~ held the equivalent rank of a sergeant. II 16a

In certain religious sects, the term designates a grade in the hierarchy of the sect. II 16a

čawgān (P) : the stick used in polo. The term is also used in a wider sense for the game itself, which originated in Persia and was generally played on horseback, though sometimes on foot; ~ was also used for any stick with the end bent back, particularly those for beating drums. II 16b

čawk : in Muslim India, a market usually located at places where four roads met. IX 800b

čay (P) : tea, introduced to sultan Mawlay Ismāʿīl in Morocco in ca. 1700; ~ is variously termed *ātāy*, *tāy*, *shāy* and *shāhī*, in different parts of the Islamic world. II 17b

♦ **čāy-khāna** : lit. tea-house, ~ covers a range of establishments in Iran serving tea and light refreshments. The term *ḳahwa-khāna* 'coffee-house' is used synonymously, although coffee is never served. S 169a

čebken → ČEPKEN

čedik (T) : an indoor shoe with a low leg, worn in the Ottoman period. It was most often made in yellow Moroccan leather, with a supple sole. V 752b

čektiri → BAS̲H̲TARDA

čelebī (T) : a term of unknown origin applied to men of the upper classes in Turkey between the end of the 13th and the beginning of the 18th century, as a title primarily given to poets and men of letters, but also to princes and heads of a ṣūfī order; ~ is the most general title of the head of the Mawlawī order of dervishes. II 19a; VI 883a; its Syrian and Egyptian variant, *s̲h̲alabī* or *d̲j̲alabī*, has the meaning of 'barbarian'. II 19a

čepken (T), or *čebken* : a short caftan with sleeves, buckled and bordered, worn as an outer garment in the Ottoman period. V 752a

čes̲h̲me (T, < P) : one of two kinds of water fountains (→ SABĪL) in Istanbul. The ~ is self-service, the water being received from a tap above a basin, while the other, called *sebīl*, is served by an attendant behind a grill. The ~s of Istanbul are mural fountains which consist of a recessed niche framed by a rectangle with a protruding basin, made of carved white marble. II 26a; VIII 682a

čewgān (T) : a crescent-shaped, jingling rattle with bells, one of two types of brass percussion supporting the drum of the musical ensemble MEHTER. VI 1008a

čeyrek (T, < P *čahāryak*) : a quarter of an hour; a coin, also known as *bes̲h̲lik*, or five piastre piece. The silver ~ had a fineness of 830, weighed 6.13 grams and measured 24 mm in diameter. II 28b

čhad̲j̲d̲j̲ā : an architectural feature found in Indian mosques, namely, the eaves pent to throw off monsoon water and increase shade. VI 690b

čhatrī (H, < San, dim. of *čhattra*) : lit. umbrella; an Indo-Muslim architectural form of the *čhattra*, sc. small, canopied structures placed at the junctions of the *chemin de ronde* of a fortification, or as decorative elements at roof level on mosque, tomb or other building, or as simple cover of an inhumation less imposing than a tomb proper. The characteristic form is that of a domed canopy supported on four strong pillars, with heavy protecting eaves. III 442b ff.; VII 195a

čhattra → ČHATRĪ

chêng (Ch) : a Chinese musical instrument which was probably not used by Islamic peoples, although known to them. The ~ was made of tubes of reed joined together. It was blown through a tube and the notes were obtained by fingerholes. VII 208b

chundawand (H) : a custom among Indian Muslims by which the group, being the sons of each wife, is entitled to its allotted portion of the inheritance until the extinction of its last member. I 172a

čift-resmi (T) : the basic land tax in the Ottoman empire paid in principle by every Muslim peasant possessing one *čift* (→ ČIFTLIK). Depending upon the fertility of the soil, it was originally levied in the lands conquered from the Byzantines in Western Anatolia and Thrace, on both Muslim and Christian peasants alike, although in other parts of the empire, the Christians were subjected to a different tax. The *Ḳānūnnāme* of Meḥemmed II specifies that the rate of the tax was 22 AKČES, the equivalent of seven services for the *tīmār*-holder (→ SERBEST). II 32a; VII 507b; VIII 486b

čifte naḳḳāre → NAḲḲĀRA

čiftlik (T, < P *djuft* 'pair' + Turkish suffix *lik*), or *čift* : farm.

In Ottoman times it designated, at first, a certain unit of agricultural land in the land-holding system, and then, later on, a large estate. Originally, it was thought of as the amount of land that could be ploughed by a pair of oxen; it applied to a holding of agricultural land comprising 60 or 80 to 150 DÖNÜMS, the size depending upon the fertility of the soil. In the Slav areas of the Ottoman empire, the term *bashtina* was often substituted for ~ . II 32b

čihra (U) : descriptive rolls for the soldiers of the Indian army, introduced by Akbar to check evasions of military obligations. S 176b

In Urdu poetry, ~ denotes the introductory verses of the elegy, *marthiya*, setting the tone with no restrictions as to details. VI 611b

čile → DEDE

čilla (P, A *al-arbaʿīniyya*) : a quadragesimal fast. I 1122a; forty days of spiritual confinement in a lonely corner or cell for prayer and contemplation; one of the five main Čishtī ṣūfī practices adopted in order to harness all feelings and emotions in establishing communion with God. II 55b; IV 991a

♦ čilla-i maʿkūs : the inverted ČILLA, performed by tying a rope to one's feet and having one's body lowered into a well, and by offering prayers in this posture for forty days. II 55b

čirāgh (T, pl. **čirāghān**) : a means of illumination, such as candle, torch or lamp. *Čirāghān* festivities, in which tulip gardens were illuminated with lamps and candles, were held at a palace on the European side of the Bosphorus of the same name. II 49a

čitr → ČATR

čizme (T) : the most widespread shoes in Turkey during the Ottoman period, with a high leg reaching up as far as the knee and a supple sole. V 752b

çöğür (T) : in music, a variant of the SĀZ 'lute', originally from eastern Turkey and Ādharbaydjān, characterised by a shorter neck and with a total length of about 100 cm. IX 120a

čorbadji̊ (T) : lit. soup-provider; the commander of eight units of infantry or cavalry, BÖLÜK, in the Galipoli ODJAḲ. I 1256a; the title applied among the Janissaries to commanders of the ORTAS and the *agha bölükleri*. The title of ~ was also given to the village notables who entertained travellers. Later, until a half-century ago, it became an appellation of merchants and rich Christians. II 61b; VIII 178b

♦ čorbadj̲ĭ kečesi : the crested headdress generally worn on ceremonial occasions by the ČORBADJ̲Ĭ, also called *ḳalafat*. Its crest was made either of cranes' feathers or of herons' feathers. II 61b

♦ čorbadj̲ĭ yamag̲h̲ĭ : the aide to the ČORBADJ̲Ĭ. II 61b

cot (P) : the pair of oxen used for labour; the work carried out by the peasant in one day. V 473a

čūb-i čīnī (P) : the china root, considered a universal cure, and which the Ṣafawid physician ʿImād al-Dīn stated cured infertility, opium addiction, baldness, rheumatism and haemorrhoids. VIII 783b

čuḳadār (T) : in the Ottoman empire, a valet-de-chambre at the palace. IX 706b

čūl : loess dune. IX 431a

čūpān (P) : 'herdsman, shepherd', a term adopted by Turkish peoples in close contact with the Iranian language-area. II 69a, where also can be found many words, chiefly plant names, in which *čoban* forms a compound

♦ čūpānbegī (P) : a tax on flocks and herds, levied in 9th/15th-century Persia. It was possibly synonomous with ḲŪBČŪR. IV 1042a

D

ḍabb (A) : in zoology, the thorn-tail lizard (*Uromastix spinipes*). II 70a

dābba (A, pl. *dawābb*) : in zoology, any living creature which keeps its body horizontal as it moves, generally a quadruped, in particular, a beast of burden or pack animal: horse, donkey, mule, or camel. II 71a

dabbāba (A) : penthouse, a siege instrument, mainly a Frankish weapon. III 473a ff.; testudine. III 472a

dabbāg̲h̲ (A) : the profession of a tanner. S 172a

dabbūs : in music, a wooden sceptre, to the head of which is attached a number of chains with jingling pieces of metal fixed loosely in the links, used by the dervish. IX 11a

In Mamlūk terminology, *fann al-dabbūs* is the mace game, one of the branches of horse-riding. II 955a

dabīḳī : a type of material, manufactured more or less everywhere but stemming originally from a locality in the outer suburbs of Damietta called Dabīḳ. II 72b

dabīr (P) : scribe, secretary, used as the equivalent in the Persian cultural world, including the Indo-Muslim one during the sultanate period, of the Arabic KĀTIB. The head of the Correspondence ministry in the Dihlī sultanate was called *dabīr-i k̲h̲āṣṣ*. IV 758b; S 173a

ḍābiṭ (A, T *zabit*) : an Ottoman term for certain functionaries and officers; later, officers in the armed forces. Originally, ~ designated a person in charge or in control of a matter or of (? the revenues of) a place. By the 11th/17th century, it was already acquiring the technical meaning of army officer, and in the 12th/18th century, it was in common use in this sense. II 74a

For ~ in the science of Tradition, → ṢAḤĪḤ

ḍabṭ (A) : the assessment of taxable land by measurement, applied under the later Dihlī Sultanate and the Mughals. II 74b; II 155b

♦ **ḍabṭiyya** (A, T *zabtiyye*) : a late Ottoman term for the police and gendarmerie. II 74b

ḍabuʿ (A, < Sem; P *kaftār*, T *ṣirtlan*, B *ifis*), and *ḍabʿ* : in zoology, the hyena. From this generic term, other terms have been derived to differentiate the male, *ḍibʿān* (alongside dhīkh), and female, *ḍibʿāna*. The cub is called *furʿul*. S 173b, where can be found other synonyms

dadjādja (A) : in zoology, the domestic fowl. II 76a

In astronomy, the constellation of the Swan, also called *al-Ṭāʾir*. II 76a

♦ dadjādjat al-baḥr, dadjādjat al-ḳubba : (in local pronunciation, *didjādja*), certain kinds of fish. II 76a

♦ dadjādjat al-māʾ → SHUNḲUB

dadjdjāl (A, < Syr) : lit. deceiver; the personage endowed with miraculous powers who will arrive before the end of time and, for a limited period of either 40 days or 40 years, will let impurity and tyranny rule the world. His appearance is one of the proofs of the end of time. II 76a; IV 408b

dādjin (A) : among the pre-Islamic Arabs, a sheep kept near the house and especially fattened for the table. II 1057b

♦ dādjina → ḲAYNA

dadjr (A), or *dudjr*, *dudjūr* : the wooden cross-beam of the ancient tiller to which the ploughshare was fixed by means of a strap of iron; sometimes the dual (*dadjrān*) can be found, because it was in two parts with one joined to the other by another strap and/or a cord. VII 22a

dafʿ (A) : in law, the reply, and, by extension, every reply made by a party in contradiction of a plea raised by his opponent. II 171b

ḍafāʾir (A, s. *ḍafīra*), or *ghadāʾir* : locks of hair. IX 312a

dafn al-dhunūb (A) : burial of offences; a nomadic practice which consists of a make-believe burial of the offences or crimes of which an Arab is accused. II 248a; IV 407a

daftar (A, < Gk; T *defter*) : a stitched or bound booklet, or register, more especially an account or letter-book used in administrative offices. According to the administrative tradition, Khālid b. Barmak introduced the register into the central administration during the reign of al-Ṣaffāḥ; until that time, records were kept on papyrus, *ṣuḥuf*. I 1090a; II 77b

♦ daftar-i awāridja : a cash-book, showing the balance of moneys in hand, one of the seven main registers on which the Īlkhānid system of book-keeping was based. II 81a

♦ daftar-i derdest : one of the auxiliary registers used in the Ottoman period alongside the DAFTAR-I KHĀḲĀNĪ to note changes, the ~ was a list of the villages or towns constituting the nucleus of the military fiefs and showing the successive changes which each fief had undergone. II 82b

♦ daftar-i idjmāl : one of the auxiliary registers used in the Ottoman period alongside the DAFTAR-I KHĀḲĀNĪ to note changes, the ~ was a summary based on the detailed register, omitting the names of the inhabitants and giving the revenues only as lump sums for each unit. II 82a

♦ **daftar-i khāḳānī** : the collection of registers in which were entered, during the Ottoman period, the results of the surveys made every 30 or 40 years until the beginning of the 11th/17th century, containing primarily lists of the adult males in the villages and towns, their legal status, their obligations and privileges, and the extent of the lands which they possessed, information on the way in which the land was used, and fiscal information with regard to revenues of the country. The ~ cannot be called a land-register; the land-register, in the modern sense of the term, was established in Turkey only from the second half of the 19th century. II 81b

♦ daftar-i mufradāt : a budget register showing the income and expenditure by cities, districts and provinces under the Īlkhānids, one of the seven main registers on which their system of book-keeping was based. II 81a

♦ daftar-i rūznāmče : one of the auxiliary registers used in the Ottoman period alongside the DAFTAR-I KHĀḲĀNĪ to note changes, the ~ was a 'day-book', into which the deeds of grants issued to new fief-holders were copied as they occurred. II 82b

♦ daftar-i taḥwīlāt : an off-shoot of the DAFTAR-I TAWDJĪHĀT, a register dealing with disbursements for stocks and running expenses in state establishments and enterprises under the Īlkhānids, one of the seven main registers on which their system of book-keeping was based. II 81a

♦ daftar-i taʿlīḳ → RŪZNĀMADJ

♦ daftar-i tawdjīhāt : a register of disbursements under the Īlkhānids, one of the seven main registers on which their system of book-keeping was based. II 81a

♦ **daftardār** (P, T *defterdār*) : keeper of the DAFTAR; an Ottoman term for the chief finance officer, corresponding to the MUSTAWFĪ in the eastern Islamic world. The title ~ seems to originate with the Īlkhānids who appointed persons to make and keep the registers. The office of ~ was renamed MĀLIYYE (Ministry of Finance) in 1253/1838, although the term remained in use for provincial directors of finances. II 83a

♦ daftarkhāne : under the Ottomans, the archives of the register-office to which the old registers were consigned each time a new survey was made. II 82b

dāgh u taṣḥīḥa (Ind.P) : a term used in Muslim India for the branding of horses and compilation of muster rolls for soldiers, introduced by Akbar in order to check all evasions of military obligations. V 685b; S 176b ḍag͟hṭa (A) : pressure; in the religious sense, the pressure applied in the tomb by the questioning asked of one's religion. I 187a

ḍaḥāʾ (A) : the period corresponding to the sun's progress over the second quarter of the diurnal arc. It comes to an end at midday. V 709b

dahān band (P) : a face veil consisting of a small, white mask covering only the mouth and chin. It was worn in the Tīmūrid period. V 749a

daḥi : a title in Serbia under the Ottomans, derived from DAYİ. IX 671b

ḍaḥiyya (A) : the name for the animal sacrificed on the occasion of the feast of the 10th day of D͟hu 'l-Ḥid͟jd͟ja. II 213a; in the Negev and other parts of former Palestine, ~ is used synonymously with *fidya* to designate a blood sacrifice made in the interests of the living for purposes of atonement. II 884a

dahnad͟j (A, P *dahna*, *dahāna*, T *dehne-i frengī*) : in mineralogy, malachite, green copper-ore. II 92a

dahol : a Kurdish bass drum which is beaten on both sides. V 478a

dahr (A) : time in an absolute sense. I 2a; infinitely extended time. II 94b

♦ **dahriyya** : holders of materialistic opinions of various kinds, often vaguely defined; philosophers of Greek inspiration. They were called the *azaliyya* by the Ik͟hwān al-Ṣafāʾ. I 128a; II 95a; II 770b

dāʿī (A) : 'he who summons' to the true faith, a title used among several dissenting Muslim groups for their chief propagandists; it became especially important in the Ismāʿīlī and associated movements, where it designated generically the chief authorised representatives of the IMĀM. The title ~ came to mean something different in each of the sects which issued from the classical Fāṭimid Ismāʿīlism. II 97b

ḍaʿīf (A, pl. *ḍuʿafāʾ*) : weak (syn. *waḍīʿ*); unable to bear arms, as opposed to S͟HARĪF. IX 330a

In the science of Tradition, the term for a weak Tradition, along with *saḳīm*, infirm. III 25a; Traditions without any claim to reliability. VIII 983b

In modern South Arabia, the plural form *ḍuʿafāʾ* denotes non-arms bearers, a group comprising builders, potters and field workers. VII 145a; and → MISKĪN

dāʾira (A) : with DUFF, a generic name for tambourine, but reserved for a round type; a round tambourine with small bells attached to the inside of the shell or body, sometimes attached to a metal or wooden rod fixed across the inside of the head. This instrument is popular in Persia and Central Asia. II 621a; and → DAWĀʾIR

♦ **dāʾira saniyya** (T) : the term used in the Ottoman empire during the last quarter of the 19th century for the administration of crown lands. S 179a

dāk͟hil → MUḤALLIL

dak͟hīl (A) : interior, inward, intimate; hence 'guest, to whom protection should be assured' and, 'stranger, passing traveller, person of another race'. II 100a; S 78b

In philology, ~ denotes a foreign word borrowed by the Arabic language. II 100a; VII 261b

In metrics, ~ is a term denoting the consonant preceding the rhyming consonant, the ~ itself being preceded by an *alif*. II 100a; IV 412a

dakka → DIKKA

dalang (Mal, Ind) : puppetmasters. IX 245a

dālāy, or *dala* : a term applied in Īlkhānid Persia to land which belonged to the ruler. The term rapidly went out of use. IV 975b

dalīl (A) : sign or indication; proof. II 101b; the demonstration of that which is not immediately and necessarily known. III 544a

In Medina, the ~ (pl. *adillā'*) is a guide who is responsible for the physical needs of the pilgrim, such as food, lodging and local transport. V 1004a

dāliya (A) : a kind of draw-well still in use in Egypt and other eastern countries for raising water for irrigation. It usually consists of two posts about five feet in height. These posts are coated with mud and clay and then placed less than three feet apart. They are joined at the top by a horizontal piece of wood, in the centre of which a lever is balanced. The shorter arm of the lever is weighted, while at the end of the longer arm hangs a rope carrying a leather pail. The peasant stands on a platform on the river bank and pulls down the balanced pole until the pail dips into the water and is filled. A slight upward push, which is helped by the counterweight, raises the bucket above the irrigation canal, into which it is emptied. V 863b

dallāl (A), or *simsār* : lit. guide; in law, ~ indicates a broker, an agent, 'the man who shows the purchaser where to find the goods he requires, and the seller how to exact his price'. Women are also found taking the part of agents. Known as *dallāla*, they act as intermediaries for harems of a superior sort. II 102b

In the Muslim West, the ~ is exclusively an intermediary who, in return for remuneration, sells by public auction objects entrusted to him by third parties. In the large towns, they are grouped in specialised guilds. II 102b

dallāla → DALLĀL

dallīna → DILLĪNA

dalw (A) : a 'water bucket', in ancient Arabia, said to be made mostly from the hides of two young camels, in which case the bucket may be called *ibn adīmayn*. I 1230a; I 1231b

In astronomy, *al-~* is the term for Aquarius, one of the twelve zodiacal constellations. VII 84a

dam (A, pl. *dimā'*) : blood; blood-guilt. S 188b

In botany, ~ *al-akhawayn* 'the blood of the two brothers' is used for dragon's-blood. IX 808b

dām → PAYSĀ

dāmād (P) : son-in-law, title used by sons-in-law of the Ottoman sultans. II 103a

ḍamān (A) : in law, ~ is the civil liability in the widest meaning of the term, whether it arises from the non-performance of a contract or from tort or negligence. In the sense of suretyship, guarantee, ~ is a liability specially created by contract. In a wider sense, it is used of the risk or responsibility that one bears with regard to property of which one enjoys the profit. II 105a; and → ḲABḌ

ḌAMĀN

In a financial sense, ~ stands for 'farming' (of taxes). The tax-farmer, *ḍāmin*, pays annually to the State a contracted sum, less than the calculated revenue from the tax, and afterwards undertakes its recovery on his own account. The State is assured of a precise and immediate return from the pockets of rich individuals but loses a portion of the money paid by the tax-payer and the control of operations. I 1144b; II 105b; III 323b; and → ḲABĀLA

♦ ḍamān al-adjīr, or *ḍamān al-ṣunnāʿ* : in law, the liability for the loss or damage caused by artisans. II 105a

♦ ḍamān al-**darak** : in law, the liability for eviction. II 105a; the guarantee against a fault in ownership. S 198a

♦ ḍamān al-ghaṣb : in law, the liability for the loss of an object taken by usurpation. II 105a

♦ ḍamān al-mabīʿ : in law, the liability for the loss of an object sold before the buyer has taken possession. II 105a

♦ ḍamān al-rahn: in law, the liability for the loss of a pledge in the possession of the pledgee. II 105a

♦ ḍamān al-ṣunnāʿ → ḌAMĀN AL-ADJĪR

ḍāmin → ḌAMĀN

dāmir (A) : a woman's jacket with short sleeves, worn in Syria and Palestine. V 740b

ḍamīr → MUḌMAR

ḍamma (A) : in grammar, ~ denotes the short vowel *u*. III 172a

dammūsa (A) : on the Arabian Peninsula, the slippery sand-swimming skink. I 541b

damūs : a brick vault. I 207b

dāna-farang (H, < P) : malachite. VIII 269a

ḍanḍī (H) : a simple kind of litter used in India for transporting people. It was essentially a hammock slung from a pole. VII 932a

dānishkada → KULLIYYA

dann, danniyya → ḲALANSUWA

dār (A) : (dwelling place), house. The two words most commonly used to designate a dwelling place, BAYT and ~ , have etymologically quite different meanings. *Bayt* is, properly speaking, the covered shelter where one may spend the night; ~ (from *dāra* 'to surround') is a space surrounded by walls, buildings, or nomadic tents, placed more or less in a circle. II 113b; palace, large dwelling complex. IV 1016b; VIII 344a

In the 5th/11th and 6th/12th centuries in Baghdad and Damascus, ~ was the name borne by the large depots with the name of the commodity for which the establishment was noted. IV 1015a

♦ **dār al-ʿahd** : 'the land of the covenant'; considered by some Muslim jurists as a temporary and often intermediate territory between the DĀR AL-ISLĀM and the DĀR AL-ḤARB. II 116a

♦ **dār al-ḍarb** : the mint, the primary function of which was to supply coins for the needs of government and of the general public. At times of monetary reforms, the ~ also served as a place where obliterated coins could be exchanged for the new issues. The large quantities of precious metals which were stored in the ~ helped to make it serve as an ancillary treasury. I 24a; II 117b; and → ḌARBKHĀNE-I ʿĀMIRE

♦ **dār al-ḥadīth** : a term first applied to institutions reserved for the teaching of ḤADĪTH in the 6th/12th century. Until these special institutions were set up, the teaching of *ḥadīth*, as of other branches of religious learning, was carried out in the mosques. II 125b; V 1129a; S 195a

♦ **dār al-ḥarb** : foreign territory. I 26a; the territories under perpetual threat of a missionary war, DJIHĀD. The classical practice of regarding the territories immediately adjoining the lands of Islam as the ~ and inviting their princes to adopt Islam under the pain of invasion, is reputed to date back to the Prophet. Classically, the ~ includes those countries where the Muslim law is not in force, in the matter of worship and the protection of the faithful and the DHIMMĪs. II 126a; II 131b

♦ **dār al-ḥikma** : 'the house of wisdom', a term used by Arab authors to denote in a general sense the academies which, before Islamic times, spread knowledge of the Greek sciences, and in a particular sense the institute founded in Cairo in 395/1005 by the Fāṭimid caliph al-Ḥākim. II 126b; II 859b; V 1125b

♦ **dār al-ʿilm** : 'the house of science', the name given to several libraries or scientific institutes established in eastern Islam in the 3rd/9th and 4th/10th centuries. The most important ~ was the one founded in Baghdad by the vizier Abū Naṣr Sābūr b. Ardashīr in the last quarter of the 4th/10th century, with more than 10,000 books on all scientific subjects. It was burnt down when the Saldjūḳs reached Baghdad in 447/1055-56. II 127a

♦ **dār al-islām** : 'the land of Islam', the whole territory in which the law of Islam prevails. Its unity resides in the community, the unity of the law, and the guarantees assured to members of the UMMA. In the classical doctrine, everything outside ~ is DĀR AL-ḤARB. II 127b

♦ dār al-kharādj : a brothel, in the Muslim West. S 134a

♦ dār al-maʿārif : schools founded by the Ottoman sultan ʿAbd al-Madjīd I in 1849. I 75a

♦ dār al-mulk : the private quarters of the caliph and his close associates in Muslim Spain. IX 45a

♦ **dār al-nadwa** : the name of a town hall in Mecca in the time of the Prophet. II 128b

♦ **dār al-salām** : 'the abode of peace', a name of Paradise in the Qurʾān; also a name for the city of Baghdad. II 128b

♦ **dār al-ṣināʿa**, or *dār al-ṣanʿa* : an industrial establishment, workshop; the term is always applied to a state workshop, e.g. under the Umayyads in Spain to establishments for gold and silver work intended for the sovereign, and for the manufacture and stock-piling of arms. The most widely-used sense is that of an establishment for the construction and equipment of warships, giving rise to the word 'arsenal' in the Mediterranean languages. II 129b; S 120a

♦ dār ṣīnī → DĀRṢĪNĪ

♦ **dār al-ṣulḥ** : 'the house of truce', territories not conquered by Muslim troops but by buying peace by the giving of tribute, the payment of which guarantees a truce or armistice. The Prophet himself concluded such a treaty with the Christian population of Nadjrān. II 131a

♦ **dār al-ʿulūm** : 'the house of sciences', an establishment for higher instruction founded in 1872 by ʿAlī Pasha Mubārak, whose aim was to introduce students of al-Azhar to modern branches of learning; the religious institutions at Deoband and Lucknow. I 817b; II 131b

darabukka : a vase-shaped drum, the wider aperture being covered by a membrane, with the lower aperture open. In performance it is carried under the arm horizontally and played with the fingers. II 135b

daradj (A) : in zoology, the courser, nearly ubiquitous in the Arabian desert. I 541b

darak → ḌAMĀN AL-DARAK

darb → SHĀRIʿ

ḍarb (A) : in prosody, the last foot of the second hemistich, as opposed to the last foot of the first hemistich, the *ʿarūḍ*. I 672b; IV 714b; VIII 747; and → IṢBAʿ

In mathematics, ~ is the term used for multiplication. III 1139b

For ~ as lithomancy, → ṬARḲ

♦ ḍarb khāne, ḍarrābkhāne → ḌARBKHĀNE-I ʿĀMIRE

♦ ḍarb al-raml → RAML

♦ ḍarb al-sadʿa : shell-divination. VIII 138b

♦ ḍarb al-silāḥ (A) : 'body piercing', one of the deeds transcending the natural order, *khawāriḳ al-ʿādāt,* practiced by the Saʿdiyya order. VIII 728b

♦ ḍarbkhāne-i ʿāmire (T), or *ḍarrābkhāne*, *nuḳrakhāne*, *dār al-ḍarb* : the Ottoman mint. II 118a

dargāh (P) : lit. place of a door; royal court, palace in Persia; in Muslim India, ~ is used to designate a tomb or shrine of a *pīr* (→ MURSHID). II 141b; IV 26a; VI 125b; VIII 954a

darī (P) : the court language, and language of government and literature, in pre-Islamic Persia. II 142a; IV 55a

In India, ~ is used to designate the normal floor-mat, a flat-woven pile-less rug of thick cotton. VIII 742a

dārī (A) : in the mediaeval eastern Muslim world, the perfume merchant. IX 100b

darība : in Muslim India, a short lane or street, usually one where betel leaves were sold. IX 800b

ḍarība (A) : a tax, applied in particular to the whole category of taxes which in practice were added to the basic taxes, ZAKĀT, DJIZYA and KHARĀDJ. Apart from *djizya*, these taxes form the basis of the official fiscal system of Islam and are essentially concerned with agriculture and stock-breeding. II 142b; S 199b; an urban tax on buildings. V 1199a

dāridja (A) : the colloquial Arabic language (syn. *al-lugha al-ʿāmmiyya*). I 561b

ḍarīḥ → ḲABR

ḍarrāb (A) : a minter, one of the craftsmen employed as staff in the mint who carried out the actual coining operation. II 118a

In Muslim Spain, ~ was the term used for night-watchman. I 687b

♦ ḍarrābkhāne → ḌARBKHĀNE-I ʿĀMIRE

dars (A) : lesson, lecture.

In mediaeval usage, ~ meant 'a lesson or lecture on law'. V 1124b

darshan (San) : the (Hindu) ceremonial appearance of a king to his subjects, adopted by the Mughal emperor Akbar and his immediate successors. It was abandoned by Awrangīb in 1078/1668. II 162a

dārṣīnī (A, < P *dār čīnī*) : Chinese cinnamon, *Cinnamomum cassia*, although it cannot be established with certainty with what original plant ~ is to be associated. In pharmacognostic texts *Cinn. cassia* is also rendered by *salīkha*, which allegedly is not identical with ~ . S 197a

dārūgha (P, < Mon) : originally a chief in the Mongol feudal hierarchy, ~ is first met in Persia in the Īlkhānid period. In his main capacities he belonged to the military hierarchy. In Ṣafawid Persia, his functions were sometimes those of a governor of town, but more commonly those of a police officer, his duties to prevent misdeeds, tyranny, brawls, and actions contrary to the sharīʿa. In the 12th/18th and 13th/19th centuries, his function at times superseded even that of the *muḥtasib* (→ ḤISBA). At the beginning of the Constitutional period, most of his duties were taken over by the municipalities and the police force. In some cases, the ~ was appointed to collect taxes or to control certain ethnic minorities; ~ was also used to denote a kind of head clerk controlling the staff of the larger government departments in Ṣafawid Persia. II 162a

In Muslim India, ~ denoted an official in the royal stables; the British used it to designate the native head of various departments and, later, the local chief of police. II 162b

ḍarūra (A), and *iḍṭirār* : necessity; in law, ~ has a narrow meaning: what may be called the technical state of necessity (resulting from certain factual circumstances which may oblige an individual to do some action forbidden by the law), and a wider sense: to describe the necessities or demands of social and economic life, which the jurists had to take into account in their elaboration of the law which was otherwise independent of these factors. The legal schools agree that prohibitions of a religious character may be disregarded in cases of necessity and danger, while most of the offences committed under the rule of necessity are excused without any form of punishment. However, murder, the amputation of a limb, and serious wounding likely to cause death, irrespective of the circumstances, are never excused. The term in its wider sense signifies practical necessity, the exigencies of social and economic life. It takes into consideration the existence of rules and whole institutions in Muslim law which reasoning by strict analogy would have condemned. II 163b

darwa (A) : a typical style of hairdressing used by an Arabic-speaking tribe of Be<u>dj</u>a origin in Upper Egypt with branches in the northern Sudan. I 1b

darwī<u>sh</u> (P) : a mendicant, dervish; a member of a religious fraternity. II 164a

daryā-begi (T), or *deryā-beyi* : 'sea-lord', a title given in the Ottoman empire to certain officers of the fleet, who usually held their appointments for life and transmitted them to their sons. II 165b

da<u>sh</u>t : steppe, e.g. *dasht-i Ḳipčaḳ*, the Ḳipčaḳ Steppe, the great plains of Southern Russia and western Kazakhstan. IX 61a; S 203b

dasim (A) : the quality of foods being oily and greasy, similarly *samīn* 'rich in fats'. II 1071b

dastabān (P, N.Afr *ḳuffāz*) : the glove used by a falconer during the hunt. I 1152b

dāstān (U, P *destān*) : in Urdu literature, a collection of short stories within a 'frame', recited to general audiences as well as to royal courts and rich households. They are the Urdu equivalents of Arab collections like *Alf layla wa-layla* and *Sīrat ʿAntar* and can be considered precursors of modern Urdu fiction. III 119a; III 375b; V 201b

In Turkish literature, the Persian term *destān* is used for the ancient popular epics in syllabic verse, transmitted orally, as well as the first verse chronicles of epic type. III 114b; IX 844a

dastūr (P, A DUSTŪR) : a Persian term which in the period of the classical caliphate came to be used as a synonym of ḲĀNŪN in the sense of 'tax-list'. IV 558a; in the Ṣafawid period, ~ is defined as a Zoroastrian priest who knows the Avesta and the Zand, the Middle Persian literature, and has the authority to command laymen (*behdīn*s) to do religious works. VII 215b

In classical Muslim administration, ~ is a copy of the *<u>dj</u>amāʿa* made from the draft. II 79a

In East Africa, ~ is the term used for custom and customary law, synonymous with ʿĀDA. I 170a

♦ dastūr al-ʿamal : a detailed assessment of revenue, prepared and sent annually by the MUSTAWFĪs of the central government in Persia to the provinces, on the basis of which the provincial *mustawfī*s allocated the tax demand among the provincial population. II 151a

daʿwa (A) : call, invitation; propaganda. II 168a; pretension. IX 432a; and → DAʿWET

In the Qurʾān, ~ is the call to the dead to rise from the tomb on the day of Judgement. II 168a

In the religious sense, ~ is the invitation addressed to men by God and the prophets, to believe in the true religion, Islam. The concept that the religion of all the prophets is Islam and that each prophet has his own ~ , was developed by the Ismāʿīlīs. II 168a

In its politico-religious sense, the ~ denotes the invitation to adopt the cause of some individual or family claiming the right to the imāmate over the Muslims, thus the ʿAbbāsid ~ , which was, strictly speaking, propaganda for a member of the Prophet's family, and Ismāʿīlī ~ , propaganda for the IMĀM, who alone could give mankind good guidance. II 168a

Among the Ismāʿīlīs, ~ is one of nine periods of instruction which completed the initiation of Ismāʿīlī neophytes. II 169b; IV 203b

♦ al-daʿwa al-djadīda, or *daʿwa djadīda* : the branch of Ismāʿīlīs, known as the Nizārīs, who refused to recognise Mustaʿlī after the death of al-Mustanṣir in 487/1094. They are now represented by the Khodjas. II 170b; III 254a

♦ al-daʿwa al-ḳadīma : the branch of Ismāʿīlīs, known as the Mustaʿlīs or Ṭayyibīs, who followed Mustaʿlī after the death of al-Mustanṣir in 487/1094. They are now represented by the Bohoras in India. II 170b

♦ daʿwat : the communal administration of the Yemeni Sulaymānī sect, which split off from the Bohoras in the 10th/16th century. I 1255a

♦ daʿwat-i samāʾ : in the Shaṭṭārī mystic ideology, the control of heavenly bodies which influenced human destiny. IX 370a

daʿwā (A) : action at law, case, lawsuit. II 170b

dawāʾ (A, pl. **adwiya**) : every substance which may affect the constitution of the human body; every drug used as a remedy or a poison. I 212b; gunpowder. I 1056a

♦ adwiya mufrada : simple drugs. I 212b; V 251b; and → ṢAYDANA

♦ adwiya murakkaba : composite drugs. I 212b; V 251b; and → ṢAYDANA

dawādār (P) : the bearer and keeper of the royal inkwell, which post was created by the Saldjūḳs. It was held by civilians. II 172b; secretary. VIII 432a; and → DĀWĀTDĀR

dawāʾir (A, s. DĀʾIRA) : circles.

In the science of metrics, the ~ are the five metric circles used by al-Khalīl for the graphic presentation of the sixteen metres. They are arranged according to the number of consonants in the mnemonic words of the metres which compose them. I 669b

In Algeria, a group of families attached to the service and person of a native chief. Before the French conquest, ~ denoted especially four tribal groups encamped to the south-west of Oran and attached to the service of the BEY of that city. They were organised as a militia. II 172b

dawār (A) : an encampment of the Arab Bedouin in which the tents are arranged in a circle or an ellipse around the open space in the middle where the cattle pass the night. In North Africa, this arrangement is called *dūwār* or *dawwār*. II 174b; S 318b

In Algeria, *douar* has lost its original meaning, and is employed to designate an administrative area, either nomad or sedentary, placed under the authority of the same chief. II 175a

According to Ibn al-Kalbī, ~ is the procession that the Arabs made around the *anṣāb* 'sacred stones', which served as replicas of the Black Stone of the Kaʿba. VIII 155b

dawāt (A) : ink-holder, inkwell; ~ is also used for *miḳlama* 'the place for keeping the pen', and for *ḳalamdān* 'penbox'. IV 471b; V 988b; S 203b

♦ dāwātdār : the keeper of the sultan of Delhi's inkpot or inkhorn. IV 759a; and → DAWĀDĀR

daʿwet (T, < A *daʿwa*) : in the science of Turkish diplomatic, the invocation composed of the formula containing the name of governor (the Bey's name), ranging from the simplest *huwa* to the longest titles. II 314b

dāwiyya (A, O.Fr *devot*) : the Knights Templars, one of the Frankish military orders, known to the Arabs from their experiences with the Crusaders. The Knights Hospitallers, known to the Arabs as *Isbitāriyya*, was another such order. S 204b

dawla (A) : turn, reversal (especially in battle); victory; the reign of the Mahdī. From the middle of the 3rd/9th century, ~ attained the meaning of 'dynasty, state', still in force today. *Al-dawla* is used as the second element in titles; its earliest usage was noted at the end of the 3rd/9th century. II 177b; IV 293b; V 621b ff.

dawm (A) : in botany, the gingerbread tree, a palm which on occasion replaces the date palm in the Gulf. I 540a; the edible fruit of the jujube, called ~ by the Bedouin of Arabia and *kunār* by the townsmen. I 540b

dawr (A, pl. *adwār*) : lit. revolution, period; the periodic movement of the stars.

In shīʿism, ~ is for the extreme sects the period of manifestation or concealment of God or the secret wisdom. S 206b

In music, ~ denotes one of two cycles which make up an ĪḲĀʿ, each of which is composed of several basic notes and a pause. S 408b

♦ dawr al-kashf : 'period of manifestation', the period for the Ismāʿīliyya before the DAWR AL-SATR, during which the twelve angels of the Zodiac kept the unadulterated pure unity of God, *tawḥīd*. At the end of time, the ḲĀʾIM will bring forth a new ~ . S 206b

♦ dawr al-satr : 'period of concealment', the period for the Ismāʿīliyya from Adam to the ḲĀʾIM, the last speaking prophet. A synonym is *al-dawr al-kabīr*. S 206b

dawsa (A) : lit. trampling; a ceremony formerly performed in Cairo by the SHAYKH of the Saʿdī order, consisting of the *shaykh* riding over the members of the order on horseback. It was believed that by such physical contact, the BARAKA of the *shaykh* was communicated to his followers. II 181b; VIII 525b; VIII 728b

dawudu : a land-leasing system in Kurdish Iran, in which the landowner, in return for supplying earth and seed, takes two-tenths of the harvest. V 473b

dawul → ṬABL

dawwār → DAWĀR

ḍayʿa (A, pl. *diyāʿ*) : estate.

In its fiscal context, ~ denotes an estate subject to tithes. The holder of the ~ was not usually its cultivator, and the peasant rents went for the greater part to the holder of the ~ . II 187b

♦ ḍiyāʿ al-khāṣṣa, *ḍiyāʿ al-sulṭān* and *ḍiyāʿ al-khulafāʾ* : the private estates of the caliph in early Islamic times. IV 972b

daydabān (A, < P *dīdebān*) : a term applied at different times to certain categories of sentinels, watchmen, inspectors, etc. II 189a

ḍayf (A) : guest; host, which meaning, however, occurred later. II 189a

dayi (T) : lit. maternal uncle; an honorific title used to designate official functions in the Regencies of Algiers and Tunis. II 189a; title of the Janissary rulers of Algiers, Tunis and Tripoli in North Africa. IX 671b

dayn (A, pl. *duyūn*) : debt; claim; in law, an obligation, arising out of a contract (loan, sale, transaction or marriage) or out of a tort requiring reparation. I 29a; S 207a

♦ dayn fī dhimma : in law, an obligation which has as its object a personal action. S 207a

♦ dayn fi 'l-ʿayn : in law, an obligation which has as its object a non-fungible, determinate thing. S 207a

♦ **duyūn-i ʿumūmiyye** (T) : the Ottoman public debt; more particularly the debt administration set up in 1881. II 677a

dayr (A, < Syr) : a Christian monastery, which continued functioning after the Arab conquest of the Middle East. They were often named after a patron saint or founder but also occasionally after the nearest town or village or a feature of the locality. II 194b

For its meaning in Somalia, → GU'

ḍaywan (A) : in zoology, the Fettered cat (*Felis ocreata*), and also used for the European wild cat (*Felis sylvestris lybica*) and the Sand cat (*Felis margarita*). IX 651b, where are listed synonyms

ḍayzan (A) : a man who marries his father's widow (the marriage is called *nikāḥ al-maḳt*), a practice which the Qurʾān disapproves of. VI 476b

dede (T) : lit. grandfather, ancestor; a term of reverence given to the heads of DARWĪSH communities. II 199b; a member of a religious order resident in one of the cells of the DARGĀH or ZĀWIYA, who has fulfilled his *čile* (period of trial) and been elevated to the rank of dervish. VI 884a

In western Turkish heroic tales, ~ is used for the rhapsodes. II 199b

In Istanbul and Anatolia, ~ was also used as a term of respect for various wonder-working holy men. II 200a

In the terminology of the Ṣafawid order, ~ denoted one of the small group of officers in constant attendance on the MURSHID. II 200a

defter → DAFTAR

deglet nūr → GHARS

deli (T) : 'mad, heedless, brave, fiery', a class of cavalry in the Ottoman empire, formed in the Balkans at the end of the 9th/15th century or the beginning of the 10th/16th century. Later, they were officially styled as *delīl* (guides) but continued to be popularly known by the their original name. Called ~ on account of their extraordinary courage and recklessness, they were recruited partly from the Turks and partly from the Balkan nations. They became brigands in the 12th/18th century and were disbanded in the 13th/19th century by sultan Maḥmūd II. II 201a

demi̊rbash (T) : lit. iron-head; the movable stock and equipment, belonging to an office, shop, farm, etc. In Ottoman usage ~ was commonly applied to articles belonging to the state and, more especially, to the furniture, equipment, and fittings in government offices, forming part of their permanent establishment. II 203b; ~ also means stubborn or persistent, and was applied by the Turks to King Charles XII of Sweden, possibly in this sense or to indicate his long frequentation of Turkish government offices. II 203b

derebey (T) : 'valley lord', the Turkish designation of certain rulers in Asia Minor who, from the early 12th/18th century, made themselves virtually independent of the Ottoman central government in Istanbul. Ottoman historians usually call them *mutaghallibe* 'usurpers', or *khānedān* 'great families'. The best known ~ families are the Ḳara ʿOthmān-oghlu of Aydi̊n, Manisa and Bergama in western Anatolia, the Čapan-oghlu of Bozok in central Anatolia, and the family of ʿAlī Pāshā of Djānīk in eastern Anatolia or Trebizond and its neighbourhood. II 206b

deryā-beyi → DARYĀ-BEGI

destān → DĀSTĀN

devedji̊ (T, P *shuturbān*) : 'cameleer', the name given to certain regiments of the corps of Janissaries. II 210b

devshirme (T) : the term in the Ottoman period for the periodical levy of Christian children for training to fill the ranks of the Janissaries and to occupy posts in the Palace service and in the administration. The earliest reference to the term appears to be contained in a sermon delivered by Isidore Glabas, metropolitan of Thessalonica, in 1395. By the end of the 10th/16th century, the system began to show signs of corrupt practices by the recruiting officers. By the beginning of the 11th/17th century, the ranks of the Janissaries had become so swollen with Muslim-born 'intruders' that frequent recruitments were no longer necessary. The system, however, continued at least till 1150/1738, but sporadically. I 36a; I 268b ff.; II 210b; II 1086a ff.

dey (Alg, < T DAYI̊) : a ruling power in Algeria, who succeeded the AGHAS of the army corps and ruled until the capture of Algiers by France. I 368a; and → DAYİ

♦ deynek (T) : a commander's baton or cane, carried by a number of high Ottoman navy officers. It was also called *ṣadafkārī ʿaṣā*, because it was encrusted with mother of pearl of different colours. VIII 565b

dhabḥ (A) : one of the two methods of slaughtering animals according to Muslim law by which the animal concerned becomes permissible as food. It consists of slitting the throat, including the trachea and the oesophagus (there are divergencies between the schools in respect of the two jugular veins); the head is not to be severed. At the moment of slaughter, it is obligatory to have the necessary intention and to invoke the name of God. Preferably the victim should be laid upon its left side facing in the direction of the ḲIBLA. II 213b

dhabīḥa (A) : in law, a victim (animal) destined for immolation in fulfilment of a vow, for the sacrifice of ʿAḲĪḲA, on the occasion of the feast of the 10th day of Dhu 'l-Ḥidjdja, or in order to make atonement for certain transgressions committed during the ḤADJDJ. II 213a; S 221b

dhabl (A) : in botany, the shell of the tortoise, highly valued for the manufacture of combs and bracelets, *masak*. IX 811a

dhahab (A) : in mineralogy, gold. II 214a

♦ dhahabiyya (A) : a Nile vessel, especially known in the 19th century. VIII 42b

dhakāʾa (A) : the strict ritual of slaughtering the DHABĪḤA which must be followed and which does not differ in form from the ritual slaughter of animals permitted as food. II 213a

dhanab (A) : tail.

In astronomy, ~ or *dhanab al-tinnīn* 'the dragon's tail' refers to the waning node, one of the points where the moon passes through the ecliptic during an eclipse of the moon. V 536a; VIII 101b; and → KAWKAB AL-DHANAB

♦ dhanab al-dadjādja → RADĪF

♦ dhanab al-ḳiṭṭ : 'cat's tail', in botany, the Bugloss (*Anchusa italica*) and the Goldylocks (*Chrysocoma*). IX 653a

♦ dhanab al-sirḥān → AL-FADJR AL-KĀDHIB

dhanb (A, pl. *dhunūb*) : sin. Synonyms are **khaṭīʾa**, *sayyiʾa*, which is an evil action, and *ithm*, a very grave sin, a crime against God. IV 1106b; and → DAFN AL-DHUNŪB

dharāʾiʿ (A) : a method of reasoning to the effect that, when a command or prohibition has been decreed by God, everything that is indispensable to the execution of that order or leads to infringement of that prohibition must also, as a consequence, be commanded or prohibited. I 276a

dharāriḥī (A) : in mediaeval ʿIrāḳ, a vagrant feigning serious wounds for begging purposes. VII 494b

dharra (A) : a term denoting in the Qurʾān the smallest possible appreciable quantity, interpreted by the commentators of the Qurʾān as: dust which remains clinging to the hand after the rest has been blown off, or weightless dust, seen when sunlight shines through a window; the weight of the head of a red ant; the hundredth part of a grain of barley; or atom. ~ was not generally used to denote the philosophical atomism of Democritus, Epicurus and the Muslim 'atomists'. In its stead, the two technical terms DJUZʾ and DJAWHAR *fard* were preferred. Modern Arabic does render atom with ~ . II 219b

dhāt (A) : thing; being, self, ego.

In philosophy, ~ is most commonly employed in two different meanings of substance and essence, a translation of the Greek οὐσία. When used in the sense of 'substance', it is the equivalent of the subject or substratum and is contrasted with qualities or predicates attributed to it and inhering in it. In the second sense of 'essence', it signifies the essential or constitutive qualities of a thing as a member of a species, and is contrasted with its accidental attributes (→ ʿARAḌ). Some Muslim philosophers distinguish, within the essence, its prior parts from the rest. II 220a; V 1262a

In Muslim India, ~ was one of the two ranks into which the *manṣabdār* (→ MANṢAB) was divided, the other being *suwār*. The rank of ~ was meant for calculating one's salary according to the sanctioned pay scale. V 686a

♦ dhāt al-anwāṭ : 'that of the suspended things', among early Muslims, the name for the SIDR tree. IX 549b

♦ dhāt al-ḥalaḳ : an armillary sphere, constructed by ʿAbbās b. Firnās in 9th-century Muslim Spain. I 11b

♦ dhātī : essential; the conceptually and ontologically prior part of the essence of a thing. II 220b; V 1262a

dhawḳ (A) : taste; insight or intuitive appreciation. II 221a; direct experience. II 1041a

In philosophy, ~ is the name for the gustatory sense-perception which, according to Aristotle, is a kind of sub-species of the tactual sense, localised in the gustatory organ, the tongue. It differs, however, from tactual sense because mere contact with skin is not sufficient for gustation to occur. II 221a

In aesthetics, ~ is the name for the power of aesthetic appreciation, something that 'moves the heart'. II 221a

In mysticism, ~ denotes the direct quality of the mystic experience. The metaphor of 'sight' is also often used, but ~ has more qualitative overtones of enjoyment. II 221a

dhawlaḳ (A) : tip (of the tongue). VIII 343a

♦ dhawlaḳī : 'pointed'; in grammar, for al-Khalīl, those consonants that are produced with the tip of the tongue, such as the *r*. VIII 343a

♦ dhawlaḳiyya, and *asaliyya* : in grammar, two terms used by al-Khalīl to indicate articulation with the tip of the tongue but specifying only the form of the tongue. III 598a

dhawwāḳ → ČĀSHNA-GĪR

<u>dh</u>ayl (A, pl. *<u>dh</u>uyūl*, *a<u>dh</u>yāl*) : 'tail', a continuation of a text, simultaneously attached to the work of which it is the 'appendix' and detached from it. IX 158b; IX 603b f.; and → MU<u>DH</u>AYYAL

♦ <u>dh</u>ayl al-ḳiṭṭ : 'long cat's tail', in botany, either the Cat's tailgrass (*Phleum pratense*) or Alfagrass (*Lygeum spartum*). IX 653a

<u>dh</u>iʾb (A) : in zoology, the wolf, and, in local usage, the jackal. II 223a

<u>dh</u>ī<u>kh</u> → ḌABUʿ

<u>dh</u>ikr (A) : 'remembering' God, reciting the names of God; the tireless repetition of an ejaculatory litany; a religious service common to all the mystical fraternities, performed either solitarily or collectively. II 164b; II 223b; II 891b; IV 94b; a discourse. IX 112a

♦ <u>dh</u>ikr al-ʿawāmm : the collective <u>DH</u>IKR sessions. II 224a

♦ <u>dh</u>ikr-i <u>dj</u>ahr : a practice of reciting the names of God loudly while sitting in the prescribed posture at prescribed times, adopted by the Či<u>sh</u>tī mystics. II 55b

♦ <u>dh</u>ikr-i <u>kh</u>afī : a practice of reciting the names of God silently, adopted by the Či<u>sh</u>tī mystics. II 55b

♦ <u>dh</u>ikr al-<u>kh</u>awāṣṣ : the <u>DH</u>IKR of the privileged (mystics who are well advanced along the spiritual path). II 224a

<u>dh</u>imma (A) : the term used to designate the sort of indefinitely renewed contract through which the Muslim community accords hospitality and protection to members of other revealed religions, on condition of their acknowledging the domination of Islam; the beneficiaries of the ~ are also collectively referred to as the ~ , or *ahl al-<u>dh</u>imma*. Originally only Jews and Christians were involved; soon, however, it became necessary to consider the Zoroastrians, and later, especially in Central Asia, other minor faiths not mentioned in the Qurʾān. II 227a In law, ~ is a legal term with two meanings: in legal theory, ~ is the legal quality which makes the individual a proper subject of law, that is, a proper addressee of the rule which provides him with rights or charges him with obligations. In this sense, it may be identified with legal personality. The second meaning is that of the legal practitioners and goes back to the root of the notion of obligation. It is the *fides* which binds the debtor to his creditor. II 231a; S 207a; abstract financial responsibility. I 27a

♦ <u>dh</u>immī : the beneficiary of the <u>DH</u>IMMA. A ~ is defined as against the Muslim and the idolater; and also as against the *ḥarbī* who is of the same faith but lives in territories not yet under Islam; and finally as against the *mustaʾmin*, the foreigner who is granted the right of living in an Islamic territory for a short time (one year at most). II 227a

<u>dh</u>irāʿ (A) : cubit, a basic measure of length, being originally the length of the arm from the elbow to the top of the middle finger. The name ~ is also given to the instrument used for measuring it. One ~ was 24 IṢBAʿ, although the cubit was not always used with great precision and a considerable number of different cubits were in common use in Islam, e.g. the legal cubit, the black cubit, the king's

cubit, and the cloth cubit. II 231b; VII 137b
A minor branch of a river, also called *khalīdj*, as distinguished from the main stream (*ʿamūd*). VIII 38a

dhrupad → BANDISH; KHAYĀL

dhubāb (A) : in zoology, the fly. II 247b

dhubbān (A) : the term used in navigation to designate the standard angular distance of four fingers, IṢBAʿs, wide, i.e. a handbreadth. IV 96b; VII 51a

dhura (A) : in botany, the great sorghum (*Sorghum vulgare*), also called Indian millet, *djāwars hindī*. IV 520a; S 249b

dhurr → ḲAMḤ

dhurriyya (A) : the descendants of ʿAlī, one of a class of noble blood, *sharaf*, that existed in Egyptian terminology of the 9th/15th century. IX 332a

dībādj (A, < P) : silk brocade. III 209b

ḍibʿān → ḌABUʿ

dibdiba (A) : any flat, firm-surfaced area; the term is related to the classical *dabdaba*, referring to the drumming sounds of hooves on hard earth. II 248b

dibs (A) : syrup, molasses; a treacle of grapes, carob, etc. I 69a; II 1062b; IX 804b

ḍidd (A, pl. *aḍdād*) : contrary; one of the four Aristotelian classes of opposites, viz. relative terms, contraries, privation and possession, and affirmation and negation. II 249a; and → AḌDĀD

diffiyya (A) : a heavy winter cloak for men, worn in Egypt. V 740b

diflā (A) : in botany, the oleander. IX 872b

dihḳān (A, < P *dehkān*) : the head of a village and a member of the lesser feudal nobility of Sasanian Persia. They were an immensely important class, although the actual area of land they cultivated was often quite small. Their principal function was to collect taxes. In Transoxania, the term was applied to the local rulers as well as the landowners. The spread of the IḲṬĀʿ system in the 5th/11th century and the depression of the landowning classes diminished the position and influence of the ~ , and the term acquired the sense of peasant, which is its meaning in modern Iran. I 15b; II 253b; V 853b

dihlīz (A) : the palace vestibule where the ruler appeared for public audience. VIII 313b

dīk (A) : in zoology, the cock, of which several kinds (*hindī*, *nabaṭī*, *zandjī*, etc.) are mentioned in the sources. II 275a

dikka (A), or *dakka* : a platform in a mosque near the MINBAR to which a staircase leads up. This platform is used as a seat for the muezzin when pronouncing the call to prayer in the mosque at the Friday service. Mosques of the Ottoman period have their ~ in the form of a rostrum against the wall opposite the MIḤRĀB. II 276a; VI 663a; and → FŪṬA
♦ dikkat al-muballigh → MUBALLIGH

ḍilʿ → DJABAL; SĀḲ; SHAYʾ

dilḳ (A) : the patched garment of ṣūfīs, also worn by clowns. V 740b

dillīna (A, < Gk), or *dallīna* : the flat mussel (*Tellina planata*). VIII 707a; its export as pickled mussels from Rosetta, in Egypt, was mentioned by the mediaeval geographer al-Idrīsī. VIII 438a

dilsiz (T, P *bīzabān*) : lit. tongueless; the name given to the deaf mutes employed in the inside service of the Ottoman palace, and for a while at the Sublime Porte. Established in the palace from the time of Meḥemmed II to the end of the sultanate, they served as guards and attendants, and as messengers and emissaries in highly confidential matters, including executions. II 277a

dīn (A, pl. *adyān*) : religion; the obligations which God imposes on man; the domain of divine prescriptions concerning acts of worship and everything involved in it. II 293b; IV 171b

For ~ as second element in titles, V 621b ff.

♦ dīn al-ḥaḳḳ : a Qur'ānic expression denoting 'the religion of Truth'; the revealed religion; the religion of the golden mean. II 294b

♦ **dīn-i ilāhī** : the heresy promulgated by the Indian Mug̲h̲al emperor Akbar in 989/1581, as a result of his discussions with learned men of all religions, which he vainly hoped would prove acceptable to his subjects. The new religion was related to earlier *alfī* heretical movements in Indian Islam of the 10th/16th century, implying the need for the reorientation of faith at the end of the first millennium of the advent of the Prophet. I 317a; II 296a

dīnār (A, < Gk; pl. *danānir)* : Muslim gold coin issued by the Umayyad caliph ʿAbd al-Malik b. Marwān, to replace the Byzantine *denarius*. There are earlier types of *dīnār*s dating from ca. 72/691-2, but the coinage reform of ʿAbd al-Malik drastically affected the style which it would henceforth have. I 77b; II 297a; V 964a ff.

dirāya (A) : the term used by al-Rāmahurmuzī to distinguish transmissions of Traditions by people who have learned to discern between all transmission minutiae, from those by people who merely transmit without paying proper heed to all sorts of crucial details in ISNĀD as well as contents of Tradition, which he terms *riwāya*. VIII 421a

dirham (A, < Gk) : the name indicates both a weight and the silver unit of the Arab monetary system, used from the rise of Islam down to the Mongol period. II 319a; V 964a ff.; VI 118a

In early mathematics, ~ was the term used for the absolute number. II 361a

dirlik (T) : living, livelihood; a term used in the Ottoman empire to denote an income provided by the state, directly or indirectly, for the support of persons in its service. It is used principally of the military fiefs, but also applies to pay, salaries, and grants in lieu of pay. II 322a; IX 656a

dirrīd̲j̲ (A) : a drum. II 135b; a lute with a long neck and plucked strings. VI 215b

dirṣ (A, pl. *adrāṣ*, *durūṣ*), and *s̲h̲ibriḳ* (pl. *s̲h̲abāriḳ*) : in zoology, the kitten of both wild and domestic cats. IX 651b

dirwa (A) : a typical style of hairdressing, which has given rise to the nickname

Fuzzy-wuzzy, practised by the ʿAbābda tribe of Upper Egypt. I 1b

dīw (P) : the name of the spirits of evil and of darkness, creatures of Ahriman, the personification of sins, whose number is legion. II 322b

dīwān (A) : a register; an office. I 801b; I 1145b; II 323a; IV 937b

In literature, a collection of poetry or prose. II 323a

For a list of *dīwān*s not listed below, II 328b ff.

♦ dīwān al-badal : under the Mamlūks, a special department established to facilitate the exchange of feudal estates of the members of the ḤALḲA against payment or compensation which had become usual after the death of the Mamlūk al-Nāṣir Muḥammad. III 99b

♦ **dīwān-begi** : the title of high officials in the Central Asian k͟hānates in the 16th-19th centuries. S 227b; among the Tīmūrids, the office of secretary of the DĪWĀN or chief of the secretariat of the *dīwān*. VIII 481b

♦ dīwān efendi : in the Ottoman empire, chancellor of the Admiralty. VIII 422a; in the Ottoman provinces, an important official attached to the *wālī*. In Egypt, under Muḥammad ʿAlī, the ~ became a kind of president of the council of ministers. VIII 481b

♦ dīwān raḳamları̊ (T) : term for the SIYĀḲAT numerals, in effect the 'written out' shapes of the numerals in Arabic, reduced to a skeletal and schematised form. IX 693a

♦ **dīwān-i humāyūn** (P) : the name given to the Ottoman imperial council founded by Meḥemmed II after the conquest of Istanbul, which, until the mid-11th/17th century, was the central organ of the government of the empire. II 337b

♦ dīwānī (A) : a form of Arabic script which consisted of letters and particular signs devised from abbreviations of the names of numbers. It was already in use during the ʿAbbāsid caliphate by the army of scribes and accountants working in the Treasury, although according to Turkish sources, the ~ script was allegedly invented for writing official documents and registers of the DĪWĀN-Ī-HUMĀYŪN. *D̲jalī dīwānī* is a variant type of ~ with the letters written within each other. It flourished from the 9th/15th century onwards. I 1145b; II 315b; IV 1125b; VIII 151b; and → TAWḲĪʿ

diya (A), or *ʿaḳl*, *maʿḳūla* : in law, a specified amount of money or goods due in cases of homicide or other injuries to physical health unjustly committed upon the person of another. It is a substitute for the law of private vengeance. In its restricted and most usual sense in law, it means the compensation which is payable in cases of homicide. I 29a; I 171b; I 338a; II 340b; V 180a

diyānay (P) : an ancient type of double reed-pipe. Its two pipes have been described as being of equal length, each of which is pierced by five finger-holes, which gave an octave between them. According to al-Fārābī, the ~ was also called the *mizmār al-mut̲hannā* or *muzāwad̲j*. VII 208a

d̲jaʿāla → D̲JUʿL

d̲jaʿba (A) : a fairly large, leather quiver having a lid fixed by means of a cord, *mik̲h̲d̲h̲af*. IV 799b

d̲jabā (T), or *d̲jabā bennāk* : in Ottoman times, married peasants possessing no land. I 1169b

d̲jābāḍūli (Mor), or *d̲jābāḍūr* : a full-length, caftan-like garment with either no buttons or a single button in front. V 745b

d̲jābāḍūr → DJĀBĀḌŪLI

d̲jabal (A, pl. **d̲jibāl**) : a massive mountain, rocky hillock; other synonyms in common use among the Bedouin in Arabia are *ḍilʿ* (pl. *ḍulūʿ*, *ḍilʿān*), *ḥazm*, which is usually lower than a ~ , *abraḳ* (pl. *burḳān*) and BARḲĀʾ (pl. *burḳ*). Promontories jutting out from the island escarpments are called *k̲h̲as̲h̲m* 'nose' (pl. *k̲h̲us̲h̲ūm*). I 536b; II 534b

d̲jabbāna (A, pl. *d̲jabbānāt*) : a piece of unbuilt land serving, i.a., as a meeting place and a cemetery. V 23a; V 347a

d̲jabbār → DJAWZĀʾ

d̲jabha → SUDJDJA

d̲jābih (A) : 'that which comes from in front', one of the technical terms designating the directions of a bird's flight, or an animal's steps, which play an important part in the application of divination known as FAʾL, ṬĪRA and ZADJR. II 760a; and → NĀTIḤ

d̲jabr (A) : compulsion. I 27b; and → DJABRIYYA

In law, ~ is compulsion in marriage exercised upon one or other of the prospective partners. S 233a

In medicine, minor or simple surgery. II 481b

♦ **al-d̲jabr wa 'l-muḳābala** : originally two methods of transforming equations, later, the name given to algebra, the theory of equations. II 360b

♦ **d̲jabriyya** (A), or *mud̲jbira* : the name given by opponents to those whom they alleged to hold the doctrine of DJABR 'compulsion', viz. that man does not really act but only God. It was also used by later heresiographers to describe a group of sects. The Muʿtazila applied it to traditionists, As̲h̲ʿarite theologians and others who denied their doctrine of ḲADAR 'free will'. II 365a; III 1142b

♦ d̲jabriyyūn : in the writings of the Ik̲h̲wān al-Ṣafāʾ (4th/10th century), the name of the representatives of the branch of mathematics called *al*-DJABR WA 'L-MUḲĀBALA. II 361b

d̲jadal → ADAB

d̲jad̲h̲aʿ → ʿATŪD

d̲jad̲h̲ba (A) : in mysticism, divine attraction. VIII 306b; IX 863a

d̲jad̲h̲īd̲h̲a (A) : in agriculture, wheat husked and crushed. II 1060b

d̲jad̲h̲r (A) : in mathematics, ~ is the term used for the square root. III 1139b

d̲jadīd (A) : new, modern. II 366a

In Persian prosody, the name of a metre of rare occurrence, said to have been invented by the Persians. I 677b

djadwal (A), or *khātim* : in sorcery, quadrangular or other geometrical figures into which names and signs possessing magic powers are inserted. These are usually certain mysterious characters, Arabic letters and numerals, magic words, the Names of God, the angels and demons, as well as of the planets, the days of the week, and the elements, and lastly pieces from the Qur'ān. II 370a

djady (A) : lit. kid; in astronomy, *al-~* is the term for Capricorn, one of the twelve zodiacal constellations. VII 84a; and → SAKHLA

dja'farī → KĀGHAD

djafna → MI'DJAN

djafr (A) : the generic name for an esoteric literature of apocalyptic character which arose as a result of the persecution which the descendants of 'Alī and Fāṭima had suffered. Later, deviating from its original form of esoteric knowledge, reserved for the successors and heirs of 'Alī, it became assimilated to a divinatory technique accessible to the wise whatever their origin, particularly mystics, consisting of speculations based on the numerical value of the Arabic letters. II 375b; IV 1129a; and → SAKHLA

djaghāna (A, < P *čaghāna*) : in music, a jingling instrument of small cymbals attached to a frame, in Europe given the name Chapeau Chinois or the Jingling Johnnie. Another name for it is *zillī māsha*. IX 10a ff.

djāgīr : land given or assigned by governments in India to individuals as a pension or as a reward for immediate services. The holder of such land was called *djāgīrdār*. II 378b; IX 581a

♦ djāgīrdār → DJĀGĪR

djāh (P) : in astronomy, the north pole, used by Islamic navigators of the Indian Ocean. V 543a

djahannam (A) : hell. I 334b; II 381b; and → SA'ĪR

djahbadh (P, pl. *djahābidha*) : a financial clerk, expert in matters of coins, skilled money examiner, treasury receiver, government cashier, money changer or collector. I 1144b; II 382b; the functionary in the Treasury whose task it was to prepare the monthly statement of income and expenditure. II 79b

djāhil (A, pl. *djuhhāl*) : 'ignorant'. Among the Druze, members of the community not yet initiated into the truths of the faith; the initiated are the *'ukkāl*. II 633a

♦ djāhilī : 'pre-Islamic'; in Sayyid Ḳuṭb's book *Ma'ālim fi 'l-ṭarīḳ*, ~ means 'barbaric', 'anti-Islamic', 'wicked', and implies apostasy from Islam, punishable by death. IX 117b

♦ **djāhiliyya** : the term for the state of affairs in Arabia before the mission of the Prophet; paganism; the pre-Islamic period and the men of that time. II 383b

djaḥmarish (A) : a term used for a female hare while suckling. S 84b

djaḥwash (A) : a child who has passed the stage of weaning. VIII 822a

djā'ifa (A) : a wound penetrating the interior of the body; a determining factor in the prescription of compensation following upon physical injury, DIYA. II 341b djaʿīla → DJUʿL

djāʾiz (A) : permissable.

In law, the term preferred by Ḥanafī authors to specify that the juridical act was legitimate or licit, in point of law, apart from its being valid, ṢAḤĪḤ, or not. Other schools also use it to denote the revocability of e.g. a contract. II 389b

In logic, ~ means what is not unthinkable. II 390a

In the vocabulary of tents, ~ is the main ridge piece, which was of considerable importance. IV 1147b

♦ djāʾiza → ṢILA

djalabī → ČELEBĪ

djalālī (P) : the name of an era founded by the Saldjūḳ sultan Malikshāh b. Alp Arslan, called after his title Djalāl al-Dawla, although it is sometimes termed *malikī*; a calendar used often in Persia from the last part of the 5th/11th century onwards. II 397b; VI 275b

In Ottoman Turkish, a term used to describe companies of brigands, led usually by idle or dissident Ottoman army officers, widely spread throughout Anatolia from about 999/1590 but diminishing by 1030/1620. IV 499a; IV 594a; S 238a

djalam (A) : shears. S 319a; a strain of sheep in the time of Djāḥiẓ found in Ṭāʾif, which was very high on its hooves and had a fleece so smooth that it appeared bald. S 318a

djalba (A, < Por/Sp *gelba*/*gelva*) : a large type of barque used by Arabs on the Arabian Sea and Indian Ocean shores. Ibn Djubayr observed that they were stitched together with coir, i.e. coconut palm fibres. VIII 811a

djalī (A), or *djalīl* : a name given to every large type of script, but more specifically used for the large type of THULUTH. It was used for large-sized frames and also for public buildings and their inscriptions. IV 1123b; V 224a

♦ djalī dīwānī → DĪWĀNĪ

djalīl → DJALĪ

djālish (A), or *shālish* : during the Mamlūk period, a special flag hoisted over the *ṭablkhāna* to make known the decision to dispatch a large expedition against a strong enemy. III 184a

djāliya (A, pl. DJAWĀLĪ) : the term used for the Arabic-speaking communities with special reference to North and South America. II 403b; II 470b

djallāb (A) : 'importer', slave-trader. I 32b; I 929a; an outer garment used in certain parts of North Africa, variant of DJALLĀBIYYA. II 404b; sheep merchant. S 316b

♦ djallābiyya : in Morocco and the west of Algeria, a hooded outer robe with long sleeves, originally worn by men only, now by both sexes. II 404b; V 745b; in Egypt, the loose body shirt still commonly worn by men, pronounced *gallābiyya*. V 741a

djallāla (A) : a 'scatophagous animal', mentioned in Tradition and developed in FIḲH with regard to the prohibition of certain foods. II 1069b

djalsa (A), and *ʿanāʾ*, *zīna* : in Morocco, the prevalent system of perpetual lease by WAḲF of dilapidated shops and workshops, whereby the tenant makes the necessary repairs, pays an annual rent and thus acquires the perpetual usufruct of the property. S 369a

♦ djalsat al-istirāḥa : in the Islamic ritual prayer, the return to the sitting position after the second inclination, RAKʿA, which practice is common among the Ḥanbalīs and the Shāfiʿīs, and now also widespread among Mālikī worshippers. VIII 929b

djalṭīṭa → FALṬĪṬA

djalwa → DJILWA

djamʿ (A), or *djamāʿa* : in grammar, the plural for units numbering three or more. II 406b; VIII 990b

djāma-dār → DJAMDĀR

djamāʿa (A) : meeting, assembly.

In religion, the community (of believers). II 411a; the common practices and beliefs of the Companions. II 295a

In North Africa, as *djemaa*, ~ denoted local administrative assemblies, which owned property collectively. II 412b; IV 362a

In Morocco, a tribal assembly of men able to bear arms, which dealt with all the business of the tribe, civil, criminal, financial and political. V 1198b

For ~ in grammar, → DJAMʿ

djamād → MAʿDIN

djāmāhāt (P, < A *djamāʿa*) : among the Shāhsewan in Persia, a community which moved and camped as a unit during the autumn migration in October and the spring migration in May, performing many religious ceremonies jointly. IX 224a

djāmakiyya (A, < P) : salary; originally, that part of the regular salary given in dress or cloth; under the Mamlūks, ~ denoted the part of the salary given in money. II 413b; a grant. IX 269a

djamal (A, Heb *gimel*) : the male camel, sometimes used equally with *ibil* for the species. III 666a

♦ djamal al-baḥr, or *ḳubaʿ* : the humpbacked whale. VIII 1022b

djamalūn (A) : in architecture, a gable roof. I 616a

djamdār (A, < P *djāma-dār* 'clothes-keeper') : 'platoon commander', the lowest commissioned rank in the Indian Army. It also denotes junior officials in the police, customs, etc., or the foreman of a group of guides, sweepers. II 421b

♦ djamdāriyya : under the Mamlūks, the keepers of the sultan's wardrobe. II 421b; VIII 432a

djāmedān (T) : a short, trimmed waistcoat without sleeves, worn as an outer garment in the Ottoman period. V 752a

djāmiʿ (A, pl. *djawāmiʿ*) : mosque; and → MASDJID DJĀMIʿ

In philosophy and science, the plural form, *djawāmiʿ*, is used to denote the compendium or handbook. VII 536b; *djawāmiʿ* is also used for the 'short' recension of Ibn Ru<u>sh</u>d's commentary on Aristotle's works. VII 539a

♦ djāmiʿ al-ḥisāb : the master-ledger of the Īl<u>kh</u>ānids, from which the annual financial reports were prepared, one of the seven main registers on which their system of book-keeping was based. II 81b

djāmiʿa (A) : an ideal, a bond or an institution which unites individuals or groups; university. II 422b; in modern usage, ~ has also been used to characterise a political, united movement; more specifically, ~ signifies the political unification of Muslim states. VIII 359b ff.

djamʿiyya (A, T *djemʿiyyet*; P *andjuman*) : society; association. This term was perhaps first used to refer to the organised monastic communities or congregations which appeared in the Uniate Churches in Syria and Lebanon. In the middle of the 19th century, ~ came into more general use, first in Lebanon and then in other Arabic-speaking countries, to refer to voluntary associations for scientific, literary, benevolent or political purposes. By the middle of the 20th century, ḤIZB had replaced ~ to refer to political movements and organisations. II 428b; III 514b ff.

djammāl (A) : camel-driver or cameleer; also an owner and hirer of camels, and a dealer in camels. S 241b

djamra (A, pl. *djimār*) : pebble. II 438a; tribe. VIII 381a; ~ is the name given to the three places (*al-djamra al-ūlā*, *al-djamra al-wusṭā*, *djamrat al-ʿaḳaba*) where pilgrims returning from ʿArafat during the pilgrimage stop to partake in the ritual throwing of stones. II 438a; III 36a; VIII 379a

♦ djamarāt al-ʿarab : tribes that never allied themselves with others. VIII 120a; the groups of Bedouin tribes. VIII 379a

djamūḥ (A) : in the terminology of horse-riding, a horse that checks its head to escape from control by the hands. II 953b

djamulyān → GÖNÜLLÜ

djāmūs (A, < P *gāv-i mī<u>sh</u>* 'bull-sheep') : in zoology, the Indian buffalo or water buffalo (*Bubalus bubalis*). S 242b

In Algeria, ~ designates women's bracelets carved from the horns of the water buffalo. S 244a

♦ djāmūs al-baḥr : the hippopotamus, to some writers. S 244a

♦ djāmūs al-<u>kh</u>alāʾ : in zoology, the African buffalo (*Syncerus caffer*), called thus by the Sudanese. It was unknown to the Arab writers. S 242b

djanāba (A) : in law, the state of major ritual impurity, caused by marital intercourse, to which the religious law assimilates any *effusio seminis*. II 440b; VIII 929a

djanāza (A) : corpse, bier, or corpse and bier, and then, funeral. II 441b

djānbāz (P, Egy *ganbādhiya*) : an acrobat, especially 'rope-dancer'; soldier; horse-dealer. II 442b

♦ djānbāzān : the name of a military corps in the Ottoman empire, serving only in time of war, in the vanguard, and charged with dangerous tasks. It was abolished towards the end of the 16th century. II 443a

d̲j̲āndār (P) : the name of certain guards regiments who provided the sovereign's bodyguard from the Sald̲j̲ūḳs on. II 444a; V 685a

djandji dalem (J) : 'the royal promise', a term in Java for the TAʿLĪḲ-ṬALĀḲ institution. I 173b

d̲j̲ang (U) : in Urdu poetry, the part of the elegy, MART̲H̲IYA, where the battle is described, with stress on the hero's valour and often including a description of his sword. VI 611b

d̲j̲anīn (A) : the term for the child in its mother's womb; foetus. VIII 821b

d̲j̲ank (A) : in music, the harp. II 1073b; IX 10a

d̲j̲anna (A) : garden; paradise. II 447a

d̲j̲anṭīṭa → FALṬĪṬA

d̲j̲ār → ID̲J̲ĀRA

d̲j̲arab (A) : in medicine, scabies. VIII 783a; IX 902b

♦ d̲j̲arab al-ʿayn → RAMAD ḤUBAYBĪ

d̲j̲arād (A) : in zoology, locusts. For the different stages of the locust's development, Arabic has special names, which, however, are variously defined. II 455a; and → ḲAYNA

d̲j̲arāʾid (Tun) : a pair of men's leather leggings. V 745b

d̲j̲aras (A, pl. *ad̲j̲rās*) : in music, the cup, bowl or cone-shape bell; the sphere-shaped bell was called the *d̲j̲uld̲j̲ul*. ~ also stood for a large bell, *d̲j̲uld̲j̲ul* meaning a small bell. A collection of these bells, on a board or chain, is known as a *ṭabla*. IX 10b f.

d̲j̲ardaḳ (A, < P), or *d̲j̲ard̲h̲aḳ* : a round bread, quite thick and cooked in an oven. V 42b

d̲j̲ard̲h̲aḳ → D̲J̲ARDAḲ

d̲j̲arf (A) : one of a number of terms for a seine or drag-net, i.e. a large pouched net used for fishing on the high seas, also called *d̲j̲ārūf*, *d̲j̲arrāfa*, *ḳaṭṭāʿa* and *baṭāna*. VIII 1021b

d̲j̲arḥ (A) : in law, the contestation that a witness is ʿADL. I 209b

♦ **al-d̲j̲arḥ wa 'l-taʿdīl** : lit. disparaging and declaring trustworthy; in the science of Tradition, a technical phrase used regarding the reliability or otherwise of traditionists. II 462a; VIII 515a

d̲j̲arīb (A) : the basic measure of area in earlier Islamic times, which, as well as being a measure of capacity for grain, etc., equal to four ḲAFĪZS, became a measure of surface area, originally the amount of agricultural land which could be sown with a *d̲j̲arīb*'s measure of seed. The extent of the ~ of area varied widely. Canonically, it was made up of 100 ḲAṢABAS, hence approx. 1600 m^2. VII 138a

d̲j̲arīd (A) : the firm central stem of the palm which, when stripped of the leaf, is used for different purposes. Used in the manner of a javelin, the ~ gave its name to DJERĪD, the well-known equestrian sport so popular in Abyssinia, the Near East and Turkey. VII 923a

♦ **djarīda** (A, pl. *djarāʾid*) : lit. leaf; a usual term in modern Arabic for a newspaper, the adoption of which is attributed to Fāris al-Shidyāḳ (syn. ṢAḤĪFA, usually used in the pl. *ṣuḥuf*). II 464b; S 247a; in Sicily, a document which set out the different legal and social levels, defining the status on the one hand of the people of the countryside, having limited rights, and on the other that of the urban classes. IX 585b

♦ al-djarīda al-musadjdjala : in classical Muslim administration, the sealed register. II 79a

♦ al-djarīda al-sawdāʾ : in classical Muslim administration, the central register of the army office prepared annually for each command, showing the names of the soldiers, with their pedigree, ethnic origin, physical descriptions, rations, pay, etc. II 78b

djāriḥ (A, pl. *djawāriḥ*) : a 'beast of prey', used in hawking. I 1152a

djarīma (A), or **djurm** : a sin, fault, offence; in modern law, the technical term for crime. II 479b

In Ottoman usage, in the forms *djerīme* and *djereme*, fines and penalties. Other prescribed fines were called *ḳinlïḳ* and *gharāmet*. II 479b; II 604a

djāriya (A) : maidservant, female slave. I 24b

djarkh (A, < P *čarkh*) : a crossbow. II 506b; an individual arbalest whose bow is drawn back by means of a wheel (whence its name); by this, very long arrows, approaching the length of javelins, could be fired. IV 798a

djarm → GARMSĪR

djarr (A), or *khafḍ* : in grammar, the genitive case. III 1008a

♦ djarr al-djiwār : a grammatical term denoting 'attraction of the indirect case'. II 558b

djarrāḥ (A) : in medicine, surgeon. II 481b

djarrār (A) : 'he who drags (someone) along'.

In the context of the pilgrimage, ~ is the name given to the few *muṭawwifūn* (→ MUṬAWWIF) who worked outside the special guild. They dealt primarily with pilgrims too poor to hire the services of a bona fide *muṭawwif*. VI 171a

djars (A, pl. *adjrās*) : in grammar, the result of the application of the articulatory organs to the place of the 'cutting', MAḲṬAʿ. III 597b

djasad (A) : body, in particular that of a higher being such as an angel. II 555a

djaʾsh (A) : a light and weak bow which, contrary to the KATŪM, vibrates when loosed. IV 798a

djaṣṣ : gypsum manufactured in the town of Siʿird, which was used in the building of local houses. IX 574b

djāsūs (A) : spy; in particular, a spy sent among the enemy. II 486b

djāti (H) : an Indian musical term for modes, constructed on heptatonic series of notes, *mūrččhanā*. III 452b; caste. III 459b

djawāb → SHARṬ

djawālī (A, s. *djālī*) : lit. émigrés; and → DJĀLIYA

As a fiscal term, ~ came to mean the poll-tax levied on non-Muslims, DJIZYA. II 490a; II 561a

djawāmiʿ → DJĀMIʿ

djāwars (A, < P *gāwars*) : in botany, millet (*Panicum miliaceum*). S 249b

djawarsh (A) : in medicine, a stomachic. IX 805a

djawf (A) : in geography, a depressed plain, sometimes replaced by *djaww*, a basin with a spring well. II 491b; VIII 1048b

djawhar (A, < P) : jewel; atom. II 494b; S 250b

In philosophy, the technical term for οὐσία 'substance'. I 784b; II 493a

djaww → DJAWF

djawwāla (A) : globetrotter. I 116a

djawz (A, < P *gawz*) : the nut in general, and the walnut (*Juglans regia*) in particular. S 264a; the walnut tree. VIII 732b; for many fruits combined with ~ , S 264b

♦ **djawzahar** (A, < P *djawz čihr* 'nut-shape'), *tinnīn*, or *ʿuḳda* (< Gk) : in astronomy, the two opposite points in which the apparent path of the moon, or all planets, cuts the ecliptic. In course of time, these points come to move on to the ecliptic. In texts dating from the 5th/11th century, ~ also indicates the *circulus pareclipticus* of the moon; and the nodes of the orbit of any of the five planets. II 501b; V 536a; VIII 101b; and → FALAK AL-DJAWZAHAR

djawzāʾ (A) : in astronomy, *al-~* is the term for Orion, the stellar figure, replaced by the translators with *al-djabbār*, and Gemini, one of the twelve zodiacal constellations, also called *al-tawʾamān*. VII 83a

djawzal (A, pl. *djawāzil*) : the chick of a sandgrouse, ḲAṬĀ. IX 744b

djayb-i humāyūn (T) : the privy purse of the Ottoman sultans, which contents provided for the immediate needs and expenses of the sovereign. II 502b

♦ al-djayb al-maʿkūs → SAHM

♦ al-djayb al-mustawī → SAHM

djaysh (A) : army. II 504a

In the south of Algeria and Morocco, *djīsh* means an armed band to go out on an ambush, GHAZW, against a caravan or a body of troops. When the ~ consisted of several hundred men, it was called a *ḥarka*. II 509b

In Morocco, *djīsh* (pronounced *gīsh*), denotes a kind of feudal organisation in the Moroccan army. II 509b

djazāʾ (A) : recompense both in a good and in a bad sense, especially with reference to the next world. II 518a

In Ottoman usage, ~ means punishment. II 518a; and → ḲĀNŪN-I DJAZĀʾĪ

For ~ in grammar, → SHARṬ

♦ djazāʾilčī : tribal levy, as e.g. that known as the Khyber Rifles, paid by the government of India for the protection of the Khyber in the late 19th century. I 238a; and → KHĀṢṢADĀR

djazīra (A) : island; peninsula; territories situated between great rivers or separated from the rest of a continent by an expanse of desert; a maritime country. II
523a

Among the Ismāʿīlīs, ~ is the name of a propaganda district. II 523a

djazīza → DJAZZĀZ

djazm (A) : in grammar, quiescence of the final ḤARF of the MUḌĀRIʿ. III 173a

djazz → IḤFĀʾ

djazzār (A) : a slaughterer of camels, sheep, goats and other animals. Today, ~ is
synonymous with *ḳaṣṣāb* and *laḥḥām*, the two terms for butcher, but in mediaeval times, they formed a distinct group of workers. S 267a

djazzāz (A) : a shearer of wool-bearers. The shears he uses are called *djalam* and
the wool obtained *djazīza*. S 319a

djebedji (T) : the name given to a member of the corps of 'Armourers of the Sublime Porte', which had charge of the weapons and munitions of the Janissaries.
The corps was closely associated with the Janissaries, and was abolished together with the latter in 1241/1826. I 1061b; S 269b

djebeli (T), or *djebelü* : an auxiliary soldier in the Ottoman empire, mostly of slave
origin. II 528b; man-at-arms. IX 656b

djedhba → ḤĀL

djerīd (A) : a wooden dart or javelin used in the game of the same name, popular
in the Ottoman empire from the 10th-13th/16th-19th centuries. The game consisted of a mock battle in the course of which horsemen threw darts at one
another. II 532a

djiʿāl → DJUʿL

djidār → LUʾAMA

djiddāba (A) : in zoology, the djeddaba kingfish, whose Arabic term is found again
in the Latinised nomenclature to specify a sub-species limited to a particular
region (*Caranx djeddaba*). VIII 1021b

djidhr (A) : root.
In mathematics, ~ is represented by the area of a rectangle having the side of the
square as its length and the unit as its width. II 360b

djiflik (T, pl. *djafālik*) : land given by Muḥammad ʿAlī and his successors to themselves or to members of their family. S 179a

djihād (A) : an effort directed towards a determined objective; a military action
with the object of the expansion of Islam and, if need be, of its defence. II 64a;
II 126a; II 538a; III 180a ff.; IV 772a; VIII 495a ff.; IX 845b

djild (A), or *adīm* : leather; parchment. Synonyms of the latter meaning are *waraḳ*,
ḲIRṬĀS, **raḳḳ** or *riḳḳ*. II 540a; VIII 407b

djilfa (A) : the nib of a reed-pen. IV 471a

djillāya (A) : an embroidered coat-like outer garment, a wedding costume, worn
by women in Syria and Palestine; in Yemen, a man's marriage caftan. V 741a

djilwa (A) : the ceremony of raising the bride's veil, and the present made by the husband to the wife on this occasion. II 542b

In mysticism, ~ (or *djalwa*) is the name of the state in which the mystic is on coming out of seclusion, KHALWA. II 542b

djimat (Mal) : an amulet, in particular a written one. II 545a

djindār (T) : the second animal in the row of mules forming the caravans that used to operate in Anatolia. IV 678b

djinn (A) : a Qurʾānic term applied to bodies composed of vapour and flame, who came to play a large role in folklore. II 546b; III 669a; V 1101a; and → ʿAMLŪĶ; ḤINN; KHUSS

djins (A, < Gk) : genus; race. II 550a; sex. II 550b

Under the Circassian rule in the Mamlūk period, *al-djins*, meaning the Race, denoted the Circassian race. II 24b

In music, ~ denotes the 'form' of the ĪĶĀʿ, whose metrical patterns were chosen by the musician by modifying the basic notes. The early music schools knew seven or eight forms. S 408b

djirāḥa → ʿAMAL BI 'L-YAD

djirāya (A) : salary, in the terminology of the Azharīs during the Ottoman period; originally, a number of loaves of bread sent daily by the Ottoman sultan to someone. II 413b

djirdjir (A) : in botany, rocket (*Eruca sativa*). IX 653a

djirga (Pash) : an informal tribal assembly of the Pathans in what are now Afghanistan and Pakistan, with competence to intervene and to adjudicate in practically all aspects of private and public life among the Pathans. I 217a; V 1079a; S 270a

djirm (A) : body, in particular the heavenly bodies. II 554b

djirrat (A) : in Čishtī mysticism, a ~ is a mystic who visits kings and their courts and asks people for money. This was considered an abuse, along with the status of a *muķallid* (a mystic who has no master), as contact with the state in any form was not permitted. II 55b

djīsh → DJAYSH

djism (A) : body. II 553b; for synonyms, → BADAN; DJASAD; DJIRM

♦ djism taʿlīmī : mathematical body; a term used by Aristotle in contrast to *djism ṭabīʿī* 'physical body'. II 555a

♦ djismiyyāt : a term employed by Abu 'l-Hudhayl to denote the corporeal pleasures of Paradise. II 449b

djisr (A, pl. *djusūr*) : a bridge of wood or of boats. II 555a; IV 555a

In mediaeval Egypt, the plural *djusūr* is used for 'irrigation dams', of which there were two types: the small irrigation dams (*al-djusūr al-baladiyya*), important for conveying water from one field to another in the village, and the great irrigation dams (*al-djusūr al-sulṭāniyya*), constructed for the provinces. V 862b

djiṣṣ (A) : plaster. II 556b

djitr → MIẒALLA

djiwār (A) : protection of another tribe; neighbourhood. I 429b; I 890b; II 558a; IX 864b; and → DJARR AL-DJIWĀR

djizya (A) : the poll-tax levied on non-Muslims in Muslim states. II 490a; II 559a

djönk (T) : a manuscript collection of folk poetry. VIII 171b

djuʿaydī → ḤARFŪSH

djubba (A) : a woollen tunic with rather narrow sleeves, worn over the shirt, ḲAMĪṢ, by both sexes in the time of the Prophet. V 733b; a coat-like outer garment worn by both sexes today in the Arab East. V 741a; in Tunisia, ~ denotes a full-length, sack-like chemise without sleeves. V 745b; a gown. IX 765a

djubn (A) : a mild cheese; its residual whey is termed *māʾ al-djubn*. S 318b

djudhām (A) : in medicine, leprosy. Other terms for the disease, depending on the symptoms, were *baraṣ*, *bahaḳ*, *waḍaḥ* and *ḳawābī*. S 270b; for more euphemisms, S 271a

djūdī (A) : a large, sea-going ship. III 324b

djuʾdjuʾ → ṢADR

djughrāfiyā (A, < Gk) : geography; in mediaeval Arabic, geography was termed *ṣūrat al-arḍ* or *ḳaṭʿ al-arḍ*, with ~ being explained as 'map of the world and the climes'. The Arabs did not conceive of geography as a science, and the use of ~ for geography is a comparatively modern practice. II 575b

djuhhāl → DJĀHIL

djuhlūl → SHUNḲUB

djūkāndār (P) : an official responsible for the care of the ČAWGĀNs and for the conduct of the game of polo. II 17a

djūkh (A), or *djūkha* : a wide-sleeved coat worn by men in the Arab East. V 741a; a long, woollen outer robe without sleeves or collar which is closed by a single button at the neck worn by men in North Africa. V 745b

djuʿl (A), or *djiʿāl*, *djaʿāla*, *djaʿīla* : in early Islamic warfare, a kind of contract, regarded as degrading, received by mercenary irregulars often drawn from tribal splinter-groups and led by their own chieftains; ~ also served to designate the sum, levied in advance, as insurance against failure to participate in an obligatory razzia. VIII 496b

djuldjul → DJARAS

♦ djuldjulān → SIMSIM

djulla → KABŪSH

djullanār (A, < P *gul-i anār*) : in botany, the blossom of the wild pomegranate tree, also called *al-mazẓ*. S 277a

djumʿa → YAWM AL-DJUMʿA

djumhūriyya → MASHYAKHA

djumla (A, pl. *djumal*) : in law, a term meaning a general Qurʾānic statement made more specific only by a ḤADĪTH which supplies a more precise definition, as opposed to NAṢṢ. VII 1029a

In grammar, a sentence. IX 526a

Its plural form *djumal* denotes a compendium or handbook, especially in grammar. VII 536b

djummār (A) : the pith of the palm-tree, eaten by pre-Islamic Arabs. II 1058b

djund (A, pl. *adjnād*) : an armed troop. Under the Umayyads, ~ was applied especially to (Syrian) military settlements and districts in which were quartered Arab soldiers who could be mobilised for seasonal campaigns or more protracted expeditions. Later, ~ took on the wider meaning of armed forces. II 601a; IX 263b

Under the Mamlūks, ~ is sometimes applied to a category of soldiers in the sultan's service, but distinct from the personal guard. II 601b

For geographers of the 3rd/9th and 4th/10th centuries, the plural *adjnād* denoted the large towns. II 601b; V 125a

djung (P) : lit. boat; an informal notebook with poetical fragments. VII 529a; VII 602a

djūnī → ḲAṬĀ

djunub (A) : in law, a person who is in a state of major ritual impurity. II 440b

djuradh (A, pl. *djirdhān*, *djurdhān*) : a term defining all rats of a large size without distinction of species. S 285b

♦ djuradhān : 'the two rats', the name of the two symmetrical dorsal muscles of the horse. S 286b

♦ djurdhāna : the name of a variety of date, in the Arabian peninsula. S 286b

djuraydī 'l-nakhl (Ir) : 'palm-tree rat', a term used in ʿIrāḳ to designate the ichneumon or Egyptian mongoose, sub-species *persicus* or *auropunctatus*. VIII 49b

djurdjunadjï (T) : a comic dancer. VIII 178b

djurm → DJARĪMA

djurnal (A) : under Muḥammad ʿAlī of Egypt, a 'daily administrative report'; the term was borrowed during the reign of Ottoman sultan ʿAbd al-Ḥamīd I to denote written denunciations. I 64a

djusūr → DJISR

djuzʾ (A, pl. *adjzāʾ*) : part, particle; a technical term used in scholastic theology (*kalām*) and philosophy to describe the philosophical atom in the sense of the ultimate (substantial) part that cannot be divided further, sometimes also called *al-djuzʾ al-wāḥid*. II 220a; II 607b

In prosody, the eight rhythmic feet which recur in definite distribution and sequence in all metres. I 669b

In the science of the Qurʾān, ~ is a division of the Qurʾān for purposes of recitation. II 607b

doʾāb (P) : lit. two waters; in the subcontinent of India, ~ is generally applied to the land lying between two confluent rivers, and more particularly to the fertile plain between the Jamna and the Ganges in present Uttar Pradesh in India. II 609b

dogāh → SHASHMAḲOM

doghandjï (T) : falconer. Hawking was a favourite traditional sport at the Ottoman court. II 614a

dokkali (B) : woollen and cotton wall covers, once a major craftsmanship in Adrar, Algeria. I 210b

dolama (T) : a caftan worn by the least important Ottoman palace servants, which had a long robe, fastened in front, with narrow sleeves. V 752a

ḍōlī (H) : a litter used in India for transporting people. It is a simple rectangular frame or bedstead, usually suspended by the four corners from a bamboo pole and carried by two or four men; when used by women there are usually curtains hanging from the bamboo. The ~ was much used for the transport of sick persons, and in war to carry casualties off the battlefield. A form where the frame is supported on two poles is used as the bier to transport a corpse to the burial-ground. VII 932a

donanma (T) : a fleet of ships, navy; the decoration of the streets of a city for a Muslim festival or on a secular occasion of public rejoicing such as a victory, and, more particularly, the illumination of the city by night and the firework displays which formed part of these celebrations. II 615a

dönüm (T, A *dūnam*) : the standard measure of area in the Turkish lands of the Ottoman empire and the Arabic lands of ʿIrāḳ, Syria and Palestine directly under Ottoman rule until 1918, originally considered to equal one day's ploughing. In Turkey it equalled 939 m^2 (approx. 1,000 sq. yards), but in the 19th century the new ~ was equated with the hectare; in 1934 the metric system of weights and measures was officially adopted by the Turkish Republic. In Syria and Palestine in recent times, the ~ is 1,000 m^2 = 0.247 acres, while in Iraq a larger ~ of 2,500 m^2 is used, despite the official adoption of the metric system in 1931. II 32b; VII 138a

dört (T) : four.

♦ dört bölük , or *bölükat-i erbaʿa* : a collective name for the four lowest cavalry regiments of the ḲAPÎ ḲULLARÎ. They were regarded as inferior in comparison to the remaining two higher divisions, the *sipāhī og͟hlanlarî* and the *silāḥdārlar*. II 1097b

♦ dörtlük : in Turkish prosody, a strophe consisting of four lines, hence synonymous with the term RUBĀʿĪ in its broader sense. VIII 580b

duʿā' (A, pl. *adʿiya*) : appeal, invocation (addressed to God) either on behalf of another or for oneself, or against someone; hence, prayer of invocation. II 617a
In the science of diplomatic, ~ is the formula of benediction for the addressee. II 302a; II 314b
In poetry, ~ is the sixth and final section of a ḲAṢĪDA, wherein the poet implores God for the prosperity of the sultan or person to whom the poem is addressed and expresses his thanks for the completion of the work. IV 715b; V 956b; V 960a

♦ duʿāk͟hʷān → BĀK͟HS͟HĪ

dūbaytī → RUBĀʿĪ

dubb al-baḥr (A) : in zoology, the sea lion, also called *asad al-baḥr* and *baḳrat al-baḥr*. VIII 1022b

dubbāʾ → ḲUTHTHĀʾ

duḏjr → DADJR

duḏjūr → DADJR

duff (A) : in music, the generic term for any instrument of the tambourine family. II 620a

ḍuḥā (A) : 'forenoon', the first part of the day, up to the moment when the sun has traversed a quarter of the diurnal arc. II 622b; V 709b

♦ ṣalāt al-ḍuḥā : a sixth prayer performed in some circles, on top of the five compulsory prayers, at the same time before midday as the ʿAṣR was performed after midday. VII 28a

duhn (A) : oil

♦ duhn al-ḥall (A), or ṣalīṭ ḏjulḏjulān, shīraḏj (P shīra) : the greasy oil of sesame. IX 615a

dūka (Tun) : a pointed bonnet for women. V 745b

dukhn (A) : in botany, the small sorghum (*Pennisetum spicatum*) widespread in the Sudan and also called Moorish millct. S 249b

dukmak (A) : in zoology, a silurus of the Nile, the Euphrates and the Niger, whose Arabic term is found again in the Latinised nomenclature to specify a sub-species limited to a particular region (*Bagrus docmac*). VIII 1021b

dūm (A) : in botany, jujube-like fruits of the *Ziziphus* trees, highly valued for food. IX 549a

duʿmūṣ (A) : the maggot. VIII 1022a

dūnam → DÖNÜM

dunyā (A) : lit. nearer, nearest; in theology, this (base) world, as opposed to DĪN and the correlative ĀKHIRA. II 295a; II 626b

durāb (A) : in zoology, the chirocentrus, whose Arabic term is found again in the Latinised nomenclature to specify a sub-species limited to a particular region (*Chirocentrus dorab*). VIII 1021b

durāda (A, < Sp *dorado*) : in zoology, the goldfish (*Sparus aurata*). VIII 1021a

durar → DURR

dūrbāsh (P) : lit. be distant; the mace or club used as an emblem of military dignity, and in Persian and Turkish usage, the functionary who carries the mace. II 627b

durḳāʿa → ḲĀʿA

durr (A), or *durar* : pearl. II 628a; artistic poetry of high quality. IX 448b; and → LUʾLUʾ

durrāʿa (A) : in Syria and Palestine, a woman's outer coat, open in front, sometimes synonymous with DJUBBA. V 741a; in North Africa, a long robe with sleeves for both sexes. V 746a

dūshāb (P) : in the mediaeval Near East, a drink from syrup or from preserves of fruit which is sometimes non-alcoholic, but which is frequently mentioned in the context of drinks which can ferment and become alcoholic. VI 720b

dūshākh (P) : a crown-like hat with a pointed rim on either side, worn by men of high rank in Saldjūḳ Persia and of Inner Asian, Turkish origin. V 748a

dustūr (A) : originally from Persian, ~ seems originally to have meant a person exercising authority, whether religious or political. Later, ~ acquired a specialised meaning, designating members of the Zoroastrian priesthood. The word occurs in *Kalīla wa-dimna* in the sense of 'counsellor'. More commonly it was used in the sense of rule or regulation, and in particular the code of rules and conduct of the guilds. In Arabic, ~ was employed in a variety of meanings, notably 'army pay-list', 'model or formulary', 'leave', and also, addressed to a human being or to invisible DJINN, 'permission'. In modern Arabic, ~ means constitution. II 638a; and → DASTŪR

Under the Ayyūbids, ~ meant a legal release from a campaign. The term gradually died out in the period of the Mamlūks. III 186b

♦ düstūr (T) : principle, precedent, code or register of rules; applied in particular to the great series of volumes, containing the texts of new laws, published in Istanbul (and later Ankara) from 1279/1863 onwards. II 640a

♦ dustūr-i mükerrem (T) : one of the honorific titles of the grand vizier of the Ottoman empire. II 638a

dūtār : an indigenous Özbeg two-stringed instrument. VIII 234b

dūwār → DAWĀR

duyūn → DAYN

duzale : a Kurdish flute with two pipes of reed or bird bone, pierced with holes and whose mouthpiece has a kind of vibratory tongue. The sound resembles that of the Scottish bagpipes. V 478a

düzen (T) : in music, the tunings [of the lute]. IX 120b

E

efendi (T, < Gk) : an Ottoman title, already in use in the 7th/13th and 8th/14th centuries in Turkish Anatolia. A 16th-century FATWĀ applied the term to the owner of slaves and slave-girls. Later, ~ became increasingly common in Ottoman usage as a designation of members of the scribal and religious, as opposed to the military, classes, in particular of certain important functionaries. During the 13th/19th century, although the Ottoman government made attempts to regulate the use of the term by law, ~ was used, following the personal name, as a form of address or reference for persons possessing a certain standard of literacy, and not styled BEY or PASHA; ~ thus became an approximate equivalent of the English mister or French monsieur. In 1934 it was finally abolished, but has remained in common use as a form of address for both men and women. I 75a; II 687a

eflāḳ (T, < Ger *Wallach*) : under the Ottomans, ~ denoted the Balkan Rumanians and those north of the Danube. II 687b; II 915a

efsane (T, < P *afsāna*) : legend; completely fantastic story, fabricated or superstitious. III 373b

elči (T) : envoy, messenger; in Ottoman diplomacy, the normal word for ambassador, although *sefīr* (< A SAFĪR) was used. II 694a; and → MAṢLAḤATGÜZĀR; SAFĪR

In eastern Turkish, ruler of a land or people. II 694a

elifi nemed (T) : a woollen initiatic girdle, worn by the Mewlewīs, so called because with its tapering end when laid out flat, it resembled the letter *alif*. They also wore a second type of woollen girdle, the *tīghbend*, during their dance, in order to hold in place the ample skirt of the garment known as the TENNŪRE. IX 167b

emānet (T) : the function or office of an EMĪN. II 695b; the system of collection of MUḲĀṬAʿA revenues directly by the *emīn*. II 147b

♦ **emānet-i muḳadesse** : the name given to a collection of relics preserved in the treasury of the Topkapı palace in Instanbul. II 695b

♦ emāneten : one of three principal ways in which mining activity was organised in the Ottoman empire, the others being ILTIZĀMEN and IḤĀLE; ~ meant the direct administration of mines or mining districts through state-appointed superintendents. V 974b

emīn (T, < A AMĪN) : an Ottoman administrative title usually translated intendant or commissioner. Primarily, an ~ was a salaried officer appointed by or in the name of the sultan, to administer, supervise or control a department, function or source of revenue. The term is used also of agents and commissioners appointed by authorities other than the sultan, and at times, by abuse, the ~ appears as tax-farmer. II 695b

emr (T, < A AMR) : a term denoting a general order issued in the name of the Ottoman sultan, as well as a special order which decreed the issue of a BERĀT. I 1170a

enderūn (T) : inside.

Under the Ottomans, ~ was used to designate the inside service (as opposed to BĪRŪN, the outside service) of the imperial household of the Ottoman sultan, comprising four departments, viz. the Privy Chamber, the Treasury, the Privy Larder, and the Great and Little Chambers. II 697b; IV 1097a

entārī (T) : a kind of caftan, worn in the Ottoman period under the real caftan and fur, descending as far as the ankle or covering the knee. V 752a

enzel (Tun, < A **inzāl**) : in law, a perpetual lease system found not only on ‘habous’ (inalienable property, the yield of which is devoted to pious purposes) but also on private, *mulk*, properties, peculiar to Tunisia. S 369a; S 423a eshām (T, < A **ashām**, s. *sahm* 'share') : the word used in Turkey to designate certain treasury issues, variously described as bonds, assignats and annuities. Although the ~ reverted to the state on the death of the holder, they could be sold, the state claiming a duty of one year's income on each such transfer. The ~ were introduced in the early years of the reign of Muṣṭafā III and the practice was continued by later sultans; their purpose and names varied from time to time. I 692b

es͟hkind͟ji (T), or *es͟hkünd͟ji* : a term in the Ottoman army denoting in general a soldier who joined the army on an expedition. As a special term, ~ designated auxiliary soldiers whose expenses were provided by the people of peasant, *reʿāyā* (→ RAʿIYYA), status. From the mid 10th/16th century, the ~ lost importance and gradually disappeared. II 714b

esrār : a pandore viol from India, with the TĀWŪS one of the two best-known examples. The ~ has a membrane on its face and has five strings played with the bow together with a number of sympathetic strings. VIII 348b

eyālet (T, < A *iyāla*) : in the Ottoman empire, the largest administrative division under a governor-general, BEGLERBEGI. An ~ was composed of SAND͟JAḲS, which was the basic administrative unit. The ~ system was replaced by that of *wilāyet* in 1281/1864. I 468b; I 906b; II 721b

ezan → AD͟HĀN

F

faḍāʾil (A, s. **faḍīla**) : lit. virtues, a genre of literature exposing the excellences of things, individuals, groups, places, regions and such for the purpose of a *laudatio*. II 728b; VI 350a

In Mamlūk terminology, ~ , or *kamālāt,* was often applied to the exercises necessary for the mastery of horse-riding. II 954b

♦ faḍāʾil al-afʿāl : in the science of Tradition, a genre consisting of Traditions that list human actions which are believed to be particularly pleasing to God. VIII 983a

fadān (A) : a word that seems to have been applied at the same time to the yoke, to the pair of oxen and to the implement that they pull to till the land, i.e. the tiller. An evolved form, FADDĀN, came to designate also the area that a pair of oxen could till in a given time. VII 21b

faddān (A) : a yoke of oxen; the standard measure of land in Egypt in former times. It was defined by al-Ḳalḳas͟handī (9th/15th century) as equalling 400 square ḲAṢABAS, i.e. 6,368 m^2. Since 1830, the ~ has corresponded to 4200.833 m^2. VII 138a

fad͟hlaka (A, < *fa-d͟hālika*) : in mathematics, the sum, total. Besides being placed at the bottom of an addition to introduce the result, ~ is also employed for the summing up of a petition, report, or other document. By extension, ~ acquired the meaning of compendium. II 727b

fadīkh (A) : drinks composed of fruits (dates, etc.) mixed in water. VI 720b; an intoxicating drink made from different kinds of dates. VII 840a

faḍīla → FAḌĀʾIL

fadjr (A) : dawn, daybreak.

♦ al-fadjr al-kādhib, or *al-ṣubḥ al-kādhib* : lit. the false dawn; the Arabic term for the column of zodiacal light which is a symmetrically converse phenomenon in the circadian cycle (syn. *dhanab al-sirḥān* 'the wolf's tail') during which prayers are forbidden. It is followed by the 'true dawn', *al-ṣubḥ al-ṣādiḳ*. VIII 928b; IX 179b

♦ ṣalāt al-fadjr : the morning prayer which is to be performed in the period from daybreak, or 'the true dawn', when faces can still not yet be recognised, until before sunrise. VII 27b; VIII 928b

faḍl → RAḤMA; ṢILA

fāfīr (Egy) : in Egypt, the term used for papyrus. VIII 261a

faghfūr (P), or *baghbūr* : title of the emperor of China in the Muslim sources. II 738a

♦ faghfūrī : Chinese (porcelain). The term has entered Modern Greek in the sense of porcelain, and also Slav languages, through the Russian *farfor*. II 738a; III 345b

fāghiya, faghw → ḤINNĀʾ

fahd (A, < Gk or L *pardus* ?; P *yūz*) : in zoology, the cheetah (*Acinonyx jubatus*). II 738b

fahl (A, pl. *fuḥūl*) : a stallion; in its plural form, a term given to powerful poets. I 405b

fahm → IDRĀK

fahrasa (A, < P *fihrist*) : the name given in Muslim Spain to kinds of catalogues, in which scholars enumerated their masters and the subjects or works studied under their direction. Synonyms of this term are: *barnāmadj*, *thabat*, *mashīkha* (*mashyakha*) and *muʿdjam*. The genre, which appears to be a particular speciality of the Andalusians, should be associated with the transmission of ḤADĪTH. I 96b; II 743b

fāʿil (A) : in grammar, the agent. VIII 384a

fāʾit (A), or *fawāt* : continuation of a work (syn. *ṣila*), but connoting discontinuity in relation to the original work. IX 604a

fāʾiẓ → AL-MĀL AL-ḤURR

faḳʿ (A) : on the Arabian Peninsula, truffles. I 540b

fakhkhār (A) : earthenware vase, pottery, ceramics, produced by practically every country in the Islamic world. II 745a

fakhr (A) : self-praise. VIII 376b

♦ fakhriyya (T, < A) : in Turkish prosody, ~ is the last but one section of a ḲAṢĪDA, wherein the poet praises himself. IV 715b fāḳiʿ (A) : said of the child who has become active, and has started to grow. VIII 822a

faḳīh (A, pl. *fuḳahāʾ*) : in its non-technical meaning ~ denotes anyone possessing knowledge, *fiḳh,* of a thing (syn. *ʿālim*, pl. *ʿulamāʾ*). II 756a

In law, ~ became the technical term for a specialist in religious law and in particular its derivative details, *furūʿ*. In older terminology, however, ~ as opposed to *ʿālim* denotes the speculative, systematic lawyer as opposed to the specialist in the traditional elements of religious law. II 756a; and → MUTAFAḲḲIH

In several Arabic dialects, forms like *fiḳī* have come to denote a schoolmaster in a KUTTĀB or a professional reciter of the Qurʾān. II 756a

faḳīr (A, pl. *fuḳarāʾ*) : a needy person, a pauper; its etymological meaning is 'one whose backbone is broken'.

In mysticism, a ~ is a person 'who lives for God alone'. Total rejection of private property and resignation to the will of God were considered essential for the ~ who aspired to gnosis. II 757b

In irrigation terminology (pl. *fuḳur*), the water outlet of a canal, ḲANĀT; a well or group of wells linked by a gallery. IV 532b

fakk → ĪWĀN

fakkāk (A) : the individual who devotes himself totally or episodically to the ransoming of Muslims held captive by infidels; in the Muslim West by the 13th century, ~ came to denote the man who liberates a captive, whether Muslim or not, as an extension of the equivalent appearing in a Christian context, called *alfaqueque* in Castillian. S 307a

faʾl (A) : an omen, appearing in varied forms, ranging from simple sneezing, certain peculiarities of persons and things that one encounters, to the interpretation of the names of persons and things which present themselves spontaneously to the sight, hearing and mind of man. II 758b

♦ **fāl-nāme** (P) : book of divination, consulted in the Muslim East (especially in Iranian and Turkish countries) in order to know the signs or circumstances that are auspicious for some decision. II 761b

fala̲d̲j̲ (A, pl. *aflā̲d̲j̲*) : the term used in Oman, Trucial Oman, and Bahrain to designate an underground aqueduct with surface apertures to facilitate cleaning. This type of aqueduct, which may be of Persian origin, is now called SĀḲĪ (pronounced *sā̲d̲j̲ī*, pl. *sawā̲d̲j̲ī*) in al-Aflā̲d̲j̲, the district in Na̲d̲j̲d which takes its name from ~ . I 233a; I 539a; IV 531b

falak (A, pl. *aflāk*) : sphere, in particular the Celestial Sphere. II 761b; VIII 101b

♦ falak al-aw̲d̲j̲ → AL-FALAK AL-K̲H̲ĀRI̲D̲J̲ AL-MARKAZ

♦ falak al-burū̲d̲j̲ : in astronomy, the term for L. *ecliptica*. II 762b

♦ falak al-̲d̲j̲awzahar : in astronomy, the massive ball into which, according to Ibn al-Hayt̲h̲am, the moon is inserted, and which carries it along as it moves. V 536a

♦ al-falak al-ḥāmil : in astronomy, the deferent. II 762b; IX 292b

♦ al-falak al-k͟hāridj al-markaz, or *falak al-awḏj* : in astronomy, the term for L. *excentricus*. II 762b

♦ al-falak al-māʾil : in astronomy, the term for L. *circulus obliquus* (or *deflectens*). II 762b

♦ al-aflāk al-māʾila ʿan falak muʿaddil al-nahār : in astronomy, the term for the circles parallel to the equator. II 762b

♦ falak muʿaddil al-nahār : in astronomy, the term for L. *circulus aequinoctialis* (the celestial equator). II 762b

♦ al-falak al-mumaththal li-falak al-burūdj : in astronomy, the term for L. *circulus pareclipticus*. II 762b

♦ al-falak al-mustaḳīm : the astronomical term for L. *sphaera recta*, the celestial sphere as appearing to the inhabitants of the equatorial region, where the celestial equator passes through the zenith. II 762b

♦ falak al-tadwīr : in astronomy, the epicycle. II 762b; IX 292b

falaḳa (A) : an apparatus used for immobilising the feet in order to apply a bastinado on the soles of the feet. The ~ existed in three different forms: a plank with two holes in it, of the pillory type; two poles joined at one end; or a single, fairly stout pole with a cord fixed at the two ends. In the Muslim East, especially among the Turks, the ~ was used as an instrument of torture, while in North Africa its use was confined to the schoolmaster. II 763b

falāsifa (A, < Gk; s. *faylasūf*) : the Greek thinkers; philosophers. II 764b

fālidj (A, pl. *fawālidj*) : the *camelus bactrianus,* or camel proper, with two humps. III 665b

In medicine, hemiplegia. VIII 111a; IX 8a

falīdja (A), and *s͟huḳḳa* : bands of hair or wool forming the awning of an Arab tent. They were sewn side-by-side and formed a rectangle. Those that were placed at the two edges, that is, those that form the larger side of the rectangle, were called *kisr* or *kasr*. IV 1147b

fallāḥ (A, pl. *fallāḥīn*) : ploughman; member of the sedentary rural population. I 575a; II 899a

fallāḳ (A, B *fellāga*) : brigands and subsequently rebels in Tunisia and Algeria. Originally the term was applied to individuals who wished to escape punishment, to deserters, and to fugitive offenders, who eventually formed bands supporting themselves by brigandage. The uprising brought about by K͟halīfa b. ʿAskar in southern Tunisia in 1915 gave new meaning to the word. Later, the incidents which occurred in Tunisia between 1952 and 1954, as well as the Algerian rebellion in 1954, made the term popular again. II 767b

fallāta : term, strictly signifying the Fulānī, used in the Nilotic Sudan for Muslim immigrants from the western *bilād al-sūdān*, and in particular those from northern Nigeria, many of whom are primarily pilgrims en route to Mecca. ~ has largely superseded the older *takārir* or *takārna*. II 767b

fals (A, pl. *fulūs*) : the name of the copper or bronze coin, regardless of its size or weight. II 768a
In astronomy, a small ring placed under the wedge at the front of the astrolabe to protect one of the movable parts of the instrument, the 'spider', and ensure a smooth turning. I 723a

falsafa (A, < Gk) : Greek thought; philosophy. ~ began as a search by Muslims with shīʿī leanings for a coherence in their intellectual and spiritual life, evolving later to grow closer to orthodox KALĀM and finally fusing with it. II 769b

falta (A) : a precipitate, arbitrary act, excusable only because God had bestowed success on it. IX 422a

falṭīṭa (A), or *djalṭīṭa*, *djanṭīṭa* : a skirt of Spanish origin worn mainly by Jewish and Andalusian women in the Muslim West. V 746a

fam → ʿAYN

fanāʾ → BAḲĀʾ WA-FANĀʾ

fanak (A, < P; pl. *afnāk*) : in zoology, the fennec-fox (*Fennecus zerda*), in the Muslim West, and the Corsac or Karagan Fox (*Vulpes corsac*, < T *ḳūrsāḳ*), in the Muslim East. However, in the imagination of all the authors who used the word, ~ must have meant the mink (*Mustela lutreola*), whose pelt was greatly esteemed in the luxury fur-trade. II 775a

fānī → PĪR

fānīd → SUKKAR

fann (A) : the modern name for art. II 775b

faʾr (A, pl. *fiʾrān, fiʾara, fuʾar*) : in zoology, the majority of types and species of the sub-order of the Myomorphs; the family of Soricids. S 285b, where can be found many synonyms and varieties
♦ faʾr firʿawn : lit. Pharaoh's rat; in Egypt, with the geographical sub-species *pharaonis*, the ichneumon or Egyptian mongoose, sometimes called *ḳiṭṭ firʿawn* 'Pharaoh's cat'. VIII 49b

farʿ (A, pl. *furūʿ*) : branch.
In fiscal law, ~ was a supplementary increase, discovered or invented in the course of history, upon the official taxes for the defrayal of attendant expenses or any other reason. I 1144a; IV 1041a
In military science, *furūʿ* are the operations by the irregulars, who do not form part of the army proper but who may play a part in the preliminaries and on the fringes of the battle. III 182a
In prosody, the *furūʿ* are the modifications in the feet of the metres, due to deviations, e.g. *mu[s]tafʿilun* becomes *mutafʿilun* when its *sīn* is lost, the 'normal' foot being part of the *uṣūl* (→ AṢL) form of the feet, and the altered foot, one of the *furūʿ*. I 671b
As a literary topos, ~ denoted thick, soft and fragrant hair. IX 313a
♦ furūʿ al-fiḳh : in law, the body of positive rules derived from the sources of legal knowledge, *uṣūl al-fiḳh* (→ AṢL). I 257b; II 889b; IX 323b

faraʿa (A, pl. *furuʿ*) : the firstling of a flock or herd, sacrificed in the pre-Islamic period during the month of Radjab as an invocation to the deities to increase the number of flocks. VIII 373b

faradjiyya (A) : a long-sleeved man's robe in Egypt. V 741a; the Moroccan variant *faražiyya* (B *tafaražit*) is a very light gown with a deep slit at the breast which may or may not have sleeves and is worn under the KHAFTĀN or garment by both sexes. It also comes in a half-length version called *nuṣṣ faražiyya*. V 746a

farāʾiḍ (A, s. *farīḍa*) : lit. appointed or obligatory portions; as a technical term, ~ means the fixed shares in an estate which are given to certain heirs according to the provisions of Muslim law. The whole of the Islamic law of inheritance is called *ʿilm al-farāʾiḍ*. II 783a; VII 106b

farāmush-khāna (P) : in Iran, a centre of masonic activities, freemasonry seemingly having come over from India where the first lodge was founded by the British in 1730. S 290a

faras (A) : in zoology, the horse (*Equus caballus*) in the sense of saddle-horse, the rider of which is termed FĀRIS. II 784b; II 800a; the chesspiece. IX 366b

In astronomy, a wedge which is fitted into a slit in the narrow end of the broadheaded pin at the front of the astrolabe to prevent the pin from coming out. I 723a

♦ faras al-baḥr : in zoology, the bellows fish (*Centriscus*). VIII 1021a

♦ **faras al-māʾ** : in zoology, the hippopotamus. S 294a

farāsha (A, P *parwāna*) : in zoology, the moth. IX 282a

faraṭ (A) : lit. dying before one's parents; a child who dies before reaching maturity. VIII 821b

fard (A, pl. *afrād*) : 'only, solitary, unique, incomplete, incomparable'.

In poetry, ~ denotes a line of verse taken in isolation (intact or reduced to a single hemistich). II 789b

In lexicography, *afrād* are the words handed down by one single lexicographer, as distinct from *āḥād* and *mafārīd*. II 790a

In the science of Tradition, ~ is synonomous with *gharīb muṭlaḳ* and means a Tradition in which the second link of the chain of those who have transmitted it is only represented by a single transmitter. II 790a; ~ is used of an ISNĀD with only one transmitter at each stage, or of a Tradition transmitted only by people of one district. III 25b

In astronomy, ~ denotes the star alpha in Hydra, *al-shudjāʿ*, and hence the most brilliant. II 790a

In arithmetic, *al-ʿadad al-fard* is the odd number (from 3 upwards, inclusive), as opposed to the even number, *al-ʿadad al-zawdj*. II 790a

In theology and philosophy, ~ denotes the species, as restricted by the bond of individuation. II 790a

In mysticism, *al-afrād* are seven in number and occupy the fourth category in the hierarchy of the saints. I 95a

farḍ (A), or *farīḍa* : lit. something which has been apportioned, or made obligatory; as a technical term in religious law, ~ is a religious duty or obligation, the omission of which will be punished and the performance of which will be rewarded. It is one of the so-called *al-aḥkām al-khamsa*, the five qualifications by which every act of man is qualified. II 790a; VIII 486b

♦ farḍ ʿayn : the individual duty such as ritual prayer, fasting, etc. II 790a; VIII 497b

♦ farḍ kifāya : the collective duty, the fulfilment of which by a sufficient number of individuals excuses others from fulfilling it, such as funeral prayer, holy war, etc. II 539a; II 790a; VIII 497b

farhang (P) : politeness, knowledge, education; dictionary.

In recent decades, ~ has come to be used also in the sense of culture, while *farhangistān* has been adopted for 'academy'. V 1095b

farhangistān → FARHANG

farīḍa → FARĀʾIḌ; FARḌ

fāridj → KATŪM

fārīna (A) : a soft variety of wheat, grown in Algeria. The indigenous hard variety, *triticum durum*, was known as *gemḥ*. IX 537b

farīr → SAKHLA

fāris (A, (pl. *fursān, fawāris*) : the rider on horseback (and thus not applicable to a man riding a camel or mule), implying, in contrast to *rākib* 'horseman', the valiant, the champion, the intrepid warrior. II 800a.

farmān (P, T *fermān*) : originally command, but by the 9th/15th century, ~ had come to denote the edict or document, as issued by the ruler, itself. There were many synonyms, such as *ḥukm, mithāl* and *raḳam*, which later came to designate a document issued by authorities of lower rank. II 309a; II 803a

♦ farmān-i bayāḍī : in the Mughal period, a confidential and important FARMĀN, not involving a sum of money, which received only a royal seal and was folded and dispatched in such a way that its contents remained private to the recipient. II 806a

farmāsūniyya (A) : freemasonry. S 296a; and → FARĀMUSH-KHĀNA

farrāsh (A) : lit. spreader of the carpets; a servant who looks after the beds and the house generally. IV 899a; an attendant in a library. VI 199a

farrūdj (A) : a robe similar to the ḲABĀʾ , but slit in the back, worn in the Prophet's time. V 733b

farsakh (P), and *farsang* : a measure of distance on a time basis, originally the distance which could be covered on foot in an hour: approx. 5.94 km for cavalry, and 4 km for foot-soldiers. In present-day Iran, the ~ is now fixed at precisely 6 km. II 812b

farsang → FARSAKH

farsha → ʿATABA

farūdiyya (A) : a square kerchief bound around the cap by women in Egypt. V 741a

farw (A), or *farwa* : a fur; a garment made of, or trimmed with, fur. Although *farwa* can mean also a cloak of camel-hair, it is likely that this term in ancient poetry refers to sheepskins with the wool left on (in Morocco called *haydūra*), used as carpets, to cover seats, or for protection against the cold. II 816b

faʾs → ḤAKMA

faṣāḥa (A) : clarity, purity.

In rhetoric, ~ is the term for the purity and euphony of language, and can be divided into three kinds: *faṣāḥat al-mufrad*, with respect to a single word when it is not difficult to pronounce, is not a foreign or rare word and its form is not an exception to the usual; *faṣāḥat al-kalām*, with respect to a whole sentence, when it does not contain an objectionable construction, a discord, an obscurity (through a confusion in the arrangement of the words) or a metaphor too far-fetched and therefore incomprehensible; and *faṣāḥat al-mutakallim*, with respect to a person whose style conforms to the above conditions. I 981b; II 824a

faṣd (A) : in medicine, bleeding. II 481b; S 303b; and → FAṢṢĀD

fas̲h̲t (A, pl. *fus̲h̲ūt*), or *ḳuṭʿa*, *nad̲j̲wa* : the term for reef in the Persian Gulf. I 535b

fāsid (A) : in law, a legal act which does not observe the conditions of validity *stricto sensu* required for its perfection; vitiated and therefore null. Only in the Ḥanafī school of law is ~ distinct from *bāṭil* 'null and void', where it denotes a legal act which lacks one of the elements essential for the existence of any legal activity. I 319a; II 829b; VIII 836a; IX 324b

fāsiḳ (A) : in theology, one who has committed one or several 'great sins'. According to the Muʿtazila, who elaborated the thesis of the so-called intermediary status, the ~ is not entirely a believer nor entirely an infidel, but 'in a position between the two' (*fī manzila bayna 'l-manzilatayn*). Al-As̲h̲ʿarī maintained the same opinion, but added that if the ~ was a believer before becoming a sinner, the 'great sin' committed will not invalidate his standing as a believer; this position was adopted by the sunnīs as a whole. II 833a

In law, ~ is the opposite of ʿADL, a person of good morals. I 209b; II 834a

fas̊il (T) : a term in Ottoman music which in its classical form can be defined as a variable selection of pieces, usually by different composers, fitting into a series of prescribed slots organised in such a way as to emphasise, within the overall unity of mode, contrast and variety. It thus alternates between instrumental and vocal, unmeasured and measured, and juxtaposes vocal pieces using contrasting rhythmic cycles. VII 1043a

faṣīl (A) : in architecture, an *intervallum*. I 616a

♦ **faṣīla** (A) : an object which is separated, like a young animal when weaned, and a palmtree sucker when transplanted; also the smallest 'section' of a tribe, the closest relatives. II 835a

fāṣila (A, pl. *fawāṣil*) : a separative.

In prosody, ~ denotes a division in the primitive feet, meaning three or four moving consonants followed by one quiescent, e.g. *ḳatalat*, *ḳatalahum*. II 834b; VIII 667b; and → SADJʿ

In Qurʾānic terminology, ~ signifies the rhymes of the Qurʾānic text. II 834b; VIII 614b

In music, ~ denotes the pause which, with the basic notes, makes up the rhythm, ĪḲĀʿ. S 408b

faskh (A) : in law, the dissolution of any contractual bond whatever, effected, as a rule, by means of a declaration of intention pronounced in the presence of the other contracting party, or by judicial process. The term is to be distinguished from *infisākh* which comes about without the need of any declaration or judicial decree. Dissolution of marriage open to the wife or her relatives is by way of ~ , while the dissolution of marriage by the man is ṬALĀḲ. II 836a; III 1056b

♦ faskha : in Mauritania, the dowry supplied by the family of the bride when she joins the conjugal home. VI 313a

faskiyya → SAHRĪDJ

faṣl (A, pl. *fuṣūl*) : separation, disjunction.

In logic, ~ is 'difference', and, in particular, 'specific difference', the third of the five predicables of Porphyry. For logicians, ~ stands both for every attribute by which one thing is distinguished from another, whether it be individual or universal, and, in transposition, for that by which a thing is essentially distinguished. II 836b; and → SHAʿĪRA

In its plural form, *fuṣūl* is employed in philosophy and science to denote aphorisms or short chapters. VII 536b

♦ al-faṣl al-ʿāmm : 'common difference', a term in logic for what allows a thing to differ from another and that other to differ from the former; equally it is what allows a thing to differ from itself at another time. This is the case of separable accidents. II 837a

♦ al-faṣl al-khāṣṣ : 'particular difference', a term in logic for the predicate which is necessarily associated with accidents. II 837a

faṣṣād (A) : lit. phlebotomist; in mediaeval Islamic society, the practitioner of *faṣd* who bled veins of the human body and performed circumcisions for men and women. A similar profession was cupping, *ḥidjāma*, which was performed by a *ḥadjdjām* but was less popular and enjoyed less status: the cupper was a much-satirised character in Arabic tales. S 303b

fatā (A, pl. *fityān*) : a boy, manservant; slave. I 24b; and → FUTUWWA

In the mediaeval Muslim East, the *fityān* (syn. *ʿayyārūn*; → ʿAYYĀR) were private groups, recruited from the depressed classes, which played the role of 'active wing' of the popular oppositions to the official authorities. I 256b; VIII 402a

In Muslim Spain, ~ was the slave employed in the service of the prince and his household, or of the ḤĀDJIB, who held an elevated rank in the palace hierarchy. II 837a

♦ al-fatayān al-kabīrān : the two majordomos under whose control the entire management of the princely household in Muslim Spain was placed. II 837a

fatḥ al-kitāb (A) : bibliomancy, a form of sorcery. VIII 138b

fatḥa (A) : in grammar, ~ denotes the short vowel *a*. III 172a

In North Africa, ~ is a slit in the D̲JALLĀBIYYA at the top of the armlets through which the bare forearm can be thrust. II 405a

For ~ in prayer, → FĀTIḤA

fatḥnāme (T) : an Ottoman official announcement of a victory; a versified narrative of exploits, written by private persons as a literary exercise. II 839a

fātiḥa (A, pl. *fawātiḥ*) : the opening (*sūra*); designation of the first SŪRA of the Qurʾān; (or *fatḥa*) a prayer ceremony in certain Arab countries, particularly in North Africa, in which the arms are stretched out with the palms upwards, but without any recitation of the first sūra. II 841a; V 425a

♦ fawātiḥ al-suwar (A), and *awāʾil al-suwar*, *al-ḥurūf al-muḳaṭṭaʿāt* : 'the openers of the SŪRAS', a letter or group of letters standing just after the BASMALA at the beginning of 29 sūras and recited as letters of the alphabet. They are generally referred to in European languages as 'the mysterious letters'. V 412a

fātik (A, pl. *futtāk*) : a killer, a syn. of ṢUʿLŪK, or category into which the *ṣuʿlūk* fell. IX 864a

faṭīm (A) : a child weaned or ablactated. VIII 822a

fatra (A) : a relaxing; an interval of time, more particularly with respect to the period separating two prophets or two successive messengers. In its more current usage, ~ is applied to the period without prophets from the time of Jesus Christ to Muḥammad. In later times, ~ was also applied, by analogy, to periods of political interregnum. II 865a

faṭṭāma → S̲H̲AMLA

faṭūr (A) : the meal marking the end of the fast of Ramaḍān. IX 94b

fāṭūs (A), or *ḥūt al-ḥayḍ* : a fabulous marine creature mentioned by mediaeval Arab authors. It shatters the ships which it encounters, but is put to flight when the sailors hang from the peripheral points of the vessel rags stained with menstrual blood, *ḥayḍ*. VIII 1023a

fatwā (A) : in law, an opinion on a point of law. II 866a; II 890a

fawāt → FĀʾIT

fawātiḥ → FĀTIḤA; IFTITĀḤ

fawd̲jār : under the Dihlī sultanate, the superintendant of elephants, who, among other things, was ordered to train them to stand firm at the sight of fire and in the noise of artillery. V 690a

fawd̲jdār : an executive and military officer, the administrative head of a district, *sarkār*, in the Mug̲h̲al administration of India. I 317a; II 868a

fayʾ (A) : in pre-Islamic times, chattels taken as booty. II 869a; in early Islam, ~ were the immoveable properties acquired by conquest, a foundation in perpetuity for the benefit of successive generations of the community, in contrast to the moveable booty, *ghanīma*, which was distributed immediately. I 1144a; IV 1031a; spoils of war. VIII 130b

In the terminology of time, ~ denotes the shade in the east which, when it moves from the west (where it is called *ẓill*) to the east, marks midday. V 709b

fayḍ → IFĀḌA

fayḍa → RAWḌA

faydj (A, < P; pl. **fuyūdj**) : a courier of the government postal service and also commercial mail serving the population at large. It was a common term all over North Africa and Egypt during the 5th/11th and 6th/12th centuries, while on the Egypt-Syria route the word *kutubī*, letter-bearer, was used. I 1044b; II 969b

♦ faydj ṭayyār : express courier. II 970b

faylasūf (A) : a philosopher; in popular language, ~ is applied in an uncomplimentary sense to freethinkers or unbelievers. II 872a

fayruzadj → FĪRŪZADJ

fāza : in Arabia, the name the Tiyāha give to a tent whose ridge-pole rests on a row of two poles. The Sbāʿ use *mgawren* or *garneyn*. IV 1148a

fazʿa (A) : a counter-attack (of a raiding group of Bedouin). II 1055b

faẓẓ (A) : water which is still drinkable, found in the stomach of camels. III 666b; and → FĪL AL-BAḤR

fellāga → FALLĀḲ

fermān → FARMĀN

fərmla (Alg) : a vest for elderly men in Algeria. V 746a

fidāʾ (A) : the redemption, repurchase, or ransoming of Muslim prisoners or slaves held by unbelievers. III 183a; VIII 502a; S 306b

fidām (A) : a piece of linen cloth which protected the mouth, worn by Zoroastrian priests, but often also by the cup-bearer, SĀḲĪ, for whom it served as a filter for tasting the drink and to help him know the precise taste. VIII 883b

fidāwī (A, < **fidāʾī**) : one who offers up his life for another. Among the Nizārī Ismāʿīlīs, ~ was used of those who risked their lives to assassinate the enemies of the sect. II 882a; VIII 442a

In Algeria, ~ means a narrator of heroic deeds. II 882a

During the Persian revolution of 1906-7, the term was applied in the first place to the adherents of the republican party, later to the defenders of liberal ideas and the constitution. II 882a

♦ fidāwiyya (Alg) : a tale or song of heroic deeds. II 882a

fiḍḍa (A) : in mineralogy, silver. II 883a

fidjār (A) : sacrilege; known particularly in the name *ḥarb al-fidjār* 'the sacrilegious war', a war waged towards the end of the 6th century A.D. during the holy months between the Ḳuraysh and Kināna on the one side and the Ḳays-ʿAylān on the other. II 883b

fidya (A) : a general designation among Syro-Palestinians for a blood sacrifice made for purposes of atonement, practised in the interests of the living. II 884a; a Qurʾānic term to denote the fast which compensates for the days of Ramaḍān in which fasting has not been practised, or to denote the impossibility of purchasing a place in Paradise. S 306b; a minor KAFFĀRA or compensation, to be paid when one has taken advantage of one of five dispensations. IX 94b

fiḳh (A) : understanding, knowledge, intelligence, and thus applied to any branch of knowledge (as in *fiḳh al-lugha*, the science of lexicography); the technical term for jurisprudence, the science of religious law in Islam. In addition to the laws regulating ritual and religious observances, containing orders and prohibitions, ~ includes the whole field of family law, the law of inheritance, of property and of contracts and obligations, criminal law and procedure, and, finally, constitutional law and laws regulating the administration of the state and the conduct of war. II 886a; IX 322b

In older theological language, ~ was used in opposition to ʿILM, the accurate knowledge of legal decisions handed down from the Prophet and his Companions, and was applied to the independent exercise of the intelligence, the decision of legal points by one's own judgement in the absence or ignorance of a traditional ruling bearing on the case in question. II 886a

fikr (A, pl. *afkār*) : thought, reflection.

In mysticism, ~ is used habitually in contrast to DHIKR: in the performance of ~ , the ṣūfī, concentrating on a religious subject, meditates according to a certain progression of ideas or a series of evocations which he assimilates and experiences, while in *dhikr*, concentrating on the object recollected, he allows his field of consciousness to lose itself in this object. II 891b

fiḳra (T) : a kind of short news item generally of entertaining nature, combining anecdote with comment on some matter of contemporary importance. VI 94b

fīl (A, < P *pīl*) : in zoology, the elephant. II 892b; the bishop in chess. IX 366b

♦ fīl al-baḥr (A) : the elephant seal; the walrus, also called *faẓẓ*. IV 648b; VIII 1022b

fiʿl (A) : act, action, opposed in noetics and metaphysics to *ḳuwwa* 'potentiality, power'. II 898a; V 578a

In grammar, the verb. II 895b; and → ISM AL-FIʿL

In logic, ~ is one of the ten categories, *actio* as opposed to *passio*. II 898a

In theology, ~ designates the action of God *ad extra*, 'what is possible (not necessary) for God to do'. II 898b

♦ fiʿl al-taʿadjdjub : in grammar, the verb of surprise. IX 528a

filāḥa (A) : lit. ploughing; the occupation of husbandry, agriculture. II 899a

♦ filāḥat al-araḍīn : agronomy. II 902a

♦ filāḥat al-ḥayawānāt : zootechny. II 902a

filawr (A), or *ḥādjūr* : in mediaeval ʿIrāḳ, a beggar or vagrant who simulates a hernia or ulcer or tumour or some similar affliction with his testicles or anus, or with her vulva, in the case of a woman. VII 494a filḳ (A), also *sharīdj* : in archery, a bow consisting of a single stave split lengthwise and spliced with glue. IV 797b

filori (T) : the Ottoman name for the standard gold coins of Europe; a local Balkan tax amounting to one ~ , imposed on the semi-nomadic Vlachs of the Balkans, in which sense it is usually referred to as *resm-i filori*. II 914b ff.; VIII 487a

filw (A) : a foal between birth and one year of age. II 785a

firandj → IFRANDJ

firāsa (A) : physiognomancy, a technique of inductive divination which permits the foretelling of moral conditions and psychological behaviour from external indications and physical states, such as colours, forms, and limbs. II 916a; V 100a

firʿawnī → KĀGHAD

firda → FURḌA

firḳ → WAKĪR

firḳate → BASHTARDA

fīrūzadj (P), or *fayruzadj* : in mineralogy, turquoise, mined in the Sāsānid period and even earlier around Nīshāpūr. There are different kinds, distinguished by colour; the best kind was considered to be the *būsḥāḳī* (i.e. *Abū Isḥāḳī*) and the finest variety of this, the sky-blue *azharī*. ~ is explained as 'stone of victory' whence it is also called *ḥadjar al-ghalaba*. II 927b; VIII 112a

firz, or *firzān* → SHAṬRANDJ

fisḳiyya (A, pl. *fasāḳī*) : a small basin which collected water from the SHADIRWĀN. IX 175b

fiṭām → SAKHLA

fitna (A) : putting to the proof, discriminatory test; revolt, disturbance; civil war. A Qurʾānic term with the sense of temptation or trial of faith, and most frequently as a test which is in itself a punishment inflicted by God upon the sinful, the unrighteous. The great struggles of the early period of Muslim history were called ~ . II 930b

fiṭra (A) : a Qurʾānic term meaning 'a kind or way of creating or of being created', which posed serious theological and legal difficulties for the commentators. II 931b; 'common to all the prophets' or 'part of the general SUNNA or religion'. IX 312b

fityān → FATĀ

♦ fityānī : a variety of couscous which is prepared by cooking grain in gravy and which is sprinkled with cinnamon. V 528a

fizr → ḲAṬĪʿ

foggara (Alg, < A *faḳḳara*; pl. *fgāgīr*) : a term used in southern Algeria to designate a *ḳanāt*, a mining installation or technique for extracting water from the depths of the earth. IV 529a; a subterranean drainage channel. S 328b

frenk-khāne (T) : in 19th-century Ottoman cities, a building in a European style, intended to house European merchants during their more or less extended stays. IX 799b frīmla (N.Afr) : a corselet for women in Algeria; an embroidered bolero in Libya. V 746a

fūdhandj (A, < P, < H *pūdana*) : mint. The Arabic nomenclature for mint is abundant; other names are *ḥabaḳ*, *nammām*, for water-mint, and *naʿnaʿ* or *nuʿnuʿ*, peppermint. S 309b

fuḍūlī (A) : in law, an unauthorised agent. VIII 836a

fūh → AFĀWĪH

fuḥsh → SUKHF

fuḥūl → FAḤL

fuḳaysha → ṢANDJ

fūḳiyya : a body shirt for men worn under the DJALLĀBIYYA in Morocco. V 746a

fuḳḳāʿ (A) : a sparkling fermented drink, almost a 'beer'. It was frequently sweetened and flavoured with fruit, so that one might call ~ the mediaeval equivalent of shandy or almost so. VI 721a; IX 225a

fūl mudammas → ṬAʿMIYYA

fūlādh → ḤADĪD

fulk (A) : a Qurʾānic term for ship, used *inter alia* of Noah's ark and the ship from which Jonah was thrown. VIII 808a

funduḳ (A, < Gk) : a term used, particularly in North Africa, to denote hostelries at which animals and humans can lodge, on the lines of caravanserais or KHĀNS of the Muslim East. II 945a; IV 1015a; IX 788b

In numismatics, an Ottoman gold coin. VIII 229b

furāniḳ : messengers in the postal service in the ʿAbbāsid period. I 1045b

furār → SAKHLA

furḍa (A) : a term used interchangeably in Ottoman documents and Arabic texts with *firda*, with reference to personal taxes; the ~ was attested in Ottoman Egypt after 1775 as one of the many illegal charges imposed on peasants by soldiers of the provincial governors. II 948a

♦ furdat (firdat) al-ruʾūs : a personal tax in Egypt under Muḥammad ʿAlī amounting to 3 per cent on known or supposed revenue of all the inhabitants, paid by all government employees, including foreigners, by employees of non-government establishments, by the *fallāḥīn* (→ FALLĀḤ), and by artisans and merchants. II 149a; II 948a

♦ firdat al-taḥrīr : in Ottoman Egypt, the name for the comprehensive levy which in 1792 replaced all the illegal charges imposed on peasants by soldiers of the provincial governors. II 948a

furdj → KATŪM

furfur → SAKHLA

furḳān (A, < Ar) : a Qurʾānic term, which poses problems of interpretation, and has been variously translated as 'discrimination', 'criterion', 'separation', 'deliverance', or 'salvation'. II 949b

furs (A) : one of two terms, the other being ʿADJAM, to denote the Persians. II 950b

furūʿ → FARʿ
furʿul → ḌABUʿ
furūsiyya (A) : the whole field of equestrian knowledge, both theoretical and practical. Treatises on ~ by actual horsemen, veterinary surgeons or riders appeared at a late stage in Arabic literature, many repeating passages from earlier works written by philologists, but also with added pages on riding, describing various methods and principles co-existing in the Muslim world. II 953b
fusayfisāʾ (A, < Gk) : in art, mosaic. I 610b; II 955a
fusṭāṭ (A, < Gk) : a small hair tent used by travellers. II 957b; IV 1147a
fuṣūl → FAṢL
fūṭa : in mediaeval Islam, a long piece of sari-like cloth originating in India and serving a variety of functions: as a loincloth, apron, and a variety of headdress. V 737b; a simple cloth with a seam, fastened in front and behind to the girdle, *tikka* (modern *dikka*). IX 676b
futuwwa (A, T *fütüwwet*) : a term invented in about the 2nd/8th century as the counterpart of *muruwwa* (→ MURŪʾA), the qualities of the mature man, to signify that which is regarded as characteristic of the FATĀ, young man; by this term it has become customary to denote various movements and organisations which until the beginning of the modern era were widespread throughout all the urban communities of the Muslim East. I 520a; II 961a
futyā (A), or *iftāʾ* : the act of giving an opinion on a point of law, FATWĀ; the profession of the adviser. II 866a
fuyūd̲j̲ → FAYD̲J̲

G

gabr (P) : a term of doubtful etymology, denoting Zoroastrians, and used generally in Persian literature. II 970b
♦ gabrī : ceramic ware developed in Persia. The ornamentation of this ware, produced by means of larger or smaller scratches in the slip that covers the body under the transparent partly coloured glaze, consists of schematic representations, recalling the ancient culture of Persia, notably of fire altars, as well as of men and beasts, birds, lions and dragons depicted in a curiously stylised manner. II 746a
gand̲j̲ : in Muslim India, a grain market. IX 800b
gandu (Hau) : the Hausa extended family, a largely self-supporting unit based on agriculture and formerly dependent on slave labour. III 277b
gandūra (N.Afr) : a full-length tunic with short sleeves, worn by men in southern Morocco and by both sexes in Algeria. V 746a
gargad̲j̲ (Ind.P) : in Mug̲h̲al India, a movable tower used in sieges. These towers

were very strong structures with solid beams covered by raw hides, tiles, or earth to protect them from the liquid combustibles thrown by the garrison; they could be destroyed only by hurling heavy stones or by a sortie. III 482a

garmsīr (P, A *djarm*) : in geography, a term used to denote hot, desert-type or subtropical lowland climates; in Arabic, ~ is particularly used for the hot, coastal region of the Persian Gulf shores and the regions bordering on the great central desert. V 183a

garneyn → FĀZA

gat → BANDISH

gaṭṭāya (B) : a kind of mat of plaited hair, which is worn very long and grown only from the top of the cranium, the remainder of the head being shaved. The wearing of the ~ is a local custom absorbed by the ʿĪsāwī order. IV 95a

gāwdār (P) : cattle-raiser. IX 682b

gaz (P) : the Persian cubit, DHIRĀʿ, of the Middle Ages, either the legal cubit of 49.8 cm or the Isfahan cubit of 79.8 cm. Until recently, a ~ of 104 cm was in use in Iran. II 232a; in 1926 an attempt was made to equate the traditional Persian measures with the metric system, so that the ~ was fixed at 1 m; after 1933 the metric system was introduced but the older measures nevertheless remained in popular use. VII 138a

In Muslim India, sixty ~ formed the side of the square BĪGHĀ, a traditional measure of area. Five thousand ~ made the length of a *kuroh* (Persian) or KROŚA (Sanskrit) , the traditional measure of road-length. S 313b

♦ gaz-i ilāhī : a measure introduced by the Mughal emperor Akbar in 994/1586, equal to ca. 32 inches. IV 1055b; S 313b

♦ gaz-i mukassar : the 'shortened' cubit of 68 cm, used for measuring cloth. II 232a

♦ gaz-i shāhī : the 'royal' cubit of 95 cm, in use in 17th-century Persia. II 232a

gečid resmi (T) : tolls levied in the Ottoman empire at mountain passes and river fords. II 147a

gedik (T) : lit. breach.

In law, a form of long-term lease arrangement of WAḲF property in Egypt, which involved, in addition to perpetual lease, the ownership and use of tools and installations of shops and workshops. S 369a; in the Ottoman period, the right to exercise a craft or a trade, either in general or, more frequently, at a special place or in a specific shop. They were inheritable if the heir fulfilled all other conditions for becoming a master in the craft. VIII 207a; IX 542a; IX 798a; S 421a

gemḥ → FĀRĪNA

geniza (Heb) : a place where Hebrew writings were deposited in order to prevent the desecration of the name of God which might be found in them. As a term of scholarship, ~ or Cairo *geniza*, refers to writings coming from the store-room of the 'Synagogue of the Palestinians' in the ancient city of Fusṭāṭ. II 987b

gersh → BILYŪN
gezme → AḤDĀTH
ghāba (A) : forest. II 991a
ghabānī (A), or *ghabāniyya* : a head scarf with an embroidered pattern of lozenges, worn by both sexes in the Arab East. V 741a
ghabn fāḥish (A) : in law, the concept of excessive loss, which is the only means by which a contract can be challenged in the case of fraud. I 319a
ghaḍaf → ḲAṬĀ
ghadāʾir → ḌAFĀʾIR
ghadāt (A) : a variant name for the *ṣalāt al-fadjr* (→ FADJR). VII 27a
ghadjar (A) : gypsies. IX 235b
ghādus (A, < L *Gadus*) : in zoology, the cod. VIII 1021a
ghaffār, ghafūr → GHUFRĀN
ghāʾib (A) : absent.
In law, usually the person who, at a given moment, is not present at the place where he should be. But, in certain special cases, the term is applied also to the person who is at a distance from the court before which he was to bring an action or who does not appear at the court after being summoned. II 995b
♦ ṣalāt al-ghāʾib : the name given to the prayer said for a dead person whose body cannot be produced. II 996a
ghāʾira → ẒĀHIRA
ghalath → ʿALATH
ghalča (P) : an imprecise designation of those mountain peoples of the Pamirs who speak Iranian languages; a term used in English for the Iranian Pamir languages. The word, though of uncertain origin, has different meanings in different languages: 'peasant' or 'ruffian' in New Persian, 'squat, stupid' in Tādjikī; in old Yaghnābi, 'slave'. II 997b
ghālī → GHULĀT; ḲĀLĪ
ghalṭa (A, pl. *ghalaṭāt*) : error.
♦ **ghalaṭāt-i meshhūre** (T) : lit. well-known errors; solecisms brought about by phonetic changes, characteristic of Turkish, producing (drastic) modifications in Arabic and Persian loan-words and branded by the purists, e.g. *bēdāwā* < *bād-i hawā*. II 997a
ghanam (A, pl. *aghnām*, *ghunūm*, *aghānīm*) : the class of small livestock with a predominance of either sheep or goats, according to country. Also, understood in the sense of 'sheep-goat patrimony'. S 316b
ghanīma (A), or *ghunm* : booty, in particular moveable booty, which was distributed immediately, as opposed to FAYʾ. I 1144a; II 1005a; S 316b
gharāmet → DJARĪMA
gharāsa (A) : the act of planting. I 135b
gharīb (A, pl. GHURABĀʾ) : lit. strange, uncommon.
In philology, ~ means rare, unfamiliar (and consequently obscure) expressions

(syn. *waḥs͟hī*, *ḥūs͟hī*), and frequently occurs in the titles of books, mostly such as deal with unfamiliar expressions in the Qur'ān and ḤADĪT͟H. I 157b; II 1011a

In the science of Tradition, ~ means a Tradition from only one Companion, or from a single man at a later stage, to be distinguished from *g͟harīb al-ḥadīt͟h*, which applies to uncommon words in the text, MATN, of Traditions. III 25b

♦ g͟harīb muṭlaḳ → FARD

g͟hārim (A), or *g͟harīm* : in law, a debtor or creditor. II 1011b; S 207b

g͟harḳad (A) : a kind of bramble. I 957b

g͟harrā' (A) : in zoology, the spotted dogfish. VIII 1022b

g͟hars (Alg) : soft dates produced in the Sūf, along with the variety known as *deglet nūr*, which are harvested for export only. IX 763b

g͟hārūḳa (A) : in law, a system whereby a debtor landowner transfers part of his plot, and the right to cultivate it, as security on a loan until redemption. Other Arabic terms for the same system were *rahn ḥiyāzī* and *bay' bi 'l-istig͟hlāl*, and in Ottoman Turkish *istig͟hlāl*. ~ is a form of usury, and as such prohibited by Islamic law. S 322b

g͟haṣb (A) : in civil law, usurpation, the illegal appropriation of something belonging to another or the unlawful use of the rights of another. II 1020a

g͟hās͟hiya (A) : a covering, particularly, a covering for a saddle; one of the insignia of royal rank carried before the Mamlūk and Sald͟jūḳ rulers in public processions. II 1020a

In the Qur'ān, ~ is used metaphorically of a great misfortune that overwhelms someone. II 1020b

g͟hāsil → G͟HASSĀL

g͟hasīl al-malā'ika (A) : 'washed by the angels', a term by which Ḥanzala b. Abī 'Āmir is known, referring to the fact that he died without having performed the G͟HUSL following sexual intercourse. IX 204b

g͟hassāl (A) : a washer of clothes and also of the dead, the latter more often known as *g͟hāsil*. The social position of the corpse-washer was higher than that of the washer of clothes. S 322b

g͟haṭā → 'ATABA

g͟haṭaṭ → ḲAṬĀ

g͟hatmā' → ḲAṬĀ

g͟hawr (A) : in geography, a depression, plain encircled by higher ground. II 1024b

g͟hawṭ (Alg, pl. *g͟hīṭān*) : a funnel-like excavation, in which date palms are planted in the Sūf. IX 763b

g͟hawt͟h (A) : lit. succour, deliverance; an epithet of the head of the ṣūfī hierarchy of saints (syn. *badal*). Some say that it is a rank immediately below the head, ḲUṬB, in the hierarchy. V 543b; S 323b

g͟hayb (A) : absence; what is hidden, inaccessible to the senses and to reason; in Qur'ānic usage, with rare exceptions, ~ stands for mystery. I 406b ff.; II 1025a

In mysticism, ~ means, according to context, the reality of the world beyond discursive reason which gnosis experiences. II 1026a

♦ **ghayba** (A) : absence, occultation; and → NĀʾIB AL-GHAYBA

In mysticism, ~ is also used for the condition of anyone who has been withdrawn by God from the eyes of men and whose life during that period may have been miraculously prolonged. II 1026a; III 51b

Among the Twelvers, ~ became a major historical period, divided into two parts: the lesser ~ (from 260/874 to c. 329/941) and the greater ~ (from the death of the fourth IMĀM onwards). II 1026a; IV 277b

In law, ~ is the state of being not present at the place where one should be. II 995b

♦ ghayba munḳaṭiʿa : in law, an absence not interrupted by information on a person's existence; the continuous absence of a plaintiff. II 995b

ghaydāḳ (A) : lit. soft or tender; a term applied to a youth or young man; when applied to a boy, ~ signifies that he has not attained to puberty. VIII 822a

ghaylam → SULAḤFĀ

ghayṭa (< Fr *guetter*), or *ghāʾita*, *ghāyṭa* : in music, a reed-pipe of two kinds, popular in Muslim Spain and North Africa. One is a cylindrical tube blown with a single reed, and the other is a conical tube blown with a double reed. The cylindrical tube instrument is known in Egypt as the *ghīṭa*. II 1027b; VII 207b

ghazal (A) : in poetry, an elegy of love; the erotic-elegiac genre. I 586a; II 1028a; S 323b

ghāzī (A, pl. *ghuzāt*) : a fighter for the faith, a person who took part in a razzia, or raid against the infidels, GHAZW; later, a title of honour, becoming part of the title of certain Muslim princes, such as the AMĪRs of Anatolia and more particularly the first Ottoman sultans; soldiers of fortune, who in times of peace became a danger to the government which employed them. I 322b; II 1043b; VIII 497a

♦ ghuzāt al-baḥr : pirates. II 526a

♦ **ghāziya** (A, pl. *ghawāzī*) : an Egyptian dancing-girl who sang and danced primarily in the streets, making a speciality of lascivious dances and often becoming a prostitute. Today both the dancing-girl and the singer are called *ʿalma* in the cities but in the rural ares the dancer is still known as ~ . I 404a; II 1048a

ghazw (A, pl. *ghizwān*) : an expedition, raid, usually of limited scope, conducted with the aim of gaining plunder. I 892a; II 509b; II 1055a

♦ ghazwa (pl. *ghazawāt*) : a term used in particular of the Prophet's expeditions against the infidels. II 1055a; VIII 497a

ghidhāʾ (A, pl. *aghdhiya*) : feeding; food. II 1057a

ghifāra → MIGHFAR

ghīla (A) : a nursing woman. VIII 824a

ghilāf (A) : a sheath. IV 518b

ghilmān → GHULĀM
ghīnā → ĶĪNĀ
ghināʾ (A) : song, singing; music in its generic sense. In Morocco, the song is divided into folk or popular song, *ķarīḥa*, and the art song, *āla* or *ṣanʿa*, while in Algeria ~ is grouped under *kalām al-hazl* and *kalām al-djidd*. II 1072b f.
ghirāra (A) : a measure of capacity for grain in central Syria and Palestine in the mediaeval period, of different size in every province, e.g. the ~ of Damascus contained 208.74 kg of wheat, whereas the ~ of Jerusalem, at least at the end of the Middle Ages, weighed three times as much. IV 520a; VI 118b
ghirbāl (A) : a parchment-bottom sieve, which in the pre-Islamic period sometimes took the place of tambourines to supply rhythm. II 1073b; and → BANDAYR
ghirnīķ (A), and *kurkī* : in zoology, the crane. I 1152b
ghīṭa → GHAYṬA
ghiyār (A) : the compulsory distinctive mark in the garb of DHIMMĪ subjects under Muslim rule, described as a piece of cloth placed over the shoulder; the garment which bears the ~ . II 1075b; V 744b
ghižak → KAMĀNDJA
ghlāla (Mor) : a sleeveless outer robe for women in Morocco. V 746a
ghubār (A) : dust.

In mathematics, ~ was the name for the immediate parents of the modern European numerals, while what are now called 'Arabic' numerals were known as 'Indian'. Sometimes the names were reversed, however, or both forms were called Indian or both called ~ . III 1140a; and → ḤISĀB AL-GHUBĀR

In calligraphy, ~ or *ghubārī* is a name given to every type of very small script difficult to read with the naked eye, but often found in the NASKH script. IV 1124a

ghubba (A, pl. *ghabīb*) : a term in the Persian Gulf for an area of deep water, of 15 fathoms or more. I 535b
ghubbān (A) : in zoology, the green scarus, whose Arabic term is found again in the Latinised nomenclature to specify a sub-species limited to a particular region (*Scarus ghobban*). VIII 1021b
ghudfa (A) : a large head shawl for women, worn in the Hebron area. V 741a
ghudwa (A), or *bukra* : in lexicography, a term used to denote the time which elapses between the morning twilight prayer, FADJR, and the sunrise. V 709b
ghufrān (A) : the verbal noun of 'to forgive', ~ refers to the two divine names, *al-ghafūr* and *al-ghaffār*. A frequent synonym is *ʿafw*. II 1078b
ghūl (A, pl. *ghīlān, aghwāl*) : a fabulous being believed by the ancient Arabs to inhabit desert places and, assuming different forms, to lead travellers astray, to fall upon them unawares and devour them. Generally, a ~ is considered a male as well as a female being in the early sources. II 1078b
ghulām (A, pl. *ghilmān*; P pl. *ghulāmān*) : a young man or boy; by extension,

either a servant, sometimes elderly and very often, but not necessarily, a slave servant; or a bodyguard, slave or freedman, bound to his master by personal ties; or sometimes an artisan working in the workshop of a master whose name he used along with his own in his signature. Rulers owned an often impressive number of slave boys who served as attendants or guards and could rise to fairly high office in the hierarchy of the palace service, as well as others who formed a component of varying importance in the armed forces. I 24b; II 1079b; VIII 821b

In falconry, a technical term for the hawker's assistant, who kept the aviary well provided with pigeons and other game-birds and was responsible for the nourishment and training of the hawks. I 1152b

♦ al-ghilmān al-khāṣṣa : the personal guard of certain ʿAbbāsid caliphs. II 1080a

♦ ghulāmān-i khāṣṣa-yi sharīfa (P) : 'slaves of the royal household', a cavalry regiment formed from the ranks of the Georgians and Circassians under the Ṣafawids. II 1083b; IV 36a; VIII 769a

ghulāmān → GHULĀM

ghulāt (A, s. *ghālī*) : 'extremists', those individuals accused of exaggeration, *ghulū*, in religion; in practice, ~ has covered all early speculative shīʿīs except those later accepted by the Twelver tradition, as well as all later shīʿī groups except Zaydīs, orthodox Twelvers, and sometimes Ismāʿīlīs. II 1093b

ghunča (P) : in botany, the rosebud, a recurring image in eastern Islamic literature. II 1133a

ghurāb (A, < L *corvus*) : in zoology, the crow. II 1096b

In navigation, a large type of mediaeval Muslim galley (< Sp *caraba*), frequently mentioned in accounts of the naval warfare between the Muslims and the Franks during Crusading and Mamlūk times. In archaic Anglo-Indian usage, it yielded the term *grab*, a type of ship often mentioned, in the Indian Ocean context, from the arrival of the Portuguese to the 18th century. VIII 810a

ghurabāʾ (A, T *ghurebā*) : an Ottoman term for the two lowest of the six cavalry regiments of the ḲAPÎ ḲULLARÎ. The regiment riding on the sultan's right side was known as *ghurebāʾ-i yemīn* and that riding on his left as *ghurebāʾ-i yesār*. II 1097b

ghurfa → AGADIR

ghurra (A) : the first day of the month, in historical works and correspondence. V 708a; a term used in Bedouin society for the young girl, who must be a virgin, white and free, given by the family of a murderer to a member of the injured family as compensation. In turn the latter forgoes his right of vengeance. VI 479b

In law, ~ is a special indemnity to be paid for causing an abortion. I 29a; VIII 823b

ghusl (A) : general ablution, uninterrupted washing, in ritually pure water, of the whole of the human body, including the hair. ~ applies also to the washing of the corpse of a Muslim. For the living, the essential ~ is that which is obligatory before performing the ritual daily prayers. II 1104a; VIII 929a

ghuṣn (A) : in prosody, separate-rhyme lines in each stanza of a MUWASHSHAḤ. VII 809b

ghūṭa (A) : the name given in Syria to abundantly irrigated areas of intense cultivation surrounded by arid land. It is produced by the co-operative activity of a rural community settled near to one or several perennial springs, whose water is used in a system of canalisation to irrigate several dozen or hundred acres. II 541a; II 1104b

ghuzāt → GHĀZĪ

ginān (H, < San *jñāna*) : in Nizārī Ismāʿīlism, a poetical composition in an Indian vernacular, ascribed to various PĪRs who were active in preaching and propagating the DAʿWA. The ~ resembles didactic and mystical poetry and is often anachronistic and legendary in nature. VIII 126a

girīz (T), or *girīzgāh* : in Turkish prosody, ~ is the passage marking the transition from the NASĪB to the main part of the ḲAṢĪDA. IV 715b; and → MAKHLAṢ

giṭūn (N.Afr) : the name given to shelters in North Africa made of sackcloth or pieces of material or of canvas produced in Europe. The name derives from the classical *ḳayṭūn* 'room in a BAYT'. IV 1149b

gīwa : characteristic foot-gear of the Bakhtiyārī tribeswomen. I 956a

gnīdra (Alg) : a light, lacy chemisette for women in Algeria. V 746a

göbak (P) : among the Shāhsewan in Persia, a 'navel' or descent group. IX 224a

♦ göbek adi̊ (T) : 'navel name'; in Turkey, a name given to a new-born child by the midwife as she cuts the umbilical cord. IV 181a

göčmen → MUHĀDJIR

gönüllü (T) : volunteer; in the Ottoman empire, ~ was used as a term (sometimes with the pseudo-Persian pl. *gönüllüyān*, in Arabic sources usually rendered *djamulyān* or *kamulyān*) with the following meanings: volunteers coming to take part in the fighting; a 10th/16th-century organised body stationed in most of the fortresses of the empire, in Europe, Asia and Egypt; and an 11th/17th-century body among the paid auxiliaries who were recruited in the provinces to serve on a campaign. II 1120b

goruta → YODJANA

göstermelik (T) : inanimate objects, without any direct connection with the shadow play, which are shown on the screen before the actual play in order to attract the interest of spectators and fire their imagination. IV 601b

göt-tikme (T) : a type of tent possessed by the Türkmen Yomut and Göklen tribes. The ~ essentially is an ÖY 'tent-house', but without the trellis walls, and regarded as inferior, though more portable. IV 1150b

gotba → ʿUDIYA

gourbi (Alg) : a shack, a fixed dwelling used in the Algerian sedentarisation of nomads in the 20th century. IX 537b

grab → GHURĀB
gu' (Somali) : the season from April to June which is the 'season of plenty' in Somalia. The other seasons are *xagaa* (July-August), *dayr* (September-November) and *jiilaal* (December-March). IX 714b
guban (Somali) : lit. burnt; a hot, dry region. IX 714a
gudhār (P) : a restricted area of a guild in which it practised its trade. IX 645b
gul (P, T *gül*) : in botany, the rose, a recurring image in eastern Islamic literature. II 1133a

Among the dervishes, *gül* signifies a particular ornament, fashioned from wedge-shaped pieces of cloth, on the top of a dervish cap, which distinguishes the head of a house of the order; in various contexts ~ is the badge of different dervish orders and of distinct grades within the orders. II 1134a

♦ **gülbaba** (T) : a title, with the sense of head of a Muslim cloister, *tekke* (→ KHĀNḲĀH), of the Bektāshī order. II 1133b

♦ **gulbāng** (P) : lit. song of the nightingale; in Turkish usage, *gülbāng* is applied to the call of the muezzin and to the Muslim war-cry. Under the Otttomans, ~ was used of certain ceremonial and public prayers and acclamations, more specifically those of the Janissary corps. II 1135a

♦ guldasta : in architecture, a shaft-like pinnacle, introduced in Tughluḳid work as a prolongation of the angle turret. VIII 315b

gūm (N.Afr, < A *ḳawm*) : the name given in the Arab countries of North Africa to a group of armed horsemen or fighting men from a tribe. They were given an official existence by the Turks in the former Regencies of Algiers and Tunis, who made them the basis of their occupation of the country, and were later used by the French to pacify the country. II 1138b

♦ gūma : a levy of GŪMs, troops; a plundering foray; sedition, revolt. II 1138b

gurīzgāh → MAKHLAṢ
guru (J) : in Malaysia and Thailand, a mystical teacher. VIII 294a; VIII 296b ff.
gzîdan (K) : a Kurdish dance performed at the occasion of a festival celebrating the gathering of the mulberry harvest, which consists of sweeping the soil under the trees before the children climb them to shake them so as to allow the women to gather the berries. V 477b

H

ḥababawar → SHAḲĪḲAT AL-NUʿMĀN
ḥabaḳ → FŪDHANDJ
ḥaballaḳ → NAḲAD
ḥabara (A) : a dark, silky enveloping outer wrap for women, worn in the Arab East. V 741a

ḥabas̲h̲ (A), or *ḥabas̲h̲a* : a name said to be of south Arabian origin, applied in Arabic usage to the land and peoples of Ethiopia, and at times to the adjoining areas in the Horn of Africa. III 2b

♦ **ḥabas̲h̲at** : a term found in several Sabaean inscriptions with apparent reference to Aksumite Abbyssinia, it has generally been assumed to apply not only to the territory and people of the Aksumite empire but also to a south Arabian tribe related to the former and in close contact with them; incense-collectors, applicable to all the peoples of the incense regions, that is, of the Mahra and Somali coasts and Abyssinia proper. III 9a

ḥabaṭ → ḤAWṬA

ḥabba (A) : lit. grain or kernel; as a unit of weight, a ~ was a fraction in the Troy weight system of the Arabs, of undefined weight. The most probable weight of the ~ in the early days of Islam was about 70-71 milligrammes (1.1 grains). III 10b

ḥabīb (A) : lit. beloved; *al-Ḥabīb* is the usual Ḥaḍramī title of a SAYYID. IX 115a; IX 333a

ḥabīs (A) : an anchorite, recluse. IX 574a

ḥabs → SID̲J̲N; ʿURWA

♦ **ḥabsiyya** (P, < A) : in Persian literature, a poem dealing with the theme of imprisonment. The genre can also be found in Urdu poetry and in the Indian tradition of Persian poetry. S 333b

ḥabs̲h̲ī : a term applied in India for those African communities whose ancestors originally came to the country as slaves, in most cases from the Horn of Africa, although some doubtless sprang from the slave troops of the neighbouring Muslim countries. The majority, at least in the earlier periods, may well have been Abyssinian (→ ḤABAS̲H̲), but the name was used indiscriminately for all Africans. In modern India, ~ is often heard applied in a pejorative sense to an Indian of dark skin, and also frequently to a man of Gargantuan appetite. III 14a

ḥadaba (A) : in the Arabian peninsula, a plain with a mantle of gravel. I 536b

ḥaḍāna (A), or *ḥiḍāna* : in law, ~ is the right to custody of the child. I 28b; III 16b

ḥadat̲h̲ (A) : in law, minor ritual impurity, as opposed to major impurity, D̲J̲ANĀBA. A person who is in a state of ~ is called a *muḥdit̲h̲* and he can regain ritual purity by means of simple ablution, WUḌŪʾ. III 19b; VIII 929a; ~ in its plural form, *aḥdāt̲h̲*, means arbitrary actions at odds with the divine Law. I 384a

ḥadd (A, pl. *ḥudūd*) : hindrance, impediment, limit, boundary, frontier.

In the Qurʾān, ~ is used (always in the pl.) to denote the restrictive ordinances or statutes of God. III 20b

In law, ~ has become the technical term for the punishments of certain acts which have been forbidden or sanctioned by punishments in the Qurʾān and have thereby become crimes against religion. The punishments are the death penalty, either by stoning or by crucifixion or with the sword; the cutting off of the hand and/or the foot; and flogging with various numbers of lashes, their intensity depending on the severity of the crime. III 20b

In theology, ~ in the meaning of limit, limitation, is an indication of finiteness, a necessary attribute of all created beings but incompatible with God. III 20b

In scholastic theology, philosophy and metaphysics, ~ is a technical term for definition, e.g. *ḥadd ḥaḳīḳī*, that which defines the essence of a thing, and *ḥadd lafẓī*, that which defines the meaning of a word. III 21a

In logic, ~ means the term of a syllogism. III 21a

In astrology, ~ denotes the term of a planet or the unequal portion, of which there are five, each belonging to a planet, into which the degree of each sign of the zodiac is divided. III 21a

Among the Druze, the main officers of the religious hierarchy are called *ḥudūd*. The five great *ḥudūd* 'cosmic ranks', adopted in a modified form from Ismāʿīlī lore, consist of the *ʿaḳl*, the *nafs al-kulliyya*, the *kalima*, the *sābiḳ*, and the *tālī*. II 632a; III 21a

ḥa<u>dh</u>a<u>dh</u> (A) : in prosody, a deviation in the metre because of the suppression of a whole *watid ma<u>dj</u>mūʿ* (→ AWTĀD), as in *mutafā[ʿilun]*. I 672a

ḥa<u>dh</u>af (A) : a strain of sheep in the time of al-<u>D</u>jāḥiẓ, with a black fleece and almost without a tail and ears, found in the Ḥi<u>dj</u>āz and Yemen. Similar to the ~ was the *ḳahd*, with a russet-coloured fleece. S 318a; a teal, or wild duck. IX 98b

ḥa<u>dh</u>f (A) : in prosody, a deviation in the metre because of the suppression of a moving and a quiescent consonant, a *sabab <u>kh</u>afīf* (→ SABAB), e.g. *mafāʿī[lun]*. I 672a

In rhetoric, the truncation of words. VIII 427a

ḥa<u>dh</u>w (A) : in prosody, the vowel immediately before the RIDF. IV 412a

hadī (A) : the name for the animal sacrificed in order to make atonement for certain transgressions committed during the ḤA<u>DJDJ</u>. II 213a

hādī (A, pl. *huddāʾ*) : the sporting pigeon; the sport of pigeon-flying (*za<u>dj</u>il, zi<u>dj</u>āl*) was very popular from the 2nd-7th/8th-13th centuries, among all the Muslim peoples. III 109a

hadia langgar (Ind, < A HADIYYA) : a gift for the permission to cast the anchor, one of the tolls and taxes known in Atjèh in relation to sea trade. S 200b

ḥadīd (A) : in mineralogy, iron; three kinds of iron were distinguished by al-Ḳazwīnī: natural iron, *al-sābūrḳān*, and artificial iron, of which there were two kinds, the weak or female, i.e. malleable iron (P *narm-āhan*) and hard or male, i.e. steel (*fūlā<u>dh</u>*). III 22b

♦ ḥadīd ṣīnī → ṬĀLIḲŪN

ḥaḍīḍ → AW<u>DJ</u>

ḥāḍira (A) : in administrative geography, 'regional capital'. IX 36b

ḥadī<u>th</u> (A) : narrative, talk; *al-ḥadī<u>th</u>* is used for Tradition, being an account of what the Prophet said or did, or of his tacit approval of something said or done in his presence. III 23b; and → AHL AL-ḤADĪ<u>TH</u>; DĀR AL-ḤADĪ<u>TH</u>; <u>KH</u>ABAR

♦ **ḥadī<u>th</u> ḳudsī**, and *ḥadī<u>th</u> ilāhī*, *ḥadī<u>th</u> rabbānī* : a class of Traditions which give words spoken by God, as distinguished from *ḥadīth nabawī* 'prophetical Tradition', which gives the words of the Prophet. III 28b

♦ ḥadīth ilāhī → ḤADĪTH ḲUDSĪ

♦ ḥadīth nabawī → ḤADĪTH ḲUDSĪ

♦ ḥadīth rabbānī → ḤADĪTH ḲUDSĪ

♦ ḥadīth al-thaḳalayn : a Tradition which refers to the two sources of guidance that Muḥammad says he is leaving behind for the Muslims: the Qurʾān and AHL AL-BAYT. IX 331b

hadiyya (A) : a gift which in the Muslim East frequently implied an effort on the part of a person on a lower level of society to get into the good graces of a recipient of a higher social status, as opposed to HIBA. In the Muslim West ~ is commonly used with the restricted meaning of a sumptuous gift offered to a sovereign, either by another sovereign or by a group of some kind, while in Morocco especially, ~ was an obligatory gift made to the sultan by his subjects, later becoming a supplementary tax. III 343a; III 346b; in Persia, ~ is a gift to an equal, and the normal expression for the exchange of presents on diplomatic missions. III 347b

ḥadjal (A) : in zoology, the partridge. IX 98b

ḥadjar (A) : stone; also applied to any solid inorganic body occurring anywhere in Nature. III 29b

hadjar (A, Eth *hagar* 'town') : the normal word for 'town' in the epigraphic dialects of pre-Islamic South Arabia, now an element in place-names given to pre-Islamic town ruins in South Arabia. III 29b

ḥadjdj (A) : the pilgrimage to Mecca, ʿArafāt and Minā, one of the five pillars of Islam. It is also called the Great Pilgrimage in contrast to the ʿUMRA, or Little Pilgrimage. One who has performed the pilgrimage is called *ḥādjdj* or *ḥādjdjī*. III 31b; III 38b; and → AMĪR AL-ḤĀDJDJ

♦ ḥadjdj al-wadāʿ : the last pilgrimage of the Prophet, in the year 10/632. III 37a

ḥadjdjām → FAṢṢĀD

ḥādjib (A) : the person responsible for guarding the door of access to the ruler, hence 'chamberlain'; a title corresponding to a position in the court and to an office the exact nature of which varied considerably in different regions and in different periods: superintendent of the palace, chief of the guard, chief minister, a head of government. III 45a; VIII 728a; S 336b

Among the Būyids, ~ was known as a military rank in the army, with the meaning of general. III 46b

In Persian prosody, the internal RADĪF, which precedes the rhyme rather than following it. VIII 369a

♦ ḥādjib al-ḥudjdjāb, or *al-ḥādjib al-kabīr* : the equivalent of the Persian *sipahsālār* (→ ISPAHSĀLĀR) or the Arabic AMĪR AL-UMARĀʾ found among dynasties like the Sāmānids, Būyids, Ghaznawids and Great Saldjūḳs. VIII 924a

♦ al-ḥādjib al-kabīr → ḤĀDJIB AL-ḤUDJDJĀB

hadjīn (A), or *shihrī* : the 'mixed breed', whose sire is better bred than the dam, one of four classifications of a horse. II 785b

hādjira → ẒĀHIRA

hādjis (A) : in Yemen, term for poetic inspiration. IX 235b

ḥadjm (A) : in medicine, cupping without or after the scarification, SHARṬ. II 481b

ḥadjr (A) : prevention, inhibition; in law, the interdiction, the restriction of the capacity to dispose; ~ expresses both the act of imposing this restriction and the resulting status. A person in this status is called *maḥdjūr* (*maḥdjūr ʿalayh*). I 27b; III 50a

♦ ḥadjra (A), or *kuffa*, *ṭawḳ* : in astronomy, the outer rim on the front of the astrolabe, which encloses the inner surface and into which a number of thin discs are fitted. I 723a

ḥādjūr → FILAWR

ḥaḍra (A) : presence; a title of respect; in mysticism, ~ is a synonym of *ḥuḍūr*, 'being in the presence of God'. III 51a

The regular Friday service of the dervishes is called ~ . III 51b

hady (A) : oblation; a pre-Islamic sacrificial offering which survived in Islam under the name ḌAḤIYYA. III 53b

haff → ḲUSHḲUSH

ḥaffāra (A) : in zoology, the wrasse, whose Arabic term is found again in the Latinised nomenclature to specify a sub-species limited to a particular region (*Chrysophrys haffara*). VIII 1021a

ḥāfiẓ (A) : a designation for one who knows the Qurʾān by heart. VIII 171a; a great traditionist. IX 608a

ḥafshrūsī → KALB AL-BAḤR

ḥāgūza (Mor) : the name of a festival celebrated in Morocco, especially in the country, at the beginning of the solar year. V 1202a

ḥāʾik (A, pl. *ḥāka*), or *ḥayyāk* : weaver (syn. *nassādj*). S 340b

In North Africa, ~ , or *ḥayk*, *taḥaykt*, is a large outer wrap, usually white, worn by both sexes. V 746a

ḥāʾir (A) : a park or pleasure-garden, or zoological garden. III 71a

ḥakam (A) : in law, an arbitrator who settles a dispute (syn. *muḥakkam*). III 72a

ḥaḳīḳa (A, pl. ḤAḲĀʾIḲ) : reality; essence, truth.

In rhetoric and exegesis, *al-ḥaḳīḳa* is the basic meaning of a word or an expression, and is distinguished from MADJĀZ, metaphor, and *kayfiyya*, analogy. III 75a

In philosophy, ~ has an ontological and a logical meaning. The ontological meaning (*ḥaḳīḳat al-shayʾ*) is best translated by 'nature' or 'essential reality'; the logical meaning (*al-ḥaḳīḳa al-ʿaḳliyya*) is the truth which 'the exact conception of the thing' establishes in the intelligence. III 75a ff.; V 1262a

In mysticism, ~ is the profound reality to which only experience of union with God opens the way. III 75b

♦ **ḥaḳā'iḳ** : the Ismāʿīlī term for their secret philosophical doctrines. I 1255b; III 71b

ḥakīm (A, pl. *ḥukamā'*; T *ḥekīm*) : sage; physician.

♦ al-ḥukamā' : the ninth degree in the ṣūfī hierarchical order of saints. I 95a

♦ **ḥekīm-bas̲h̲i̊** (T) : in the Ottoman empire, the title of the chief palace physician, who was at the same time head of the health services of the state. III 339b

ḥaḳḳ (A, pl. **ḥuḳūḳ**) : something right, true, just, real; established fact; reality. I 275a; III 82b; and → AHL-I ḤAḲḲ; DĪN AL-ḤAḲḲ; RASM

In law, ~ is a claim or right, as a legal obligation. Religious law distinguishes *ḥaḳḳ Allāh*, God's penal ordinances, with *ḥaḳḳ al-ādamī*, the civil right or claim of a human. III 82b; III 551b; *ḥuḳūḳ*, when used of things in law, signifies the accessories necessarily belonging to them, such as the privy and the kitchen of a house, and servitudes in general. III 551b

In mysticism, ~ *al-yaḳīn* is the real certainty which comes after the acquisition of visual certainty and intellectual certainty. *Ḥuḳūḳ al-nafs* are such things as are necessary for the support and continuance of life, as opposed to the *ḥuẓūẓ*, things desired but not necessary. III 82a-b; III 551b

♦ ḥaḳḳ ʿaynī : in law, a real right, as opposed to *ḥaḳḳ s̲h̲ak̲h̲ṣī* 'personal right'. IX 495a

♦ ḥaḳḳ al-d̲jahābid̲h̲a → MĀL AL-D̲JAHĀBID̲H̲A

♦ ḥaḳḳ-i ḳapan → ḲAPAN

♦ ḥaḳḳ-i ḳarār (T) : a fixed charge in the Ottoman empire on parcels of land known as ČIFTLIK, which a peasant had to pay in order to obtain permission to sell or give up his land. II 907a; VIII 486a

♦ ḥaḳḳ s̲h̲ak̲h̲ṣī → ḤAḲḲ ʿAYNĪ

♦ ḥuḳūḳ bayt al-māl : assets of the Treasury; those monies or properties which belong to the Muslim community as a whole, the purpose to which they are devoted being dependent upon the discretion of the IMĀM or his delegate. I 1142a

ḥakma (A) : in the terminology of horse-riding, the curb-chain of the bit, which is also composed of branches, *s̲h̲ākima*, and a mouthpiece, *fa's*. II 954a

ḥakw (A) : a binding for a waist wrapper, worn by both sexes in the Arabian peninsula (syn. *brīm*). V 741a

ḥāl (A, pl. *aḥwāl*) : state, condition; in mysticism, a spiritual state; the actualisation of a divine 'encounter'. III 83b; trance; among the Ḥmāds̲h̲a in North Africa, ~ is used for a light, somnambulistic trance, while a deeper, wilder trance is called *d̲jed̲h̲ba*. S 350b

In medicine, ~ denotes 'the actual functional (physiological) equilibrium' of a being endowed with NAFS. III 83b

In grammar, ~ is the state of the verb in relation to the agent, its 'subjective' state. III 83b; circumstantial qualifier. IX 527b

In scholastic theology, ~ is the intermediate modality between being and non-being. III 83b; a technical term employed by some 4th-5th/10th-11th century Baṣran scholastic theologians, *mutakallimūn*, to signify certain 'attributes' that are predicated of beings. I 411a; II 570b; S 343b

♦ ʿilm-i ḥāl : a genre in Ottoman literature, forming a kind of catechism of the basic principles of worship and of behaviour within the family and the community. VIII 211b

ḥāla (A, pl. *ḥuwal*) : a term in the Persian Gulf for a low sandy islet which may be covered at high tide. I 535b

ḥalaḳ → DHĀT AL-ḤALAḲ

ḥalāl (A) : in law, everything that is not forbidden. III 660b

ḥalam → ḲIRDĀN

ḥalāwī (A) : in zoology, the guitar fish, whose Arabic term is found again in the Latinised nomenclature to specify a sub-species limited to a particular region (*Rhinobatus halavi*). VII 1021b

ḥalazūn (A) : in zoology, the general term for snail. VIII 707a

ḥalf → ḲASAM; MUSALSAL AL-ḤALF

ḥalfāʾ (A) : in botany, alfa-grass (*Stipa tenacissima*) and esparto-grass (*Lygoeum spartum*), two similar plants found in North Africa. The former is called in Tunisia ~ *rūsiyya* or *geddīm*. A field of alfa is sometimes called *zemla*. III 92a, where can also be found dialectal terms used in the harvesting of both plants

ḥalīb (A) : fresh milk, straight from the animal. S 318b

halīladj (P, San), or *ahlīladj*, *ihlīladj* : in botany, myrobalanus, the plum-like fruit of the *Terminalia chebula*-tree, found in South Asia and the Malayan archipelago. The Arabs knew five kinds of myrobalanus. S 349a

In mathematics, ~ , but especially its variant *ihlīladj*, was used to designate an ellipse. S 349b

ḥālim (A) : a boy who has attained to puberty, or virility. VIII 822a

ḥalḳ → ISTIḤDĀD

ḥalḳa (A) : a circle; gathering of people seated in a circle; gathering of students around a teacher, hence 'course'. I 817a; III 95a; V 1129a

Among the Ibāḍī-Wahbīs of the Mzāb, ~ was a religious council made up of twelve recluses, *ʿazzāba*, presided over by a SHAYKH. III 95a

Under the Ayyūbids and Mamlūks, a term for a socio-military unit which, during most of the period of Mamlūk rule, was composed of non-Mamlūks. Under Ṣalāḥ al-Dīn it seems to have constituted the elite of his army. I 765b; III 99a; and → AWLĀD AL-NĀS

In military science, ~ was the term used for the encirclement of the enemy in an increasingly tightening ring, a strategy employed by the Turkish and Mongol tribes in the field of battle. The same tactics were also very common in hunting, especially in the early decades of Mamlūk rule. III 187b

In astronomy, part of the suspensory apparatus of the astrolabe, the ~ is the ring which passes through the handle, ʿURWA, moving freely. I 723a

ḥalḳiyya (A) : in grammar, a term used by al-Khalīl to denote the laryngeals. III 598a

ḥallāḳ (A) : a barber, hairdresser (syn. *muzayyin*). S 350a

ḥālūsh → KALB AL-MAYY

hām, hāma → ṢADĀ

hamada (Alg) : silicified limestone. S 328a

ḥamal (A) : lamb; in astronomy, *al-~* is the term for Aries, one of the twelve zodiacal constellations, also called *al-kabsh* 'the ram' because of its 'horns'. VII 83a; S 319a

♦ ḥamalat al-ʿilm (A), or *naḳalat al-ʿilm* : lit. bearers of learning; among the Ibāḍiyya, the ~ were teams of missionaries who were sent out after completion of their training to spread propaganda in the various provinces of the Umayyad caliphate. III 650b

ḥamām (A, pl. *ḥamāʾim*, *ḥamāmāt*) : in zoology, any bird 'which drinks with one gulp and coos', that is, any of the family of the Columbidae: pigeons and turtledoves. In the restricted sense, ~ denotes the domestic pigeons. III 108b, where are found many terms, in the different countries, for the many different types of birds

ḥamāsa (A) : bravery, valour; in literature, the title of a certain number of poetic anthologies which generally include brief extracts chosen for their literary value. III 110b; the boasting of courage, a subject of occasional verse. I 584b; the genre of the epic poem, although ~ has been replaced today by MALḤAMA in this sense. III 111b

In Persian literature, ~ has come to denote a literary genre, the heroic and martial epic. III 112a

♦ ḥamāsiyya : in Turkish literature, ~ indicates an epic poem. III 114b

hamasāla (P) : allocations on the revenue of specific villages or districts, according to which the taxpayers paid their taxes, up to the amount stipulated, to the holder of the ~ instead of to the government tax-collector. IV 1045a

ḥamd (A) : praise; on the Arabian Peninsula, a bush and a prime source of salt needed by camels. I 540b

In Urdu religious literature, specifically praise of God. V 958a

♦ **ḥamdala** (A) : the saying of the formula *al-ḥamdu li 'llāh* 'Praise belongs to God'. III 122b

ḥāmiḍ → ḲĀRIṢ

ḥamla (A) : in the Ottoman empire, the term used to designate the group of people at the rear of the Baghdad-Aleppo caravan. IV 679a

ḥammāda (N.Afr) : large areas which are the outcrops of horizontal beds of secondary or tertiary limestone or sandstone (or calcareous or gypso-calcareous crusts of the quaternary era). III 136b

ḥammāl (A) : street-porter, bearer, who transports packages, cases, furniture, etc. on his back in towns and cities. In Istanbul, if two or more porters are required, a long pole, called *sırık* in Turkish, is used to carry the heavy load. In Fās, the ~ mostly carries cereals; the Berber word for porter, of which there is a special guild, is *zərzāya*. III 139a

ḥammām → MUKAYYIS; WAḲḲĀD; ZABBĀL

hamsāya (Pash) : in Afghanistan, a client attached to and living under the protection of a tribe. I 217a

ḥamūla (A) : a group of people who claim descent from a common ancestor, usually five to seven generations removed from the living. III 149b

hāmūr (A) : in the Persian Gulf, term for the grouper. I 541b

ḥanak (A), or *taḥnīk al-ʿimāma* : a turban which was distinctively wound under the chin. Originally, the ~ was worn by the chief eunuchs of the Fāṭimid court, who were the AMĪRs of the palace. The caliph al-ʿAzīz was the first ruler to appear in the ~ . This fashion was introduced into the East by the Fāṭimids from North Africa, where it still may be seen, especially in southern Algeria and Morocco. V 738a

ḥanbal (A) : a rug made of coarse wool. IX 764b

hanbala (A), or *hunbuʿa* : the swaying and limping gait of the hyena, as described in pre-Islamic poetry. S 174a

handasa → ʿILM

ḥanfāʾ → AṬŪM

ḥanīf (A, pl. *ḥunafāʾ*) : in Islamic writings, one who follows the original and true (monotheistic) religion. In the Qurʾān, ~ is used especially of Abraham. III 165a; later Islamic usage occasionally uses ~ as the equivalent of MUSLIM. III 165b

♦ ḥanīfiyya : the religion of Abraham, or Islam, especially when used by Christian writers. III 165b

ḥāniṭ (A) : the child who has reached the age of reason. VIII 822a

ḥan<u>sh</u>al (A, s. *ḥan<u>sh</u>ūlī*) : small parties of Bedouin on foot. II 1055a

han<u>sh</u>īr → ʿAZĪB

ḥantam → IKLĪL AL-MALIK

ḥanūṭ (A) : a perfume or scented unguent used for embalming (**ḥināṭa**), consisting of sweet rush or some mixture (*<u>dh</u>arīra*), musk, ʿANBAR, camphor, Indian reed and powdered sandal wood. III 403b f.

ḥāra (A) : a quarter or ward of a town; in Morocco, used as a synonym of MALLĀḤ, a special quarter for Jews. II 230a; III 169b; and → <u>SH</u>ĀRIʿ

ḥaraka (A) : motion.

In philosophy, ~ is used for the Aristotelian notion of motion. III 170a

In grammar, ~ is a state of motion in which a ḤARF 'letter' exists when not in a state of rest, *sukūn*. It implies the existence of a short vowel, *a*, *i*, or *u*, following the letter. III 172a

♦ ḥarakī (A) : in modern-day terminology, 'activist', as in *tafsīr* ~ 'activist exegesis'. IX 118a ḥaram (A) : among the Bedouin, a sacred area around a shrine; a place where a holy power manifests itself. I 892b; III 294b; III 1018a; the sacred territory of Mecca. I 604a; IV 322a; V 1003a

♦ **al-ḥaramayn** : the two holy places, usually Mecca and Medina, but occasionally, in Mamlūk and Ottoman usage, Jerusalem and Hebron. III 175a

♦ ḥaramgāh → ḤARĪM

haram (A, pl. *ahrām, ahrāmāt*) : pyramid, pre-eminently the pyramid of Cheops and Chephren. III 173a

ḥarām (A) : a term representing everything that is forbidden to the profane and separated from the rest of the world. The cause of this prohibition could be either impurity (temporary or intrinsic) or holiness, which is a permanent state of sublime purity. IV 372b

ḥarb (A) : war. III 180a

♦ ḥarba → ʿANAZA

♦ ḥarbī (A), or *ahl al-ḥarb* : a non-Muslim from the DĀR AL-ḤARB. I 429b; II 126b; III 547a; VII 108b; IX 846a

ḥareket ordusu (T) : 'investing' or 'marching' army. I 64a; the name usually given to the striking force sent from Salonica on 17 April 1909 to quell the counter-revolutionary mutiny in the First Army Corps in Istanbul. III 204a

ḥarf (A, pl. *ḥurūf, aḥruf*) : letter of the alphabet; word. III 204b; articulation of the Arabic language, a phoneme. III 597a; a Qurʾānic reading; dialect. III 205b

♦ ḥarf ʿilla, or *muʿtalla* : a 'weak' consonant, viz. the semi-vowels *alif, wāw, yāʾ*. III 1129b; VIII 836b; VIII 990b

♦ ḥarf mutaḥarrik : individual 'moving' consonant; a consonant with a vowel, as opposed to *ḥarf sākin*; a short syllable. I 669b

♦ ḥarf sākin → ḤARF MUTAḤARRIK

♦ **ḥurūf al-hid̲j̲āʾ** : the letters of the alphabet. III 596b

♦ ḥurūf al-muʿd̲j̲am : properly, those letters with diacritical points, but in practice ~ has become a synonym for *ḥurūf al-hid̲j̲āʾ*, the letters of the alphabet, but referring solely to writing. III 597a

♦ al-ḥurūf al-muḳaṭṭaʿāt → FAWĀTIḤ AL-SUWAR

♦ al-ḥurūf al-muṭbaḳa → IṬBĀḲ

♦ ʿilm al-**ḥurūf** : onomatomancy, a magical practice based on the occult properties of the letters of the alphabet and of the divine and angelic names which they form. III 595b

ḥarfūs̲h̲ (A, pl. *ḥarāfīs̲h̲, ḥarāfīs̲h̲a*), sometimes *k̲h̲arfūs̲h̲* : vagabond, ne'er-do-well, often used in the sense of ruffians, rascals, scamps. The term frequently appears from the 7th/13th to the 10th/16th century in chronicles and other works dealing with the Mamlūk domains of Egypt and Syria, where it denotes the lowest element in the strata of Mamlūk society. During the Ottoman period ~ was replaced by *d̲j̲uʿaydī* as a general term for vagabond, beggar. III 206a

ḥarīd (A) : in zoology, the parrot fish, whose Arabic term is found again in the

Latinised nomenclature to specify a sub-species limited to a particular region (*Scarus harid*). VIII 1021b

harim → PĪR

hārim (A, pl. *hawārim*) : a (female) camel which feeds from the *harm* bush. I 541a

ḥarīm (A), also *ḥaramgāh*, *zanāna* : a term applied to those parts of the house to which access is forbidden; hence more particularly to the women's quarters. III 209a

ḥarīr (A, Ott *ipek*) : silk (syn. *ibrīsam*, *ḳazz*); ~ occurs in the Qurʾān, where it is said that the raiment of the people of Paradise will be silk, but Tradition and the schools of law traditionally forbid the wearing of silk to men, allowing it to women. III 209b

♦ ḥarīra (A) : a gruel made from flour cooked with milk, eaten by pre-Islamic Arabs. II 1059a

harīr → KHURŪR

ḥarīsh → KARKADDAN

ḥarka → DJAYSH

ḥārr → ḲĀRIṢ

ḥarra (A, pl. *ḥirār*) : a basalt desert in Arabia, which owes its origin to subterranean volcanoes which have repeatedly covered the undulating desert with a bed of lava. I 535a; III 226a; III 362a; IX 817a

ḥarrāḳa (A) : 'fire ship'; ~ presumably denoted in origin a warship from which fire could be hurled at the enemy, but was soon used for passenger-carrying craft in Mesopotamia and also on the Nile. VIII 811a

ḥarrāthā → KALB AL-MAYY

ḥarṭānī (A, < B ?; pl. *ḥarāṭīn*) : name given in northwest Africa to a sedentary population of the oases in the Saharan zone; ~ is not applied in dialect exclusively to human beings, but is variously used for a horse of mixed breed, an ungrafted tree, a wilding, or a holding of land that is not free. III 230b

ḥarūn (A) : in the terminology of horse-riding, a horse that refuses to walk forward. II 953b

ḥarz → ʿIBRA

ḥasab (A) : nobility, possessed by one (*ḥasīb*) either with noble ancestry or acquired by the performance of memorable deeds of prowess or the display of outstanding virtues. III 238b

ḥasan (A) : good.

In the science of Tradition, one of three kinds of Traditions, in between ṢAḤĪḤ 'sound' and ḌAʿĪF 'weak' or *saḳīm* 'infirm'. ~ Traditions are not considered as strong as *ṣaḥīḥ* Traditions, but are necessary for establishing points of law. III 25a; a 'fair' Tradition, a genuine euphemism for mostly poorly authenticated Traditions. VIII 983a

♦ **ḥasanī** : the name given in Morocco to the money minted on the orders of Mawlay al-Ḥasan from 1299/1881-2 onwards. A ~ , or *dirham ḥasanī*, is a coin with the value of a tenth of a douro. III 256a

ḥas͟harāt (A) : insects.

♦ ḥas͟harāt al-arḍ, or *k͟has͟hās͟h* : small animals which live on the ground. III 307b

hās͟hima (A) : a fracture of a bone; a determining factor in the prescription of compensation following upon physical injury, DIYA. II 341b

hās͟himiyya (A) : a term commonly applied in the 2nd-3rd/8th-9th centuries to members of the ʿAbbāsid house and occasionally to their followers and supporters. III 265a

ḥas͟hīs͟h (A) : a narcotic product of *Cannabis sativa*, hemp. III 266a

♦ ḥas͟hīs͟hat al-sanānīr : 'herb for cats', in botany, the labiate Balm (*Melissa officinalis*). IX 653a

♦ **ḥas͟hīs͟hiyya** : the name given in mediaeval times to the followers in Syria of the Nizārī branch of the Ismāʿīlī sect. Carried by the Crusaders from Syria to Europe, the name appeared in a variety of forms in Western literature, and eventually found its way in the form of 'assassin' into French and English usage with corresponding forms in Italian, Spanish and other languages, used at first in the sense of devotee or zealot. III 267b

ḥās͟hiya (A, pl. *ḥawās͟hī*) : margin; marginal note, super-commentary on the commentary, S͟HARḤ; gloss. I 593a; I 816b; III 268b; the entourage of a ruler. III 269a

ḥas͟hm, or *ḥas͟hm-i ḳalb, afwād͟j-i ḳalb, ḳalb-i sulṭānī* : a term used in the 7th/13th century to denote the Dihlī cavalry, or the standing army at the capital. III 199a; V 685a

♦ ḥas͟hm-i aṭrāf : a term denoting the cavalry which the IḲṬĀʿ-holders recruited from the regions in which they were posted, or from the garrisons under their command. Later, it was called the *ḥas͟hm-i bilād-i mamālik*. V 685a

ḥas͟hr (A) : resurrection. VIII 372a

♦ ḥas͟hr ʿāmm → ḤAS͟HR K͟HĀṢṢ

♦ ḥas͟hr k͟hāṣṣ : 'specific resurrection'; among the Imāmīs, the resurrection that will involve believers and unbelievers only from Muḥammad's community, and not from earlier communities, in contradistinction to the Resurrection, *ḥas͟hr ʿāmm*. VIII 372a

has͟ht bihis͟ht (P) : lit. eight paradises; a technical term in Mug͟hal architecture used for a special nine-fold plan of eight rooms (four oblong [open] axial porches and four usually double-storeyed corner rooms) arranged around a central (often octagonal) domed hall. VII 795a; IX 46b

ḥas͟hw (A) : 'stuffing'; 'farce', hence 'prolix and useless discourse'. I 671b; III 269b; and → ṢILA

In prosody, ~ is a collective name for the feet of a verse other than the last foot of the first hemistich and the last foot of the second hemistich. I 671b

♦ **ḥas͟hwiyya** : lit. those that stuff; a contemptuous term with the general meaning of 'scholars' of little worth, particularly traditionists. It is used of the *aṣḥāb al-ḥadīth* (→ AHL AL-ḤADĪTH) who recognise as genuine and interpret literally the crudely anthropomorphic Traditions. I 410b; III 269b; IX 879b

ḥāṣil (A), or *bā'ika* : in mediaeval Islam, a warehouse. IX 788b; IX 793b

ḥatār (A), or *ḥitr*, *hutra* : a band placed vertically around the awning of an Arab tent, in order to fill the space which separates it from the ground. IV 1147b

hātif (A) : an invisible being whose cry rends the night, transmitting a message; a prophetic voice which announces in an oracular style a future happening. III 273a; in modern Arabic, a telephone. III 273b

ḥaṭīm (A) : a semi-circular wall of white marble, opposite the north-west wall of the Kaʿba. The semi-circular space between the ~ and the Kaʿba, which for a time belonged to the Kaʿba, is not entered during the perambulation. IV 318a

hawā'iyya → HĀWĪ

ḥawāla (A) : lit. draft, bill; ~ is the cession, i.e. the payment of a debt through the transfer of a claim. III 283a; IV 405b; IX 770a

In finance, ~ is an assignation on a MUḲĀṬAʿA, tax payment, effected by order of the ruler in favour of a third party. The term is used both for the mandate and for the sum paid. III 283b

In Ottoman Turkish, ~ has the sense of a tower placed at a vantage-point; these towers were sometimes built for blockading purposes near castles which were likely to put up a long resistance. III 285a

ḥawāmīm (A), or *ḥawāmīmāt* : a name for the SŪRAs that begin with the initials *ḥā-mīm*: xl-xlvi. IX 887b

ḥawāntī (A) : in Muslim Spain, a shopkeeper in the SŪḲ, as opposed to the major trader, *tādjir*. IX 789a

ḥawārī (A, < Eth) : apostle; a bird in Sumatra, 'smaller than a pigeon, with a white belly, black wings, red claws and a yellow beak', mentioned by al-Ḳazwīnī. IX 699b f.

♦ ḥawāriyyūn : a collective term denoting twelve persons who at the time of the 'second ʿAḳaba' are said to have been named by Muḥammad (or those present) as leaders of the inhabitants of Mecca. III 285a

hawāy : a bird, which 'speaks better than a parrot', recorded in Mozambique by al-Ḳazwīnī in the 13th century. Presumably a mynah bird is meant. IX 699b

hawbar → ʿAWBAR

ḥawḍ (A, pl. *aḥwāḍ*, *ḥiyāḍ*) : a cistern or artificial tank for storing water; drinking trough, wash-basin. III 286b; V 888a

In eschatology, the ~ is the basin at which on the day of the resurrection Muḥammad will meet his community. III 286a

♦ ḥawḍ al-sabīl → SABĪL

hawda : a term used in India to designate the litter on working and processional elephants, either a long platform from which the passengers' legs hang over each side, or a more elaborate boxed-in structure with flat cushions which afforded more protection during tiger and lion hunts. The seat on the back of processional elephants has the ~ covered by a canopy, often jewelled, and is known as *ʿamārī*. VII 932b

ḥawfī (A) : a type of popular poetry peculiar to Algeria, consisting of short poems of between two and eight verses which are sung by girls or young women. The genre is more commonly called *taḥwīf*, which means the act of singing the ~ . III 289b; IX 234a

ḥāwī (A, pl. *ḥāwiyyūn, ḥuwā*) : a snake-charmer or itinerant mountebank. III 291a

hāwī (A) : 'pertaining to air'; in grammar, an attribute of the letter *alif* which according to Sībawayh 'has some [exhaled] air'. For al-K͟halīl, the *alif*, *wāw*, and *yāʾ* were *hawāʾiyya*, that is to say *fi 'l-hawāʾ* 'in the air [exhaled]', which could be said to be slightly different. III 291a

ḥawlī (A) : a foal between one and two years of age. II 785a

♦ ḥawliyya : a term used in the Sudan and the horn of Africa to denote a feast held in honour of a saint. VI 896b

ḥawma : a district. IX 473a

ḥawrāʾ (A, pl. *ḥūr*) : white, applied in particular to the very large eye of the gazelle or oryx; by extension, ~ signifies a woman whose big black eyes are in contrast to their 'whites' and to the whiteness of the skin. III 581b

In eschatology, the plural **ḥūr** 'houris' is used in the Qurʾān for the virgins of Paradise promised to the believers. II 447b; III 581b

ḥaws͟h (A) : an unroofed burial enclosure, typically Cairene. IV 429b; in mediaeval Islam, an enclosed area, urban or suburban, of rural aspect, a yard of beaten earth, where cattle or poor immigrants could be accommodated. IX 788b

ḥaws͟hab → K͟HUZAZ

ḥawṭ (A) : in southern Arabia, a red and black twisted cord which a woman wears round her hips to protect her from the evil eye. III 294a

♦ **ḥawṭa** (A), or *ḥabaṭ* : enclave, enclosure; in southern Arabia the name given to a territory placed under the protection of a saint and thus considered sacred. III 294a

ḥawz (A, > Sp *alfoz* 'district'; pl. *aḥwāz*) : in North Africa, particularly Morocco, the territory, suburb, environs of a large town; in Tunisia, ~ had a fiscal sense. With *al-*, ~ denotes exclusively the region of Marrakesh, the Haouz, a wide embanked plain drained by two wadis. III 300b

hayʾa (A) : shape, form, state, quality; configuration; in philosophy, predisposition, disposition. III 301a

♦ **ʿilm al-hayʾa** : in astronomy, (a branch of) astronomy, dealing with the geometrical structure of the heavens. III 302a; III 1135a; VIII 105b; VIII 785b

ḥayāt (A) : life. III 302a

ḥayawān (A) : the animal kingdom; an animal or animals in general, including man, who is more precisely called *al-ḥayawān al-nāṭiḳ*. III 304b

ḥayḍ (A) : menstruation; menstrual blood. A discharge which exceeds the legal duration fixed for the menses is called *istiḥāḍa*. III 315b; VIII 1023a

ḥaydar (A) : 'lion'; by-name given to ʿAlī b. Abī Ṭālib. III 315b

ḥayderī (T) : a short dervishes' garment without sleeves, stopping at the waist. V 752a

haydūra → FARW

ḥayk → ḤĀʾIK

haykal (A, pl. *hayākil*) : in mysticism, the physical world as a whole as well as the planets. II 555a

hayr (A, pl. *hayarāt*) : the name for the Great Pearl Banks, which stretch along nearly the entire length of the Arabian side of the Persian Gulf. I 535b

ḥayra → TAḤAYYUR

ḥays (A) : a mixture of dates, butter and milk, associated with the tribal tradition of the Ḳuray<u>sh</u> and said to be among the favourite dishes of the Prophet. II 1059a; S 366b

hays → SILB

hayūlā (A, < Gk) : substance, primary matter; ~ is sometimes substituted for *mādda* and sometimes distinguished from it, but frequently the two terms are considered virtually synonymous. II 554a; III 328a

ḥayy (A) : clan, i.e. the primary grouping in nomadic life. I 306a; III 330a; in certain modern dialects, a quarter in a town or settlement, in particular that inhabited by the same ethnic or tribal element. III 330b

ḥayya (A) : in zoology, snake, a generic name of the ophidians, embracing all kinds of reptiles from the most poisonous to the most harmless. III 334b

ḥayyāk → ḤĀʾIK

haza<u>dj</u> (A) : in prosody, the name of the sixth Arabic metre. I 670a; a metre of quantitative rhythm composed of a foot of one short and three longs repeated three times, hence four equal feet. VIII 579a

hazārāt : millenary cycles, a theory of Indian astronomy. I 139b

ḥazawwar (A) : said of a boy who has become strong, and has served, or one who has nearly attained the age of puberty. VIII 822a

ḥāzī (A, < Ar) : an observer of omens; a generic term covering different divinatory and magical practices. IV 421b; one who divines from the shape of the limbs or moles on the face. I 659b

ḥāzir (A) : sour milk, despised by pre-Islamic Arabs. II 1057b

ḥazm → <u>DJ</u>ABAL

ḥazzāb (A) : a person attached to certain mosques in Algeria, who had to recite a defined portion of the Qurʾān, ḤIZB, twice a day so as to achieve a complete recitation of the Qurʾān in one month. III 513b

he<u>dj</u>e (T) : in Turkish prosody, syllabic metre, usually of 11 syllables divided 6-5 with no caesura. VIII 2b

heello → BELWO

hees → MAANSO

ḥekīm → ḤAKĪM

herbed (P) : a Zoroastrian who knows the Avesta and has been initiated as a priest. VII 215b

hiba (A) : a gift, especially that from a more highly placed person to one on a lower level of society, in contrast to HADIYYA. III 342b

In law, ~ is a gift *inter vivos*, a transfer of the ownership of a thing during the lifetime of the donor, and with no consideration payable by the donee. III 350a

♦ hiba bi-s̲h̲arṭ al-ʿiwaḍ : a gift with consideration, whereby the donee undertakes to compensate the donor. III 351a

ḥibāla (A, pl. *ḥabāyil*), or *uḥbūla* : in hunting, a snare with a draw-net. IX 98b

ḥibāra (A) : in early Islam, a striped garment similar to the BURDA and said to be the favourite garment of the Prophet; also, a fabric. V 734a

ḥibr → MIDĀD

ḥidāʾ (A) : in zoology, the kite. I 1152b

ḥidd (A, pl. *ḥudūd*) : a term in the Persian Gulf for a sand bank. I 535b

hid̲j̲āʾ (A) : a curse; an invective diatribe or insult in verse, an insulting poem; an epigram; a satire in prose or verse. III 352b; a trivial mocking verse of an erotic and obscene content. VIII 376b; and → ḤURŪF AL-HID̲J̲Āʾ

ḥid̲j̲āb (A) : the veil. I 306b; III 359a; the curtain behind which caliphs and rulers concealed themselves from the sight of their household, also known as *sitāra*, *sitr*. III 360a; an amulet which renders its wearer invulnerable and ensures success for his enterprises. III 361a

In medicine, ~ is a membrane which separates certain parts of the organism, e.g. *ḥid̲j̲āb al-bukūriyya* 'hymen', *al-ḥid̲j̲āb al-ḥād̲j̲iz* or *ḥid̲j̲āb al-d̲j̲awf* 'diaphragm', *al-ḥid̲j̲āb al-mustabṭin* 'pleura'. III 359a

In mysticism, ~ represents everything that veils the true end, all that makes man insensitive to the Divine Reality. III 361a

ḥid̲j̲āma → FAṢṢĀD

hid̲j̲ar → HID̲J̲RA

ḥid̲j̲r → ḤIṢĀN

hid̲j̲ra (A) : the emigration of Muḥammad from Mecca to Medina in September 622; the era of the ~ , distinguished by the initials A.H., beginning on the first day of the lunar year in which that event took place, which is reckoned to coincide with 16 July 622. III 366a; ~ implies not only change of residence but also the ending of ties of kinship and the replacement of these by new relationships. VII 356a

In the context of Saudi Arabia, ~ (pl. **hid̲j̲ar**) is a Bedouin settlement, many of which were established by ʿAbd al-ʿAzīz b. ʿAbd al-Raḥmān Āl Suʿūd to promote the sedentarisation of the Bedouin of Saudi Arabia during the first quarter of the 20th century. III 361b; III 1064b; IX 904b

In law, emigration to the DĀR AL-ISLĀM, by Muslims residing in the DĀR AL-ḤARB. S 368a hid̲j̲wiyya (T, < A) : in Turkish literature, a satirical ḲAṢĪDA attacking an enemy or someone of whom the poet disapproves. IV 715b

ḥikāya (A) : 'imitation', hence tale, narrative, story, legend. III 367a; in the *Fihrist*, ~ is used in the sense of a textual copy as well as an account of the facts, equivalent to RIWĀYA. III 368b; and → K̲H̲ABAR

In the science of Tradition, ~ implies a literal quotation, a verbatim reproduction, as in the expression *ḥakaytu ʿanhu 'l-ḥadīt̲h̲ᵃ ḥikāyatᵃⁿ*. III 368b

In grammar, ~ means the use in a narrative of the verbal form which would have been used at the time when the event narrated took place. III 368b

♦ ḥikāyat iʿrāb : in grammar, the exact repetition of a word used by a speaker with a vowel of declension no longer appropriate to its function in the new context. III 368b

♦ ḥikāyat ṣawṭ : onomatopoeia. III 368b

ḥikma (A) : wisdom; science and philosophy. III 377b; IX 879b; and → DĀR AL-ḤIKMA

ḥikr (A) : in law, one of the various forms of long-term lease of WAḲF property, common in Egypt and Syria. Similar forms were called D̲J̲ALSA, ENZEL, GEDIK, ID̲J̲ĀRATAYN, K̲H̲ULUWW AL-INTIFĀʿ and NAṢBA. S 368b

hilāl (A) : the new moon, the crescent. III 379a

ḥilf (A) : a covenant, compact, especially that between quite separate tribes, conducing to the amalgamation of these tribes; friendship, and, by extension, oath. III 388b

In pre-Islamic Arabia, the ~ was an institution which merged with that of WALĀʾ, the admission of an individual to a clan; a second type of ~ consisted of the agreement between the clans within one tribe through which they settled on a common line of conduct; a third type of ~ could also be arranged between opposing clans within one group, or between different groups, for the accomplishment of a particular object. III 388b

ḥill (A) : in law, freedom of action in sexual matters. I 27a

ḥilm (A) : justice and moderation, forbearance and leniency, self-mastery and dignity of bearing, as contrasted with *d̲j̲ahl*, the fundamental characteristic of the D̲J̲ĀHILIYYA, and *safah* or *safāha*. III 390b; discretion. IX 332b

ḥiltīt (A) : 'devil's dirt'; the latex of the asafoetida (*and̲j̲ud̲h̲ān*) which, when exposed to the air, hardens into a dirty-yellow gum resin. VIII 1042b

ḥimā (A) : lit. 'protected, forbidden place'; in Arabia, an expanse of ground, with some vegetation, access to and use of which are declared forbidden by the man or men who have arrogated possession of it to themselves. II 1005b; III 294b; III 393a; VIII 495a; IX 817a

ḥimār (A) : in zoology, the donkey (fem. *atān*, *ḥimāra*). III 393b

♦ ḥimār hindī : 'white donkey', a term used by al-D̲j̲āḥiẓ for the rhinoceros, translated from the Greek. IV 647b

ḥimāya (A) : 'protection', from the pre-Islamic period given, in return for financial compensation, by a nomadic tribe to the settled inhabitants (syn. KHAFĀRA), or the protection by a superior of the property of the inferior, from whose point of view it is called TALDJIʾA. The institution of ~ is almost unrecognised by Islamic law, but was in fact important in classical Islamic society. III 394a

In the context of mediaeval Islamic taxation, a supplementary tax levied by the police for their services. I 1144a; II 143b; III 394b

In politics, ~ refers to various bilateral treaty agreements, particularly those contracted between Great Britain and the sheikhly rulers of states on the western seaboard of the Persian Gulf. III 395a

In North Africa, ~ has been used officially of the protection exercised by a foreign Christian power over certain individuals, then over states. III 395a

ḥiml (A) : lit. load, a measure of capacity used in mediaeval Egypt for great quantities of various commodities. The ~ was reckoned at 600 Egyptian RAṬLS, i.e. 266 kg, but as far as spices were concerned it consisted of 500 *raṭl*s only, i.e. 222.45 kg. VI 119b

ḥināḍ (A) : horses thinned down for horse-racing by being covered with blankets so that excessive weight was sweated off. II 953a

ḥināṭa → ḤANŪṬ

hind (A) : in geography, ~ denoted regions east of the Indus as well as practically all the countries of Southeast Asia; only when used together with *sind*, which referred to Sind, Makran, Baluchistan, portions of the Panjab and the North-West Frontier Province, was the whole of mediaeval India meant. III 404b

hindibāʾ (A) : in botany, cultivated endive (*Cichorium endivia*), particularly widespread in the Muslim West and known there under its Mozarabic name *sharrāliya* or its arabicised form *sarrākh*; in Morocco, the Berber term *tīfāf* is mainly used. S 370b; chicory, one of the Prophet's preferred vegetables. II 1058a

hindū (A) : name given to the largest religious community of India. III 458b

hing → ANGŪZA

ḥinn (A) : an inferior species of DJINN, belief in which is accepted by the Druze. S 371a

ḥinnāʾ (A) : in botany, henna (*Lawsonia alba*), the whitish flower of which was called *fāghiya* or *faghw*. III 461a

ḥinṭa → ḲAMḤ

ḥirbāʾ (A) : in zoology, the chameleon. The female is most often called *umm ḥubayn*, while the male is referred to by a number of KUNYAS, the most frequent in Muslim Spain being *abū barāḳish*. The idea of 'chameleonism', i.e. the ability to become invisible by turning the same colour as that of any object on which it happens to be, is termed *talawwun*. II 1059b; III 463a

ḥirfa → ṢINF

hirkūl (A), or *manāra* : in zoology, the finback. VIII 1022b

hirmīs → KARKADDAN

hirr → SINNAWR

ḥirz (A) : in law, safe keeping, either by the guarding by a watchman or by the nature of the place, e.g. a private house. IX 62b

ḥisāb (A) : computation; in the Qur'ān, the 'reckoning' which God will require on the Day of Judgement, YAWM AL-ḤISĀB. III 465a

♦ **ḥisāb al-ʿaḳd**, or *ḥisāb al-ʿuḳad* or *al-ʿuḳūd*, *ḥisāb al-yad*, and *ḥisāb al-ḳabḍa bi 'l-yad* : dactylonomy, digital computation, the art of expressing numbers by the position of the fingers. III 466a

♦ **ḥisāb al-djummal** : a method of recording dates by chronogram, consisting of grouping together, in a word or a short phrase, a group of letters whose numerical equivalents, added together, provide the date of a past or future event. III 468a

♦ **ḥisāb al-ghubār** : calculation by means of dust, a Persian method which owes its name to the use of a small board on which the calculator spread a fine layer of dust in which he drew GHUBĀR numerals. III 468b

♦ ḥisāb hawāʾī → ḤISĀB MAFTŪḤ

♦ ḥisāb al-hind : calculation by means of the Indian numerals. III 466b

♦ ḥisāb maftūḥ, or *ḥisāb hawāʾī* : mental calculation. III 469a

♦ ḥisāb al-nīm : a divinatory procedure based upon the process of adding the numerical value of all the letters forming a word (in this case a proper name), by which it can be predicted which of the two rulers at war will be the victor and which the vanquished. III 468b

♦ **ʿilm al-ḥisāb** : arithmetic. III 1138a

ḥiṣān (A) : a term used to distinguish the pure-bred stallion from the pedigree brood-mare, which is called *ḥidjr*, since the word for horse, FARAS, is not specific. II 785a

ḥiṣār (A) : in military science, siege. III 469a

In Turkish use, a castle, fortress, citadel, stronghold, a common component of place-names in Turkey. III 483a

ḥisba (A) : the duty of every Muslim to 'promote good and forbid evil'; the function of the person, *muḥtasib*, who is effectively entrusted in a town with the application of this rule in the supervision of moral behaviour and more particularly of the markets. III 485b; VIII 402b; religious magistrature, judgeship. I 27b

For the Ottoman empire, → IḤTISĀB

ḥiṣn (A) : fortress, a fairly common element in place-names. III 498a

ḥiss (A) : in philosophy, sense-perception, sometimes used with the meaning of (individual) sense. III 509a

ḥitr → ḤATĀR

ḥiyal (A, s. *ḥīla*) : artifices, devices, expedients, stratagems; the means of evading a thing, or of effecting an object; mechanical artifices, automata; tricks of beggars and conjurors, etc. III 510b; S 371b

In law, circumventions of the law. I 28a; legal devices; the use of legal means for extra-legal ends. I 123b; III 159b; III 511a

In military science, ~ (with synonyms *makāʾid* and *ādāb*) is a technical term for strategems of war. III 510b

ḥiyāṣa (A) : a cloth belt with a silver plaque in the centre, worn by men in the Arab East. V 741a

ḥiyāza → ḲABḌ

ḥizām (A) : a belt or sash worn about the waist by both sexes in the Arab East. V 741a

ḥizb (A, pl. *aḥzāb*) : a group, faction, a group of supporters; part, portion. III 513a; in modern Arabic, a political party. III 514a

In Qurʾānic studies, ~ indicates a definite portion of the Qurʾān which a believer binds himself to recite. In certain countries, e.g. Egypt and those of North Africa, the Qur'ān is divided into 60 *ḥizb*s, which are half the length of the 30 DJUZ's attested from a very early period. III 513b

In mysticism, ~ or *wird* denotes the recitation of Qurʾānic verses and prayers composed by the founder of the order at the beginning of the DHIKR session. II 224a; in Egypt, ~ denotes a religious fraternity, as well as the 'office' of each fraternity, consisting of the above-mentioned recital during the Friday service. From this meaning, ~ has come to mean formulae of 'supererogatory liturgy'. III 513b

hoca → KHWĀDJA

ḥol (Mal) : a term used in Malaysia to denote a feast held in honour of a saint. VI 896b

horde (Eng, < T ORDU) : name given to the administrative centre of great nomad empires, particularly also to the highly adorned tent of the ruler; then to such nomad confederacies themselves, insofar as they formed a tenuous association linked to no particular place, substantially different in their way of life and government from the settled population, and inflicting considerable damage on this population by their marauding attacks. III 536a

hoz → TIRA

ḥubāra (A), or *ḥubārā* : in zoology, the bustard. I 541b; II 1058b; IX 98b

ḥubūs → WAḲF

ḥudāʾ (A), or *ḥidāʾ* : the camel driver's song. II 1073a

hūdabarī (P) : in the time of the Tīmūrids, term used in conjunction with SOYŪRGHĀL if the latter was on a permanent basis and not renewed annually. IX 732a

hudhud (A) : in zoology, the hoopoe. III 541b

ḥudjariyya (A, < *ḥudjra* 'room') : a term used in Egypt for the slaves who were lodged in barracks near to the royal residence. Under the Fāṭimids, they were organised into a sort of military bodyguard. II 507a; II 1080a; III 545b

ḥudjdja (A) : a Qurʾānic term meaning both proof and the presentation of proof, ~ is applied to a conclusive argument attempting to prove what is false as well as what is true; dialectical proof. III 543b

In shīʿī theology, the ~ refers to that person through whom the inaccessible God becomes accessible, and sometimes to any figure in a religious hierarchy through whom an inaccessible higher figure became accessible to those below. In its more specialised meaning, ~ referred to a particular function within the process of revelation, sometimes identified with the role of Salmān as witness to ʿAlī's status as IMĀM. III 544b

Among the Ismāʿīliyya, ~ is a rank in the hierarchy, coming under the BĀB. The ~ conducted the DAʿWA, and was one of the greater DĀʿĪs, of whom there were twelve, or occasionally twenty-four. Each seems to have been in charge of a district. In some works, the ~ is also called the *lāḥiḳ*. I 832b; II 97b; III 544b

Among the Nizārīs, ~ was used for Ḥasan-i Ṣabbāḥ as visible head of the movement when the IMĀM was hidden; later, it developed into one ~ who alone, by divine inspiration, could fully perceive the reality of the *imām*; eventually the ~ became simply the *imām*'s heir-apparent. III 544b

ḥudjra (A) : room, apartment; with *al-*, especially the room of ʿĀʾisha where the Prophet, Abū Bakr and ʿUmar were buried, now one of the holiest places of Islam. III 545b

hudna (A) : peace agreement; truce. I 24a; III 546b

In law, ~ is equivalent to 'international treaty', whose object is to suspend the legal effects of hostilities and to provide the prerequisite conditions of peace between Muslims and non-Muslims, without the latter's territory becoming part of the DĀR AL-ISLĀM. III 547a

ḥudūd → ḤADD

ḥuḍūr → ḤAḌRA

ḥudūth (A) : the verbal noun of *ḥadatha*, which means 'to appear, to arise, to take place'. III 548a

♦ **ḥudūth al-ʿālam** : in philosophy, both the existence of a thing, after its non-existence, in a temporal extension; and contingency, i.e. the fact of a being's existing after not having existed, but in an ontological or essential extension, which does not necessarily involve time. III 548a

ḥukamāʾ → ḤAKĪM

ḥuḳḳa → IBRA

ḥukm (A, pl. *aḥkām*) : decision, judgement. I 257a; effect. I 318b; injunction. VIII 667a; and → FARMĀN

For ~ in law, → AḤKĀM

In philosophy, ~ means the judgement or act by which the mind affirms or denies one thing with regard to another, and thus unites or separates them. III 549a; also, sensory intuition, where assent of the mind immediately follows perception. III 549b

In grammar, ~ means the specific activity of a word, the proper function which the word performs at its basic position, *martaba*, in which it is placed. III 550a

In Ottoman Turkish, ~ is also used in the sense of a special type of order, the documents of which were to be dealt with separately by the administration and which, at present, are registered in the Turkish archives as a separate archival item, *aḥkām defterleri*. I 1170b

♦ ḥukm-i ḥāṣil : the sharing of the harvest; one of three methods of collecting land revenue under the Dihlī sultanate. II 273a

♦ ḥukm-i misāḥat : the measurement of the area under cultivation and assessment according to a standard rate of demand per unit area according to the crop sown; one of three methods of collecting land revenue under the Dihlī sultanate. II 273a

♦ ḥukm-i mus̲h̲āhada : the estimating of the probable yield of the harvest; one of three methods of collecting land revenue under the Dihlī sultanate. II 273a

ḥuḳna (A) : in hunting, the covered-over pit-trap, also called *ug̲h̲wiyya*, *mug̲h̲awwāt*, *wad̲j̲ra* and *dafīna*. IX 98b

ḥukr (A) : a tax on the lands used for pasture, paid by shepherds in Morocco during the Marīnid period. VI 573b

ḥuḳra → SH̲ĀWĪ

ḥuḳūḳ → ḤAḲḲ

ḥukūma (A) : the act or office of adjudication by a sovereign, a judge or an arbitrator. I 384a; III 551b

Under the Sald̲j̲ūḳs, and in the Ottoman period, ~ denoted the office or function of governorship, usually provincial or local. III 552a

In the Kurdish lands, the term *ḥukūmet* stood for a number of regions listed among the components of certain Ottoman EYĀLETS. III 552a

In modern Arabic, ~ means government, which sense seems to have been first used in 19th-century Turkey. In Persia, *ḥukūmat* still has the more general sense of political authority. III 552a

♦ ḥukūmat, ḥukūmet → ḤUKŪMA

ḥulā (A) : ornaments, personal jewellery. III 568b

ḥulalliyya : a large dark wrap wound around the body with the upper parts pulled down over the shoulders and secured with pins, worn in Egypt. V 741a

ḥulla (A) : a word which in the mediaeval period used to refer to a suit consisting of two or more garments. Today, it means 'a western suit of clothes'. V 737a

ḥullān (A), or *ḥullām* : the lamb or kid born of a Caesarian section. S 319a

ḥulm → RUʾYĀ

ḥulūl (A) : the act of loosing, unfastening, untying; resolving a difficulty; in scholastic theology and mysticism, an infusion of substance, the incarnation of God in a creature. In the thought of al-Ḥallād̲j̲, ~ means an intentional complete union (in love), in which the intelligence and the will of the subject are acted upon by divine grace. III 102b; III 571a,b; IV 283a

In grammar, ~ denotes the occurrence of the accident of inflection, IʿRĀB. III 571b

In law, ~ denotes the application of a prescription. III 571b

In philosophy, ~ denotes both the inhesion of an accident in an object and the substantial union of soul and body. III 571b

ḥulwān (A) : a succession tax paid by those heirs of the tax farmers (→ MÜLTEZIM) who desired to inherit tax farms. It was one of the taxes which formed an additional source of revenue for the Egyptian government in the years immediately preceding the Napoleonic invasion of 1798. II 148b; 'douceur', 'donative'. III 572a

humā (P) : in zoology, the bearded vulture (*Gypaetus barbatus*), the largest of the birds of prey in the Old World. III 572a

humāyūn (P) : 'fortunate, glorious, royal'; used as an epithet of the ruler, but has in recent years become obsolete. III 574a

ḥumra (A) : in medicine, erysipelas. IX 9b

ḥums (A) : in pre-Islamic times, the holy families serving the local sanctuaries. II 1059a; people observing rigorous religious taboos, especially Ḳuraysh and certain neighbouring tribes. Although ~ is the plural of *aḥmas* 'hard, strong (in fighting or in religion)', one of the ~ is called *aḥmasī*, fem. *aḥmasiyya*. The observance of the taboos was called *taḥammus*. III 577b

hunbuʿa → HANBALA

ḥūr → ḤAWRĀʾ

ḥurḍa (A) : the archer in a game of MAYSIR. VI 924a

hurmizd → MUSHTARĪ

ḥurriyya (A, T *ḥurriyyet*) : an abstract formation derived from *ḥurr*, 'free'. In a legal sense, ~ denotes freedom as opposed to slavery; through mysticism, where ~ appears as one of the guide-posts on the mystical path, and denotes basically the freedom of the mystic from everything except God and the devotion to Him, ~ came to occupy a significant position in Muslim metaphysical speculation. III 589a

ḥurūf → ḤARF

ḥūsh (A) : the country of the DJINN, into which no human ventures; a fabulous kind of camels, which are the issue of a cross between ordinary camels and *djinn* stallions. III 637b

♦ ḥūshī → GHARĪB

ḥusn (A) : loveliness, excellence; and → BAYĀN; TAKHALLUṢ

ḥūt (A, pl. *aḥwāt*, *ḥītān*, in dialect, *ḥiyūta*) : a term often used to designate fish in general, but applied primarily to very large fish and cetaceans. VIII 1020b; and → SAMAK

In astronomy, *al-~* is the term for Pisces, one of the twelve zodiacal constellations. VII 84a

♦ ḥūt al-ḥayḍ → FĀṬŪS

♦ ḥūt mūsā, or *ḥūt mūsā wa-yūshaʿ* : lit. the fish of Moses [and of Joshua], a name for the common sole (*Solea vulgaris*). VIII 1020b

♦ ḥūt sīdnā sulaymān : lit. the fish of our master Solomon, a name for the common sole (*Solea vulgaris*). VIII 1021a

♦ ḥūt sulaymān : lit. the fish of Solomon, a name for the salmon. VIII 1023a
♦ ḥūt Yūnus : lit. the fish of Jonah, a name for the whale. VIII 1022b
♦ ḥūtiyyāt : in zoology, the marine mammals or cetaceans. VIII 1022b

ḥutra → ḤATĀR

huwa huwa (A) : lit. he is he, or it is it; in logic, ~ means what is represented as entirely identical; modern logicians express this equation with ≡ . III 642b
In mysticism, ~ is the state of the saint whose perfect personal unity testifies to divine unity in the world. III 642b

huwayriyya → WARDJIYYA

huwiyya (A) : ipseity, an abstract term formed to translate the Plotinian category of identity, ταὐτότης, and the Aristotelian ὄν 'being', although for the latter ~ is used interchangeably with ANNIYYA and *wudjūd*. I 514a; III 644a
In modern Arabic, ~ means 'identity'. III 644a

hūwiyya (A) : the most characteristic part of the ritual surrounding the yearly occasion of retreat of the Demirdāshiyya order, in which the head of the order, a number of leaders and some members form a circle turning anti-clockwise while calling *hū, hū*. S 208b

ḥuẓūẓ → ḤAḲḲ

I

ʿibādāt (A, s. *ʿibāda*) : submissive obedience to a master, and therefore religious practice, corresponding, in law, approximately to the ritual of Muslim law. III 647a; 'the religious acts which bring the creature into contact with his creator', while its counterpart, MUʿĀMALĀT, signifies relations between individuals. VI 467a; acts of worship. IX 323b
♦ **ʿibādat-khāna** (Ind.P) : a house of worship built by the Mughal emperor Akbar (1542-1605) where learned men of all religions assembled to discuss theological problems. I 317a; S 378a

ʿibādī (A) : Christian. I 196a

ibʿādiyya → ABʿĀDIYYA

ibāḥa (A) : originally, 'making a thing apparent or manifest', hence 'making a thing allowable or free to him who desires it'; in law, ~ was first used with regard to those things which every one is permitted to use or appropriate (and → MUBĀḤ); in a narrower sense, ~ denotes the authorisation, given by the owner, to consume (part of) the produce of his property. III 660b
In theology, ~ is a term that is commonly applied to antinomian teachings (or actions) of certain shīʿī and ṣūfī groups, as in the accusation *ibāḥat al-maḥārim* 'allowing the forbidden'. II 136b; III 662a; VIII 146a

♦ ibāḥiyya → SHUYŪʿIYYA

ibdāʿ (A) : absolute creation; primordial innovation; the bringing into existence with nothing preceding, as opposed to KHALḲ, the bringing into existence from an existing thing. III 663b

ibdāl (A) : replacement, mutation; in grammar, a term indicating both morphological features involving a mutation of a phonetic character, and doublets, e.g. *madaḥa* and *madaha*, which have the same meaning but differ from each other by a single consonant. III 665a; VIII 836b

ibil (A) : in zoology, the collective noun for the dromedary (*camelus dromedarius*) and the camel proper (*camelus bactrianus*). III 665b; and → BAʿĪR; DJAMAL

ibn (A, pl. ABNĀʾ) : son. III 669b; descendant. VIII 163a

♦ ibn adīmayn → DALW

♦ ibn awbar : in botany, the sand truffle. III 670a

♦ ibn ʿirs (A) : in zoology, the ferret (*Mustela putorius furo*). II 739b; weasel. III 670a

♦ ibn yaʿḳūb : lit. the son of Jacob, in zoology, a name for the common sargo (*Diplodus sargus*). VIII 1021a

ibra (A) : a term used in navigation denoting the needle of a compass, *ḥuḳḳa*. The rose of the compass was known as *bayt al-ibra* and consisted of a circle divided into thirty-two rhumbs (*akhnān*) which were named after prominent stars whose risings and settings were approximately on these rhumbs. VII 51b

♦ ibrat al-rāʿī, or *ibrat al-rāhib* → SHAWKA

ibrāʾ → ṢULḤ AL-IBRĀʾ

ʿibra (A) : the assessed value of the revenue on an estate. III 1088b; IV 557a; ~ may have originated simply as an extension of MASĀḤA and MUḲĀSAMA, the average annual value of the crop over a number of years, usually three, assessed by whatever method, being taken as the basis on which the tax was calculated. The term ~ is not met with after the early centuries and appears to have been replaced by *ḥarz*, which, in the later centuries, seems usually to have meant not an average calculation made on the basis of three or more years, but an arbitrary valuation arrived at by the tax-collector, sometimes, but not always, after an inspection of the crop during growth or harvest time. IV 1038a

ibrīḳ (A) : in art, a term used for any kind of ewer, irrespective of function or material, but generally a vessel for pouring water or wine. Other terms for specific kinds of ewers are *bulbula* or *kubra*. S 406a

ibrīsam → ḤARĪR

ibtidāʾ (A) : introduction, prologue; in rhetoric, the ~ is one of the three sections of the poem or composition which should receive particular attention and should conform to certain criteria of style and content. The other two sections are TAKHALLUṢ ‘transition’, and the **intihāʾ** ‘conclusion’. III 1006a; III 1246a

In law, ~ is used as a technical term in the expression *ibtidāʾan*, meaning ‘per se’. I 339a; and → ISTIʾNĀF

ič oghlāni (T), or *ič agha* : lit. lad of the interior; the name given to the ʿADJAMĪ OGHLĀN after he was appointed to the sultan's household. I 206b; Ottoman term for those boys and youths, at first slaves, recruits and occasionally hostages, later free-born Muslims, who were selected for training in the palaces in Edirne and Istanbul in order to occupy the higher executive offices of the state. I 394a; III 1006b

icazetname → IDJĀZA

ʿīd (A, < Ar) : festival. III 1007a

♦ **ʿīd al-aḍḥā**, and *ʿīd al-ḳurbān*, *ʿīd al-naḥr* : the 'sacrificial festival' during the yearly pilgrimage on 10 Dhu 'l-Ḥidjdja. This festival is also known as *al-ʿīd al-kabīr* 'the major festival' as opposed to *al-ʿīd al-ṣaghīr* 'the minor festival, another name for ʿĪD AL-FIṬR. III 1007b; S 317a; and → LEBARAN

♦ **ʿīd al-fiṭr** : the 'festival of breaking the fast' of Ramaḍān on 1 Shawwāl. III 1008a; and → ʿĪD AL-AḌḤĀ; LEBARAN

♦ ʿīd al-ḳurbān → ʿĪD AL-AḌḤĀ

♦ ʿīd al-naḥr → ʿĪD AL-AḌḤĀ

iʿdādī (T) : 'military preparatory' schools, founded by the Ottoman sultan ʿAbd al-Madjīd I in 1845. I 75a

iḍāfa (A, P *ezāfe*, T *izâfet*) : in grammar, the uniting of one term with another, the determinative complement or 'construct state', by which possession, material, etc. is expressed. The first term is called *al-muḍāf*, the second *al-muḍāf ilayhi*. III 1008a

idāra (A) : common name in the modern Islamic languages for administration, acquiring its technical significance during the period of European influence. III 1010b

ʿidda (A) : in law, the duration of widowhood, or the legal period of abstention from sexual relations imposed on widows or divorced women, or women whose marriages have been annulled, providing the marriage was consummated, before remarriage. I 28a; I 172b; III 1010b; VIII 28a; VIII 836a

iddighām → IDGHĀM

ʿīdgāh → MUṢALLĀ

idghām (A), or *iddighām* : in grammar, the contraction of two similar consonants in a geminate. III 1013a; assimilation. VIII 121a; VIII 344a; VIII 836b

idhāʿa (A) : broadcasting (*mudhīʿ* 'broadcaster', *midhyāʿ* 'microphone'), inaugurated in the Islamic world in Turkey in 1925. III 1014a

idhār → LIDJĀM

ʿidhār (A), or *khaṭṭ* : the down of a young man. IX 313b

idhn (A) : authorisation, in particular, in law, the authorisation necessary to enable certain types of incapable persons to conclude isolated legal transactions, and the general authorisation to carry out commercial transactions in a normal way. III 1016a

In religious law, a safe conduct given by non-Muslims to a Muslim in their territory. For its opposite, → AMĀN. I 429b

īdjāb → BAYʿ

idjāba (A) : 'answer-poem', a genre of Arabic poetry. VIII 805a

īdjār (A), and *idjāra* : in law, a contract to hire, the contract by which one person makes over to someone else the enjoyment, by personal right, of a thing or of an activity, in return for payment. III 1017a; the hiring out of a service and of movable objects, with the exception of ships and beasts which are used for transportation. V 126b; and → KIRĀʾ

idjāra (A) : the granting of protection to a stranger according to ancient Arab practice; to ask for protection is *istadjāra*, and the *djār* (pl. *djirān*) is mostly the person protected, but may also be the protector. III 1017b; and → ĪDJĀR; IDJĀZA

♦ idjāratayn (A, T *idjāreteyn*) : a form of long-term leasing of WAḲF property, common in Anatolia and all countries formerly part of the Ottoman empire since the 16th or 17th century. ~ contracts involved immediate payment of a lump sum as well as yearly, variable, rather low rents. S 368b; a 'double rent' agreement, whereby a relatively high entry fine was paid, in exchange for which the tenant was allowed a lease which his heirs might inherit. IX 542a

iʿdjāz (A) : lit. the rendering incapable, powerless; since the second half of the 3rd/9th century, the technical term for the inimitability or uniqueness of the Qurʾān in content and form. III 1018a; V 426b; IX 887a

īdjāz (A) : in rhetoric, terseness. VIII 614b

idjāza (A) : authorisation, licence; and → RIḲĀʿ

In the science of Tradition, ~ means, in the strict sense, one of the methods of receiving the transmission of a Tradition, whereby an authorised guarantor of a text or of a whole book gives a person the authorisation to transmit it in his turn so that the person authorised can avail himself of this transmission. III 27a; III 1020b

In modern Persian and in Ottoman Turkish, as *icazetname*, the term has come into modern use to mean 'certificate of fitness' (to teach). III 1021a

In prosody, ~ (or *idjāra*) is used for the substitution of an unrelated letter for the RAWĪ, the rhyme letter. IV 412b

In rhetoric, ~ is used both when a poet builds some lines or even a whole poem on a single line or hemistich suggested by somebody else, often a ruler, and when two poets compose alternately a hemistich or one or more lines of the same poem. When this is done in the form of a contest, the term *tamlīṭ* (*mumālaṭa*, *imlāṭ*) is found. III 1022a

idjdhāb → TAḤAYYUR

idjmāʿ (A) : in law, the third, and in practice the most important, of the sources of legal knowledge, being the unanimous agreement of the community on a regulation imposed by God. Technically, ~ is the unanimous doctrine and opinion of the recognised religious authorities at any given time. I 259b; II 182b; II 887b; III 1023a; V 239a; IX 324b idjmāl (A) : a summary register. IX 123b f.

idjtihād (A) : lit. effort; in law, the use of individual reasoning; exerting oneself to form an opinion in a case or as to a rule of law, achieved by applying analogy to the Qurʾān and the custom of the Prophet. The opposite is called *taḳlīd*, the unquestioning acceptance of the doctrines of established schools and authorities. I 259b; III 1026a; IX 324b

idjtimāʿ (A) : in astronomy, the conjunction (mean or 'true') of the sun and moon. In astrology, ~ is sometimes employed to refer to the conjunction of the planets, although *ḳirān* is preferred. IV 259a

In human psychology, ~ is the intermediary between the faculty of desire and the active power, the decision which follows after a hesitation between action and no-action, as a result of which one of the two prevails. According to others, ~ is the desire to act at its maximum intensity. V 577b

idmāʾ → SHIʿĀR

iḍmār (A) : concealing; in grammar, ~ is used in the sense of 'imply'; it is used by grammarians when speaking about an unexpressed grammatical element, supposedly existent and active. Its opposite is *iẓhār*. With Sībawayh, ~ refers to the personal pronoun, which later became *al*-MUḌMAR, which was preferred over *al-maknī*, the Kūfan term. III 1027b

In prosody, ~ has taken on a technical meaning, denoting 'the quiescence of the *tāʾ* of *mutafāʿilun* in the *Kāmil*'. I 672a; III 1028a

idrāk (A, P *dar-yāftan*) : sensory perception; comprehension (syn. *fahm*); in philosophy, ~ implies an *adaequatio rei et intellectus*. The whole philosophical problem of ~ is to find out what this adequation is, and how and where it is achieved. III 1028a

iḍṭirār (A) : compulsion, coercion, as opposed to IKHTIYĀR, freedom of choice. In theology, human actions carried out under compulsion were distinguished from those carried out of free choice; the latter were voluntary and the results of an acquisition, *iktisāb* (→ KASB). With al-Ashʿarī, the opposite correlatives became no longer *iḍṭirār-ikhtiyār*, but *iḍṭirār-iktisāb*. In later Ashʿarite theology, ~ is reserved for an action that, of itself, cannot take place. III 1037b; and → ḌARŪRA

ifāḍa (A) : a term used for the running of the pilgrims from ʿArafāt on the evening of the 9th of Dhu 'l-Ḥidjdja after sunset in which they trace the road by which they had come from Mecca. III 36a; along with *fayḍ* 'course made in an enthusiastic manner', ~ is used for the other courses than SAʿY. IX 97b; and → ṬAWĀF AL-IFĀḌA

ifrād (A) : in the context of the pilgrimage, one of three methods of performing it, consisting of making the ḤADJDJ alone, at the prescribed time, the ʿUMRA being performed outside the month of the pilgrimage or simply neglected. III 35a; III 53b

ifrandj (A), or *firandj* : the Franks. The name was originally used of the inhabitants of the empire of Charlemagne, and later extended to Europeans in general. In mediaeval times, ~ was not normally applied to the Spanish Christians, the Slavs or the Vikings, but otherwise it was used fairly broadly of continental Europe and the British Isles. Between the 16th and the 19th centuries, ~ came to designate European Catholics and Protestants. III 1044a

ifrāṭ (A) : among the shīʿīs, exaggeration in religion. IX 163b

ifrīḳiya (A, < L) : the eastern part of the Maghrib, whence the name adopted by some modern historians for Eastern Barbary. It was sometimes confused with the whole of the Maghrib and sometimes considered as a geographically separate region. III 1047a

ʿifrīt (A, pl. *ʿafārīt*) : an epithet expressing power, cunning and insubordination, ~ occurs only once in the Qurʾān, in the sense of rebellious. Later, in its substantive form, it came to mean a class of particularly powerful chthonian forces, formidable and cunning. In the popular tales, the ~ is a DJINN of enormous size, formed basically of smoke; it has wings, haunts ruins and lives under the ground. ~ may be used of humans and even animals, and then expresses cunning, ingenuity and strength. In Egyptian Arabic, ~ also has the meaning of the ghost or spirit of a person deceased. III 1050a; IX 406b

ifsintīn → AFSANTĪN

iftāʾ → FUTYĀ

iftitāḥ (A) : in the science of diplomatic, the introduction or introductory protocol of documents, whose individual parts (*fawātiḥ*), according to al-Ḳalḳashandī, are the *basmala*, *ḥamdala*, *tashahhud*, *ṣalwala* (*taṣliya*), *salām*, and *baʿdiyya* (*ammā baʿdu*). II 302a; and → ṬIRĀZ

īghāl → MUBĀLAGHA

īghār (A) : in classical Muslim administration, both an exemption or a privilege with respect to taxes, and the land which was covered by this privilege. The term became absorbed in that of IḲṬĀʿ in later centuries. III 1051a

igherm → AGADIR

ightāla → TAḌABBABA

iğretileme → ISTIʿĀRA

iḥāle (T) : one of three principal ways in which mining activity was organised in the Ottoman empire, the others being EMĀNETEN and ILTIZĀMEN. ~ meant the long-term concessionary leasing of state lands for purposes of mining exploration to licensed individuals or mining companies. V 974b

īhām (P) : in Persian poetry, *double entendre*. IX 90b

iḥdāth (A) : an innovation in time; the act of bringing into existence a thing that is preceded by a time. III 1051a

iḥfāʾ (A), or *djazz* : moustache. The verb used in cutting the ~ is *ḳaṣṣ*. IX 312a f.

ihlīladj → HALĪLADJ

iḥrām (A) : the state of temporary consecration of someone who is performing the pilgrimage, ḤADJDJ or ʿUMRA. The entering into this holy state is accomplished by the statement of intention, accompanied by certain rites, and for men, by the donning of the ritual garment. A person in this state is called *muḥrim.* III 1052b

iḥṣāʾ (A) : 'enumeration'; among the Nuḳtawiyya sect, ~ is used to designate the process of how, when a being rises or descends from one level of existence to another, the traces of his former existence are still visible and can be discerned by the insightful. VIII 115a

iḥsān (A) : in Mauritania, a contract for the loan of a lactiferous animal, the hiring of a young camel for the purpose of following a she-camel so that she continues to give milk. VI 313a; and → IKHLĀṢ

iḥṣān → MUḤṢAN

iḥtisāb (A, T) : an official term in the administration of the Ottoman empire, its basic meaning being the levying of dues and taxes, both on traders and artisans and also on certain imports, but it came to denote the whole aggregate of functions that had devolved upon the *muḥtasib* (→ ḤISBA). III 489a

iḥtiyāṭ (A) : in Turkish military usage, reserve of the regular army, to be contrasted with the *redīf* (→ RADĪF) 'reserve army' or militia, created in 1834. VIII 370a
In law, prudence in legal matters, characteristic of the Shāfiʿī school. IX 812b

iḥyāʾ → MAWĀT

īḳāʿ (A) : a term denoting musical metrics or rhythm in the sense of measuring the quantity of notes. The early Islamic ~ can be considered as a forerunner of mediaeval European mensura. S 408b

iḳāla (A) : in law, *mutuus dissensus*, a mutual agreement between the parties to put an end to a contract. I 319b; III 1056b

iḳāma (A) : the second call to the ṢALĀT, pronounced by the muezzin in the mosque before each of the five prescribed daily *ṣalāt*s and that of the Friday service. I 188b; III 1057a; VIII 927b

iḳdāda (A) : a white KĀFIYYA worn in summer in the Arab East. V 741a

ikerzī (B) : a Berber turban consisting of a white cloth wound about the head leaving the crown uncovered. V 746a

ikfāʾ (A) : in prosody, the substitution of a cognate letter for the rhyme letter, RAWĪ, e.g. *nūn* for *mīm*. IV 412b

ikhāwa → KHĀWA

ikhlāṣ (A) : 'dedicating, devoting or consecrating oneself' to something; ~ is preeminently an interior virtue of the faithful Muslim, whose perfection of adherence, and witness, to his faith is gauged by ~ and *iḥsān* 'uprightness in good'. The opposites of ~ are *nifāḳ* 'hypocrisy' and *shirk* 'associating others, or other things, with God'. III 1059b; VIII 547a

ikhshīd (P) : a title given to local Iranian rulers of Soghdia and Farghāna in the pre-Islamic and early Islamic periods. III 1060b

ikhtilādj (A) : spontaneous pulsations, tremblings or convulsions of the body, particularly the limbs, eyelids and eyebrows, which provide omens the interpretation of which is known as *ʿilm al-ikhtilādj* 'palmoscopy'. III 1061a

i<u>kh</u>tilāf (A) : ‘difference, inconsistency’; in law, the differences of opinion among the authorities of law, both between schools and within each of them. III 1061b

i<u>kh</u>tiyār (A) : choice; and → IḌṬIRĀR

In philosophy, ~ means free preference or choice, option, whence power of choice, free will. III 1037a; III 1062a

In law, ~ has the meaning of opinion freely stated. III 1062a

In treatises on the IMĀMA, where ~ has the meaning of choice or election, it is customary to contrast the *ahl al-i<u>kh</u>tiyār* with the *ahl al-naṣṣ*, the supporters of free election with the supporters of textual determination. III 1063a

♦ **i<u>kh</u>tiyārāt** : ‘hemerologies and menologies’ (L. *electiones*); in divination, hemerology, an astrological procedure whose aim is to ascertain the auspicious or inauspicious character of the future, dealing with years, months, days and hours. III 1063b; VIII 107b

In literature, ~ is a synonym of MU<u>KH</u>TĀRĀT ‘anthologies’. III 1064a; VII 528b

♦ **i<u>kh</u>tiyāriyya** (T, < A) : the elite or veterans of an Ottoman guild or army unit. S 409b

i<u>kh</u>wān (A) : brethren; the term most commonly used for DARWĪ<u>SH</u> in Morocco and Algeria. II 164a; a religious and military movement of Arab tribesmen which had its heyday from 1912-1930 in Arabia. III 1064a

♦ i<u>kh</u>wāniyyāt : friendly invitations to profit from the pleasure of love and drink. IV 1005b; a poetic genre in which protestations of friendship are found integrated with the theme of youth and of old age. IX 387a

iḳlāba (A) : in modern Mecca, the ceremony held to celebrate when a boy has read through the whole of the Qurʾān (the ceremony after the half or one-third is called *iṣrāfa*). IV 1113a

iklīl al-malik (A) : in botany, the melilot (*Melilotus officinalis*) (infrequent syn. *nafal*, *ḥantam*, *<u>sh</u>a<u>dj</u>arat al-ḥubb*). In Muslim Spain, ~ was known under the Romance name *ḳurunīlla*. S 410a

iḳlīm (A, < Gk) : in geography, clime, climate; region. I 658a; III 1076b; V 398a

In administrative geography, ~ was used for province or canton, the equivalent or a subdivision of a KŪRA. This usage is peculiar to Syria and Upper Mesopotamia. III 1077b; V 398a; zone. IX 36b

In al-Masʿūdī, ~ is used for the Persian *ke<u>sh</u>war*, which refers to the seven great kingdoms of the world. III 1077b

ikrāh (A) : in law, duress, of which there are two kinds: unlawful (*ikrāh <u>gh</u>ayr ma<u>sh</u>rūʿ*) and lawful (*ikrāh bi-ḥaḳḳ*). Only the former is recognised by the Qurʾān and has legal effects. I 319a; S 410b

iḳrār (A) : in law, affirmation, acknowledgement; recognition of rights. The declarant is called *al-muḳirr*, the beneficiary *al-maḳarr lahu*, and the object of the recognition *al-muḳarr bihi*. I 28b; III 511b; III 1078a; IX 845b

Among the Bektā<u>sh</u>īs, the ceremony of initiation. IX 168a

iksīr (A, < Gk; pl. *akāsīr*) : originally the term for externally applied dry-powder or sprinkling-powder used in medicine, ~ came to be used for the elixir, the substance with which the alchemists believed it possible to effect the transformation of base metals into precious ones. III 1087b

♦ iksīrīn (A) : in medicine, an eye-powder. III 1087b

iḳṭāʿ (A) : in fiscal administration, a form of grant, often (wrongly) translated as 'fief'; the delegation of the fiscal rights of the state over lands to the military. I 1353a; II 508a; III 1088a; IV 975a; IV 1043b

iḳtibās (A) : 'to take a live coal (*ḳabas*) or a light from another's fire', hence to seek knowledge; in rhetoric, ~ means to quote specific words from the Qurʾān or from Traditions without indicating these as quoted, found both in poetry and prose. III 1091b

iḳtirān (A) : in astronomy, conjunction. VIII 105a

iktisāb → KASB

iḳwāʾ (A) : in prosody, faulty rhyme. II 1073b; the change of the vowel MAD̲J̲RĀ, e.g. *u* with *i*. IV 412b

il (A, T *il*; pl. ĪLĀT) : in Turkish, empire; district over which authority is exercised, territory; people; peace. III 1092a; in the Republican period, *il* was introduced to replace *vilāyet* for province. III 1092b; VIII 189a

In Persian, ~ was used of 'tribesfolk' (syn. *ulus*), and by the 7th/13th century had become current with the meaning 'submissive, obedient'. III 1092b

īlāʾ (A) : in law, an 'oath of continence', the husband swearing in the name of God not to have sexual relations with his wife for at least four months. When this time had passed without a resumption of conjugal relations, the marriage was not automatically broken up except in Ḥanafī law, the other schools allowing the wife to judge the occasion for the severance, which would take place by a repudiation that the husband would pronounce, or that the ḲĀḌĪ would formulate in his place. IV 689a; VI 478a; VIII 28a

īlāf (A) : a Qurʾānic term which probably refers to economic relations entered into by the Ḳuray*s̲h̲*īs well before the advent of Islam; the lexicographers define ~ as 'pact guaranteeing safety, safe conduct, undertaking to protect'. III 1093a

ilāh (A, pl. *āliha*) : deity; in pre-Islamic poetry, *al-*~ was an impersonal divine name although for Christians and monotheists, it denoted God; by frequency of usage, *al-*~ became Allāh. III 1093b

♦ **ilāhī** (A) : in Turkish literature, a genre of popular poetry of religious inspiration, consisting of poems sung, without instrumental accompaniment, in chorus or solo during certain ceremonies, and distinguished from other types of popular religious poetry by its melody and use in ritual. III 1094a; 'divine [hymn]'. VIII 2b; and → TAʾRĪK̲H̲-I ILĀHĪ

♦ ilāhiyyāt (A) : in philosophy, ~ gained currency as denoting the whole mass of questions concerning God. I 415a

ʿilal (A, s. **ʿilla** 'cause') : diseases, defects.

In poetry, one of two groups of metrical deviations (the other being ZIḤĀFĀT), ~

appear only in the last feet of the two halves of the lines, where they alter the rhythmic end of the line considerably, and are thus clearly distinct from the ḤASHW feet. As rhythmically determined deviations, ~ do not just appear occasionally but have to appear regularly, always in the same form, and in the same position in all the lines of the poem. I 671b
In the science of ḤADĪTH, ~, usually rendered 'hidden defects', is a main approach of ISNĀD criticism; it highlights links between certain pairs of transmitters which are subject to dispute. VIII 515a

īlāt (P) : nomadic or semi-nomadic tribes, term first used in Īlkhānid times. Early Islamic geographers and historians refer to these tribes by the generic term *al-akrād*, by which they mean not necessarily people of Kurdish race but non-Arab and non-Turkish tent dwellers and herdsmen. III 1095b f.

ʿilb → SIDR

ilçe (T) : district. VIII 189a

ildjāʾ → TALDJIʾA

ilḥād → MULḤID

ilhām (A) : lit. to cause to swallow or gulp down; a Qurʾānic term denoting God's revelation to men individually, as opposed to His revelation to men generally by messages sent through the prophets, *waḥy*. III 1119b

ilidja (T) : 'hot spring'; a bath served by a hot spring. Other synonyms are ḲAPLIDJA, used primarily of the baths served by thermal springs in Bursa, and *bāna*. II20b

ilḳāʾ → ṬARḤ

ʿilla (A, pl. *ʿilal*) : cause. III 1127b; and → ḤARF ʿILLA; SABAB

ʿilliyyūn (A, < Heb *ʿelyōn*) : a Qurʾānic term meaning both the 'place in the book where the deeds of the pious are listed' and 'an inscribed book'. III 1132b

ʿilm (A) : knowledge; the result of laborious study. III 1133a; and → ḤAMALAT AL-ʿILM

♦ ʿilm ʿamalī : in philosophy, practical knowledge, which comprises, according to al-Khwārazmī, ethics, domestic economy and politics. I 427b; in theology, the knowledge of religious obligations, complete only when these obligations are fulfilled, as opposed to *ʿilm naẓarī* 'the knowledge of things'. III 1133b

♦ ʿilm al-ʿazāʾim : the talismanic art, consisting of calling upon DJINNS and angels for the performance of some project. IV 264b

♦ **ʿilm al-djamāl** : aesthetics. III 1134a

♦ **ʿilm al-handasa** : geometry. S 411b

♦ ʿilm al-ḳāfiya : rhyme theory. VIII 894a

♦ ʿilm naẓarī → ʿILM ʿAMALĪ

♦ ʿilm sharʿī : revealed knowledge. I 427b

For other expressions with *ʿilm*, → the final component.

♦ **ʿilmiyye** (T) : the body of the higher Muslim religious functionaries in the Ottoman empire, especially those administering justice and teaching in the religious colleges. III 1152a iltibās → SABAB

iltizām (A) : a form of tax-farm used in the Ottoman empire. III 1154a; and → MÜLTEZIM

For ~ in prosody, → LUZŪM MĀ LĀ YALZAM

iltizāmen (T) : one of three principal ways in which mining activity was organised in the Ottoman empire, the others being EMĀNETEN and IḤĀLE. ~ meant the farming out of mining revenues to investors on a short-term contract basis. The usual term for these contracts in the mining context was six years. V 974b

īmāʾ → ISHĀRA

ʿimād → ʿAMĪD

imāla (A) : in the science of phonetics, ~ stands for inflection, a palatalisation, produced by a rising movement of the tongue towards the prepalatal region. III 1162a; the inclination of the vowel *a* towards *i*. VIII 343b

imām (A) : leader of the official prayer rituals, the ṢALĀT. From the earliest days of Islam, the ruler was ~ as leader in war, head of the government and leader of the common *ṣalāt*. Later, as the ruler's representatives, the governors of the provinces became leaders of the *ṣalāt*, just as they were heads of the KHARĀDJ. They had to conduct ritual prayer, especially the Friday *ṣalāt*, on which occasion they also delivered the sermon, KHUṬBA. Starting from ʿAbbāsid times, the office devaluated; the ~ no longer represented a political office, but came to belong to the personnel of the mosque. Each mosque regularly had one. He had to maintain order and was in general in charge of the divine services in the mosque. VI 674b; VIII 927b

In religious practice, the ~ is the transveral bead of a larger size on a rosary that separates the groups of beads. IX 741b

In mathematics, ~ is the number with which the numerator of a fraction is in relationship. IV 725b

♦ imām al-difāʿ : among the Ibāḍiyya, an IMĀM invested by the people living in a state of secrecy, *ahl al-kitmān*, to defend them in misfortune. III 658a

♦ **imām-bārā** (U) : lit. enclosure of the IMĀMS; a term used in Muslim India for the buildings where the shīʿīs assemble during Muḥarram and recite elegies on the martyrdom of Ḥasan and Ḥusayn. III 1163a

♦ **imāma** : the imamate, 'supreme leadership' of the Muslim community. III 1163b

♦ imāmān : in mysticism, assistants of the ḲUṬB, the second category in the hierarchy of the saints. I 95a

♦ **imāmzāda** (P) : the designation for both the descendant of a shīʿī IMĀM and the shrine of such a person. III 1169b

īmān (A) : in theology, faith (in God). III 1170b; IV 171b ff.

ʿimāret (T, < A *ʿimāra* 'foundation') : soup kitchen, erected as a public convenience in Ottoman times. IV 1152a

imḍā (T), or *tewḳiʿ-i ḳāḍī* : in Turkish diplomatic, the legal formula which was usually placed on the right side close to the first lines of the text of a copy stating (usually in Arabic) the conformity of the copy with the original. II 315b; and → PENČE

imlāṭ → IDJĀZA

immar, immara → SAKHLA

imsāk (A) : in religious law, abstinence, e.g. from things which break the fast. IX 94b; and → IMSĀKIYYA

♦ imsākiyya : modern religious time tables distributed for the whole month of Ramaḍān. They indicate in addition to the times of prayer, the time of the early morning meal, *suḥūr*, and the time before daybreak (called the *imsāk*) when the fast should begin. VII 30b

imtiyāzāt (A) : commercial privileges, (Ottoman) capitulations granted to non-Muslims living outside the DĀR AL-ISLĀM. III 1178b

imẓad (B) : hair, fur; ~ denotes a musical instrument once in use among the Touareg noblewomen, generally compared to a violin, but held by the player on her thighs as she sat low down, just above the ground, with her legs tucked back. III 1195b

in shāʾ allāh → ISTITHNĀʾ

ʿīna → BAYʿ AL-ʿĪNA

i̊naḳ (T) : a title which existed in various Turkic and Mongol states, belonging to the close retinue of the ruler. S 419a

inʿām (A) : lit. favour, beneficence; applied more specifically to donatives, largesse, given to troops. III 1200b; VIII 398b

In Persia, ~ was a present, usually of money, given from superiors to inferiors. III 347b

ʿinān (A) : in law, ~ is best rendered as a limited investment partnership in which relations between the partners are based on mutual agency alone and not mutual suretyship; one of the two classes of commercial partnership among the Ḥanafīs, the other being MUFĀWAḌA. VII 310a; *sharikat ʿinān* means partnership in traffic, contracted when each party contributes capital. IX 348b; and → LIDJĀM

iʿnāt → LUZŪM MĀ LĀ YALZAM

ʿināya (A) : providence. III 1203a

In ʿAbd al-Razzāḳ al-Ḳāshānī's mystical thought, ~ covers ḲAḌĀʾ and ḲADAR both, just as they contain everything that is actual; it is the divine knowledge, embracing everything as it is, universally and absolutely. I 90a

In mysticism, ~ is used with the more precise meaning of divine 'benefaction' or of a 'gift granted' by God. III 1203a

indjīl (A, < Gk) : gospel; in the Qurʾān, ~ is used to refer to the Revelation transmitted by Jesus as well as the scripture possessed and read by the Christian contemporaries of Muḥammad, i.e. the four Gospels; in current usage extended to mean the whole of the New Testament. III 1205a

īndjū (T) : the term applied to royal estates under the Mongols. III 1208a; land primarily, though not exclusively, granted to the ruler's family and supporters. Gradually the concept of ~ land became assimilated to existing concepts of crown lands and came to signify land over which the ruler had full rights of disposal and which he granted on a heriditary title to his family and others. Whether the grantees then had full rights of disposal themselves is not clear. IV 975b

infaḥa (A) : rennet used to make cheese. S 318b

infisākh → FASKH

inḥirāf → SAMT

inḥiṣār (T, < A), and *ḥaṣīr* : monopolies and restrictive practices of Ottoman guilds, the full term being *inḥiṣār-i beyʿi ve shirā*. These monopolies included restrictions concerning the number or kind of people allowed to perform a trade or profession, as well as limitations imposed on production or on commerce. S 421a

inkār (A) : in law, denial, as when a person who is summoned by law to acknowledge a debt denies that he owes it. The transaction which puts an end to the legal conflict is called *ṣulḥ ʿalā inkār*. III 1236b; IX 845b

inṣāf (A) : equity; in poetry, a genre, or at least a theme, also called *ashʿār al-naṣaf* or *ashʿār munṣifa*, indicating verses in which the poets praise the fervour and the valour in war of the rival clan and acknowledge that victory has been hard-won. III 1236b

In ethics, ~ came to mean impartiality, objectivity, integrity, in short a complete ethical code for the activity of the man of learning; also, a method of argument in which, instead of immediately asserting the inferiority or error of that which is being attacked in comparison with that being defended, both are placed on a fictitious equal footing although it is granted that one or the other is inferior or wrong. III 1237a

insān (A) : man. III 1237a

♦ **al-insān al-kāmil** : in mysticism, the concept of the Perfect Man. I 117b; III 1239a

inshāʾ (A) : the composition of letters, documents or state papers; later, a form of literature in which were included style-books for chancery scribes, copy-books and letter manuals. II 306b; III 1241b; VIII 749b; and → MUNSHĪ

insī (A) : the part of the point of the nib of a reed-pen to the left of the incision, called thus, 'human', because it is turned towards the writer. IV 471a

intaḍat (al-sinn) → ITHTHAGHARA

intihāʾ → IBTIDĀʾ

intiḥār (A) : suicide. In Tradition literature, ~ is used to designate suicide by piercing or cutting one's throat. III 1246b

inzāl → ENZEL; ṢĀḤIB AL-INZĀL

ʿīr → KĀRWĀN

iʿrāb (A) : a technical term in grammar, sometimes translated as inflexion; however, there is no adequate term directly to translate ~ . By ~ Arab grammarians denoted the use of the three short vowels at the end of the singular noun. I 569b; III 1248b

irāde (T) : lit. will; a term adopted in Ottoman official usage from 1832 to designate decrees and orders issued in the name of the sultan. Later, under the constitution, the sultan's function was limited to giving his assent to the decisions of the government and ~ remained in use for this assent. III 1250a

ʿirāfa (A) : in divination, the knowledge of things unseen or of things to come, on the basis of things visible or present. IV 421b

In administrative terminology, a unit headed by an ʿARĪF. I 629a

ʿirāḳ → SHASHMAḲOM

♦ ʿirāḳ ʿadjamī (A) : from the late mediaeval period on, ~ indicated Iranian Media (called *al-djibāl* by the ancient geographers), to distinguish it from *ʿirāḳ ʿarabī*, ʿIrāḳ proper. I 206b

♦ ʿirāḳiyya (A), or *ʿirāḳya* : a kind of reed-pipe which may have been the forerunner of the European rackett. It has a cylindrical pipe and is played with a double reed. VII 208a

iram (A) : in geography, a pile of stones erected as a way-mark. III 1270a

ʿirḍ (A, pl. *aʿrāḍ*) : a term corresponding approximately to the idea of honour, but somewhat ambiguous and imprecise; a strong army; a valley covered with palm trees. At the present day, ~ has become restricted to the woman and her virtue. IV 78a ff.; VI 475a

In Tradition literature and poetry, ~ also has the meaning of the body of animals, or even of men; the parts of the body which sweat; the smell of a man or a woman. IV 77a

irdabb (A) : a measure of capacity for grain. Originally a Persian measure, the ~ was used in Egypt for a long time under the Ptolemies and the Byzantines, and is still in use today. The actual weight of the ~ varied depending on time and place. VI 119a

irdāf (A) : in rhetoric, a term denoting implication, e.g. *ṭawīl al-nidjād* 'with long crossbelt', meaning 'tall in stature', because the one cannot go without the other. V 117a

ʿirḳ (A, pl. *ʿurūḳ*) : vein; root; race, stock. IV 78b

In Tradition literature, ~ is found with the indiscriminate sense of artery and vein, blood; certain anomalies of birth. IV 78b

In geography, ~ is used to describe the form masses of sand can take in Saudi Arabia. I 537a; in sub-Saharan Africa, ~ (Eng *erg*) designates great stretches of dunes, clothed with a herbaceous vegetation which stabilises the sands. VIII 837a

♦ ʿirḳ al-ḥayya : 'serpent's root', a root of the melilot introduced from Syria into the Arab West and used there as an antidote against poisonous snakebites. S 410a

♦ ʿirḳ (ʿurūḳ) al-luʾluʾ : 'the veins of the pearl', designation for the mother-of-pearl. VIII 707a

irsāl (A) : the legislative function of prophecy. IX 812b; and → ḲABḌ

♦ **irsāliyye** (T), or *māl-i irsāliyye* : an Ottoman financial term applied to the annual 'remittances' of cash and kind sent to the personal treasury of the sultan in Istanbul by the holders of the non-feudal SANDJAḲS as well as by the governors of the non-feudal Arab provinces. The latter consisted of the balance left in each provincial treasury after the provincial expenditures and governor's salary were paid. IV 79b

irtidād → MURTADD

irtidjāʿ → RADJʿIYYA

irtidjāl (A) : in pre- and early Islam, the improvising, extemporising of a poem or a speech. A synonym is *badīha*, with the slight difference being that in the case of *badīha*, the poet allows himself a few moments of thought. IV 80b

iryāla → RIYĀLA

ʿiṣāb → LIDJĀM

♦ ʿiṣāba (A) : a headband worn by women in the Arab East. V 741a

ʿīsāwiyya (A) : in Morocco, a simple, wide tunic consisting of a hole in the centre for the head and one at each side for the arms, made of striped wool and worn by men; also, a very ample blouse of strong cotton worn over other clothing. V 746a

iṣbaʿ (A), or *aṣbaʿ* : finger.

As a measurement of length, ~ is the breadth of the middle joint of the middle finger, conventionally 1/24 of the cubit, DHIRĀʿ. IV 96b; a fingerbreadth and subdivision of the ḲABḌA, which is made up of four ~ . II 232a

In Arab navigational texts, ~ is the unit of measurement of star altitude. It was considered to be the angle subtended by the width of a finger held at arm's length against the horizon. IV 96b

In astronomy, ~ or *iṣbaʿ al-kusūf* refers to the twelve equal parts, called fingers, which divided the diameter of the sun or of the moon in order to obtain a standard for measuring the amount of an eclipse. In the West one spoke of 'digits'. V 537a

In music, ~ denotes the tonal mode; the rhythmic mode is called *ḍarb*. II 1074a

iṣbahbadh → ISPAHBADH

iṣbahsalār → ISPAHSĀLĀR

isbitāriyya → DĀWIYYA

iṣfahsalār → ISPAHSĀLĀR

isfirnī (A, < Gk *Sphyraena*), or *safarna*, *safarnāya* : in zoology, the spet or barracuda. VIII 1021a

ʿishāʾ (A) : evening or beginning of the night; a variant name given to the *ṣalāt al-maghrib*. VII 26b

♦ ṣalāt al-ʿishāʾ : the evening prayer which is to be performed, according to the law books, from the last term mentioned for the *ṣalāt al-maghrib* (→ MAGHRIB)

till when a third, or half of the night has passed, or till daybreak. VII 27b; VIII 928b

ishān (P) : in mysticism, ~ was formerly used in Central Asia in the sense of SHAYKH or MURSHID, teacher or guide, in contrast to MURĪD, disciple or pupil. Since the very existence of *ishān*s was strongly disapproved of by the Soviet and Chinese authorities, the term is now obsolescent, if not obsolete. IV 113a

ishʿār (A) : in pre-Islamic times, the custom of making an incision in the side of the hump of the camel marked for the sacrifice during the pilgrimage and letting blood flow from it. III 32b

ishāra (A) : gesture, sign, indication; in rhetoric, ~ acquired the technical meaning of allusion. IV 113b

In mysticism, ~ is the esoteric language of the inexpressible mystical experience. IV 114b; symbolic expression. VIII 139b; a silent gesture or sign (syn. *īmāʾ*, *ramz*). VIII 428b

For ~ in grammar, → ISM AL-ISHĀRA

ishbāʿ (A) : in metrics, one of the six vowels of the rhyme, to wit, the vowel of the DAKHĪL. IV 412a

In prosody, the lengthening of short syllables, and the shortening of long syllables, especially in end position. VII 811a

ishdād (A) : a woven, woollen belt, worn by both sexes in the Arab East. V 741a

īshīk-āḳāsī (P) : a Ṣafawid administrative term meaning 'usher'. The ~ was a minor court official who operated in two different branches of the administrative system, namely, the DĪWĀN and the ḤARAM. IV 118b

ʿishḳ (A) : love, passion; the irresistable desire to obtain possession of a loved object or being. III 103a; IV 118b

ishḳīl (A) : in botany, the sea onion, a plant whose leaves are wide and thick, bent back, covered with a sticky liquid and whose ends are thorny. VIII 687b

ishrāḳ (A) : illumination; the name given to illuminative Wisdom, advocated by Shihāb al-Dīn Suhrawardī. IV 119b

♦ **ishrāḳiyyūn** : adepts of Shihāb al-Dīn Suhrawardī's illuminative Wisdom, ISHRĀḲ, used first, however, in a text by Ibn Waḥshiyya in the 4th/10th century to denote followers of a hermetic tradition who had received some illumination which had placed their works above those of the Peripatetics, *mashaʾiyya*. The term can be applied without hesitation, however, to all of Suhrawardī's followers, who still exist in Iran today. IV 120b

ishtiḳāḳ (A) : in grammar, translated approximately as etymology or derivation by means of analogy, ḲIYĀS. In its general sense, ~ signifies 'taking one word from another', under certain defined conditions. IV 122a; IX 528a

ishtirākiyya (A) : socialism. The word seems to have been first used in this sense in 19th-century Turkish, but fell into disuse, and was replaced by *sosyalist*. Adopted in Arabic, it soon gained universal currency in the Arab lands. IV 123b

īshūrūni → LĀSHŌN
iskemle (T) : stool.
♦ iskemle aghasi̊, or *iskemledjiler bashi* (T) : in Ottoman court life, an officer chosen from among the oldest grooms, whose duty was to carry a stool plated with silver which the sultan used in mounting his horse, when he did not prefer the assistance of a mute who went on his hands and knees on the ground. VIII 530b
isḳumrī (A, < Gk *Scomber*) : in zoology, the mackerel. VIII 1021a
iṣlāḥ (A) : reform, reformism; in modern Arabic, ~ is used for 'reform' in the general sense; in contemporary Islamic literature it denotes more specifically orthodox reformism of the type that emerges in the doctrinal teachings of Muḥammad ʿAbduh, in the writings of Rashīd Riḍā, and in the numerous Muslim authors who are influenced by these two and, like them, consider themselves disciples of the Salafiyya. IV 141a
islām (A) : submission, total surrender (to God). IV 171b
In European languages, it has become customary to speak of Islam to denote the whole body of Muslim peoples, countries, and states, in their socio-cultural or political as well as their religious sphere. Modern Arabic often uses *al-islām* in a similar sense. IV 173b
♦ islāmī → ASLAMĪ; MUSLIM
ism (A, pl. *asmāʾ*), also *ʿalam*, *ism ʿalam* : name; in Arabic-Islamic usage the full name of a person is usually made up of the following elements: the *kunya*, usually a name compound with *abū* 'father of', or *umm* 'mother of'; the ~ ; the *nasab*, or pedigree, a list of ancestors, each being introduced by the word *ibn* 'son of' (the second name of the series is preceded by *bint* 'daughter of', if the first name is that of a woman); and the *nisba*, an adjective ending in *ī*, formed originally from the name of the individual's tribe or clan, then from his place of birth, origin or residence, sometimes from a school of law or sect, and occasionally from a trade or profession. A certain number of persons are also known by a nickname, *laḳab*, or a pejorative sobriquet, *nabaz*, which when the name is stated in full, comes after the *nisba*. IV 179a
In grammar, ~ is the technical term used to signify the noun. IV 181b
♦ ism ʿayn : in grammar, the term used for a word denoting a concrete individual, as opposed to an *ism djins*, a generic word. I 785a
♦ ism djins → ISM ʿAYN
♦ ism al-fiʿl : in grammar, the nominal verb. IX 528a
♦ ism al-ishāra, or *al-ism al-mubham* : in grammar, the demonstrative noun. IX 527b
♦ ism mawṣūl : in grammar, a relative noun. IX 528a
♦ **al-asmāʾ al-ḥusnā** : lit. the most beautiful names, being the 99 names of God. I 714a
ʿiṣma (A) : in theology, a term meaning immunity from error and sin, attributed by

sunnīs to the prophets and by shīʿīs also to the IMĀMS. IV 182b; IX 423a; ~ denotes also infallibility, in sunnism in respect of the community and in shīʿism in respect of the *imāms*. IV 184a; VIII 95a

ismākiyya (A) : systematic ichthyology. VIII 1020b

isnād (A) : in the science of Tradition, the chain of authorities (syn. *sanad*) going back to the source of the Tradition, an essential part of the transmission of a Tradition. III 24a; IV 207a; VIII 514b

In grammar, ~ denotes the relationship between the *musnad* 'that which is supported by (the subject)', and the *musnad ilayhi* 'that which supports (the subject)', the relationship of attribution or predication. VII 705a

In the science of diplomatic, ~ means the decisive words *an yuʿhada ilayhi*, etc. in letters of appointment. II 302a

♦ isnād ʿālī : lit. a high *isnād*, when there are very few links between the transmitter and the Prophet, or between him and a certain authority. Such a Tradition, the quality of which is known as *ʿuluww*, is considered a valuable type on the ground that the fewer the links, the fewer the possible chances of error. III 26a; IX 607b

♦ isnād nāzil : lit. a low *isnād*, when there are many links between the transmitter and the Prophet, or between him and a certain authority. The quality of such Traditions is called *nuzūl*. III 26a

ispahbadh (P, A *iṣbahbadh*) : army chief; the Islamic form of a military title used in the pre-Islamic Persian empires and surviving in the Caspian provinces of Persia down to the Mongol invasions. IV 207a

ispahsālār (P, A *iṣbahsalar, isfahsalar*), and *sipahsālār* : army commander; the title given to commanders-in-chief and general officers in the armies of many states of the central and eastern mediaeval Islamic world. II 210b; IV 208a; VIII 769b; VIII 924a; in Muslim India, governor or viceroy. IX 738b

ispendje (T, < Sl *yupanitsa*), or *ispenče* : the Ottoman name of a poll tax levied on adult non-Muslim subjects and amounting usually to 25 AḲČES a year. Originally, ~ was a feudal peasant household tax in the pre-Ottoman Balkans; it extended into eastern Anatolia from 1540 onwards. II 146b; IV 211a; VIII 487a

isrāʾ → MIʿRĀDJ

iṣrāfa → IḲLĀBA

israʾīliyyāt (A) : a term covering three kinds of narratives: those regarded as historical, which served to complement the often summary information provided by the Qurʾān in respect of the personages in the Bible, particularly the prophets; edifying narratives placed within the chronological (but entirely undefined) framework of 'the period of the (ancient) Israelites'; and fables belonging to folklore, allegedly (but sometimes actually) borrowed from Jewish sources. IV 211b

iṣṭabl (A, < Gk; pl. *iṣṭablāt,* rarely *aṣābil*) : stable, i.e. the building in which mounts and baggage animals are kept tethered; the actual stock of such animals belonging to one single owner. IV 213b

istār (A) : a weight in the apothecary's or troy system, taken over from the Greeks and usually estimated according to two different scales. On the one hand are the equations: 1 *istār* = 6 DIRHAM and 2 *dānaḳ* = 4 MIT͟HḲĀL (an apothecary's stater); on the other, 1 *istār* = 6 1/2 *dirham* = 4 1/2 *mit͟hḳāl* (commercial ~ in the East). IV 248b

istiʿād͟ha (A) : the practice for protecting oneself from the evil influence of Satan, by pronouncing *aʿūd͟hu bi 'llāhi min al-s͟hayṭān al-rad͟jīm*. IX 408b

istiʿāra (A, T *iğretileme*) : in rhetoric, the term commonly used in the sense of metaphor. In the early period, ~ is used occasionally in the sense of 'borrowing of a theme by one author from another'. IV 248b; in Turkish literature, ~ is a class of trope in which the comparative elements of the relationship between objects are stressed in various degrees. V 1028a

♦ istiʿāra-i makniyya (T *kapalı iğretileme*) : in Turkish literature, an implicit metaphor, in which the comparison is achieved by reference to an attribute of an object without mentioning the object itself, 'a cool stream *sang lullabies*'. V 1028a

♦ istiʿāra-i muṣarraḥa (T *açık iğretileme*) : in Turkish literature, an explicit metaphor, in which the comparison is achieved by direct reference to an object, 'our *lions* are off to the battlefield'. V 1028a

istibḍāʿ (A) : a form of intercourse forbidden by the Prophet, consisting of a man who, fearing that he himself could not sire a robust offspring, placed his wife in the hands of a better progenitor. S 133a

istibdād (A) : absolutism. I 64a

istibdāl (A) : in law, dation in payment. S 207b

In Ottoman WAḲF administration, a case in which the *waḳf* administrator is authorised to divest the foundation of properties which are no longer useful and to acquire others in their stead. IX 542a

istibrā' (A) : confirmation of emptiness; in law, ~ is a) the temporary abstention from sexual relations with an unmarried female slave, in order to verify that she is not pregnant, on the occasion of her transfer to a new master or a change in her circumstances; and b) an action of the left hand designed to empty completely the urethra, before the cleaning of the orifices which must follow satisfaction of the natural needs. I 28a; I 1027a; IV 252b

istidlāl (A) : in logic, proof by circumstantial evidence. VII 1051a; reasoning. I 1326b; argumentation. VIII 894a; inference. I 410b

istifhām (A) : in grammar, interrogation, indicated simply by the intonation of the sentence or by two interrogative particles. IV 255a

istig͟hlāl → G͟HĀRŪḲA

istiḥāḍa → ḤAYḌ

istiḥdād (A) : shaving the pubis, *ʿāna*. The syn. *ḥalḳ* is used for shaving the buttocks (*ḥalḳat al-dubur*). IX 312b

istiḥḍār (A) : the invocation of D͟JINNs and angels and making them perceptible to the senses; spiritism. IV 264b; and → ISTIKH̲DĀM

istiḥḳāḳ (A) : in eschatology, 'merit' which, in Muʿtazilī thinking, is attached to human deeds, bringing reward. III 465b

istiḥsān (A) : in law, arbitrary personal opinion. I 730a; a method of finding the law which for any reason is contradictory to the usual ḲIYĀS, reasoning by analogy. III 1237a; IV 255b; juristic preference. IX 324b

istiḳbāl (A) : in astronomy, the opposition of sun and moon, that is, the situation wherein their elongation from each other amounts to 180 degrees. IV 259a

In astrology, ~ is sometimes employed to refer to the diametric aspect of the planets, although in general MUḲĀBALA is preferred. IV 259a

istik̲h̲āra (A) : the concept which consists of entrusting God with the choice between two or more possible options, either through piety and submission to His will, or else through inability to decide oneself, on account of not knowing which choice is the most advantageous one. The divine voice expresses itself either by means of a dream or by rhapsodomancy, ḲURʿA. IV 259b

In literary texts, ~ is merely a pious formula for a request to God for aid and advice, with no ritual character. IV 260a

istik̲h̲dām (A) : making a spirit do a certain thing, one of three procedures of spiritism. The other two are *istinzāl* 'making a spirit descend in the form of a phantom' and *istiḥḍār* 'making a spirit descend into a body'. IX 570b

istik̲h̲rād̲j̲ (A) : in classical Muslim administration, the amount actually received, as opposed to the estimate, AṢL. II 78b; extracting money by force or violence. VII 724a

istiḳlāl (A) : separate, detached, unrestricted, not shared, or sometimes even arbitrary; in Ottoman official usage, ~ acquired the meaning of unlimited powers, e.g. in the terms of appointment of a provincial governor or military commander. In both Turkish and Arabic in the late 18th and early 19th centuries, ~ is commonly used in the sense of the independence of the holder of power from the restraints by either subjects or suzerain. IV 260b

During the same period, under the influence of European political thought and practice, ~ began to acquire the modern meaning of political sovereignty for a country or nation and, in Arabic, became primarily associated with the national independence movements among the Arabs. IV 260b

istiḳrār (A) : in classical Muslim administration, an inventory of the army supplies remaining in hand after issues and payments have been made. II 79a

istiḳsām (A) : in divination, belomancy, consultation of the throw of darts, three types of which were practised by the ancient Arabs. IV 263b

isṭīl (A) : in mediaeval ʿIrāḳ, a vagabond who pretends to be blind for begging purposes. VII 494a

iṣṭilāḥ (A, pl. *iṣṭilāḥāt*) : in the works of early grammarians, in the discussion on language, ~ was used in the sense of a social institution tacitly accepted by its users; when opposed to *aṣl al-lug̲h̲a* 'language', ~ denoted metalanguage. V

805b; Arabic words or calques from the Greek which have assumed a technical meaning. II 765b

istimnāʾ (A) : masturbation. IX 566a

istimṭār → ISTISḲĀʾ

istiʾnāf (A) : lit. recommencement, renewal; in law, in modern Arabic, appeal; in classical law, ~ is used with its sense of recommencement with regard to the ʿIBĀDĀT, the religious duties, especially prayer, i.e. when the entire prayer, which has been interrupted by the occurrence of a ritual impurity, has to be begun again. In Mālikī law, ~ is called *ibtidāʾ*. IV 264a

istindjāʾ (A) : in law, the purification incumbent upon the Muslim after the fulfilment of his natural needs. IV 264b

istinshāḳ (A) : in law, the inhaling of water through the nostrils at the time of the ablutions, WUḌŪʾ and GHUSL. IV 264b

istinzāl (A) : in divination, hydromancy. IV 264b; and → ISTIKHDĀM

istiʿrāḍ (A) : the mustering, passing in review and inspecting of troops, also known as *ʿarḍ*, the official charged with this duty being known as the ʿARĪḌ. IV 265a

Among the Khāridjites, ~ is a technical term meaning the interrogation to which the enemies of these sectarians were subjected on falling into their hands; used, in a general sense, of religious murder, the putting to death of Muslims and pagans who objected to their still rudimentary doctrine. IV 269a

istiṣḥāb (A) : in law, the principle by which a given judicial situation that had existed previously was held to continue to exist as long as it could not be proved that it had ceased to exist or had been modified. I 276a; IV 269b; IX 324b

istisḳāʾ (A), or *istimṭār* : a supplication for rain during periods of great droughts, a rogatory rite still practised at the present day (notably in Jordan and Morocco) and dating back to the earliest Arab times. I 109a; IV 269b; VIII 931a

istiṣlāḥ (A) : in law, like ISTIḤSĀN, a method by which the otherwise usual method of deduction, analogy, is to be excluded in the preparation of legal decisions. IV 256b

istiṭāʿa (A) : in theology and scholastic theology, the term for the 'capacity' to act created by God in the human subject. I 413b; III 1063a; IV 271a

istithnāʾ (A) : in a religious context, ~ refers to the saying of the formula 'if God wills', *in shāʾ Allāh*. III 1196a; VII 607a

In grammar, ~ signifies 'exception', i.e. that one or more beings are excepted from the functions exercised in a complete sentence, as in 'everyone came except Zayd'. IV 272b

istiwāʾ (*khaṭṭ al-*) (A) : the line of equality, of equilibrium, that is to say, the equator, which divides the earth into two hemispheres, the northern and the southern, and joins together all those points of the globe where day and night are equal. IV 273a

īṭāʾ (A) : in prosody, a defect of the rhyme occurring when the same word in the same meaning is repeated in the rhymes of lines belonging to the same poem. It is permissable under certain circumstances. IV 413a

ītār (A) : in archery, the act of stringing or bracing the bow. IV 800a

itāwa (A, < *atā*) : lit. gift; a general term met with, especially in pre- and proto-Islamic times, meaning a vague tribute or lump payment made, for example, to or by a tribe or other group; later, the word describes, sometimes in a denigrating way, a tip or bribe. IV 276a

itb (A) : a loose gown worn by women in the Arabian peninsula. V 741a

itbāʿ (A) : a particular form of paronomasia, constituted by the repetition of a qualifying term to which there is added a metaplasm, i.e. the deliberate alternation of a radical consonant, usually the first, but never the third, e.g. *ḥasan basan* 'wonderfully attractive'. The first element is called *matbūʿ* or *mutbaʿ*, and the second *tābiʿ*. VII 823a

iṭbāḳ (A) : in grammar, velarisation; the *ḥurūf al-muṭbaḳa* are 'the emphatic consonants', that is, *ṣād*, *ẓāʾ*, *ṭāʾ* and *ḍād*. III 598b

ithbāt (A) : to witness, to show, to point to, to demonstrate, to prove, to establish, to verify and to establish the truth, to establish (the existence of something); in mysticism, ~ is the opposite of *maḥw*, the effacement of the 'qualities of habit', and denotes the fact of performing one's religious obligations. IV 277a

ithm → DHANB

iththaghara (A) : a verb which means '[a boy] bred his central milk teeth or front teeth, or he bred his teeth after the former ones had fallen out' (Lane). Several terms refer to different stages of this process: *shakka*, *ṭalaʿa*, *nadjama*, *nasaʿa*, *intaḍat (al-sinn)*, *adrama (al-ṣabiyy)*, *aḥfara*, *abdaʾa*. VIII 822a

iʿtibār (A) : in the science of Tradition, the consideration of whether a transmitter who is alone in transmitting a Tradition is well known, or whether, if the Tradition is solitary by one authority, someone in the chain has another authority, or whether another Companion transmits it. III 26b

iʿtiḳād (A) : the act of adhering firmly to something, hence a firmly established act of faith. In its technical sense, the term denotes firm adherence to the Word of God. It may be translated in European languages by the words 'croyance', 'belief', 'Glauben', with the proviso that this 'belief' is not a simple opinion or thought, but is the result of deep conviction. IV 279a

iʿtikāf (A) : a period of retreat in a mosque, a particularly commended pious practice which can be undertaken at any time. IV 280a

iʿtimād (A) : in archery, the holding firmly in the left hand the grip or handle of the bow while the right-hand fingers make a good locking of the string, the two hands exerting equal force. IV 800b

♦ **iʿtimād al-dawla** (A) : lit. trusty support of the state, a title of Persian viziers during the Ṣafawid period and subsequently. IV 281b

ʿitḳ (A) : emancipation (of slave). The freedman is called *ʿatīḳ* or *muʿtaḳ*. I 29b

♦ ʿitḳ al-sāʾiba : in Mālikī and Ḥanbalī law, an ancient type of enfranchisement of the slave without patronage, which term refers to the pre-Islamic custom of turning loose in complete freedom one particular she-camel of the herd, protected by taboos. I 30b

♦ **ʿitḳnāme** (T), *ʿitiḳnāme, ʿitāḳnāme* : an Ottoman term for a certificate of manumission, given to a liberated slave. IV 282b

iṭlāḳāt (A) : in the science of diplomatic, the name given to documents reaffirming decisions of former rulers; sometimes, however, they were simply called TAWḲĪʿ. II 303b; II 306b

iṭlāḳiyya (A) : one of two main headings in the monthly and yearly accounting registers of the Īlkhānids, under which fell payments by provincial tax-farmers made to members of the court, palace servants, and the military. III 284a; and → MUḲARRARIYYA

ʿiṭr → AFĀWĪH

ʿitra → AHL AL-BAYT

ittibāʿ (A) : 'active fidelity' to the Traditions of both the Prophet and the SALAF, a term preferred by reformists to *taḳlīd*, which denoted the servile dependence on traditional doctrinal authorities that they rejected. IV 152a

ittiḥād (A) : unity, association, joining together; in theology, the Christian incarnation of the Word in the person of Jesus, which concept is rejected by Muslims as being contradictory. IV 283a

In mysticism, the mystic union of the soul with God. IV 283a

ittiṣāl (A), or *wiṣāl* : in mysticism, a union of man and God which excludes the idea of an identity of the soul and God. IV 283a

ityān al-mayta (A) : necrophilia. IX 566a

ʿiwaḍ (A) : exchange value, compensation, that which is given in exchange for something; in law, ~ is used in a very broad sense to denote the counterpart of the obligation of each of the contracting parties in onerous contracts which are called 'commutative', that is, contracts which necessarily give rise to obligations incumbent on both parties. Thus in a sale, the price and the thing sold are each the ~ of the other. IV 286a

In unilateral contracts, ~ (*badal* and *thawāb* are also used) is employed in a more restricted sense: it is applied to the compensation offered by one of the two parties who is not absolutely obliged to give any. IV 286a

īwān (P, T *eyvān*) : in architecture, a chamber or a hall which is open to the outside at one end, either directly or through a portico; an estrade or a raised part of a floor; a palace or at least some sort of very formal and official building; any one of the halls in a religious building, MADRASA or mosque, which opens onto a courtyard. Art historians and archaeologists have given ~ a technically precise meaning, that of a single large vaulted hall walled on three sides and opening directly to the outside on the fourth. IV 287a; a room enclosed by three walls, opening out in the whole width of the fourth side, like an enormous gaping flat-based ledge, and generally roofed by a cradle vault (semi-cylindrical). Although not without similarity to the Greek *prostas*, the ~ does seem to be a genuinely Iranian creation. It became a characteristic theme of Sāsānid architecture. II 114a; and → LĪWĀN

In the terminology of horse-riding, a light bit. Two other types of bit were used: the *fakk*, a snaffle bit, and the *nāzikī*, seemingly the equivalent of the modern bit used by the Spahis. II 954a

iwazz (A) : in zoology, wild geese. IX 98b

ʿiyāfa (A) : animal omens (zoomancy) and, in the strict sense, ornithomancy, that is to say, the art of divining omens in the names of birds, their cries, their flight and their posture. IV 290b

iyāla → EYĀLET

izār (A), *azr, miʾzar, īzār* : a large sheet-like wrap worn both as a mantle and as a long loin cloth or waist cloth by pre-Islamic Arabs. III 1053a; V 732b; a large, enveloping body wrap for women in the Arab East or for both sexes in North Africa. V 741a; V 746a; a fringed shawl worn by Jewish women in Morocco. V 746a; and → RIDĀʾ

iẓhār → IḌMĀR

ʿiẓlim → NĪL

J

jawi → PEGON

jiilaal → GUʾ

K

ḳāʿa (A) : in modern dwellings in Egypt, the principal room in the ḤARĪM, with a central space and lateral extensions. The walls surrounding the central space rise to the level of the terraces and carry a lantern which lights the interior. II 114b; an elongated hall with two axial ĪWĀNs and a sunken central area, usually square, known as the *durḳāʿa*. IV 428b; VIII 545b

♦ ḳāʿa muʿallaḳa : in architecture, a raised hall, a living unit located on the second floor. VIII 545b

ḳaʿada (A) : term for the designation of the quietists. I 207a

ḳaʾan → KHĀḲĀN

kaʿb (A) : in mathematics, ~ , or *mukaʿʿab*, denotes the third power of the unknown quantity. II 362a; the cube root. III 1139b

♦ kaʿb kaʿb : in mathematics, the term for the sixth power. III 1140b

kaʿba (A) : the most famous sanctuary of Islam, called the temple or house of God, and situated in the centre of the great mosque in Mecca. The name ~ is connected with the cube-like appearance of the building. In former times the word also used to designate other similarly shaped sanctuaries. IV 317a

ḳaba zurna → ZURNA

ḳabā → ḲABĀʾ

ḳabāʾ (A, < Sp *capo* or *capa*), or *ḳabā* : a cloak or cape worn by soldiers. III 100a; V 739b; V 743b; a luxurious, sleeved robe, slit in front, with buttons, made of fabrics such as brocade. V 733b; V 748a ff.

kabāʾir (A, s. *kabīra*) : the 'grave sins', mentioned in the Qurʾān, the exact definition of which remained variable. The ~ are distinguished from the *ṣag͟hāʾir* 'lesser sins'. IV 1107b

kabaḳ (A), or *ḳabaḳ* : in archery, a small target. II 954a; in Mamlūk terminology, a 'gourd' game, one of the branches of horse-riding. II 955a

ḳabāla (A) : in law, a guarantee, used mainly in connection with fiscal practice. It concerns the levying of the land-tax, K͟HARĀD͟J, and that of special taxes, *mukūs* (→ MAKS). Local communities were held jointly responsible by the Treasury for the payment at the required time of the full amount of land-tax demanded. When individuals had difficulty in finding the necessary ready money immediately, an application was made to a notable to advance the sum required. The matter having generally been agreed in advance, this notable acted as a guarantor for the debt of the locality in question. This procedure constitutes the contract of ~ , the offer being called *taḳbīl* and the person named *mutaḳabbil*. I 1144a; IV 323a

Alongside its use with regard to taxation on land, ~ , as well as ḌAMĀN in this context, occurs in a more permanent sense to signify the farming of special revenues, generally of *mukūs* (→ MAKS), especially in towns, such as the sale of salt or the management of baths or even of a local customs office. IV 324a

ḳabas → IḲTIBĀS

kabāt͟h (A) : the ripe fruit of the thorn tree *arāk* (*Capparis sedata*). II 1058b

kabd → KABID

ḳabḍ (A) : lit. seizure, grasping, contraction, abstention, etc., and used in the special vocabulary of various disciplines.

In law, ~ signifies taking possession of, handing over. In Mālikī law *ḥiyāza* is more frequently used. *Tasallum* is also employed to mean the act of handing over. Taking possession is accomplished by the material transfer of the thing when movable goods are involved; by occupation when it is a question of real estate, but also symbolically by the handing over of the keys or title deeds of the property. III 350a; IV 325b

In mysticism, ~ is a technical term used to denote a spiritual state of 'contraction' as opposed to 'expansion', BASṬ. I 1088b; IV 326a

In prosody, ~ is the suppression of the fifth quiescent letter in the feet *faʿūlun* and *mafāʿīlun* which occurs in the metres *ṭawīl*, *hazadj*, *muḍāriʿ* and *mutaḳārib*, so that these feet are reduced to *faʿūlu* and *mafāʿilun* respectively. A foot suffering this alteration is called *maḳbūḍ*. I 672a; IV 326b

In the Islamic ritual prayer, ~ is the position assumed after the saying of the words '*allāhu akbar*'. The hands are placed on the base of the chest, the right hand over the left. The Imāmīs and the Mālikīs let the arms fall at this point: the position of *sadl* or *irsāl*. VIII 929a

♦ ḳabḍ amāna : in law, the term used for when the trustee, in regard to contracts which involve the temporary transfer of something from one contracting party to the other, is only held responsible if he has been at fault or in transgression, TAʿADDĪ, of the rules of the contract or of the customary dealings in such matters. IV 326a

♦ ḳabḍ ḍamān : in law, the term used for when the trustee, in regard to contracts which involve the temporary transfer of something from one contracting party to the other, is held responsible for any loss arising in respect of the object, even through chance or circumstances over which he has no control. IV 326a

♦ ḳabḍa : a measure of length, equalling a handsbreadth, or one-sixth, of the cubit, DHIRĀʿ. The ~ , in turn, consisted of four IṢBAʿs. II 232a; VII 137b

In treatises on archery, ~ means grasp, sc. the position of the left hand (for a right-handed person) on the grip or handle of the bow. In order to distinguish this technique from that of the ʿAḲD, the authors sometimes call this more precisely *al-ḳabḍa bi 'l-shamāl*. IV 800b

kabid (A, according to lexicographers the only correct form), or *kabd*, *kibd* : liver; through contiguity of meaning, ~ is also used to designate the parts of the body in the vicinity of the liver. Thus, for instance, in classical Arabic ~ can denote the surfaces of the body more or less close to the liver as well as the chest and even the belly. In the same way ~ is also frequently used to cover the middle, centre, interior (we would say heart) of something. IV 327a

ḳābiḍ (A) : the quality of food being astringent. II 1071b

ḳābila (A) : in alchemy, the part known as the 'receiver' of the distilling apparatus. I 486a

ḳabīla (A) : a large agnatic group, the members of which claim to be descended from one common ancestor; this word is generally understood in the sense of tribe. IV 334a

kabīr (A) : lit. large; designation for a tribal chief. IX 115b; and → ṢAGHĪR

ḳabr (A) : tomb; ~ was first applied to the pit used as a burial place for a corpse (as was the term *ḍarīḥ*), giving rise to its habitual use in the text of numerous epitaphs containing the expression *hādhā ḳabru...* 'this is the grave of...'. Originally distinguished from the term *ṣandūḳ* 'cenotaph', ~ had the more general meaning of the tumulus or construction covering the grave to bring it to notice, a custom current in Islamic countries from early times. IV 352a

kabsh → ḤAMAL; SINNAWR
ḳabūl → BAYʿ
kabūsh (A), and *shalīl* : in the terminology of horse-riding, a cloth worn by the horse. The terms *tashāhir* and *djulla* are confined to stable-cloths. II 954a
ḳačḳun → YAWA
ḳaḍāʾ (A, T *ḳażāʾ*) : originally meaning 'decision', ~ has in the Qurʾān different meanings according to the different contexts, e.g., doomsday, jurisdiction, revelation of the truth, and predestination, determination, decree. IV 364b
In theology, ~ means God's eternal decision or decree concerning all beings, that must be fulfilled in all circumstances, and the execution and declaration of a decree at the appointed time; sudden death. IV 364b
In a religious context, ~ is the technical term for the neglected performance of religious duties, e.g. repeating prayers to make up for having omitted them at the appointed time, as opposed to ADĀʾ. I 169b; IV 365a; IX 94b
In law, ~ stands for both the office and the sentence of a ḲĀḌĪ 'judge'; ~ is also found in legal terminology with the meaning 'payment of a debt. IV 364b ff.
In ʿAbd al-Razzāḳ al-Ḳashānī's mystical thought, ~ means the existence of the universal types of all things in the world of the Universal Reason. I 89b
In the Ottoman empire, *ḳażāʾ* meant not only the judgement of the ḲĀḌĪ but also the district which his administrative authority covered. The term ~ , denoting an administrative district, has remained in use in the Turkish republic. IV 365a
♦ **al-ḳaḍāʾ wa 'l-ḳadar** : when combined into one expression, these two words have the overall meaning of the Decree of God, both the eternal Decree (the most frequent meaning of ḲAḌĀʾ) and the Decree given existence in time (the most frequent sense of ḲADAR). Other translations are possible, for example, *ḳaḍāʾ*, predetermination; *ḳadar*, decree or fate, destiny, in the sense of determined or fixed. It is also possible to use *ḳaḍāʾ* alone for decree in its broadest sense and define *ḳadar* more precisely as existential determination. The expression combining them is in general use and has become a kind of technical term of scholastic theology. I 413a; II 618a; IV 365a
In Persian literature, *ḳaḍāʾ u ḳadar* is a genre of poetry devoted to stories about the working of fate, fashionable in the 10th-11th/16th-17th centuries. VI 834b; VIII 776a
♦ ḳaḍāʾ u ḳadar → AL-ḲAḌĀʾ WA 'L-ḲADAR
ḳadam → ATHAR
ḳadar (A) : measure, evaluation, fixed limit; in its technical sense, ~ designates determination, the divine decree in so far as it sets the fixed limits for each thing, or the measure of its being. III 1142b; IV 365b; and → AL-ḲAḌĀʾ WA 'L-ḲADAR
In ʿAbd al-Razzāḳ al-Ḳashānī's mystical thought, ~ is the arrival in the world of the Universal Soul of the types of existing things; after being individualised in order to be adapted to matter, these are joined to their causes, produced by

them, and appear at their fixed times. I 89b

ḳadāsa (A) : holiness; beings that are pure, wholly unsullied or in touch with the divine. IV 372a

ḳaḍb → ḲATT

♦ ḳaḍba (A) : a quiver made from the *nabʿ* wood (*Grewia tenax*). IV 800a

kaddād (A, pl. *kawādīd*) : a tiller of the soil. I 233b

ḳadḥ (A) : in medicine, the operation for cataract. II 481b

kaḏḥḏḥāb → ṢĀLIḤ

ḳaḏḥḏḥāf (A) : oarsman, part of the crew of the warships in the Muslim navy. S 120a

ḳaḏḥf (A) : in law, a slanderous accusation of fornication, ZINĀʾ, or of illegitimate descent; in the latter case, it amounts to accusing the mother of fornication. I 29b; IV 373a

ḳāḍī (A) : judge; a representative of authority, invested with the power of jurisdiction. In theory, the head of the community, the caliph, is the holder of all powers; like all other state officials, the ~ is therefore a direct or indirect delegate, NĀʾIB, the delegate retaining the power to do justice in person. The objective being the application of the law, which is essentially religious, the function of the judge is a religious one. In theory, his competence embraces both civil and penal cases, and includes the administration of mosques and pious endowments. His competence in penal matters, however, is restricted to the very few crimes envisaged by the law, their repression being currently undertaken by the police. II 890b; IV 373b

♦ **ḳāḍī ʿaskar** : judge of the army; an institution dating from the 2nd/8th century. Under Saladin, this institution was called *ḳāḍī leshker*. The position began to lose its importance after the middle of the 10th/16th century, when power passed into the hands of the grand MUFTĪ of Istanbul. It was finally abolished under the Turkish republic. IV 375a

♦ ḳāḍi ʾl-djamāʿa : ḲĀḌĪ of the community of Muslims; a title which ʿAbd al-Raḥmān gave, between 138/755 and 141/758, to the *ḳāḍī* of the Spanish territory already conquered, until then known as *ḳāḍi ʾl-djund* ʻḳāḍī of the military districtʼ. Later, ~ became an institution similar to that of the ḲĀḌI ʾL-ḲUḌĀT. IV 374b; VI 2a

♦ ḳāḍi ʾl-djund → ḲĀḌĪ ʾL-DJAMĀʿA

♦ ḳāḍi ʾl-ḳuḍāt : ʻthe judge of judgesʼ; the highest position in the system of judicial organization of the Islamic state, which, when combined with the institution of the *wizāra* (→ WAZĪR), was the highest step under the authority of the caliph. The institution of ~ was an adaptation of the Persian *mōbedān-mōbed*. I 164b; IV 374a; VI 2a

♦ ḳāḍī leshker → ḲĀḌĪ ʿASKAR

ḳaḍīb (A) : rod (syn. *ʿaṣā*), one of the insignia of the sovereignty of the caliph. IV 377b

In archery, ~ signifies a bow made of a stave all of a piece and unspliced, sc. a self-bow. IV 798a

In music, a wand which supplied rhythm. II 1073b; a percussion stick. VIII 852b; IX 10b

ḳadīd (A) : in pre-Islamic Arabia, meat cut into thin strips and left to dry in the sun. II 1059a

ḳadi̊n → KHĀṢṢEKĪ

ḳādi̊rgha → BASHTARDA

kadkhudā → KETKHUDĀ

ḳadriya (A) : cedar-oil, extracted from cedarwood. IV 772b

ḳafā (A) : nape of the neck. IX 312b

kafāʾa (A) : equality, parity and aptitude; in law, ~ denotes the equivalence of social status, fortune and profession (those followed by the husband and by the father-in-law), as well as parity of birth, which should exist between husband and wife, in default of which the marriage is considered ill-matched and, in consequence, liable to break up. I 27b; IV 404a; IV 1116b; and → KUFU

kafāla (A) : in law, an institution corresponding to some extent to the surety-bond, with the difference that thc jurists distinguished two types of surety-bond: that for which the surety, *kafīl*, is binding to secure only the appearance in court of the debtor, *aṣīl* or *makfūl*; known as the *kafāla bi ʾl-nafs*, it is an institution peculiar to Islamic law. And, secondly, the *kafāla bi ʾl-māl*, by means of which the surety stands as a pledge to the creditor, *makfūl lahu*, that the obligation of the principal debtor will be fulfilled. IV 404b

ḳafesī (T) : a dome-shaped ḲAVUḲ 'cap', worn with a long turban forming folds fastened towards the base with a fine thread or pin. It was worn in Ottoman Turkey from the 17th century by the functionaries of the Defter (→ DAFTAR). V 751b

kaff (A) : palm, paw; in divination, *ʿilm al-~* is a process which belongs to the realm of physiognomy, designating more specifically chirognomy or the art of deducing the character of a person according to the shape and appearance of the hands. But the use of the term has become general. It also covers both chiromancy (the study of the lines of the hand), dactylomancy (prognostications drawn from the observation of the finger joints), and onychomancy (divination from the finger nails). IV 405b

In prosody, ~ is a deviation in the metre because of the suppression of the 7th consonant, e.g. the *nūn* of *fāʿilātu[n]*. I 672a

♦ kaff al-hirr (A) : in botany, the Corn crowfoot (*Ranunculus arvensis*) and the Asiatic crowfoot (*R. asiaticus*). IX 653a

kaffāra (A) : Qurʾānic term for an expiatory and propitiatory act which grants remission for faults of some gravity. IV 406b; IX 94b

kāfī (Pu) : a genre of Muslim Punjabi literature, comprising a lyric consisting of rhymed couplets or short stanzas having a refrain repeated after each verse, and normally following the usual Indian poetic convention whereby the poet assumes a female persona, typically that of a young girl yearning to be united with her husband/love, allegorically to be understood as an expression of the soul's yearning for God. VIII 256a

kafīl → KAFĀLA

ḳāfila → KĀRWĀN

kāfir (A) : originally, 'obliterating, covering', then, 'concealing benefits received', i.e. ungrateful, which meaning is found even in the old Arab poetry and in the Qur'ān; the development of meaning to 'infidel, unbeliever' probably took place under the influence of Syriac and Aramaic. IV 407b

♦ **kāfirkūb** (A, < *kāfir* + P *kūbīdan*) : lit. heathen-basher, i.e. a club; the term is testified, only in the plural *kāfirkūbāt*, in ʿIrāḳ from the end of the 2nd/8th century, although al-Ṭabarī cites it when describing the incidents arising in 66/685 during the revolt of al-Mukhtār. It seems to be a term born of a particular period and in a relatively circumscribed area which swiftly became obsolete. IV 44b; IV 411a

ḳāfiya (A, pl. *ḳawāfin*) : in prosody, rhyme. Originally, the word meant 'lampoon', then 'line of poetry', 'poem'. These earlier senses survived in Islamic times after the word had also come to be used in the technical sense of 'rhyme'. The native lexicographers believe that 'rhyme' is the original and that 'line of poetry', 'poem' are secondary. IV 411b; and → SADJʿ

♦ ḳāfiya muḳayyada : fettered *ḳāfiya*, a rhyme in which the rhyme consonant is not followed by a letter of prolongation. IV 412a

♦ ḳāfiya muṭlaḳa : loose *ḳāfiya*, a rhyme in which the rhyme consonant is followed by a letter of prolongation or by a short vowel and a vowelled or quiescent *hāʾ*. IV 412a

kāfiyya (A), or *kūfiyya* : a head scarf worn by both sexes in the Arab East. V 741a

ḳafīz (A) : a measure of capacity used in ʿIrāḳ and caliphal Persia for weighing small quantities of grain. Its actual weight varied. VI 119b f.

ḳafla → ʿAḲD

ḳaftān → KHAFTĀN

kāfūr (A, < H *karpūra*, *kappūra*, Mal *kapur*) or *ḳāfūr, ḳa(f)ūr* : camphor, the white, translucent substance which is distilled together with camphor oil from the wood of the camphor tree (*Cinnamomum camphora*) indigenous to east Asia (China, Formosa, Japan). IV 417b; VIII 1042b

The same word ~ (variants *kufurrā*, *kifirrā*, *djufurrā* etc.) also designates the integument of the palm leaf or of the grapevine. IV 418a

kāghad (A, < P), or *kāghid* : paper. After its introduction in Samarḳand by Chinese prisoners in 134/751, various kinds of paper were then made and it must be supposed that paper achieved some importance as early as the second half of the 2nd/8th century. Names for the different kinds of paper are: *firʿawnī*, *sulaymānī*, *djaʿfarī*, *ṭāhirī*, and *nūḥī*. IV 419b

ḳag͟han → KH̱ĀḲĀN
kāg͟hān (A) : in mediaeval ʿIrāḳ, a boy who acts as a male prostitute. VII 494a
♦ kāg͟hānī : in mediaeval ʿIrāḳ, a vagrant who gives out that he is demoniacally possessed or an epileptic. VII 494a
kāg͟hid → KĀG͟HAD
kag͟hnî (T) : a Byzantine wagon, used in medieval Turkicised Anatolia. I 205b
ḳaḥba (pl. *ḳiḥāb*) → BAG͟HIYY
ḳahd → ḤAD͟HAF
kaḥḥāl (A) : in medicine, an oculist. I 388a
kāhin (A) : a term of controversial origin. It appears to have been used by the 'Western Semites' to designate the possessor of a single function with related prerogatives: the offering of sacrifices in the name of the group, the representing of this group before the deity, the interpretation of the will of the deity, and the anticipation and communication of his wishes. The Arab ~ combined the functions of sacrificer and guardian of the sanctuary, and those of the *mantis* and the *augur*; hence, it is possible to render ~ by 'priest', in the sense of agent of the official cult. But the predominance of nomadism, where it was usually the head of the family or tribe who offered sacrifices and in which frequent migrations prevented the establishment of an official form of worship and fixed places of worship, weakened the first role of the ~ while favouring the development of the second, more in keeping with the expectations of most of his fellow-tribesmen. Thus it is virtually necessary to translate ~ as 'diviner' with the dual meaning of the Latin *divinus*, that is to say, 'one inspired' and 'prophet', without excluding his strictly priestly role in places where social conditions allowed it, such as at Mecca. IV 420b; and → ʿARRĀF
ḳāhiriyya (A) : omnipotence (of God). I 89b
kāhiya → KETK͟HUDĀ
kahramān → KĀRIM
kahrubā (P), also *kāhrabāʾ* : yellow amber; today, ~ also used for electricity. IV 445b
ḳahwa (A) : coffee; originally a name for wine, ~ was transferred towards the end of the 8th/14th century to the beverage made from the berry of the coffee tree; the word for coffee in Ethiopia, *būn*, has passed into Arabic in the form *bunn*, as a name of the coffee tree and berry. IV 449a
♦ ḳahwa-k͟hāna → ČĀY-K͟HĀNA
kahya → KETK͟HUDĀ
ḳāʾid (A, pl. *ḳuwwād)* : an imprecise term, but one always used to designate a military leader whose rank might vary from captain to general. II 507b; IV 456a; designation for a tribal chief (referring to the chief's leadership in war). IX 115b
♦ ḳāʾid raʾsih : 'governor of himself', a powerful ḲĀʾID who was removed from office and compelled to live at court, with the honour due to his rank. IV 456b

ḳāʿid (A) : lit. sitter; in shīʿī terminology, the 'sitting' members of the family of the Prophet, who refused to be drawn into ventures of armed revolt, in contrast to the ḲĀʾIM. IV 456b

ḳaʿīd (A), and *khafīf* : a term applied to a wild animal or bird which approaches a traveller or hunter from the rear, one of the technical terms designating the directions of a bird's flight, or an animal's steps, which play an important part in the application of divination known as FAʾL, ṬĪRA and ZADJR. I 1048a; II 760a

ḳāʾif (A, pl. *ḳāfa*) : a physiognomist. I 28b

ḳāʾila → ẒĀHIRA

ḳāʾim (A) : lit. riser, the SHĪʿĪ MAHDĪ, referring both to the member of the family of the Prophet who was expected to rise against the illegitimate regime and restore justice on earth, and to the eschatological Mahdī. Synonyms in shīʿī terminology are: *ḳāʾim āl Muḥammad, al-ḳāʾim bi 'l-sayf, al-ḳāʾim bi-amr Allāh, ḳāʾim al-ḳiyāma*. IV 456b; V 1235b

Among the Ismāʿīliyya, ~ is the name of the seventh 'speaking' prophet who will abrogate Muḥammad's sharīʿa and restore the pure unity, *tawḥīd*, of the times before Adam's fall. IV 203b; IV 457a; S 206b

♦ ḳāʾim bi-aʿmāl : in the science of diplomacy, the term for *chargé d'affaires*. VIII 813a; and → MAṢLAḤATGÜZĀR

♦ **ḳāʾim-maḳām** (T) : the title borne by a number of different officials in the Ottoman empire. The most important of them was the *ṣadāret ḳāʾim-maḳāmi̊* or *ḳāʾim-maḳāmi̊ pasha* who stayed in the capital as deputy when the grand vizier had to leave for a military campaign. The ~ enjoyed almost all the authority of the grand vizier, issuing *fermāns* (→ FARMĀN) and nominating functionaries, but he was not allowed to intervene in the area where the army was operating. IV 461b

In 1864 the ~ became the governor of an administrative district, and under the Republican regime he continued to be administrator of such a distict. IV 461b

In Ottoman Egypt, ~ was applied to the acting viceroy before Muḥammad ʿAlī Pasha, and under the latter to specific grades in the military and administrative hierarchies. IV 461b

ḳāʾime (T, < A) : the name formerly used for paper money in Turkey, an abbreviation for *ḳāʾime-i muʿtebere*. Originally, the word was used of official documents written on one large, long sheet of paper. IV 460a

kaʿk (A) : in the mediaeval Middle East, a pastry, to which dough SAWĪḲ was added. IX 93b

ḳaʿḳāʿ (A) : a man whose foot-joints can be heard cracking as he walks; often found as a proper name in the early days of Islam. IV 463b

ḳalʿa (A) : castle, fortress. IV 467a; citadel. IX 411a; and → AGADIR

ḳalafat → ČORBADJI̊ KEČESI

ḳalāḳil (A) : a name for the SŪRAs that begin with *ḳul* 'say:': lxxii, cix and cxii-cxiv. IX 887b

kalām (A) : a word; in the Qurʾān, ~ is found in the expression *kalām allāh* 'the Word of God'. IV 468b; ~ , or **ʿilm al-kalām**, is also the term for 'theology', one of the religious sciences of Islam and the discipline which brings to the service of religious beliefs discursive arguments. III 1141b ff.; a rational argument, defensive apologetics, or the science of discourse (on God). I 694a; IV 468b
For ~ in music, → GHINĀʾ

ḳalam (A, < Gk κάλαμος 'reed') : the reed-pen used for writing in Arabic script. It is a tube of reed cut between two knots, sliced obliquely (or concave) at the thicker end and with the point slit, in similar fashion to the European quill and later the steel-pen. IV 471a

In Ottoman usage, ~ (pronounced *ḳalem)* was used figuratively to designate the secretariat of an official department or service; it then came to be the normal term for an administrative office. This usage has survived in modern Turkish, and is also current in Arabic. IV 471b

♦ ḳalamdān → DAWĀT

♦ **ḳalamkārī** (< P *ḳalam* 'pen' + *kār* 'work') : the hand-painted and resist-dyed cottons of India, known as chintz. IV 471b

ḳalān : a Mongolian tax, apparently a general term for occasional exactions of a specifically Mongol rather than Islamic character, imposed on the sedentary population by the Mongols and including some kind of corvée. VII 233b

ḳalandar (T, < P ?) : 'a vagabond of scandously offensive behaviour'; the name given to the members of a class of wandering dervishes which existed formerly, especially in the 7th/13th century, in the Islamic world, within the area extending from Almalïk in Turkestan in the east to Morocco in the west, practising in its extreme form the antinomian way of life of Malāmatiyya mysticism. ~ passed into Arabic also in the form *karandal*. IV 58b; IV 472b; VI 225b

♦ ḳalandariyyāt : in Persian literature, a genre of poetry, named after the ḲALANDAR. Poems of this genre can be quatrains or may have a form intermediate between the ḲAṢĪDA and the GHAZAL. They are characterised by the use of antinomian motives referring to the debauchery of beggars and drunks. IV 58b; IX 4b

ḳalansuwa (P), and *ḳalansuwa ṭawīla*, *ṭawīla* or *danniyya* : a distinctive, tall, conical Persian hat, resembling a long amphora-like wine jar known as *dann*, worn in the mediaeval Islamic period. Its top was pointed. IV 940a; V 737b; a pointed bonnet for men in Algeria and Tunisia. V 746a

kalāntar (P) : a term used in the 8th/14th and 9th/15th centuries to mean 'leader', occurring especially with reference to the tribal and military classes. From the late 9th/15th century onwards, ~ designates (i) an official belonging to 'civil' hierarchy in charge of a town or district or the ward of a town, (ii) the head of a guild, and (iii) the head of a tribe or sub-tribe. In its first sense, which is now obsolete, ~ sometimes overlapped or was synonymous with RAʾĪS, DĀRŪGHA, and KETKHUDĀ. IV 474a kalawta (A), or *kalūta* : a kind of cap which is first mentioned in the Fāṭimid period. It was to become a standard item in Ayyūbid and Mamlūk times. V 738a

kalb (A) : in zoology, the domestic dog (*Canis familiaris*). IV 489b; wood-eating worms. IV 491b

For ~ in astronomy, IV 492a; IX 471b

♦ kalb al-baḥr, or *ḥafshrūsī* : in zoology, the white whale. VIII 1022b; the dog-fish, also called the *kawsadj* or *lakhm*. IV 491b

♦ kalb al-māʾ : in zoology, the otter; in the western Islamic world, ~ is the name for the beaver. IV 491b

♦ kalb al-mayy : in zoology, the mole-cricket (*gryllotalpa vulgaris*), also called *ḥālūsh* or *ḥarrāthā*. IV 491b

ḳalb (A, pl. *ḳulūb*) : heart. IV 486a; and → ḤASHM

ḳāldjiyān (T) : in Ottoman times, the worker in the mint who prepared the standard ingots by melting the metal. II 119a

ḳalghay : a title best known as indicating the deputy or heir apparent of the KHĀNs of the Crimean Khānate. Its linguistic origins are uncertain. IV 499b

ḳālī (T) : a type of carpet (variants *ghālī*, *khālī*) manufactured at Ḳālīḳalā (now Erzerum). Although ~ is generally considered to be Turkish in origin, it is unattested in ancient Turkish texts. It may therefore be of Iranian origin. S 136a

ḳalʿī (A), or *ḳalaʿī* : tin; the Arabic name, either after Kalah, a well known port on the peninsula of Malacca, or *kaling*, the Malayan word for tin, bears witness to the fact that tin had to be imported. IV 502a; V 964b; ~ is also used for a type of sword which is often mentioned, especially in early Arabic poetry. This kind of sword is generally considered to be of Indian origin. IV 502b

kalima (A) : the spoken word, utterance; ~ can also be extended to mean 'discourse' and 'poem'. IV 508a; VIII 532a

In Druze hierarchy, ~ is the third of the five cosmic ranks in the organisation. II 632a

ḳālīte → BASHTARDA

kallābazī : the master of the hawking-pack, assisting the falconer or hawker, who sets his greyhounds on the gazelle or the hare. I 1152b

ḳallāvī (T) : a headdress reserved for dignitaries with the rank of pasha which, from the 18th century, became official head-gear in Ottoman Turkey. It was a ḲAVUḲ with the body of a cone, worn with a white turban rolled around, draped and bulging in four places, decorated with a gold band. V 751b

ḳalpaḳ (T) : busby, a kind of bonnet of lamb's fleece or woollen cloth decorated with lamb's fleece, worn by men and women in Ottoman Turkey. V 751b

ḳalūḳ (A) : in the terminology of horse-riding, a horse of uncertain temper. II 954a

kalūta → KALAWTA

kalym : the purchase of the fiancée, a custom among the Čerkes tribes of the Caucasus which could only be avoided by resorting to abduction in case of refusal by the parents. The pretence of forcible abduction remains an essential rite in the marriage ceremony. II 23a

ḳāma → BĀʿ

kamāla (A) : a renewable seasonal contract covering two seasons, either summer-autumn or winter-spring, which engages a shepherd or goatherd. S 319b; and → FAḌĀʾIL

kamān (P) : bow; a violin bow. VIII 346b; VIII 348a

♦ kamāna : in India, a bamboo bow, used to cut marble. VIII 269a

♦ kamān<u>dj</u>a (A, < P *kamānča*, dim. of *kamān*), or more rarely *<u>sh</u>ī<u>sh</u>ak* (A, < P, T *<u>gh</u>ičak*, *<u>gh</u>ižak*, etc., < San *<u>gh</u>o<u>sh</u>aka* ?) : the hemispherical viol, perhaps the best known form of viol in the Islamic east. The body consists of a hemisphere of wood, coconut, or a gourd, over the aperture of which a membrane is stretched. The neck is of wood, generally cylindrical, and there is a foot of iron, although sometimes there is no foot. In texts where both the *<u>gh</u>ižak* and the ~ are described, the former is a larger type of the latter, having, in addition to its two ordinary strings, eight sympathetic strings. In Egypt, the hemispherical viol is nowadays called *rabāb miṣrī*. VIII 348a

kamar (P) : a broad belt often red in colour, worn by men in the Arab East. V 741a; IX 167b

ḳamar (A) : in astronomy, the moon; the full moon is termed *badr*. IV 518a

ḳamḥ (A) : the name for wheat in Syria and Egypt; in Iraq ~ is called *ḥinṭa* and in Arabia *<u>dh</u>urr*. IV 519b

ḳamil → ḲAML

kāmil (A) : in prosody, the name of the fifth Arabic metre. I 670a

kamīn (A) : the rear-guard (of a raiding group of Bedouin). II 1055b; in military science, an ambuscade by a detachment of the army drawn up in a carefully chosen position near the rear-guard. III 202b

ḳamīṣ (A, < late L *camisia*), or *ḳamīṣa* : a shirt-like dress worn by both sexes all over the Arab world. V 733b ff.

ḳaml (A) : lice; some maintain that ~ applies only to females and that for males the term is *ṣuʾāb* (pl. *ṣiʾbān*, which actually designates nits). All species of lice, including head-lice and body-lice, fall within this term. A man more prone than others to give rise to lice is called *ḳamil*. IV 521b

kammūn (A) : in botany, cumin (*Cuminum Cyminum*); ~ was also used as a generic term for other plants which bore aromatic or medicinal seeds: *kammūn armanī* or *rūmī* was in fact caraway (*Carum Carvi*), also called *kammūn barrī* ‘wild cumin’. ~ *ḥulw* was one of the names for aniseed, while ~ *aswad* was fennel-flower, properly called *<u>sh</u>ūnīz*. IV 522a, where can be found more variants; *kammūn kirmānī* is wild cumin (*Lagoecia cuminoides*). IX 653a

kamulyān → GÖNÜLLÜ

ḳāmūs (A, < Gk) : dictionary; during the time of the Prophet, ~ was used for ‘the bottom, the very deepest part of the sea’, and later, following Ptolemy, geographers applied the term, in the form *uḳiyānūs*, to 'the mass of water surrounding the earth', more particularly the Atlantic Ocean. Al-Fīrūzābādī used ~ metaphorically as the title of his great dictionary, which name stuck, still carrying the sense of 'fullness, exhaustiveness' in contrast to *muʿdjam* 'lexicon'. IV 524a

kān wa-kān (A) : in literature, one of the seven post-classical genres of poetry. The genre was devised by the Baghdādī poets and its name derives from the formula used by story-tellers to open their narratives: 'there was and there was', i.e. 'once upon a time'. A ~ poem is in monorhyme with a long vowel after the rhyme letter. IV 528a

kanʿad (A) : in the Persian Gulf, term for the king mackerel. I 541b

ḳanāt (A, pl. *ḳanawāt, ḳanā, ḳunī, aḳniya*) : a canal, irrigation system, water-pipe. Used also for a baton, a lance, etc., ~ originally meant reed. IV 528b

In Persian, ~ is used today especially for underground water pipes, a mining installation or technique using galleries or cross-cuts to extract water from the depths of the earth. By means of a gently sloping tunnel, which cuts through alluvial soil and passes under the water-table into the aquifer, water is brought by gravity flow from its upper end, where it seeps into the gallery, to a ground surface outlet and irrigation canal at its lower end. IV 529a

kanbiyaṭūr (A) : Campeador (< L *campeator*), a title in Castilian Spain given to el-Cid. IX 533a

kanbūsh → ḲUMĀSH

kandūri (P), or *kandūra* : a leather or linen table-cloth; in India, ~ means also a religious feast held in honour of a venerated person like Fāṭima, and as such was imported into the Indonesian archipelago, where it has become a feast given with a religious purpose, or at least in conformity with religious law. IV 540a; religious meal. IX 154a

kanīsa (A, < Ar; pl. *kanāʾis*) : synagogue, church, temple; syn. *bīʿa*, which unlike ~ is found once in the Qurʾān. IV 545a

kannās (A) : lit. sweeper; a sanitary worker in the mediaeval Near East who swept public squares and other places such as prisons, dungeons and latrines, and transported garbage in boats or by other means to places outside the cities. The term is synonymous with *kassāḥ*; other terms used for the same occupation are *sammād* and *zabbāl* 'dung collectors'. IV 547b

kannis → SHUNḲUB

ḳanṭara (A, pl. *ḳanāṭir*) : a bridge, particularly one of masonry or stone; an aqueduct (especially in the plural), dam; high building, castle. IV 555a

kantu : a type of salt in the salt works near Bilma, in Niger, ~ is moulded into loaves in hollowed out palm-trunks and used chiefly for the feeding of animals. I 1222a

ḳānūn (A, < Gk; pl. *ḳawānīn*) : a financial term belonging to the field of land-taxes; a code of regulations, state-law (of non-Muslim origin). IV 556a

In fiscal administration, ~ refers both to the principles on which was based the assessment of taxes and to the resulting sum due from the taxpayer, either in the case of a single property or all the properties in one district taken together. In those provinces where many lands were assessed by the procedure of ~ , this word came to mean a kind of fiscal cadaster. II 79a; IV 557a

In law, *ḳawānīn* were at first regulations issued by the guardians of public order (especially the governors) in the fields of common law and penal law where the s̲h̲arīʿa was silent. Under the Ottoman sultans, ~ came to be applied mainly to acts in the domain of administrative and financial law and of penal law. Nowadays, in all Middle Eastern countries, ~ denotes not only those codes and laws which are directly inspired by western legislation, such as civil and commercial law, administrative and penal law, but also those laws and codes which are confined to reproducing, albeit simplifying, the provisions of the s̲h̲arīʿa. The word ~ , however, has been replaced by *lāʾiḥa* (pl. *lawāʾiḥ*) in Egypt and by NIẒĀM or *tartīb* elsewhere. IV 556b

In organisations, e.g. guilds in Ottoman times, ~ was used also for the statutes, which were drawn up by the guildsmen and registered with the ḲĀḌĪ. IV 558b

Among the Berbers, especially in Kabylia and the Aurès, ~ was adopted to mean the customs, mainly as regards penal matters, pertaining to a particular village. IV 562a

In music, the ~ is the present-day psaltery of the Arabs and Turks, a stringed musical instrument with a shallow, flat, trapezoidal sound-chest. It has fallen into disuse in Spain and Persia, where it was once very popular. It is, however, still a great favourite in North Africa, Egypt, Syria and Turkey, where it is to be found strung trichordally with from 51 to 75 strings. VII 191a

♦ al-ḳānūn al-asāsī (A, T *ḳānūn-i esāsī*, P *ḳānūn-i asāsī*) : ‘basic law’, the constitution. II 651b; II 659b; in Turkey, *ḳānūn-i esāsī* was replaced by *anayasa* during the linguistic reforms in the Republic. II 640a ff.; IV 558b

♦ ḳānūn-i d̲j̲azāʾī (T) : in Ottoman usage, a penal code. II 518b

♦ ḳānūn (al-k̲h̲arād̲j̲) : ‘Domesday Book of the Empire’; the most important register of the tax office and the basic survey of land and taxable crops and in accordance with which the K̲H̲ARĀD̲J̲ is collected. II 78b

♦ **ḳānūnnāme** (T) : in Ottoman usage, ~ generally referred to a decree of the sultan containing legal clauses on a particular topic. In the 9th/15th century the term *yasaḳnāme* had the same meaning. ~ was occasionally extended to refer to regulations which viziers and pashas had enacted, to laws which a competent authority had formulated or to reform projects. However, a ~ was like any normal ḲĀNŪN in that only a sultan’s decree could give it official authority. IV 562a; Ottoman tax register. VIII 203b

ḳānungo : in the Mug̲h̲al empire, one of the three chief PARGANA officials, the others being the *amīn* and the *s̲h̲iḳdār* (→ S̲H̲IḲḲDĀR), who were responsible for the *pargana* accounts, the rates of assessment, the survey of lands, and the protection of the rights of the cultivators. VIII 271a ḳapan (T, < A *ḳabbān* 'a public balance', 'a steelyard') : an Ottoman term used to designate the central 'markets' for basic commodities, which were established in Istanbul in order to ensure the authorities' control of the importation and distribution of the raw materials needed by the craftsmen and of the foodstuffs to provision the people, and in order to facilitate the collection of the tolls and taxes due to the state. IV 226b

In Ottoman fiscal administration, ~ (or *ḥaḳḳ-i ḳapan*, *resm-i ḳapan*) was also the name for weighing duties levied at the public scales, paid in kind on cereals and dried vegetables, and in cash on other produce. II 147a; III 489b

ḳapani̲d̲j̲a (T) : a sumptuous fur worn by the Ottoman sultan, with a large fur collar, narrow or short sleeves, decorated with fur below the shoulders, with straight supplementary sleeves, laced with frogs and loops in front. V 752a

ḳapi̊ (T) : lit. gate; by extension the Ottoman Porte, that is, the sultan's palace; ~ is also used for the grand vizier's palace and the seat of government. IV 568a

♦ ḳapi̊ ag̲h̲asi̊ → ḲAPU AG̲H̲ASI̊

♦ ḳapi̊ kāhyasi̊ → ḲAPI̊ KETHÜDASI̊

♦ ḳapi̊ kethüdasi̊, or *ḳapi̊ kāhyasi̊* : an agent, 'close to the Porte', of a high dignitary of an Ottoman subject or vassal. IV 568a

♦ ḳapi̊ ḳullari̊ : lit. slaves of the Porte; the sultan's troops. I 35b; IV 568a

♦ **ḳapi̊d̲j̲i** : the guard placed at the main gates of the Ottoman sultan's palace in Istanbul.IV 568a

♦ ḳapi̊ya čikma : the appointment of ʿAD̲J̲AMĪ OG̲H̲LĀNs to the palace service. I 206b

ḳapli̊d̲j̲a (T), or *i̊li̊d̲j̲a*, *kaplud̲j̲a*, *ḳablud̲j̲a* : the general term used in Turkey for a place where a hot spring is roofed over, as in a bath house. III 1120b; IV 569b, where are listed many more synonyms; and → I̊LI̊D̲J̲A

ḳaptan → ḲAPUDAN; ḲAPUDAN PAS̲H̲A

ḳapu ag̲h̲asi̊ (T), or *ḳapi̊ ag̲h̲asi̊* : the chief white eunuch and the senior officer in the Ottoman sultan's palace, until the late 10th/16th century. He was the sole mediator between the sultan and the world outside the palace, and had the authority to petition the sultan for the appointment, promotion and transfer of palace servants, AG̲H̲AS and IČ OG̲H̲LANs. II 1088a; IV 570b; IV 1093a

ḳapudan (T, < It *capitano*), or *ḳaptan* : any commander of a ship, small or large, foreign or Turkish. VIII 564b

♦ **ḳapudan pas̲h̲a**, or *ḳaptan pasha, ḳapudan-i deryā* : the title of the commander-in-chief of the Ottoman navy, becoming current only ca. 975/1567. Earlier titles were *deryā begi* and *ḳapudan-i deryā*. The squadron-commander was known as *ḳaptan*, and the individual commander as *reʾīs* (→ RAʾĪS). I 948a; IV 571b; VIII 564b

In the 10th/16th century, the ~ became as well the governor of an EYĀLET, which consisted of a group of ports and islands. II 165

♦ ḳapudan-i deryā → ḲAPUDAN PAS̲H̲A

♦ ḳapudana bey : one of three grades of admiral, instituted when the naval hierarchy was organised under ʿAbd al-Ḥāmid I, or later under his successor Selīm III. The other two were *patrona bey* 'vice-admiral' and *riyāla bey* 'rear-admiral'. VIII 566b ff.

kār (A, T) : a form of music known in Turkey (*kiār*). I 67a; and → ṢINF

ḳarʿ → ḲUTHTHĀʾ

♦ ḳarʿa (A) : in alchemy, the part known as 'cucurbit' of the distilling apparatus. I 486a

ḳarā (T) : black, dark colour; strong, powerful. The former meaning is commonly meant when ~ is a first component of geographical names; the latter with personal names, although it may refer to the black or dark brown colour of hair or to a dark complexion. IV 572b

ḳarāba (A) : kinship; as a technical term, ~ seems to be of post-HIDJRA usage. In the Qurʾān, and pre-Islamic poetry, the preferred term is *ḳurba*. The superlative *al-aḳrabūn* is also found, with the meaning of the closest relatives, those who have a claim to inherit from a man. IV 595a

ḳarabataḳ (T) : a performance practice associated exclusively with the Ottoman music ensemble, MEHTER, consisting of the alternation of soft passages played by a partial ensemble with thunderous tutti passages. VI 1008a

karābīsī : clothes-seller. IV 596a

ḳarāghul (Ott, < Mon; mod.T **karakol**) : lit. black arm; in Ottoman times, a patrol during military campaigns, sent out apart from the vanguard forces, *čarkhadjï*, by the Ottoman army. The maintenance of security and order in different quarters in Istanbul was carried out by Janissary orders called *ḳulluḳ*. In modern Turkish, ~ became *karakol*, which is the common term for police station or patrol. IV 611a

♦ ḳaraghulām (T) : in the Ayyūbid army under Ṣalāḥ al-Dīn, a second grade cavalryman. I 797b; VIII 468a

ḳaragöz (T) : lit. black eye; in literature, ~ is the principal character in the Turkish shadow play, and also the shadow play itself, which is played with flat, two-dimensional figures, manipulated by the shadow player, which represent inanimate objects, animals, fantastic beasts and beings, and human characters. IV 601a

karakol → ḲARĀGHUL

ḳaraḳul : lambskin. I 506a

karam → SHARAF

karāma (A, pl. *karāmāt*) : a marvel wrought by a saint, mostly consisting of miraculous happenings in the corporeal world, or else of predictions of the future, or else of interpretation of the secrets of hearts, etc. IV 615a

ḳaran (A) : in archery, a quiver made from pieces of leather put together in such a way that the air can circulate through interstices left so that the fletchings of the arrows do not deteriorate. IV 800a; and → ḲIRĀN

karandal → ḲALANDAR

ḳaranful (A) : in botany, the clove. IV 626b

ḳarārīṭ → ḲARRĪṬA

ḳarasṭūn (P ?) : an instrument made up of a long beam which has at one of its ends a stone as a weight. If the Armeno-Persian origin of the word is correct, the ~ must be a kind of lever or balance, very similar to the SHĀDŪF, the contrivance used for raising water and still in use in certain eastern countries. IV 629a; the Roman balance or steelyard. IV 629a; VII 195b

ḳaraẓ (A) : in botany, the acacia fruit. S 172a

kārbānsālār → KĀRWĀN

ḳarbūṣ (A, pl. *ḳarābīṣ*) : the pommel of a horse saddle, the cantel, or back pommel, being called *muʾakhkhara* or *ḳarbūṣ muʾakhkhar*. II 954a; IX 51a; the saddle rested on a pad, *mirshaḥa*, held in position by girths, *ḥizām*, and a breast-strap, *labab*. II 954a

ḳarḍ (A), or *salaf* : in law, the loan of money or other fungible objects. I 633a; VIII 899b; the loan of consummation. I 26b

♦ ḳarḍ ḥasan : in law, an interest-free loan. VII 671b; VIII 899b

kardūs (A, pl. *karādīs*) : in military science, a squadron, an innovation which is said to have been introduced by Marwān II. III 182b; VIII 794a

ḳarīb (A) : lit. near; in Persian prosody, the name of a metre, of rare occurrence, said to have been invented by the Persians. I 677b

ḳāriḥ (A) : a foal between four and five years of age. II 785a

ḳarīḥa → GHINĀʾ

kārim (A) : yellow amber, in Egypt (syn. *kahramān)*; also, a fleet, especially a merchant fleet. IV 640b

♦ **kārimī** (< KĀRIM ?) : the name of a group of Muslim merchants operating from the major centres of trade in the Ayyūbid and Mamlūk empires, above all in spices. IV 640a

ḳarīn (A) : a companion; in pre-Islamic usage, and in the Qurʾān, a term for a man's spirit-companion or familiar. IV 643b; IX 407a

♦ ḳarīna : in Arabic literary theory, one of the terms used to indicate SADJʿ rhyme. VIII 737b; and → ḲAYNA

In Persian literature, ~ , or *ḳarīna-yi ṣārifa*, was used for a clue required to express the relationship between a MADJĀZ 'trope', and the corresponding ḤAḲĪḲA 'literal speech'. Such a clue is either implied in the context or specifically added, e.g. in *shīr-i shamshīrzan*, where the adjective points to the actual meaning of 'valiant warrior'. V 1027a

ḳāriṣ (A) : the quality of food being piquant, not always interchangeable with *ḥārr* 'hot' or *ḥāmiḍ* 'sour'. II 1071b

kārīz : a term used in eastern and south-eastern Persia, Afghanistan, and Balūčistān to designate a *ḳanāt*, a mining-installation or technique for extracting water from the depths of the earth. IV 529a

♦ kārīzkan → MUḲANNĪ

karkaddan (A, < P *kargadān*) : in zoology, the rhinoceros; ~ is the term for three varieties: the Indian rhinoceros, also called *mirmīs*, *ziba'rā/zib'arā* and *sinād*; the rhinoceros of Java; and the rhinoceros of Sumatra (P *nis͟hān*). The African species was known to the Arabs well before Islam: the Black rhinoceros was called *ḥarīs͟h* or *k͟hirtīt* (also one of the many terms for the rhinoceros' horn), and Burchell's rhinoceros, *hirmīs*, *abū ḳarn*, *umm ḳarn* and *'anaza*. IV 647a

♦ karkaddan al-baḥr (A), or *ḥarīs͟h al-baḥr* : in zoology, the narwhal (*Monodon monoceros*). IV 648b; VIII 1022b

ḳarḳal (A) : in Mamlūk times, the small receptacle in which water falls before flowing over the S͟HADIRWĀN; the channel itself was called *silsal*. IX 175b

karkūr (N.Afr, B *akəkur*), more exactly *kərkūr* : a heap of stones, and, more especially, a sacred heap of stones. The cult of heaps of stones seems to come from a rite of transference or expulsion of evil; the individual, picking up a stone, causes the evil of whatever kind that afflicts him to pass onto it and gets rid of it by throwing it or depositing it with the stone on a place suitable for absorbing it. The accumulation of these expiatory pebbles forms the sacred piles of stones which rise all along the roads, at difficult passes and at the entrances to sanctuaries. IV 655b

karm (A) : in botany, the vine, grapevine. IV 659a; in art, *karma* is a vine-scroll frieze. I 611b

ḳarmāṭī → KŪFĪ

karōh → KROŚA

karr (A) : attack.

♦ al-karr wa 'l-farr : in military science, the tactic of withdrawal and counterattack. VIII 131a

ḳarrīṭa (Alg, < It *carretta*) : a cart and wagon; in the 16th century, its plural *ḳarārīṭ* was used to designate Portuguese wagons. I 206a

kars͟hūnī (A, < Syr) : the name of the Syriac script used by the Christians of Syria and Mesopotamia for writing Arabic. IV 671b

In India, ~ is applied to the Syriac script used for writing Malayalam, the vernacular language of the Malabar Christians. IV 671b

kārvān-kes͟h → KĀRWĀN

kārwān (A, < P) : a caravan, composed of horses, mules, donkeys, and especially camels; in India, caravans for the bulk transport of grain were pulled by oxen. In the pre-Islamic period, the Arabs had for long used the word *'īr*, and later the more usual word *ḳāfila*, which at the beginning of the 1st/7th century was current for gatherings of traders, as the equivalent of ~ . IV 676b

In the Ottoman period, the leader responsible for organising the ~ was called *kervān-bas͟hi̊* (in Persia and India, *kārvān-kes͟h* or *kārbānsālār*). IV 677b

♦ kārwānsarāy (P) : caravanserai. IX 44; and → ḲAYSĀRIYYA

ḳarwas͟ha (A) : originally, the name of the argot of the Moroccans practising the trades of sorcerer and treasure-seeker in Egypt, today applied to the secret language of the Dakārna (s. Dakrūnī) of Sudanese origin installed in the Village of the Sudanese close to Madāmūd in Upper Egypt and elsewhere. A part of the vocabulary is of Moroccan origin, while the grammar is that of the spoken language of the region of Luxor. IV 679b

ḳarya (A, T *ḳarye*; pl. *ḳurā*) : a town, village; and → NĀḤIYE

As a Qurʾānic term, ~ indicates an important town. Mecca, Medina, Sodom, Nineveh, and the coastal town are so called. IV 680a

♦ al-ḳaryatayn : a Qurʾānic term for Mecca and Medina. IV 680a

♦ umm al-ḳurā : 'the mother of towns'; a Qurʾānic term for Mecca. IV 680a

kās → ṢAND̲J̲

♦ kāsatān → MUṢAFFAḤĀT

ḳaṣab (A) : any plant with a long and hollow stem like the reed (*Arundo donax*), to which the term is especially applied. IV 682a; a coloured linen cloth manufactured at Tinnīs, or a white one made at Damietta, or sometimes a cotton cloth made at Kāzarūn, out of which women's fine veils were woven, some set with precious stones. It can also mean a silken material, as well as a kind of brocade encrusted with little strips of gold or silver. IV 682b

♦ ḳaṣab al-bardī, or *al-bardī* : the papyrus reed. IV 682a

♦ ḳaṣab al-d̲j̲arīra : the sweet flag (or fragrant rush). IV 682a

♦ ḳaṣab ḥulw → ḲAṢAB AL-SUKKAR

♦ ḳaṣab al-maṣṣ → ḲAṢAB AL-SUKKAR

♦ ḳaṣab al-sukkar, also *ḳaṣab al-maṣṣ* or *ḳaṣab ḥulw* : the sugar cane. IV 682b

ḳaṣaba (A, mod. T *kasaba*) : originally, the essential part of a country or a town, its heart. This usage occurs especially in the Muslim West, where it is also applied to the most ancient part of a town (syn. *al-madīna*); later, a fortified castle, residence of an authority in the centre of a country or a town; principal town. III 498b; IV 684b

In North Africa, ~ occurs in the sense of fortress-citadel (dialect: *ḳaṣba*). IV 685a

In the Turkish Republic, a *kasaba* is a town with from 2000 to 20,000 inhabitants. I 974b

As a basic measure of length, ~ equalled a number of cubits varying between five and eight, but giving an average length of four metres. VII 137b; the ~ was predominantly used in surveying. In 1830 the ~ was established at 3.55 metres. II 232b

ḳasam (A), and *yamīn*, *ḥalf* : an oath. IV 687b

In the Qurʾān, ~ or its verb *aḳsama* apply, in general, to the oaths pronounced by God himself. IV 687b

In law, ~ is the extrajudiciary oath by which a person binds himself to do or not to do a certain specific physical or juridicial act, by invoking the name of God or one of the divine attributes. IV 687b ḳasama (A, < ḲASAM) : in law, an oath by which is asserted the guilt or innocence of an individual presumed to have killed someone, repeated fifty times, either by the ʿAṢABA of the victim of a murder (Mālikī school of law, where it is a procedure of accusation), or by the inhabitants of the place of the crime (Ḥanafī school of law, where it is a procedure for the defence of the one presumed guilty). IV 689b

kasb (A) : in economic life, gain. IV 690b

In theology, ~ means acquisition, appropriation. The verb *kasaba* is frequently found in the Qurʾān, mainly with the sense of acquiring those rewards or punishments which are the fruit of moral acts. ~ has had a long history in the scholastic theology, especially in the As͟hʿarī school, where ~ and *iktisāb* were employed to define that which reverted to man in a 'freely' accomplished and morally qualified act. III 1063a; IV 692a

ḳaṣba → ḲAṢABA

kas͟hf (A) : in mysticism, the act of lifting and tearing away the veil (which comes between man and the extra-phenomenal world). IV 696b; VIII 429a

Under the Mamlūks, the term ~ was used to designate a mission of AMĪRs from Cairo to Upper Egypt that consisted in guaranteeing security during harvests, inspecting the condition of the canals, and, to a growing extent, controlling the Bedouin. VIII 865a

kās͟hī (P, T, < *Kās͟hānī*) : the tiles or trimmed pieces of faïence serving to cover completely or partially the main fabric of buildings in a design principally decorative but also, at times, to protect them against humidity. IV 701a

♦ kās͟hī-kārī : a process of tile-decorating, whereby the design is reproduced on tiles of baked earth which are then painted, generally with different metal oxides, to become polychromatic, then rebaked. IV 702a

♦ kās͟hī-yi muʿarraḳ-kārī, or simply *muʿarraḳ-kārī* : a technique of tile-decorating, which consists of cutting, according to precise forms, pieces of monochrome ~ of different colours to compose a polychrome design. IV 701b

kās͟hif (A) : under the Ottomans, a district prefect. VIII 235a; ~ is still in use today in Egypt. VIII 865b

ḳās͟hiḳ : in music, a rattle instrument, made up of two wooden spoons attached to each other, in the hollow of which are a number of small bells, used in Persia and Turkey. IX 11b

ḳas͟hḳa (T) : in western Turkish, the name given to a blaze on the forehead of animals such as horses, sheep and cattle; in Čag͟hatay the word also means 'brilliant', 'gallant'. It is probable that *ḳas͟hḳāy*, the name of a Turkish people living in the Fārs province of Iran, is related to one of these meanings. IV 705b

kas͟hkūl (P) : an oval bowl of metal, wood or coconut (calabash), worn suspended by a chain from the shoulder, in which the dervishes put the alms they receive and the food which is given them. IV 706b

In modern Arabic, ~ is sometimes used for a kind of album or collection of press cuttings, as well as denoting a 'beggar's bowl'. IV 706b

ḳas̲h̲s̲h̲āba (Mor) : a long sleeveless outer gown for men, and a long-sleeved flowing tunic with a deep slit down the breast for women, worn in Morocco. V 746a

kas̲h̲ūt̲h̲ rūmī → AFSANTĪN

kāsib (A, pl. *kawāsib*) : a carnivore. II 739b

ḳaṣīda (A) : in poetry, a polythematic ode which numbers at least seven verses, but generally comprises far more. It consists essentially of three parts of variable length: (1) an amatory prologue (NASĪB) in which the poet sheds some tears over what was once the camping place of his beloved now far off; (2) the poet's narration of his journey (*raḥīl*) to the person to whom the poem is addressed; (3) the central theme, constituted by the panegyric of a tribe, a protector or a patron, or in satire of their enemies. The Arabic ~ is a very conventional piece of verse, with one rhyme and in a uniform metre. From the end of the 2nd/8th century onwards, the classical ~ gave birth to a whole series of autonomous poetic genres. All these genres are represented in independent pieces, to which the name of ~ continues often to be given, even though incorrectly. I 583b; I 668a; IV 713b

The Persian ~ is a lyric poem, most frequently panegyric. Quantitatively, a poem cannot be a ~ unless the number of its distichs exceeds fifteen and does not exceed thirty. The ~ comprises three parts: the exordium, the eulogy, and the petition. It is first and foremost a poem composed for a princely festival, especially the spring festival and the autumn one, and was connected with courtly life in Persia. IV 57b; IV 714a

The Turkish ~ has the same rhyme scheme and metric patterns as the ~ in Arabic and Persian. The usual length of a Turkish ~ is between 15 and 99 couplets, but in fact, some longer ones exist. Theoretically, a complete Turkish ~ should contain six sections: NASĪB, TAG̲H̲AZZUL, GIRĪZGĀH, MADḤIYYA, FAK̲H̲RIYYA and DUʿĀʾ, but invariably do not contain all of them. Very often, one or more are left out, the most frequent omissions being the *tag̲h̲azzul*, *fak̲h̲riyya* and *duʿāʾ* sections. IV 715b

In Swahili, ~ normally refers to a poem praising the Prophet. V 963a

♦ ḳaṣīda simṭiyya → MUSAMMAṬ

♦ ḳaṣīda zad̲j̲aliyya → MALḤŪN

♦ ḳaṣīda-yi madīḥa → MADĪḤ

kāsir (A, pl. *kawāsir*) : a rapacious predator, used in hawking. I 1152a

ḳaṣīr (A) : in North Africa, a refugee, like the ṬANĪB, but one entitled to make use of his prestige among his former group with which he has not severed all relations. S 78b; among contemporary nomads like the Ruwalāʾ, ~ indicates a mutual relationship between members of different tribes by which each grants protection against his fellow-tribesmen. III 1018a

ḳasm (A) : a term for a land tax, in Syria and Palestine in the 10th/16th century, coming to a fifth, sometimes as much as a third, of the produce. VII 507b

kasr (A) : in mathematics, ~ is the term for a fraction. IV 725a
In medicine, ~ signifies a fracture. II 481b
In grammar, ~ denotes the sound of the vowel *i*. IV 731a
For ~ in Bedouin culture, → FALĪDJA

ḳaṣr (A) : palace, used in particular for Umayyad desert palaces and frontier forts. IX 44a; and → AGADIR
♦ ḳaṣriyya : the palace guard of the Fāṭimids. IX 685b

kasra (A) : in grammar, ~ denotes the vowel *i*, more specifically the written sign itself, KASR denoting the sound in question. III 172a; IV 731a

ḳāṣṣ (A, pl. *ḳuṣṣāṣ*) : a popular story-teller or preacher, deliverer of sermons whose activity considerably varied over the centuries, from preaching in the mosques with a form of Qur'ānic exegesis to downright charlatanism. IV 733b; an older, if not the primary meaning of ~ is 'a kind of detective responsible for examining and interpreting tracks and marks on the ground'; thus is it found twice in the Qur'ān. V 186a; jester. IX 552b

ḳaṣṣāb → DJAZZĀR

kassāḥ → KANNĀS

ḳassām (T, < A) : the title given in Ottoman law to the trustee who divided an estate between the heirs of a deceased person. Ottoman law recognised two types of ~ , those under the *ḳāḍī 'asker* 'judge of the army', and the others employed locally in each ḲĀḌĪ's court. The local ~ was called *shehrī* or *beledī*. IV 735b; VI 4b
♦ ḳassāmlïḳ → ḲISMA

ḳaṣṣār (A) : a fuller; bleacher. IV 1161a; V 89b; a term in the Persian Gulf for a projecting rock. I 535b

ḳaṣṣāṣ → ḲIṢṢA-KHWĀN

ḳassī (A) : a striped fabric from Egypt containing silk, one of seven things forbidden by Muḥammad in a Tradition. V 735b

ḳāt (A) : in botany, a smooth-stemmed shrub (*Catha edulis, Methyscophyllum glaucum*) which grows in East Africa and southwestern Arabia; its leaves are used as a drug. IV 741a

ḳaṭ' (A) : lit. cutting off.
In the science of Qur'ānic reading, ~ or *waḳf* was the pause in reading, based on the sense or otherwise. Later, a distinction was made between the short pause for breath, and the other pauses, based on the sense; according to some, ~ indicated only the first; according to others only the second. IV 741b
In grammar, ~ is used in the term *alif al-ḳaṭ'* for the disjunctive *hamza* which, opposed to the *hamzat al-waṣl*, cannot be elided. ~ further indicates the deliberate cutting, for a special purpose, between elements of a sentence which syntactically are closely connected. IV 742a
In prosody, ~ indicates cutting short the ending of certain metrical feet, e.g., the shortening of the metrical *fā'ilun* to *fā'il*. This shortened form is then called *maḳṭū'*. IV 742a

In mathematics, ~ is used in many terms: *ḳaṭʿ zāʾid* 'hyperbola', *ḳaṭʿ nāḳiṣ* 'ellipse', *ḳaṭʿ mukāfī* 'parabola', and *ḳaṭʿ mukāfī mudjassam* 'paraboloid'. IV 742a
In astrology, ~ indicates scission. IV 742a
In the science of diplomatic, ~ refers to the format of paper. *Al-ḳaṭʿ al-kāmil* was an in-folio format used for treaties, *al-ḳaṭʿ al-ʿāda*, a small ordinary format used for decrees and appointments of the lowest rank. IV 742b
In logic, ~ means 'to assert something decisively or refute someone completely'. IV 743a
In medicine, ~ is the excision of soft diseased substance. II 481b
In art, *ṣanʿat-i ḳaṭʿ* was the art of cutting silhouette, brought from Persia to Turkey in the 10th/16th century, and to the west in the 11th/17th century, where at first, as in the east, light paper on a dark gound was always used. II 755b
♦ ḳaṭʿ al-ṭarīḳ, or *muḥāraba* : highway robbery or robbery with violence, which in certain circumstances is punished with death. IV 770a; IX 63a

ḳaṭā (A, pl. *ḳaṭawāt, ḳaṭayāt*) : in zoology, the ornithological family of Pteroclididae or sandgrouse. The term is onomatopaeic for their cry. Three species are distinguished: the *kudrī* or *ʿarabī* (*Pterocles Lichtensteini*), the *djūnī* or *ghaḍaf*, *ghatmāʾ* (*Pterocles orientalis*), and the *ghaṭaṭ* (*Pterocles alchata*). IV 743a

kataba 'l-kitāb (A) : lit. he has written the book; a fabulous marine creature mentioned by mediaeval Arab authors. It lives in the Indian Ocean, and its juice produces an invisible ink legible only at night. VIII 1023a

katar (P) : a type of levelling board used in central Iran for the preparation of irrigation check banks, and operated by two men, one pulling and the other pushing. II 905b

ḳaṭf (A) : in prosody, a deviation in the metre because of the suppression of a *sabab khafīf*, a moving and a quiescent consonant, and the preceding vowel, e.g. in *mufāʿal[atun]*. I 672a

ḳaṭīʿ (A) : a family flock of ten to forty animals, called *fizr* if there are only sheep, and *ṣubba* if there are only goats. S 319a
♦ **ḳaṭīʿa** (A, pl. *ḳaṭāʾiʿ*) : a Muslim administrative term designating, on the one hand, those concessions made to private individuals on state lands in the first centuries of the HIDJRA, and, on the other hand, the fixed sum of a tax or tribute, in contradistinction to taxation by proportional method or some variable means. III 1088a; IV 754b; IV 973a
In early Islam, ~ was a unit of land, often a sizable estate, allotted to prominent individuals in the garrison cities founded at the time of the conquests. V 23a

kātib (A, pl. *kuttāb*) : a secretary, a term which was used in the Arab-Islamic world for every person whose role or function consisted of writing or drafting official letters or administrative documents. In the mediaeval period, ~ denoted neither a scribe in the literary sense of the word nor a copyist, but it could be applied to private secretaries as well as to the employees of the administrative service. It can denote merely a book-keeper as well as the chief clerk or a Secretary of State, directly responsible to the sovereign or to his vizier. IV 754b

In law, an author or compiler of legally-watertight formulae for use in *shurūṭ* (→ SHARṬ). IX 359a

In Western and Spanish Arabic, ~ is an alternative name for the planet Mercury. VIII 101a

katif (A, pl. *aktāf*) : shoulder.

♦ ʿilm al-katif, or *ʿilm al-aktāf* : scapulomancy or omoplatoscopy, i.e. divination by the use of the shoulder-bones. This art forms a part of the practices of physiognomy. It is universal in scope, inasmuch as it provides for the foretelling of what will happen in the different regions of the earth towards which the four sides of the scopula are pointed according to the signs revealed by it. IV 763a

ḳātil al-nimr → AḲŪNĪṬUN

ḳatīl al-raʿd (A) : lit. victim of the thunder; a name for the quail, as ancient belief held that the quail would be inevitably struck down by stormy weather. VIII 1006b

ḳātir (P) : in tribal Persia of the 19th century, a sum of money, which was increased or diminished according to the prosperity or otherwise of the tribes and the power of the government to exercise authority over them. III 1105b

ḳaṭirān → ḲAṬRĀN

katkhudā → KETKHUDĀ

ḳatl (A) : killing, putting to death, used in the two principal meanings of the word, sc. the crime of murder and the punishment of execution. IV 766b

katm (A) : a black dye which masks the red of the henna. IX 383b

katra : in Muslim India, a term for a market, usually known after the commodity sold there. IX 800b

ḳaṭrān (A), or *ḳiṭrān, ḳaṭirān* : tar obtained by dry distillation of organic substances; the residuum left after the distillation of tar, i.e. liquid pitch; cedar-oil extracted from cedarwood. The substance is obtained from several kinds of coniferous trees, especially the *Cedrus Libani*, and was used as a medicine. IV 772b

kātriya (Tun) : a lieutenant in the army in the Regency of Tunis. IX 657a

ḳatt (A), and *ḳaḍb, barsīm* : in botany, alfalfa, a common crop raised in the shade of date palms in the Gulf. I 540a

ḳaṭṭaʿa → DJARF

katūm (A), and *fāriḏj, furḏj* : in archery, a bow made from a single stave, hence it does not vibrate when loosed. IV 798a

katun : in Ottoman Greece, a semi-permanent settlement of Albanian or Vlach cattle breeders. VIII 169b

ḳaṭwa → NAṬṬĀLA

ḳavuḳ (T) : a rather high, variously-shaped cap, with a headband wound round it, worn by officers of the Janissaries; other professions had their own special ~, some with specific names. IV 806a ff.; the ~ , whose height varied, normally had the form of a contracted or enlarged cylinder, flat or bulging; but there were also those which resembled a truncated cone or a cupola. The highest *ḳavuḳs* (40 to 60 cm) were kept rigid by means of a construction of metal bars or a kind of basket. They had a smooth or quilted surface and were trimmed with cotton to give the effect of relief or a dome shape with the quilting. V 751a

ḳawābī → DJUDHĀM

ḳawad → ḲIṢĀṢ

ḳawāzib → BARMĀʾIYYŪN

kawkab (A, pl. *kawākib*) : star; according to context, ~ can mean 'planet' specifically. VIII 97b; and → MURĀHIḲ

♦ kawkab al-dhanab, or (*kawkab*) *dhu dhanab* : 'star with a tail', a comet. VIII 102b

♦ (al-kawākib) al-mutaḥayyira : in the 'scientific' period of Arabic-Islamic astronomy which was based on translations from Greek, the common term for the five planets (Mercury, Venus, Mars, Jupiter, and Saturn) without the Sun and Moon. VIII 101a

♦ (al-kawākib) al-sayyāra : in the 'scientific' period of Arabic-Islamic astronomy which was based on translations from Greek, the common term for the five planets plus the Sun and Moon. VIII 101a

♦ al-kawākib al-sufliyya : the lower planets (below the Sun), Moon, Mercury and Venus. VIII 101b

♦ al-kawākib al-thābita : the fixed stars, known as simply *al-thawābit*. VIII 98a

♦ al-kawākib al-ʿulwiyya : the upper planets (beyond the Sun), Mars, Jupiter and Saturn. VIII 101b

♦ kawkaba (pl. *kawkabāt*), or *ṣūra*, pl. *ṣuwar* : constellation. VIII 98b

ḳawḳan (A) : in Hispano-Arabic, the usual term for snail. VIII 707a

ḳawl (A) : in music, a vocal form, at present in India a form of religious song. III 453a

♦ ḳawlī : the 'word-member', one of two classes of the ordinary members of the AKHĪ organization, YIGIT, who made a general profession only, as opposed to the active 'sword-member', *sayfī*. I 323a

ḳawm (A) : people. IV 780b; a term of tribal provenance used to denote a group of people having or claiming a common ancestor, or a tribe descended from a single ancestor. IV 781a; VIII 234a

In Atjeh, ~ has acquired a peculiar form, *kawōm*, and is used to mean 'all those who descend from one man in the male line'. IV 781a

In North Africa, the ~ (*goum*) means a contingent of cavalry levied from a tribe, a practice continued by the French. IV 784b

Under the Circassian rule in the Mamlūk period, *al-ḳawm*, meaning the People, was applied only to the Circassians. II 24b

In India, ~ is a term for the social division among the non-Muslim population, denoting different groups such as the Bhaṭṭī, Tarkhān, Pindjārā; it is debatable whether these should be called castes or not. III 411a

♦ **ḳawmiyya** : nationalism. IV 781a

ḳawmā → ḲŪMĀ

kawn (A, pl. *akwān*) : generation, especially in the phrase *kawn wa-fasād*, generation and corruption, which renders Aristotle's *De generatione et corruptione.* IV 794b

In scholastic theology, ~ is the advent in nature of the existent thing, the existentialisation of all corporal beings. IV 795a

kawōm → ḲAWM

ḳaws (A) : the bow, a term used both in archery, of which there were numerous types. IV 795b; and in music. VIII 346a

In astronomy, *al-~* is the term used for the bow of Sagittarius (cross-bow), one of the twelve zodiacal constellations. VII 83b; VIII 842a

♦ **ḳaws ḳuzaḥ** : rainbow. IV 804a

♦ ḳaws al-ridjl (wa 'l-rikāb) : the most common name in the Mamlūk period for the cross-bow type of weapon; it seems to have been given to cross-bows of various sizes, including those employed in sieges. III 476a

♦ ḳaws al-ziyār : the 'wheel cross-bow', which was operated like the ordinary cross-bow to shoot a powerful arrow, but requiring several men to operate it. III 469b

kawsadj → KALB AL-BAḤR

ḳawṭ → ḲĪNĀ

kawthar (A) : a Qur'ānic word for the name of a river in Paradise or a pond which was shown to the Prophet at the time of his ascension to the Throne of God. IV 805b

ḳawuḳlu (T) : lit. the man with the ḲAVUḲ; a character of the Turkish ORTA OYUNU theatre. IV 806a

ḳawwāl → ZADJDJĀL

ḳawwās (A), or occasionally *ḳawwāṣ* : a bowman, later, musketeer, 'policeman-soldier', especially the one in the service of high-placed Turkish officials and foreign ambassadors. From this term is derived the French *cawas* and the German *Kawasse*. IV 808b

In colloquial usage, both in Turkey and in other Islamic states, ~ denotes the servants and guards of foreign embassies. IV 808b

kayfiyya → ḤAḲĪḲA

ḳayl (A) : among the Sabaeans, in the pre-Islamic period, the leader of the SHAʿB, the grouping in their social organisation constituted of a number of clans; the ~ came from the dominant clan, but was himself subordinate to the king. IV 819a; a kinglet. IX 162b

ḳayn (A) : an artisan, workman; blacksmith. However, since the men working at this trade usually belonged to the lowest stratum of the population, ~ became a deprecatory term applied to slaves and was used as an insult in the desert. IV 819a

♦ **ḳayna** (A, pl. *ḳaynāt, ḳiyān*) : female singing slave. I 32b; IV 820b; other terms for the professional singing girl were *dādjina, muddjina, musmiʿa, ḳarīna, ṣadūḥ* (and *ṣādiḥa*), and *djarāda*. II 1073a; IV 820b

ḳayṣar (A, < Gk) : the usual name in early Islam for the Roman and Byzantine emperor. It is always used without the article, like a proper name. IV 839a

ḳaysāriyya (A, < Gk), also *ḳayṣariyya* : the name of a large system of public buildings laid out in the form of cloisters with shops, workshops, warehouses and frequently also living-rooms, originally distinguished from the SŪḲ probably only by its greater extent, and by having several covered galleries around an open court, while the *sūḳ* consists only of a single gallery. At the present day, ~ is not infrequently quite or almost identical in meaning with the Persian word *kārwānsarāy*. IV 840a; IX 796b; in mediaeval Islam, an imperial establishment for the protection of stages on major commercial routes. IX 788b

In Algiers at the present day, ~ means barracks; after the first half of the 17th century it was used to denote the Janissaries' barracks. IV 841a

ḳayṣūm → SHĪḤ

ḳayṭūn → GĪṬŪN

kayy (A) : in medicine, cauterization by fire with the object of surgical incision. II 481b

ḳayyān (A), or *muḳayyin* : a profession in mediaeval Islam, consisting of acquiring young slaves fit to become *ḳiyān* 'female singing slaves', in forming them under strict rules and in hiring out their services to private persons. IV 822b

kayyās → MUKAYYIS

ḳayyim (A) : lit. he who stands upright; with *bi, ʿalā, li* or the genitive alone, 'he who takes something upon himself, takes care of something or someone and hence also has authority over them'. This meaning of supervisor is found in all possible applications: administrator of a pious foundation, of baths, superintendent of a temple, caretaker of a saint's grave, etc. IV 847b; lessee of the steam bath. III 140b

In eschatological literature, ~ denotes a provider, a husband, of a woman. IV 847b

ḳażāʾ → ḲAḌĀʾ

ḳazaḳ (T) : independent; vagabond. IV 848a

Under the Tīmūrids, ~ signified the pretenders in contrast to the actual rulers, and also their supporters, who led the life of an adventurer or a robber at the head of their men. At the same time, ~ began also to be applied to nomad groups which separated from their prince and kinsmen and so came into conflict with the state; later, ~ had also the meaning of nomad, in contrast to the sedentary Sart population in Central Asia. IV 848b

The status of ~ is also regarded as a very old social institution of the nomad

Turkic peoples. The word became the name of a political unit and later an ethnic designation by having been applied in the former meanings to those groups of the Özbek tribal confederacy that had abandoned the KHĀN Abu 'l-Khayr and migrated to the north-east steppes of Turkistān, where they formed the core of the population of the present Kazakhstan. IV 848b

ḳazz → ḤARĪR

ḳeblī → SAMŪM

kehledān (T) : in Ottoman times, the worker in the mint who made the ingots into plates to be minted. II 119a

kelek (T, A, < Akk *kalakku*), or *kellek, kelik* : a curious raft made of bags of goat's hair, which is already known from the sculptures of Nineveh and has hardly changed in the course of centuries. Particularly mentioned by travellers in Mesopotamia and Persia, ~ is said to be typical for the upper part of the Tigris. IV 870a; VIII 810b

kemān (T), or *yay* : a bow-like instrument used by Ottoman carders to separate the cotton fibre from the seed by beating with it, in order to make the cotton clean and fluffy. V 559a

kenīz (P) : a female slave. I 24b

kervān-bashi̊ → KĀRWĀN

keshif (T) : in Ottoman administration, a detailed protocol compiled after damages to WAḲF-owned buildings, e.g. a BEDESTĀN, due to fire, determining the expenses involved in reparation. IX 542b

keshwar → IḲLĪM

kəskās (N.Afr) : a conical vessel made of earthenware or plaited alfalfa, used in North Africa for the preparation of couscous. V 528a

kəswa kbīra (Mor) : an elegant wedding and festivity dress of Jewish women consisting of several parts, derived from the 15th-century Spanish dress style. V 746a

ketkhudā (P, > T *kʸahya*), or *katkhudā* : master of the house, head of the family; husband, chief of a tribe, headman of a village; tithe-officer in a town. IV 8b; IV 893b; steward. I 278a; and → KALĀNTAR

In Ottoman administration, ~ designated someone who looked after the affairs of an important government official or influential person, i.e. an authorised deputy official. IV 893b

In Ottoman and Persian guilds, ~ was the head of a guild, who dealt with the material and administrative aspects of guild life. He was chosen by the guild nobles and his appointment was confirmed by the ḲĀḌĪ. IV 894a; IX 645b

In North Africa, the form *kāhiya* was current in Tunisia until recent times to designate the subordinates of the caïds, governors at the head of particular administrative divisions. In a more general way, *kāhiya* was in general use with the sense of 'assistant to a high official, president or director'. In Algeria, the *kahya* was a bey's lieutenant, but also a police superintendent and even a simple corporal in the army of AMĪR ʿAbd al-Ḳādir. The use of the term for a subordinate endowed it with the pejorative meaning of 'inferior quality'. IV 894b

khabar (A, pl. *akhbār, akhābir*) : a report, piece of information, especially of a historical, biographical or even anecdotal nature. IV 895a; VI 350a; from the 8th/14th century onwards, ~ is used interchangeably with ḤADĪTH and ḤIKĀYA in the sense of 'story'. III 369a; and → ṢĀḤIB AL-KHABAR; SHIʿR

In the science of Tradition, ~ refers both to Traditions that go back to Muḥammad and to Traditions that go back to the Companions or Successors. III 23b; IV 895a

In Arabic grammar, ~ refers to the constituent parts of the nominal phrase, e.g. *zayd^{un} karīm^{un}*, where *zayd*, the first term, is MUBTADAʾ, and *karīm*, the second one, is ~ . IV 895b; predicate. VIII 384a

♦ **khabar al-wāḥid** : in the science of Tradition, a Tradition going back to a single authority. Synonyms are *khabar al-āḥād* (→ ĀḤĀD, and III 25b), *khabar al-infirād* and *khabar al-khāṣṣa*. IV 896a

khabn (A): in prosody, a deviation in the metre because of the loss of the second consonant of a foot, e.g. the *sīn* in *mu[s]tafʿilun*. I 672a

khabrāʾ (A, pl. *khabārī*) : a silt flat, as is common in the Syrian desert, which comprises part of Syria, Jordan and northern Saudi Arabia and is mostly composed of highly dissected terrain. The rainfall, which usually occurs in the form of sudden cloudbursts, picks up a large amount of material from the erosion remnants and carries it inland downstream at high velocities. When such a stream reaches a gently sloping and wide open area, the ensuing loss in the velocity of the water stream causes the silts to be deposited. A ~ is the resulting silt flat. II 248b; IV 897b

In Arabia, ~ is a hollow with an impervious bottom holding water for while after rain. I 538a

khabūṭ (A) : in the terminology of horse-riding, a horse that stamps its fore-feet. II 953b

khadd al-ʿadhrāʾ (A) : lit. virgin's cheek; the name for the anemone in mediaeval ʿIrāḳ. IX 248b

khaḍḍār → BAḲḲĀL

khādim (A) : a (free) servant, domestic; eunuch. I 33a; IV 899a; a female slave. I 24b

In North Africa, ~ has acquired the specialised meaning of negress, while *khdīm* is used for a domestic servant. I 24b; IV 899a

♦ **khādim al-ḥaramayn** : lit. servant of the two holy places (that is, Mecca and Medina), a title used by a number of Mamlūk and Ottoman sultans. IV 899b

khadīra (A) : a productive palm tree which has lost its dates when they were still green. VII 923b

kh^{w}ādja (P, pl. *kh^{w}ādjagān*) : a title used in many different senses in Islamic lands. In earlier times it was variously used of scholars, teachers, merchants, ministers and eunuchs. In mediaeval Egypt it was a title for important Persian and other foreign merchants. In Sāmānid times, with the epithet *buzurg* 'great', it designated the head of the administration; later, ~ was a title frequently accorded to viziers, teachers, writers, rich men, and merchants. In the Ottoman empire it was used of the *ulema*, and in the plural form *kh^w^ādjegān* designated certain classes of civilian officials. In modern Turkey, pronounced *hodja* (modern orthography *hoca*) it designates the professional men of religion, but is used as a form of address for teachers in general. In Egypt and the Levant (pronounced *khawāga* or *khawādja*), it was used for merchants, then more particularly for non-Muslim merchants, and then as a more or less polite form of address for non-Muslims in general. IV 907a; IV 1092b

In India, ~ designates those Ismāʿīlīs who follow the Agha Khān. IV 907a; as **khōdja**, the name of an Indian caste consisting mostly of Nizārī Ismāʿīlīs and some sunnīs and Twelver shīʿīs split off from the Ismāʿīlī community; in a looser sense, *khōdja* refers to the Indian Nizārīs in general. V 25b

♦ **kh^w^ādja-i djahān** : a title of high dignitaries in various sultanates of India, notably the sultanate of Dihlī, the Bahmanids, and the sultanate of Madura. IV 907b

khafāra (A) : protection, used, often together with ḤIMĀYA, to designate certain social practices. Orginally, it primarily denoted the protection which Arab tribes extended to merchants, travellers and pilgrims crossing their territories, often in return for payment or as part of an agreement. Later, the word's usage became extended to the 'protection' in return for an obligatory payment exacted by various social groups from other groups or from richer individuals. IV 913a

khafḍ (A), or *khifāḍ* : female excision, corresponding to *khitān*, the circumcision of boys. Under Islam, ~ has never been regarded as obligatory, but has been considered as recommended. IV 913a; VIII 824b

For ~ in grammar, → DJARR

khafīf (A) : in prosody, the name of the eleventh Arabic metre. I 670a; and → ḲAṢĪD

khafiyye (T, < A) : lit. secret (police); under the Ottoman sultan ʿAbd al-Ḥamīd II, ~ came to mean a network of espionage and informing, and included the whole range of informers and spies from the highest social levels to the lowest. I 64a

khaftān (P), or *ḳaftān, ḳuftān* : an ample, full-length robe with sleeves that buttons down the front. This originally Persian garment became extremely popular throughout the Arab world. V 737b

khāḳān (Mon *ḳaghan* or *khaghan*) : a title borrowed by the Turks from the Juan-juan meaning (supreme) ruler. It was applied by the Turks and the mediaeval Muslim geographers and historians to the heads of the various Turkish confederations, but also to other non-Muslim rulers such as the Emperor of China. IV 915a; VIII 621b; in the form *ḳa'an* it was borne by the successors of Čingiz-Khān, the Mongol Great Khāns in Ḳaraḳorum and Peking. IV 915a

♦ khāḳānī (A) : a beggar in the time of al-Djāḥiẓ, who painted over his face in order to make it swell up; possibly a male prostitute. VII 494b

khāl (A, pl. *akhwāl*) : maternal uncle, whether a full, consanguineous or uterine one. The paternal uncle is *ʿamm* (pl. *aʿmām*). IV 916a; and → SHĀMA

khalʿ (A) : in medicine, luxation. II 481b; exclusion of a tribe-member from his tribe by his kinsmen. IX 864b

khalaf → AL-SALAF WA 'L-KHALAF

khālī → ḲĀLĪ

khalīʿ (A, pl. *khulaʿāʾ*) : in early Islam, one who has been disowned by his kinsmen for fear of accepting the consequences of his crimes, acquiring soon the meaning of SHĀṬIR 'a rebel who makes a conscious decision to practise evil'. IX 864a

khalīdj (A) : a canal from a river. IX 659a; and → DHIRĀʿ

khalīfa (A) : caliph. As a title, after the first four caliphs, Abū Bakr, ʿUmar, ʿUthmān and ʿAlī, ~ passed to the Umayyads, then to the ʿAbbāsids. But it was also assumed by the Spanish Umayyad ʿAbd al-Raḥmān III and his successors as well as by shīʿī Fāṭimids, the Ḥafṣids and the Marinids. ~ was never officially transferred to the Ottoman sultans. IV 937a; ~ was also used as a title during the Sudanese Mahdist period (1881-1898). IV 952b

In political theory, ~ is the title of the leader of the Muslim community. The full title is *khalīfat rasūl allāh* 'successor of the messenger of God'. IV 947b

In mysticism, ~ may have any of the following meanings, all carrying the idea of vicarship: the ḲUTB or perfect man, *al-insān al-kāmil*, around whom the spheres of being evolve, upon whom the Muḥammadan Reality, which is the hidden side of his own reality, irradiates; the successor of the (alleged) founder of an order or of the deceased leader of a group of mystics; a MURĪD who, after having reached a certain stage of mystical perfection, is granted permission by his spiritual master to initiate novices and to guide them on the mystical path; the deputy of the head of an order in a particular area; the pre-eminent representative and principal propagator of an order in a particular area acting independently. IV 950a

Among the Bektāshiyya, ~ refers to a rank of spiritual achievement which could be attained only by those who had been ordained as *bābā*, head of a *tekke* (→ KHĀNḲĀH). IV 951b

Among the Sanūsiyya, ~ may denote the representative of the head of the order who has been sent on a mission to a ZĀWIYA. IV 952a

Among the Nizārī Ismāʿīlīs, a plenipotentiary of the long-hidden IMĀM. I 353b

khalīlī (A) : name of highly esteemed grapes in the region of Samarḳand. IX 110b

khāliṣa (P, < A; pl. *khāliṣadjāt*) : in Persia, crown lands, and lesser rivers, ḲANĀTS and wells belonging to the crown. IV 972b

Under the Dihlī sultanate, ~ land was an area under direct revenue administration from which the troops could be paid in cash. II 272b

khalḳ (A) : creation. IV 980a; and → IBDĀʿ

♦ khalḳdjilik (T) : democracy. VIII 219a

♦ khalḳ al-insān (A) : human anatomy. IX 394b

khalwa (A) : privacy, seclusion.

In mysticism, ~ means 'retirement, seclusion, retreat', and, more specifically, 'isolation in a solitary place or cell', involving spiritual exercises. IV 990a; IX 300a

In law, the theory of ~ is that consummation between husband and wife is presumed to have occurred if they have been alone together in a place where it would have been possible for them to have had sexual intercourse. III 1011a

In North Africa, ~ is used for a heap of stones where women, for purposes of a mystical nature, attach rags to reeds planted between the stones and where they burn benzoin and styrax in potsherds. IV 381b; V 1201b

khalwātiyya (A) : a variety of ʿABĀʾ made in Ḥasbaya. V 741a

khamīra (A) : yeast. III 1087b

khamīs (A) : in military science, the five elements into which the army is divided: the centre, right wing, left wing, vanguard, and rear guard. III 182a; and → KHAMSA WA-KHAMĪS

khamīṣa (A) : a black garment with edging. IX 313a

khamriyya (A) : in poetry, a Bacchic or wine poem. This name does not seem to be attested in the mediaeval nomenclature of the genres. The usual expressions *al-ḳawl fī 'l-khamr*, *lahu maʿānī fī 'l-khamr*, *waṣṣāf li 'l-khamr*, indicate the existence of themes, but do not include any willingness to organise them into an independent poem. IV 998a

khamsa (A) : five; also, a piece of jewellery called 'the hand of Fatma' which is used as an amulet. I 786a; IV 1009a

In Persian and Turkish literature, a set of five MATHNAWĪ poems, e.g. the five epic poems of Niẓāmī of Gandja. IV 1009b

♦ khamsa wa-khamīs : a formula said against the evil eye. IV 1009a

khān (T, P) : in Turkish, a title first used by the Tʿu-chüeh apparently as a synonym of *ḳaghan*, the later KHĀḲĀN, with which its relationship is obscure; ~ was afterwards normally applied to subordinate rulers. The term was applied to various ranks throughout Islamic history, surviving into modern times in much the sense of the English 'esquire'. IV 1010b; and → SULṬĀN

In military science, ~ was used for a commander of ten thousand soldiers. IV 1019b

In India today, ~ is a common affix to the names of Muslims of all classes and is often regarded as a surname. IV 1010b

Of Persian origin, ~ designates both a staging-post and lodging on the main communication routes, and a warehouse, later a hostelry in the more important urban centres. IV 228a; IV 1010b; sometimes the urban ~ would be not a structure, but a group of several specialised markets, like the Khān al-Khalīlī in

Cairo, a collection of shops enclosed by two large gateways. IV 1015b

♦ khān khānān : a high military title in mediaeval Indo-Muslim usage, the highest title conferred on an officer of the state. IV 1019b; V 629b

♦ khānazād : under the Mughals, a noble belonging to families previously connected with imperial service. VII 322a

♦ khānedān → DEREBEY

♦ **khānḳāh** (P, pl. *khawāniḳ, khānḳāhāt*) : a building usually reserved for Muslim mystics belonging to a dervish order. The terms RIBĀṬ, *tekke* and ZĀWIYA refer to establishments with similar aims. The usual translation of 'monastery' does not convey the complexity of the institution. IV 433a; IV 1025a; VIII 494a

khandaḳ (A, < P) : ditch, trench, moat. Its most famous use is in the 'expedition of the ~', in which Muḥammad foiled a Meccan attempt to storm Medina in 5/627. IV 1020b; another expedition involving a ~ was in 327/939 in Muslim Spain before Simancas at the river of Alhándega (< *al-khandaḳ*). IX 304a

khāniḳ (A) : choking.

♦ khāniḳ al-dhiʾb → AḲŪNĪṬUN

♦ khāniḳ al-fuhūd : in botany, a variety of aconite (*Doronicum pardalianches*), also called *khāniḳ al-namir* (→ AḲŪNĪṬUN); by metonymy, ~ has been extended to mean the effects of poisoning induced by this plant. II 740b

♦ khāniḳ al-nimr → AḲŪNĪṬUN

khannāḳ (A) : in mediaeval Islam, a category of thieves, the strangler or assassin, who may have worked by suffocating his victim but may also have been a disembowler, *bāʿidj*, or one who pounded his victim's head with a stone, *rāḍikh*. V 769a

khʷānsālār (P) : the overseer of the food at the court of the Muslim sovereigns. II 15a; VIII 954a; steward. VIII 924b

khār čīnī → ṬĀLIḲŪN

kharā (A) : human excrement, used as fuel in the public baths of Ṣanʿāʾ. IX 2b

kharadj (A), and *khaṣaf, naṣīf* : a term in the vocabulary of colour meaning a mixture, a combination of two colours sometimes regarded as opposites. V 699b

kharādj (A, < Gk) : tax, more specifically, land tax. IV 1030b; in mediaeval Persian usage and in the Ottoman empire, ~ also meant a tribute, taken from e.g. the peace agreements made after the victories of the Ottomans in the West. IV 1034a; IV 1055a

In Ottoman usage , ~ denoted both the land tax and the poll-tax on the state's non-Muslim subjects. IV 1053b

In the Muslim West, ~ was the tax imposed upon prostitutes, who were called *kharādjiyyāt* or *kharādjayrāt*. S 134a; and → DĀR

For ~ in India, → MUWAẒẒAF

kharbaḳ (A) : in botany, the hellebore. IX 434b; IX 872b

khardja → MUWASHSHAḤ

khardjlik (T) : in the Ottoman period, a sum (usually 50 AKČE per person) collected annually by the ESHKINDJI 'auxiliary soldier', from an assistant, YAMAḲ, to join the sultan's army on an expedition. II 714b

khārfūsh → ḤARFŪSH

khargāh : a trellis tent, serving as a private chamber for the Mongol ruler. IX 45b

khārib (A, pl. *khurrāb*) : a camel thief. V 768b; IX 864b

kharīf (A) : in India, the harvest collected after the end of the rains. II 909a

kharīr → KHURŪR

kharkhara → KHURŪR

kharrūba (Sic) : a small-sized stellate coin introduced in Sicily by the Fāṭimids, whose weight was theoretically 0.195 gr but which in practice varied between 0.65 and 1.25 gr. IX 590a

khartāwī (T) : a high, pointed ḲAVUḲ, worn with a turban rolled around, whose end was often left free. It was worn in Turkey from the 17th century on. V 751b

kharūf → SAKHLA

♦ kharūf al-baḥr (A), or *umm zubayba* : the manatee, one of the sirenian mammals or 'sea cows'. VIII 1022b

kharwār (P) : a donkey's load, a unit of weight which was widespread in the Persian lands in all periods. The Būyid ruler ʿAḍud al-Dawla fixed it at 96.35 kg, but in later times a heavier ~ was introduced, weighing 288 kg; at present a ~ of 297 kg is widespread, although others are used. VI 120b

khaṣaf → KHARADJ

khashab (A) : wood. IV 1085a

♦ khashaba (A, pl. **khashabāt**; T *lawḥ*) : a plate of wood through which a knotted string was threaded, the only instrument for measurement used in mediaeval Islamic navigation. The ~ was used for measuring the altitude of a star above the horizon. It was held at fixed distances from the eye using the knots placed on the string, and this enabled the height of the plate to measure different angular altitudes. The ~ originally represented the hand of the navigator held at arm's length. VII 51a

In the plural, *khashabāt* was the name given to wooden pillars which in mediaeval times were driven into the seabed at the place where the Shaṭṭ al-ʿArab empties into the Gulf, to guide sailors in danger of being drawn into a dangerous whirlpool and also on occasion to signal the approach of pirates. IV 1086a

khashāsh → ḤASHARĀT

khashkhāsh (A) : in botany, the oppyx, or poppy (*Papaver somniferum*). I 243a; IX 249a; IX 615a

khashm → DJABAL

khaṣī (A, pl. *khiṣyān*) : castrate, the man or animal who has undergone the ablation of the testicles; the complete eunuch, deprived of all his sexual organs, is a *madjbūb*. I 33a; IV 1087a

khaṣmān (A, s. *khaṣm*, pl. *khuṣūm* or *khuṣamāʾ*) : in law, the (two) parties to a lawsuit, whereby each party is the *khaṣm* of the other. II 171a

khāṣṣ (A, fem. *khāṣṣa*) : 'personal, private, pertaining to the state or ruler', a term used in Ottoman administration. At first used interchangeably, later, *khāṣṣa* came to be used for the services and matters concerning the ruler and his palace, while ~ was used rather for the private estates of the ruler. IV 972b; IV 1094a; and → MAMLAKA

In magic, **khāṣṣa** (pl. *khawāṣṣ*), also *khāṣṣiyya* (pl. *khāṣṣiyyāt*), in the meaning of 'sympathetic quality', is a recurring theme, indicating the unaccountable, esoteric forces in animate and inanimate Nature. It was believed that all objects were in relation to one another through sympathy and antipathy and that diseases could be caused and cured, good and ill fortune be brought about as a result of the relations of these tensions. IV 1097b

Al-khāṣṣa also denotes the elite, the notables, or the aristocracy, and is frequently mentioned in one breath with its counterpart *al-ʿāmma*, which signifies commonalty, the plebs, or the masses. I 82b; I 491a; IV 1098a; IX 232a; in Ismāʿīlī usage, the *khāṣṣ* were the elite who knew the BĀṬIN, and the *ʿāmm*, the ignorant generality. I 1099a

For ~ in Indian administration, → DABĪR; KHĀṢṢA-NIWĪS

♦ khāṣṣ al-khāṣṣ : 'specific difference' or 'the particular of the particular', a term in logic for what constitutes the species. It is the simple universal attributed to the species in reply to the question: what is it in its essence in relation to its genus. II 837a

♦ khāṣṣa → KHĀṢṢ

♦ khāṣṣa-niwīs (Ind.P) : in the Dihlī sultanate, the secretary attached to the court or on court duty. IV 759a

♦ khāṣṣat al-shams : in astronomy, the mean solar anomaly. IX 292a

♦ **khawāṣṣ al-ḳurʾān** : the art of drawing prognostications from verses of the Qurʾān to which beneficial effects are attributed. IV 1133b

♦ ʿilm al-khawāṣṣ : the knowledge of the natural properties of the letters, based on alchemy. III 595b

khāṣṣadār : a tribal levy; in the 1920s paid by the government of India to replace the Khyber Rifles, to ensure safety of the Khyber Pass. I 238b; and → DJAZĀʾILČĪ

khāṣṣakiyya (A) : under the Mamlūks, the sultan's bodyguard and select retinue, considered to be the most prestigious body within the Mamlūk military aristocracy. IV 1100a

khāṣṣekī (T, < P *khāṣṣagī*, < A *khāṣṣ* 'private, special, confidential') : a term applied to persons in the personal service of Ottoman rulers, both in the palace from the 10th/16th to the 13th/19th centuries, e.g. the sultan's concubines, whose number varied between four and seven. The favourites were honoured by the title of *ḳadi̊n*. Those who bore him a child were called *khāṣṣekī sulṭān*; and in the military organisation, where the 14th, 49th, 66th, and 67th companies or *orta*s of the Janissary corps were called *khāṣṣekī ortalari̊*. IV 1100a

♦ khāṣṣekī sulṭān → KHĀṢṢEKĪ

khaṭʾ → KHAṬAʾ

khaṭaʾ (A) : a mistake, which is made in thought, speech or action; hence in the field of knowledge, error; in that of action, omission, failure, all this, of course, unintentional. IV 1100b

In logic, ~ denotes an error; the opposite is *ṣawāb*. IV 1101a

In law, ~ or *khaṭʾ* is an unintentional action, an act contrary to law, in which the intention of committing an illegal act is lacking, while the action itself may be deliberate; the opposite is *ʿamd*. IV 768b; IV 1101b

khātam (A), or *khātim* : a seal, signet, signet-ring; the impression (also *khatm*) as well as the actual seal-matrix. ~ is applied not only to seals proper, engraved in incuse characters with retrograde inscriptions, but also to the very common seal-like objects with regular inscriptions of a pious or auspicious character; indeed, anything with an inscription stamped upon it may be called ~ . II 306a; IV 1102b

In Morocco, at the present time, ~ denotes also any kind of ring worn on the finger. IV 1105b

khaṭīʾa → DHANB

khaṭīb (A, pl. *khuṭabāʾ*) : among the ancient Arabs, the name for the spokesman of the tribe, often mentioned along with the *shāʿir*, the poet. The distinction between the two is not absolutely definite, but essentially is that the *shāʿir* uses the poetic form while the ~ expresses himself in prose, often, however, also in SADJʿ 'rhymed prose'. IV 1109b; designation for a tribal chief. IX 115b

In early Islam, with the advent of the *khuṭba*, the address from the MINBAR in the mosque, the ~ was given a specifically religious character. IV 1110a; preacher of the Friday sermon. VIII 955a

khātim → DJADWAL; KHĀTAM

khatm → KHĀTAM

khatma (A), or *khitma* : the technical name for the recitation of the whole of the Qurʾān from the beginning to end. IV 1112b

In classical Muslim administration, ~ is the statement of income and expenditure prepared and presented monthly by the DJAHBADH to the DĪWĀN. II 78b

♦ al-khatma al-djāmiʿa : in classical Muslim administration, the annual statement. II 78b

khaṭṭ (A) : writing. IV 1113a; and → ʿIDHĀR

In divination, ~ (or *raml*) is the line which the geomancer traces on the sand when he is practising psammomancy; also, the black or white lines on the hooves of wild cattle or on the flanks and the backs of stags. IV 1128b

♦ khaṭṭ al-idjāza → RIḲĀʿ

♦ khaṭṭ-i muʿammāʾī : an artificial script used in both Persia and Turkey, ~ is the re-arrangement of a ḤADĪTH or some other important saying in a way which is difficult to read. IV 1126b

♦ khaṭṭ-i shadjarī : 'tree-like writing', a name given by western scholars to an artificial script, applied to THULUTH and used both in Persia and Turkey for writing book titles, in which the letters bear a resemblance to the branches of a tree. IV 1126b

♦ khaṭṭ-i sünbülī : 'hyacinth script', a script invented by the Turkish calligrapher ʿĀrif Ḥikmet (d. 1337/1918), in which the letters resemble a hyacinth and are also reminiscent of DĪWĀNĪ letters. IV 1126b

♦ al-khaṭṭ bi-raml : Arab geomancy. IV 1128b

khaṭṭāra (Mor, pop. *khettara* or *rhettara*) : a term used to designate the underground draining system, existing especially in Marrakesh, with wells sunk to a depth of 40 m. IV 532b

khātūn : a title of Soghdian origin borne by the wives and female relations of the Tʿu-chüeh and subsequent Turkish rulers. It was employed by the Saldjūḳs and Khʷārazm-Shāhs and even by the various Čingizid dynasties. It was displaced in Central Asia in the Tīmūrid period by *begüm*, which passed into India and is still used in Pakistan as the title of a lady of rank (→ BEGAM). IV 1133a

khāwa (A, < *ikhāwa* 'brotherliness') : a term formerly used in the Arabian peninsula for payments made in return for the right to enter alien territory and for protection while staying there. Similar payments made by pilgrim caravans on the way to the Holy Cities were called *ṣurra*. IV 1133a

khawāriḳ al-ʿādāt (A) : among the Saʿdiyya Ṣūfi order, deeds transcending the natural order, such as healing, spectacles involving body piercing, *ḍarb al-silāḥ*, and, best known, the DAWSA. VIII 728b

khawāṣṣ al-ḳurʾān → KHĀṢṢA

khawātim (A, s. *khātima*) : in the science of diplomatic, the concluding protocal of documents, consisting of the ISTITHNĀʾ, the *taʾrīkh* (dating), and the *ʿalāma* (signature). II 302a

khawf → ṢALĀT AL-KHAWF

khawkha (A) : private entrance to the mosque. IX 49b

khawr (A) : in the Arabian peninsula, a term for an inlet in the Arabian shores of the Persian Gulf; a submarine valley. I 536a; also, a desert well with water too salty for humans to drink from. I 538b

khawtaʿ → KHIRNIḲ

khayāl (A) : figure. IV 602b

In Indian music, ~ is the most important song form in the classical repertoire. It arose as a reaction to the traditional rigid and austere composition *dhrupad*. Its content deals primarily with religious and amorous themes, and consists of a relatively short set piece employed as the basis for improvisation. III 453b; IV 1136a

♦ **khayāl al-ẓill** : the shadow-play, possibly brought over from south-east Asia or India and performed in Muslim lands from the 6th/12th to the present century. IV 602b; IV 1136b khayāshīm (A, s. *khayshūm*) : the nasal cavities. VIII 121a

khaylāniyyāt (A), or *banāt al-māʾ* : in zoology, the sirenian mammals or 'sea cows'. VIII 1022b

khayma (A) : a tent; ~ was originally used to denote a rudimentary shelter, circular in construction, erected on three or four stakes driven into the ground with supporting cross-members covered with branches or grass. IV 1147a

♦ khaymānegān (T) : lit. people living in tents.

In Ottoman administration, any wandering subject who might come and exploit the land on a temporary basis, paying rents or tithes to the owner. VI 960a

khayr (A) : charity, gifts in money or kind from individuals or voluntary associations to needy persons. In Islam, to make such gifts is a religious act. The word has the sense of freely choosing something, i.e. virtue or goodness, a service to others beyond one's kin. It also means goods such as property or things that have material value. IV 1151a

♦ khayr wa-khidmat : among the AHL-I ḤAḲḲ, an offering of cooked or prepared victuals, like sugar, bread etc., which with raw offerings of male animals (→ NADHR WA-NIYĀZ) is an indispensable feature of a DHIKR session. I 261b

khaysh (A, pl. *khuyūsh, akhyāsh*, n. of unity, *khaysha*) : a coarse, loose linen made with flax of poor quality and used in the manufacture of sacks, wrappings and rudimentary tents; also, a kind of fan, still used in ʿIrāḳ, where it is now called by the Indian name *pānka*. IV 1160b

khayyāṭ (A) : a tailor, dressmaker. IV 1161a

khayzurān (A) : a rod, one of the insignia of sovereignty of the Umayyad caliphs in Muslim Spain. IV 377b; bamboo. IV 682a; VIII 1022a

khāzin (A, pl. *khuzzān, khazana*) : lit. he who keeps safe, stores something away; a term for a quite menial and lowly member of the ʿAbbāsid caliphal household. IV 1181b; a keeper of books or librarian. IV 1182a; VI 199a

As a term of mediaeval Islamic administration, ~ stands for certain members of the financial departments and also of the chancery; an archivist. III 304b; IV 1181b

The plural *khazana* is found in the Qurʾān and denotes the angels who guard Paradise and Hell. IV 1181b

khazīne (T, < A *khazīna*) : the Ottoman state treasury. IV 1183b; the annual income of a province sent to Istanbul. IV 1184b

In popular language, ~ gradually took the form of *khazne*, and came to be used as a place for storing any kind of goods or for storing water. IV 1183b; and → KHZĀNA

khazīr (A), or *khazīra* : a gruel generally made from bran and meat cut up into small pieces and cooked in water, eaten by pre-Islamic Arabs. II 1059a

khazne → KHAZĪNE

khazz (A) : a term for a mixture of silk and wool, but sometimes also used for silk. III 209b; floss silk. S 341a khazzān (A) : a type of sedentary merchant in mediaeval Islam, who, by means of stocking or de-stocking, plays on variations of price as influenced by space, time and the quantities of the commodities traded. IX 789a

khel → TIRA

khettara → KHAṬṬĀRA

khibāʾ (A) : a kind of tent, probably similar to the BAYT in size, but distinguished from it by the camel hair (*wabar*) or wool that was used to make the awning. Apparently, it was the usual dwelling of the cameleer nomads. It is impossible to be certain whether the distinction between ~ and *bayt* corresponds to a different geographical distribution, to a contrast between two large categories of nomads in Arabia, or simply to different levels of life within one tribe. IV 1147a

khibyāra → BAṬRAKH

khidāʿ (A) : trickery. IX 567b

khiḍāb (A) : the dyeing of certain parts of the body (and especially, in regard to men, the beard and hair) by means of henna or some similar substance. V 1b; IX 312a; IX 383b

khidhlān (A) : in theology, a term applied exclusively to God when He withdraws His grace or help from man. Its opposite is LUṬF. I 413b; V 3b

khidīw (A, < P) : khedive, the title of the rulers of Egypt in the later 19th and early 20th centuries. In a way, ~ was a unique title among the vassals of the Ottoman sultan, which the ambitious viceroy of Egypt sought precisely in order to set himself apart and above so many other governors and viceroys of Ottoman dominions. V 4a

khidmet (T) : one of seven services to be rendered by the RAʿIYYA to the TĪMĀR-holder (→ SERBEST) such as the provision of hay, straw, wood, etc. II 32a; and → KHAYR WA-KHIDMET

♦ khidmet aḳčesi̊, or *maʿīshet* 'livelihood' : in the Ottoman tax system, service-money which government agents were allowed to collect for themselves as a small fee for their services. VIII 487b

khidr (A, pl. *khudūr*) : the section inside the Arab tent reserved for women. The term derives from the name of the curtain which separated this section from the rest of the tent. IV 1148a

khifāḍ → KHAFḌ

khilʿa (A, pl. *khilaʿ*) : a robe of honour, also called *tashrīf*. Throughout much of the mediaeval period, the term did not designate a single item of clothing, but rather a variety of fine garments and ensembles which were presented by rulers to subjects whom they wished to reward or to single out for distinction. These robes were normally embellished with embroidered bands with inscriptions known as ṬIRĀZ and were produced in the royal factories. I 24a; V 6a; V 737a

♦ khilʿet behā (T) : lit. the price of a KHILʿA, a sum of money given in place of the robe of honour to Janissary officers upon the accession of a sultan in the Ottoman empire. V 6b kh̲īmī (A, < Gk) : a kind of edible mussel, probably the *Chana Lazarus* L., the juice of which is said to get the digestion going. VIII 707a

kh̲innaws (A, pl. *kh̲anānīs*) : in zoology, a piglet. V 8a

kh̲inzīr (A, pl. *kh̲anāzir*) : in zoology, the pig. In North Africa, *ḥallūf* is preferred, while the Touaregs use *aẓubara*, or *taẓubarat*. V 8a

In medicine, the plural form *kh̲anāzir* denotes scrofulous growths on the neck. V 9b

♦ kh̲inzīr al-baḥr : 'sea-pig', in zoology, the dolphin and porpoise, also called *bunbuk*. V 9b; VIII 1022b

kh̲īrī (A) : in botany, the stock. IX 435a

kh̲irḳa (A) : the patched robe of the ṣūfīs, synonymous with *dilḳ*. V 737a; V 741a; a veil, head scarf, worn by women in the Arab East. V 741a; in Turkey, a full, short caftan with sleeves. V 752a; and → MANDĪL

In mysticism, from the original meaning of cloak, ~ has been broadened to designate the initiation as such. V 17b; followed by a noun complement, it may serve to define various categories or degrees of initiation to the mystical path, e.g. *kh̲irḳat al-irāda*, *kh̲irḳat al-tabarruk*. V 18a

♦ kh̲irḳat al-futuwwa : the act of investiture originally conferred by the ʿAbbāsid caliphs and later by the Ayyūbid sultans, which was one of the features marking out the chivalric orders of the Islamic world before they spread into Christendom. V 18a

♦ kh̲irḳa kh̲iḍriyya : 'investiture by al-Kh̲iḍr', an expression describing those cases in which some contemplatives are said to have received spiritual direction directly from the powerful and mysterious person who, in the Qurʾān, shows a wisdom superior to the prophetic law. V 17b

♦ kh̲irḳa-yi saʿādet (T) : under the Ottomans, the annual ceremony held on 15 Ramaḍān of honouring the collection of relics preserved in the treasury of the Topkapı palace in Instanbul. II 695b; and → KH̲IRḲA-YI SH̲ERĪF

♦ **kh̲irḳa-yi sh̲erīf** (T), or KH̲IRḲA-YI SAʿĀDET : one of the mantles attributed to the Prophet, preserved at the Topkapı palace in Instanbul. II 695b; V 18a

kh̲irniḳ (A, pl. *kh̲arāniḳ*), or *kh̲awtaʿ* : in zoology, the leveret, a young hare. S 84b

kh̲irtīt → KARKADDAN

kh̲itān (A) : (male) circumcision. V 20a; VIII 824b

♦ al-kh̲itānāni : the two circumcised parts, i.e. that of the male and the female. V 20a

kh̲iṭba (A) : 'demand in marriage', betrothal. ~ does not involve any legal obligation and is not a legal act, but certain effects nevertheless follow from it, although the law schools differ: the right of seeing the woman, and the right of priority, in that once a woman is betrothed to a man, that woman cannot be sought in marriage by another man. V 22b; a solicitation, which usually prefaces the marriage contract. VIII 27b

kh̲itma → KH̲ATMA

khiṭr (A) : a flock of two hundred sheep or goats. S 319b; and → NĪL

khiṭṭa (A, pl. *khiṭaṭ*) : a piece of land marked out for building upon, a term used of the lands allotted to tribal groups and individuals in the garrison cities founded by the Arabs at the time of the conquests. V 23a

khiyāna (A) : in law, embezzlement. IX 62b

khiyār (A) : in law, the option or right of withdrawal, i.e. the right for the parties involved to terminate the legal act unilaterally. V 25a

♦ khiyār al-madjlis : in law, a Meccan doctrine, later taken up by al-Shāfiʿī, whereby an offer in a transaction can be withdrawn after it has been accepted, as long as the two parties have not separated. I 1111b; III 1017a

♦ khiyār al-sharṭ : in law, *jus paenitandi*, a clause by means of which, in certain legal acts (in particular, contracts), one of the parties, or both of them, reserve the right to annul or to confirm, within a specified time, the legal act which they have just drawn up. I 319b; V 25a; IX 359a

♦ khiyār al-taʿyīn : in law, a clause allowing the one making the stipulation to make his final choice between the different objects of one and the same obligation. V 25b

khnīf → AKHNIF

khō shāb → SHERBET

khōdja → KHWĀDJA

khoṭoz (T) : a popular feminine head-gear in the form of a conical KÜLĀH or hood decorated with a fine scarf or shawl and trimmed with feathers, precious stones and ribbons, worn in Ottoman Turkey. V 751b

khudāwendigār (P) : a title used for commanders and viziers during the Saldjūḳ period. As an attribute, the term was also used for mystics like Djalāl al-Dīn Rūmī. V 44b

In Ottoman usage, the term was used as the title of Murād I, and as the name of the SANDJAḲ and province of Bursa. V 44b

khūdja (Tun) : a secretary in the army in the Regency of Tunis. IX 657a

khuff (A) : a sort of shoe or boot made of leather, worn in early Islamic times. V 735b; a leather outer sock, still worn in the Arab East. V 741a

khulʿ (A) : in law, a negotiated divorce. III 19a; IV 286a; a divorce at the instance of the wife, who must pay compensation to the husband. VI 477b

khulāṣa (A) : in literature, a technical term referring to a selection made from an extensive work. VII 528b

khuld (A, < Ar; pl. *khildān*) : in zoology, the Mole rat or Blind rat (*Spalax typhlus*). S 287b

khuluww al-intifāʿ (A) : in law, a system in Egypt and Palestine for repairs and setting up of installations, whose main features were a loan made to the WAḲF and the right of the *waḳf* at any time to repurchase the property and repay the tenant the added value. S 368b

In Algeria and Tunis, ~ was rather like *ḥikr*, long-term leasing of WAḲF property, and involved perpetual usufruct or even 'co-proprietorship' with the *waḳf*. S 368b

khumāsiyy (A) : 'a boy five spans in height, said of him who is increasing in height' (Lane). VIII 822a

khumbara (T), or *ḳumbara* : bombs, used in Ottoman warfare. There is mention in the sources of bombs made of glass and of bronze: *shīshe khumbara*, *tundj khumbara*. I 1063a

♦ **khumbaradji** (T, < P) : in the Ottoman military, a bombardier, grenadier. I 1062a; V 52b

khums (A) : lit. one-fifth; in early Islam, the fifth of war booty reserved to the Prophet. I 1142a; II 869b; IX 420a; one of five tribal departments into which Baṣra was divided under the Umayyads. I 1085b

khunyāgar (P) : pre-Islamic Persian minstrels (*gōsān* in the Parthian period, *huniyāgar* in Middle Persian) who performed as storytellers, singers and musicians as well as improvising poets. From the 5th/11th century on, the performing artist became increasingly referred to by *rāmishgar* or *muṭrib*. IX 236b

khurāfa (A) : a fabulous story; superstition, fairy tale, legend. III 369b

khurūdj (A) : in prosody, the letter of prolongation following the *hāʾ* as WAṢL (as in *yaḳtuluhū*). IV 412a

khurūr (A), or *kharīr*, *kharkhara*, *harīr* : the purring of a cat. IX 651b

khuss (A) : the son of a man and of a *djinniyya*. III 454b

♦ khussān : according to Ibn Durayd, the stars around the (North) Pole that never set, i.e. the circumpolar stars. VIII 101a

khusūf → KUSŪF

khuṭba (A) : sermon, address by the *khaṭīb*, especially during the Friday service, on the celebration of the two festivals, in services held at particular occasions such as an eclipse or excessive drought. V 74a; a pious address, such as may be delivered by the WALĪ of the bride on the marriage occasion. VIII 27b; and → LAYṬ

khuwān (A) : a solid, low 'table', synonymous with *māʾida*. S 99b

khuwwa (A) : protection-money, paid to pass through regions safely or to protect property. I 483b; IX 316b; S 305a

khuzām al-ḳiṭṭ (A) : 'cat's mignonette', in botany, the varieties *Astralagus Forskallii* and *Astralagus cruciatus* of the genus Milk vetch. IX 653b

khuzaz (A, pl. *khizzān*, *akhizza*), or *ḥawshab*, *ḳuffa* : in zoology, the male hare, or buck. S 84b

khzāna (Mor) : the official tent of state authorities, of conical design and made of unbleached cloth decorated with black patterns. IV 1149

kiai → KYAHI

kibd → KABID

ḳibla (A) : the direction of Mecca (or, to be exact, of the Kaʿba or the point between the *mīzāb* 'water-spout', and the western corner of it), towards which the worshipper must direct himself for prayer. IV 318a; V 82a; V 323b; VIII 1054a In many Muslim lands, ~ has become the name of a point of the compass, according to the direction in which Mecca lies; thus ~ (pronounced *ibla*) means in Egypt and Palestine, south, whereas in North Africa, east. V 82b; V 1169a

kibrīt (A, < Akk) : sulphur. V 88b

ḳidam (A) : in philosophy and theology, the term for eternity. V 95a

ḳig̲h̲ad̲j̲ (A, < T *kiğaç* 'slope, incline') : a term denoting either an exercise in which an archer, shooting parallel with his left thigh, shoots at a ground target, or else any kind of downwards shot made from horseback. Possibly, it also means shooting rearwards by a group of cavalrymen at full gallop. IV 801b

kik̲h̲a (K) : an elected chief of a Kurdish village. V 472a

ḳilāda (A) : in the terminology of horse-riding, a collar worn by a horse. II 954a

kilīm (T, < P *gilīm*) : a woolen rug generally long and narrow in shape. S 136a

ḳily (A, < Ar) : potash, potassium carbonate [K_2CO_3], but also soda, sodium carbonate [NA_2CO_3]; ~ thus indicates the salt which is won from the ashes of alkaline plants, but is also confusingly used for the ashes themselves and the lye. Synonyms are *shabb al-ʿuṣfūr* and *shabb al-asākifa*. V 107a

ḳīma (A) : in law, the market value (of the victim of bloodshed). I 29b

ḳimar (A) : gambling, strictly prohibited according to Islamic law. V 108b

ḳīmī (A) : in law, non-fungible. S 55a

ḳinā (A) : a flock of one to two hundred sheep; such a flock for goats is called *g̲h̲īnā* or *ḳawṭ*. S 319b

kināya (A) : in rhetoric, a term corresponding approximately to metonomy and meaning the replacement, under certain conditions, of a word by another which has a logical connection with it (from cause to effect, from containing to contained, from physical to moral, by apposition etc.); ~ constitutes a particular type of metaphor. V 116b

ḳinbār (A) : coconut palm fibre. VIII 811a

ḳindīl (A, < Gk) : a cylindrical quiver in which the arrows are placed with their heads downwards, as opposed to the procedure with the D̲J̲AʿBA. IV 799b; (oil) lamp. IX 282a; IX 288a; IX 665a

ḳi̊nli̊ḳ → DJARĪMA

ḳinna (A) : galbanum, the desiccated latex of *Ferula galbaniflua*, used as a spice and medicine. VIII 1042b

kirā᾽ (A) : in law, a term meaning the leasing or hiring out of things, in particular immovable property and ships and beasts which are used for transportation. V 126b

ḳirā᾽a (A) : reading; in the science of the Qur᾽ān, ~ means recitation; a special reading of a word or of a single passage of the Qur᾽ān; a particular reading, or redaction, of the entire Qur᾽ān. V 127a

ḳirāḍ → MUḌĀRABA

ḳirān (A) : in astrology, the conjunction; without further qualification, this refers to the mean or true conjunction of Saturn and Jupiter. V 130b; VIII 833a

In astronomy, ~ is sometimes used in place of *idjtimāʿ*, the conjunction of the sun and moon. IV 259a

In the context of the pilgrimage, ~ denotes one of three methods of performing the pilgrimage, viz. when the *ʿumra* 'Little Pilgrimage' and the *ḥadjdj* 'Great Pilgrimage' are performed together. The other two methods are IFRĀD and TAMATTUʿ. III 35a; III 53b

In the terminology of ploughmen, ~ (or *ḳaran*) refers to a rope passing over the oxen's head and attached to the beam of the tiller. VII 22b

For ~ in numismatics, → ṢĀḤIB ḲIRĀN

ḳīrāṭ (A, < Gk) : a unit of weight. 24 *ḳīrāṭ*s made up a *mithḳāl*, which was equal to 60 barley grains. VI 118a; on the other hand, sometimes 4 barley grains made a ~ . III 10b; V 11b

ḳirdān (A), and *ḥalam* : in zoology, a sort of moth. IV 522a

kirkira → ṢADR

ḳirṣ → ḲURṢ

ḳirsh (A, < It *grosso*; pl. *ḳurūsh*) : a piastre. IX 269b; a silver coin, called *thaler* upon its first issue in Europe. IX 599a

♦ ḳirshiyyāt (A) : in zoology, fish of cartilaginous skeleton, in other words the selachians or squalidae. VIII 1022b

ḳirṭās (A, < Gk) : papyrus, papyrus roll; parchment; rag paper. IV 742a; V 173b; VIII 261b; VIII 407b; bag. V 174a

In medicine, ~ refers to a dressing, and a kind of absorbent gauze. V 174a

kīs → MUKAYYIS

ḳiṣāṣ (A) : in law, retaliation (syn. *ḳawad*), which is applied in cases of killing (*ḳiṣāṣ fī 'l-nafs*), and of wounding which do not prove fatal (*ḳiṣāṣ fī-mā dūn al-nafs*). I 29a; IV 770a; V 177a

kishk (A) : a preparation of barley and milk, used in medicine as an antidote to fever and, when the body was washed with it, as a treatment for exhaustion as it opened the pores. IX 225a

ḳishlaḳ (T, < *ḳïsh* 'winter') : winter quarters, originally applied to the winter quarters, often in warmer, low-lying areas, of pastoral nomads in Inner Asia, and thence to those in regions like Persia and Anatolia. V 182b

In Čaghatay Turkish of Central Asia, the sense of ~ evolved from that of 'the khān's residence, winter quarters of the tribe' into the additional one of 'village'. V 182b

In Ottoman usage, ~ meant 'barracks' and it spread thus with the form *ḳïshla* into the Balkan languages. This meaning has in fact passed into the Arabic colloquials of Syria and Egypt, as has also that of 'hospital, infirmary', so that in Egyptian Arabic we have both *ḳushlāḳ* 'barracks' and *ḳashla* 'hospital'. V 182b

ḳishriyyāt → SARAṬĀN

ḳisma (A, T *ḳismet*) : fate, destiny; in this final sense, and especially via Turkish, *ḳismet* has become familiar in the West as a term for the fatalism popularly attributed to the oriental. V 184a
In mathematics, ~ is the term used for division of a number. III 1139b
In Ottoman usage, *ḳismet* was also a technical term of the *ḳassāmlıḳ*, the official department of state responsible for the division of estates between the various heirs, *resm-i ḳismet* denoting the payment which the ḲASSĀM received from the heirs of a deceased person in payment for the trusteeship of the estate. IV 735b; V 184b

ḳismet → ḲISMA

kisr → FALĪDJA

ḳiṣṣa (A, pl. *ḳiṣaṣ*) : the term which, after a long evolution, is now generally employed in Arabic for the novel, while its diminutive *uḳṣūṣa* (pl. *aḳāṣīṣ*) has sometimes been adopted as the equivalent of novella, short story, before being ineptly replaced by a calque from the English 'short story', *ḳiṣṣa ḳaṣīra.* V 185b; used of every kind of story, but applied particularly to edifying tales and stories of the prophets. III 369a; V 186b
In the science of diplomatic, ~ was the term for petition. II 306a
♦ ḳiṣṣa-khʷān (T) : the Turkish equivalent of Arabic *ḳaṣṣāṣ*, a teller of stories about the pre-Islamic prophets, the champions of Islam or the great mystic figures. III 374a; V 951a; IX 409a; and → SHAYYĀD

ḳisṭ (A) : a measure of weight used for olive oil in Egypt during the period of the Umayyad and ʿAbbāsid caliphs. Its actual weight varied. VI 119a

ḳisṭās (A, < Gk or Ar) : the Qurʾānic word for the common balance. VII 195b

ḳiṭʿa (U, < A; pl. *ḳiṭaʿ*) : in Urdu literature, a short poem, consisting of as few as one or two verses. IX 470a

kitāb (A) : 'letter, book'; in the Qurʾān, the transaction of contractual enfranchisement, consisting of the master's granting the slave his freedom in return for the payment of sums (*kitāba*) agreed between them. In law, ~ became later known as *mukātaba* or *kitāba*. The slave freed thus is called *mukātab*. I 30a
♦ kitāba → KITĀB
♦ kitābiyya (A) : a Muslim slave woman. VII 474b

ḳitār, ḳitarā → ḲITHĀRA

ḳiṭār (A) : in classical Arabic, a train of camels drawn up one behind the other, now used with modified meaning to designate a railway train. I 572b

ḳithāra (A), or *ḳitarā* : a musical instrument of the lyre family. It first appears in Arabic literature on music in the 3rd/9th century to denote a Byzantine or Greek instrument of this type. It was made up of a richly-decorated rectangular sound box, two vertical struts fastened together by a yoke and (twelve) strings which were left free at their greatest width. The ~ and the *lūrā* were variants of the same instrument, but the ~ was the instrument for professionals, while the *lūrā* was a smaller instrument played by beginners and amateurs. At a later period,

the term, as *ḳitār*, was used to denote a different instrument, the guitar. V 234a
ḳiththā' al-ḥimār (A) : in botany, *Ecballium elaterium.* IX 872b
kitmān (A) : secret.
Among the Ibāḍiyya, a state of secrecy, the condition in which they were to do without an imāmate, because of unfavourable circumstances. III 658a
ḳiṭmīr : the name of the dog in SŪRA xviii in the Qur'ān; among the Turks of East Turkistan, as in Indonesia, it was still customary in recent times to inscribe letters which it was desired to protect from loss, with ~ instead of 'registered'. I 691b
ḳiṭr → NUḤĀS
♦ ḳiṭrān → ḲAṬRĀN
ḳiṭṭ → SINNAWR
♦ ḳiṭṭ-namir → WASHAḲ
ḳiyāfa (A) : in divination, the science of physiognomancy (*ḳiyāfat al-bashar*), and the examination of traces on the ground (*ḳiyāfat al-athar*). V 234b; VIII 562a
ḳiyāma (A) : in theology, the action of raising oneself, of rising, and of resurrection. V 235b
♦ yawm al-ḳiyāma : the Day of Resurrection, which with the Last Hour (*al-sā'a*) and the Day of Judgement (*yawm al-dīn*) constitute one of the necessary beliefs of Islam. V 235b
ḳiyās (A) : in law, judicial reasoning by analogy, the fourth source of Islamic law. It is the method adopted by the jurisconsults to define a rule which has not been the object of an explicit formulation. III 1026a; V 238b
In grammar, ~ indicates the 'norm', meaning the instrument which enables the grammarian to 'regulate' the morphological or syntactical behaviour of a word, where this is not known through transmission or audition, on the basis of the known behaviour of another word, by means of a certain kind of analogy. It is synonymous with *miḳyās*. V 242a
In logic, ~ is the general name for syllogism. I 1327a; II 102b; IX 359b
♦ ḳiyās ḥamlī : in logic, the attributive or predicative syllogism, as opposed to *ḳiyās sharṭī*, the conditional or hypothetical syllogism. IX 359b
kiyūniyā (A, < Gk) : 'columella', the interior of the Purpura and of the trumpet-snail, which used to be burned for its etching power. VIII 707a
ḳïz (T) : 'girl, unmarried female', but often used with the more restricted meanings of 'daughter, slave girl, concubine'. In mediaeval usage, one of its denotations was 'Christian woman', doubtless influenced by the meanings 'slave girl, concubine'. V 242b
kiẓāma (A, pl. *kaẓā'im*) : in the Ḥidjāz, an underground canal used for extracting water from the depths of the earth; especially a series of wells sunk at a certain distance from one another and linked by a gallery laid out at a level that does not tap the underground water. IV 532b
ḳïzïl-bāsh (T) : lit. red-head; in its general sense, ~ is used loosely to denote a wide

variety of extremist shīʿī sects, which flourished in Anatolia and Kurdistān from the late 7th/13th century onwards. The common characteristic was the wearing of red headgear. In its specific sense, ~ was a term of opprobrium applied by the Ottoman Turks to the supporters of the Ṣafawid house, and adopted by the latter as a mark of pride. I 262a; III 316a; IV 34b ff.; V 243a; V 437b

kneze (Serb) : lit. prince; under the Ottomans, a local strongman. IX 671a

ḳol (T) : one of three 'arms' of a postal route; also a technical term in administrative language. I 475a; an actor's guild. IX 646b

♦ ḳol aghasĭ : a military rank intermediate between those of *yüzbashĭ* and BIÑBASHĬ; commander of a wing. I 246a

♦ ḳolu (P) : in pre-Tīmūrid Persia, a headman of a craft, appointed as such by the members. IX 645b

köle → KUL

kontosh (T) : a fur (or caftan) with straight sleeves and a collar, worn in Ottoman Turkey. V 752a

ḳopi : a salt-bed. IX 832a

köprü ḥaḳḳi (T) : a bridge-toll levied in the Ottoman empire. II 147a

kopuz : the lute of the Oghuz, which they brought into Asia Minor, the ancestor of the present SĀZ. It seems to have had three strings, a long neck and a soundboard of hide. IX 120a

kōs → KROŚA

kös (T) : a large copper kettledrum, which could measure one-and-a-half metres at the top. It was taken on Ottoman military campaigns and played at official occasions. VI 1008a

ḳosh-begi (T) : the title of high officials in the Central Asian khānates in the 16th to 19th centuries, probably with the meaning 'commander of the (royal) camp, quartermaster'. V 273a; S 419b

köshk (T, < P *kūshk*) : a pavilion in a pleasance which could be merely a modest shelter or have several rooms. It was rarely a substantial building. The term gave rise to the English 'kiosk'. V 274a

In Ottoman naval terminology, ~ was the name given to the after-deck or poop cabin. V 274a

ḳoshma (T) : originally a general term for poetry among the Turkish peoples, later, applied to the native Turkish popular poetry, in contrast to the classical poetry taken from the Persian and based on the laws of Arabic metrics. V 274b; a folk-musical form, which varies in different parts of Anatolia and Azerbaijan, but which contains typically an instrumental introduction, followed by a vocal recitative and melody. V 275b

kōtwāl (H) : a commander of a fortress, town, etc. V 279b; IX 438b; in India, before and under the Mughals, and in British India for approximately a century more, ~ was used in the sense of 'official responsible for public order and the maintenance of public services in a town'. V 280a

ḳoyun resmi (T), or *ʿādet-i ag͟hnām* : the most important tax levied on livestock in the Ottoman empire at the rate of 1 AKČE for two sheep, collected directly for the central treasury. II 146b

krośa (H, later *kōs*, P *karōh*) : lit. earshot, this term later became the standard term for describing distance. It has been differently reckoned at different periods and in different regions, and has almost everywhere a distinction between a larger and a smaller measure. VII 138b

ḳūba (A) : in medicine, eczema. III 291a

ḳubaʿ (A) : in zoology, one of the multiple names for the ray or skate (→ RĀYA). VIII 1022b; and → D͟JAMAL AL-BAḤR

ḳubba (A, T *ḳubbe*) : a hide tent, in pre-Islamic Arabia. IV 1147a; a tomb surmounted by a dome. IV 352b; V 289a; the general name for the sanctuary of a saint. VI 651b

In the construction of scales and balances, the ~ was the housing for the pointer (*lisān*), often used also as a carrying handle. V 295b

In geography and astronomy, ~ , *ḳubbat al-ʿālam, ḳ. al-arḍ, ḳ. Arīn* are expressions used to denote the geographical centre of the earth at the zenith of which exists the dome of the heavens, *ḳubbat al-samaʾ* or *wasaṭ al-samāʾ*. The ~ is defined as being equidistant from the four cardinal points, and thus situated on the equator. V 297a

♦ ḳubbat al-k͟haḍrāʾ : term best translated as ‘Dome of Heaven’, ~ was the name of the palace erected at Damascus by Muʿāwiya and recurs frequently in early Islamic times for other palaces. IX 44b

♦ **ḳubbe wezīri** (T) : lit. vizier of the dome, the name given, under the Ottomans, to the members of the *dīwān-i humāyūn* who came together on several mornings each week around the grand vizier in the chambers of the Topkapı Palace called *ḳubbe altı̊* because it was crowned by a dome. This institution was abandoned under Aḥmed III. V 299b

ḳūbčūr (Mon) : a tax of Mongolian origin. Originally, a tax on flocks and herds, payable by the Mongol nomads to their ruler, and later, a poll-tax to be paid by the subject population. The animal-levy continued to be paid by the Mongols until it was abolished by G͟hāzān; it is sometimes referred to as *ḳūbčūr-i mawās͟hī* to distinguish it from the poll-tax. IV 1050a; V 299b

kubra → IBRĪḲ

kudrī → ḲAṬĀ

ḳudsī → ḤADĪT͟H ḲUDSĪ

kuffa → ḤAD͟JRA

ḳuffa → K͟HUZAZ

ḳuffāz → DASTABĀN

kūfī (A) : a term used to designate the angular form of Arabic script, as opposed to the flexible *nask͟hī* script. It continued to be in use for some five centuries after the advent of Islam, especially for writing Qurʾāns. Moreover, it was used for writing the titles of manuscripts and their sections and the BASMALAS at their beginnings until almost the end of the 7th/13th century, often as an element of decoration. IV 1121a ff.; V 217a ff. The best distinguished types of ~ styles of writing are *māʾil* (used in the Ḥidjāz in the 2nd/8th century), *mashḳ* (used in the Ḥidjāz and Syria), western (with round shapes), and eastern ~ (also called *ḳarmāṭī*, characterised by its edgy forms). Later direct developments of these ~ script styles are *maghribī* (used in al-Andalus and till the present day in the MAGHRIB) and *sūdānī* (used in sub-Saharan West Africa). VIII 151a

kūfiyya → KĀFIYYA

kufr (A) : unbelief.

The following kinds of unbelief are distinguished: *kufr al-inkār* (neither recognising nor acknowledging God); *kufr al-djuḥūd* (recognising God, but not acknowledging Him with words, that is remaining an unbeliever in spite of one's better knowledge); *kufr al-muʿānada* (recognising God and acknowledging him with words but remaining an unbeliever (obdurate) out of envy or hatred); *kufr al-nifāḳ* (outwardly acknowledging, but at heart not recognising God and thus remaining an unbeliever, that is a hypocrite). IV 408a

♦ kufriyyāt : in literature, a genre of blasphemous or heretical poems. III 355b

kufu (Sw, < A *kafāʾa*) : in East Africa, a husband of equal socio-economic class. VIII 34a

kuḥl (A) : traditionally translated as antimony sulphide (stibnite), the Arabic word, the origin of our word alcohol, was used in mediaeval Arabic and Persian texts to indicate both an eye cosmetic, an eye ungent and a lead mineral found at Isfahan. From the fine powder used to stain the eyelids, the word was applied to an essence obtained by distillation. The process needed for the production of alcohol itself was probably introduced into the Islamic world from Europe, where it was first discovered in the 7th/13th century. I 1089a; V 356a; also used in a much wider sense for the 'science and art of caring for the eyes', the equivalent of the ophthalmology of the West at the present day. I 785a

kuhūla (A) : the period of age following that of SHABĀB. IX 383a

ḳūḳī (A) : in numismatics, the term for the early DĪNĀR in North Africa and Spain. II 297b

kūkra (A) : in zoology, the talitrus, a small leaping crustacean, also known as the sand-flea (*Talitrus saltator*), and often used as bait in fishing. VIII 1021b

ḳul (T, pl. *ḳullar*), or *köle* : an old Turkish word which came, in Islamic times, to mean 'slave boy, male slave', also in a religious sense 'slave of God'. However, the original meaning of ~ was that of 'servant, vassal, dependent', slavery in the Islamic juridical sense not existing among the ancient Turks. I 24b; V 359a

Under the Ottomans, the plural *ḳullar* became the standard designation for the Janissaries. V 359a

♦ ḳullar aghasi̊ : the title given to the commander-in-chief of the sovereign's slave forces under the Ottomans and the Persian Ṣafawids alike. V 359b; VIII 770a

♦ **ḳul-og͟hlu** : lit. son of a slave, in Ottoman usage, more specifically the son of a Janissary, admitted to the pay-roll of the corps. In the period of Turkish domination in Algeria and Tunisia, ~ (as *ḳulug͟hlī*, *kulug͟hlī* and, with dissimilation, *ḳurug͟hlī*, *kurug͟hlī* : the French *koulougli* and variants) denoted those elements of the population resulting from marriages of Turks with local women. I 371a; V 366b

ḳula (A) : a children's game mentioned in ancient poetry and described as played with two small wooden boards, one twice as long as the other and the one being hit with the other. The Prophet's uncle al-ʿAbbās is described as having played ~ as a boy, this being in an anecdote intended to show his innate decency. V 615b

külāh (T) : a cap, hat, a very widespread masculine and feminine head-gear in Ottoman Turkey, of which several dozen variants existed. They could be made from felt or woollen cloth combined with other materials such as cotton, fur, small turbans, scarves and trimmings. As to their shape, the most common were caps, head-dresses in the shape of a dome, cone, cylinder broadening towards the top, tube, helmet, brimmed hats with flaps and straps. V 751b

kulliyya (A, T *fakülte,* P *dānis͟hkada*) : lit. completeness. In the 19th century ~ acquired the technical meaning of faculty as a unit of teaching and learning, mostly at the university level, according to branches of learning. II 423a; V 364a

külliyye (T) : in Ottoman usage, the complex of buildings with varying purposes centred round a mosque. The concept of a ~ was inherent in the earliest form of the mosque where one building housed the place of prayer and teaching as well as serving as a hostel. Later, other services were incorporated under one foundation document, and each was housed in its own building within an enclosure. V 366a

ḳulluḳ (T) : one of seven services, to be rendered by the RAʿIYYA to the TĪMĀR-holder (→ SERBEST), such as the provision of hay, straw, wood, etc. II 32a; and → ḲARĀG͟HUL

ḳulug͟hlī, kulug͟hlī → ḲUL-OG͟HLU

ḳūmā (A), or *al-ḳawmā* : the name of one of the seven types of post-classical poetry. It was invented by the people of Baghdad, and it is connected with the *saḥūr*, the last part of the night when, during the month of Ramaḍān, it is still permitted to eat and drink and to take meals at that time. The ~ , which is always in Arabic colloquial, has only been cultivated in ʿIrāḳ, where it has been used to express various themes, such as those of love, wine-drinking, of flower-description, etc. Technically, there are two types: the first is made up of strophes of four hemistichs, of which three (the first, second and fourth) are the same in length and rhyme with each other, while the third is longer and does not rhyme with the rest; and the second is made up of three hemistichs of the same rhyme, but of increasing length. V 372b

ḳumāsh (A, pl. *aḳmisha*) : cloth, any woven stuff, synonymous with the classical words *bazz* and *thiyāb*. V 373b
Under the Mamlūks, ~ took on the specialised meaning of 'dress uniform' although this sense is not found in any dictionary. The Mamlūk ~ must have been a heavy garment, as Mamlūk soldiers threw off their armour and ~ when fleeing the battlefield. V 373b; ~ (pl. *ḳumāshāt*) was also sometimes used in Mamlūk terminology as a synonym for *kanbūsh* or 'caparison' of a horse. V 374b

ḳumbara → KHUMBARA

ḳumbāz (A) : an overgarment, gown, made of striped silk, worn by both sexes in the Arab East. V 741a

kümbed → TURBA

kumis (Rus, < T *ḳi̊mi̊z*) : koumiss, fermented mare's milk, the staple drink of the steppe peoples of Eurasia from the earliest time. V 375b

ḳūmis (A, < L *comes*) : a title which in al-Andalus denoted the Christian responsible to the state for the *muʿāhidūn* or Scriptuaries, or at least, for the Christian Mozarabs. I 491a; V 376a; VIII 834a; ~ was also applied to the counts of the Christian kingdoms. V 377a

ḳummal (A) : a Qurʾānic term usually translated as 'lice', but commentators define it as either crickets or a sort of moth. IV 522a

kunak : the swearing of brotherhood, a custom among the Čerkes tribes of the Caucasus by which a man became a member of another clan. II 23a

kunār → DAWM

kündekārī (T) : a woodwork technique consisting of tongue-and-groove panelling of polygons and stars set in a strapwork skeleton. VIII 968a

kundur → LUBĀN

ḳunfudh (A) : in zoology, the hedgehog and the porcupine. V 389b; and → LAYLAT AL-ḲUNFUDH

- ḳunfudh al-baḥr : in zoology, the edible sea-urchin. V 390b; VIII 1021a
- ḳunfudh baḥrī : in zoology, the beaver. V 390b

kūniya (A), or *ḳūniyā* : the wooden setsquare (syn. *afādhān*) and level used by carpenters and land surveyors in mediaeval times. VII 198b; VII 202a

ḳunnāḥa (A) : a polo-stick and, in general, a curved piece of wood.
In the terminology of ploughmen, ~ refers to a kind of joining pin used to connect the ploughshare (or rather the cross-beam) to the beam, SILB. VII 22b

ḳunūt (A) : 'standing', 'a prayer during the ṢALĀT', a term with various meanings, regarding the fundamental signification of which there is no unanimity among the lexicographers. V 395a; VIII 930b

kunya (A) : patronymic, an onomastic element composed of *abū* 'father' or *umm* 'mother' plus a name, in principle, the eldest son's name, but the ~ can also be composed of the name of a younger son or even of a daughter. IV 179a; V 395b

ḳūpūz (T) : an open chest viol with two strings, which is very popular in Turkestan. VIII 348b

ḳur᾽ (A, pl. *ḳurū᾽*) : a Qur᾽ānic word which is defined both as the inter-menstrual period and as synonymous with *ḥayḍ* 'menstrual indisposition' by the Qur᾽ān commentators. III 1011a; IV 253a

kura (A) : in astronomy, the sphere, globe. V 397a

♦ al-kura al-muḥarriḳa : the burning-glass. V 397b

♦ laʿb al-kura (A) : the game of polo, also called *laʿb al-ṣawlad̲j̲ān* or *al-ḍarb bi 'l-kura*, one of the branches of horse-riding. II 955a

kūra (A, < Gk) : in geography and mediaeval administration, an administrative unit within a province, a district. V 397b; IX 308b; a pagarchy. I 330a; I 1340b; a province. VIII 636a; IX 305b

ḳurʿa (A) : the drawing of lots, whatever form this may take. V 398a

In divination, rhapsodomancy, the interpretation of verses or parts of verses or prophetic words encountered by chance on opening the Qur᾽ān or the *Ṣaḥīḥ* of al-Buk̲h̲ārī. V 398b

ḳurba (A) : an act performed as a means of coming closer to God. VIII 712a; and → ḲARĀBA

ḳurbān (A) : a sacrifice, a sacrificial victim. V 436b

In Christian Arabic, ~ means the eucharist. V 437a

ḳūrči (P, < Mon *ḳorči* 'archer') : a military term with a variety of different meanings: he who bears arms, the sword, chief huntsman; armourer, sword-cutler, troop of cavalry, captain of the watch; leader of a patrol, commandant of a fort, gendarmerie in charge of a city's security; sentry, sentinel, inspector. V 437b

In Ṣafawid usage, ~ denoted a member of the Turcoman tribal cavalry which formed the basis of Ṣafawid military power, and in this sense was therefore synonymous with ḲÏZÏL-BĀS̲H̲. V 437b

ḳūrïltāy (Mon *ḳurilta*) : an assembly of the Mongol princes summoned to discuss and deal with some important questions such as the election of a new K̲H̲ĀN. IV 499b; V 498a

ḳurḳ (N.Afr, pl. *aḳrāḳ*) : cork-soled sandals, distinctly Mag̲h̲ribī. V 743b

kurkī → G̲H̲IRNĪḲ

kurkum (A) : in botany, curcuma. III 461a

kurkūr (A, < Gk, pl. *karākīr*) : a type of large ship used especially for freight, known to the pre-Islamic poets and mentioned still in mediaeval Mesopotamia. VIII 811a

ḳurmūṣ → TIMRĀD

kurr (A) : a measure of capacity used in ʿIrāḳ and Persia in the classical period for weighing great quantities of grains. Its actual weight varied. VI 119b

ḳurra (A) : in pre-Islamic times, a mixture of flour mixed with hair, obtained from spreading the flour on the head and then shaving it, which people in times of famine ate. IV 521b

ḳurṣ (A), or *ḳirṣ* : a metallic cap or crown, often studded with jewels, worn on top of a woman's headdress in the Arab East. V 741a

kursī (A, < Ar) : a seat, in a very general sense (chair, couch, throne, stool, even bench). In the daily life of mediaeval Muslims, it refers more specifically to a stool, i.e. a seat without back or arm-rests. V 509a; a wooden stand with a seat and a desk, the desk for the Qur'ān and the seat for the reader. VI 663b

Among the other objects designated by ~ , the following are examples: a support (stool) on which the turban is deposited during the night; a chair of particular design used by women in childbirth; a stool for daily ablutions; in mediaeval Egypt, a seat for flour-sellers; an astrolabe-stand; a slab into which a pointed instrument is implanted, through the base; in Mecca, a kind of moving ladder (or staircase) near the Kaʿba; among the Persians, a kind of stove (a low 'table', under which a fire is lit. Blankets are laid on this table and then wrapped round the knees to provide warmth); the base of a column, pedestal; a plate supporting the powder compartment and percussion mechanism of the flint-lock rifle; in Spain, small pieces of silver or gold worn by women in their collars and known in Spanish as *corci*; the seat of the bishop, his see, diocese etc. V 509b

In the Qur'ān, ~ tends to be accorded the sense of throne by the commentators, since its function is to bestow a particular majesty on the one who sits there. Nevertheless, ~ need not indicate a seat in the usual sense of the word. There are other interpretations of the term, some allegorical, e.g. the absolute knowledge of God, or his kingdom, some literal, e.g. footstool, a bench set before the throne. V 509a

In astronomy, ~ denotes a triangular piece of metal which is firmly attached to the body of the astrolabe. I 723a

In orthography, ~ signifies each of the characters (*alif*, *wāw*, *yā'*) on (or under) which the *hamza* is placed; in calligraphy, a kind of embellishment in square form. V 509b

♦ kursī al-sūra : the place where the ritual reader of the Qur'ān sits cross-legged in the mosque, not to be confused with DIKKA. II 276a

ḳurṭum (A), and *ʿuṣfur* : in botany, safflower. III 461a

ḳurug̲h̲lī, kurug̲h̲lī → ḲUL

ḳuruḳ (P) : the prohibition of men and boys from any place where the king's wives were to pass. The consequences to those who failed to get out of the way were sometimes fatal. Though probably not a new practice, it was rigorously enforced in Persia under the Ṣafawids. VI 856b

ḳurūn al-sunbul (A) : in botany, ergot. IX 872b

kurūr (A) : the reincarnation of souls, a doctrine professed by the Muʿtazilī Aḥmad b. Ḥābiṭ, which, although differing from Muʿtazilī teachings, found with him justification in the Qur'ān. Its corollary, also professed by him, was the doctrine of the TAKLĪF of animals. I 272a

kurziyya (N.Afr) : a simple winding cloth for the head, distinctly Mag̲h̲ribī. V 743b

ḳus̲h̲aḳ (T) : the ceremony of the girding, carried out during the initiation of apprentices to Turkish tanners' guilds in Anatolia, Rumelia and Bosnia. I 323b

ḳū<u>sh</u>d<u>j</u>i (T) : the profession of falconer, in Ottoman times. I 393a
kū<u>sh</u>k : mud-brick buildings with a central court or domed hall surrounded by living quarters and used as residences of the feudal aristocracy of Central Asia. IX 44b
ḳu<u>sh</u>ḳu<u>sh</u> (A) : the sand-smelt, a small fish, also called *balam* and *haff*. VIII 1023a
kuskusū (A, < B) : couscous, a culinary preparation containing semolina which is the national dish of the peoples of North Africa. The equivalent term among the majority of the Bedouin tribes of Algeria and at Tlemcen is *ṭʿām* used alone, elsewhere it is *ʿay<u>sh</u>*, *mʿā<u>sh</u>*, or *noʿma*. V 527b
kust (P) : quadrant. IX 682b
kusūf (A), or *<u>kh</u>usūf* : the eclipse of the sun or of the moon. *Al-kusūf* is used alike for the eclipse of the moon (*kusūf al-ḳamar*) and for that of the sun (*kusūf al-<u>sh</u>ams*), but they are often distinguished as *al-<u>kh</u>usūf*, eclipse of the moon, and *al-kusūf*, of the sun. V 535b; VIII 931b
♦ ṣalāt al-kusūf : a communal prayer held in the mosque in the event of an eclipse (of the sun or the moon). VIII 931b
ḳuṭʿa → FA<u>SH</u>T
ḳuṭb (A, pl. *aḳṭab*) : a pole, a pivot around which something revolves, e.g. the pivot for mill stones. V 542b
In astronomy, ~ designates the axis of the celestial east-west movement and, more specifically, its two poles. In modern terminology, the terrestrial poles are also called ~ (with adjective *ḳuṭbī* 'polar'). Apart from this, in the construction of the astrolabe ~ (also *miḥwar*, *watad*) signifies the central pivot, or axis, which keeps together its different discs, the spider, and the rule. I 723a; V 542b
In mysticism, ~ denotes either the most perfect human being, *al-insān al-kāmil*, who heads the saintly hierarchy, or else the universal rational principle, *al-ḥaḳīḳa al-muḥammadiyya*, through which divine knowledge is transmitted to all prophets and saints, and which manifests itself in *al-insān al-kāmil*. Each of the various ranks in the saintly hierarchy has also been conceived of as being headed by a ~ . IV 950a; V 543a
ḳu<u>th</u><u>th</u>āʾ (A) : (a kind of) cucumber, one of the Prophet's preferred vegetables, along with some other gourds: *dubbāʾ* 'a kind of marrow' and *ḳarʿ* 'marrow'. II 1058a,b
ḳuṭr (A) : in mathematics, the diameter of a circle or of any section of a cone and the diameter of a cone; the diagonal of a parallelogram or of any quadrilateral; the hypotenuse of the so-called umbra triangle. V 566b
ḳuṭrub (A) : the male of the SIʿLĀT, considered thus by those sources who do not consider the *siʿlāt* to be the female of the <u>GH</u>ŪL, a fabulous being. II 1078b; the werewolf. V 566b
kuttāb (A) : a type of beginners' or primary school; an appellation for the Islamic traditional school, also known as *maktab*. V 567b; VI 196b; and → KĀTIB
kuṭṭaka (H) : 'dispersion'; in mathematics, a method of continued fractions, referred to as early as the 5th century by Āryabhaṭa. I 133a

kutubī → FAYDJ

ḳuʿūd (A) : sitting; the sitting posture in prayer which is the penultimate component of a *rakʿa*. V 572a

ḳuwwa (A) : 'strength, power'; also, a thread which is part of a rope. In its sense of power, ~ plays a role in the discipline of Qurʾānic studies, theology, philosophy, medicine, and human psychology. V 576a

kūz (Egy, pl. *kīzān*) : a long and narrow vessel, often fitted with a handle, which, among its other functions, was used for the preparation or storage of FUḲḲĀʿ, a sparkling drink. VI 721a; bowls. VI 721b

kuzbara : in botany, coriander. IX 615a

kyahi (J), or *kiai* : in Indonesia, a religious teacher, respected old man. VIII 294a; VIII 296b

L

laashin (Somali, pl. *laashinno*) : in the southern, mainly agriculturalist clans of Somalia, specific reciters of poetry who often recite in an extemporised manner. IX 725b

labab → ḲARBŪṢ

labad → ṢŪF

laban (A) : milk. In certain dialects, the distinction has arisen between ḤALĪB, milk, and ~ , fully or partially curdled milk. II 1057b; VI 722a; buttermilk. S 318b

♦ al-labaniyya : a mediaeval dish containing meat and leeks or onion, cooked in milk together with a little powdered rice. VIII 653a

labān → ṢADR

labbāda → LIBDA

lăbda → LIBD

labin (A), or *libn* : unfired brick whose use in building dates back to the earliest antiquity. The ~ generally has a geometric, fairly regular shape, that of a parallel-sided rectangle. The wooden mould into which the dampened clay is put is called *milban*. V 584b

la<u>dj</u>ʾa (A) : in botany, ~ *<u>kh</u>aḍrāʾ* is the green turtle or true chelon (*Chelonia mydas*) and ~ *sahfiyya* is the imbricated chelon (*Chelonia imbricata*). IX 811a

lā<u>dj</u>ward : lapis lazuli. VIII 269a

laffa (A) : a man's turban cloth in the Arab East. V 741a

lafīf (A) : in law, an 'unsifted' witness, neither a virtuous man nor a professional, more a 'man in the street'. I 428a; and → <u>SH</u>AHĀDAT AL-LAFĪF

lafūt (A) : in zoology, a term used for two different types of fish: the lophot

(*Lophotes*) and the unicorn fish (*Lophotes cepedianus*). VIII 1021a; VIII 1021b

lag̲h̲ïm (T) : explosive mines of various types and sizes, an instrument of war used in the Ottoman empire. I 1063a

♦ lag̲h̲ïmd̲j̲ïlar : in Ottoman military, the sappers who, with the aid of the large labour forces set at their disposal, prepared the trenches, earthworks, gun-emplacements and subterranean mines indispensable in siege warfare. I 1062a

lag̲h̲w → ṢILA

♦ lag̲h̲w al-yamīn → YAMĪN

lāgmī : 'palm-wine', a drink in Arabia, extracted from the sap rising in the palm trunk. This very sweet and refreshing liquid ferments quite quickly, becoming charged with alcohol which renders it intoxicating. VII 923b

laḥḥām → D̲J̲AZZĀR

lahīb : in medicine, congestion (there is question as to its exact meaning). IX 9b

lāḥiḳ → ḤUD̲J̲D̲J̲A

laḥn (A) : a manner of speaking.

In grammar, dialectical or regional variation, which was judged contrary to the grammarians' instinctive conception of the norm. Thus, ~ takes on the sense of 'deed of committing faults of language', then of 'perverted use (solecism, barbarism, malapropism, etc.)', and becomes a synonym of K̲H̲AṬAʾ. V 606b; V 804a

In rhetoric, ~ 'letter riddle' is seen as one of the different types of *taʿmiya* 'mystification'. VIII 427a

♦ **laḥn al-ʿāmma** : lit. errors of language made by the common people; in lexicography, a branch designed to correct deviations by reference to the contemporary linguistic norm, as determined by the purists. The treatises which could be classed under this heading, correspond, broadly speaking, to our 'do not say ... but say ...', the incorrect form generally being introduced by 'you say' or 'they say', and the correct form by *wa 'l-ṣawāb* 'whereas the norm is ...'. V 605b; S 388a

lāhūt (A) : divinity, the antithesis of *nāsūt*, humanity. V 611b

In the mystical thought of al-Ḥallād̲j̲, ~ means the incommunicable world of the divine essence, the world of absolute divine transcendence, and therefore absolutely superior to all other 'spheres of existence'. I 351a; V 613a

lāʾiḥa → ḲĀNŪN

lāʾit → LŪṬĪ

laḳab (A, pl. *alḳab*) : nickname or sobriquet, and at a later date under Islam and with more specific use, honorific title. It is usually placed after the NISBA. IV 180a; IV 293b; V 618b; VIII 56a

laḳāniḳ (A, < L), or *naḳāniḳ* : mutton sausages, containing little semolina and sold by *naḳāniḳiyyūn*. II 1063b

lak̲h̲m → KALB AL-BAḤR

lak̲h̲nāʾ → BAẒRĀʾ

laḳīṭ (A) : a foundling, a human child whose parentage and whose status (free or slave) is unknown. I 26a; V 639a; VIII 826b

laksamana → BENDAHARA

laḳwa (A) : facial paralysis. VIII 111b

lala (P) : in Ṣafawid times, a ḲÎZÎL-BĀSH provincial governor, responsible for the physical and moral welfare of the royal prince, in particular the heir-apparent, under his charge, and for training him for his future responsibilities. IV 37a; VIII 770b; a preceptor or tutor. IX 211a

lāla → SHAḲĪḲAT AL-NUʿMĀN

lalamiko (Sw) : in Swahili literature, an elegy. VI 612b

lālla (Mor) : the name for women saints of Berber origin in Morocco. V 1201a

lamṭ (A) : in mediaeval Islam, the oryx of the Sahara. The term is now obsolete. V 651b

lanḍaī → MIṢRĀʿ

landj (A, < Eng 'launch'), or *lansh* : in Kuwayt, a motor launch provided with one or two sails, and employed, though not a great deal, along the Bāṭina, whereas in the Red Sea, the term is found from ʿAḳaba to as far as Ghardaḳa and Port Sudan. VII 53b

langgar (J) : in Indonesia, a small mosque serving for the daily cult and religious instruction alone. VI 700a; the little prayer-cabin near the house. VII 103b

lansh → LANDJ

lārī (P), or *lārīn* : the larin, a silver coin current in the Persian Gulf and Indian Ocean in the 16th and 17th centuries. It takes its name from the town of Lār, the capital of Lāristān at which it was first struck. It weighed about 74 grains, and its shape was a thin silver rod about 4 inches long, doubled back and then stamped on either side. II 120b; V 683b

lāsa (A) : a woman's head scarf of white silk or cotton net into which flat metal strips have been decoratively hammered, worn in Syria and Palestine. V 741b

lashkar (P) : the term normally used by the Indian Muslim rulers for army. V 685a

lāshōn (< Heb, 'tongue, language') : a form of slang used by Jewish traders and artisans. Occasionally it was called *īshūrūni*. This slang was based on the utilisation of a basically Hebrew vocabulary in accordance with completely Arabic morphology and syntax. IV 301b

lāṭī → LŪṬĪ

laṭīm (A) : 'knocked out of the enclosure by a blow', the name for the ninth horse in a race, according to the order of finishing. II 953a

♦ laṭīma (A) : silk. IX 865a

lāṭis (A), or *lūṭis* : in zoology, the Nile perch (*Lates nilotica*). VIII 1021a

lawāṭa-kār → LŪṬĪ

lawḥ (A, pl. *alwāḥ*) : board, plank; tablet, table; school-child's slate; blackboard. V 698a; and → KHASHABA

In the Qurʾān and the pseudoepigraphical literature, ~ has the specific meaning

of the tablet as the record of the decisions of the divine will, which is kept in heaven. It can also mean the tablet as the original copy of the Qurʾān. V 698a
Among the Bahāʾīs, ~ is the name for a letter sent by Bahāʾ Allāh. I 911b

lawn (A) : the general term used to express the concept of colour. Besides this precise sense, it also denotes 'shade', 'aspect', 'type', 'dish (of food)', etc. V 699b

layālī → LAYL

layḳ (A) : ink well. VIII 52a

layl (A, pl. *layālin*) : nighttime, night. V 707b; and → ṢĀḤIB AL-LAYL

♦ laylat al-barāʾa : 'the night of quittancy', i.e. forgiveness of sins, a religious festival, marking the night of mid-Shaʿbān. I 1027b; IX 154a

♦ laylat al-harīr : 'the night of clamour', the name of a violent conflict, on 10 Ṣafar 37/28 July 657, between ʿAlī and Muʿāwiya after a week of combat. I 383b

♦ laylat al-kashfa : in early literature on the Shabak and Ṣarlīs, term referring to the three annual nightly celebrations, in which both sexes take part. IX 153b

♦ laylat al-ḳunfudh, or *laylat al-anḳad* : 'the hedgehog's night', a night racked by insomnia. V 390a

♦ laylat al-maḥyā : a night made alive by devotional activity, MAḤYĀ, which came to denote: 1) the night of 27 Radjab, when religious gatherings were held at the shrine of ʿAlī, in early 8th/14th-century al-Nadjaf, 2) the night of 27 Ramaḍān, when the Ḥarīriyya order commemorated the death of the order's founder, and 3) the night of mid-Shaʿbān in several parts of the Islamic world. VI 88a

♦ layālī (A) : in music, a solo melodic modal improvisation entrusted to the human voice without written music. VI 97a

♦ al-layālī al-bulḳ, or *al-ayyām al-bulḳ* : the forty 'mottled' days, which, in two series of twenty, immediately precede and follow AL-LAYĀLĪ AL-SŪD and during which the cold is less severe. V 708a

♦ al-layālī al-sūd : lit. the black nights, e.g. the very cold period which begins in December and ends forty days later. V 708a

layṭ (A), and *nadjr, khuṭba* : a term applied to a dirty colour, a mixture of two blended colours. V 699b

lāzim (A) : in law, 'binding'. I 319b; VIII 836a

lebaran (Ind) : 'end, close'; the name generally used in Indonesia for the ʿĪD AL-FIṬR, the 'minor festival'. The expression *lebaran haji* is sometimes used for the ʿĪD AL-AḌḤĀ, the 'major festival'. V 714b

leff (A) : a term used in the Berber-speaking regions of central and southern Morocco (a different term is used in a similar way in Berberophone regions of northern Morocco, and *ṣoff* appears to be its equivalent in Kabylia) to denote a kind of political alliance or party, which were invoked, like military alliances, when violent conflict occurred: members of the same ~ were expected to give support to each other, when any one of them became involved in conflict with opponents from the other ~ . V 715a

lewend (T, < ? It *levantino*) : two kinds of Ottoman daily-wage irregular militia, one sea-going (*deñiz*), the other land-based (*ḳarā*), both existing from early times. The land-based ~ were further divided into *ḳapîlî lewend*, *ḳapîsîz lewend*, and *mīrī lewend*. V 728a

liʿān (A) : 'cursing', 'oath of imprecation'; in law, the oath which gives a husband the possibility of accusing his wife of adultery without legal proof and without his becoming liable to the punishment prescribed for this, and the possibility also of denying the paternity of a child borne by the wife. It frees the husband and wife from the legal punishment for respectively ḲADHF and incontinence. I 1150b; IV 689a; V 730b

libās (A, pl. *lubus*, *albisa*) : clothing, apparel. V 732a; in Egypt, ~ acquired the general meaning of 'drawers' for men. IX 677b

libd (A, pl. *lubūd*), or *labad* : felt; moquette saddle, or a piece of felt put under the saddle. V 798a

♦ lăbda : in Morocco, a small felt carpet, favoured by the middle classes for performing the *sudjūd*. ~s are especially used by FAḲĪHs and have almost beome one of their distinctive marks. VIII 741a

♦ libda, or *labbāda* : a felt cap worn by men in the Arab East. V 741b

libn → LABIN

libna (A) : in astronomy, a large mural quadrant. VIII 574a

lidjām (A) : the harness of the horse, which includes the reins, *ʿinān*, the cheek straps, *idhār*, and the browband, *ʿiṣāb*. II 954a; also, the curb bit, used to rein horses suddenly or make swift turns. II 953a

līḳ (A) : the black powder of collyrium. VIII 52a

liman reʾīsi (T) : 'captain of the port', an admiral in the Ottoman navy. He was also commander of the midshipmen (*mandedji*). VIII 565b

līmanda (A) : in zoology, the dab, the nomenclature of which was drawn directly from Greco-Roman (*Limanda*). VIII 1021a

līmī (A) : in zoology, the umbra limi, whose Arabic term is found again in the Latinised nomenclature to specify a sub-species limited to a particular region (*Umbra limi*). VIII 1021b

limma (A) : in zoology, the limma ray, whose Arabic term is found again in the Latinised nomenclature to specify a sub-species limited to a particular region (*Raia lymma*). VIII 1021b; and → ṢUDGH

lisān (A) : tongue; language. V 805a; an oral message. VIII 532a

In the language of scales and balances, ~ is the pointer (on a scale). V 295b

♦ ʿilm al-lisān, or *lisāniyyāt* : linguistics. V 806b

liṣṣ (A, P *duzd*, Ott *khayrsîz*, T *hırsız*; pl. *luṣūṣ*) : thief, robber (syn. *sāriḳ*). V 767b; IX 866a

lithām (A, Touareg *tegulmust*, *shāsh*) : the mouth-veil, a piece of material with which the Bedouin concealed the lower part of the face, the mouth and sometimes also part of the nose. It served the practical purpose of protecting the organs of respiration from heat and cold as well as against the penetration of dust. It also made the face unrecognisable, and thus formed a protection against the avenger of blood. The ~ has no considerable importance for Islam from the purely religious point of view. V 744a; V 769a

liwā → LIWĀʾ

liwāʾ (A, T *liwā*) : a banner, flag, standard. I 349a; an army brigade, both under the Ottomans and in the Iraqi army, *amīr al-liwāʾ* being a brigadier (as in Egypt until 1939). V 776a; VIII 370b

Under the Ottomans, *liwā* indicated a province, several of which were at a certain moment joined into an EYĀLET, later *wilāyet*. Synonymous with *sandjaḳ*, ~ was mainly used in official documents. Accordingly, *mīr liwā* (< A *amīr al-liwāʾ*) stood for *sandjaḳ begi*, the governor and military commander of a ~ . Of all the states issued from the Ottoman empire, only Iraq kept the term ~ (up till 1974) to indicate a province. V 776a

♦ liwāʾ-i sherīf → SANDJAḲ-I SHERĪF

līwān (A) : at times the spoken Arabic form of ĪWĀN, generally furnished with carpets and divans. II 114b; in India, ~ is the usual name for the western end of a mosque, directed towards Mecca. VI 689b

liwāṭ → LŪṬĪ

lol (Kash) : a love lyric in Kashmiri poetry. S 333a

luʾama (A) : a rather imprecise term which would designate on the one hand all the parts of the tiller, whether of wood or iron, and on the other hand only the ploughshare, which is not very likely, or, more probably, like *silb*, the beam tied to the cross-beam at a point called *djidār*. VII 22b

lubān (A), and *kundur* : frankincense. V 786a; VIII 1042b

lūd (Tun) : a boat devised by the islanders of Ḳarḳana, an archipelago lying off the eastern coast of Tunisia, where the shallows extend very far out to sea. The ~ is broad, without a keel and therefore well adapted to the contours of the sea-bed. IV 651b

luffāḥ → SIRĀDJ AL-ḲUṬRUB

lugha (A) : speech, language. IV 122a; V 803a

♦ (ʿilm al-)lugha : lexicology or, more exactly, the science of the datum of the language. IV 524a; V 806a; lexicography. VIII 614a

♦ fiḳh al-lugha : a synonym of *ʿilm al-lugha*, but it seems likely that this was a more specialised branch of the same discipline, that is, the study of the semiological distinctions and affinities which exist between the elements of vocabulary. IV 524a; V 806a

♦ al-lugha al-makhzaniyya : the language of the Moroccan government, a correct Arabic intermediate between the literary and the spoken Arabic, composed of official formulae, regular clichés, courteous, concise and binding to nothing. VI 136b

lughz (A, pl. *alghāz*) : enigma, a literary play on words. The ~ is generally in verse, and characteristically is in an interrogative form. Thus, for *falak* 'heavenly firmament' : 'What is the thing which in reality has no existence, but nevertheless you see it in existence wherever you confront it [...] and if we cut off its head (= *fa*), it will be yours (= *lak*)?'. V 806b

luḥma → SADĀ

lukāṭ (A) : in art, a mosaic of coloured tiles, as found in the Alhambra. I 500a

luḳaṭa (A) : in law, an article found. V 809b

lüle (T) : a measure of capacity traditionally defined as the amount of water passing through a pipe of given dimensions in 24 hours, or approximately 60 m^3. V 882a

luʾluʾ (A, pl. *laʾāliʾ*, *laʾālī*), and *durr* : pearl. The difference between the two synonyms cannot be defined with precision, although some say that the ~ is a pierced pearl and the *durr* the unpierced one. V 819a; the word for pearl-trader can only be derived from ~ : *laʾʾāl* or *laʾʾāʾ*. V 820a

lūra (A), or *lūrā* : a wooden, pear-shaped instrument of five strings, played by the Byzantines and identical with the *rabāb* of the Arabs. VIII 347b; and → ḲITHĀRA

luṭf (A) : a Qurʾānic term, derivatives of which are used in the two senses of 'kind' and 'subtle', the opposite of KHIDHLĀN. V 833b

In theology, ~ is applied to the notion of divine grace, favour or help, being developed by the Muʿtazila to deal with an aspect of human freedom and its relation to divine omnipotence. Divine favour makes it possible for man to act well and avoid evil. V 833b

luthgha (A) : in grammar, a deviation in the pronunciation of a number of phonemes (not exclusively *ghayn*, as is often believed). V 804a

lūṭī (A, pl. *lāṭa*), or *lāʾiṭ* : a homosexual playing the active part in the act of sodomy, *liwāṭ*, as opposed to the *maʾbūn*, the passive partner, who practices *ubna*. V 776b

In current Persian, ~ (also *lāṭī*, *lawāṭa-kār*) denotes an itinerant entertainer accompanied by a monkey, bear or goat, which dances to the sound of a drum and coarse songs. This, however, appears to have been a late restriction of the meaning of the term, deriving perhaps from its earlier use to describe a jester attached to a royal or princely court. In other contexts, it is equivalent to a loose liver, gambler, and wine-bibber. V 839a

lūṭis → LĀṬIS

luṭṭ (A) : in zoology, the burbot (*Lota lota*). VIII 1021a

luzūm mā lā yalzam (A), and *iʿnāt*, *iltizām* : 'observing rules that are not prescribed'; in prosody, the term commonly used for the adoption of a second, or even a third or fourth, invariable consonant preceding the rhyme consonant, *rawī*, which, at least in classical poetry, remains itself invariable. The term is also used in dealing with rhymed prose, *sadjʿ*. In later Arabic and Persian literary theory the term also covers a variety of other devices which have nothing to do with the end rhyme. V 839b

In Persian rhetoric and prosody, the terms ~ and *iʿnāt* are used, as in Arabic, for the adoption of a second invariable consonant in prose and in poetry, and the reduplication of the rhyme consonant. In addition, however, the two terms are used for the repetition of two or more words in each hemistich or line of poetry, and for the use of internal rhyme. V 841a

M

māʾ (A) : water. V 859b; and → DJUBN

In medicine, ~ is used as a technical term for cataract: *māʾ nāzil fī ʾl-ʿayn*. I 785b

maʿād (A) : lit. place of return, a technical term in religious and philosophical vocabulary, bringing together the two senses of return and recommencement: return to the source of being which is God, and a second creation which is the Resurrection. V 894b; a synonym of ĀKHIRA, the Hereafter. I 325a; eschatology. IX 208b

maʿānī (A, s. MAʿNĀ) : meanings; contents. I 784b; V 320b ff.

♦ **al-maʿānī wa ʾl-bayān** (A) : two of the three categories into which, since the time of al-Sakkākī (d. 626/1229), the study of rhetoric has often been divided, the other being BADĪʿ. *ʿIlm al-bayān* can be best translated with ‘science of figurative speech’, as it only deals with the simile (as an introduction to the discussion of metaphor), the metaphor, the analogy, the metonymy and the allusion, and statement by implication. *ʿIlm al-maʿānī* indicates a set of rather strict rules governing the art of correct sentence structure, the purpose of which was to demonstrate that changes in word order almost invariably lead to changes in meaning. I 858a; I 1114a; V 898a; VIII 894a

♦ al-maʿānī al-thāniya → MAʿNĀ

maanso (Somali) : a genre of poetry, handling serious themes, sometimes referred to as ‘classical poetry’ by English-speaking scholars. Less ‘serious’ poetry, such as work and dance songs, is called *hees*. ~ is composed by named individuals. IX 725b

maʿārif (A, s. MAʿRIFA) : education, public instruction. The term was already used in mediaeval times to denote the secular subjects of knowledge or culture in general, in opposition to the religious sciences, *ʿulūm* (→ ʿILM). Starting from the 19th century, ~ came into use in Egypt and Iran to denote public education and kept this notion until the 1950s; ~ in the sense of education has died out in official usage, steadily being replaced by *tarbiya*. It seems that the same process is taking place in non-official usage. V 902b

maʾāṣir → MARĀṢID; MAʾṢIR

maʿaskar → ʿASKAR

maʾāt̲h̲ir → MAT̲H̲ĀLIB

mā baʿd al-ṭabīʿa (A, < trans. Gk τὰ μετὰ τὰ φυσικά), or *mā baʿd al-ṭabīʿiyyāt* : metaphysics, an expression which denotes either the discipline which one embarks upon after physics, utilising the results of the natural sciences, or else it can be one whose goal lies beyond the apprehendable objects which are the concern of physics. V 841a

mābeyn (T, < A *mā bayn* 'what is between') : the intermediate apartments of the Ottoman palace, lying between the inner courts of the palace and the harem, a place where only the sultan, the eunuchs and the womenfolk could penetrate and where the corps of select pages known as *mābeynd̲j̲is* waited on the monarch for such intimate services as dressing and shaving him. V 938b

mablūʿ → ʿANBAR

mabsūṭ (A) : a literary type which multiplies detail and argument, in contrast to MUK̲H̲TAṢAR, which synthesises and compresses. IX 324a

maʾbūn → LŪṬĪ

maḍāfa → MANZIL

madar (A) : the term designating in classical Arabic the mortar used to point unfired brick. It is made of earth with an admixture of lime or ash. ~ also refers to the construction of earth and *labin*, unfired brick. V 585a; and → AHL AL-MADAR

♦ madara : a village built of *labin*, unfired brick. V 585a

madār (A) : in the science of Tradition, a term used to indicate that certain MATNs, or *matn* clusters, are due to one particular transmitter who is held responsible for disseminating these to a number of pupils. VIII 517a

madd (A), and *nazʿ al-watar* : in archery, the draw, drawing of a bow. This consists of bringing the bow-string back towards oneself. This technique has variants in terms of the anchor-point selected, which can be at different levels: eyebrow, earlobe, moustache, chin, sternum. IV 800b

In music, the sustaining of notes. IX 101a

♦ **al-madd wa 'l-d̲j̲azr** : lit. the ebb and the flow, the name given to the phenomenon of the tide. V 949b

mādda → HAYŪLĀ

maddāḥ (A, T *meddāḥ*) : lit. panegyrist; in Ottoman usage, the professional storytellers of the urban milieux. The Persians used ~ in the same way, but more rarely; as for the Arabs, they used it, in a fairly late period, to designate the 'begging singers of the streets'. III 367b; V 951a; in Egypt, a folk poet, associated primarily with a religious repertory. IX 235b

In North Africa, the *məddāḥ* is a kind of religious minstrel who goes to festivals to sing the praises of saints and of God, and holy war, and who is accompanied on the tambourine and flute. V 951a

maddūḥ (A) : a drink made by Bedouin, when dying of thirst in the desert, from a slaughtered camel's blood, which had been beaten carefully so as to separate the sediment from the serum, which was then drunk. S 189b

madḥ → MADĪḤ

madhhab (A, pl. *madhāhib*) : a way of thinking, persuasion; the four schools of law in orthodox Islam, viz. the Ḥanafī, Mālikī, Shāfiʿī and Ḥanbalī. Some other later schools, such as the Ẓāhiriyya founded by Dāwūd b. Khalaf al-Ẓāhirī, the traditionists and a short-lived one founded by al-Ṭabarī, were also called ~ . II 890a; IX 323a

Among the Wahbi Ibāḍiyya, who call themselves *ahl al-madhhab* or *ahl al-daʿwa*, ~ is the equivalent of DAʿWA. II 170a

♦ madhhab al-ḥaḍarāt : the name for the Plotinian scheme of dynamic emanation. III 51b

madḥiyya (T, < A) : in Turkish prosody, the ~ or eulogy is the couplet which comprises the central part of the ḲAṢĪDA. IV 715b; ~ also is used to designate any poem composed for the purpose of extolling an individual, including the *nefes* or *ilāhī* types of poems written or uttered by members of the mystic orders to eulogise God or leading personalities of these religious brotherhoods, and the secular poems circulated by the literary innovators of the last century. V 957a

maʾdhūn (A) : in law, a slave authorised by his master either to conclude an individual sale, or generally to engage in trade. I 29a; I 1112a; III 50b

Among the Ismāʿīlīs, ~ was the name for subordinates to a DĀʿĪ who were licensed to preach. II 97b

māḍī (A) : in grammar, the preterite, a technical term used to denote the verbal form that normally, but not solely, is devoted to the expression of past time. V 954b

madīd (A) : in prosody, the name of the third Arabic metre. I 670a

madīḥ (A, P *ḳaṣīda-yi madīḥa*), or *madḥ* : the genre of the panegyric poetry in Arabic and other Islamic literatures, the individual poem being usually referred to as *umdūḥa* (pl. *amādīḥ*) or *madīḥa* (pl. *madāʾiḥ*). A panegyric can be an independent unit as well as a component of a larger literary work, usually the ḲAṢĪDA. In the latter case, ~ is the technical term used to refer to the section of the poem devoted to the praise of God, the Prophet, the sultan, the grand vizier, etc. IV 714b; V 931a; V 955a ff.

In Urdu poetry, the specifically secular eulogy, addressed to rulers, governors, nobles, and other rich or influential lay persons, was usually termed *madḥ* rather than ~ . Other terms were *taʿrīf* and *sitāʾish*. ~ could also refer to a eulogy of religious persons, living or dead, although praise of God, the Prophet, ʿAlī and subsequent shīʿī IMĀMs had their own terminology. V 958a

maḍīḳ (A) : shallows or a ford. I 215a

maʿdin (A, pl. *maʿādin*) : mine, ore, mineral, metal. In modern Arabic, however, ~ is mostly used for metal, *mandjam* meaning mine, *muʿaddin*, miner, and *djamād*, mineral. V 963b

madīna (A) : the lower town (L *suburbium, pars inferior civitatis*). IX 411a; and → ḲAṢABA

maḍīra (A) : a dish of meat cooked in sour milk, sometimes with fresh milk added, and with spices thrown in to enhance the flavour. This dish seems to have been quite well sought-after in mediaeval times. V 1010a

mad̲j̲āz (A) : interpretation, paraphrase. I 158b

In rhetoric, a term meaning trope and, more generally, the use of a word deviating from its original meaning and use, its opposite being ḤAḲĪḲA. III 898b; V 1025b

♦ mad̲j̲āz-i mursal (P, T) : free trope, or the trope that is not based on a similarity of form but on abstract relationships (between a condition and the place where it manifests itself, a whole and its parts, a cause and its effects, etc.). V 1027a ff.

mad̲j̲būb → K̲H̲ĀṢĪ

mad̲j̲būr (A) : in later As̲h̲ʿarite theology, the term for when human free choice, which is only acquisition, also remains without true ontological freedom, and is thus compulsory. III 1037b

mad̲j̲d → S̲H̲ARAF

mad̲j̲d̲h̲ūb (A) : lit. the attracted one, a term in mysticism for the name for the representative of a type of piety which is chiefly of a passive nature, in contradistinction to the more active 'striding one', *sālik*, a characteristic which is expressed in numerous pairs of oppositions. While the ~ , on the way to God, may abandon himself to be drawn by divine attraction, the *sālik* depends on his own exertions, which is, however, in the same way as the attraction, a gift of God. Usually, mixed forms occur, as in 'the strider who is attracted' and the 'attracted one who is striding'. In more recent literature in particular, ~ is a frequently used extenuating and exculpating designation of eccentric ecstatics, love-maddened persons, holy fools, and despisers of the law. V 1029a

mad̲j̲dūḥ (A) : the blood of a sacrificed camel. III 666b

mad̲j̲hūl (A) : in the science of Tradition, a traditionist who is unknown either as regards his person, or his reliability. III 26b; VIII 516b

In grammar, the ~ is the verb whose agent is not known or, if known, remains unexpressed and cannot be expressed. II 897a

mad̲j̲hūra (A) : 'voiced'; in grammar, ~ signifies the manner of articulation of the letters of the alphabet. Its opposite is *mahmūsa* 'unvoiced'. III 598a

mad̲j̲lis (A, pl. *mad̲j̲ālis*) : a term meaning a meeting place, meeting assembly, a reception hall (of a caliph, high dignitary or other personage) and a session which is held there, a hall in which a professor's courses are given or a judge's sentences delivered (hence 'praetorium, tribunal'), or further where the debates of an assembly take place (hence 'council'). V 1031a; ~ assumed the modern connotation of parliament in the 19th century, as the concept of parliamentarism became widespread, thanks to the impact of Western influence on the Middle East. V 1033b

Among the Ismāʿīlīs, ~ referred to a formal session of religious instruction, the place of it, and also to the lecture or sermon read in it by a DĀʿĪ to the faithful. V 1033a

Among the Indian shīʿīs, ~ is especially used for the shīʿī mourning assemblies held during Muḥarram to commemorate the tragedy of Karbalāʾ. V 1033a; the collective term for the stationary shīʿī commemorative rituals is *madjālis al-ʿazāʾ*. VIII 465a

♦ madjlis al-ʿaḳd : in law, the contractual meeting, in which and at which time the contract must be concluded. I 319a

♦ madjlis ḥīrī : in architecture, a portico with three doors fronting the T-shaped reception hall common in ʿAbbāsid residences from Sāmarrā to Egypt, called after the city of al-Ḥīra. VIII 545a

♦ **madjlis al-shūrā** : the name given to extraordinary, ad hoc consultative assemblies in the Ottoman empire, taking place between the Russo-Ottoman war of 1768-74 and, roughly, the abolition of the Janissaries in 1826. V 1082b

madjmaʿ (A, pl. *madjmāmiʿ*) : lit. a place of collecting, a place in which people collect, assemble, congregate. Whereas *madjlis* had been the current term in earlier Arab civilisation for [the place of] an informal literary gathering and developed the meaning of 'council', ~ came to be used in the second half of the 19th century for private academies and clubs which met to discuss language and literature as well as other problems. Although they were short-lived, they eventually gave rise to the founding of still-existing official academies all over the Middle East. V 1090a

madjmūʿa (A, T *medjmūʿa*) : in Persian literature, a technical term most often referring to a volume of prose texts by more than one author. VII 528b; in Turkish literature, *medjmūʿa* was used until the Tanẓīmāt period to represent the genre of anthology, as well as a collection of either verse or prose or a mixture of both. After the Tanẓīmāt, ~ meant a periodical or journal, but now *dergi* is used for this purpose. VII 531a

madjnūn (A, pl. *madjānīn*) : possessed, mad, madman; DJINN-possessed. V 1101a

madjrā (A), or *mudjrā* : in prosody, the vowel of the *rawī*, rhyme letter. IV 412a

A measure of distance, ~ measures at the most 150 km/100 miles. II 1121b

maʿdjūn (A) : in medicine, an electuary. IX 805a

madjzūʾ (A) : in prosody, a deviation consisting of one DJUZʾ missing in each of the two hemistiches. I 671a; VIII 421a

maḍmūn (A) : in law, the thing for which one is liable or responsible, occurring in the following connections: *maḍmūn bihi* 'thing pawned', *maḍmūn ʿanhu* 'debtor', *maḍmūn lahu* or *ʿalayhi* 'creditor'. V 1121b; and → ḌAMĀN

maḍrab (A) : in music, a wooden stick covered with tow or cotton and held by the musician between thumb and index finger, used with the SANṬŪR 'dulcimer'. IX 19b

madraḳa (A) : a variety of tunic, THAWB, worn by Jordanian women. V 741b

madrasa (A) : a school, in the sense of both institution and place of learning.

In modern usage, ~ is specifically the name of an institution and place of learning where the Islamic sciences are taught, i.e. a college for higher studies, as opposed to an elementary school of traditional type, *kuttāb*. In mediaeval usage, ~ was essentially a college of law in which the other Islamic sciences, including literary and philosophical ones, were ancillary subjects only. I 593a; V 1123a; in Persia in the 5th/11th century, ~ could mean a centre for ṣūfis. IV 1025b

In Indonesia, ~ is also used for the traditional boarding school, *pesantren*. III 1227b

maʿdūm → SHAYʾIYYA

mafākhir → MATHĀLIB

mafārīd → FARD

mafḳūd (A) : in law, a person who at a given moment is not present at the place where he should be and concerning whose existence there is uncertainty. Without the uncertainty, he is called *ghāʾib*. If his absence extends to a period when persons of the same generation as him are dead, the judge declares him dead; his estate then goes to his heirs and his marriage or marriages are dissolved. II 995b

mafradj (A) : in Yemeni architecture, the top storey of a multi-storey tower house, used as a second reception room and for the daily afternoon ḲĀT-chewing ritual. IX 2b

mafrash → MIFRASH

mafrūk (A) : lit. twisted; in archery, ~ denotes a way of loosing an arrow, involving a light, partial draw, a brief moment at rest, and then a sudden end to the draw followed immediately by the loose. IV 800b

mafṣūl (A, < *vassal* ?) : a term used to denote certain juridical categories of landed estates in Syria in the time of the Mamlūks. V 1159a

mafʿūl bihi (A) : in grammar, the direct object. VIII 384a

mag (Somali) : in Somali society, the payment of blood money, traditionally in livestock. IX 713b

maghānī (A), or *aghānī* : a pair of loggias that flank a reception hall on both sides and which were intended for the singers and musicians, who traditionally performed behind curtains or screens. VI 719a

maghāriba (A) : the Arab-speakers of the Muslim West, as opposed to the *mashāriḳa*, those of the East. The frontier between the two major groupings, which includes Muslim Spain, in spite of its special circumstances and its separate destiny, was, and still is, located to the east of Tripoli, at Lebda. V 1159a

maghāzī (A), also *maghāzī ʾl-nabī*, *maghāzī rasūl allāh* : a term which signifies in particular the expeditions and raids organised by the Prophet Muḥammad in the Medinan period. In a broader sense, it refers to the Prophet's general biography and background. V 1161b; VIII 53a

maghnam (A) : either the mass of the booty or that part of it which goes to the central government. II 1005a; VIII 496b

maghnāṭīs (A, < Gk) : magnetite (lodestone, magnetic iron ore, Fe_3O_4); compass, also called *ḥuḳḳ al-ḳibla* (box for the *ḳibla*), *bayt al-ibra* (house of the needle), and the modern *ḥikk*. V 1166b

maghrib (A) : that part of Africa which Europeans have called Barbary or Africa Minor and then North Africa, including Tripolitania, Tunisia, Algeria and Morocco; the west, the setting sun. V 1183b; Morocco, which name is a deformation of the southern metropolis of the kingdom, Marrākush. The country's full name is *al-mamlaka al-maghribiyya*. V 1184a; and → MAṬLAʿ

♦ ṣalāt al-maghrib : the sunset prayer which is to be performed, according to the law books, in between the time after sunset and the time when the red twilight, *shafaḳ*, has disappeared. There are small deviations only, in connection with a predilection for the first term. VII 27b; VIII 928b

♦ maghribī → KŪFĪ

magnahuli : a kind of WAḲF, in favour of women only, existing on the island of Great Comore. I 170a

mahā → BAḲAR

maḥabba (A) : love of the soul and of God. III 84a; IV 94b; and → AKLAT AL-MAḤABBA

In the Čishtī mystical doctrine, the following kinds of ~ are distinguished: *maḥabbat-i islāmī* 'love which a new convert to Islam develops with God on account of his conversion to the new faith', *maḥabbat-i khāṣṣ* 'love which is the result of cosmic emotion, and which should be developed by the mystic', and *maḥabbat-i muwahhibī* 'love which a man develops as a result of his 'effort' in the way of following the Prophet'. II 55b

maḥāla (A, pl. *maḥāl*) : the huge pulley which is used for raising water from wells. In Egypt, the word is also used to denote a water-wheel for irrigation, comparable to the NĀʿŪRA. V 864a

maḥall (A) : lit. place of alighting, settling, abode. V 1214b; in philosophy, the thing qualified. III 571a

In the Mughal empire, a subdivision (syn. PARGANA) of a *sarkār* 'district' and the lowest fiscal unit. I 317a; also in the context of Islamic India, ~ is widely used in the sense of 'palace pavilion' or 'hall', and more particularly of private apartments in the palace, the *maḥall-sarā*; hence also a queen or consort. V 1214b; IX 46b

♦ **maḥalla** (A, T *maḥalle*) : a place where one makes a halt, where one settles (for a longer or shorter time); a quarter of a town, especially in Turkish, Persian and Urdu. IV 229b; V 1220b; characteristically, the Ottoman *maḥalle* consisted of a religious community grouped around its mosque (or church or synagogue) and headed by its religious chief. V 1222b

In North Africa, ~ designates a movable camp, then, by extension, the troops on campaign within the territory at least nominally dependent on the sovereign who commands them or entrusts the command to the heir apparent, another member of the royal family or, exceptionally, to a confirmed war commander. V 1220b

maḥāra → SARAṬĀN

maḥāris → MANĀẒIR

al-maḥāsin wa 'l-masāwī (A) : lit. merits and faults. A literary genre which developed in the course of the first centuries of the Islamic period, having originated within the Arabo-Muslim heritage, although some scholars have concluded, ill-advisedly, that it was inspired by an ancient Iranian model. Two categories of ~ may be distinguished: MUNĀẒARA 'theological debate' and MUFĀKHARA, MUNĀẒARA 'secular debate'. V 1223b

maḥḍar (A) : decree. I 117a; and → SIDJILL

mahdī (A) : lit. the rightly guided one. The name of the restorer of religion and justice who, according to a widely-held Muslim belief, will rule before the end of the world. Throughout Islamic history there has been a recurrence of Mahdī movements. In early days, the best known Mahdī was Ibn Tumart, the founder of the Almohad movement; in modern times, the Sudanese Muḥammad al-Mahdī. In radical shīʿism, belief in the coming of the Mahdī of the family of the Prophet became a central aspect of the faith. V 1230b; V 1247b

mahdjar (A) : the name given to places in Northern, Central and Southern America to which Lebanese, Syrians, Palestinians and other Arabs have emigrated. V 1253a

maḥdjūr → ḤADJR

maḥfil (A) : the term for a freemason lodge. S 286a

maḥfūr (A, pl. *maḥāfīr*) : common to the Syrian desert, an open, ring-shaped storage dam built along the edges of a silt flat, KHABRĀʾ, with an up-stream opening, where, after the central hollowed-out depression has been coated with silt, the water can be naturally stored for a long time, occasionally lasting throughout the entire dry summer season. IV 897b

♦ maḥfūra : a carpet that is decorated with a relief design. S 136a

maḥfūẓ (A) : lit. committed to memory; in the science of Tradition, an acceptable Tradition which, when compared with one which is SHĀDHDH, a Tradition from a single authority which differs from what others report, is considered of greater weight. III 26b

māhī zahrah (P) : lit. fish poison; in botany, *Anamirta cocculus* or *Menospirmum cocculus*. IX 872b

māhin → MIḤNA

māhiyya (A) : quiddity; in logic, that which replies to the question: what is this? I 513b; V 1261a

In theology and metaphysics, ~ is that through which a thing is what it is. In this sense, the term is synonymous with essence, *dhāt*, and with reality, *ḥaḳīḳa*. V 1261a

maḥkama (A) : a court of justice. VI 1a

maḥlūl (A) : vacant. In Ottoman administration, ~ is used in the registers of a grant or office which has been vacated by the previous holder, by death, dismissal, or transfer, and not yet re-allocated. The term is also used more generally for land and other assets left without heir. VI 44b

maḥmal (A) : a type of richly decorated palanquin, perched on a camel and serving in the past to transport people, especially noble ladies, to Mecca. VI 44b
In a more restricted and precise, political sense, ~ designates palanquins of this same type which became political symbols and were sent from the 7th/13th century by sovereigns with their caravans of pilgrims to Mecca (or the principal caravan when it was split up) in order to bolster their prestige. VI 44b

mahmūsa → MADJHŪRA

mahr (A) : in law, the gift which the bridegroom has to give the bride when the contract of marriage is made and which becomes the property of the wife. I 209a; VI 78b; VIII 27b
In the pre-Islamic period, the ~ was the purchase price of the bride and was handed over to her legal guardian; the bride received none of it. She was given the **ṣadāḳ**, a voluntary gift, not as a result of the contract. In the period shortly before Muḥammad, however, the ~ , or at least a part of it, seems already to have been given to the women. According to the Qur'ān, this is already the prevailing custom. By this amalgamation of ~ and *ṣadāḳ*, the original significance of the ~ as the purchase price was weakened and became quite lost in the natural course of events. VI 79a
♦ mahr al-mithl : a bridal gift fixed by the ḲĀḌĪ according to the circumstances of the bridegroom, when the *mahr* is not fixed at the conclusion of the marriage contract and when the parties cannot agree upon it. VIII 27b

maḥras → MASHLAḤ

maḥrem (A), or *mḥarram* : the compartment in a Bedouin tent reserved for the womenfolk. Here, the cooking is done and the provisions stored. The other compartment is for receiving menfolk. IV 1148b

mahriyya (A) : the méhara, a species of camel famed for its speed and the slimness of its limbs and body. III 666a

maḥsūsāt (A) : sensibilia. III 509a; VI 87a

māḥūz (A) : 'space between two armies'; ~ could be applied to a maritime forward post in relation to the city by which it was controlled and was used to describe the port of two small cities on the Palestinian coast, Ghazza and Azdūd. VIII 502a

maḥw → ITHBĀT

maḥyā (A) : in mysticism, a communal nightly liturgical ritual in which the recital of supplications for divine grace for the Prophet is central. VI 87b; the name among the Demirdāshiyya order for their ḤAḌRA. S 208b; and → LAYLAT AL-MAḤYĀ

mai (Kanuri) : term for a Muslim ruler among the Sefawa in Central Africa, the first of whom was probably from the 5th/11th century. IV 567a

♦ mai wallafa wakoki, or *mai waka* (Hau) : a Muslim poet. IX 244a

mā'ida → KHUWĀN

mā'il → KŪFĪ

ma'īshet → KHIDMET AKČESĪ

mā'iza (A) : in zoology, the goat, with *shiyāh al-ma'z*. S 316b

makā'id → ḤIYAL

maḳāla (A, pl. *maḳālāt*) : an article, published in a newspaper or periodical, in Arabic, Persian and Turkish. V 90a; originally, an oral message. VIII 532a
In Persian, ~ has been used to denote a collection of discourses, spoken or written, on a given subject; it was used in reference to spoken discourses and sermons up to the late 19th century. ~ has also been used to designate a book's inner divisions, while its plural, *maḳālāt*, has also been used for the utterances, statements and dictations of ṣūfī SHAYKHs. VI 91b

maḳām (A, pl. *maḳāmāt*) : lit. place, position, rank.
In music, ~ began to appear in Islamic musical treatises at the end of the 'Abbāsid period, to designate Arabo-Irano-Turkish and assimilated musical modes, and is still predominantly used today. VI 96b; VIII 2b
In mysticism, *maḳāmāt* are the progressive stations that the soul has to attain in its search for God. III 83b
In architecture, ~ can denote a little chapel and a saint's tomb. VI 651b
♦ al-maḳām al-'irāḳī : a typically 'Irāḳī genre whose poem is entrusted to a solo singer and the accompaniment to an instrumental quartet from the beginning to the finale. VI 101b

maḳāma (A, pl. *maḳāmāt*) : an Arabic literary genre of rhymed prose, created by al-Hamadhānī (358-98/968-1008). Translation of ~ with 'assembly' or 'session' does not convey exactly the complex nature of the term. The structure of the ~ is characterised by the existence of a hero, whose adventures and eloquent speeches are related by a narrator to the author who, in turn, conveys them to his readers. Many later imitators of al-Hamadhānī, however, were to dispense with the hero, if not with both characters. VI 107a ff.

maḳbūḍ → ḲABḌ

maḳbūl (A) : in the science of Tradition, an acceptable Tradition which fulfils the requirements, and is either *ṣaḥīḥ* 'sound' or *ḥasan* 'good'. III 26b

makfūl → KAFĀLA

ma'khadh (A) : in music, the initial note. The final note is termed *rakz*. IX 101a

makhāridj → MAKHRADJ

makhazza → MU'ARNIBA

makhlaṣ (P, < A), or *gurīzgāh* : the transitional distich between the prologue and the panegyric of a Persian ḲAṢĪDA, which must skilfully introduce the name of the person being eulogised. IV 57b; IV 714b; nom-de-plume. VIII 3a; IX 354a

makhradj (A, T *makhredj*; pl. *makhāridj*) : place of exit.
♦ **makhāridj al-ḥurūf** (A) : lit. the place of emission of the letters; in gram-

mar, the points of articulation of the 29 phonemes of Arabic. III 598a; VI 129b

♦ **makhredj** : an Ottoman term used in education and law.

In Ottoman education, ~ was used in reference to two schools in the 19th century, of which one prepared students for employment in Ottoman administrative offices (*makhredj-i aḳlām*), the other for military schools (*makhredj-i mekātib-i ʿaskeriyye*). VI 133a

In Ottoman law, ~ had two meanings. Certain judicial districts in the empire were referred to as *makhredj mewlewiyyeti*. The name derived from a common attribute of the judges appointed to these districts. All were judges 'going out' to their first appointment after teaching in schools. The judges who had completed this appointment and were awaiting assignment to a higher ranking judicial district were called *makhredj mewālīsi*. VI 133b; in Ottoman inheritance law, ~ was the term for the denominator which was used to divide an inheritance among heirs. VI 133b

makhrūṭ (A) : cone.

In astronomy, the shadow of the earth during an eclipse of the moon. V 536a

makhzan (A) : in Morocco, the government; at first ~ was applied more particularly only to the financial department, the Treasury. VI 133b; and → AL-LUGHA AL-MAKHZANIYYA

makhzen (Mor) : a garrison placed in a stronghold. II 510a

makkārī : 'for hire', a term used in the Ottoman empire to designate small caravans operating between cities, which would transport merchants and travellers for a fare. IV 678b

makkās (A) : probably a tax-farmer under the Ḥafṣids; collector of the MAKS. II 146a

makkī (A) : in the mediaeval Near East, a beggar who pretends to be a rich merchant who has been robbed of his goods. VII 494b

makkūk (A) : a measure used for weighing grains in northern Syria and Upper Mesopotamia. Its actual weight varied, e.g. that of Aleppo and Tripoli contained 83.5 kg of wheat and that of Ḥamāt 92.77 kg. IV 520a; VI 118b

maḳlūb (A) : 'transposed'; in the science of Tradition, a term used when a Tradition is attributed to someone other than the real authority to make it an acceptable GHARĪB Tradition, or when two Traditions have the ISNĀD of the one with the MATN of the other. III 26a

maknī → IḌMĀR

makrūh (A) : a reprehensible action, an action disapproved of; one of the five juridical qualifications of human actions according to Islamic law. VI 194b

maḳrūn, maḳrūna → ZUMMĀRA

makrūna (A) : a head scarf worn by Bedouin women in the Arabian peninsula. V 741b

makrūs (Alg, pl. *makārīs*) : an adolescent of 12-14 years; in the Mzāb, ~ means an adult fit to carry arms. III 98a

maks (A, < Ar; pl. *mukūs*) : octroi duties. II 146a; a toll, custom duty. VI 194b; tax unsanctioned by the s͟harīʿa; non-canonical tax. VIII 71b; VIII 955a

maḳṣūra (A, pl. *maḳāṣir*) : in poetry, the name given to a poem whose rhyme is constituted by an *alif maḳṣūra*. VI 195b

In architecture, the ~ is a box or compartment for the ruler built in a mosque, near the MIḤRĀB, introduced at the beginning of the Umayyad period either to protect the ruler from hostile attacks or for the purpose of teaching and performing the ṢALĀT. VI 661b ff.

maḳṭaʿ (A) : in Persian prosody, the term for the last distich, BAYT, which in the G͟HAZAL contains the nom-de-plume of the author. II 1033b; IV 715a

In grammar, a 'cutting' in the resonance emitted from the chest as it rises in the throat to produce the ḤARF. III 597b

maktab (A, pl. *makātib*) : originally, an appellation for the Islamic traditional school frequently known also as *kuttāb*. In Egypt, the Copts too used ~ to denote their own traditional schools; a school; bureau, department; office; agency. VI 196b

In modern Persian usage, in addition to its basic meaning of 'school', ~ has acquired also the connotation of an 'instructing manual'. VI 197a

♦ maktab al-sabīl → SABĪL

maktaba (A, P *kitāb-k͟hāna*) : library. VI 197b

maḳtal (A) : a genre in Turkish narrative literature denoting works commemorating miracles and happenings around the martyrs of the house of the Prophet, particularly his grandson Ḥusayn. III 374a; V 193b

makt͟h (A) : stop, stay.

In astronomy, ~ means the phase in which the moon is eclipsed. For the case of total eclipse, the place where it begins is called *awwal al-makt͟h* and where the moon begins to emerge from the shadow, *āk͟hir al-makt͟h*. V 536b

maḳṭūʿ (A) : in the science of Tradition, a Tradition going back to a Successor regarding words or deeds of his. III 25b; an ISNĀD which is 'cut off' at the level of the Successor, thus without mention of either the Prophet or a Companion. VII 631a

In Ottoman Turkey, a form of poll-tax, D͟JIZYA, which was fixed by agreement, and which amount thus could not be altered. It was extensively applied. II 563b

For ~ in prosody, → ḲAṬʿ

maʿḳūla → DIYA

mal → BAVIK

māl (A, pl. *amwāl*) : possession, property, referring among the Bedouin particularly to camels, but also to estates and money, and in any case to concrete things. The word is formed from *mā* and *li* and means properly anything that belongs to anyone. VI 205a; taxes. II 148a; IV 1034a; VI 205a; capital. II 361a; and → S͟HARIKAT AMWĀL

In mathematics, ~ was used for the unknown quantity in an equation; in this meaning it was afterwards replaced by *s̲h̲ay*ʾ. Used for the unknown in quadratic equations, it became the word for the square of a number. The fourth power is called *māl al-māl*, the fifth *māl*ᵘ *kaʿb*ⁱⁿ, the square of the cube. II 361a; VI 205b

♦ **māl al-bayʿa** (also *ḥaḳḳ al-bayʿa*, *rasm al-bayʿa* and *ṣilat al-bayʿa*) : a term used for the payments made to army officers at the time of the swearing of the oath of allegiance, BAYʿA, to a new ruler. VI 205b

♦ māl al-d̲j̲ahābid̲h̲a, or *ḥaḳḳ al-d̲j̲ahābid̲h̲a* : the fee of the D̲J̲AHBAD̲H̲ for his services to the government, levied as a charge on the taxpayer. II 382b

♦ al-māl al-ḥurr : one of the three main sources of revenue for the Egyptian government in the years immediately preceding the Napoleonic invasion of 1798, ~ was composed of the MĪRĪ, a fixed tax, and the *fāʾiẓ*, a tax which went to the concessionaries of tax farms and was fixed by the terms of the concession. All the land taxes were farmed out by the government to *multazim*s (→ MÜLTEZIM), who collected them through their agents. II 148a

♦ māl al-kus̲h̲ūfiyya : one of the three main sources of revenue for the Egyptian government in the years immediately preceding the Napoleonic invasion of 1798, ~ were taxes which paid for the military and administrative expenses within the Egyptian provinces. II 148a

♦ māl manḳūl → ʿAḲĀR

♦ māl nāṭiḳ → MĀL ṢĀMIT

♦ māl ribawī : in law, goods capable of usury and interest, RIBĀ. VIII 492b

♦ māl ṣāmit : dumb property, in contrast to *māl nāṭiḳ* 'speaking money', applied to slaves and cattle. VI 205a

♦ māl-i ād̲h̲arūy (P) : rent paid for fire-temple premises or land by Zoroastrians in 4th/10th-century eastern Persia. IX 683a

♦ māl-ı̊ muḳātele (T) : 'fighting money', revenue from land grants, DIRLIK. IX 656a

malāhī (A, s. *malhā*) : a term which, in a figurative sense, is used as the equivalent of 'musical instruments', sometimes being replaced by *ālat al-lahw* or linked with the word *lahw* 'game, pastime, amusement'. VI 214a

malāḥim → MALḤAMA

mālaḳ (A), or *mimlaḳa* : a wide board that the ploughman presses on with all his weight and is pulled along by two oxen, the ~ is a rudimentary implement for levelling the earth after ploughing and burying completely the seed which was sown there before the ploughshare turned over the soil. The word is an equivalent of the Egyptian *zaḥḥāfa*. VII 22b

malaka (A) : in philosophy, ~ is used to translate the Greek *hexis* 'a being in a certain state or habit'. It is contrasted with privation, ʿADAM, in translations and commentaries on Aristotle. VI 220a

malakī (A) : in numismatics, a variety of DĪNĀR instituted in 479/1086 under the Ṣulayḥids in Yemen. IX 816b

malam (Hau, < A *muʿallim*; pl. *malamai*) : ~ was formerly used to designate a man versed in the Arabic language and Islamic sciences to whatever extent. Nowadays, although the traditional ~ remains a familiar feature of Hausa society, the term itself has been debased to the point where (like the Arabic term *al-sayyid*) it merely serves the function of the English 'Mr'. In the phrase *shehu malami*, it is used as an epithet for a distinguished exponent of the Islamic sciences. VI 223a; IX 244a

malang (P ?) : a term with uncertain etymology, used in Muslim India, to denote wandering dervishes of the Ḳalandarī, BĪ-SHARʿ or antinomian type. VI 228b

malḥama (A, pl. *malāḥim*) : an epic; in the Islamic Middle Ages, ~ meant a writing of a divinatory character, specifically the *Malḥamat Dāniyāl*, a collection of meteorological signs with their divinatory meanings. VI 247a; VIII 106a

In its plural form, *malāḥim*, it is applied to a literature consisting of predictions of a historical character. II 377a; VI 216a

malḥūn (A), or *ḳaṣīda zadjaliyya* : a term designating a language which sprang from the local North African dialects which served for the expression of certain forms of dialectal poetry, as well as this poetry itself. I 571b; VI 247b

malik (A, pl. *mulūk*) : king; government.

As a kingly title, the term appears repeatedly in pre-Islamic inscriptions from southern Arabia and the Syrian desert fringes. Islam, however, presented a new order in which God alone was the King. Considered to be a term of abuse, ~ was not officially assumed by Muslim rulers in the early centuries of Islam, but towards the middle of the 4th/10th century, the Būyids began adopting the title, as did Sāmānid, Khwārazmī, Ghaznawid, Saldjūḳ, Fāṭimid, Ayyūbid and Mamlūk rulers after them. ~ was also freely applied to princes, viziers and provincial governors, which rendered the term less majestic, the title *sulṭān* being considered superior as it conveyed a sense of independent sovereignty. VI 261a

♦ **malik al-shuʿarāʾ** : 'king of the poets', an honorific title of a Persian poet laureate. It was the highest distinction which could be given to a poet by a royal patron. Like other honorifics, it confirmed the status of its holder within his profession and was regarded as a permanent addition to his name which sometimes even became a hereditary title. VI 276a; IX 241b

♦ **malik al-tudjdjār** : 'king of the big merchants', an office and a title which existed in Iran from Ṣafawid times, and probably earlier, until the end of the Ḳādjār period. The ~ was chosen by the prominent merchants of each big town and nominated by the authorities to be the link between the trading community and the authorities. He also settled disputes between the Iranian merchants and their customers, between the merchants themselves, and between local and foreign merchants and trading-firms. VI 276b

♦ malikī → DJALĀLĪ

♦ **mulūk al-ṭawāʾif** : 'the kings of the territorial divisions', the Arabic phrase used by Muslim historians originally for the regional rulers of the Parthian or Arsacid period in pre-Islamic Persia; the rulers of the principalities which arose on the ruins of the Umayyad empire of al-Andalus at the end of the 5th/11th century. VII 551a; VII 552a

mālik (A) : in law, owner (of a slave). I 24b

♦ **mālikāne** (< A *mālik* and P *-āne*) : in law, intangible property, i.e. fiscal revenues, whenever the enjoyment of them is connected with full ownership. The term's content has nonetheless changed over the centuries. VI 277b; VIII 405b

♦ mālikiyyat al-māl (A) : in law, patrimonial ownership. I 27a

malīkh (A), or *masīkh* : 'completely insipid'; in the terminology of food, one of the degrees of insipidity, along with *tafih* 'without either real sweetness, acidity or bitterness'. II 1071a

malīl → MALLA

maliṣa → AṬŪM

māliyye (T, < A) : a term used in the 19th and 20th centuries, in Arabic and Turkish, to refer to financial affairs and financial administration. In the Ottoman empire, and in various of its successor states, the term has also acquired a more specific reference to the Ministry of Finance. VI 283b

malḳaf (Egy) : (wind) catcher; the usual term for the ventilation shaft known as *bādahandj* in mediaeval Arabic. S 115b

malla (A), or *malīl* : 'hot ash', a loaf of bread cooked under ashes, eaten in ancient Arabia by Bedouin. V 41b

mallāḥ (A) : the name given to the place of residence, quarter, assigned to the Jews of Morocco. There is a difference between the urban ~ and the rural ~ . The former is a quarter adjacent to the Muslim city, integrated within it or shifted to the nearby periphery, yet enclosed within a separate enclave defended by a wall and a fortified gateway. The latter is an 'open' village exclusively inhabited by Jews, situated some distance from the nearest *ḳṣar* or fortress of the protector. VI 292b

maʾluka (A) : an oral message. According to the Arab lexicographers, ~ derives from the root *aluka* which signifies 'to champ the bit' when used in reference to a horse. VIII 532a

malūsa (A) : a large Turkish-style turban worn by religious dignitaries in Tunisia. V 746a

mamālik → MAMLAKA

mamlaka (A, pl. *mamālik*) : absolute power over things and especially over beings: to begin with, that of God over creation as a whole, and then, that of any individual, in certain circumstances; ~ is also applied to the place either in origin or by application, of the power under consideration. In this latter sense, the most current denotation of ~ is a piece of territory under the control of some authority; a kingdom. VI 313b

In geographical literature, ~ refers to the Islamic world. VI 313b
In Ṣafawid Persia, the plural *mamālik* referred to provinces and regions alienated from the direct control of the central government, in contrast to KHĀṢṢA, provinces and districts under its direct administration. VI 16b; VIII 751a; state lands. IV 36a

mamlūk (A) : lit. thing possessed, hence 'slave', especially used in the sense of military slave. The term is especially known in relation to the Mamlūk sultanate established and maintained by *mamlūks* in Egypt (1250-1517) and in Syria (1260-1516); and in relation to the role of their sucesssors, the neo-Mamlūks, in Ottoman Egypt. I 24b; VI 314a

mamsūkh → MASKH

maʾmūma → ĀMMA

maʾmūr (A) : in the late Ottoman empire and Turkish republic, a civil official. VI 340b

maʿnā (A, pl. MAʿĀNĪ) : 'meaning, what the speaker intends to say'.
In grammar, ~ indicates the semantic counterpart of *lafẓ*, the linguistic expression. VI 346a
In philosophy, ~ is used to translate a number of Greek expressions, to denote e.g. concept, thought, idea, meaning, entity. VI 347a
In poetry, ~ meant both the meaning of a word or proposition in a certain given verse, and the meaning of a trope. VI 347b
In Nuṣayriyya terminology, ~ is 'the Essence', a name for God. VIII 148a
♦ al-maʿānī al-thāniya : in philosophy, the five predicables (genus, species, difference, property, accident), also known as *al-alfāẓ al-khamsa*. II 550a

manākh (A) : war for territory, one of the Bedouin's warlike activities. II 1055a

manāḳib (A, s. MANḲABA) : a plural substantive, rendered approximately by 'qualities, virtues, talents, praiseworthy actions', featuring in the titles of a quite considerable number of biographical works of a laudatory nature, which have eventually become a part of hagiographical literature in Arabic, in Persian and in Turkish. Immediately following the development of mysticism and the cult of saints, the subjects preferred are the marvellous aspects of the life, the miracles or at least the prodigies of a ṣūfī or of a saint believed to have been endowed with miraculous powers; hence, ~ ultimately acquires the sense of 'miracles' or 'prodigies'. VI 349a

manāḳirī (A) : 'beak-ambergris', according to mediaeval authors, the term for a variety of ambergris which contains the claws and beak of a bird which alights on the lumps and being unable to get away perishes on them. In actuality, ambergris frequently contains the hard mandibles of a cuttle-fish which serves as food to the spermwhale. I 484a

manām → RUʾYĀ

manār (A), or **manāra** : lighthouse; an elevated place where a light or beacon is established; the means of marking (with fire, originally) routes for caravans or for the army in war; lampstand; certain kinds of 'arms' (arm-rests of seats, thrones, etc.); minaret, i.e. the tower alongside (or on top of) a mosque, used to call the faithful to prayer (in this sense normally *manāra*). VI 358b

In East Africa, ~ (Sw *mnara*, pl. *minara*) also refers to the pillar tombs which are an architectural peculiarity of the eastern African coast. VI 370a

For ~ in zoology, → HIRKŪL

manāzil → MANZIL

manāẓir (A), or *ʿilm al-manāẓir* : the science of optics. VI 376a

In travel, ~ was used to designate the fires and their sites, near the sea, which guided ships and gave warning of the arrival of an enemy (by lighting the fire in the direction of the town). Some fires were lit on the Mediterranean coast from Alexandria as far as the regions of North Africa. It is even recorded that opposite the Palestinian coast an exchange of signals of this kind was made between ships and the coast. Synonyms are *nīrān*, *mawāḳīd* and *maḥāris*. VI 359a

mandala (J) : in East and Central Java, a rural Hindu-Buddhist type of school, where ascetical *guru*s imparted religious doctrine and mystical wisdom to students residing together in a communal setting. It is thought by some scholars to be the precursor of the PESANTREN. VIII 296b

mandara (A) : a large room in an Egyptian house, whose central part, a substitute for the courtyard, is paved, adorned with a fountain and surrounded by two or three ĪWĀNs. II 114b

mandedji → LIMAN REʾĪSI

mandī : in Muslim India, a market where different commodities, particularly corn, were brought from outside and sold in bulk. During the Dihlī sultanate, the officer who looked after the market in general was called *shaḥna-i mandī*. IX 800b f.

mandīl (A, < L *mantellum*), normalised *mindīl* : handkerchief, napkin, towel; piece of cloth, used for many other purposes, such as covering or carrying something or serving, attached to the body, as an untailored part of dress. Synonyms in Arabic are e.g. *mashūsh*, *minshafa*, *khirḳa*. VI 402b

In Syria and Palestine, ~ is the name for a woman's head scarf, veil. V 741b

In Iraq, ~ denotes an embroidered kerchief hung from the waist sash by men. V 741b

mandjālī (Telugu) : a measure of weight in South India, being the equivalent of a seed notionally used, of about 260 mg. VI 122a

mandjam → MAʿDIN

mandjanīḳ (A, < Gk) : mangonel; a general term for any kind of stone-throwing siege-engine. The expressions ~ and *ʿarrāda* are both used for this kind of machine, and although the *ʿarrāda* may have been the smaller of the two, the expressions often seem to be interchangeable. III 469b; III 472b; VI 405a

mandūb (A) : in law, a meritorious and recommended action. VI 408a

mandrāghūras → SIRĀDJ AL-ḲUṬRUB

mangh (Sin), or *mungh* : in Sind, wind catchers, from around 1 m square and up to 2 m high, which rise above the flat roofs of houses to catch the summer wind. IX 638a

manghïr (T) : an Ottoman copper coin. II 118a; VIII 229a

manhūk (A) : in prosody, a deviation in the metre consisting of a line being 'weakened to exhaustion', i.e. when it is reduced to a third of its size. I 671a

māni (T, < A *ma'nā*) : a form of Turkish popular poetry, most usually a piece of poetry made up of heptasyllabic verses rhymed on the pattern *a a b a*, but there are also some rhymed *b a c a*; each quatrain may be sufficient to fulfil a certain function or to transmit a certain message. VI 420b

♦ kesik māni : 'truncated *māni*', a MĀNI reduced to the schema *a b a* by the disappearance of the first verse. VI 420b

manḳaba (A, pl. MANĀḲIB) : a narrow street between two houses; a difficult path on the mountain; a noble action. VI 349b

♦ manḳabat (U) : in Urdu poetry, praise of the fourth caliph, 'Alī, and of subsequent shī'ī IMĀMs. V 958a; VIII 776a

manḳāna (A) : a clock, constructed in the 9th century in Muslim Spain by 'Abbās b. Firnās. I 11b

mann (A) : the standard weight for small quantities of dry (and even liquid) commodities in most provinces of Persia. VI 120a; in Egypt, the ~ was used to weigh spices such as cinnamon, nutmeg, mace, cloves, cubeb and borax. VI 119a

manṣab (Ind.P) : a term of the military system of the Mughals in India, denoting a rank, the holder of which was termed *manṣabdār*. Personal or DHĀT rank was expressed numerically in even-numbered decimal increments and could vary from as low as 20 *dhāt* to a maximum of 7000 *dhāt* for the highest nobles. *Dhāt* determined the *manṣabdār*'s relative status and his pay. *Manṣabdār*s could simultaneously hold trooper, or SUWĀR, ranks. VI 422b

manṣabdār → MANṢAB

manshūr (A, pl. *manshūrāt*, *manāshīr*) : lit. spread out, ~ has come to mean a certificate, an edict, a diploma of appointment, and particularly, a patent granting an appanage. VI 423a

In Egypt in the early Arab period, ~ was a pass which the government compelled the peasants to have, designed to curb increasing movement away from the land. II 303a; VI 423a

In 'Abbāsid times, ~ was given to grants of fiefs, while under the Fāṭimids (and Ayyūbids) it denoted certain letters of appointment. Under the Mamlūks, ~ became restricted to feudal grants, in different grades according to size and writing. II 303a; VI 423b; VIII 814b

In modern Egypt, edicts of the government are called ~ . In many Arabic states, serial publications now are called *manshūrāt*. VI 424b

In mathematics, ~ means prism. VI 424b

In astronomy, *manshūrāt* denotes spherical prisms; according to Ptolemy, 'sawn pieces' or 'disks' comprised between two circles parallel to and equidistant from the equator of a sphere. II 763a

manshūrāt → MANSHŪR

manṣūb (A) : the chief agent in India of the Yemeni Sulaymānī sect, which split from the Bohorās in the 10th/16th century. I 1255a; IX 829b

For ~ in grammar, → NAṢB

In its plural form, *mansūbāt*, lit. set-ups, was the term for the numerous problems in the game of chess. IX 366b

manṭal (A) : in Yemeni architecture, the 'long drop', where the fuel, human excrement, for heating the bath is kept. IX 2b

manṭiḳ (A) : logic. VI 442a

mantū : a steamed dumpling, one of the Özbeg noodle dishes for which their cuisine is known. VIII 234b

manzil (A, pl. *manāzil*) : a halt; a temporary stay; stage of a journey. VI 454b; hospice or night lodging intended for travellers. I 1225a; VI 455a; at the present time, ~ denotes a lodging, a house and even an apartment. V 455a

At the end of the Ottoman period, ~ signified a private hostelry, as opposed to the *maḍāfa*, which was communal. VI 455a

In Iran and, especially, in Hindūstān, ~ came to designate a camp, characteristically the royal camp. VI 456a

In astronomy, *manāzil*, or, more fully, *manāzil al-ḳamar*, are the lunar mansions, or stations of the moon, a system of 28 stars, groups of stars, or spots in the sky near which the moon is found in each of the 28 nights of her monthly revolution. I 523a; VI 374a

In mysticism, ~ is the stage in the spiritual journey of the soul. III 84a; VI 454b

♦ manzila → MAWḌIʿ

♦ **al-manzila bayn al-manzilatayn** (A) : a theological term used by Wāṣil b. ʿAṭāʾ and the later Muʿtazila for designating the salvational status of the mortal sinner. They held that any Muslim guilty of a serious sin is neither believer nor non-believer, and is liable to punishment in the Fire. I 694b; VI 457b

marāfiḳ (A, s. *marfiḳ*) : lit. benefits, favours, one of several terms used for bribes, douceurs. This form of bribery became institutionalised in the ʿAbbāsid caliphate with the establishment of a special office, the *dīwān al-marāfiḳ*, in which were placed bribes and money from commissions collected from aspiring candidates for office. II 325a; VI 498a

marāʿī (P) : a pasture tax in Persia. IV 1042a; in 19th-century usage in Kāshān, ~ was a tax on sheep and goats levied at so much per animal which bore young and was in milk. IV 1042b

marak (A), or *maraḳa* : in the terminology of food, a broth. II 1059a

maʿraḳa → ʿARAḲIYYA

marāṣid (A), or *maʾāṣir* : customs, dues and tolls which exist on the frontiers, on the international trade routes, and the ports. II 143a; and → MAʾṢIR

marāsim (A) : official court ceremonies, both processional and non-processional. Synonyms are *rusūm*, especially for the whole range of ceremonial, including protocol and etiquette, MAWSIM and *mawkib* (→ MAWĀKIB). VI 518a

marātib (A, s. *martaba*) : lit. ranks, degrees, a term applied especially in Muslim India to the drums and standards, *aṭbāl wa ʿalamāt*, borne by the sultan or conferred by him on the great AMĪRS, later elaborated as 'standards, kettledrums, trumpets, bugles and reedpipe' as carried by two ships among the fifteen of the governor of Lāharī Bandar. The ~ could function as battle ensigns. VI 536b

marbaṭ (A, pl. *marābiṭ*), or *marbiṭ* : the place where domestic animals are tethered. Among the nomads, the ~ simply involves tying the animal's halter to some bush or a large stone buried in the sand. For sedentary and urban populations, the ~ takes the form of a kind of shelter, beneath which animals can shelter from the sun. By extension, ~ very soon took on the general sense of stables. VI 537b

In Saudi Arabia and the United Arab Emirates, ~ and *mirsal* are also the names of the 'leash' which holds the falcon down to its perching-block or on the falconer's gauntlet. VI 537b

mardjaʿ-i taḳlīd (P) : a title and function of a hierarchical nature denoting a Twelver jurisconsult who is to be considered during his lifetime, by virtue of his qualities and his wisdom, a model for reference, for 'imitation' or 'emulation' by every observant Imāmī shīʿī (with the exception of other MUDJTAHIDS) on all aspects of religious practice and law. VI 548b; S 103b

mardjān → BUSSADH

mardūd (A) : in the science of Tradition, a 'rejected' Tradition, more particularly a Tradition from a weak transmitter which contradicts what authorities transmit. III 26b

mardūf → RIDFA

marfiḳ → MARĀFIḲ

marfūʿ (A, pl. *marfūʿāt*) : lit. lifted up.

In the science of Tradition, a Tradition traced back to the Prophet whether or not the ISNĀD is complete. Transmitters who developed the habit of frequently 'raising' ISNĀD strands 'to the level' of *marfūʿāt* were called *raffāʿūn*. III 25b; VIII 384a; and → MUTTAṢIL; RAFʿ

marḥala (A, pl. *marāḥil*) : in mediaeval Islamic usage, a stage of travel, normally the distance which a traveller can cover in one day; it was, therefore, obviously a variable measurement of length, dependent on the ease or difficulty of the terrain to be crossed. VI 558b

mārid (A) : a term found once in the Qurʾān, meaning rebel, but, with ʿIFRĪT, ended by being used of one particular class of fantastic beings from the nether regions. The popular tales represent the ~ as being superior to the *ʿifrīt*: he is forty times stronger and has at his command a thousand auxiliaries. III 1050a; IX 406b maʿriḍ (A) : ‘place of display’, term in some countries for a public slave market which every big town had in the mediaeval period. I 32b

maʿrifa (A) : knowledge, cognition. III 1133a; VI 568b

In grammar, ~ designates the definite noun, as opposed to *nakira*, indefinite noun. VI 569a

In onomastics, ~ is the appellative formed of Ibn followed by the ISM, LAḲAB or NISBA of the father or of an ancestor, sometimes celebrated but more often obscure. This is also called *s̲h̲uhra*. III 670a

māristān (A) : a lunatic asylum. I 500b

māriyya (A) : the pearl-grey tone of the plumage of sandgrouse. IV 744a

markab (A) : lit. conveyance; in early Arabic usage, the most general word for ‘ship’ . The term was, however, used in the first place for travel by land, with such specific meanings as ‘riding-beast’, ‘conveyance drawn by animals’. VIII 808a

marḳaba (A) : the mountain refuge of a brigand-poet. IX 865b

markaz → MUWAS̲H̲S̲H̲AḤ

markūb (A) : pointed men’s shoes of thick red morocco, worn in Egypt. V 741b

marnab (A) : in zoology, the Brown rat (*Mus decumanus*) or ‘Sewer rat’. S 285b

marṣad (A) : observatory. VI 599b

marsūm (A) : in the science of diplomatic, a grade of appointment used for military personnel in Mamlūk times only. Distinction is made between major and minor appointments: *mukabbara* is the appointment of the commander of a fortress and military persons of medium rank, and *muṣag̲h̲g̲h̲ara* is the appointment for the lower ranks. II 303a

martaba → ḤUKM; MARĀTIB

martak (A) : in mineralogy, yellow lead. IX 872b

mart̲h̲āt → MART̲H̲IYA

mart̲h̲iya (A, pl. *marāt̲h̲ī*), or *mart̲h̲āt* : elegy, a poem composed in Arabic (or in an Islamic language following the Arabic tradition) to lament the passing of a beloved person and to celebrate his merits. IV 1027a; VI 602b

In Urdu poetry, the ~ is almost always religious and usually about the Karbalāʾ martyrs, although a secular type exists. V 635b; VI 610b

martolos (T, < Gk) : a salaried member of the Ottoman internal security forces, recruited predominantly in the Balkans from among chosen land-owning Orthodox Christians who, retaining their religion, became members of the Ottoman ʿASKARĪ caste. By 1722 the institution was merged with the Muslim local security police. VI 612a

maʿrūf (A) : in the science of Tradition, a weak Tradition confirmed by another weak one, or a Tradition superior in MATN or ISNĀD to one called MUNKAR; also, a traditionist when two or more transmit from him. III 26b

marumakkatyam : in southern India, a law of inheritance whereby the children of the sister inherit, practiced by the Moplas. I 172a maryūl (N.Afr) : a short, embroidered shift for women in Libya. V 746a

marzpān (P, A *marzubān*) : warden of the march, markgrave; the title of a military governor of a frontier province under the Sāsānids in the 4th or 5th centuries AD. By mid-6th century, the ~ had become a high-ranking military and administrative official. After the decline of the Sāsānid empire, *marzubān* survived at Marw and Marw al-Rūd as the title of local Iranian officials under Muslim rule. It came to be used as a proper name and was also used metaphorically in poetry for a ruler or master, or for a leader of the Magians. VI 633a

masāʾ (A) : originally, 'evening twilight', but today applied to the evening, as opposed to *ṣabāḥ* 'morning'. It also comes to designate the period which begins at noon and encroaches upon the night. V 709b

maṣāff (A) : a line of troops. II 1080a

♦ maṣāffiyya : a corps of slaves, probably originating from those employed to form a line of troops in the reception rooms of the ʿAbbāsid court, under the command of the Chamberlain and numbering 10,000 men. In 317/929, the ~ forced the caliph al-Ḳāhir to flee. They were massacred in 318/930. II 1080b

masāḥa (A) : one of three ways of assessing land tax, KH̲ARĀD̲J, the other two being MUḲĀSAMA and MUḲĀṬAʿA. The amount due was based on the measurement of the land, but ~ did not, however, involve a comprehensive cadastral survey. Usually only the land sown was taken into account. It differed from the *muḳāsama* system in that the tax demand did not vary in a good year or a bad year. Known in the early centuries, it continued to be used down to modern times. IV 1037b

masāʾil → MASʾALA

masak → D̲H̲ABL

masʾala (A, pl. *masāʾil*) : question, problem.

♦ al-masʾala al-minbariyya : in law, a particular problem of inheritance, which ʿAlī is reported to have solved off-hand when it was submitted to him while he was on the MINBAR. I 765a

♦ al-masʾala al-**surayd̲jiyya** : in law, a hotly debated problem of repudiation to which Ibn Surayd̲j, the S̲h̲āfiʿī jurist, gave his name. III 949b; IX 893b

♦ **masāʾil wa-ad̲jwiba** : lit. questions and answers, a technique of argumentation in mediaeval Islam which has strongly influenced, both in form and content, numerous Arabic writings in virtually all fields of knowledge. Unsolved problems, or questions and objections propounded by a third person, are followed by answers or explanations and refutations. Sometimes the author, at the request of a third person, composed a monograph on a group of themes, and even dedicated it to him. The pattern of questions and answers often became a literary topos, and, finally, the pattern also turned into a technique of scientific research or presentation, without any dialogue between teacher and pupil or between two opponents. VI 636a

♦ masāʾil mulaḳḳaba : in law, a category of questions 'called by special names', to which e.g. the AKDARIYYA belongs. I 320a

maṣāliḥ → AFĀWIH; MAṢLAḤA

maṣdar (A) : in grammar, the verbal noun. IX 528a

masd̲j̲id (A) : mosque. The modern Western European words (Eng *mosque*, Fr *mosquée*, Ger *Moschee*, It *moschea*) come ultimately from the Arabic via Spanish *mezquita*. VI 644b

The word is used in the Qurʾān for sanctuary, especially the Meccan sanctuary; ~ is also applied to pre-Islamic sanctuaries. Even as late as Ibn K̲h̲aldūn, ~ is used in the general meaning of a temple or place of worship of any religion. VI 644b

♦ masd̲j̲id d̲j̲āmiʿ : in early Islam, the common name used for the chief (Friday) mosque in a certain place, but by the time of al-Maḳrīzī (9th/15th century), the word *d̲j̲āmiʿ* meant any mosque of some size. VI 656a

♦ **masd̲j̲idī** (A, pl. *masd̲j̲idiyyūn*) : an adjective specifically concerning the Friday mosque of Baṣra in the time of al-D̲j̲āḥiẓ and used to designate groups of adults or young people who were accustomed to meet together in that building, near the gate of the Banū Sulaym, as well as of poets, popular story-tellers, and transmitters of religious, historical and literary Traditions, in particular those regarding poetic verses. VI 709a

mʿās̲h̲ → KUSKUSŪ

al-masḥ ʿalā ʾl-k̲h̲uffayn (A) : lit. the act of passing the hand over the boots; a term designating the right whereby sunnī Muslims may, in certain circumstances, pass the hand over their shoes instead of washing their feet as a means of preparing themselves for the saying of the ritual prayer. VI 709b

mās̲h̲āʾ allāh (A) : a phrase occurring in the Qurʾān and widely used in the Islamic lands of the Middle East with the general meaning of 'what God does, is well done'. The formula denotes that things happen according to God's will and should therefore be accepted with humility and resignation. In a cognate signification, the phrase is often used to indicate a vague, generally a great or considerable, but sometimes a small, number or quantity of time. The phrase is also the equivalent of the English 'God knows what', and, as signifying 'what God has willed', expressing admiration or surprise. VI 710b

mas̲h̲ād̲j̲in (A) : water-driven trip-hammers, i.e. stones fitted to axles which are installed on running water for pounding e.g. ores or flax for paper. V 969b

mas̲h̲aʾiyya → IS̲H̲RĀḲIYYŪN

mas̲h̲ʿar (A, pl. *mas̲h̲āʿir*) : a place or thing which puts one in the presence or gives a feeling of the sacred or of a divinity; a place where the rites of sacrifice were performed. The journey between ʿArafa and Minā and that between al-Ṣafā and al-Marwa is called *al-mas̲h̲ʿar al-ḥarām*. IX 424b, where are found synonyms

mas̲h̲āriḳa (A) : the Arabs and Arabised peoples of the East in contrast to those of the West called MAG̲H̲ĀRIBA. VI 712a

mas̲h̲āyik̲h̲ → S̲H̲AYK̲H̲

mashdūd → SHADD

mashhad (A) : any sacred place, not necessarily having a construction associated with it; a tomb in general, the burial place of an earlier prophet, saint or forerunner of Muḥammad or of any Muslim who had had pronounced over him the profession of faith; a martyrium; any small building with obvious religious features like a MIḤRĀB. V 289a; VI 713b

mashhūr (A) : in the science of Tradition, a well-known Tradition transmitted via a minimum of three different ISNĀDs. III 25b; VI 717a

In law, the 'predominant' opinion, as opposed to the isolated or "anomalous' opinion, SHĀDHDH. I 428a

mashīkha → FAHRASA; MASHYAKHA

mashḳ → KŪFĪ

mashla (A) : a variety of ʿABĀʾ made in Baghdad. V 741b

mashlaḥ (A), or *mushallaḥ*, *mashlakh*, *maḥras* : an undressing and rest room found in the steam bath. III 141a

mashlakh → MASHLAḤ

mashraba (A) : a niche attached to lattice wooden windows known as MASHRABIYYA where the water jars were kept cool and fresh for drinking. VI 717b

mashrabiyya (A) : a technique of turned wood used to produce lattice-like panels, like those which were used in the past to adorn the windows in traditional domestic architecture. The ~ technique is a speciality of Cairo, where it was used with a latitude of patterns and combinations. The panels are composed of small pieces of wood which are turned in various forms and are fixed together without glue or nails, but simply by being inserted into each other, thus giving the panel more resistance towards the flexibility of the wood with the change of temperature. V 1153a; VI 717b

mashriḳ (A) : the East; for the Arab world, all the lands to the east of Egypt. VI 720a; and → MAṬLAʿ

♦ **mashriḳ al-adhkār** (A) : a term used in the Bahāʾī movement for four related concepts: a). In Iran (loosely) to describe early morning gatherings for reading of prayers and sacred writings. b). Generally of any house erected for the purpose of prayer. c). Most widely, to refer to Bahāʾī temples. d). In its widest application, to refer to a central temple in conjunction with various dependencies regarded as intrinsic to the overall institution. These include a school for orphans, hospital and dispensary for the poor, home for the aged, home for the infirm, college of higher education, and traveller's hospice. With the exception of a home for the aged in Wilmette, Illinois, no dependencies have as yet been established. I 918a; VI 720a

mashrūʿ (A) : in law, the lawful act, as a term sometimes used in place of DJĀʾIZ as e.g. in the contract of crop-sharing and in the contract of association. II 390a

mashrūṭ (A) : inferior marriage, a legal institution characteristic of North Africa, called AMAZZAL among the Zemmur in Morocco. I 171b maṣhṭūr (A) : in prosody, a deviation in the metre consisting of the suppression of a complete half, *shaṭr*, as e.g. when the RADJAZ is reduced to one hemistich. I 671a

maṣḥūb → ṢĀḤIB

masḥūra → ARGHŪL

mashūra → MASHWARA

mashūsh → MANDĪL

mashwara (A, T *meshweret*), or *mashūra* : consultation, in particular by the ruler of his advisers, the latter being variously defined. The term sometimes also appears to mean some kind of deliberative gathering or assembly.

Among Ottoman historians, ~ was commonly used to denote ad hoc meetings and councils of military and other dignitaries to consider problems as they arose. The sultan was not normally present at such gatherings.

In the course of the 19th century, ~ or *meshweret* was much used by Turkish and Arabic authors, first to describe European representative institutions, and then to justify their introduction to the Islamic lands. VI 724a

mashyakha (A), or *mashīkha* : a plural of SHAYKH and an abstract noun denoting a *shaykh*'s position or authority. VI 725b

In the Muslim West ~ was used to designate the collectivity of urban elders and notables often wielding considerable political influence in the cities and hence carrying the sense of a 'municipal council'. VI 725b

During Bonaparte's Egyptian expedition, ~ acquired a new meaning. Seeking an Arabic expression for 'republic', Bonaparte's orientalist experts came to use ~ . This was apparently an intended allusion to the Directoire of five who were governing France at the time. In the second half of the 19th century, ~ in the sense of republic gave ground to **djumhūriyya**. II 594a; VI 725b; and → FAHRASA

masīkh → MALĪKH; MASKH

ma'ṣir (Akk ?) : a technical term of fiscal practice in the hydraulic civilisation of early Islamic ʿIrāḳ, doubtless going back to earlier periods there. From being a barrier across the river to halt shipping, ~ soon acquired the meaning of 'customs house where tolls are collected' and then the actual tolls themselves. VI 728b

♦ maʾāṣiriyyūn : a body of officials attached to the police guard of Baghdad in the caliphate of al-Muʿtaḍid (279-89/892-902) who collected tolls from river traffic on the Tigris. VI 729a; and → MARĀṢID

maskh (A) : the metamorphosis of men into animals. The product of the metamorphosis is called ~ (*miskh*) or *masīkh* (*mamsūkh*). II 95b; III 305b; VI 736b

maskūk (A, pl. *maskūkāt*) : coined money. IX 592a

maṣlaḥa (A, pl. *maṣāliḥ*) : the concept in Islam of public interest or welfare. II 254b; VI 738b

In law, ~ in the sense of 'general good' and 'public interest' is used as a basis for legal decisions. I 276a; VI 738b; IX 324b

♦ maṣlaḥatgüzār (T) : in Ottoman diplomacy, the term for *chargé d'affaires*. II 694a; and → ḲĀʾIM BI-AʿMĀL

maslūb (A) : castrated by evulsion. IV 1087a

maṣnaʿa (A, pl. *maṣāniʿ*) : a Qurʾānic word meaning 'notable palaces, fortresses and edifices in which special endeavours are invested'. IX 626a

masraba (A) : beginning of the stomach. IX 312a

mast (A), or *mazz, mazd, mizz* : a long stocking of soft, yellow leather; inner shoe worn by both sexes in the Arab East. V 741b

mastaka (J), or *mustaka* : an ornament on top of a sphere on the roof of a Javanese mosque. In later times, this ornament was crowned by a crescent as the decisive symbol of Islam. VI 700b

masūmi (A) : a fine ʿABĀʾ of white wool for men, produced in Baghdad. V 741b

maṭāf (A) : the term for the pavement on which the circumambulation of the Kaʿba is performed. IV 318a

maṭāliʿ → MAṬLAʿ

maṭar (A) : a measure of capacity for liquids, e.g. olive oil, used in mediaeval Egypt. According to a Venetian source, the ~ contained, in the later Middle Ages, about 17 kg of olive oil. VI 119b

maṭārif (A) : items of streaked silk originating from Yemen. IX 866a

matbūʿ → ITBĀʿ

maṭfara (A, pl. *maṭāfira*) : in music, a place of 'jumping' towards higher notes. IX 101a

mat͟hal (A, pl. *amt͟hāl*) : a proverb, popular saying. VI 815b; the proverbial saying, also comprising the extensive group of comparisons involving a comparative in the form *afʿal^{u} min*; adages (gnomes, dicta); set turns of speech; parable, fable. III 369b; VI 816a; a figurative expression. IV 248b

mat͟hālib (A, s. *mat͟hlaba, mat͟hluba*) : lit. faults, vices, defects; disgrace.
In early Islam, ~ was broadly applied to what were regarded as subjects of shame for the tribes, the ethnic groups or even clans, rather than separate individuals; ~ was used in poetry in connection with themes in satire to denigrate or revile an enemy. Later, ~ appeared in the titles of a number of works usually written by genealogists and collectors of historical Traditions and can be contrasted with *maʾāt͟hir* or *mafāk͟hir* 'exploits, feats, glorious titles' and MANĀḲIB. I 892a; VI 828a

mat͟hānī (A) : a technical term used in the Qurʾān, the precise meaning of which is unclear. It refers to the revelation sent down to Muḥammad and commentators have usually understood it to refer to the (seven) verses of the Fātiḥa, the first chapter of the Qurʾān. Another interpretation is that ~ refers to the punishment-stories, which may have once formed a collection separate from the Qurʾān. V 402a

mat͟hnāt (A) : an expression, mentioned by al-D̲jawharī, that may refer to the quatrain. It is said to be equivalent to 'what is called in Persian DŪBAYTĪ, which is singing (*al-ghinā'*)'. VIII 583b

mathnawī (A) : a term used in Persian, Turkish and Urdu for a poem written in rhyming couplets. In Arabic such a poem is called MUZDAWIDJ. The single characteristic which separates the ~ from all other classical verse forms is its rhyming scheme *aa bb cc*, etc. Otherwise, the name is given to poems differing greatly in genre as well as in length and composition; this form is eminently suitable for epic and didactic verse because of the freedom allowed in rhyming. I 677a; IV 58a ff.; V 201a; VI 832a

maṭlaʿ (A, pl. **maṭāliʿ**) : in astrology, the rising point of a celestial body, usually a star, on the local horizon. This concept was important in Islamic folk astronomy, as distinct from mathematical astronomy, because it was by the risings and settings of the sun and stars that the ḲIBLA, the direction of Mecca, was usually determined in popular practice. The terms used for the rising and setting points of the sun were usually *mashriḳ* and *maghrib*, ~ being generally reserved for stars. The term ~ was also used to denote the 'time of rising' in the expression *maṭlaʿ al-fadjr*, daybreak or the beginning of morning twilight. VI 839a

In poetry, ~ refers to the first distich of a poem, which opens the poem and signals all the areas of expression. IV 714b

Its plural, *maṭāliʿ*, denoted ascensions, an important concept in mediaeval spherical astronomy and astronomical timekeeping. ~ represent a measure of the amount of apparent rotation of the celestial sphere, and are usually measured from the eastern horizon. Two kinds were used: (1) right ascensions, or ascensions in *sphaera recta*; and (2) oblique ascensions, or ascensions in *sphaera obliqua*. Right ascensions refer to the risings of arcs of the ecliptic over the horizon of a locality with latitude zero, and were called in mediaeval scientific Arabic *maṭāliʿ fi 'l-falak al-mustaḳīm*. Oblique ascensions, associated with a specific latitude, were called *maṭāliʿ al-balad* or *al-maṭāliʿ al-baladiyya*. VI 792b

maṭlūb → ṬĀLIB

maṭmūra (A, pl. *maṭāmīr*) : a natural or man-made cavity used for the concealment of victuals or of riches; a silo. VI 842a; a cave, large or small and very deep, in which prisoners or Christian slaves were confined; subterranean prison. VI 843a

Al-Djāḥiẓ calls the (subterranean ?) cells of monks by the plural form, *maṭāmīr*. VI 842b

matn (A) : text, especially the text of a book as distinguished from its oral explanation or its written or printed commentary. VI 843a; castration by incising and at the same time cauterising the scrotum by means of a red-hot blade of iron and removing the testicles. IV 1088a

In the science of Tradition, ~ denotes the content or text itself, as distinct from the chain of traditionists who have handed it down, ISNĀD. VI 843a; VIII 514b

maṭrāḳ (A) : a contest with a stick, cudgel or rapier for the purpose of training and knight-errantry. VI 843b

maṭrūḥ (A) : in the science of Tradition, a rejected Tradition, held by some to be synonymous with a Tradition that is MATRŪK, by others to be a separate class of Traditions less acceptable than ḌAʿĪF, but not so bad as *mawḍūʿ* 'fictitious', the worst type of all. III 26b

matrūk (A) : a technical term of Ottoman Turkish law concerning a category of land called *arāḍī-yi matrūka* 'assigned lands'. VI 844b

In the science of Tradition, ~ is a Tradition from a single transmitter who is suspected of falsehood in Tradition, or is openly wicked in deed or word, or is guilty of much carelessness or frequent wrong notions. III 26b

maʿṭūf → ʿAṬF

maʿūna (A, pl. *maʿūnāt, maʿāwin*) : lit. assistance; an administrative term of early Islamic history with several meanings. In texts relating to the pre-ʿAbbāsid period, it refers to allocations comparable with, but distinct from, stipends and rations. ~ was sometimes a gratuity paid to those who were not in receipt of stipends, sometimes a bonus supplementary to stipends, and sometimes a regular (more precisely, annual) payment made to those in receipt of stipends and rations alike; *maʿūnāt* was even used as a global term for private income from public funds. From the 3rd/9th century onwards, the leader of the ~ was charged with police duties. The actual police building was called ~ too, at least by the time of the Geniza documents. VI 848b

mawākib (A, s. *mawkib*) : processions, specifically solemn processions; audience. VI 518a; VI 849b; in Turkish usage, *mawkib*, or *mewkib-i hümāyūn*, was used for the prince's procession while for the sultan either *rikāb* or *binish* were common. VIII 529a

mawāḳīd → MANĀẒIR

mawālid → MAWLID

mawāliyā (A, pl. *mawāliyāt*), or *mawāliyyā, mawālī* and *muwālayāt* : a non-classical Arabic verse form which was well established by the 6th/12th century, when it always occurs as four hemistichs of BASĪṬ, all with the same rhyme. Later, it was elaborated into a variety of multi-rhyme compositions. VI 867b

As folk-verse, ~ is a favourite in Arab lands. In common parlance the composition itself is almost always called a *mawwāl*, although ~ is still used, especially in writing. III 289b; VI 868a

In music, *mawwāl* also stands for an interpretative freesong, with no set tune. VI 868b

mawāshī (P), and *mawāsh* : taxes in Persia levied on cows, mules and asses at so much per head. IV 1042b

mawāt (A) : in law, dead lands, land which is uncultivated or merely lying fallow, which belongs to nobody and which is, in general, far from centres of population. Legal scholars use **iḥyāʾ** 'bringing to life' to mean putting such a piece of land to use. III 1053b; IV 1036a; VI 869b

mawḍiʿ (A) : place; in ethics, the 'place' of an act as determining its goodness or badness. IX 527a

In the grammar of Sībawayhi, ~ *fī 'l-kalām* 'place in speech' denotes the position in which a speech element is used. The correlative of ~ is *manzila*, which represents status on the paradigmatic axis, and a third term in this set, *mawḳiʿ*, denotes simply the occurrence of an element in the string without regard to its function. IX 527a

♦ mawḍiʿ al-s͟hams : in astronomy, the true solar longitude. IX 292a

mawḍūʿ → MAṬRŪḤ

māwī : a caste of Hindū highway robbers, members of which were recruited by the Mug͟hal emperor Akbar to guard the palace and to control highway robbery. V 686b

mawḳiʿ → MAWḌIʿ

mawkib → MAWĀKIB

mawḳif (A) : place of standing; specifically the place where the WUḲŪF, the halt, is held during the pilgrimage, viz. ʿArafāt and Muzdalifa or D̲jamʿ. VI 874a

In eschatology, the ~ is the place where, on the day of resurrection, several scenes of the last judgment will take place. V 236a; VI 874a

In pre-Islamic times, ~ was one of the terms used to designate the religious shrines, usually in the form of stones, to be found along tracks and at camping sites, of the nomadic tribes. VI 874a

mawḳūf (A) : in the science of Tradition, a Tradition going back only to a Companion. III 25b; VII 631a; VIII 384a

In law, a state of suspense between parties and equally as regards any third party; a category of contract which is neither valid nor invalid. I 319b; III 1016b; VIII 836a

mawlā (A, pl. *mawālī*) : a person linked by proximity to another person; patron; client; freedman; a party to an egalitarian relationship of mutual help, that is, a kinsman, confederate, ally or friend. IV 44a; VI 874a

In the Qurʾān and in Traditions, ~ is applied to God with the meaning of tutor, trustee and lord. VI 874a

♦ **mawlāy** : lit. my lord, an honorific title borne by the Moroccan sultans of the S͟harīfian dynasties (Saʿdids and ʿAlawids) who were descended from al-Ḥasan b. ʿAlī, with the exception of those who were called Muḥammad and whose title was therefore SAYYIDĪ or *sīdī*. VI 888b

In mysticism, ~ is a title frequently used in connection with saints, especially in North Africa. VI 874b

mawlid (A, pl. *mawālid*), or *mawlūd* : the time, place or celebration of the birth of a person, especially that of the Prophet Muḥammad or of a saint; a panegyric poem in honour of the Prophet. VI 895a; a great festival, of which there are three in Egypt: on the 17th or 18th of January, on or about the vernal equinox, and about a month after the summer solstice. I 281a

♦ **mawālid** : genethlialogy, i.e. the art of deducing portents from the position of the stars at the time of birth, an area of judicial astrology. VIII 106a

♦ **mawlidiyya** or *milādiyya* : a poem composed in honour of the Prophet on the occasion of the anniversary of his birth and recited as a rule before the sovereign and court after ceremonies marking the *laylat al-mawlid.* VI 897b

mawlūd → MAWLID

mawna → BA<u>SH</u>TARDA

mawsim (A) : market, especially in connection with the markets of early Arabia; festival, generally with a religious basis. When such a festival signifies the birthday of a prophet or local saint, the term more generally used is MAWLID, but often some other event in a holy man's life, or even his death, may be celebrated, often at a date which shows continuity with some ancient nature festival or other rite; also, season. Thus in Lebanon, ~ denotes the season of the preparation of silk, while in India and in European terminology referring to these parts of the world, it has required the meaning of 'season' in connection with the weather conditions special to those regions, such as the regularly returning winds and rain periods. *Monsoon*, *mousson*, *moesson* and other corruptions of the term are found in this literature. VI 902a; pilgrimage. I 159b

mawṣūl → ṢILA

mawwāl → MAWĀLIYĀ

mawz (A) : the banana (tree). VIII 732b

maydān (A, pl. *mayādīn*) : a large, open, demarcated area, flat and generally rectangular, designed for all kinds of equestrian activity; the exercises of mounted formations; in figurative usage, the confrontation of two parties; like the English 'field', ~ is extended to the broad sense of 'domain of activity', physical, intellectual or spiritual. VI 912b ff.; hippodrome. II 954b

♦ maydānī : in archery, an arrow of a specified pattern. VI 912b

may<u>kh</u>ān (Mon) : a low tent requiring little wood for its construction and in recent times covered with cotton cloth purchased from Chinese traders. IV 1151a

mayl (A) : declination, an important notion in spherical astronomy. It is a measure of the distance of a celestial body from the celestial equator. Muslim astronomers tabulated either the declination and right ascensions of stars or their ecliptic coordinates. Also of concern to them was the solar declination, *mayl al-<u>sh</u>ams*, of which there were two kinds, *al-mayl al-awwal* and *al-mayl al-thānī.* VI 914b

♦ al-mayl al-aʿẓam, or *al-mayl al-kullī* : the obliquity of the ecliptic, the basic parameter of spherical astronomy. VI 914b

♦ mayl ṭabīʿī : in physics, natural inclination; also a current philosophical term. I 112a

maysir (A) : an ancient game of chance, using arrows to win parts of a slaughtered beast. It was forbidden by the Qurʾān. VI 923b

mayta (A) : dead (used of irrational beings); as a substantive, ~ means an animal that has died in any way other than by slaughter. In later terminology, the word means firstly an animal that has not been slain in the ritually prescribed fashion, the flesh of which therefore cannot be eaten, and secondly all parts of animals whose flesh cannot be eaten, whether because not properly slaughtered or as a result of a general prohibition against eating them. II 1069a; VI 924b

maẓāhir → MAẒHAR

maẓālim → MAẒLIMA

mazar (A), or *mizr* : in the terminology of food, the word for various fermented drinks. II 1061a; and → NABĪDH

mazār : in Muslim India, a term used for signifying a *pīr*'s (→ MURSHID) tomb, especially for the smaller wayside shrine. VI 125b

mazd → MAST

mazhar (A), or *mizhar* : in music, a round tambourine with or without jingling rings. The former in Persia was called the DĀʾIRA. ~ is also said to be the term for a lute, but this is doubtful. II 620b f.

maẓhar (A, pl. *maẓāhir*) : lit. place of outward appearance, hence 'manifestation, theophany', a technical term used in a wide variety of contexts in shīʿism, ṣūfism, Bābism, and, in particular, Bahāʾism, where it is of central theological importance. At its broadest, the term may be applied to any visible appearance or expression of an invisible reality, reflecting the popular contrast between the exoteric (*ẓāhir*) and the esoteric (BĀṬIN). In its more limited application, however, it refers to a type of theophany in which the divinity or its attributes are made visible in human form. VI 952a

♦ maẓhar ilāhī, or *maẓāhir-i ilāhiyya* : the Bahāʾī technical term for manifestations of God which feature through the prophets, never cease and are successive. I 916a; VI 953a

mazīdī (A) : in mediaeval ʿIrāḳ, a beggar who gives out that he just needs a little more money to purchase what he needs. VII 494a

maẓlima (A, pl. **maẓālim**) : an unjust or oppressive action, an antonym of ʿADL. Its plural form, *maẓālim*, came to denote the structure through which the temporal authorities took direct responsibility for dispensing justice. *Maẓālim* sessions were held regularly under the ʿAbbāsid caliphs al-Mahdī and al-Hādī. VI 933b; IX 325a; the name of a tax under the Aghlabids. II 145b

maẓlūm (A, P) : someone or something treated or used wrongfully, unjustly, injuriously, or tyrannically. In Persian, ~ also means 'mild, gentle, modest'. VI 958b

In shīʿī, especially Twelver, Islam, ~ is an attribute characterising the IMĀMs, especially al-Ḥusayn b. ʿAlī and ʿAlī al-Riḍā, who are ready for martyrdom. VI 958b

mazraʿa (A) : arable land, a field, for grain production as opposed to pasture, vineyard, orchard, etc.

In Ottoman administration, ~ designates a periodic settlement or a deserted village and its fields. To register a piece of land as ~ , it was required that it be checked whether the place had a village site in ruins, its own water supply and a cemetery. VI 958a

mazraba (A) : the net which is used, especially in Tunisia, for tunny fishing. It involves a huge enclosure formed of meshed cloth with which the tunny bed is surrounded. VIII 1021b

mazz → MAST

maẓẓ → DJULLANĀR

mḍamma (Mor) : a leather belt worn by men, women and children in Morocco. V 746a

meddāḥ, məddāḥ → MADDĀḤ

medin : a silver coin, based on the half-dirham, struck by the Burdjī Mamlūks and continued by the Ottomans after their conquest of Egypt and Syria. VIII 228b ff.

medjelle (T, < A *madjalla*) : originally, a book or other writing containing wisdom; in its best-known application, ~ refers to the civil code in force in the Ottoman empire and briefly in the Turkish Republic from 1869-1926. Known in full as the *Medjelle-yi Aḥkām-i ʿAdliyye*, it covers contracts, torts and some principles of civil procedure. VI 971a

medjīdiyye (T) : in numismatics, Ottoman coins of 20 piastres. I 75a

medjmūʿa → MADJMŪʿA

mehter (P 'greater') : an Ottoman musical ensemble consisting of combinations of double-reed shawms (*zurna*), trumpets (*boru*), double-headed drum (*ṭabl*), kettle-drums (*naḳḳāre, kös*) and metallic percussion instruments. The ~ was an analogue of the wind, brass and percussion ensembles used for official, municipal and military purposes in other Islamic states. The Ottoman ~ was outlawed in 1826. VI 1007a

mela → PETH

melayu → PEGON

mēlmastyā → PASHTŪNWALĪ

mensūkhāt (A, s. *mensūkh* 'annulled') : an expression used in the Ottoman empire, after the abolition of certain early Ottoman army units, in the 11th/ 17th century, for the fiefs and other grants these units had previously held. These were referred to as *mensūkhāt timari* 'annulled fiefs'. VI 1017a

məntān (N.Afr), or *məntāl* : a man's waistcoat with long, straight sleeves, worn in Morocco, Algeria and Tunisia. V 746b

meshweret → MASHWARA

mewlewiyyet (T), or *mollaliḳ* : a title given to certain judicial districts in the Ottoman empire. VI 1029b; a generic term used in the Ottoman empire to designate the positions held by the MOLLĀS in civil and religious administration, which embraces simultaneously the rank, the duties or jurisdiction and the tutorial functions of the *mollā*. VII 222a

mgawren → FĀZA

mḥarram → MAḤREM

miʾa (A) : hundred; in the plural, *al-miʾūn* refers to all SŪRAs other than the 'seven long ones', AL-SABʿ AL-ṬIWĀL, with over 100 verses: x-xii, xvi-xviii, xx, xxi, xxiii, xxvi and xxxvii. IX 887b

midād (A) : ink. In Middle Eastern manuscripts, two types of black ink were generally used, both of which date from pre-Islamic times. One was prepared on the basis of carbon and oil, and the other one from gall-nuts and ferrous components, the former originally being designated as ~ , the latter as *ḥibr*. Later, the two words were used as synonyms. VI 1031b

mid̲h̲yāʿ → ID̲H̲ĀʿA

miʿd̲j̲an (A) : 'the trough', a depression in the pavement on which the circling of the Kaʿba is performed, just opposite the door. According to legend, Ibrāhīm and Ismāʿīl mixed the mortar used in building the Kaʿba here. IV 318a

In the mediaeval kitchen, a wooden bowl in which the dough for bread was mixed, also called *d̲j̲afna*. VI 808a

mid̲j̲wāl (A) : a piece of white fabric, used in the game of MAYSIR, which was held over the archer's hands so that he could not see the arrows in the quiver. VI 924a

midraʿa (A) : a woolen, sleeved tunic worn only by the very poor in mediaeval times. V 737a

miḍrab (A) : among the pre-Islamic Bedouin, a tent under which important people camped when travelling. IV 1147a

mifras̲h̲ (A, P *mafras̲h̲*, T *mifres̲h̲*) : a travelling pack for bedding. The term is now generally applied to the woven rectangular bedding packs still used by nomads, and normally made in pairs to balance on either side of the camel carrying them. VII 1a

mifres̲h̲ → MIFRAS̲H̲

mig̲h̲far (A), or *g̲h̲ifāra* : a cap or headcloth of mail worn on military expeditions in early Islam. Over it a ḲALANSUWA or a helmet known as *bayḍa* (so-called because of its resemblance to an ostrich egg) was worn. The Prophet wore a ~ on the day Mecca surrendered. V 735a

miḥlab (A) : a wooden container in which yeast was kept, used in the mediaeval kitchen. VI 808a

miḥmal (A) : scales for gold. VII 195b

mihmindār (P) : the title of the 18th dignity, out of the 25 at the Mamlūk sultan's court; part of his duties was to receive ambassadors and delegations of Bedouin. VII 2a

miḥna (A, pl. *miḥan*) : a testing, trial. More particularly, it signifies the procedure adopted by the caliph al-Maʾmūn in 218/833, and officially applied under his two immediate successors, for the purpose of imposing the view that the Qurʾān had been created. V 1124a; VII 2b

mihna (A, pl. *mihan*) : a profession, service and handiness, mostly domestic (syn.

ṢINĀʿA); *aṣḥāb al-mihan* are artisans, *māhin* is one who serves others skilfully, a servant. IX 626b

miḥrāb (A, pl. *maḥārīb*) : the prayer niche in the mosque, indicating the direction of prayer. It is made up of an arch, the supporting columns and capitals, and the space between them. Whether in a flat or recessed form, it gives the impression of a door or a doorway. VII 7a

mihragān (P) : the name of an Iranian Mazdaean festival, traditionally celebrated in Iran around the autumn equinox; also, the name of some musical themes whose origin goes back to the Sāsānid period. VII 15a ff.; ~ and NAWRŪZ are celebrated by the Nuṣayrīs as the days when the divinity of ʿAlī is manifested in the sun. VIII 146b

miḥrāth (A, pl. *maḥārīth*), and *miḥrath* (pl. *maḥārith*) : a plough. In mediaeval times, however, ~ was more specifically applied to the tiller, which is not equipped with wheels or a mould-board or a coulter, but consists essentially of a ploughshare, a crossbeam, a handle and a pole (or beam). Although it goes back to the earliest antiquity, this agricultural implement is still in use, without modification of note, throughout the Islamic world. VII 21b

mihtar (A) : in Mamlūk Egypt, the head of the *rikāb-khāna*, the depot for harness and in general for all the material required for horses and stables. VIII 530a

miḥwar → ḲUṬB; ẒILL

mīḳāt (A, pl. *mawāḳīt*) : appointed or exact time.

In law, ~ is applied to the times of prayer and to the places where those who enter the ḤARAM are bound to put on the IḤRĀM. VII 26a

In astronomy, *ʿilm al-mīḳāt* is the science of astronomical timekeeping by the sun and stars and the determination of the times of the five prayers. VII 27b; and → MUWAḲḲIT

♦ mīḳātī : an astronomer who specialised in spherical astronomy and astronomical timekeeping, but unlike the MUWAḲḲIT, was not necessarily associated with any religious institution. Mention of such astronomers appeared for the first time in Egypt in the 7th/13th century. VII 29b

mikhdhaf → DJAʿBA

mikhlāf (A, pl. *makhālīf*) : in mediaeval administrative geography, an 'administrative province' or 'rural area', a term used particularly in Yemen. In the early 6th/13th century, ~ is defined with the restricted sense of the settled and cultivated lands around a fortress. From the period of Ayyūbid rule in Yemen onwards, ~ gradually falls out of use there and it is no longer used at the present time. VII 35a; IX 166a

miḳlā (A), and *miḳlāt* : a pan generally used for frying fish and the like, made of iron and used in the mediaeval kitchen. A stone-made ~ was used for other purposes, although the distinction between the two is unclear. VI 808a

miḳlama → DAWĀT

miḳran (A) : a piece of wood fixed on the oxen's head, when they plough, by means of a rope called *taw<u>th</u>īḳ*. VII 22b

miḳṭara (A) : the occasional name for an apparatus, more often called a FALAḲA, used for immobilising the feet in order to apply a bastinado on the soles of the feet. II 763b

miḳyās (A) : measurement, means of measuring; any simple measuring instrument; in Egypt the name of the Nilometer, i.e. the gauge in which the annual rise of the river can be measured. VII 39b; the gnomon of the sundial, also called *<u>sh</u>a<u>kh</u>ṣ* or *<u>sh</u>ā<u>kh</u>iṣ*. VII 210a; and → ḲIYĀS

mīlād (A) : time of birth, in contradistinction to MAWLID, which may denote also 'place of birth'; Christmas. VII 40b; in South Africa, festival celebrating the birthday of the Prophet. IX 731a

mīlādiyya → MAWLIDIYYA

milāḥa (A) : navigation, seamanship; seafaring. VII 40b

milal → MILLA

milban (A) : a wooden mould used to fabricate unfired brick, composed essentially of dampened, shaped clay, which is then turned into the ~ without a bottom or cover, packed tight and finally dried in the sun; the clay is fined down with sand, gravel, chopped straw or potsherds in fixed proportions to prevent its crumbling and cracking. Once taken out of the ~ , the brick is left for a while longer in the sun. V 585a

milḥafa (N.Afr), and *mlaḥfa, tamǝlḥaft* : a large, enveloping outer wrap worn by women in the Arab East and by both sexes in North Africa. V 741b; V 746a

milk (A, pl. *amlāk*) : private property.

In law, ~ denotes ownership, which is distinguished from possession, *yad*. The characteristic feature of ~ is its perpetual nature. I 28b; VII 60b

♦ amlāk-i salṭanatī : a term used under the Ḳā<u>dj</u>ārs in contradistinction to *amlāk-i <u>kh</u>āṣṣa*, private estates. IV 973a; after the grant of the Persian Constitution, the ~ were the personal estates of the ruler, also referred to as *amlāk-i <u>sh</u>āhī*. IV 979b

♦ amlāk-i <u>sh</u>āhī → AMLĀK-I SALṬANATĪ

milla (A, pl. *milal*, P *millat*, T **millet**) : religion, sect; with the article, *al-milla* means the true religion revealed by Muḥammad and is occasionally used elliptically for *ahl al-milla*, the followers of the Islamic religion. II 294b; VII 61a

In the Qurʾān, ~ always means 'religion', e.g. the religion of the Christians and Jews, the religion of Abraham. II 294b; VII 61a

In Ottoman Turkish, *millet* came to denote the internally-autonomous religious groups within the Ottoman empire (Jews, Armenians, Greek Orthodox, etc.). VII 61a ff.

In modern Persian and Turkish, ~ means 'nation, people'. VII 61a

♦ **al-milal wa 'l-niḥal** (A) : one of the stock phrases employed, in the heresiographical literature, to denote an enumeration of religious and occasionally philosophical doctrines, as well as the various groups or schools which profess them. VII 54a

millat → MILLA

millet → MILLA

mimʿār-bas̲h̲ï (T) : a local master-builder, not to be confused with the Ottoman's Chief Architect officiating in Istanbul. IX 540b

mimlaḳa → MĀLAḲ

mīnā → BĀZĀR

mīnāʾī (P ?) : enamel. IV 1167a; a type of ceramics with polychrome under- and over-glaze painting produced during the late 6th/12th and early 7th/13th centuries. The precise mediaeval name of this ware is uncertain. Iranian authors of the 11th/14th centuries link the term to translucent or luminous substances such as the sky or wine vessels; ~ is also used by them to describe a type of glass. Later authors use the term to describe glass vessels that had been painted and gilded. VII 72b

minbar (A) : the raised structure or pulpit from which solemn announcements to the Muslim community were made and from which sermons were preached. VII 73b

mindīl → MANDĪL

mind̲j̲al → ZABR

mind̲j̲am (A) : the tongs and the beam of the common balance. VII 195b

minhād̲j̲ → S̲H̲ARĪʿA

mins̲h̲afa (A) : a large, white head veil for women in the Arab East. V 741b; and → MANDĪL

minṭaḳat al-burūd̲j̲ (A), and *minṭaḳat falak al-burūd̲j̲* : the zodiac; the ecliptic circle. VII 81b

mintān (T) : a short caftan without sleeves, stopping at the waist, worn in Ottoman Turkey. V 752a

mīr (P, < A AMĪR) : a Persian title applied to princes, but also borne by poets and other men of letters. In India and Pakistan, SAYYIDs sometimes call themselves by the title. It also occurs in official titles in both the Dihlī sultanate and in Mug̲h̲al administration, e.g. *mīr baḥr* 'naval commander'. VII 87b; IX 333a

♦ mīr-āb → MĪRĀB

♦ **mīr-āk̲h̲ūr** : under the Ottomans, the master of the stables, the official given charge of all aspects relating to the supply and maintenance of the Ottoman sultan's stables. VII 88a; VIII 529a and → AMĪR ĀK̲H̲ŪR

♦ mīr-ʿalem : under the Ottomans, the 'standard-bearer'. VIII 529a

♦ mīr bak̲h̲s̲h̲ī : quartermaster-general. Under the Mug̲h̲al emperor Akbar, the ~ was administrative head of the military department and responsible for all transport arrangements during campaigns. He could be placed in command of an army in the field. I 316b

♦ mīr sāmān : under the Mug̲h̲al emperor Akbar, the ~ was in charge of the

BUYŪTĀT department and was responsible for the organisation of the factories, workshops and stores maintained by the emperor. I 316b

♦ mīr-zāda → MĪRZĀ

♦ mīr-i farsh : the term usually applied to stone weights, often of marble carved and inlaid with semi-precious stones, used to hold down a pall over a grave. VII 88a

♦ **mīr-i mīrān** : 'supreme commander', a military and political term used in 18th-century Ottoman Turkish administrative practice as being virtually synonymous with BEGLERBEGI 'provincial governor', and then increasingly used to denote the honorary rank of *beglerbegi*, although this last title was considered as somewhat superior to that of ~ . In the 19th century, ~ also became a civil service rank. VII 95b; VIII 280b

♦ **mīrī** (T, < A *amīrī*) : 'belonging to the government'. Under the Ottomans, ~ was singled out to designate assets that belong of right to the highest Muslim authority, the sultan. Throughout Ottoman history, it was used as a noun meaning 'lands belonging to the government', 'land tax' levied from them, as well as 'the public treasury'. II 148a; VII 125a

♦ al-mīrī (Ir) : the government. VII 88a

mīrāb (P), and *mīr-āb* : an official of the Ṣafawid state responsible for the distribution of the water of a ḲANĀT. IV 531a; V 872b

mirabbaʿ → RUBĀʿĪ

miʿrādj (A), and *isrāʾ* : originally, a ladder, then 'ascent'; in particular, the Prophet's ascension to Heaven. VII 97b

mirbāʿ → RĀBIʿ

mirfaʿ (A) : a footstool, an ink-stand and the base of the small oriental table. In certain texts it may be replaced by KURSĪ. V 509a

mīrī → MĪR

mirʿizz (A) : flock, tuft of wool. S 317a

mirkās (A), or *mirḳās* : 'merguez', a North African kind of fried sausage made from minced leg of mutton with the addition of various spices and ingredients, such as pickle, pimento, dried coriander, nard and cinnamon. VII 126a

mirmīs → KARKADDAN

mirrīkh (A) : the planet Mars. VII 127a

mirsal → MARBAṬ

mirshaḥa → ḲARBŪṢ

mirwad (A) : a small probe or stick with a rounded end used by women to apply cosmetic to their eyebrows, eyelashes or the edges of their eyelids. In mediaeval times, the sticks were commonly of bronze. V 356b

mirwaḥa (A) : fan, vane. Large fans are called *mirwaḥat al*-KHAYSH, hand fans *mirwaḥat al-khūṣ* 'palm-leaf fan'. VII 127b ff.

In music, a jingling instrument used by Christians. IX 11a

mīrzā (P), and *mirzā* : 'born of a prince', a title given to noblemen and others of good birth. Since the time of Nādir S̲h̲āh's conquest of India, it has been further applied to educated men outside of the class of *mullā*s or *ʿulamāʾ* (→ MOLLĀ). In modern times, but not formerly, the title is placed after the name of a prince; when placed before the name of other persons bearing it, it is equivalent to 'Mr'. VII 129a

In Indian usage, it is given, from Mug̲h̲al times onwards, to kinsmen of the Mug̲h̲als, the Tīmūrids, the Ṣafawids, members of other royal houses and to certain Mug̲h̲al nobles. In modern times in India and Pakistan, the prefixed ~ is particularly used by men of the Mug̲h̲al division of AS̲H̲RĀF Muslims. VII 129b

mirzam (A) : in astronomy, *al-~* designated β Canis Maioris, β Canis Minoris and γ Orionis; in modern times in Central Arabia, *el-mirzem* is used for Sirius. IX 471b; and → NUḤĀM

misabbaʿ → SABʿĀNĪ

misāḥa (A) : the measurement of plane surfaces; survey, the technique of surveying. VII 137b; and → MUḲĀSAMA

♦ **ʿilm al-misāḥa** : the science of measurement, plane and solid geometry. VII 135a

misalla (A, pl. *masāll*) : an obelisk. VII 140b

miṣbāḥ → SIRĀD̲J̲

misḥ (A) : a coarse cloth. IX 677a

mis̲h̲mis̲h̲ (A) : the apricot-tree and its fruit (*Prunus armeniaca*). VII 141b

mis̲h̲ṭāḥ (A) : a place where flour is sifted by shaking. IX 361b

misk (A) : musk. VII 142a

misk̲h̲ → MASK̲H̲

miskīn (A, pl. *masākīn, miskīnūn*) : poor, destitute; miserable, humble. II 757b; VII 144b

In modern South Arabia, ~ denotes the top layer of the population subject to the tribesmen, comprising the petty traders and artisans, constituting the layer above the *ḍuʿafāʾ* (→ ḌAʿĪF). VII 145a

In ʿIrāḳī Kurdistan, *miskēn* denotes villagers who do not claim tribal origin, a class of lowly social status and often oppressed by tribal neighbours. VII 145a

miṣr (A, pl. *amṣār*) : in earliest Islam, the settlements developing out of the armed encampments established by the Arabs in the conquered provinces outside Arabia and then, subsequently, the capital towns or metropolises of the conquered provinces; the land of Egypt and its capital city. VII 146a ff.

As a geographical term, ~ is defined as an administrative unit, a large urban centre where a ruler or governor resides and which has located there the administrative organs, treasury, etc. of the province. VII 146b

miṣrāʿ (A) : in poetry, one of two clearly distinct halves of a line of poetry. I 668a; VIII 579a; in Afghan poetry, a lyrical distich in a peculiar metre, also called *lanḍaī*. I 221a

miss → NUḤĀS

misṭara (A) : a ruler. VII 198b
miswāk → SIWĀK
mīt̲h̲āḳ → ʿAḲD
mit̲h̲āl → FARMĀN
mit̲h̲ḳāl (A) : the oldest Arab unit of Troy weight. III 10b; an apothecary's stater equalling two *dānaḳ*; a gold DĪNĀR. IV 248b; a standard weight unit, which was not everywhere the same. VI 118a
miʾūn → MIʾA
miyāḳis (A, < Gr) : in zoology, the common mussel (*Mytilus edulis* L.), a popular foodstuff. VIII 707a
miyān (T), or *miyān-k̲h̲āne* : in Turkish poetry, the third line of each stanza of the S̲H̲ARḲĪ. IX 354a
mīzāb → ḲIBLA
mizād̲j̲ (A) : mixture; temperament. VIII 100a
In metaphysics, the final qualitative pattern resulting from definite proportions of the constituents of a given mixture, i.e. hot, cold, moist and dry. I 1084a
miʿzaf (A, pl. *maʿāzif*), and *miʿzafa* : a term denoting today any string or wind instrument or even, more restrictedly, a piano, but one which was employed in mediaeval Islamic times to instruments with 'open strings', which were played with the fingers or a plectrum. VII 189b
miẓall (A) : a canopy, a portable but firm construction, serving as well as the general's tent, insignia of command, rallying point and headquarters on campaign. In the Muslim West, much confusion is caused because of the resemblance in both form and meaning between ~ and MIẒALLA. VII 192a
miẓalla (A) : lit. an instrument or apparatus for providing shade, *ẓill*, apparently synonymous with the S̲H̲AMSA, *s̲h̲amsiyya*, lit. an instrument or apparatus for providing shelter for the sun, probably therefore referring to the sunshade or parasol borne on ceremonial occasions and processions over early Islamic rulers. In Mamlūk sources this appears as *d̲j̲itr*, *s̲h̲itr* (< P *čitr*, → ČATR) denoting the parasol as one of the insignia of royalty; VII 191b; among the pre-Islamic Bedouin, a large tent, often made of goat's hair. V 1147a; VII 192b
mīzān (A) : balance, scales; in eschatology, the Qurʾānic 'balance' which weighs the deeds of an individual. III 465b
In the scientific thought of D̲j̲ābir b. Ḥayyān, ~ forms a fundamental principle meaning a.o. specific gravity, the metaphysical principle *par excellence,* and a speculation on the letters of the Arabic alphabet. II 358b
In mathematics, ~ means, among other things, testing the correctness of any calculation. VII 198b
In divination, in magic squares, ~ stands for the sum of the largest and smallest figures; it is half the total of the vertical row, horizontal row or of the diagonals. VII 198b
In astronomy, *al-~* is the term for Libra, one of the twelve zodiacal constellations. VII 83b

♦ ʿilm al-mīzān : alchemy. VII 198b

miʾzar → IZĀR

mizhar → MAZHAR

mizmār (A) : lit. an instrument of piping. In the generic meaning, it refers to any instrument of the wood-wind family, i.e. a reed-pipe or a flute. In the specific sense, ~ refers to a reed-pipe (i.e. a pipe played with a reed) as distinct from a flute. In Persian, the equivalent of ~ in this sense is NĀY. VII 206b

♦ mizmār al-mut͟hannā → DIYĀNAY

mizr → MAZAR; NABĪD͟H

mizwad (A, pl. *mazāwid*) : a food-bag, made by the Tuaregs from cheetah skin if they can catch the animal. II 740a

mizwala (A), and *sāʿa s͟hamsiyya* : in modern Arabic, a sundial. In mediaeval Islam, horizontal sundials were called *ruk͟hāma* or *basīṭa,* vertical sundials *munḥarifa.* VII 210a

mizwār (A, < B *amzwaru* 'he who precedes, he who is placed at the head') : in North Africa, chief of a religious brotherhood, the superintendent of a ZĀWIYA or the chief of a body of *s͟horfā* (→ S͟HARĪF), equivalent to the Arabic MUḲADDAM. In those districts of Morocco where the old Berber organisation has survived, mainly in the Great Atlas and Central Atlas, *amzwār* is sometimes the equivalent of *anflūs*, the political adviser to a body. VII 211b

mizz → MAST

mōbad͟h (P) : chief of the Mad͟jūs, a title for a type of Zoroastrian priest which in the Sāsānid state had a variety of ritual, judicial and administrative responsibilities. By the 4th or 5th century, a three-level hierarchy had developed of local *mōbad͟h*s, grand *mōbad͟h*s of provinces or regions and a supreme *mōbad͟h* over the entire state. The function of ~ continued to exist in Islamic times but it is not always clear whether ~ is used as a generic term for any priest or is used in a specifically technical sense in sources referring to Islamic Iran; this term is also used somewhat loosely in modern scholarship for Zoroastrian priests in early Islamic times. VII 213b

mōbedān-mōbed → ḲĀḌI 'L-ḲUḌĀT

mohur (Eng, < P *muhr*, < San *mudrā*) : an Indian gold coin. VII 221a

mollā (P, < A MAWLĀ), or *mullā* : a title of function, of dignity or profession, and of rank, limited, with a few exceptions, to the Turco-Iranian and Indian world, ~ indicates in the first instance any Muslim scholar who has acquired a certain degree of religious education and the aptitude to communicate it. In current usage, ~ is most often applied to the *ʿulamāʾ*, the religious scholars. Distinguished by his clothing and physical appearance, his prestige and claim to knowledge, the ~ in Iran today has succeeded in occupying a wide range of functions at many different levels. Exercising the basic prerogatives in matters of education, ritual functions (prayers, marriages, funerals etc.) and judicial functions, the *mollā*s constitute the basis of what has been called, erroneously in the view of some, a veritable clergy. VII 221a; and → MEWLEWIYYET

♦ mollalïḳ → MEWLEWIYYET

mposa (Sw) : in East Africa, the proposer of a marriage, a senior member of the family who is usually but not necessarily from the groom's family. VIII 33b

muʾaddib (A) : a later appellation than MUDARRIS or MUʿALLIM for teacher in the Arab lands; in some cases, the ~ was a higher rank, namely, the more learned or the private tutor. V 568a

muʿaddin → MAʿDIN

muʾa**dh****dh**in (A), and *munādī* : originally, among the Arab tribes and in the towns, the crier making important proclamations and invitations to general assemblies. From the beginning of Islam, ~ and *munādī* have been used to designate the official whose main function is to summon the believers to public worship on Friday and to the five daily prayers. Both terms are used quite indiscriminately. VI 675b

muʾadjdjal (A) : in law, yearly, variable, rather low rents. S 368b; in India, 'deferred dower', the remainder of the MAHR after a token amount has been paid at the time of marriage, becoming payable when the wife is divorced or widowed. I 172b

muʿadjdjal (A) : in law, a lump sum paid immediately. S 368b; in India, 'prompt dower', a token amount of the MAHR paid at the time of marriage. I 172b

muʿāf (A) : one of five classes, that of 700 men-at-arms excepted from taxation, into which the population of Eastern Transcaucasia was divided in the late 18th century under Muḥammad Ḥasan. IX 255a

♦ muʿāfī (P) : under the Ṣafawids, a temporary (but renewable) grant of immunity. Another similar grant was called the *musallamī*. IX 732b

muʿāhad (A) : a non-Muslim under the protection of the Islamic state. IV 768a

♦ **muʿāhada** : treaty, agreement. VII 250a

muʿāḳaba (A) : in prosody, the obligatory alternation of the shortening of two adjacent cords. This phenomenon occurs in the *madīd*, *ramal*, *khafīf*, and *mudjtathth* metres. The apparent reason for the existence of this phenomenon is to avoid a sequence of four moving letters. VIII 747b

muʿākama (A) : a term denoting a scantily dressed woman, var. *mukāʿama*, which also means pressing one's lips on the lips of a person of the same sex. IX 566b

muʿāḳara (A) : a term denoting the action of two or more friends who drink together; also, a meal taken with friends. VII 850a

muʾākhāt (A) : brothering, a practice found in the early days of Islam by which two men became 'brothers'. VII 253b

muʿālidj (A) : lit. treating, developing; in Muslim Spain, ~ had the sense of 'retailer of fruit and vegetables'. I 961b

muʾallaf → BASĪṬ

♦ **al-muʾallafa ḳulūbuhum** (A) : lit. those whose hearts are won over; the term applied to those former opponents of the Prophet Muḥammad who are said to have been reconciled to the cause of Islam by presents of 100 or 50 camels from Muḥammad's share of the spoils of the battle of al-Ḥunayn after Muḥammad's forces had defeated the Hawāzin confederation. VII 254a

muʿallaḳ (A) : suspended.

In the science of Tradition, ~ is used when there is an omission of one or more names at the beginning of the ISNĀD, or when the whole *isnād* is omitted. III 26a

muʿallal (A) : in the science of Tradition, ~ applies to a Tradition with some weakness in ISNĀD or MATN. Al-Ḥākim calls it a Tradition mixed with another, or containing some false notion of the transmitter, or given as MUTTAṢIL when it is MURSAL. III 26a

muʿallim (A) : teacher. A synonym was MUDARRIS, and later MUʾADDIB. V 568a; in guild terminology, master-craftsman. VIII 871b; IX 168b

♦ al-muʿallim al-t͟hālit͟h : lit. the third teacher; an appellation for Mīr Muḥammad Bāḳir b. S͟hams al-Din Muḥammad al-Ḥusaynī al-Astarābādī, known as (Ibn) al-Dāmād. II 103b

♦ al-muʿallim al-t͟hānī : lit. the second teacher; an appellation for Abū Naṣr al-Fārābī. I 631a

muʿāmalāt (A) : in law, transactions concerning credit granted by a donor to a beneficiary; also, the bilateral contracts, as opposed to the ʿIBĀDĀT which constitute the 'ritual of Islamic law'. In this general sense, the ~ define juridico-human relations and ensure that the Muslim's behaviour conforms to juridico-moral theories. VII 255b; interpersonal acts. IX 323b

muʾāmara (A) : in classical Muslim administration, an inventory of orders issued during the period of the general issue of pay, *ṭamaʿ*, bearing at its end a signed authorisation by the sultan. II 79a

muʿammā (A) : lit. something made obscure, hidden; a word puzzle, verbal charade, a kind of literary play upon words (syn. LUG͟HZ and UḤD͟JIYYA); the ~ is distinguished by the absence of the interrogatory element and by the fact that the sense of the passage had been made 'blind' by various procedures; also, secret writing, code. V 806b; VII 257a; VIII 217a

muʿammar (A) : an appellative of legendary and historical people who are alleged to have lived to an exceptionally great age. VII 258a

muʿanʿan (A) : in the science of Tradition, an ISNĀD where *ʿan* ('on the authority of') is used with no clear indication of how the Tradition was received. III 26a; *isnād*s omitting the established transmission methods and with only one or more times the preposition *ʿan* between two transmitters are called ~ . Closely connected with this is the *isnād* which is *muʾannan*, which introduces the information transmitted by an older to a younger authority simply by means of the conjunction *anna* 'that'. VII 260a

muʾannan → MUʿANʿAN

muʾannat͟h → MUD͟HAKKAR

muʿāraḍa (A) : opposition.

In literary theory, ~ indicates imitation or emulation; the poet composes his work in the same rhyme and metre, and in doing so, often tries to surpass the original. The imitating of someone's work was also used sometimes as a deliberate act of homage. VII 261a; IX 463b; 'counter-poem'. VIII 805a; and → NAḲĀʾIḌ

As a technique in manuscript production, ~ has the meaning of collation, i.e. the textual comparison of a manuscript with another of the same work, preferably with one from which it was copied. A synonym is MUḲĀBALA. VII 490b

muʾarniba (A, < *arnab*), or *murniba* : regions where (adult) hares are plentiful; the regions where young hares are predominant are called *ma<u>kh</u>azza* or *mu<u>kh</u>arniḳa*. S 85a

muʿarrab (A) : an arabicised loan or foreign word, in theory, only those which were integrated into the Arabic of pre- and early Islamic times; those of the post-classical period are called MUWALLAD. However, *muwallad* does not only refer to loan words, but to all kinds of linguistic neologisms which came up in post-classical Arabic. The difference between ~ and *muwallad* is not taken into consideration by all philologists, and so ~ often is the general term for 'loan word, foreign word'. VII 261b

muʿaskar → ʿASKAR

muʿāṭāt (A) : in law, a mutual delivery of the object of sale and of the sale price. I 318b

muʿāwaḍa (A) : barter, exchange.

In law, ~ stands for a contract which is based on a mutual obligation, in opposition to a contract with a one-sided obligation. Examples are contracts of sale, lease and marriage. VII 263b; and → ṢULḤ AL-IBRĀʾ

muʿawwi<u>dh</u>atān (A), and *muʿawwi<u>dh</u>āt* : the name given to the last two SŪRAs of the Qurʾān, because they both begin with the words 'Say: I seek refuge in the Lord'. VII 269b; IX 887b

mubaʿʿaḍ (A) : 'partial', a term for a slave held in joint ownership and enfranchised by one of the owners, who, however, is not wealthy enough to compensate his fellow-owners for the value of their shares. I 30a

In mathematics, ~ is a subdivided fraction, or a fraction of a fraction. IV 725b

mübādele (T, < A *mubādala*) : exchange, used in Ottoman Turkish for the exchange of commodities and of values, the exchange of prisoners of war, the exchange of ambassadors, and the exchange of populations. VII 275a

mubāḥ (A) : 'licit, authorised', one of the five juridical qualifications of human acts. VII 276a; 'indifferent', neither obligatory or recommended, nor forbidden or reprehensible. III 660b

mubāhala (A) : a term indicating both the spontaneous swearing of a curse in order to strengthen an assertion or to find the truth, and a kind of ordeal, invoked for the same purpose, between disputing individuals or parties, in which the instigation or call to the ordeal is more important than the execution; also, ~

is the name of a 'historical' ordeal which is said to have been proposed in 10/632-3 by the Prophet to a deputation of the Christian Nadjrānīs. VII 276a

mubālagha (A) : in grammar, ~ is used to denote the intensive meaning of a number of morphemes and syntagmas. Most consistently it is applied to the intensive participles of the forms *faʿūl*, *faʿʿāl*, etc. VII 277a

In literary theory, ~ came to mean hyperbole, intensification. Ḳudāma (d. 337/948) uses ~ to denote a very specialised type of emphasising (*īghāl* with later authors) in which a poetic idea is rounded out by a pertinent little exaggeration at the end of the line. VII 277a; emphasis. VIII 614b

muballigh (A) : a participant in the Friday or feast-day prayers with a loud voice. While saying his prayer, he has to repeat aloud certain invocations to the IMĀM, for all to hear. In mosques of any importance, he stands on a platform, DIKKA, and is therefore called *dikkat al-muballigh*. II 276a

mubāra'a (A) : in law, a form of divorce by mutual agreement by which husband and wife free themselves by a reciprocal renunciation of all rights. I 1027a

mubāriz (SpA), or *barrāz* : 'the champion who comes out of the ranks, when two armies are ranged against one another, to challenge an enemy to single combat'. IX 533a

mubashshir → NADHĪR

mubayyiḍa (A) : 'those clothed in white', i.e. ʿAlids and their supporters at the battle at Fakhkh in 169/786, as opposed to their opponents, *al-musawwida* 'those clothed in black', ʿAbbāsids and their supporters. III 617a; (< P *safīd-djāmagān*) followers of a semi-secret organisation devoted to the cult of Abū Muslim who proclaimed the imminent return of Zoroaster and wore white garments. They were involved in a number of revolts in eastern Iran and Transoxania in the 2nd/8th century. IV 16b; VII 500a

mubham (A) : 'obscure'; in the science of Tradition, ~ is used of an ISNĀD when a transmitter is named vaguely, e.g., *radjul* (a man), or *ibn fulān* (son of so and so). III 26a; and → ISM

mubtada' (A) : beginning, start.

In grammar, ~ is generally translated as 'inchoative'. It designates the first component part with which one begins the nominal phrase, whose second component is the predicate, KHABAR. VII 283a

In history, ~ is employed in particular with regard to the beginning of the creation and also to biblical history in general. VII 283b

mubtadi' → ADJĪR

mudabbadj (A) : 'variegated, embellished'; in the science of Tradition, the term used when two contemporaries transmit Traditions from one another. III 26a

mudabbar → TADBĪR

muḍāf → BARRĀNĪ; IḌĀFA; MUFRAD

mudallas (A) : in the science of Tradition, a Tradition with a concealed defect, TADLĪS, in the ISNĀD. III 26a

muḍāraba (A), and, in S̲h̲āfiʿī and Mālikī sources, **ḳirāḍ**, *muḳāraḍa* : in law, a commercial association whereby an investor entrusts capital to an agent who trades with it and shares with the investor a pre-determined proportion of the profits. Losses incurred in the venture are the responsibility of the investor; the agent loses his time and effort, and any profit he would have gained were it successful. VII 284b; profit-sharing. IX 348b

mudārāt (A) : in Imāmī tradition, a practice of treating others in a friendly manner while concealing your true attitude towards them. IX 206a

muḍāriʿ (A) : similar.

In grammar, ~ is the verbal form characterised by the prefixing of one of four augments, marks of the person, *hamza*, *tāʾ*, *yāʾ* and *nūn*. It is devoted to the expression of the present and future, and is the opposite of MĀḌĪ, characterised by the suffixing of personal markings and allocated to the expression of the past. VII 285b

In prosody, ~ is the name of the twelfth Arabic metre, said to be invented by Abu 'l-ʿAtāhiya. I 108a; I 670a

mudarris (A) : a teacher, instructor; in mediaeval usage, when used without a complement, a professor of law at a MADRASA. The same term with a complement was sometimes used to designate other professors. V 1124b; V 1131a

mudawwara (A) : lit. something circular; a term used in the central and western parts of the Arab world in the later Middle Ages to denote a large tent of rulers and great men, used especially when the army was on the march. VII 286a

mudd (A) : a measure (of various weights) of capacity. The ~ was (about) 1.05 litres in ʿIrāḳ, 3.673 litres in Syria, and 2.5 litres in Egypt. VI 117b

♦ mudd al-nabī : the MUDD of Medina, forming the basis for establishing the value of the ṣāʿ (4 ~ is 1 ṣāʿ). VIII 654a

muddaʿī (A) : in law, the plaintiff in a lawsuit. II 170b

♦ muddaʿā ʿalayh : in law, the defendant in a lawsuit. II 170b

♦ muddaʿā bihi : in law, the object of the claim in a lawsuit. II 171a

muddaṯh̲ṯh̲ir (A) : the title of the 74th SŪRA of the Qurʾān, derived from the first verse which may be translated 'O you covered in a cloak'. VII 286a; and → MUZZAMMIL

muddjina → ḲAYNA

mud̲h̲akk (A) : a term for a foal older than five years of age. II 785a

mud̲h̲akkar (A) : masculine.

In grammar, a technical term for one of the two states of a noun, whose opposite is *muʾannat̲h̲* 'feminine'. VII 289b

♦ mud̲h̲akkarāt : in poetry, poems composed about boys. IX 8b

mud̲h̲ayyal (A) : a complex chronogram, whereby the principal chronogram is completed by a supplementary chronogram, *d̲h̲ayl*, the sum of the two providing the date. III 468a

mud̲h̲īʿ → IDHĀʿA

mūḍiḥa (A) : a wound laying bare the bone, a determining factor in the prescription of compensation following upon physical injury, DIYA. II 341b

mudīr (A, T *müdīr*) : the title of governors of the provinces of Egypt, an office created by Muḥammad ʿAlī shortly after 1813. The chief task of the ~ is the controlling of the industrial and agricultural administration and of the irrigation, as executed by his subordinates. At the present time, Egypt comprises 25 *mudīriyya*s or governorates. VII 290a; and → SĀḲĪ

♦ mudīriyya : administrative district. IX 166b; and → MUDĪR

mudjabbir (A) : in medicine, a bone-setter, bone-healer. II 481b

mudjaddara → ARUZZ MUFALFAL

mudjaddid (A) : renewer (of the century), a term used for the renovator whom God will send to the Muslim community at the turn of each century, in order to explain matters of religion. VII 290a

mudjahhiz (A) : a type of merchant in mediaeval Islam, the purveyor who supplies travellers with all that they need. IX 789a

mudjāhid (A, pl. *mudjāhidūn*) : a fighter for the faith, one who wages war against the unbelievers. VII 290b

In Muslim India, the *mudjāhidīn* were the rebellious forces of Aḥmad Brēlwī (d. 1831), who fought the Sikhs to oust them from the Pandjab. I 282b; IV 196b; VII 290b

In Saudi Arabia, the *mudjāhidūn* is the popular name for the National Guard, made up of detachments of the Ikhwān. III 1068a

mudjallī (A), or *muḳaffī* : a name for the third horse in a horse-race, according to the order of finishing. II 953a

muʿdjam → FAHRASA; ḤURŪF AL-MUʿDJAM; ḲĀMŪS

mudjarrad → RABBĀNĪ

mudjāwara (A) : 'proximity, association'; in rhetoric, one of three types of metaphor as defined by al-Sakkākī, as e.g. the container for the contained: *zudjādja* 'bottle' = 'wine'. V 117a

mudjāwir (A) : neighbour; a person, who, for a shorter or longer period of time, settles in a holy place in order to lead a life of asceticism and religious contemplation and to receive the BARAKA 'blessing' of that place. VII 293b; VIII 495b; the permanently-appointed personnel of places of pilgrimage (guards, cleaners, guides, etc.) who in general belong to the local population. VII 294b

In Egypt until today, ~ may indicate any student of the Azhar who comes from outside and lives in the premises of al-Azhar. VII 293b

mudjāzāt → SHARṬ

mudjbira → DJABRIYYA

mudjdiba (A) : in geography, a term applied to terrain covered with moving sands and totally waterless. VIII 845b

muʾdjiza (A) : lit. that by means of which (the Prophet) confounds, overwhelms his opponents; the technical term for miracle. It does not occur in the Qurʾān, which denies miracles in connection with Muḥammad, whereas it emphasises his 'signs', *āyāt*, later taken to mean the verses of the Qurʾān. ~ and ĀYA have become synonyms; they denote the miracles performed by God in order to prove the sincerity of His apostles. The term KARĀMA is used in connection with the saints; it differs from ~ in so far as it denotes nothing but a personal distinction granted by God to a saint. VII 295b

mudjrā → MADJRĀ

mudjtahid (A) : in law, one who possesses the aptitude to form his own judgement on questions concerning the sharīʿa, using personal effort, IDJTIHĀD, in the interpretation of the fundamental principles of the law. III 1026b; VII 295b; and → MUṬLAḲ

mudjtathth (A) : in prosody, the name of the fourteenth Arabic metre. Theoretically, it comprises three feet: *mustafʿilun / fāʿilātun / fāʿilātun* to each hemistich, but in practice there is just one single *fāʿilātun*. This metre is not used by the ancient poets. I 670a; VII 304a

mudjūn (A) : a word whose meaning ranges from jest and frivolity to the most shameless debauchery, including vulgarity, coarseness, impudence, libertinage, obscenity and everything that may provoke coarse laughter, such as scatological humour, ~ nourished, from a literary viewpoint, entertaining works full of more or less obscene anecdotes. VII 304a

♦ mudjūniyyāt : poetry of sexual perversion. IX 453b

muḍmar (A) : implicit.

In grammar, ~ (syn. *ḍamīr*) designates a noun in which the person is disguised by means of a mark. This term is the converse of *muẓhar* 'explicit', designating a noun in which the person is revealed in a clear manner. The category of the implicit noun corresponds to that of the personal pronoun in Western grammar. VII 304b; IX 527b

mudradj (A) : 'inserted'; in the science of Tradition, ~ is used of a gloss in the MATN, or of giving with one ISNĀD texts which differ with different *isnād*s, or of mentioning a number of transmitters who differ in their *isnād* without indicating this. Generally, ~ is used of inserting something in the *isnād* or the *matn* of one Tradition from another to make this appear part of it. III 26a

muḍṭarib (A) : 'incongruous'; in the science of Tradition, ~ is used when two or more people of similar standing differ with one another in their version of a Tradition. The difference may affect ISNĀD or MATN. III 26a

♦ muḍṭarib al-ḥadīth : a man whose Traditions are confused. III 26a

mufākhara (A, pl. *mufākharāt*) : in poetry, a genre consisting of self-praise, but hardly ever separated from HIDJĀʾ, taunting and deriding the rival. VII 308b; a contest for precedence and glory, usually taking place between groups, tribes and clans in pre-Islamic Arabia, although in post-Islamic times, there were caliphs who were not ashamed to take part in them. VII 309b

mufakhkham → TAFKHĪM

mufalfil (A) : in the mediaeval Near East, a beggar who pretends to have been the victim of a robbery. The ~ works together with a confederate. VII 494b

mufāwaḍa (A) : in law, a form of commercial partnership, most prominently associated with the Ḥanafī school, and in a lesser degree with the Mālikīs. For the Ḥanafīs, the ~ is one of two classes of commercial partnership, ʿINĀN being the other, and is perhaps best translated as a universal, or unlimited, investment partnership. VII 310a

In the context of Mālikī law, ~ denotes a partnership in which each of the contracting parties confers on the other an unqualified mandate to dispose of their joint capital in any acceptable manner designed to benefit their common enterprise. VII 311a

mufrad (A, pl. *mufradāt*) : in grammar, ~ denotes the singular, usually when applied to the 'simple' noun, in opposition to the dual and plural forms. II 406b; VII 313a; in morphology, ~ means 'simple', as opposed to MURAKKAB 'compound', and designates a noun made up of a single element. In syntax, ~ means 'in isolation', as opposed to *muḍāf* 'in annexation' and designates a noun which is not followed by a determinating complement. VII 313b

In lexicography, more often used in the plural *mufradāt*, ~ denotes the words taken in isolation in the lexicon. I 1083a; VII 313b

In mathematics, ~ denotes simple or ordinary fractions. IV 725b

♦ al-mufradūn : the ninth degree in the ṣūfī hierarchical order of saints. I 95a

muftī (A) : the person who gives an opinion on a point of law, FATWĀ, or is engaged in that profession. II 866a; IX 325a

mug͟haffal (A) : in early Islam, an 'irresponsible wit'. IX 552b

mug͟hārasa (A) : in law, a lease for agricultural planting, one of the most-used forms of contract. Under its terms, the owner of a piece of land charges a person with the planting of trees on it under a co-ownership basis, and in return, he agrees to grant the planter ownership of a predetermined proportion of the whole crop. The lessee thus becomes an owner; and he can put an end to the common ownership by demanding a division of the land. VII 346b

al-mug͟hayyabāt al-k͟hams (A) : lit. the five mysteries, things concealed in the unseen.

In theology, ~ are regarded as known to God alone as part of His prescience and foreknowledge of all aspects of nature and human activity. They are usually identified with the five things known to God as expounded in Q xxxi:34 : the hour of the Last Judgement; when rain will be sent down; what it is in the womb (i.e. the sex and number of children); what a man will gain, of his sustenance, on the morrow; and when a man shall die. VII 346b

mug͟hnam → WAKĪR

muḥabbar (A) : fabric of high quality manufactured in Yemen; artistic poetry of high quality. IX 448b

muḥabbat-i kull (Ind.P) : absolute love, the highest station of spiritual attainment in the religious thought of the Mug̲h̲al emperor Akbar. IX 846b

muhādana → MUWĀDAʿA

muḥāḍara (A, pl. *muḥāḍarāt*) : a gathering in the course of which the participants converse and exchange information, quotations and stories. VII 851b

In the mystical thought of al-Ḳus̲h̲ayrī, ~ is getting oneself into position vis-à-vis the objective sought, the first of three stages in the progression towards Reality. This stage remains 'behind the veil', the lifting of which belongs to the second stage. IV 697a

muḥaddit̲h̲ (A) : the usual term for a technical specialist in Traditions. I 259a

muḥadjdjar (P) : balustrade. IX 191b

muhādjir (A, pl. **muhādjirūn**) : lit. one who migrates.

In Turkey and Ottoman lands, ~ was used for refugees and the victims of the population exchanges in the early years of the Republic; by 1933 the term was replaced by the neologism *göčmen*. VII 350b

In India, ~ has been used to describe those Muslims from the Indo-Pakistan subcontinent who migrated from their homes in order to protect their religion and to safeguard their interests as Muslims, the first group leaving in the early decades of the 20th century and the second group in 1947. VII 354b

In early Islam, the plural *muhādjirūn* stands for the Emigrants, those Meccan Muslims who emigrated from Mecca to Medina either just before Muḥammad himself or in the period up to the conquest of Mecca in 8/630. VII 356a; members of Arab tribes, who settled at Medina after their conversion to Islam and thus renounced returning to their tribes, are also designated as ~ . VIII 828a

muḥāfaẓa (A) : governorate. IX 166b

muḥākāt (A) : in the poetics of the philosophers, symbols, mimeses, enigmas. IX 459a

muḥakkak (A) : 'strongly expressed (word); tightly-woven (cloth)'; ~ is a form of Arabic script, whose main characteristic is the feature that the left corner of twenty-one letters are angled. This script was used for long-page format Qurʾāns and also for frames. After the end of the 11th/17th century, ~ yielded place to T̲H̲ULUT̲H̲. IV 1123a; VIII 151b

muḥakkam → ḤAKAM

muḥakkima (A) : the phrase *al-muḥakkima al-ūlā* stands for the cry *lā ḥukm illā li 'llāh*, raised at Ṣiffīn by those who protested against arbitration. I 384a

muḥallabiyya (A) : a popular rice pudding dish; the mediaeval version of it was made with meat or chicken, sweetened with honey and seasoned with spices to which saffron-coloured rice is added. VIII 653a

muḥallil (A) : in early Islam, a horse entered into a competition, whose owner made no wager and gained the whole amount staked by all the other entrants if his horse won (syn. *dāk̲h̲il*). II 953b; in gambling, a 'legaliser', i.e. someone who did not contribute to the stakes, which made the gambling legal, although the law schools differ as to the legality of this procedure. V 109b muḥammadī (A) : in numismatics, the name given in the reign of the Ṣafawid Muḥammad K͟hudābanda to the double *s͟hāhī*, or 100 dīnārs. In 1888 it was renamed *dō s͟hāhī*. VIII 790a; IX 203b

muḥammira (A, P *surk͟h-d͟jāmagān*) : 'wearers of red', the name for the K͟hurramiyya, a religious movement founded in the late 5th century AD by Mazdak and the various Iranian sects which developed out of it. VII 664a

muḥāraba → ḲAṬʿ AL-ṬARĪḲ

muḥarraf (A) : 'altered'; in the science of Tradition, ~ is used of a change occurring in the letters of a word. III 26a

muḥarram (A) : the first month of the Muslim year. The name was originally not a proper name but an adjectival epithet qualifying Ṣafar I, the first month of the pre-Islamic Meccan year. VII 464a

muḥāsaba (A) : lit. accounting.

In classical Muslim administration, ~ is the term given to the comprehensive accounting presented by an ʿĀMIL on relinquishing his appointment when it is not approved by the authority to whom he presents it. When it is approved, it is called MUWĀFAḲA. II 78b

In Ottoman finance, ~ referred to financial accounting. VII 465b

In mysticism, ~ , more precisely *muḥāsabat al-nafs*, denotes 'inward accounting, spiritual accounting'. VII 465a

muḥaṣṣil (A) : a term used under the Anatolian Sald͟jūḳs and Ottomans for various types of revenue collectors. It acquired special significance amid extensive Ottoman financial reforms of 1838-9. VII 467b

muḥdit͟h → ḤADAT͟H

muḥīl (A) : in law, the transferor, i.e. one who has a debt to A and a claim against B, and settles his debt by transferring his claim against B to the benefit of A. In this case, A is the creditor, *al-muḥtāl*, and B is the cessionary, *al-muḥtāl ʿalayhi*. III 283a

muḥillūn (A) : lit. those who make lawful (what is unlawful); an expression used in early Islamic historical texts to denote those who had shed the blood of al-Ḥusayn b. ʿAlī. VII 470a

muḥkam → MUTAS͟HĀBIH

muhmala (A) : a gloss signifying the unpointed ḤARF, e.g. *ʿayn muhmala*. III 597a

muhr (P) : a seal, signet or signet-ring. VII 472a

In Arabic, the term for a foal at birth; from then on, it is given different names, determined by the stage of development of the teeth. II 785a

♦ muhrdār (T *mühürdār*) : the keeper of the seals, 'private secretary', in Persian and Ottoman administration. VII 473a

muḥrim (A) : the pilgrim who has entered the state of ritual purity. II 1069a; III 1052b

muḥṣan (A) : in law, a term denoting a certain personal status: married (and the marriage has been duly consummated), free, and Muslim. The quality of *iḥṣān* resides in each spouse when both satisfy all three criteria. VII 474b

muḥtāl (A) : in mediaeval Islam, a category of thieves, one who worked by stratagems and who did not kill in the course of his crimes and was therefore looked down on by his more desperate and violent confrères. V 769a; and → MUḤĪL

muḥtalim (A) : dreaming, and particularly dreaming of copulation and experiencing an emission of the seminal fluid in dreaming. VIII 822a

muḥtasib → ḤISBA

muʿīd (A, T) : in the Ottoman school system, a repétiteur. IX 702b

mukaʿʿab → KAʿB

mukāʿama → MUʿĀKAMA

muḳābal (A) : a pair of complimentary opposites, e.g. absence and presence. III 84a

♦ **muḳābala** : in astronomy, ~ is used as the term for the opposition of a planet and the sun or of two planets with one another. In opposition, the difference in longitude between the heavenly bodies is 180 degrees. ~ may be used to refer to the opposition of sun and moon, although the usual technical expression for this phenomenon is *al-iṣtiḳbāl*. VII 490a

In astrology, the diametric aspect of the planets. IV 259a

As a technique in manuscript production, ~ has the meaning of 'collation', i.e. the textual comparison of a manuscript with another of the same work, preferably with one from which it was copied. A synonym is *muʿāraḍa*. VII 490b

In literary theory, ~ refers to a type of antithesis, in which both sides of the opposition consist of two or more terms. VII 491b

♦ muḳābeledji (T) : clerk. VIII 291a

mukabbara → MARSŪM

muḳābeledji → MUḲĀBAL

mukābir (A) : in mediaeval Islam, a category of thieves, the robber with violence. V 769a

muḳaddam (A) : lit. placed in front; the chief, the one in command, e.g. of a body of troops or of a ship (captain). In the dervish orders, ~ is used for the head of the order or the head of a monastery. VII 492a

In logic, ~ means the protasis in a premise in the form of a conditional sentence. VII 492a

In mathematics, ~ means the first of two numbers in a proportion, or in other words, the divided number in a simple division. VII 492a; and → TĀLĪ

mukaddī (A, pl. *mukaddūn*, ? < P *gadā*) : in mediaeval Islam, a wandering beggar or vagrant, who, with a remarkable talent for plausible lying and a knowledge of certain effective dodges, succeeds in opening up the purses of those simple persons who allow themselves to be taken in by his eloquent but mendacious words. VII 494a

muḳaddima (A) : the foreword, preface or introduction to prose works; as a literary genre, the independent development of the preface, which had a stereotyped form consisting of initial commendations, a middle part and closing praises, was developed in particular by al-D̲j̲āḥiẓ and Ibn Ḳutayba. VII 495b

mukaddis (A) : in mediaeval ʿIrāḳ, a beggar who makes a collection for buying a shroud. VII 494a

muḳaffī → MUD̲J̲ALLĪ

mukallaf (A) : in law, one who is obliged to fulfil the religious duties. I 993b

♦ mukallafa : in Egypt, the term used to designate the land survey registers. II 79b

muḳallid → D̲J̲IRRAT; TAḲLĪD

muḳannī (A) : a specialist in constructing a ḲANĀT, a mining installation for extracting water from the depths of the earth, called *kārīzkan* in Afghanistan. IV 529b

muḳanṭarāt (A) : in astronomy, the parallel circles at the horizon, normally called circles of height or parallels of height. This term was borrowed in the Middle Ages by Western astronomers, under the term *almícantarat*. VII 500b

muḳāraʿa → MUK̲H̲ĀRAD̲J̲A

muḳāraḍa → MUḌĀRABA

muḳarbaṣ (A), or *muḳarbas* : in architecture, a term denoting a technique of craftmanship used in the mediaeval Muslim West, yielding Sp. *mocárabe*. It can be defined as 'work formed by a geometric combination of interlocking prisms, externally cut in concave surfaces and used as decoration in vaults, cornices etc.'. It forms a counterpart to, but is different in execution from the MUḲARNAS technique of the Muslim central and eastern lands. The ~ was carved in jesso, brick, wood, marble or stone and was frequently coloured. VII 500b

mukārī (A) : lit. hirer; a dealer in riding beasts and beasts of burden, usage being extended from the person buying and selling and hiring to the muleteer or other person accompanying a loaded beast. VII 501b

muḳarnas (A, < Gk) : in architecture, 'stalactites', a type of decoration typical for Islamic architecture all over the central and eastern parts of the Muslim world, composed of a series of niches embedded within an architectural frame, geometrically connected and forming a three-dimensional composition around a few basic axes of symmetry. The essential function of the ~ is ornamental. Its counterpart in the Muslim West is MUḲARBAṢ. I 1229a; II 863b; VII 501a

muḳarr → IḲRĀR

muḳarrariyya (A) : one of two main headings in the monthly and yearly accounting registers of the Īlk̲h̲ānids, under which fell the regular (*muḳarrar*) payments made every year by order of the sovereign from the *dīwān-i aʿlā* to ḲĀḌĪS, S̲H̲AYK̲H̲S, SAYYIDS, students, financial officials, etc. III 284a; and → IṬLĀḲIYYA

mukarrib (A) : lit. unifier; in ancient Yemen, a sovereign superior to the kings. IX 91a; IX 675b

muḳāsama (A) : lit. dividing out; a system of raising the land tax, involving the levy, by agreement, of a percentage or share of the crops, usually taken when these last had ripened. The early sources on law and finance distinguished it from the system of MISĀḤA, the assessment of a fixed lump sum on the land according to its fertility, location, etc., and from the system of MUḲĀṬAʿA, which implied a fixed annual sum payable without regard to the variations of prosperity and harvest and often the subject of a tax-farming contract. Known in the early centuries, it continued to be used down to modern times. IV 1032a ff.; VII 506b

In the Ottoman empire and in India, ~ is one of two terms describing the land tax (the other is MUWAẒẒAFA); the *kharādj muḳāsama* refers to a certain proportion of the produce accruing to the state from every field. II 158a; IV 1055b; VII 507b

mukāshafa (A) : in mysticism, ~ means illumination, epiphany. In the mystical thought of al-Ḳushayrī, ~ is the lifting of the veil, a 'raising of the curtain' on to the world of mystery, the second of three stages in the progression towards Reality. IV 697a

mukāsir (A) : among the Ismāʿīlīs, the name of one of the subordinates who assists the DĀʿĪ. II 97b

muḳāṭaʿa (A) : in the mediaeval taxation system, ~ was used for the sum handed over by a tax farmer in return for the collection and management of the revenue from a given province or district. IV 1038a; VII 508a

In the Ottoman empire, ~ denoted tax farm, especially used by the Ottomans in connection with taxation imposed on the traffic in commodities in and out of the empire or at the entry to the big towns. VII 508a

mukātab(a) → KITĀB

muḳātil (A) : in Western and Spanish Arabic, *al-~* is an alternative name for the planet Saturn. VIII 101a

muḳaṭṭaʿāt (A) : one of the names given to the mysterious letters placed at the head of 26 SŪRAs of the Qurʾān. VII 509a

In poetry, ~ are fragmentary pieces, very often topical poems, such as elegies, chronograms and satires. III 58a

muḳayyin → ḲAYYĀN

mukayyis (A), or *kayyās* : the 'masseur', one who wields the *kīs*, a bag of tow used to massage the clients, in a **ḥammām** 'steam bath'. III 140b

muḳbulā (A) : a term for a fish stew, also known as *munazzalat al-samak*, based on eel or carp. VIII 1023a

mukhaḍram (A, pl. *mukhaḍramūn*) : a person who lived in the DJĀHILIYYA and in the time of Islam, applied in particular to poets; *al-mukhaḍramūn* constitute the class of pagan poets who died after the proclamation of Islam, although the meaning has been extended to poets living in the Umayyad and the ʿAbbāsid period. VII 516a

In the science of Tradition, ~ signifies a transmitter who accepted Islam but had not seen the Prophet. VII 516a

♦ mukhaḍramū 'l-dawlatayn : 'the poets of the two dynasties', a term for poets living in the Umayyad and the ʿAbbāsid period. VII 516a

mukhallefāt (T, < A) : 'things left behind (at death)', an Ottoman financial-judicial term alluding to the property of deceased officials and of those who died without heirs that the Ottoman treasury confiscated. The inheritances of the minors or the mentally handicapped who could not oversee their shares were also seized and kept until they reached puberty; the treasury also approved the expenditure of the money for them. I 1147b; VII 517a; for compound terms having to do with clerks, departments, etc. of Ottoman administration involved in ~ , VII 517a

mukhammas (A) : in Arabic, early Persian and Turkish poetry, a five-line MUSAMMAṬ, a stanzaic form of poetry, with either four lines of separate rhyme and one line with common rhyme, or blocks of five rhyming lines, e.g. *aaaaa bbbbb* etc. VII 660a ff.; and → TAKHMĪS

mukhannathūn (A) : in mediaeval Spain, ~ were (male) singers disguised as women, and considered deviants. V 778a

mukhāradja (A) : the game of mora, morra, or mication (L *micatio*, It *mora*), played all around the shores of the Mediterranean, and also in Arabia and Iraq. It is a game of chance and is in principle forbidden by Islam. Synonyms are *muḳāraʿa*, *munāhada* and *musāhama*, followed by *bi 'l-aṣābiʿ* 'with the fingers'. VII 518a

mukharniḳa → MUʾARNIBA

mukhāṭara (A) : a legal device, familiar in mediaeval European mercantile circles in its Latin garb *mohatra*, which is a form of 'a double sale', *bayʿatān fī bayʿa*. Its purpose was to circumvent the prohibition of any form of interest on a capital loan. VII 518b; and → BAYʿATĀN FĪ BAYʿA

mukhattam (A) : a pattern of lines in cloth, from silks to woolen materials, forming quadrangular compartments, i.e. checks. Such cloths seem to have been woven almost everywhere in the Islamic lands. VII 519a

mukhtalas (A) : 'snatched'; in archery, a way of loosing an arrow, by drawing rapidly and loosing immediately without any break in time. IV 800b

mukhtalif (A) : in mathematics, disjunct fractions which do not have the same denominator. IV 725b

mukhtalis (A) : in law, a thief who comes secretly but goes away openly. IX 63a

mukhtār (A) : lit. chosen person; in the late Ottoman empire and some of its successor states, the headman of a quarter or village, appointed by the central government and charged with a variety of duties. VII 519a

In law, (an act done) by choice, not under compulsion. VII 635b

♦ mukhtārāt : an anthology, selection of poetry. VII 526b

mukhtaṣar (A) : a handbook or an abridged manual, usually condensed from a longer work. VII 536a, where is also found a list of approximately equivalent terms; an epitome, a concise exposition. IX 324a

mukḥula → NAFFĀṬ

muḳīm (A) : a term denoting 'a person domiciled in the place and satisfying the stipulations of the law'; in Indonesia, the Friday communal prayer is only valid, according to the Shāfiʿī school of law, if 40 *muḳīm*s are present, and since the population was rarely numerous enough to allow this, ~ acquired the meaning of 'department, circle' because of the custom of grouping several villages together. I 741a

muḳla (A) : a very wide turban worn by *ʿulamāʾ* (→ FAḲĪH) in Egypt. V 741b

muḳrif (A) : the 'approacher', whose dam is of better breeding than the sire, one of the four classifications of a horse. II 785b

muḳṭaʿ (A) : holder of a fief, IḲṬĀʿ. V 862b; a provincial governor under the Dihlī sultanate, transferable at will, who commanded the local military forces and was paid personally by the grant of a revenue assignment or by a percentage of the provinical revenues. II 272b

muḳtaḍab (A) : 'untrained' or 'extemporised'. IX 10b

In prosody, the name of the thirteenth Arabic metre, in fact little used. I 670a; VII 540

mulāʾa (A) : a large, enveloping outer wrap worn by women in the Arab East. V 741b

mulaḥḥin (Yem) : in the northern Yemeni tribal system, a composer or singer of folk poetry. IX 234b

mulammaʿāt (A) : in Persian literature, ~ are macaronic verses, a mixed composition of Arabic, Persian and sometimes Turkish elements used to obtain a humorous effect. III 355b

mülāzemet (T, < A *mulāzama*) : in Ottoman administration, the certificate of eligibility for office. VII 545a; and → MULĀZIM

mulāzim (A, T *mülāzim*) : in Ottoman administration and military, a candidate for office in the Ottoman learned hierarchy (the ʿILMIYYE). VII 545b; also, a tax-farmer, part of a special corps to collect the poll-tax in certain districts; one of 300 special mounted bodyguards whom sultan Süleymān I selected from among his household to accompany him on campaigns, so-called because they were preparing for important administrative posts which came by way of reward for their services to the sultan. VII 545a; the personal bodyguard to the Ṣafawīd shāh. I 8a; reserves for posts in the Ottoman palace and guild system. VII 545b

In the Ottoman military, ~ applied to the lowest two ranks of officers after the reorganisation of the army in the 19th century, corresponding to the rank of lieutenant. VII 545b

mulḥam (A) : a fabric with a silk warp and a woof of some other stuff. V 737a

mulḥid (A) : a deviator, apostate, heretic, atheist. There is no evidence of pre-

Islamic usage in a religious meaning, which arose in the ʿAbbāsid period on the basis of Qurʾānic verses. Under the Umayyads, ~ had been synonymous with *bāg͟hī* 'rebel' and *s͟hāḳḳ al-ʿaṣā* 'splitter of the ranks of the faithful', denoting the desertion (*ilḥād*) of the community of the faithful and rebellion against the legitimate caliphs. VII 546a

In Ottoman usage, ~ and *ilḥād* were commonly employed to describe subversive doctrines among the s͟hīʿīs and ṣūfīs. VII 546b

mulimm → MUTARAʿRIʿ

mulkiyya (A, T *mülkiyye*) : a title to property (→ MILK). VII 547a

Under the Ottomans, *mülkiyye*, or more precisely *idāre-i mülkiyye*, had by roughly the 1830s become the customary Ottoman term for civil administration. VII 547a

mullā → MOLLĀ

multazam (A) : the name for the part of the wall of the Kaʿba between the Black Stone and the door of the Kaʿba, so-called because the visitors press their breasts against it while praying fervently. IV 318a

mültezim (T, < A *multazim*) : in Ottoman administration, a tax-farmer who, from the mid-16th century on, collected taxes and dues on behalf of the Ottoman treasury. The ~ could either deliver all the proceeds while drawing a salary, or he could buy the right to retain the proceeds himself by paying the treasury an agreed sum in advance; this latter system was known as *iltizām*, which differed from the other term used for a tax-farm, *muḳāṭaʿa*, in that it referred to the collection of revenues from the imperial domains. *Muḳāṭaʿa* was applied to the collection by contract of other revenues. VII 550b

mulūk al-ṭawāʾif → MALIK

mulūk͟hiyya → ṬAʿMIYYA

mumālaṭa → ID͟JĀZA

mumayyiz (A) : in law, the 'discerning minor', a stage in the transition from the status of minor to that of major. I 993b; VIII 836a

♦ mümeyyiz (T) : in the Ottoman empire, a clerk who examined every matter to be put before the S͟HAYK͟H AL-ISLĀM as to correctness of presentation. II 867a

mūmis → BAG͟HIYY

mūmiyāʾ (A, P *mūmiyāʾī*) : bitumen, mineral tar (L *Mumia naturalis persica*), a solid, black, shining mineral liquid which trickles from rock-caves. In ancient medicine, it was mainly used against lesions and fractures. It is to be distinguished from the *Mumia factitia var. humana*, the bituminous substance of the Egyptian mummies, which is called *biṣṣasfalṭus* (and variants). VII 556a

mumsika (A) : a bit of metal, projecting from the outer rim of the astrolabe and fitting into an exactly corresponding indentation on the edge of each disc, which prevents the discs from turning. I 723a

muʾna (N.Afr) : a special allowance for food, to which members of a GŪM were entitled when on active service. II 1138b

munādī (A) : town crier, herald.
In the Qurʾān, ~ is used for the one who will proclaim the Last Day and give the summons to Judgement, in popular Islam usually identified with the angel Isrāfīl. VII 557a

munādjāt (A) : a whispering to, talking confidentially with someone.
In religion, 'extempore prayer', as opposed to the corporate addressing of the deity in the ṢALĀT. VII 557b; a doxological supplication. IX 213a
In mysticism, the ṣūfīs' communion with God. VII 557b

munadjdjim → AḤKĀMĪ

munaffidh → ṢĀḤIB AL-ASHGHĀL

munāfiḳūn (A) : a Qurʾānic term usually translated with 'hypocrites', to refer to dissenters within the community, whether openly or in secret. VII 561a

munāghāt (A) : term for the beggars' jargon of the Banū Sāsān. IX 70b

munāhada → MUKHĀRADJA

munāḳaḍāt → NAḲĀʾIḌ

munʿaḳid (A) : in law, a contract which fulfils all the conditions necessary to its formation. II 836a

munaḳḳila (A) : a fracture with displacement of a bone, a determining factor in the prescription of compensation following upon physical injury, DIYA. II 341b

munakkis (A) : in the terminology of horse-riding, a horse with bad head carriage. II 954a

munāsaba (A), or *tanāsub* : in rhetoric, correspondence between words in regard either to their pattern or to their meaning. II 825b

munāṣafa (A) : in law, reciprocal property-sharing by two co-owners, each of them holding the half of a one and undivided object, a special form of co-ownership. VII 564a
In the context of Muslim-non-Muslim relations, ~ historically became particularly important in the juridicial, fiscal and administrative organisation of border regions between Islamic and Frankish Crusader states in 12th and 13th-century Syria. The *raison d'être* of a ~ was to arrange a compromise on disputed border territories which neither the Frankish nor the Muslim neighbouring states were able to control completely. VII 564a

munāshada (A) : a set form of oath, at the beginning of a prayer of petition, sometimes involving a threat or coercion, directed at God. VII 564b

munāẓara (A, pl. *munāẓarāt*) : a scientific, in particular theological-juridical, dispute between Muslims and adherents of the AHL AL-KITĀB, and between Muslims themselves. V 1130b; V 1223b; VII 566b; VIII 363b
In literature, a literary genre in which two or more living or inanimate beings appear talking and competing for the honour which of them possesses the best qualities. VII 566b

munāziʿ (A) : in the terminology of horse-riding, a horse that takes the bit in its teeth and jerks the hands. II 953b

munazzalat al-samak → MUḲBULĀ

munfaṣil (A) : in the science of Tradition, ~ is applied to a Tradition with several breaks in the ISNĀD, to distinguish it from MUNḲAṬIʿ. III 26a

munfatiḥa (A) : open, disengaged.

In grammar, a term meaning non-velar, indicating all the letters of the Arabic alphabet except for *ṣād*, *ẓāʾ*, *ṭāʾ*, and *ḍād*. III 596b

mungh → MANGH

munḥarifa → MIZWALA; SAMT

munḳalib (A) : in the science of Tradition, a term used by some to indicate a Tradition which has a slight transposition in the wording. III 26a

munkar (A, pl. *munkarāt, manākīr*) : 'unknown, objectionable'; in the science of Tradition, a Tradition whose transmitter is alone in transmitting it and differs from one who is reliable, or is one who has not the standing to be accepted when alone. When one says of a transmitter *yarwi 'l-manākīr* 'he transmits ~ Traditions', this does not involve the rejection of all his Traditions; but if he is called *munkar al-ḥadīth*, they are all to be rejected. III 26b; VII 575b

munḳaṭiʿ (A) : in the science of Tradition, applied commonly when there is a break in the ISNĀD at any stage later than the Successor; ~ has also been used of an *isnād* including unspecified people, or one later than a Successor who claims to have heard someone he did not hear. III 25b

munkhafiḍa (A) : 'lowered'; in grammar, those letters whose pronunciation does not require the elevation of the back of the tongue, i.e. all but the emphatic consonants, *ḥurūf al-muṭbaḳa*, and *ḳāf*, *ghayn*, and *khāʾ*. III 596b

munsalakh (A), or *sarār* : the last day of the month, in historical works and correspondence. V 708a

munṣarif → MUTAMAKKIN

munsariḥ (A) : in prosody, the name of the tenth Arabic metre. I 670a

munshī (A), or more correctly *munshiʾ* : in the Persian and Indo-Muslim worlds, a secretary in the ruler's chancery, an exponent of the high-flown epistolary style general in mediaeval Islamic chanceries from the 2nd/8th century onwards known as INSHĀʾ. VII 580b; VIII 481b

munshid (A) : a reciter of poems. IX 229a; in Egypt, a folk poet, associated primarily with a religious repertory. IX 235b

munṣif (A) : lit. one who metes out justice; a term used in Indo-Muslim administration, and then in that of British India, to denote a legal official or judge of subordinate grade. VII 580b; sub-judge. I 287b

♦ **munṣifa** : the name given by mediaeval Arabic critics and anthologists to those poems in which a description of the fights between tribes is accompanied by a recognition, with equity, of the opponent's valour and the sufferings endured by the poet's own side. VII 580b

muntahib (A) : in law, a robber who falls upon someone and robs him at a place where help is available. IX 63b muntasib (A) : in mathematics, a fraction of relationship. IV 725b, where an example in modern notation is given

murābaḥa (A) : in law, a permissible form of sale that allows a purchaser to buy with the intention of subsequently reselling to a designated buyer with a fixed profit rate. IX 471a

murābaṭa → MURĀBIṬ

murabbaʿ (A) : a lute with a quadrangular sound box. V 234a

In poetry, a four-line MUSAMMAṬ, a stanzaic form of poetry, composed of three lines with separate rhyme and one line with common rhyme. VII 660b; VIII 584b; IX 353b

In mathematics, ~ , or MĀL, denotes the second power of the unknown quantity. II 362a

♦ murabbacılık (T) : a land-leasing system in Turkey, in which, in exchange for his work, the farmer only touches one-fourth of the harvest. V 473b

murābiṭ (A, pl. *murābiṭūn*) : marabout. Originally, a warrior in the holy war, DJIHĀD or RIBĀṬ, who was slain fighting against the infidel. V 1200b; a type of warrior-monk who inhabited a *ribāṭ*, a fortified convent on the frontiers of Islam. VII 583b; hence a saint, who never took part in a *djihād* in his lifetime. Of the words used for saint in Morocco: *walī*, *sayyid*, *ṣāliḥ*, ~ is the only one applied to the descendants of a saint, who possess the BARAKA, miraculous powers, of their ancestor. V 1200b

♦ **al-murābiṭūn** : the Almoravids, a dynasty of Berber origin which ruled in North Africa and then Spain during the second half of the 5th/11th century and the first half of the 6th/12th century. VII 583b

♦ murābaṭa : 'measures of vigilance', in al-Ghazālī's mystical thought, a fundamental concept made up of six degrees, outlined in his exposition 'On spiritual surveillance and inward accounting' in Book 38 of his *Iḥyā*ʾ. VII 465a

muraddaf (A) : in Persian prosody, a poem with RADĪF, a word or whole phrase that follows the rhyme letter, not to be confused with the term *murdaf*, which means 'provided with a RIDF', a letter of prolongation immediately preceding the rhyme letter. VIII 369a

muraghghabāt (A) : in shīʿī law, the daily and non-daily supererogatory prayers. VII 879a

murāhiḳ (A) : in law, the minor on the point of reaching puberty, a stage in the transition from the status of minor to that of major. I 993b; as a term connected with a child's development, 'he was, or became, near to attaining puberty or virility' (Lane) (syn. *kawkab*). VIII 822a

murāḳaba (A) : 'spiritual surveillance', in al-Ghazālī's mystical thought, the second of the six degrees making up the 'measures of vigilance', *murābaṭa* (→ MURĀBIṬ). It is an examination of the motives of the action and the soul's hidden intentions, in order to reject everything that would serve to satisfy egoism or any passion and that is not performed with a view to God alone. VII 465a; a practice of absorption in mystic contemplation, adopted by the Čis͟htī mystics in order to harnass all feelings and emotions in establishing communion with God. II 55b

muraḳḳa*ʿ* (A) : an album, in which paintings and drawings, alternating with specimens of calligraphy, were mounted. No actual examples earlier than the 16th century have survived, but the period of the ~ would appear to be coterminous with that of classical Persian painting. VII 602b; VIII 787b

In mysticism, the patched mantle worn by ṣūfīs. VIII 742b

murakkab (A) : composite; and → BASĪṬ

In grammar, the construct state of the noun. I 1083b; the singular, when applied to the 'compound' noun. II 406b; and → MUFRAD

In medicine, the compound of the constituents. I 1083b

muraṣṣaʿ (A) : in the Ottoman empire, a very prestigious, high-degree order or decoration, NIS͟HĀN, that was elaborately adorned with diamonds or brilliants, usually worn with a sash across the breast. VIII 58b

murattab (A, pl. *murattabūn*) : in mediaeval Islam, an official in the postal service. I 1044b

For the Turkish *müretteb*, → NIẒĀM

murdaf → MURADDAF

murdjiḳāl (A) : 'bat'; an apparatus for ascertaining differences of level. It consists of an equilateral triangle with a plumb-line which hangs from the middle of one side. The triangle is suspended by this side. Two rods, an ell in length, are erected to ten ells apart; a rope is passed from the top of one to the top of the other and the ~ is suspended in its centre by two threads. If the plumb-line goes through the triangle, both places are on the same level. VII 203a

murīd (A, P *s͟hāgird*) : lit. he who seeks; in mysticism, the novice or postulant or seeker after spiritual enlightenment by means of traversing the ṣūfī path in obedience to a spiritual director. VII 608b

murniba → MUʾARNIBA

murr (A) : myrrh, a gum resin from the bark of several varieties of thorny scrubs of *Commiphora abyssinica*. VIII 1042b

♦ murrī : a condiment, made with barley flour. IX 225a

mursal (A) : without a specific textual basis. IX 364b; in the science of Tradition, a Tradition in which a Successor quotes the Prophet directly, that is, the name of the Companion is lacking in the ISNĀD. III 26a; VII 631a; VIII 384a

♦ mursal al-ṣaḥābī : a Tradition in which a Companion describes some event involving the Prophet at which he/she could not possibly have been present. VII 631a

murs͟hid (A), and **baba**, PĪR, S͟HAYK͟H : lit. one who gives right guidance; in mysticism, the spiritual director and initiator into the order of the novice who is following the ṣūfī path. VII 631b

♦ murs͟hid-i kāmil (P) : 'perfect spiritual director', a title assumed by the S͟HAYK͟Hs of the Ṣafawiyya ṣūfī order in the 8th/14th century, demanding complete obedience from all their adherents. The title was adopted by the Ṣafawid shāhs, the temporal monarchs in Persia during the 10th-early 12th/16th-early 18th centuries. VII 632a

murtadd (A) : 'one who turns back', especially from Islam, an apostate. Apostasy is called *irtidād* or *ridda*; it may be committed verbally by denying a principle of belief or by an action, e.g. treating a copy of the Qur'ān with disrespect. IV 771a; VII 635a

murtāḥ (A) : a name for the seventh horse in a horse-race, according to the order of finishing. II 953a

murtahisha → RAHĪSH

murtaththth (A) : lit. he who is worn out, a warrior of the type that is not allowed special burial rites because his death is not a direct and immediate result of his wounds. IX 205a

murtaziḳa → RIZḲ

murūʾa (A), or *muruwwa* : a term used especially in pre-Islamic and early Islamic usage, the meaning of which is imprecise. There is reason to believe that ~ originally describes the sum of the physical qualities of man and then by a process of spiritualisation and abstraction his moral qualities. After Islam, its meaning was extended thanks to the now pre-dominating moral focus. Broadly speaking, with the rightly-guided caliphs, ~ means chastity, good nature and observance of Qurʾānic laws, with the Umayyads, ~ implies politics, diplomacy, work, dignity and compassion, and with the early ʿAbbāsids, ~ implies merit and is contrasted with abjectness; with the moralists, ~ is identified with ADAB in the meaning of good conduct. Becoming more and more abstract, ~ finally came to mean virtue. VII 636b ff.

In law, ~ indicates the fact of abstaining from any act capable of offending religion although not constituting an illicit act. VII 637b

In the spoken language of today, ~ means 'energy' in Egypt (*miriwwa*) and Syria (*muruwwa*), as in the expression 'so-and-so has not the ~ to accomplish such a thing'. VII 637b

mürurnāme (T) : in the Ottoman period, a special authorisation from the sultan given to the MUSTAʾMIN proposing to travel. This document was obtained through the intermediary of his ambassador. III 1181b

muruwwa → MURŪʾA

musabbiḥāt (A) : the name given to SŪRAS lvii, lix, lxi, lxii and lxiv, because they begin with the phrase *sabbaḥa* or *yusabbiḥu li 'llāh*. VII 650b; IX 887b

muṣādara (A) : in mediaeval administration, ~ is firstly 'an agreement with someone over the payment of taxation due'. The most frequently found meaning is, however, 'the mulcting of an official of his (usually) ill-gotten gains or spoils of office'. The latter meaning was also found in the Ottoman empire, but here ~ was extended to the property of non-officials as well as to deceased persons. II 152b; VII 652b

In mathematics, ~ are premisses or postulates. VII 652b

muṣaddar → ṢADR

musaddas (A) : in Arabic, early Persian and Turkish poetry, a six-line MUSAMMAṬ, a stanzaic form of poetry, with either five lines of separate rhyme and one line with common rhyme, or blocks of six rhyming lines, e.g. *aaaaaa bbbbbb* etc. VII 660a ff.

In later Persian and Indo-Muslim poetry, a type in which the first four lines rhyme with one another, while the remaining two lines rhyme among themselves, e.g. *aaaa bb*, *cccc dd*, *eeee ff* etc. This type is often called a TARKĪB-BAND. VII 662a

muṣaffaḥāt (A) : in music, 'clappers', known in Persia and Turkey as *čarpāra* (lit. four pieces') or *čālpāra*, in Egypt as *aḳlig͟h*, and in Spain as *kāsatān* (whence perhaps castanet). IX 10b

musāfiḳ → ṢANDJ

muṣag͟hg͟hara → MARSŪM

musāhama → MUK͟HĀRADJA

muṣaḥḥaf (A) : 'mistaken'; in the science of Tradition, ~ is used of a slight error in the ISNĀD or MATN, commonly confined to an error in the dots. III 26a

musahibu (Sw, < A **muṣāḥib**) : a term of East African Muslim court life. It is possible that the literary word *musahibu* is simply *ṣāḥib* with the *mu*-prefix (in Swahili morphology to be placed before all words denoting persons and also trees), but in some of the Swahili chronicles and the older epics, *musahibu* occurs in a special meaning, that of the close companion of the sultan. He is usually a half-brother or cousin. He has, among other things, to accompany the ruler wherever he goes and to protect him against treason. VII 657b

musāhim → SAHM

musāḳāt (A) : in law, a lease of a plantation for one crop period, with profit-sharing. The contract for such a lease is between the owner of the plantation and a husbandman, who undertakes to tend the trees or vines of the plantation for one season, at the end of which the proceeds of the crop are divided in agreed portions between the two contracting parties. The landowner's portion constitutes his rent. VII 658b

muṣālata (A) : the wholesale lifting of other people's poems, as distinguished from the other kind of plagiarism: taking up, and playing with, existing and attributable motifs. IX 56a

musālima (A) : the term used for Spanish converts adopting Islam in the first generation. Thereafter, they were called *muwalladūn* (→ MUWALLAD). VI 881a

muṣallā (A, P **namāzgāh**) : any place of prayer, therefore also mosque. VI 653b; the place where the ṢALĀT is performed on certain occasions; VII 658b; the sanctuary or covered area in a mosque; the open space, usually outside a settlement, used during the two festivals (ʿĪD AL-AḌḤĀ and ʿĪD AL-FIṬR) by the entire Muslim community; a directional indicator either entirely isolated in a huge open space, or set in a long wall. VII 659b

In North Africa, the ~ is a large threshing floor, with a wall provided with a MIḤRĀB and an elevated place for the speaker, used for the rites of 10 Dhu 'l-Ḥidjdja. VII 659a

In India, *namāzgāh* is an alternative name for *ʿīdgāh*, the open structure built usually to the west of a town, consisting solely of what in a mosque would be the western wall, with MIḤRĀB(S) and MINBAR and, essentially, within a spacious enclosure which should be capable of accommodating the entire adult male Muslim population. The structure is used only for the celebration of the two ʿĪD festivals, and no special sanctity attaches to it. VII 947a

musallam → SALAM

♦ musallamī → MUʿĀFĪ

musallī (A), or *ʿāṭif* : the name for the fifth horse in a horse-race, according to the order of finishing. II 953a

muṣallī (A) : the name for the fourth horse in a horse-race, according to the order of finishing. II 953a

musallim → SALAM

musalsal (A) : lit. strung together.

In the science of Tradition, ~ is applied when the transmitters in an ISNĀD use the same words, or are of the same type, or come from the same place. III 26a

In calligraphy, ~ is a term for the letters of the THULUTH script when joined to each other. It was sometimes practised by calligraphers to show off their skill. IV 1124a

♦ musalsal al-ḥalf : in the science of Tradition, a Tradition in which each transmitter swears an oath. III 26a

♦ musalsal al-yad, and *al-musalsal fī 'l-akhdh bi 'l-yad* : in the science of Tradition, a Tradition in which each transmitter gives his hand to the one to whom he transmits the Tradition. III 26a; III 977a

musāmaḥāt (A) : in the science of diplomacy, documents of a primarily business nature concerning tax-relief, probably only in Mamlūk times, divided into large, issued in the name of the sultan, and small, in the name of the governor. II 303a

musammaṭ (A), also *ḳaṣīda simṭiyya* : an originally Arabic (then also Hebrew, Persian, Turkish) stanzaic form of poetry, whose single stanzas, normally all of the same structure, consist of two elements: first, a fixed number of lines that rhyme with each other, the rhyme, however, changing from one stanza to the next (separate rhymes), followed by a stanza-closing line that rhymes with the end lines in all other stanzas of the poem. This rhyme that runs through the whole poem (common rhyme) is called *ʿamūd al-ḳaṣīda* by the Arab authorities. The lines correspond to the hemistichs in normal poetry. The rhyme scheme of a simple ~ is thus e.g. *bbb a*, *ccc a*, *ddd a*, etc. VII 660a

muṣannaf (A, pl. *muṣannafāt*) : in Arabic literature, an early technical term applied to a collection of religious learning organised upon an abstract, structured subdivision in chapters, hence the opposite of MUSNAD, a collection arranged according to the first or oldest transmitter. III 24a; VII 662b

muṣāriʿ → ṢURʿA

musarwal (A) : a pigeon with feathered legs, a horse with white legs, or a tree with branches down on the trunk. IX 677b

musāwāt (A) : equality. In modern times, ~ has been used for the political concept of human equality. VII 663a

musawwad (A) : a term found in pre-Islamic South Arabian inscriptions to indicate an aristocratic group in Ḥaḍramawt; ~ is used to this day to denote the SAYYIDs, the descendants of the Prophet. S 338b

musawwida (A) : lit. the wearers, or bearers, of black; the name given to the partisans of the ʿAbbāsids at the time of the DAʿWAs of Abū Muslim al-Khurāsānī and Abū Salama al-Khallāl against the Umayyads, apparently from the black banners these rebels wore. VII 664a; and → MUBAYYIḌA

musayyaḥa (A) : a silk KĀFIYYA worn in the Arabic East. V 741b

müsellem (A) : 'exempt'; in the Ottoman military, provincial landed cavalrymen, excused from any dues or taxes on land initially granted them, who later became transformed into auxiliary forces no longer employed in actual fighting but in discharging duties such as dragging guns, levelling roads, digging trenches, carrying provisions and casting cannon balls. Then, as the Ottoman state required them to pay taxes rather than serve in the army, they lost their privileged status and dissolved into the tax-paying populace. VII 665a; VIII 404b

mushāʿ (A) : in law, common and repartitional ownership by the entire village community of all agricultural lands of the village. I 661a; VII 666b

mushāʿara (A) : in Muslim India, a poetical contest; in Urdu usually pronounced *mushāʿira*, ~ has come to be applied in its wider aspect to denote an assembly where Urdu poets come together to recite their compositions. VII 667b; IX 434a

mushaʿbidh → SHAʿBADHA

mushadjdjara → BAYT

muṣḥaf (A) : a complete text of the Qurʾān considered as a physical object. The term ~ is not always consistently used to refer to the Qurʾānic text said to be completed in the time of ʿUthmān, while *ṣuḥuf* was reserved, again not consistently, for the first collection, said to be undertaken in the time of Abū Bakr. VII 668b; a collection of written leaves placed between two covers, or a collection of a complete assemblage of leaves, each leaf being called a *ṣaḥīfa*, or a collection of pieces, of documents, a corpus, or vulgate. VIII 835a

mushāhada (A) : in the mystical thought of al-Ḳushayrī, ~ is direct vision, the 'presence of the reality', the third of three stages in the progression towards Reality. IV 697a

mushaʿʿib (A) : in mediaeval ʿIrāḳ, a person who maims a child at birth in order to make use of it at a future time for begging purposes. VII 494a

mushākil (A) : in Persian prosody, the name of a metre, of rare occurrence, said to have been invented by the Persians. I 677b

mushallaḥ → MASHLAḤ

mushāraka (A) : in law, 'participation financing', a contractual partnership. Its essence is joint exploitation of capital (or, in full or in part, of the work and skills of the partners or of the credit for partnership investment) with joint participation in profits and losses. Unlike the MUFĀWAḌA, the ~ is a limited investment partnership in which the core of the investment is money. VII 671b

mushāraṭa (A) : agreement, arrangement.

In al-Ghazālī's mystical thought, the first of the six degrees making up the 'measures of vigilance', *murābaṭa* (→ MURĀBIṬ). It is the anticipatory accounting of the soul made in the morning every day, which consists of instructing it in the engagements that it is to fulfill. VII 465a

mushāwar (A) : an adviser, in Muslim Spain especially used for an adviser of judges. IX 505b

♦ müshāwir (T) : a technical adviser, whether a foreigner or not, synonym of *müsteshār* (→ MUSTASHĀR). VII 733a

mushīr (A) : lit. one who points out, advises, hence 'counsellor, adviser' in administrative usage, in recent times also acquiring in military usage the connotation of 'field-marshal' in both the Arab and Turkish worlds. According to some authorities, ~ was at first (before the ʿAbbāsids) the title of the ministers (later WAZĪR) or secretaries of state (KĀTIB). However, with a few exceptions, this older and broader conception did not survive. VII 677a

mushrif (A) : lit. overseer, supervisor, controller; the title of an official, whose office seems basically to have been a financial one, and who appears at various times and with various duties in the history of the ʿAbbāsid caliphate and its successor states, from North Africa to the eastern Islamic lands. I 389b; VII 678b; VIII 702b

In the early Ghaznawid sultanate, the ~ was, next to the financial officer, also spy and internal intelligence agent. VII 679a

In Egypt and Syria of the Ayyūbids and Mamlūks, ~ was used for the official in charge of the royal kitchens, watching over the food cooked there. VII 679b

Under the Ḥafṣids, the ~ was head of the maritime customs. II 146a

mushtarī (A, P *hurmizd*) : the planet Jupiter. A synonym is *bardjīs*. VII 680a; VIII 101a

mushtarīk (A), or *mushtarik* : in grammar, homonym. I 184b; as used by modern linguists, ~ denotes 'polysemy', i.e. it qualifies a noun which can have several meanings. VII 680b

muslim (A) : the person who professes Islam, *islāmī* being exclusively used today for what is relative to Islam. VII 688b

musmiʿa → ḲAYNA

musnad (A) : in early Islam, any inscription in the pre-Islamic South Arabian script. VII 705a

In grammar, ~ is defined by later classical Arabic grammarians as 'that which is leant upon (or propped against) (the headword or subject), is supported by (it)'. They define *musnad ilayhi* as 'that which supports', i.e. the headword or subject. The relationship between them is termed ISNĀD 'the act of leaning (one thing against another)', 'the relationship of attribution or prediction'. However, the terms have a different, almost reversed, meaning in Sībawayh. VII 705a

In the science of Tradition, ~ indicates a work in which each Companion's Traditions were collected together, an arrangement that was not very convenient since the Traditions were not arranged by subject. III 24a; VII 705b; ~ is also applied to an ISNĀD that goes back all the way to the Prophet without a link missing. VII 705b; VIII 384b

mustadrak (A) : a continuation of a work, characterised by both continuity and discontinuity: it follows the line of the original work but amends it by means of reflection on the basis of the constitutive principles of the latter; omissions of the author of the original work are corrected. IX 604a

mustafād (A) : a collective name for indirect taxes under the ʿAlawīs. II 146a

mustafī (A) : in law, the person who asks for an opinion on a point of law, FATWĀ. II 866a

mustafīḍ (A) : in the science of Tradition, a Tradition which is treated by most as an intermediate class between Traditions with two transmitters, MAS̲H̲HŪR, and Traditions with many transmitters, MUTAWĀTIR, although some treat a ~ Tradition as being equivalent to either the one or the other. III 25b

mustaḥabb (A) : in law, a recommendable action, corresponding largely to MANDŪB. VII 722b

mustaḥfiẓ (A) : in Turkish military usage, the territorial army. VIII 371a

mustaka → MASTAKA

mustaḳarr (A) : lit. permanent; among the Fāṭimids, ~ denotes IMĀMs descended from ʿAlī and Fāṭima. II 851b

mustaḳfī (A) : in mediaeval Islam, a cut-purse who follows and steals up behind a person to rob him. V 768b

mustak̲h̲ridj̲ (A) : in mediaeval administration, the person responsible for collecting money, such as that of the poor-tax or land-tax. VII 724a; and → ISTIK̲H̲RĀDJ̲

In Muslim Spain, the ~ was the official who collected on behalf of the Muslim state the taxation due from the Mozarabs. VII 724a

mustakris̲h̲ (A) : a child who has become large in his stomach or hard in his palate, and has begun to eat. A syn. to the verb *istakras̲h̲a* is *tazakkara*.VIII 822a

muṣṭalaḥa (A) : the term for a technical term. I 572a

mustaʿliya (A) : 'raised'; in grammar, those letters whose pronunciation requires the elevation of the back of the tongue, i.e. the emphatic consonants, *ḥurūf al-muṭbaḳa*, and *ḳāf*, *g̲h̲ayn*, and *k̲h̲āʾ*. III 596b; VIII 343b

mustaʾmin (A) : a non-Muslim, not living on Muslim territory, who has been given a safe conduct or pledge of security and thereby becomes protected by the sanctions of the law in his life and property for a limited period. I 429b; II 341b

mustamlī (A) : a Tradition transmitter's clerk, the earliest representatives of this professional class emerging in the course of the first half of the 2nd/8th century. His function was to write the Tradition down from dictation and to reiterate the Tradition in a way audible to the audience. V 1133b; VII 725b

mustaraḳa → ANDARGĀH; ṬABAḲA

mustaʿriba (A) : lit. arabicised.

In genealogy, the name of one of the three groups into which the population of Arabia is divided, the other groups being the *ʿarab ʿāriba* (the, for the most part, extinct original Arabs of pure stock) and the MUTAʿARRIBA. Like the latter, ~ is applied to tribes who were not originally Arabs. They trace their descent from Maʿadd b. ʿAdnān, a descendant of Ismāʿīl. All the north Arabian tribes are included among the ~ , so that the Ḳuraysh, to which Muḥammad belonged, are one of them. VII 732b

In Muslim Spain, ~ was applied to the Christian Spaniards who retained their religion under Islam (Eng Mozarab). VII 732b

mustashār (A, T *müsteshār*) : counsellor.

Under the Ottomans, the general secretary to a ministry or the under-secretary of state. The function was retained under the Turkish Republic and each ministry has its ~ ; also, the name given to the 'counsellors' of Turkish or foreign embassies or legations. VII 732b

mustashriḳ (A, pl. **mustashriḳūn**) : an orientalist, one who studies the Orient; one becoming like the Oriental. VII 735b

mustathnā (A) : lit. excepted, separated; in mathematics, excepted fractions, separated by the subtraction sign. IV 725b

♦ **müstethna eyāletler** (T) : in Ottoman administration, those provinces of the Ottoman empire separated from the 'normally-administered' ones of the Anatolian and Rumelian heartland. VII 756a

mustawdaʿ (A) : under the Fāṭimids, a trustee or guardian of the imāmate, whose function was to 'veil' the true IMĀM, MUSTAḲARR, in order to protect him, and who acted by right of an assignment which so to speak allowed him to enter the family of the true *imām*s. II 851b

mustawfī (A) : in mediaeval administration, an official who was in charge of official accounts and thus acted as an accountant-general. IV 977b; VII 753b

For the Ottoman empire, → DAFTARDĀR

mustawḳad (A) : 'fire-place', a major cooking contrivance found in the mediaeval kitchen. It was designed to accommodate several cooking pots and/or pans side-by-side at the same time. It was erected to about half-a-person's height, giving easy access to the cooking food and was provided with vents allowing for an intake of air over the coals and for the expulsion of smoke. VI 808a

mustazād (A) : lit. additional; in Persian and kindred literature, principally Turkish and Urdu, a poem of which each second hemistich is followed by a short metrical line which has some bearing on the sense of the first hemistich without altering the meaning. All these lines rhyme together throughout the poem. I 677b; VII 754b

müsteshār → MUSTASHĀR

müstethna eyāletler → MUSTATHNĀ

müsweddedji (T) : a clerk in the Ottoman empire who drafted in hypothetical terms every matter for the SHAYKH AL-ISLĀM, who had no contact with litigants nor their advocates. II 867a

mutʿa (A) : lit. enjoyment; in law, temporary marriage, also called *nikāh al-mutʿa*, a marriage which is contracted for a fixed period. It was authorised at the beginning of Islam but forbidden later by the SUNNA; shīʿism tolerates it, however. VI 476a; VII 757a; VIII 28b; also, the indemnity payable to a divorced wife when no dowry has been stipulated. VII 759a

mutaʿarriba (A) : 'those who seek to become Arabs'; in genealogy, the term applied to the descendants of Ḳaḥṭān who were regarded as 'having become Arabs' in contrast to the supposedly indigenous 'pure' Arab tribes. They settled in southern Arabia. VII 759b

mutaʿashshā (A) : in mediaeval Islam, the name for the places where pilgrims stopped for the evening meal on the pilgrim highway running from ʿIrāḳ to the Holy Cities. S 198b

muṭābaḳa (A) : in literary theory, a contrast between two single contraries; antithesis. VII 491b

mutabarriz (A) : the name for the second horse in a horse-race, according to the order of finishing. II 953a

muṭabbikh (A) : said of a young man who is full (or plump). VIII 822a

mutadārik (A) : in prosody, the name of the sixteenth Arabic metre. It does not seem to have been used by the poets before Islam or the first century AH. It is made up, in each hemistich, of four *fāʿilun*, which may be reduced to *faʿilun* or even *faʿlun*. I 670a; IV 412b; VII 759b

mutafaḳḳih (A) : a student of FIḲH 'undergraduate', as opposed to FAḲĪH 'doctor of the law' or 'graduate student'. V 1124b

mutaghallibe → DEREBEY

mutaḥayyir → KAWKAB

muʿtaḳ → ʿITḲ

mutaḳabbil → ḲABĀLA

mutakallim → ḤĀL

mutaḳārib (A) : in prosody, the name of the fifteenth Arabic metre, comprising in each hemistich, four feet made up of one short and two longs (*faʿūlun*). A certain number of licences are possible, in particular, the omission of the fourth foot, the shortening or even the cutting out of the third syllable of a foot, etc. I 670a; VII 763a mutakāwis (A) : in prosody, the situation in which the two quiescent consonants of the rhyme letter, *rawī*, are separated by four vowelled consonants (as in *faw[ḳa ḳadami]h*). IV 412b

mutak͟hayyila (A) : in the poetics of the philosophers, a faculty responsible for the re-actualisation of images which have been perceived in the past. IX 458b

muṭālaba (A) : in law, the 'exaction of payment' (Ger *Haftung*). I 29a

muʿtalla → ḤARF ʿILLA

mutamakkin (A) : in grammar, 'having full freedom of movement', i.e. a masculine noun declinable in three cases, a synonym of *munṣarif*. IX 53a

mutammima (A, pl. *mutammimāt*) : the generic term for the genre of complements in Arabic literature. IX 603b

mutanad͟jd͟jis → NAD͟JIS

mutarādif (A) : in prosody, the situation in which the two quiescent consonants of the rhyme letter, *rawī*, come in immediate succession (as in *ḳāl*). IV 412b

mutarad͟jd͟jila (A) : a woman who tries to resemble men in clothing habits and ornaments. IX 566b

mutāraka → MUWĀḌAʿA

mutarākib (A) : in prosody, the situation in which three vowelled consonants stand between the two quiescent consonants of the rhyme letter, *rawī* (as in *fī[d͟jabali]y*). IV 412b

mutaraʿriʿ (A), or *mulimm* : a child 'almost or quite past the age of ten years, or active' (Lane). VIII 822a

mutaṣaddī : in Muslim India, the functionary in the Dihlī sultanate who issued both permits to merchants who brought their merchandise into the market for sale and passes for goods which were taken out of the city. IX 801a

mutaṣaddir → ṢADR

mutasallik → ṢĀḤIB AL-LAYL

mutasalṭin (A) : a petty prince. IX 849a

mutaṣarrif (A, T *müteṣarrif*) : in Ottoman administration, the chief administrative official of the SAND͟JAḲ or LIWĀʾ, the second highest in the hierarchy of administrative districts, as defined by the provincial administration laws of 23 Rabīʿ I 1284/25 July 1867 and S͟hawwāl 1287/1871. With the transformation of the old *sand͟jaḳ*s into *wilāyet*s (→ EYĀLET) in 1921, ~ passed out of use as a designation for a type of local official. VII 774a; IX 13b; governor. VIII 1b

♦ mutaṣarrifiyya : a synonym of SAND͟JAḲ, an (administrative) regime, as e.g. created in Lebanon in 1861. V 794a; V 1253a

mutas͟hābih (A) : in Qurʾānic science, the term for the 'ambiguous' verses, whose picturesque style, if taken literally, would seem to ascribe human attributes or acts to God, distinct from the *muḥkam* verses, whose sense is clearly established. I 409a ff.

mutaṭawwiʿa (A), or *muṭṭawwiʿa* : lit. those who perform supererogatory deeds of piety, those over and above the duties laid upon them by the s͟harīʿa.

In military contexts, ~ was used as a designation for volunteer fighters, especially to be found on the frontiers of the Islamic world, where there were great opportunities to fight a holy war against the pagans. From around the 5th/11th century, ~ was replaced more and more by GHĀZĪ and MUDJĀHID for the concept of volunteer warriors for the faith. VII 776b; VIII 795b; volunteers who served in the early Islamic armies without regular stipends, but who shared in the plunder. VIII 568b

In present-day Bedouin society, elders responsible for order and decency. V 768a

In contemporary Saudi Arabia, *muṭawwiʿ* (a modern formation from the same root) is used to designate the religious police who enforce the closure of shops during the times of public prayer, oversee morals, etc. VII 777b

mutawakkiliyya (A) : a plant, or dish, forbidden by al-Ḥākim in addition to the classical food prohibitions. II 1070a

mutawallī (A) : in Mughal India, a manager of land-grants. VIII 751b

mutawātir (A) : 'uninterrupted'. IX 371a; in the science of Tradition, a Tradition (or, in general, any report) with so many transmitters that there could be no collusion, all being known to be reliable and not being under any compulsion to lie. III 25b; VII 781b

In prosody, ~ is applied to the rhyme in which only one moving letter intervenes between the last two quiescents. VII 781b

♦ mutawātir bi 'l-lafẓ : in the science of Tradition, a Tradition in which the texts appended to the various chains are identical in wording. VII 781b

♦ mutawātir bi 'l-maʿnā : in the science of Tradition, a Tradition in which the texts are identical in meaning only, as opposed to *mutawātir bi 'l-lafẓ*. VII 781b

muṭawwiʿ → MUTAṬAWWIʿA

muṭawwif (A, pl. *muṭawwifūn*) : the pilgrim's guide in Mecca. His task is to assist the pilgrim by supplying his material needs and in performing the rites of the pilgrimage. The *muṭawwifūn* are organised in a special guild, which is divided in sub-guilds. An alternative term sometimes encountered is *shaykh al-ḥadjdj*. VI 170b; VII 782a

muṭayyin (A) : in the mediaeval Near East, a beggar who smears himself with mud and feigns madness. VII 495a

mutazawwidja (A) : an appellative for women in early Islam who have had several husbands. I 308b

mutbaʿ → ITBĀʿ

muṭbaḳa → IṬBĀḲ

müteferriḳa (T) : under the Ottomans, a corps of mounted guards, or member of the guard, who were especially attached to the person of the sultan. VII 794a

muthallath (A) : in mathematics, a triangle.

In astronomy, *kawkab al-muthallath* is the constellation of the (northern) Triangle. The star at the apex is an astrolabe star and is called *ra's al-muthallath*. VII 794b

In astrology, *muthallatha* is used for each of the four divisions of the zodiacal circle, each of which includes three signs 120 degrees apart. VII 84b; VII 794b

muthamman (A) : octagon, octagonal.

In architecture, plan figures and buildings of eight equal sides. VII 795a

♦ muthamman baghdādī : in Mughal architecture, the irregular octagon with four longer and four shorter sides, which may assume the shape of a square or rectangle with chamfered corners. VII 795a

muthannā (A) : in grammar, the dual. II 406b

In prosody, *muthannayāt*, or *thunāʾiyyāt*, are used for short-lined quatrains with rhyme scheme *a b a b*. VIII 584b

mutḳin (A) : 'exact'; in the science of Tradition, a quality of a reliable transmitter of Tradition. II 462a

muṭlaḳ (A) : 'absolute', as opposed to restricted, *muḳayyad*; 'general', as opposed to KHĀṢṢ. VII 799b

In grammar, *mafʿūl muṭlaḳ* denotes the absolute object (cognate accusative), i.e. a verbal noun derived, mostly, from the verb of a sentence and put in the accusative to serve as an object, even if the verb is intransitive. VII 799b

In law, ~ is applied to the MUDJTAHIDs of the heroic age, the founders of the schools, who are called *mudjtahid muṭlaḳ*, an epithet which none after them has borne. VII 799b

In dogmatics, ~ is applied to existence, so that *al-wudjūd al-muṭlaḳ* denotes God as opposed to His creation, which does not possess existence in the deepest sense. VII 799b

muṭrib → KHUNYĀGAR

muttaṣil (A) : contiguous.

In the science of Tradition, an unbroken ISNĀD traced back to the source. III 25b; VIII 384b

♦ muttaṣil marfūʿ : in the science of Tradition, an unbroken ISNĀD going back to the Prophet. III 25b

♦ muttaṣil mawḳūf : in the science of Tradition, an unbroken ISNĀD going back to a Companion. III 25b; VIII 384b

muṭṭawwiʿa → MUTAṬAWWIʿA

muwādaʿa (A) : a truce of friendship. IX 373b; peace between Muslim and non-Muslim communities, also called *muhādana*, for a specific period of time. IX 845a f.

In Mālikī law, a system for ensuring that a female slave observe the period of sexual abstinence, ISTIBRĀʾ, by giving the slave into the hands of a trustworthy person, preferably a woman, who forbade the new owner to come near her until the period had elapsed. IV 253b

muwāḍaʿa (A) : understanding.

In law, ~ means the rescission of a sale or transaction. A synonym is *mutāraka*. VII 801a; a covering document in a transaction which sets out the real relationship of the parties to each other and the real purport of their agreement, intended to prevent one party from using a document on which the transaction is recorded to its exclusive advantage and for a purpose contrary to the aim of the whole of the agreement. III 511b

In mediaeval administration, ~ denotes the contract of service of officials. VII 801a

muwāfaḳa (A) : in administration, a term for the comprehensive accounting presented by an ʿĀMIL on relinquishing his appointment when it is approved by the authority to whom he presents it. If they differ, it is called *muḥāsaba*. II 78b

♦ al-muwāfaḳa wa ʾl-d̲jamāʿa : in administration, the comprehensive accounting presented by an ʿĀMIL on relinquishing his appointment, one of the many records and registers of a Muslim administrative office of the 4th/10th century. II 78b

muwaḥḥidūn (A, s. *muwaḥḥid*) : 'unitarians'; a name by which the Druze call themselves. II 631b; the name given to the adherents of the reformist movement of which the principal element was the divine unicity, *tawḥīd*, which ruled during the 6th/12th and 7th/13th centuries in North Africa and Spain, known in the West as the Almohads. VII 801b

muwaḳḳit (A) : a professional astronomer associated with a religious institution, whose task it was to ascertain the ḲIBLA and the times of prayer. Mention of such astronomers appeared for the first time in Egypt in the 7th/13th century. VI 677b; VII 29b

muwālāt → WALĀʾ

muwālayāt → MAWĀLIYĀ

muwallad (A) : a hybrid, of mixed blood, a word originally belonging to the vocabulary of stock-breeders; hence, a cross-breed, half-caste or even 'one who, without being of Arab origin, has been born among the Arabs and received an Arabic education'. VII 807a; originally meaning home-born slaves. VI 881a

In Muslim Spain, the descendants of non-Arab neo-Muslims, brought up in the Islamic religion by their recently-converted parents, thus the members of the second generation, the sons, and, by extension, those of the third generation, the grandsons. The sons of an Arab father and indigenous mother were not regarded as ~ . I 85b; I 491a; VII 807b; original population of Spain. IX 232a

In grammar and literary theory, ~ refers to a word, linguistic phenomenon, or literary feature not found in classical Arabic of pre- and early Islamic times, thus 'post-classical'. VII 808b; and → MUʿARRAB

muwāraba (A) : ambiguity.

In rhetoric, ~ denotes the ability to remedy a gaffe or an offensive phrase by repeating the expression in an attenuated form, if not radically modified, or else by trying to make the person addressed believe that he has not properly understood what has been said to him. VII 808b

Among the G̲h̲umāra, a Berber tribe of northwestern Morocco, a 5th/11th-century custom consisting of a recently-married bride, still a virgin, being carried off clandestinely by the young men of the locality and held far from her husband for a month or even more, sometimes several times in succession if very beautiful. This custom was flattering to the woman. VII 809a

muwāṣafa (A) : in mediaeval administration, a list showing the circumstances and causes of any changes occurring in the army. II 79a

muwashshaḥ (A), or *muwashshaḥa* : in literature, a genre of stanzaic poetry, which, according to indigenous tradition, developed in al-Andalus towards the end of the 3rd/9th century. It is reckoned among the seven post-classical genres of poetry in Arabic. Its fundamental characteristics were the arrangement in strophes and the addition of a final part, *khardja* (also called *markaz*), in vernacular Arabic or Romance mixed with the vernacular. I 595b; I 601a; VII 809a

muwaththiḳ (A), or *shurūṭī* : in law, the profession of drafting deeds. IX 208a

muwāṭin (A) : citizen, a modern word coined around the turn of the 20th century. VII 812b

muwaẓẓaf(a) (A), or *waẓīfa* : in mediaeval administration, a form of land tax depending on the return that the land was capable of yielding, and being due whether the land was tilled or not. For Muslim writers or historians of India, the ~ is always meant when KHARĀDJ is mentioned. IV 1055b; VII 507b

For the Turkish *muwaẓẓafe*, → NIẒĀM

muzammilātī (A) : in mediaeval Cairo, the attendant of the waterhouse, SABĪL, who was in charge of cleaning its premises and its utensils, and of raising the water from the cistern and serving it to the thirsty. VIII 679b ff.

muzāraʿa (A) : in law, a lease of agricultural land with profit-sharing, in which contract the owner of the land arranges with a husbandman for the latter to have the use of his land for a specified period, during which the husbandman sows, tends and harvests an agricultural crop. When the crop is harvested, the two parties to the contract divide the proceeds in agreed shares, the share of the landowner constituting the rent for the lease of his land. II 905b; V 871b; VII 822b

muzāwadj → DIYĀNAY

♦ **muzāwadja** (A) : coupling.

In literary theory, ~ means paranomasia, a play on words consisting in the coupling of two terms which are similar in external form or in meaning and linked by the conjuction *wa-*, e.g. (*bayna-hum*) *hardj wa-mardj* ‘between them there are disagreements’, where the two elements have an independent existence. VII 823a

In rhetoric, ~ denotes the ‘coupling’ of two themes conveying comparable effects by means of two parallel expressions. VII 823b

muzayyin → ḤALLĀḲ

muzdawidj (A) : double.

In grammar, the use of two terms in which the form of one is changed to make it resemble that of the other. VII 825b

In rhetoric, ~ consists in establishing a kind of alliteration between two adjacent words having the same form, the same metrical quantity and the same rhyme. VII 825b

In prosody, a poem with rhyming couplets, usually written in the RADJAZ metre which has either eleven or twelve syllables. In Persian and Turkish, it is called MATHNAWĪ. I 2b; I 108a; VI 832b; VII 825b; VIII 376a

♦ muzdawidjāt : a poem in the RADJAZ metre consisting of strophes of five hemistichs in which the first four hemistichs rhyme together and the fifth ones have a common rhyme. Sometimes the strophe has only four hemistichs, the first three rhyming together and the fourth rhyming jointly. VII 825b

muẓhar → MUḌMAR

muzzammil (A) : the title of the 73rd SŪRA of the Qurʾān, derived from the first verse which may be translated 'O you covered in a cloak'. VII 286a; and → MUDDATHTHIR

myron : sacred oil, in the Cilician-Armenian kingdom. IX 679a

N

nabʿ (A) : *Grewia tenax*, a wood from which the pre-Islamic Arabs made their bows, still used today in Somalia. IV 797b

nabaʾ (A) : a Qurʾānic term for 'news, announcement', which meaning ~ has retained until today; also, an edifying tale, a story of a prophet. III 369a

nabaʿ (A) : a shallow water source. I 100a

nabāt (A) : plants. VII 831a; and → SUKKAR

♦ nabātī : a strong yellow-coloured paper preferred by Cairo printers. IV 420a

nabaṭī (A) : the name given to the popular vernacular poetry of Arabia. VII 838a

nabaz (A) : in onomastics, an unpleasant sobriquet, LAḲAB, such as that of Marwān I (*al-ḥimār* 'the ass'). IV 180a; V 618b

nabbāl → AḲŪNĪṬUN

nabbāsh (A) : lit. burrower, excavator; in mediaeval Islam, a category of thieves, said to be well-known and presumably a man who dug up a people's buried treasure hoards. V 769a

nabīdh (A) : intoxicating drinks, several kinds of which were produced in early Arabia, such as *mizr* (from barley; and → MAZAR), BITʿ (from honey or spelt) or FAḌĪKH (from different kinds of dates). These ingredients were steeped in water until they were fermented, and the result of the procedure was a slightly intoxicating drink. Sometimes ~ was consumed mixed with strong intoxicating ingredients like cannabis. IV 996a; VII 840a nabḳ (A) : in botany, the fruit of the SIDR tree. IX 549b

nabl (A) : in archery, a wooden or Arab arrow, one of the three main words denoting the arrow, the others being *sahm* (an arrow made from a reed, or of hard, solid wood) and *nus̲h̲s̲h̲āb* (Persian arrow). IV 799a

nad̲h̲īr (A) : 'warner'; a Qurʾānic term, whose opposite is *bas̲h̲īr*, *mubas̲h̲s̲h̲ir*. Both ~ and *bas̲h̲īr* are applied to the prophets, the former when they are represented as warners, the latter as announcers of good tidings. ~ is used as an epithet of Noah, the great warner before the Deluge, and of Muḥammad himself. VII 845a

nad̲h̲r (A, pl. *nud̲h̲ūr*) : 'vow', a procedure which was taken over into Islam from the pre-Islamic Arabs, for whom the vow always had more or less the character of a self-dedication, and underwent modification. In Islam the vow and the oath are treated together. VII 846a ff.

♦ nad̲h̲r wa-niyāz : among the AHL AL-ḤAḲḲ, raw offerings, including animals of the male sex, oxen, sheep, cocks, intended for sacrifice, which with cooked or prepared victuals (→ K̲H̲AYR WA-K̲H̲IDMAT) is an indispensable feature of a D̲H̲IKR session. I 261a

nadīm (A, pl. *nidām*, *nudamāʾ*, *nudmān*) : drinking companion, and, by extension, friend, courtier (or confidant) of kings or of wealthy persons; his function is to entertain them, eat and drink in their company, play chess with them, accompany them in hunting and participate in their pastimes and recreations. VII 849b

nādira (A), pl. *nawādir* : lit. rare thing, rarity; a pleasing anecdote containing wit, humour, jocularity and lively repartee, of the type which has never ceased to be an integral feature of all social gatherings, whether intimate or official. VII 856a

In grammar, the plural form *nawādir* also denotes compounds containing *abū*, *umm*, *ibn* etc., and dual forms. VI 823a

naʿd̲j̲a (A) : a reproductive ewe. S 319a

nad̲j̲ama → IT̲H̲T̲H̲AG̲H̲ARA

nad̲j̲āsāt → NAD̲J̲IS

nad̲j̲is (A) : impure, the opposite of *ṭāhir*. In law, *nad̲j̲āsāt* are things impure in themselves and cannot be purified; *mutanad̲j̲d̲j̲is* is applied to those things which are defiled only. The law schools differ in their definitions of what is impure. VII 870a

nad̲j̲l (A) : progeny. VIII 821b

nad̲j̲m (A, pl. **nud̲j̲ūm**) : star; an alternative name for the Pleiades, otherwise called *al-t̲h̲urayyā*. VIII 97b

♦ **nud̲j̲ūm (aḥkām al-)** : 'decrees of the stars', astrology. VIII 105b; the art of drawing omens from the position of the stars at a person's birth. VIII 705b

nad̲j̲r → LAYṬ

nad̲j̲wa → FAS̲H̲T

nad̲j̲wā (A) : under the Fāṭimids, a tax which had to be paid by those who were present at the Ismāʿīlī learned meetings which were held at the palace, abolished by al-Ḥākim. III 81a

nafādh (A) : in prosody, the vowel of the *hāʾ* serving as WAṢL. IV 412a

nafaḳa (A) : in law, maintenance for a divorced woman. III 1011b; VIII 433a

nafal (A, pl. *anfāl*) : in early Islam, a bonus share given to those warriors who distinguished themselves (in the battle). II 1005b; VIII 800b; and → IKLĪL AL-MALIK

naffāṭ, naffāṭa → NAFṬ

nāfidh (A), or *sālik* : through-way, e.g. *shāriʿ nāfidh* or *ghayr nāfidh* 'cul-de-sac'. IX 320b

nāfila (A, pl. *nawāfil*) : in theology, supererogatory work; those works which are supererogatory in the plain sense, in contradistinction to other works which have become a regular practice, *sunna muʾakkada*. VII 878a

In law, ~ is used for the supererogatory ṢALĀT as well as for the whole class of supererogatory *ṣalāt*s. VII 878b; VIII 931a

nafīr → NEFĪR

nafs (A, pl. *anfus*, *nufūs*) : soul; self, person. VII 880a; and → RŪḤ

In divination, ~ is a term of geomancy, being the first 'house' of the *ummahāt*, because it guides to problems concerning the soul and spirit of the inquirer, and to the beginning of affairs. VII 883a

♦ al-nafs al-kulliyya : in Druze hierarchy, the second of the five cosmic ranks in the organisation. II 632a; in Abū Bakr al-Rāzī's thought, ~ is the Universal Soul, the 'second Eternal' of five, which shook and agitated Matter in order to produce the world, without success. III 328a

nafṭ (A, P *naft*) : the purest form of Mesopotamian bitumen. I 1055b; a generic, vague appellation for a substance which is basically petroleum. VII 884a; 'Greek fire', a liquid incendiary compound which was hurled at people, the various siege weapons which were made of wood, and ships. I 1055b; VII 884a; fireworks; gunpowder. I 1056a; oil, in the modern sense of the word. VII 886b

♦ naffāṭ, or *zarrāḳ* : a specialist in discharging 'Greek fire' in the form of a jet, by means of a special copper tube, called the *naffāṭa*, *zarrāḳa*, or *mukḥula*. I 1055b

nafūd (A) : a sandy area, in the north of the Arabian peninsula; in the south it is called a *ramla*. I 537a; dune desert; Arabian sand seas. II 91b; VII 891a

nafūr (A) : in the terminology of horse-riding, a horse that swerves and shies. II 954a

nafy (A) : in grammar, negation. VII 895b

nahār (A) : a day, which extends from sunrise to sunset. V 707b; the ~ begins at the moment that the upper edge of the sun appears on the horizon, just as the night and the official day begin when the opposite edge, now uppermost, disappears. V 709b

nahdj → SHĀRIʿ

nāḥiye (T, < A *nāḥiya* 'district, vicinity') : in Ottoman administration, the subdivisions of a *wilāyet* 'province' (→ EYĀLET); the rural subdivision of a ḲAḌĀʾ. The subdivisions of a ~ are called *ḳarye* 'village'. In the Turkish Republic, the ~ is a subdivision of the *ilçe* or district. VII 906a

nahr (A, pl. *anhār, anhur*) : running water, hence a perennial watercourse, river, stream of any size, thus opposed to a *wādī* 'a watercourse filled only at certain times of the year' or a *sayl* 'periodic torrent'; artificially-contrived running water-courses, i.e. canals and navigations. VII 909b

naḥr (A) : in law, one of the two methods of slaughtering animals, by which the animal concerned becomes permissible as food. The term applies to camels only, and consists of driving the knife in by the throat without it being necessary to cut in the manner prescribed for the DHABḤ, the camel remaining upright but at the same time facing the ḲIBLA. II 213b

naḥs → SAʿD WA-NAḤS

naḥw (A) : path, way; fashion, manner. V 913a; a type of expression. V 804a

In grammar, the term for 'grammar' (to be contrasted with LUGHA 'lexical studies') and, more specifically, 'syntax' (the counterpart of ṢARF or *taṣrīf* 'morphology', so that for 'grammar' one also finds the phrase *naḥw wa-ṣarf*). VII 913a; VIII 894a

♦ naḥwī (pl. *naḥwiyyūn*) : grammarian. V 1133b; in its plural form ~ refers to an (anonymous ?) group of participants in the grammatical debate in which Sībawayhi was involved. IX 525b

nāʾib (A) : substitute, delegate, any person appointed as deputy of another in an official position; and → SAFĪR

In the Mamlūk and Dihlī sultanates, the ~ is the deputy or lieutenant of the sultan; the governor of the chief provinces. VII 915a

In law, a judge-substitute, or delegate of the ḲĀḌĪ in the administration of law. VII 915b

In politics, a parliamentary deputy. VII 915b

♦ nāʾib al-ghayba : under the Mamlūks, the temporary governor of Cairo (or Egypt) during the absence of the sultan. II 996a; VII 915a

♦ nāʾib khāṣṣ → SAFĪR

♦ nāʾib al-salṭana : under the Mamlūks, a sort of Prefect of Upper Egypt, a post created in 780/1378 and inaugurated at Asyūṭ. VIII 865a; a viceroy. I 138a

♦ al-nāʾib al-ʿumūmī : in modern legal usage, the public prosecutor. VII 915b

nāʾiba (A) : an occasional tax in kind, levied by the first Saʿdīs; it later became more or less permanent and payable in cash. II 146a

nāḳa (A) : the female camel, a term also found in the Qurʾān, where it appears in the edifying stories of Ṣāliḥ, the Thamūd, etc. III 666a

♦ nāḳa al-baḥr → AṬŪM

♦ ṣāḥib al-nāḳa : 'the man with the she-camel'; a popular nickname for Yaḥyā b. Zikrawayh, an Ismāʿīlī agitator. VIII 831a

naḳāʾ (A) : a term connected with *nuḳāwā*, a generic noun denoting alkaline plants utilised for washing linen and whitening cloths; a 'rite of reconciliation', used in the Ḥidjāz for righting injuries, whereby an offender pronounces a formula on the doorstep of the aggrieved person, who then appears, covers the former's hand with a cloth, and kills a sheep to celebrate the reconciliation. VII 920a

In the Arabian peninsula, ~ or *naḳā* (pl. *niḳyān*) denotes a large dune bare of vegatation. II 537a; and → ṬIʿS

naḳad (A) : a strain of sheep in Bahrain in the time of al-Djāḥiẓ, which was stunted but a good wool producer. Other small-sized sheep were the *ḥaballaḳ*, which is still bred, and the *ṭimṭim*, with shorn ears and a woolly dewlap under the throat, found in Yemen. S 318a

naḳāʾiḍ (A, s. *naḳīḍa*) : in prosody, a form of poetic duelling in which tribal or personal insults are exchanged in poems, usually coming in pairs, employing the same metre and rhyme, synonymous with *munāḳaḍāt*. Sometimes *naḳīḍa* is used for what is more properly termed a *muʿāraḍa*, a poem with the same metre and rhyme as another, made by way of emulation or in order to surpass, without the invective element. VII 920a

naḳāniḳ → LAḲĀNIḲ

naḳarāt (T) : lit. peckings; in Turkish poetry, the refrain, that is, the ultimate line or ultimate and penultimate lines of each stanza of the SHARḲĪ. IX 354a

naḳb (A, pl. *nuḳūb*) : an underground tunnel; in military science, mining, a system of siege warfare which reached the peak of its success in the late 6th/12th and the 7th/13th centuries. After the Crusades, mining declined considerably. III 473b

In mediaeval Islam, ~ gave rise to the designation *aṣḥāb al-naḳb* or *naḳḳābūn*, thieves who burrowed into cellars and vaults from the outside or from adjacent houses. V 768b

naḳd (A) : the portion of the dowry handed over at the conclusion of a marriage. In modern Arabic, ~ signifies 'money'. VII 921a

naḳḍ (A) : 'refutation', in particular when used in reference to a book. VIII 363a; and → RADD

♦ **naḳḍ al-mīthāḳ** (A) : in shīʿism and, more commonly, Bahāʾism, the act of violating a religious covenant. VII 921a

nakhkhās (A) : 'cattle-dealer', a term in the mediaeval period for a slave merchant. I 32b; in Muslim India, a market where slaves as well as animals were sold. IX 800b

nākhudāh (A, < H *nāo* and P *khudā*) : in navigation, a term for 'captain'. VII 41b

naḳīʿ (A) : drinks composed of fruits (dates, etc.) mixed in water. VI 720b

naḳīb (A, pl. *nuḳabāʾ*) : chief, leader, of a tribe or other group.

In early Islam, the Medinans negotiating with Muḥammad about the HIDJRA were asked to appoint 12 *nuḳabāʾ* as representatives. Both the number 12 and the sense of ~ as representative were repeated in the preparatory stages of the

ʿAbbāsid revolution. VII 926a
During the Dihlī sultanate, the ~ was an official of lower rank than the *ḥādjib*, chamberlain, probably best translated 'usher'. VII 926a
Under the Mamlūks, the *nuḳabāʾ* were the military police, responsible for seeing that the members of the expeditionary force, despatched against a strong enemy, presented themselves on time and in the appointed place. III 184a
In mysticism, *al-nuḳabāʾ* are the 300 'chiefs', the seventh degree in the ṣūfī hierarchical order of saints. I 95a; for the Demirdāshiyya order, S 208b; in modern Egyptian usage, the *nukabāʾ* are ṣūfīs who run the brotherhood's regional cells on behalf of the regional deputy, KHALĪFA. The *shaykh*'s closest associate is called *naḳīb al-sadjdjāda*. VIII 744a
In guild terminology, the ~ was the master's assistant and the master of ceremonies. IX 168b; and → AKHĪ

♦ **naḳīb al-ashrāf** : lit. the marshal of the nobility; under the ʿAbbāsids, the office of head of the community of ʿAlid descendants. VII 926b; IX 333b; his function was to investigate all claims to descent from the Prophet's family and to keep rolls of the legitimate descendants of the Prophet, for they were entitled to a lifetime pension. The ~ for the sunnīs was called the *naḳīb al-hāshimiyyīn*, for the shīʿīs, the *naḳīb al-ṭālibiyyīn*. V 1131b; IX 333b

♦ naḳīb al-hāshimiyyīn → NAḲĪB AL-ASHRĀF

♦ naḳīb al-sadjdjāda → NAḲĪB

♦ naḳīb al-ṭālibiyyīn → NAḲĪB AL-ASHRĀF

naḳīḍa → NAḲĀʾIḌ

nakira → MAʿRIFA

naḳḳāb(ūn) → NAḲB

naḳḳāra (A, T *naḳḳāre*) : a medium-sized kettle-drum made of copper, one of the instruments of the military band, NAḲḲĀRA-KHĀNA. The two parts of the ~ were tuned differently to produce bass and treble tones, and were struck with sticks of uniform shape. VI 1008a; VII 927b

♦ čifte naḳḳāre (T) : a 'double drum'. VIII 178b

♦ **naḳḳāra-khāna** (P) : a kind of military band, composed of various instruments, kettle-drums, horns, trumpets, and reed-pipes. VII 927b

naḳḳāsh (A) : die-sinker, one of the craftsmen employed as staff in the mediaeval mint, whose professional activity was restricted to engraving only. II 118a; an artist who embellishes surfaces; an illuminator of manuscripts; an embroiderer; a wall decorator. VII 931a

♦ naḳḳāshī (A) : a term which covers drawing and painting, whether representational or decorative. VIII 451b

♦ **naḳḳāsh-khāna** (T, < A and P) : the name of the Ottoman royal painting atelier. VII 931a

naḳsh ḥadīda (N.Afr) : the name given to the sculpturing of plaster applied, with an iron tool, more or less thickly on the wall. II 556b

nāḳūs (A, < Syr; pl. *nawāḳīs*) : a kind of rattle once used and in some places still used by Eastern Christians to summon the community to divine service. It is a board pierced with holes which is beaten with a rod. I 188a; VII 943a; a percussion slab. IX 10b

naʿl (A) : in early Islam, a sandal which could be of palm fibre, smooth leather, or leather with animal hair. V 735b; a general word for shoe used throughout the Middle East today. V 741b; and → SIKKA

namāzgāh → MUṢALLĀ

namir (A), or *nimr* : in zoology, the panther (*Panthera pardus*), better known, in Africa, by the name of 'leopard'. VII 947b; VIII 120a

♦ namira : in early Islam, a man's wrap with strips of varying colours which give it the appearance of a tiger's skin. V 734a; the black ink of the writing contrasting with the white of the page. VII 950a

nammām → FŪDHANDJ; ṢANDAL

nāmūs (A) : originally, a transcription of the Greek νόμος, which was left untranslated in Ibn Hishām. It is also a true Arabic word, with such varied meanings that only some can be considered old and original. In the modern vernacular, ~ has survived as 'midge', with *nāmūsiyya* as 'mosquito net'. VII 953b; the bearer of a favourable secret. II 486b

In religion and philosophy, ~ , from the Greek loanword, is used frequently for 'divine law', revealed through the prophets. VII 954a; for the Ikhwān al-Ṣafāʾ, ~ meant a kind of divine being. VII 954b

In magic, ~ is used for magical formulae, particularly those which are based on illusions of the senses. VII 955a

In zoology, ~ is a noun used in the collective sense denoting the totality of dipterous, nematoceratous insects or mosquitos. VII 955b

♦ nāmūsiyya → NĀMŪS

naʿnaʿ → FŪDHANDJ

nanawātai → PASHTŪNWALĪ

nār (A, pl. *nīrān*) : fire. VII 957b; for ~ in compounds, VII 958a ff.; and → MANĀẒIR

nard (P) : the game of backgammon; any kind of dicing. VII 963a

nardjis (A, T *nergis*, P *nargis* and *ʿabhar*) : in botany, the narcissus. In al-Andalus, three terms were used: *nardjis ḳādūsī* (the meadow narcissus), *nardjis aṣfar* (jonquil) and *bahār* (< *ʿabhar* ?). VII 963b f.

narkh (P) : in the Ottoman empire, the prices determined by official authorities for various goods, especially food, shoes and some other basic goods. VII 964a

narm-āhan → ḤADĪD

nasaʿa → ITHTHAGHARA

nasab (A) : kinship, the relationship, particularly ancestral, i.e. the genealogy of an individual or a tribe. The list of ancestors is introduced either by *ibn* 'son of' or by *bint* 'daughter of', if the first name is that of a woman. III 238b; IV 179b; VII 967a; VIII 56a

naṣārā (A, s. *naṣrānī*) : Christians in the Muslim Arab world. In the Qur'ān, where it is found fifteen times, ~ denotes Christians in general, in the eastern groups known to the Muslims of the Nestorians, Melkites and Jacobites. Other words for Christians are *masīḥī*, *rūm* (specifically, the Byzantine Christians) and *ifrandj* (the western Christians). VII 970a

naṣb (A) : setting up, raising.

In grammar, the accusative and subjunctive cases, because both take *-a* and are thus *manṣūb* 'raised'. III 1249a; VII 974b

In music, a secular song, which in pre-Islamic Arabia found expression on all occasions of joy, and would include wedding songs, children's songs and lullabies, although it is said to be no more than a refined camel driver's song, ḤUDĀ'. II 1073a

♦ naṣba : a form of long-term lease arrangement of WAḲF property in Tunis, which involved, in addition to perpetual lease, the ownership and use of tools and installations of shops and workshops. S 369a

nas<u>h</u>am (A) : in botany, *Chadara velutina*, used in the construction of pre-Islamic Arab bows. IV 797b

nas<u>h</u>īd (A, pl. *anā<u>sh</u>īd, na<u>sh</u>ā'id, an<u>sh</u>ād*) : a piece of oratory, a chant, a hymn and a form of vocal music. This type of ~ is always placed at the head of a vocal composition, or at the start of a musical performance in the guise of a prelude leading to the main theme, borrowing from it the fragment of text which is essential to its development; the sources assign different lengths to it. II 1073a ff.; VII 975b; in the contemporary period, ~ is employed as the equivalent of 'hymn', e.g. *na<u>sh</u>īd waṭanī* 'national anthem'. VII 976a; with *in<u>sh</u>ād*, *un<u>sh</u>ūda*, the measured (*mīzān al-<u>sh</u>i'r*) type of solo, chorus or antiphon, the unmeasured (*<u>gh</u>ayr mawzūn*) being called *tartīl*. II 1073a

na<u>sh</u>īṭa (A) : casual plunder obtained while journeying to meet the enemy. II 1005a

nasī' (A) : intercalary month, intercalation, or person (pl. *nasa'a*) charged, in pre-Islamic Mecca, with the duty of deciding on intercalation. The Arabic system of ~ can only have been intended to move the ḤA<u>DJDJ</u> and the fairs associated with it in the vicinity of Mecca to a suitable season of the year. It was not intended to establish a fixed calendar to be generally observed. VII 977a

In Judaeo-Islamic societies, ~ (Heb) is an honorific title used to designate descendants of the house of David, who were accorded particular respect. VII 977b

nasīb (A) : in literature, a generic term applied in mediaeval sources to love poetry. In its modern understanding it denotes the amatory prologue of the ḲAṢĪDA, the polythematic ode. Disregarding individual attempts to change the character of the ~ , and innovations limited to a particular period, the generic features are to be defined as follows: an elegiac concept of love, the evocation of memories, and a Bedouin setting alluded to by generic signals. IV 715b; VII 978a

naṣīf → KHARADJ

naṣīḥāt al-mulūk (A) : lit. advice for rulers; in pre-modern Islamic literature, the genre which consists of advice to rulers and their executives in politics and statecraft, the ruler's comportment towards God and towards his subjects, the conduct of warfare, diplomacy and espionage, etc., corresponding to the genre of mediaeval European literature known as that of 'mirrors for princes' or *Fürstenspiegel*. VII 984b

al-nāsikh wa 'l-mansūkh (A) : a term for the doctrine of abrogation, a synonym of NASKH. VII 1009b

naskh (A) : the act of cancellation, abrogation; in Qur'ānic exegesis, in the science of Tradition, and in law, ~ is the generic label for a range of theories concerning verses and Traditions which, when compared, suggest frequent, serious conflict. VII 1009b

In calligraphy, ~ , or *naskhī*, is used to designate the flexible, rounded script which in the post-Umayyad period was a favourite script of the scribes. It is sometimes called 'broken' kūfic, and in the far Iranian provinces was used especially for personal inscriptions on pottery. IV 1122a; V 221a; VIII 151a ff.

♦ naskh-i taʿlīḳ, naskh-taʿlīḳ → NASTAʿLĪḲ

♦ naskhī → NASKH

nasnās (A, pl. *nasānis*), or *nisnās* : in mediaeval Arabic literature, a 'demi-man' with human face and vertical stance, without a tail and possessing the faculty of speech, but also covered with a thick fleece, usually russet-coloured; in all likelihood, the ~ was nothing other than an anthropomorphic ape observed by seafaring Arab merchants of the Indian Ocean. V 133a

naṣrānī → NAṢĀRĀ

naṣrī (A) : in numismatics, a square silver coin of Ḥafṣid Tunisia, which remained in use after the Ottomans conquered the Maghrib. VIII 228b

naṣṣ (A) : text. III 1062b; designation. IX 423a; and → IKHTIYĀR

In law, a text whose presence in either Qur'ān or Tradition must be demonstrated to justify an alleged ruling. VII 1029a

In the science of Tradition, ~ is the 'raising' of a Tradition, i.e. its attribution to its originator, not necessarily the Prophet. VII 1029a

Among the Bohorās sect in India, ~ denotes the appointment of the head of the sect. I 1254b

♦ naṣṣ wa-taʿyīn : the shīʿī principle that the Prophet had designated ʿAlī to be his successor. VII 1029a

nassādj (A) : weaver, textile worker, synonymous with *ḥā'ik* although less derogatory. VII 1029b; and → TANAWWUṬ NASSĀDJ

♦ nassādjī : a Persian tax levied on every man or woman living in the village who had a loom. IV 1042b nastaʿlīḳ (P), or *naskh-i taʿlīḳ, naskh-taʿlīḳ* : a script, which is said in the works on calligraphy to have been formed by joining NASKH and TAʿLĪḲ, which compound gradually came to be pronounced as ~ . The invention of this script goes back as far as the 7th/13th century. In Turkey and in Arabic countries it is erroneously called *taʿlīḳ*. IV 1124a; VIII 151b; and → SHIKASTA TAʿLĪḲ

nāsūkhiyya → TANĀSUKH

nāsūt → LĀHŪT

naʿt (A) : qualification.

In poetry, ~ denotes a ḲAṢĪDA praising and expressing devotion to the Prophet Muḥammad. IV 715b; an encomium of the Prophet. IX 213a

In grammar, ~ is a technical term used to designate a qualifying adjective and its function as an epithet, synonymous with ṢIFA and *waṣf*. VII 1034a; IX 527b

In onomastics, ~ means a personal name. The Umayyads considered an ISM and KUNYA sufficient, but the use of LAḲAB and ~ became current under the ʿAbbāsids. II 302a

naṭʿ → SUFRA

natīdja (A) : in logic, the conclusion resulting from the combination of the two premisses, *muḳaddimāt*, in the syllogism, ḲIYĀS. In place of the usual ~ we also find RIDF or *radf* 'deduction'. VII 1034b

nātiḥ (A) : a term applied to a wild animal or bird which approaches a traveller or hunter from the front. I 1048a

nāṭiḳ (A) : among the Ismāʿīliyya, one of seven 'speaking' prophets, each of whom reveals a new religious law. The seventh ~ , the ḲĀʾIM, will abrogate Muḥammad's sharīʿa and restore the pure unit, *tawḥīd*, of the times before Adam's fall. IV 203a; S 206b; and → ṢĀMIT

In poetry, a didactic poem in which each verse is sung to another mode, popular in the 16th and 17th centuries. IX 101a

naṭrūn (A) : in mineralogy and pharmacology, a compound of sodium carbonate ($NaCO_3$) and sodium bicarbonate ($NaHCO_3$) with several impurities, obtained partly from natural crystallisations occurring in sodium-containing lakes and partly artificially. VII 1035a; S 130b

In modern Morocco, ~ (var. *litrūn, liṭrūn*) indicates a mixture of gypsum and rock salt. VII 1035a

naṭṭāla (A) : an artificial irrigation contrivance, still in use in Egypt, as well as in many African countries. Two men stand face to face, each holding two cords of palm-fibre ropes to which is attached a wide, shallow waterproof basket. This basket, made from twisted palm leaves or leather, is known in Egypt by the name *ḳaṭwa*. The two men holding the ropes bend slightly toward the water, dip the basket and fill it. Then they straighten while turning to the field, thus raising the basket which is emptied into the mouth of the irrigation canal. V 863b

nāʿūra (A, pl. *nawāʿīr*) : 'noria', a current-driven, water-raising wheel, sometimes confused with SĀḲIYA. It is mounted on a horizontal axle over a flowing stream so that the water strikes the paddles that are set around its perimeter. The water is raised in pots attached to its rim or in bucket-like compartments set into the rim. The large norias at Ḥamāt in Syria can still be seen today. I 1232a; V 861a; VII 1037a

nawā → SHA<u>SH</u>MAḲOM

nawāb → NAWWĀB

nawādir → NĀDIRA

nawba (A) : 'turn'; in its non-technical meaning, appearing in the *Ag<u>h</u>ānī* by al-Iṣbahānī of the 4th/10th century, ~ refers to the practice of having a given musician perform regularly at court on a particular day of the week, or to several musicians taking turns to sing during a single sitting; in the art-music of the Islamic Middle East and North Africa, ~ denotes a complex form made up of a number of individual pieces arranged in a standard sequence. VII 1042a

♦ nawbat : in Muslim India, a large orchestra consisting of wind and percussion instruments. These usually played at regular periods in the gateways of palaces and shrines. III 452b

nawḥ (A) : in music, the elegy. II 1073a

♦ nawḥa (A) : in Persian literature, a genre of strophic poems in classical metres which are sung on occasions involving breast-beating or self-flagellation with chains. They often have unconventional rhyme-schemes and arrangements of lines and refrains within the stanza. The number and placement of stresses in each line are important, those for breast-beating having a more rapid rhythm than those for chain-flagellation. VI 609b

In Urdu literature, a short elegy on the theme of the Karbalāʾ martyrs, also called SALĀM. VI 610b

nawriyya (A) : in literature, a genre of poetry devoted to the description of flowers, which, however, is practically impossible to separate, as a genre, from the *rawḍiyya* or *rabīʿiyya* (descriptions of gardens or of the spring, respectively). VII 1046a; VIII 357a

nawrūz (P) : the first day of the Persian solar year, marked by popular festivities. It begins at the vernal equinox. VI 523a ff.; VII 1047a; VIII 146b

nawwāb (P, < A *nuwwāb*), or *nawāb* : in Muslim India, a title originally granted by the Mug<u>h</u>al emperors to denote a viceroy or governor of a province, certainly current by the 18th century. A ~ might be subordinate to another governor and the title tended to become a designation of rank without necessarily having any office attached to it. In the later 18th century, the term was imported into English usage in the form Nabob, applied in a somewhat derogatory manner to Anglo-Indians who had returned from the subcontinent laden with wealth. It eventually passed into other languages, including French. VII 1048a

nāy (P) : a term used by the Persians in early days to designate the reed-pipe (A *mizmār*). The flute was called *nāy narm* 'soft *nāy*'. Later, they called the reed-pipe the *nāy siyāh* 'black *nāy*', and the flute the *nāy safīd* 'white *nāy*', because of the colour of the instruments. VII 207a

nayzak → SHIHĀB

naz' al-watar → MADD

naẓar (A) : theory, philosophical speculation; and → 'ILM NAẒĀRĪ

In philosophy, a term which probably not until the 9th century AD received the meaning of research in the sense of scientific investigation as translation of the Greek θεωρία. VII 1050a

In dialectical theology, ~ meant 'reflection', 'rational, discursive thinking'. VII 1051a

♦ naẓariyya : the theoretical sciences, as determined by the philosophers. I 427b

nāzikī → ĪWĀN

nāzila (A, pl. *nawāzil*) : in law, especially Mālikī law, a specific case, case in question, distinguished from the FATWĀ by the fact that it is not, properly speaking, a juridical consultation but a case which is set forth as a real case. VII 1052a

nāẓim → ṢŪBADĀR

naẓīr (A) : in astronomy, ~ denotes the nadir, the bottom, the pole of the horizon (invisible) under the observer in the direction of the vertical; also, the deepest (lowest) point in the sphere of heaven; originally (and generally), the point diametrically opposite a point on the circumference of a circle or the surface of a sphere. VII 1054a

naẓm (A) : the arrangement of pearls in a necklace; poetry with perfect order and symmetry; composition. IX 449a; IX 458a; in western and central Sudanic prosody, the versifying of an existing prose text. IX 243b; in Urdu poetry, a thematic poem. IX 162a

nāẓūr (A) : a term used in Muslim Spain and certain parts of North Africa in mediaeval times to denote a look-out or watch-tower of one kind or another, and, in parts of 19th-century North Africa at least, a lighthouse; originally, the man whose business it was to keep watch. VII 1056a

nefes (T, < A *nafas* 'breath') : a type of poem written or uttered by members of Turkish mystic orders to eulogise God or leading personalities of the orders. V 275a; V 957a; VIII 2b

nefīr (A), or *nafīr* : in Ottoman usage, a term alluding to a musical instrument similar to a horn. The person playing the instrument was referred to as *nefīrī*. VIII 3b; a trumpet, chief instrument of the cylindrical tube type. I 1291b; and → BORU

In military usage, ~ alludes to a body of men assembled for a common purpose. VIII 3b

♦ nefīr-i 'āmm : in the Ottoman empire, the recruitment of volunteers by a general call to arms, in contrast with *nefīr-i khāṣṣ*, the mobilisation of a certain well-defined group of people. VIII 3b

♦ nefīr-i khāṣṣ → NEFĪR-I 'ĀMM

nemče (T, < A *al-nimsā*) : 'mute', a term borrowed from the Slavonic used by the Ottomans to indicate the Germans. In a broader sense, they also used it for the territory of the Holy Roman Empire, which lasted until 1806, and in a restricted sense for the territories under Habsburg rule within the boundaries of modern Austria. VIII 4a

nidāl (A) : in archery, a long bow. II 954a

nifāḳ → IKHLĀṢ

nīfuk (N.Afr) : a slit for the elbow at the lower extremity of the armlets in the DJALLĀBIYYA. II 405a

nihāya (A) : in philosophy, a term denoting that which forbids access to something beyond a certain limit. The concept of ~ applies to such realities as time, space, and the division of bodies. VIII 24a

niḳāba (A) : 'trade union', i.e. association for defending the interests of and promoting the rights of wage and salary earners; ~ can also denote the liberal professions and even those of employers. The term's usage became general after the First World War. VIII 25b

♦ niḳābiyya : syndicalism. VIII 25b

nikāḥ (A) : marriage (properly, sexual intercourse); ~ is used both for stable and temporary unions. VI 475b; VIII 26b

♦ nikāḥ al-khidn : concubinage, which is prohibited by the Qur'ān. VI 476a

♦ nikāḥ al-maḳt : marriage to the father's widow, which is prohibited by the Qur'ān. VI 476a

♦ nikāḥ al-mutʿa → MUTʿA

♦ nikāḥ al-raḥt : a form of polyandry forbidden by the Prophet, whereby a woman takes a group of husbands (less than ten) and, if she has a child, attributes the paternity to one of this group, who is unable to refuse it. S 133a

al-niḳris al-ḥārr (A) : in medicine, feverish gout. IX 9b

nīl (P, < San *nīla* 'blue'), or *nīlādj* : the oldest known organic dye, *Indigo tinctoria* L., *Indigoferae*; the main component of natural indigo, which can be obtained from various kinds of indigofera (*Isatis tinctoria*, *Cruciferae*) and from the knotweed (*Polygonum tinctorium*, *Polygonaceae*). VIII 37b

In the Middle Ages, the Arabs used ~ , actually indigo, to indicate woad (Dioscurides' ἰσάτις). The constant confusion between the two plants led to a series of Arabic synonyms, like *ʿiẓlim*, *wasma* (*wāsima*), *khiṭr*, *nīla*, *tīn akhḍar* etc. which were used indifferently for the two plants. VIII 37b

nīlādj → NĪL

nīlūfar : in botany, lotus seeds. IX 615a; in Turkish, *nīlūfer* are water-lily flowers. IX 417a

nīm-fatḥa (P) : in Persian prosody, an extra short vowel, added to words ending in two consonants (*nūn* excepted) preceded by a short vowel, or one consonant preceded by a long vowel. I 677a

nim-ling (P) : in archery, a quiver made of various skins sewn together. IV 799b nimʿa → RAḤMA

nimekare (P) : a land-leasing system in Kurdish Iran, in which the landowner leases out the irrigated lands and supplies the seed, and the peasant supplies the work, with the landowner taking three-fifths of the harvest and the peasant two-fifths. V 473b

nimr → NAMIR

nims (A, pl. *numūs*, *numūsa*) : the ichneumon or Egyptian mongoose (*Herpestes ichneumon*). In some parts of the Islamic world such as the Maghrib and Lebanon, ~ has been erroneously applied to the weasel (*Mustela nivalis*). As a result of similar confusion, some Arabic dialects employ ~ to identify various other members of the sub-family Mustelidae such as the stone-marten (*Martes foina*), the polecat (*Mustela putorius*) and the ferret (*Mustela putorius furo*); the term is even found erroneously applied to the civet (*Genetta genetta*). VIII 49b ff.

In botany, ~ is given to two plants: *al-nims* is, in the Maghrib, Downy koelaria (*Koelaria pubescens*); *biṭṭīkh nims* 'ichneumon melon' or *biṭṭīkh ʿayn al-nims* 'ichneumon's eye melon' is a nickname given to the watermelon (*Citrullus vulgaris*, of the variety *ennemis*). VIII 50b

nīrān → MANĀẒIR

nīrandj (A, < P *nayrang*, *nīrang*) : the operations of white magic, comprising prestidigitation, fakery and counter-fakery, the creating of illusions and other feats of sleight-of-hand, ḤIYAL. VIII 51b; amulets which have an extraordinary power over men and over natural phenomena; acts done by magicians. VIII 52b

niṣāb (A) : in law, the definite minimum value. IX 62b

nīsān : the seventh month in the Syrian calendar, which corresponds to April of the Roman year and like it has 30 days. VIII 53b

nisba (A) : in grammar, the adjective of relation. VIII 53b

In onomastics, the element of a person's name, consisting of an adjective ending in *ī*, formed originally from the name of the individual's tribe or clan, then from his place of birth, origin or residence, sometimes from a MADHHAB or sect, and occasionally from a trade or profession. In Arabic, the ~ is always preceded by the definite article, which in Persian disappears. IV 180a; VIII 54a

niṣf (A) : half.

In numismatics, the term for the half DĪNĀR, or *semissis*, struck in North Africa and Spain during the transitional period and in the early years of the 2nd/8th century. The third *dīnār*, *thulth*, or *tremissis*, was also struck, while the quarter *dīnār*, *rubʿ*, was introduced by the Aghlabids in North Africa early in the third quarter of the 2nd/8th century. II 297b

♦ **niṣf al-nahār** (A) : 'half of the day', 'midday'; in astronomy, used in the expression which denotes the 'meridian circle' (*dāʾirat* ~). VIII 56b

nishān (P) : sign, banner, seal (and hence letter of a prince); order, decoration; under the Ottomans, ~ designates all orders from the sultan, without any restriction of subject, that were provided with the sultan's signature. Since the 10th/

16th century, this category denoted especially those orders, concerning financial matters, which were drawn up by the highest financial department of the empire. I 1170b; in Ottoman Turkish, ~ basically denoted a sign or a mark and also designated the sultan's signature, *ṭughra*, and, by extension, a document bearing it; the standards of the Janissaries; the insignia on military, naval and other uniforms; and, later, decorations bestowed by the sultan. In 19th and 20th-century literary Arabic, ~ had essentially the same connotations. The ~ are to be distinguished clearly from medals. VIII 57b ff.; and → KARKADDAN

♦ nishān-i humāyūn → ṬUGHRA

♦ **nishāndji** (T) : under the Ottomans, secretary of state for the sultan's signature, ṬUGHRA; chancellor. VIII 62a

Under the Saldjūḳs and Mamlūks, an official for drawing the sultan's signature, also called *tewḳīʿī*. VIII 62a

nisnās → NASNĀS

nitādj (A) : the parturition of pregnant sheep. S 319a

nithār (A) : in the pre-modern Middle East, the showering of money, jewels and other valuables on occasions of rejoicing, such as a wedding, a circumcision, the accession of a ruler, the victorious return from a military campaign etc. VIII 64a

In numismatics, the Mughal silver (sometimes also gold) coin scattered at weddings, processions and other public spectacles. VII 345a; other terms for largesse-coins were *nūr afshān* and *khayr ḳabūl*. VIII 64b

♦ nithārī : in numismatics, for a short time the name of the quarter-rupee during the reign of the Mughal ruler Djahāngīr. VIII 64b

niṭʿiyya (A) : in grammar, a term used by al-Khalīl for the prepalatals. III 598a

niyāḥa (A) : lamentation; the term is used to designate the activity of professional mourners who play a great role in funeral ceremonies all around the Mediterranean. VIII 64b

niyāz → NADHR WA-NIYĀZ

niyya (A) : intention. Acts prescribed by Islamic law, obligatory or not, require to be preceded by a declaration by the performer that he intends to perform such an act. This declaration, pronounced audibly or mentally, is called ~ . Without it, the act would be null, *bāṭil*. VIII 66a

niẓām (A) : in Muslim India, an honorific title which became characteristic of the rulers of the state of Ḥaydarābād, derived in the first place from the fuller title ~ *al-mulk*. VIII 67a; and → ḲĀNŪN

In Turkish military usage, ~ or *niẓāmiyye*, *ʿasākir-i niẓāmiyye*, *ʿasākir-i muwaẓẓafe* was used in the strict sense for an active or regular army (standing army) and in the wider sense for regular or disciplined troops (syn. *müretteb*). VIII 370a

nḳāb (N.Afr) : a face veil for married women in Morocco and Algeria, often synonymous with LITHĀM. V 746b noʿma → KUSKUSŪ

noyan (pl. *noyad*) : a Mongolian title, rendered in the Muslim chronicles of the Mongol and Tīmūrid periods in the Arabic script as *nūyān*, *nūyīn*, *nuyīn* etc. In the pre-Činggisid period the *noyad* were the hereditary clan chieftains. Under Činggis Khān and his successors, the title was granted initially as a military rank, and it came to mean 'commander'. Under the Yüan regime in China, ~ was used to refer to all officials serving in public posts. VIII 87a

nubuwwa (A) : prophecy. VIII 93b

nudjabāʾ (A) : in mysticism, the seventy 'pre-eminents', the sixth degree in the ṣūfī hierarchical order of saints. I 95a

nudjūm → NADJM

nuffār (A) : a term for those who took part in the siege of the house of the caliph ʿUthmān b. ʿAffān in 35/655, which culminated in his assassination. I 382b; II 415a

nuḥāf → NUḤĀM

nuḥām (A) : the Greater Flamingo, *Phoenicopterus ruber roseus* or *antiquorum* of the order of the Phoenicopteridae (*nuḥāmiyāt*) which resemble waders with their long legs and palmipeds with their webbed feet. Other mediaeval names for the flamingo were *mirzam* and *turundjān*, which refers to its striking colour, while in Egypt, it is called *basharūsh* (< O.Fr *becharu*), becoming in Tunisia *shabrūsh*. Also found are the terms *nuḥāf*, *niḥāf*, *surkhāb* and *rahū 'l-māʾ* 'aquatic crane'. VIII 110b

nuḥās (A) : the term most often used in Arabic for copper (Cu). Other terms, according to al-Bīrūnī, were *al-miss* (in ʿIrāḳ and Khurāsān) and *al-ḳiṭr* (i.e. brass). VIII 111b

nūḥī → KĀGHAD

nuḳabāʾ → NAḲĪB

nuḳāwā → NAḲĀʾ

nukhūd → ʿASHRAFĪ; TŪMĀN

nuḳrakhāne → ḌARBKHĀNE-I ʿĀMIRE

nuḳṣān (A) : in mathematics, ~ is the term used for subtraction. III 1139b

nuḳta (A) : in mathematics, the term for the geometrical point. II 220a

nuʿmān → SHAḲĪḲAT AL-NUʿMĀN

♦ nuʿmānī → SABʿĀNĪ

nūn (A) : the 25th letter of the Arabic alphabet. VIII 120b

♦ nūn ghunna : in Indian phonetics, the final form of *nūn* written without its diacritical point, used when a nasalised long vowel stands finally in a word, or even morpheme. VIII 121b

♦ ṣāghir nūn (T) : in Ottoman Turkish, the term for the Persian *gāf*, which was used in writing to convey the gutterally pronounced /ñ/. VIII 121a

nūr (A) : light. VIII 121b

♦ nūra (A) : lime, used to make a depilatory paste. IX 312a f.

nū<u>sh</u>ādir (A, < ? Pah) : sal-ammoniac. In the earliest Latin translations (*nesciador*, *mizadir*), the transliteration of the Arabic name is still used; in the Latin forms *aliocab*, *alocaph* is also found the general term *al-ʿuḳāb*. VIII 148a

nu<u>sh</u><u>sh</u>āb → NABL

nus<u>kh</u>a (A) : 'transcript', 'copy'; in the manuscript era, 'manuscript'. VIII 149a; a certified verbatim copy of an original document. IX 359a

nuṣūb (A, pl. *anṣāb*) : in the plural (more often used), the blocks of stone on which the blood of the victims sacrificed for idols was poured, as well as sepulchral stones and those marking out the sacred enclosure of the sanctuary. Among sedentary populations, the ~ , a rough stone, has become the ṢANAM, a stone carved with the image of the idols of the Kaʿba. VIII 154b

nūtī (A, pl. *nawātiya*) : a sailor; on a mediaeval Islamic warship, the ~ made up the crew, along with the oarsmen (ḲA<u>DH</u><u>DH</u>ĀF), craftsmen and workmen (*<u>dh</u>awu 'l-ṣināʿa wa 'l-mihan*), fighting men (e.g. NAFFĀṬ) and the marines. S 120a

nuwayḳsa → ṢAN<u>DJ</u>

nuzha (A) : in music, a rectangular type of psaltery of greater compass than the ḲĀNŪN. It was invented in the 7th/13th century; 108 strings were mounted in the instrument. VII 191a

nuzūl → ISNĀD NĀZIL

O

oba, or *obā* : among the Kurds, a temporary association of stock-breeders from different villages, formed in the spring to lead the herds to the pastures and to return at the end of the autumn. Neither kinship nor tribal relations are necessary to be a member of the ~ , which system is particular to the semi-nomadic tribes and makes its appearance towards the end of the 19th and the beginning of the 20th century. V 472a; among the <u>Sh</u>āhsewan in Persia, a herding unit of three to five households. IX 224a; in eastern Anatolia, the grazing area of a nomadic household. VI 961b; a clan. VIII 608a

ocak-zāde → O<u>DJ</u>AḲ

ōda (Ir) : in modern Iraqi architecture, two small rooms flanking the ĪWĀN. II 114a

o<u>dj</u>aḳ (T, > A *wu<u>dj</u>āḳ*) : fireplace, hearth, chimney; in modern Turkish, *ocak* replaced the traditional name for the month of January by law in 1945. VIII 161b Under the Ottomans, an army unit. I 368a; VIII 161b; IX 657a; S 409b; family. I 1267a; VIII 161a

In mysticism, a religious order. IV 167b; among the Bektā<u>sh</u>iyya, and the Mawlawiyya, ~ had a special place in their *tekke*s (→ <u>KH</u>ĀNḲĀH). VIII 161b

♦ ocak-zāde : among the Alevis of Anatolia, an ~ is a spiritual guide who belonged to one of the lineages stemming from the twelve IMĀMS. VIII 161b

♦ odjaḳ oghlu : 'son of a good house'. VIII 163a

♦ odjaḳlïḳ : in the Ottoman empire, a system whereby a given region was responsible for supplying an arsenal with one particular ship-building commodity. I 947b; an accounting system applied for securing gunpowder supplies, a special fund allocated for purchases and requisitions of essential supplies such as sulphur and saltpetre. V 979a; a special sort of *tīmār* (→ SERBEST). VIII 161a; family succession. I 1267a

oghlan → OGHUL

oghul (T) : 'offspring, child', with a strong implication of 'male child', as opposed to ḲÏZ 'girl'; ~ is very frequently found in family names where it takes the place of the Persian *zāde* or the Arabic IBN. VIII 163a

♦ oghlan : an original plural, which evolved into an independent singular, meaning 'youth', 'servant', 'page', 'bodyguard'. From ~ comes the German *Uhlan*, the name for light cavalry. VIII 163a

okka (T) : in the Ottoman empire, a measure of weight equal to 1.283 kg. VI 120b

ordu (T, Mon *orda*) : 'the royal tent or residence', 'the royal encampment', a term which became widespread in the mediaeval Turco-Mongol and then in the Persian worlds, acquiring from the second meaning that of 'army camp'. VIII 174a; in Turkish military usage, army corps. VIII 370b

For Indo-Persian usage, → URDU

♦ ordu-yu hümāyūn : under the Ottomans, a general term for the imperial army. VIII 174b

♦ ordudju bashï/aghasï : the chief of a staff of tradesmen and technicians who accompanied the Janissaries on their campaigns away from the capital. VIII 174b

ʿörf (T), or *ʿörfī* : under the Ottomans, a large, dome-shaped headdress, ḲAVUḲ, worn with a white turban rolled around and which, draped, forms harmonious folds. It was worn from the 18th century by the religious classes. V 751b

orta (T) : lit. centre; in Ottoman military terminology, the equivalent of a company of fighting men in the three divisions of which the Janissary corps was eventually composed. VIII 178b

♦ **orta oyunu** : 'entertainment staged in the middle place', a form of popular Turkish entertainment so-called because it takes place in the open air, *palanka*, around which the spectators form a circle. VIII 178b

ʿösher → ʿUSHR

otlaḳ resmi → YAYLAḲ RESMI

öy (T) : among the Türkmen Yomut and Göklen tribes, a type of tent, either *aḳ öy* 'white house' (taken from the colour of the covering felts when new) or *ḳara öy* 'black house' (from the colour of the felts when old and blackened by smoke). The ~ has a trellis wall, with a doorway in it, circular in plan, with a roof wheel supported by struts from the top of the trellis wall. IV 1150b

ozan (T) : a Turkish bard; the term ~ was replaced in the late 9th/15th century by ʿĀSHIḲ. I 697b; nevertheless, in certain contemporary dialects of Anatolia, ~ has survived with the meaning 'poet', 'singer', as also as an element of the terms *ozanlama* 'assonantal sayings, proverbs', *ozancı* 'garrulous person', *ozanlık* 'pleasantry' and *ozannama* 'improvised story, song'. In Turkmen, ~ is archaic and is replaced by *bagsı* 'popular poet', but at the present day, in modern Turkish, ~ has replaced the Arabic term *shāʿir* (*şair*). VIII 232a; folk poet. IX 239a

♦ ozancı → OZAN

♦ ozanlama → OZAN

♦ ozanlık → OZAN

♦ ozannama → OZAN

P

paččī-kārī → PARČĪN-KĀRĪ

pādishāh (P) : the name for Muslim rulers, especially emperors. VIII 237a
In Turkish folklore, the chief of the DJINN. II 548a

pahlawān (P, < *pahlaw* 'Parthian'; A *bahlawān*) : in pre-modern Persian and thence in Turkish, 'wrestler', 'one who engages in hand-to-hand physical combat', subsequently 'hero', 'warrior', 'champion in battle'. VIII 239a
In Arabic, *bahlawān* is clearly a secondary development, and has in more recent times acquired the meaning of 'acrobat', 'tightrope walker in a circus' etc. In the most recent colloquial of Cairo, it has become a pejorative term for 'tricky person'. VIII 239a

pāʾī (H 'quarter', > Eng 'pie') : in numismatics, the smallest copper coin of British India = one-twelfth of an anna. Originally, the ~ was the quarter of an anna or pice (→ PAYSĀ); after the Acts of 1835, 1844 and 1870, the pie was one-third of a pice. VIII 239b

paisā → PAYSĀ

pālāhang (P) : lit. string, rope, halter, cord; ~ is applied to the belt worn around the waist by dervishes, especially the Bektāshīs, and on which is fixed a disc of stone with twelve flutings at the edge. VIII 244a

palanka → ORTA

palkī (H ?) : 'palanquin', an enclosed variety of litter used in India for transporting people, its central pole having an upward curve to afford more head-room for the passenger. In its common form it was in use for considerable journeys. A more elaborate form, with its carriage and pole covered with plates of silver, was in use in royal processions. VII 932a

pān (H ?) : in Mughal cuisine, a heart-shaped green leaf smeared with lime and catechu, to which is added slices or granules of betel-nut with aromatic spices, sometimes camphor, musk, or costly perfumes. A ~ was often presented to a courtier as a mark of royal favour. VI 814b

♦ pāndān : betel-boxes. I 299b

panghulu → PENGHULU

pānka → KHAYSH

pāra (P) : 'piece', 'fragment'; in numismatics, a Turkish coin of the Ottoman and early Republican periods. The ~ was originally a silver piece of 4 AḲČEs, first issued early in the 18th century; it soon replaced the *aḳče* as the monetary unit. With the post-World War II inflation, the ~ eventually disappeared from use; in present-day Turkey, *para* has acquired the general meaning of money. VIII 266b

parčīn-kārī (P, U *paččī-kārī*) : a technique of inlay-work, usually set in marble, used in the architecture of the Indo-Pakistan subcontinent. VIII 267a

parda-dār (P) : lit. the person who draws the curtain; 'court chamberlain', a term used among the dynasties of the eastern Islamic world from the Saldjūḳ period onwards as the equivalent of Arabic ḤĀDJIB. III 48b; VIII 270

pargana (H, < San) : in Indo-Muslim administrative usage, a term denoting an aggregate of villages, a subdivision of a district (syn. MAḤALL). In later Anglo-Indian usage, the term was often rendered as *pergunnah*. VIII 270a

parī (P, T *peri*) : in folklore, a fairy, belonging to the realm of supernatural tales; in Turkish everyday speech as well as in stories of fantastic adventures and tales of the supernatural, *peri* is often taken as a synonym of DJINN. II 547b; VIII 271a

♦ parīkhʷān → BĀKHSHĪ

parias (< L) : in the mediaeval Iberian peninsula, a tribute paid by one ruler to another in recognition of his superior status. VIII 272a

parmaḳ (T) : under the Ottomans, a measure of length equivalent to one and a quarter inches. I 658a

♦ parmaḳ ḥisābi̊ (T) : the original Turkish method of versification, wherein the verses are based not on quantity but on the number and stress of the syllables. IX 353b

parwāna (P), or *parwānača* : in mediaeval Persian administration, the term used for the document 'related' by the official to the chancery, PARWĀNAČĪ. VIII 277a; and → FARĀSHA

♦ **parwānači** : 'relater', in mediaeval Persian administration, a term used for the official who noted down the instructions for the promulgation of deeds, and who forwarded them to the chancery. The function is recorded for the first time under Tīmūr. VIII 276b

pās-i anfās (P) : a practice of regulating the breath, adopted by the Čishtī mystics in order to harnass all feelings and emotions in establishing communion with God. II 55b

pasazh (T) : in 19th-century Ottoman cities, a shop-lined covered street, a modern version of the *ārāsta*. IX 799b

pasha (T, < P *pādishāh*) : under the Ottomans, the highest official title of honour, used in Turkey until the advent of the Republic and surviving for sometime after that in certain Muslim countries originally part of the Turkish empire (Egypt, ʿIrāḳ, Syria); ~ was military rather than feudal in character, although it was not reserved solely for soldiers but was also given to certain high civil (not religious) officials. VIII 279b

♦ **pashalik** (T) : the office or title of a PASHA; the territory under the authority of a *pasha* (in the provinces). VIII 282a

pāshīb (Ind.P) : in Mughal siegecraft, a raised platform constructed by filling the space between the top of the fort wall and the base of the besieger's camp below, with bags of sand and earth. III 482a

pashtūnwalī (Pash) : the special social code of the Afghans, the main pillars of which are *nanawātai* 'right of asylum', BADAL 'revenge by retaliation, vendetta', and *mēlmastyā* 'hospitality'. I 217a

pat̲hān → ASHRĀF

patrona (T, < It) : in the Ottoman navy, a 'galley carrying the lieutenant-general or the next in command to the chief of the squadron'; the term is also applied to Christian ships. VIII 565a;

♦ patrona bey : in the Ottoman navy, 'vice-admiral'. VIII 566b

patuḳ (P) : a habitual location for a guild. IX 646a

patwāri : in the Mughal empire, the village accountant, whose functions resembled those of the ḲĀNUNGO in the administrative unit PARGANA. VIII 271a

pawlā : the name given in the Mughal emperor Akbar's monetary system to the quarter-*dām* (quarter-PAYSĀ). VIII 288a

pāyak (Ind.P) : in the Dihlī sultanate, the footsoldiers who were maintained within the infantry contingents and who were mostly Hindūs. They were good archers and were generally arrayed in front of the lines of horses, or around the elephants in order to prevent them from fleeing. V 686b

paysā (H, Eng 'pice'), or *paisā* : in numismatics, a copper coin of British India, equalling 3 pies or 1/4 anna. Under the Mughals, ~ became applied to the older *dām*, introduced by Shīr Shāh, 40 of which went to the rupee, as the unit of copper currency. In the currencies of modern India and Pakistan, 100 ~s equals one rupee, and in that of Bangladesh, one taka. VIII 288b

pāzār → BĀZĀR; ČARSHI̊

pegon (Mal), *jawi* or *melayu* : in Indonesia, the name for Arabic characters that were adapted for the vernaculars. III 1217a; VIII 153a

penče (T, < P *pandja* 'palm of the hand') : in the science of diplomatic, a sign placed on a document issued by higher Ottoman officials, used instead of the ṬUGHRA. It was usually placed not at the beginning but on the left hand or right hand margin or at the foot of the scroll. Sometimes it was called *imḍā* or erroneously *ṭughra*. II 314b; VIII 293b

pendjik (T, < P *pandj yak* 'fifth') : in Ottoman financial and administrative usage, a term denoting the fifth which the sultan drew as the ruler's right (equivalent to the Arabic *khums*) from booty captured in the DĀR AL-ḤARB. VIII 293b

♦ pendjikči bashi : the official in charge of the process of extracting the sultan's fifth. VIII 293b

penghulu (Ind, Mal; Sun *panghulu*) : lit. headman, chief, director; used in southeast Asia as a title for secular and religious leaders. VIII 294a; IX 852a; the highest official in a mosque in Java, often a learned man who has studied theology and is a pupil of the *pesantren*, the Indonesian religious school, or of the modern MADRASA; he may even have studied in Mecca. VI 701a

penyair → SHĀʿIR

pergunnah → PARGANA

peri → PARĪ

pertaapan → PONDOK

pesantren (J) : in Indonesia, the educational institution where students, *santri*, study classical Islamic subjects and pursue an orthoprax communal life. PONDOK is an alternative term, preferred in Malaysia and the Patani region of southern Thailand. Sometimes the two terms are combined in Indonesia, when the speaker means to make clear that a traditional Islamic boarding school, a '*pondok pesantren*', and not merely a religious day school (such as the more modern *madrasa*), is meant. VIII 296a

peshdār (T) : in the Ottoman empire, the term for the third animal of a mule caravan operating in Anatolia. IV 678b

peshek (T) : in the Ottoman empire, the term for the leading animal of a mule caravan operating in Anatolia, which kept some way ahead of the others and carried a smaller load. IV 678b

pēshwā (P) : 'leader'; in onomastics, a title for one of the ministers of the Bahmanī sultans of the Dakhan and, more specifically, the hereditary ministers of the Marāṭhā kings of Satara. VIII 300b

peth, or *mela* : in Muslim India, an occasional or seasonal market. IX 800b

peyk (T) : in the Ottoman military organisation, a messenger. IX 712b

pīr (P) : lit. old person, elder; in Islamic law, used for people in their fifties or even in their forties, while those even older are often qualified as *harim*, *fānī* 'decrepit, worn out'. VIII 306a

In general Persian usage, ~ is often, as with Arabic SHAYKH, used in compound expressions by metonomy, e.g. *pīr-i dihḳān* 'well-matured wine'. VIII 306a

For ~ in mysticism, → MURSHID

♦ pīr awtār (Ind.P) : the daily allowance paid to FĀḲIRs from collective village sources. VIII 306b

♦ pīr bahn (Ind.P) : a woman owing spiritual allegiance to the same spiritual mentor and therefore a sister. VIII 306b

♦ pīr bhāi (Ind.P) : a disciple of the same spiritual mentor and therefore a brother. VIII 306b

♦ pīr kā nayza (Ind.P) : a standard carried in procession to the grave of some saint. VIII 306b

♦ pīr pāl (Ind.P) : land endowed for assistance of the *pīr* or for maintenance of some mausoleum. VIII 306b

♦ pīr zāda (Ind.P) : the son of the *pīr*. VIII 306b

♦ pīr-i kharābāt (Ind.P) : in popular Indo-Muslim usage, a *pīr* free from the bonds of sharīʿa law; owner of a tavern. VIII 307a

♦ pīr-i mughān (Ind.P) : lit. chief priest of the Magi, but generally the term used for a tavern keeper. VIII 306b

♦ pīr-i ṣuḥbat (Ind.P) : a saint from whose company one derives spiritual benefit. VIII 306b

♦ pīr-i ṭarīḳat (Ind.P) : a saint to whom one owes spiritual allegiance. VIII 306b

♦ pīrān (Ind.P) : charity lands bestowed on the poor in honour of a saint. VIII 306b

pīrāhan (P) : a close-fitting, long-sleeved robe, covering the entire body down to the feet, worn by women in Tīmūrid Persia. V 749a

pīrān → PĪR

pīshkāsh (P) : a present from an inferior to a superior; from the Mongol period onwards, ~ denoted a form of tribute to the Persian sovereign from the governors. III 347b; as a technical term, ~ denotes a 'regular' tax and an *ad hoc* tax levied by rulers on provincial governors and others, and an *ad hoc* impost laid by governors and officials in position of power on the population under their control. VIII 312b

♦ pīshkāsh-niwīs : 'registrar of presents'; under the Ṣafawids, the official of the royal secretariat who recorded their number and value. This official is found until the second half of the 19th century. VIII 312b

pīshtāḳ (P) : lit. the arch in front; in Muslim Indian architecture, a portal in the form of a monumental arched niche in a rectangular frame. VI 683a; VIII 313b

pīshwā (P) : chief. IX 499b

pist (P) : a kind of food compounded of the liver of gazelles or almonds, etc. A daily portion of the size of a pistachio, *pista*, is taken by derwishes and others who undertake long fasts and is sufficient to maintain life. VIII 316b

piştmala (K) : a kind of praetorian guard of the Kurdish chiefs who are recruited in all the fractions, TIRA, of the tribe and who, in the past, had almost the status of slave. V 472a

pondok (Mal, < A *funduḳ*), or *pertaapan* : hut, cottage; lodgings; by extension, an Islamic religious boarding school. VIII 294a; VIII 296a; and → PESANTREN

post : in India, the decoction of the poppy-husks to make opium. I 243a

pōst → PŪST

posta (T, A, < It *posta*) : a term borrowed in the 19th century to designate the new conception of European-style postal services in the Near East. In more recent times, it has been replaced at the formal level by BARĪD, but *būsta* and *būstadjī* 'postman' continue in use in the Arab Levant at the informal level, and *posta* remains the standard term in Modern Turkish. In modern Persian, also *post*, from the French *poste*, is used. VIII 325b; postage stamps. VIII 325b

pōstakī → PŪST

potur (T) : a pair of trousers, full as far as the knee and straight from the knee to the ankle, worn in Ottoman Turkey. V 752b

♦ potur og̲h̲ullarï : in the Ottoman period, Bosnian Muslim lads recruited for the Janissaries. A document dating from 998/1589 defines them as 'circumcised but ignorant of Turkish'. II 211b

♦ potur ṭā'ifesi → POTURNĀK

♦ poturnāk : the name for Bosnians who converted to Islam. The reference occurs as early as 921/1515; in a separate document dated 981/1573, they are called *potur ṭā'ifesi*. II 211b

prang sabil (Mal, *prang* 'war') : the name of the holy war, D̲J̲IHĀD, in East Asia. VIII 333a

prem-gāthā (H) : lit. love song; a school of writing in Awadhi (Eastern Hindi), of ṣūfī inspiration, comprising narrative love stories. III 456b

pūs̲h̲ī → BŪS̲H̲Ī

pūst (P, T *pōst* or *pōstakī*) : 'skin'; a tanned sheepskin, used as the ceremonial seat or throne of the head, *pīr* or *s̲h̲ayk̲h̲*, of a dervish order. VIII 343b

♦ **pūst-nes̲h̲īn** : lit. the one sitting on the (sheep's) skin; the title given to the *baba* or head of a dervish *tekke* (→ K̲H̲ĀNḲĀH) in Persian and Ottoman Turkish ṣūfī practice. VIII 343b

R

rabʿ (A, pl. *ribāʿ*) : home, domicile, home town or home country; in mediaeval Islam, facilities for temporary accommodation in cities concentrated in a single building. IX 788b

In Cairene architecture, ~ designates a type of urban dwelling which is a rental multi-unit building founded for investment; ~ can also refer to the living quarters belonging to a religious institution. VIII 344a

rabāʿ (A) : a name for a foal between three and four years old. II 785a

rabāʿa (A), or *magʿad al-rid̲j̲āl* : the compartment in a Bedouin tent reserved for receiving menfolk. In the middle, a hearth is scraped out and used for making coffee. IV 1148b

rabāb (A) : in music, the generic name for the viol, or any stringed instrument played with a bow. VIII 346a; the instrument known as rebeck. I 1124a; in Egypt, a two-string spike-fiddle. IX 235b

♦ rabāb miṣrī → KAMĀND̲J̲A

♦ rabāb turkī → ARNABA

♦ rabāba : in music, the Arabian one-string spike-fiddle. IX 235a

rabaḍ (A, pl. *arbāḍ*) : district or quarter of a town situated outside the central part. This term lies at the origin of the Spanish word *arrabal*, which has the same meaning. VIII 348b

In Muslim Spain, ~ was given to the civil quarter situated below the strictly military quarter; ~ was also applied to the quarters of the lepers and of prostitutes, while among the Spanish Christians it designated a parish. VIII 348b

rabāʿī → ʿATŪD

rabb (A, pl. *arbāb*) : lord, God, master of a slave. Pre-Islamic Arabia probably applied this term to its gods or to some of them. In pre-Islamic times, ~ also was one of the titles given to certain of the KĀHINS. VIII 350a

♦ rabbānī (A) : among the mystical order ʿĪsāwā, the slow introductory section of their ecstatic dancing, a form of invocation, during which the dancers, standing in line, hold hands and perform vertical bending movements together with lateral motions. It is followed by a more rapid section, the *mudjarrad*, and the dance often ends in displays of fakirism. IV 95a

♦ arbāb al-sadjādjīd, and *mashāyikh al-sadjdjāda* : in Egypt, from the end of the 11th/17th century, applied to the leaders of Egypt's major ṣūfī *ṭuruḳ* (→ ṬARĪḲA) and *ṭuruḳ*-linked institutions. ~ , however, seems to have been reserved for the four family-based *ṭuruḳ* which traced themselves back to the Rightly-Guided Caliphs and the Companions, namely, *al-Bakriyya*, *al-ʿInāniyya*, *al-Khudayriyya*, and *al-Wafāʾiyya*. VIII 743b

rābiʿ (A), or *sayyid al-mirbāʿ* : a designation for tribal chief (from the chief's entitlement to a quarter of captured booty). IX 115b

rabīʿ (A) : the name of the third and fourth months of the Muslim calendar. Originally, ~ means the season in which, as a result of the rains, the earth is covered with green; this later led to the name ~ being given to spring. VIII 350b; in Muslim India, ~ is the harvest collected at the end of the winter. II 909a

♦ rabīʿiyya (pl. **rabīʿiyyāt**) → NAWRIYYA

rābiṭa (A, > Sp *rábida* 'monastery') : 'bond'; in mysticism, ~ originally meant the relationship of a MURĪD to his master, and hence a close friendship; a hermitage which was a place of retreat for persons considered to be saints, accompanied by their disciples. VIII 359b; VIII 503b; liaison of the disciple's heart, in imagination, with that of his SHAYKH. IX 156a

In Muslim Spain, a fortified enclosure, a bastion constructed on the coast to deter enemy attacks from the sea; ~ sometimes served as a substitute for RIBĀṬ. VIII 359a

In 19th-century Ottoman usage, ~ became a political notion in the sense of 'league' and with *islāmiyya* attached to it, ~ soon rendered the European word Pan-Islam. VIII 359b

♦ **al-rābiṭa al-islāmiyya** : lit. the Islamic league. VIII 359b

rabṭ (A) : in medicine, ligature (of veins). II 481b

raḍāʿ (A), *riḍāʿ* or *raḍāʿa* : suckling; in law, the suckling which produces the legal impediment to marriage of foster-kinship. VIII 361a; the suckling is called *raḍīʿ*. VIII 822a

♦ raḍāʿ al-kabīr : the suckling of non-infants. VIII 361b

radd (A) : 'return'; a response to an adversary, intended to refute his statements or opinions. Another term in frequent use is *naḳḍ* 'refutation', although *naḳḍ* is principally employed in reference to a book. VIII 362b

In mathematics, ~ denotes reduction and refers to the operation (division) by which an integral coefficient is reduced to unity. II 361a

♦ radd al-ʿadjuz ʿalā 'l-ṣadr : in prosody, the rhetorical figure of anticipating the rhyme word in the first half (at times even the beginning of the second half) of the line. VIII 747b

radf → NATĪDJA

raḍīʿ → RAḌĀʿ

radīf (A, T *redīf*) : lit. one who rides behind, 'pillion rider'.

In grammar, the plural *rawādif* signified the last two groups of the ABDJAD terms, which consisted of the consonants peculiar to Arabic, as opposed to the first six groups which preserve faithfully the order of the 'Phoenician' alphabet. I 97b

In astronomy, *al-~* , or *al-ridf*, is the ancient Arabic name for *dhanab al-dadjādja*, the star Deneb (α Cygni); ~ also refers to a star or constellation that is rising at sunrise, while its opposite (*raḳīb*) is setting. VIII 368b

In Persian prosody, the adjunction of a word or a short phrase, always shorter than a hemistich, to the rhyme letter and its repetition thoughout the poem. It is very frequently used in GHAZALs. IV 57a; VIII 368b

In Turkish military usage, *redīf* was the name given by Maḥmūd II to the reserve army, 'militia', created in 1834. The *redīf* was made up of battalions (*tabur*). VIII 370a

♦ radīf mutadjānis : in Persian prosody, a special artifice with complete paronomasia between RADĪFs, resulting from the fact that the *radīf* does not have the same meaning throughout the poem (which it is supposed to have). VIII 369a

rāḍikh → KHANNĀḲ

radjʿa (A) : return.

In shīʿī dogma, ~ is the return to life, which will precede the universal resurrection and gathering; only the virtuous will take part in it under the guidance of the Mahdī of the last times. I 334b; IV 457a; V 236a; VIII 372b; the passing of the soul into another body either human or animal; the transmigration of the spirit of holiness from one IMĀM to the next, more usually known as *tanāsukh*; return of power to the shīʿa; return from concealment, usually of a particular *imām* at the end of his occultation. VIII 371b

In classical Muslim administration, a requisition issued by the paymaster for certain troops stationed in outlying areas, for one issue of pay. II 79a

♦ al-radjʿa al-djāmiʿa : in classical Muslim administration, a global requisition issued by the head of the army office for each general issue of arm pay, rations, etc. II 79a

radjab (A) : the seventh month of the Islamic calendar, observed in the DJĀHILIYYA as a holy month in spring. VIII 373b

♦ radjabiyya : a special pilgrim caravan which set off from Cairo in the month of RADJAB, mentioned from time to time in the 8th/14th century chronicles. III 35a; and → 'ATĪRA

♦ al-radjabiyyūn : in mysticism, the tenth degree in the ṣūfī hierarchical order of saints. I 95a

radjaz (A) : tremor, spasm, convulsion (as may occur in the behind of a camel when it wants to rise); thunder, rumble, making a noise. VIII 375b; the oracular utterance of war. VIII 733a

In prosody, the name of the seventh Arabic metre, the simplest, and according to tradition, the oldest metre. It has a rising rhythm and is dipodically bound. This metre is most often used for short poems and improvisations in pre-Islamic and early Islamic times. A poem composed in this metre is called *urdjūza*. I 670a; I 673b; IV 80b; VIII 376a; poetry defined by 'halved', i.e. three-foot, lines without caesura. VIII 378b

In Urdu poetry, ~ refers to the hero's battle oration which forms part of the MARTHIYA. VI 611b

radjfa (A) : in the Qur'ānic story of Shu'ayb, commonly glossed as 'earthquake'. IX 491a

radjīm (A) : lit. stoned; for explaining the Qur'ānic expression *al-shayṭān al-radjīm*, it has been suggested that ~ is an Ethiopic loan word meaning 'accursed'. IX 408b

radj'iyya, or *irtidjā'* : the term coined in modern Arabic for reaction in the political sense. VIII 379a; with *aṣḥāb al-radj'a*, adherents of any of the shī'ī doctrines described under RADJ'A. VIII 372b

radjm (A) : stoning; the casting of stones at Minā, one of the pre-Islamic rites preserved by Muḥammad and inserted among the ceremonies of the pilgrimage. VIII 379a

In law, a ḤADD punishment of death which occurs in certain cases of immorality. IV 770a; VIII 379a

raḍkh (A) : a bonus share (of the booty given at the discretion of the IMĀM to those bondmen, women, and DHIMMĪs who may in some way have contributed to victory). II 1006b

raf' (A) : elevation, the act of raising something.

In grammar, the nominative and indicative cases, because both take *-u* and are thus *marfū'* 'raised'. III 1249a; VIII 383b

For ~ in the science of Tradition, → MARFŪ'

ra'fa → RAḤMA

rāged → RĀḲID

raghīf (A) : a round bread, quite thick and cooked in an oven. V 42b

raḥā (A) : in Muslim Spain, a water mill. I 492a
rahbāniyya (A) : monasticism. VIII 396b
rāhdār (P), or *tutḳavul* : the 'guardian of the roads' in the Īlkhānid and Djalāʾirid periods, paid by the central government and under the orders of a senior military commander. I 861a
raḥḥāl (A), or *raḥḥāla* : the person endowed with skill in the saddling of a camel, or one who travelled much. The form *raḥḥāla* neatly translates as 'globetrotter'. VIII 528a
raḥīl (A) : 'travelling by camel', in Arabic poetry applied to themes involving a desert journey. In its specific meaning ~ denotes a section of the polythematic ḲAṢĪDA, following the NASĪB, where the poet describes his camel and his travels. IV 713b; VIII 397b
rahīsh (A), or *murtahisha* : in archery, a bow whose string, at the moment of loosing, strikes the part called the *ṭāʾif*, the torus; such a bow, usually slim and light, vibrates when loosed. IV 798a
raḥma (A) : a Qurʾānic term, denoting either kindness, benevolence (syn. *raʾfa*) or, more frequently, an act of kindness, a favour (syn. *niʿma* or *faḍl*). Almost invariably, ~ is applied to God. VIII 398a
rahn (A) : in law, pledge, security; *rāhin* is the giver, and *murtahin* the taker of the pledge. VIII 400a
♦ rahn ḥiyāzī → GHĀRŪḲA
rahū 'l-māʾ → NUḤĀM
raʾī → ṢĀḤIB
raʾīs (A, pl. *ruʾasāʾ*, T *reʾīs*) : head, chief, leader of a recognisable group (political, religious, juridical, tribal, or other). The term goes back to pre-Islamic times and was used in various senses at different periods of Islamic history, either to circumscribe specific functions of the holder of the office of 'leadership' or as an honorific title. VIII 402a; IX 115b
In the scholastic community, ~ was applied to any scholar who had reached the summit of his field in his locality. V 1131b; and → KALĀNTAR
In the Ottoman navy, the term *reʾīs* was used for an individual commander. I 948a; VIII 403b; in modern Turkish, *reis* means 'captain of a small merchant vessel, skipper; able-bodied seaman'. VIII 403b
♦ raʾīs al-balad : in the mediaeval Near East, a kind of mayor, whose influence counterbalanced, and sometimes exceeded, that of the ḲĀḌĪ 'judge'. I 256a
♦ raʾīs al-baladiyya → AMĪN AL-ʿĀṢIMA
♦ reʾīs efendi → REʾĪS ÜL-KÜTTĀB
♦ reʾīs kesedāri̊ : in the Ottoman empire, pursebearer to the REʾĪS EFENDI. VIII 422a
♦ **reʾīs ül-küttāb** (T, < A), or *reʾīs efendi* : properly, 'chief of the men of the pen', a high Ottoman dignitary, directly under the grand vizier, originally head of the chancery of the Imperial Dīwān, later secretary of state or chancellor and Minister of Foreign Affairs. VIII 481b

♦ reʾīs al-ʿulemāʾ (T) : the supreme religious head of Bosno-Herzegovinian Muslims, as well as the highest religious authoritative body; an Ottoman office created in 1882 in order to gain control over Muslim religious institutions. I 1274a

rāʿiyat al-shayb (A) : the first white hair which appears on the head. IX 383a

raʿiyya (A, pl. *raʿāyā*; T pl. *reʿāyā*) : lit. pasturing herd of cattle, sheep, etc., a term which in later Islam came to designate the mass of subjects, the tax-paying common people, as opposed to the ruling military and learned classes. I 712a; VIII 403b

rakʿa (A) : lit. the act of bowing, bending; in the act of worship, a sequence of utterances and actions performed during the prayer. VIII 406b; VIII 929a,b

raḳāʿa (A) : burlesque, a genre of literature, closely akin to SUKHF, practiced a.o. by al-Ṣaymarī. S 16b

raḳaba (A, T *raḳabe*) : lit. neck, nape of the neck; term frequently used in the Qurʾān for 'slave'. I 24b; the original title to land. II 900b; the freehold ownership of agricultural lands in the Ottoman empire. II 906b

In law, the 'physical person'. I 29a

raḳam → FARMĀN

raḳīb (A) : 'guardian, vigilant one who knows everything that takes place'; one of the names of God. VIII 406b

In Arabic love poetry, the person who, by watching or simply being present, prevents the lovers from communicating with each other. VIII 406b

For ~ in astronomy, → RADĪF

rākib → FĀRIS

rāḳid (A, N.Afr *rāged* or *bū mergūd*) : lit. sleeping child; a foetus which is considered to have stopped its development, continuing to stay in the womb in an unchanged condition for an indefinite period of time, after which it may 'wake up' again and resume its development until it is born. VIII 407a

raḳīḳ (A) : the generic term for slave. I 24b

raḳḳ → DJILD

rakkād (A) : a type of merchant in mediaeval Islam, the itinerant trader who owes his profits to his knowledge of the differences in purchase and sale prices according to the places where the transactions take place. IX 789a

raḳḳāṣ (A, Fr *rekkas*) : in Muslim Spain, a runner, generally Sudanese, employed by the postal service in the 4th/10th century. I 1046a; a messenger who travels on foot long distances in order to carry official or private mail; nowadays, an occasional messenger, above all in time of war. VIII 415a

Other technical senses are: pendulum; hand of a watch; trigger of a fire-arm; part of a mill which produces a noise through the movement of the millstone. VIII 415a

raḳḳī (A, < *Raḳḳa*) : in the mediaeval Muslim world, a well-known kind of coarse soap, similar to date-palm paste, from which lozenges were made in Damascus. VIII 693a rakwa (A) : a leather bowl, one of the ṣūfī paraphernalia. VIII 742b

rakz → MAʾKHADH

ramad (A) : in medicine, ophthalmitis, inflammation of the eye, or ophthalmia (conjunctivitis), inflammation of the conjunctiva. VIII 417a

♦ ramad ḥubaybī, or *djarab al-ʿayn* : one of the medical terms for trachoma. I 785b

♦ ʿilm al-ramad : originally only meaning 'conjunctivitis', ~ now embraces eye diseases of all types. I 785a

ramād (A) : ordinary ashes; ashes for washing. VIII 419b

ramaḍān (A) : name of the ninth month of the Muslim calendar, the only month to be mentioned in the Qurʾān. VIII 417b

ramaka (A) : a term for a mare of mixed breed. II 785a

ramal (A) : in prosody, the name of the eighth Arabic metre. I 670a; VIII 421a

In music, a rhythmic mode said to have been invented by Ibn Muḥriz, a famous Meccan musician of the 1st-2nd/7th-8th centuries. III 883a; VIII 421b

ramas, ramaṣ → RAMATH

ramath (A) : in the Gulf area, a raft or a sort of raft made of tree trunks or lengthy pieces of wood tied together by coconut fibre. It has variant names in other parts of the Middle East: *ramaṣ*, *ramas*, and SAFĪNA, which is the classical term for ship in general. VII 53b

rāmishgar → KHUNYĀGAR

raml (A, pl. *rimāl*, *armul*) : sand.

In divination, ~ , and *ḍarb al-raml* mean geomancy (→ KHAṬṬ); also, in Persian usage, divination by means of dice. II 761b; VIII 138b; VIII 423b

♦ ramla → NAFŪD

ramm (A, pl. *rumūm*) : a geographical term employed by al-Iṣṭakhrī to denote a tribal district in Persia in the early centuries. III 1096b

ramūḥ (A) : in the terminology of horse-riding, a horse that kicks. II 953b

ramz (A, pl. *rumūz*) : allusion; code; sigla; and → TAʾRĪKH

In rhetoric, ~ 'circumlocution' denotes a specific subcategory of KINĀYA. VIII 427a

For ~ in mysticism, → ISHĀRA

In modern Arabic literature, ~ became an exact equivalent of the Western term 'symbol'. VIII 430a; according to al-Ṭabarī, ~ in pre-Islamic poetry also meant an unintelligible murmur or whisper. VIII 428b

rank (P) : lit. colour, dye, a term used in mediaeval Arabic sources primarily to designate the emblems and insignia of AMĪRs and sultans in Egypt, Syria, and al-Djazīra. Mamlūk historians occasionally also use it as a generic term for emblem in general, such as e.g. the ~s of merchants' guilds and those of Bedouin chieftains in Tunisia. VIII 431b

rapak (J) : a technical term for the charge made by the wife, at the court for matters of religion, that the husband has not fulfilled the obligations which he took upon himself at the TAʿLĪḲ of divorce. VIII 433a

raʾs (A, pl. *ruʾūs, arʾus*) : head; and → MUTHALLATH
In astronomy, ~ , or ~ *al-tinnīn* 'the dragon's head', refers to the crescent node, one of the points where the moon passes through the ecliptic, during an eclipse of the moon. V 536a; VIII 101b
In geography, ~ is the common word for 'cape', but it also used with the meaning of 'headland, promontory'. VIII 433b
♦ **raʾs al-ʿām** : New Year's Day, lit. beginning of the year, i.e. 1 al-Muḥarram. VIII 433b
♦ raʾs al-hirr : 'cat's head', in botany, the Hemp nettle (*Galeopsis*). IX 653a
♦ raʾs al-māl → SALAM

rasan (A) : the bozal, a bit preferred to the curb bit by Arab horsemen in the East. II 953a

raṣāṣ (A), or *usrub* : in mineralogy, lead, which was mostly obtained from galena (lead sulphide). V 967a
♦ raṣāṣa : a gauge, used before the Nilometer was built to measure the rising of the Nile. VII 39

rashād (A) : in botany, cress or rocket, forbidden by al-Ḥākim in addition to the classical food prohibitions. II 1070a

rashwa (A, pl. *rushā*) : in law, 'bribe', which is strictly forbidden by law. VIII 451a

rasm (A, T **resm**) : the act of drawing, a drawing, not always distinguished from painting. VIII 451b
In Ottoman usage, *resm* (pl. *rüsūm*) means state practices and organisations as distinguished from those based on Islamic principles and traditions, specifically taxes and dues introduced by the state called *rüsūm-i ʿurfiyye*. ~ was sometimes called *ḥaḳḳ* in the sense of legal right, as in the term *ḥaḳḳ-i̊ ḳarār*, a fee which feudal cavalryman took when vacant MĪRĪ land was assigned to a peasant. The term ~ is also used synonymously with ḲANŪN, *teklīf* and ʿADĀT. A ~ is called *ʿadāt* whenever it originates from a locally-established custom. VIII 486a; for specific taxes, → BĀD-I HAWĀ; ČIFT-RESMI; FILORI; ḲAPAN; ḲISMA; YAYLAḲ RESMI
♦ rasm al-ṣadārat : in Tīmūrid Persia, a specific tax which was raised as a percentage on WAḲF-revenues, and which made up the financial support for the ṢADR, also called *sahm al-ṣadārat*. VIII 750a

rass (A) : in prosody, the vowel (always *a*) immediately before the *alif* of the TAʾSĪS, the *alif* of prolongation placed before the rhyme letter. IV 412a; and → AṢḤĀB AL-RASS

rāst → SHASHMAḲOM

rasūl (A, pl. *rusul*) : messenger, apostle; in the secular sense, diplomatic envoy, ambassador. VIII 454b

ratha : in Muslim India, the bullock-cart with a domed canopy used particularly by women on journeys; their escorts may walk on foot beside them. VII 932b

rātib (A, pl. *rawātib*) : a word meaning what is fixed and hence applied to certain non-obligatory ṢALĀTS or certain litanies, such as the DHIKR. VIII 459a

rātīnadj → ṢAMGH

raṭl (A, < Ar) : in the mediaeval Near East, the most common weight of capacity, used for small quantities of various commodities. The actual weight of a ~ varied depending on time, place and type of commodity. The ~ of Baghdad, which was equal to 401.674 g (according to others, 397.26 g), was considered the 'canonical' ~ of the Muslims, because it was used from the days of the first caliphs. VI 117a ff.; VIII 654a

rattī (< San *raktikā*) : 'red one', in Muslim India, a measure of weight used for small quantities of various commodities, e.g. jewels. Its name derives from the seed of a small red-flowered leguminous creeper, *Abrus precatorius*; the actual weight of such a ~ seed varies from 80 to 130 mg, its notional weight, at least up to the 8th/14th century, being 116.6 mg. Abu 'l-Faḍl calls the ~ *surkh*. VI 122a

rawādif → RADĪF

rawḍa (A) : lit. garden; in Arabia, a basin or hollow whose bottom does not hold water, so that wild vegetation may be fairly abundant there. In the north it is called *fayḍa*. I 538a

In Muslim India, a monumental tomb within an enclosure, not necessarily of a *pīr* (→ MURSHID). VI 125b

♦ **rawḍa-khwānī** : a shīʿī Persian mourning ritual commemorating the suffering and martyrdom of Ḥusayn, the grandson of the Prophet Muḥammad, and other shīʿī martyrs. VIII 465a

♦ rawḍiyya → NAWRIYYA

rawī (A) : in prosody, the rhyme letter which, since it occurs in every type of rhyme, is considered its principal consonant after which famous poems are often named, e.g. the *Lāmiyya* of al-Shanfarā. IV 412a; VIII 368b

rāwī (A, pl. *ruwāt*) : reciter and transmitter of poetry, as also of narrative Traditions and ḤADĪTH. There is an intensive form *rāwiya*, explained as 'copious transmitter', used in mediaeval sources as a synonym to *rāwī*. In modern research ~ is applied, as a rule, to the learned collectors of Bedouin poetry in the 8th century. VIII 466b; IX 236a

rāwiya → RĀWĪ

rawk (? < Dem *ruwkh* 'land distribution') : in Egyptian administration, ~ means a kind of cadastral survey which is followed by a redistribution of the arable land. VIII 467b

rawwāgh (A) : in the terminology of horse-riding, a horse that shies. II 953b

raʾy (A) : personal opinion; the result of independent excercise of the intelligence. In law, the decision of legal points by one's own judgement in the absence or ignorance of a traditional ruling bearing on the case in question. I 730a; II 886a; IX 878b; and → AHL AL-RAʾY

rāya (A) : a term for flag, used during the Prophet's lifetime along with LIWĀʾ and,

less commonly, *ʿalam*. Some Traditions contrast the ~ , the Prophet's black flag, with his *liwāʾ*, which was white. The use of the ~ does not seem to be confined to Muslims, since at Badr, Ṭalḥa carried the ~ of the idolaters. I 349a
In zoology, ~ (< *Raia*) or *radja* means 'ray' or 'skate'. VIII 1021a; for other synonyms, VIII 1022b
♦ rāyat-i aʿlā (U) : title used by the Sayyid kings of Dihlī. IX 119b

rayb → SHAKK

rayd (A, pl. *aryād, ruyūd*) : a ledge of a mountain, resembling a wall, or a resting upon ledges of mountains. At least in the Ḥaḍramawt, ~ is the term for the centre of the territory of a Bedouin tribe, which is generally a depression in the rocky plateau. VIII 470a

rayḥān, rayḥānī → RĪḤĀN

rāziyānadj → BASBĀS

razḳa → RIZḲ

reʿāyā → RAʿIYYA

redīf → RADĪF

reg → RIḲḲ

reʾīs → RAʾĪS

resimcılık (T) : a land-leasing system in Turkey, in which the amount of the rent depends on the situation and fertility of the soil, the rentability of the cultivation and the degree of the dependence of the peasant. V 473b

resm → RASM

rezza (Mor) : a small, rather flat turban, worn in Morocco. V 746b

ribā (A) : lit. increase; in law, usury and interest, and in general any unjustified increase of capital for which no compensation is given. The exact meaning of ~ is unknown, but it entailed, evidently, a condemnation, from a moral point of view, of those who grew rich through the misery of others, without the loan granted helping the borrower in any way to retrieve his fortunes, such as lending dates to a starving man, etc. I 111b; IV 691b; VIII 491a; VIII 915a

ribāṭ (A) : in Qurʾānic usage, the preparations made with the mustering of cavalry, with a view to battle; after the great conquests, ~ was used to denote a fortified edifice, normally situated in hazardous regions. VIII 493b
In mystical terminology, the urban residence of ṣūfīs, in the East and in Egypt more commonly known as *khānḳāh*. VIII 493b; and → KHĀNḲĀH; MURĀBIṬ; SIKKA

riḍā (A) : lit. the fact of being pleased or contented; contentment, approval; a term found in mysticism and also in early Islamic history. VIII 509a

ridāʾ (A) : a piece of white seamless cloth, draped around the upper half of the wearer's chest, which, with the IZĀR, makes up the garment worn by men during the pilgrimage. I 1053a

riḍāʿ → RAḌĀʿ

ridda → MURTADD

ridf (A) : in prosody, the *wāw* and *yāʾ* immediately preceding the rhyme letter as letters of prolongation or to mark the diphthongs *aw* en *ay*, and the *alif* as letter of prolongation in the same position. IV 412a; VIII 369a; and → NATĪDJA; RADĪF

♦ ridfa (A), or *shadjara* : alternate.

In prosody, with regard to the MAWĀLIYĀ as folk-verse, the sestet of alternating rhymes which are added, as a form of elaboration, after the *farsha* (→ ʿATABA), the first three lines; ~ is also used for each of the two rhymes. The verse is then said to be *mardūf* or *ṣaʿīdī* 'Upper Egyptian'. VI 868a

♦ ridf-i zāʾid : in Persian prosody, a consonant intervening between the RIDF and the rhyme letter. VIII 369b

ridjāl (A, s. *radjul*) : men; as a technical term, the transmitters of ḤADĪTH 'Muslim Tradition'. VIII 514b

♦ ridjāl al-ghayb : 'the men of the mystery', the hierarchy of saints, in which there are ten categories, crowned by the ḲUṬB. I 94b; II 1025b

♦ **ʿilm al-ridjāl** : the science devoted to the study of the persons figuring in ISNĀDs, with the purpose of establishing their moral qualities, the bibliographical details which will provide the necessary checks on either the materials transmitted or the *isnād*s themselves, and the exact identification of the names, to prevent confusion between persons of the same name. III 1150b

ridjl (A) : foot; and → SĀḲ

♦ ridjl ghurāb : 'crow's foot'; in the science of diplomatic, the popular term for the signature, ʿALĀMA, of the person drawing up the document, used with great lack of respect. II 302a

♦ ridjl al-ḳiṭṭ, or *ridjl al-hirr*, *ẓufr al-ḳiṭṭ* : in botany, the Cat's foot (*Antennaria dioica*). IX 653a

riḍwān (A) : in the Qurʾān, God's grace, favour, which believers will meet in the hereafter. VIII 509a; VIII 519a

rīf (A, pl. *aryāf*) : countryside; a food-producing fringe of a river traversing arid country. VIII 521b; VIII 562a

In Morocco, ~ denotes, in the circle of tents, those which are on the periphery. By extension (?), certain Berberophone groups of the Middle Atlas use it to define a group of tents held together by a close relationship in the male line. VIII 521b

rifāda (A) : the institution of providing food for the pilgrims in Mecca. I 9a; I 80a

rīḥ (A) : wind; in music, a musical phrase. S 351a

♦ rīḥ al-sabal : in medicine, an eye complaint, to be cured by the roasted flesh of the scorpion. I 344a

riḥāla (A) : in early Islam, a camel saddle made of wooden bows joined together with leather thongs and adorned with skins. III 667a

rīḥān (A), or *rīḥānī*, *rayḥān*, *rayḥānī* : basil; and → ʿABAYTHARĀN

In Persian calligraphy, ~ is a smaller version of the Arabic script called MUḤAḲḲAḲ, used for copying Qurʾāns, and like *muḥaḳḳaḳ*, starting to go out of circulation after the 11th/17th century in favour of NASKH. IV 1123a; VIII 151b

riḥiyyāt (N.Afr) : flat, leather slippers worn by both sexes in North Africa. V 746b riḥla (A) : a journey, voyage, travel; a travelogue; originally, the word ~ connoted the act of saddling one or more camels. VIII 528a

ri̊ḳʿa (T), *ri̊ḳʿī* or *ruḳʿa* : in Turkish calligraphy, a script probably invented during the second half of the 12th/18th century. The main characteristics of ~ are that its letters are less rounded and more straight than in the DĪWĀNĪ script; ~ was used along with *dīwānī* in the DĪWĀN-i̊ HUMĀYŪN, and like Persian SHIKASTA *nastaʿlīḳ*, it also became a standard form of hand-writing among Turks, used for letters and every kind of correspondence. When written rapidly and without adhering to the rules, ~ is called *ri̊ḳʿa ḳi̊rmasi̊*. IV 1126a; a more common variant of this script has now become the cursive for daily use throughout the Middle East. VIII 151b

riḳāʿ (A) : in Persian calligraphy, a smaller version of the TAWḲĪʿ script. Formerly used for writing letters, epics and stories, ~ later came to be used for writing the final pages of Qurʾāns and especially those of learned books. The Ottoman calligraphers called this script *idjāza* or *khaṭṭ al-idjāza*. IV 1123b; VIII 151b

rikāb (A) : lit. stirrup; in Persian and Turkish usage at Muslim courts, 'the sovereign himself or his presence, the foot of the throne'. VIII 528b

In Turkish usage, ~ was also applied to the imperial cavalcade and the procession formed on this occasion; the audience given by the sultan, whether or not he was in procession; and the service of the sultan or simply his presence, which was not necessarily immediate. ~ and *rikāb-i̊ hümāyūn* were also used in the sense of interim or substitute. VIII 529a

♦ rikāb aghalari̊ : name applied to a certain number of important officers or dignitaries of the Ottoman palace (from 4 to 11, according to the different sources). VIII 529a

♦ rikāb ḳāʾimmaḳāmi̊ : the substitute for the grand vizier, who was appointed to the Ottoman sovereign when the grand vizier moved from place to place. VIII 529a

♦ rikāb solaghi̊ : the name given to the eight *solaḳ* lieutenants who walked by the Ottoman sultan's stirrup in the great procession. VIII 529a

♦ **rikābdār** (P, < A RIKĀB), or *rikībdār* : 'one put in charge of the stirrup, one who holds the stirrup, when his master mounts'; in a wider sense, ~ meant a kind of squire, groom or riding attendant who had charge of the care and maintenance of harness and saddlery and of everything required for mounting on horseback. The term was used especially in Egypt and Turkey. In Persia it was replaced by its Turkish synonym *üzengi* (or *zengü*) *ḳurčisi*. Synonyms in Arabic were *rikābī* and *ṣāḥib al-rikāb*. VIII 529b ff.

In 19th and early 20th-century Egyptian usage, *rikib-dār* or *rakbdār* means 'jockey groom'. VIII 530a

♦ rikābī → RIKĀBDĀR

♦ rikāb-i̊ hümāyūn → RIKĀB

♦ rikāb-i̊ hümāyūnde : 'with the (Ottoman) sultan', a term used in speaking of the troops of the capital or of the grand vizier insofar as he was endowed with the full powers of the sultan. VIII 529a

♦ rikāb-k͟hāna : in Mamlūk Egypt, the depot for harness and in general for all the material required for horses and stables. VIII 530a

rik͟hl → SAK͟HLA

rīk͟hta : in Bengali literature, half-Persian, half-Bengali poetry, introduced by Nūr Ḳuṭb al-ʿĀlam. VIII 125a

rik͟hwa (A) : 'relaxed'; in grammar, a division equivalent in modern phonetics with 'constrictive', designating the letters *h*, *ḥ*, *g͟h*, *k͟h*, *s͟h*, *ṣ*, *ḍ*, *z*, *s*, *ẓ*, *t͟h*, *d͟h*, *f*. III 599a

riḳḳ (A) : an abstract term for 'slavery'. I 24b; and → DJILD

In geography (Eng **reg**), 'dessicated terrain, terrain where water has disappeared, at least on the surface'. VIII 481a

rind (P, pl. *runūd*, *rindān*) : 'scamp, knave, rogue, drunkard' or 'a debauchee', a name given to groups of young men who were considered elements of disorder in mediaeval Baghdad from the time of the Saldjūḳs. In the terminology of poetry and mysticism, ~ acquired the positive meaning of 'one whose exterior is liable to censure, but who at heart is sound'. II 961b; VIII 531a

risāla (A) : originally, the oral transmission of a message; message, mission; missive, letter, epistle, monograph; from the 5th/11th century onwards ~ could also be a synonym of MAḲĀMA. VIII 532a; and → BARĀʾA; PARWĀNAČI

In Ottoman Turkish, ~ also denoted 'a piece of cloth fixed to the front of a dervish's *tādj* or cap' and, by the 19th century, 'a booklet or a weekly or monthly journal'. VIII 544a

rit͟hāʾ (A) : 'lamentation'; in prosody, the corresponding literary genre. VI 603a

riwāḳ (A, pl. *arwiḳa*, *riwāḳāt*) : the moveable screen of the nomadic tent. II 113b; in architecture, the space between two rows of pillars. VI 661b; ~ was later used for 'student lodgings', because of the many students living in the halls of mosques. VI 662b; that part of a structure that forms its front. Depending on the type of structure, a ~ could be a gallery, an ambulatory, a portico, a colonnade, a porch, or a balcony. ~ was also used to indicate the Greek stoa, such as the stoa attributed to Aristotle in Alexandria. VIII 545a

♦ al-riwāḳiyyūn : the Stoics. VIII 545a

riwāya (A) : in literature, the oral transmission of a Tradition, a poem or a story; also the authorised transmission of books. In modern Arabic, ~ has been adopted to mean a story, a novel, a play or a film. III 369b; VIII 545b; and → DIRĀYA; ḤIKĀYA

riyāʾ (A) : ostentation, hypocrisy. VIII 547a

riyāḍiyyāt (A), or *riyāḍa* : mathematics. VIII 549b

riyāfa (A, < RĪF) : in divination, the water-diviner's art which estimates the depth of water under the earth through the smell of the earth, its vegetation and the instinctive reactions of certain creatures, in particular, the hoopoe. VIII 562a

riyāl (A, < Sp *real*) : in numismatics, a name used for a silver coin in a number of Islamic countries, first recorded in the East in Persia in 1609. The ~ is still in use today in Yemen, Saudi Arabia, Oman, the United Arab Emirates, Dubai and Qatar. III 256a; VIII 563b

♦ **riyāla** (T, < It *reale*), *riyāle*, *riyāla bey*, or *iryāla* : a general officer of the Ottoman navy who commanded the galley of the same name, later 'rear-admiral'; the rank of ~ was at first known among the Turks only as applied to officers of the navies of Christendom, coming into use among the Turkish sailors in the time of Meḥemmed IV, 1058-99/1648-87. VIII 564a ff.

rizḳ (A, pl. *arzāḳ*) : lit. anything granted by someone to someone else as a benefit, hence in theology and the Qurʾān, 'bounty, sustenance, nourishment'. I 204a; VIII 567b

In military terminology, ~ is used to designate the regular payments, in cash and in kind, made to those soldiers registered on the DĪWĀN of earliest Islamic times and, by the ʿAbbāsid period, on the more elaborate *dīwān al-djaysh*, hence equivalent to ʿAṬĀʾ or ṬAMAʿ. Those soldiers drawing regular allowances were called *murtaziḳa*. A single pay allotment was termed *razḳa* (pl. *razaḳāt*). VIII 568b

rōk (Dem) : a kind of cadastral revision, under Ṣalāḥ al-Dīn, of which the object was to measure the surface area of all the lands in Egypt, to assess their value in terms of land tax, *kharādj*, and to distribute them to officers and soldiers as a substitute to salaries. VII 164b

rū band (P) : a rectangular white veil fastened over the *čādur*, the all-enveloping wrap worn outside, and falling over the face. The ~ , an innovation in the Ṣafawid period, had a small slit covered with netting over the eyes to permit vision. V 749b

rubʿ (A) : lit. quarter; in astronomy, quadrant. VIII 574a; and → NIṢF

♦ rubʿ āfāḳī : the universal horary quadrant, known in mediaeval Europe as *quadrans vetus*. VIII 574b

♦ rubʿ mudjayyab : the sine quadrant, with markings resembling modern graph-paper, developed from the *rubʿ al-sāʿāt*. VIII 574b

♦ rubʿ al-muḳanṭarāt : a quadrant in the form of one-half of the markings on an astrolabe plate, the rete being replaced with a thread with movable bead attached at the centre. VIII 575a

♦ rubʿ al-sāʿāt : the horary quadrant, marked with a radial solar scale and curves for the hours. VIII 574b

rubāb (P) : a stringed Persian instrument which was played with the fingers or plectrum. It might be the origin of the instrument RABĀB. VIII 346a

rubāʿī (A, pl. *rubāʿiyyāt*), and *mirabbaʿ*, *du-baytī*, *tarāna* : a verse form; in Persian prosody, the shortest type of formulaic poem, usually but inaccurately called 'quatrain', said to have been the earliest of the verse forms invented by the Persians. It is derived from no less than twenty-four varieties of the HAZADJ metre. The ~ is defined not only by the number of lines but also by its pattern of rhyme (*a a b a*, less commonly *a a a a*) and its metre. In Arabic, this verse form is called *rubāʿiyya*. I 677a; IV 58a; VI 868a; VIII 578b ff.

♦ rubāʿiyya (A) : in literary theory, a literary work in four parts, translating both tetralogy and quartet. VIII 585a; and → RUBĀʿĪ

rūdhbār (P), or *rūdbār* : lit. a district along a river, or a district intersected by rivers. VIII 586a

rudjūʿ (A) : in theology, return (to God). VIII 587a

rughām (A) : mucus (of sheep). S 317b

rūḥ (A) : in early Arabic poetry, 'breath', 'wind'; in the Qurʾān, ~ denotes a special angel messenger and a special divine quality. In post-Qurʾānic literature, ~ is equated with NAFS and both are applied to the human spirit, angels and DJINN. VII 880a

rūḥāniyya (A) : 'spirituality', 'spiritual being'; in angelology, the *spiritus rector*, the angel who rules each of the celestial spheres. VIII 593b

ruḥla (A) : the destination of a journey; a rarer meaning is that of a noble or learned man to whom one may travel. VIII 528a

ruḳʿa (A) : a piece of clothing; an administrative document; a sealed, personal message. VIII 835a; and → RİḲʿA

rukh (A) : redistribution of land. VII 164b

rukhāma → MIZWALA

rukhkh (A) : a huge ostrich-like bird (*Aepyornis maximus*), now extinct, probably existing well into historical times as a peculiar species in Madagascar. Though early Arab seafarers could conceivably have seen the bird face-to-face, Arabic tradition soon turned the ~ into a fabulous creature embellishing it with all kinds of strange details. VIII 595a

In chess, the term for rook, castle. IX 366b

rukhṣa (A, pl. *rukhaṣ*) : lit. permission, dispensation.

In law, ~ is a legal ruling relaxing or suspending by way of exception under certain circumstances an injunction of a primary and general nature. Its counterpart is ʿAZĪMA. VIII 595a; IX 778a

♦ rukhṣat (U, < A) : in Urdu poetry, the part of the elegy where the martyr-hero bids farewell to his nearest and dearest. VI 611b

ruḳḳ (A) : a term in the Persian Gulf for a shoal. I 535b

rukn (A, pl. *arkān*) : lit. corner, support, pillar.

In law, a condition in a contract. I 319a

In natural science and alchemy, ~ denotes cardinal point, part, direction, and, in particular, element. VIII 596b

In religious usage, the plural *arkān* is commonly found in the expression *arkān al-dīn* or *arkān al-ʿibāda*, denoting the basic 'pillars' of religion and religious observance. These so-called 'pillars of Islam' are usually enumerated as: profession of faith (SHAHĀDA); the pilgrimage (ḤADJDJ); the worship (ṢALĀT); fasting (ṢAWM); and almsgiving (ZAKĀT, ṢADAḲA). To these some authorities add a sixth, perpetual warfare against infidels (DJIHĀD). VIII 596b

ruḳya (A) : enchantment, magical spell, permitted in exceptional cases, on condition that it brings benefit to people and does not harm anyone. VIII 600a

rūm (A) : name for the Romans, the Byzantines, and the Christian Melkites interchangeably. VIII 601a

♦ **rūmī** : a designation for the Turks from Byzantium, *al-rūm*, which was once under the Eastern Roman Empire. VIII 612a

In Ottoman art and architectural ornamentation, ~ also indicated a special motif in the form of a leaf or stylised animal designs. VIII 612b

♦ rūmiyya : a tribute paid by some groups of the Banū ʿĀmir to the Spanish in the 16th century. IX 537a

rumḥ (A) : the game of lance, also called *th̲aḳāfa* or *th̲iḳāf*, one of the branches of horse-riding. II 955a

rūpiyya (< San *rūpya*) : in numismatics, an Indian coin, a rupee. VIII 618a

rūsak̲h̲tad̲j̲ : in chemistry, antimony. VIII 111b

rus̲h̲d (A) : in law, discretion or responsibility in acting. I 993b; mental maturity. VIII 821b

♦ rüs̲h̲diyye (T) : under the Ottomans, the secondary school of six grades (ages 11 to 16), created during the reign of Maḥmūd II (1801-39). I 75a; V 904a

rustāḳ (A, pl. *rasātīḳ*; < Mid.P *rōstāg*) : lit. rural district, countryside; in mediaeval administrative usage, ~ designated a district or canton centred on a town. VIII 636a

In wider literary usage, ~ , or *rustā*, was contrasted with the urban centres, and its populations regarded as country bumpkins compared with the more sophisticated town-dwellers. VIII 636a

rusūm → MARĀSIM; RASM

ruṭab → TAMR

rutaylāʾ (A) : in zoology, the tarantula. IX 873a

ruṭūbāt (A) : in medicine, dyscratic juice in the stomach. IX 432a

ruʾyā (A) : lit. vision, nocturnal vision, dream. Muslim tradition distinguishes between ~ , the true dream, the dream inspired by God, and *ḥulm*, the false dream, resulting from the passions and preoccupations of the soul, or inspired by Satan. VIII 645a

In its philosophical-mystical meaning, the term, like *manām*, describes the dream as a means to transmit fictitious observations or, in the best instances, information and knowledge which convey another, higher reality. VIII 647a

♦ **ruʾyat al-hilāl** : in astronomy, the sighting of the lunar crescent, of particular importance for the fixing of the beginning and end of Ramaḍān and the festivals. VIII 649b

rūznāma (P) : lit. record of the day, hence acquiring meanings like 'almanac, calendar, daily journal' etc; in mediaeval administration, the daily record of payments and receipts of the treasury; also called *daftar-i taʿlīḳ* under the Īlk̲h̲ānids. II 78b; the form *rūznāmad̲j̲* points to an origin in Sāsānid administra-

tion. The keeper of the ~ under the Ottomans was called **rūznāme<u>dj</u>i**. VIII 652a
In Fāṭimid and early Ayyūbid Egypt, ~ was used in a sense contrary to its etymological meaning and its usage in the eastern Islamic world, sc. for the rendering of accounts every ten days. VIII 652a

♦ rūznāme<u>dj</u>i → RŪZNĀMA

ruzz (A), or *aruzz*, *uruzz* : rice, *Oryza sativa* L., one of two major cultivated species, the other being the indigenous African variety *O. glaberrima*, both of
which spring from perennial rice. VIII 652b; and → ARUZZ

S

ṣāʿ (A) : a measure of capacity which was used in the Ḥi<u>dj</u>āz in the days of
Muḥammad, equal to 4 MUDDs. The ~ did not spread to other countries, except
perhaps in Algeria and Tunisia where it is still used, with varying equivalences.
V 118a; VIII 654a

sāʿa (A) : lit. hour, hence 'clock'. VIII 654a

For the ancient Arabs, ~ meant nothing more than 'a moment, a brief lapse of
time', as they did not divide the day into 24 hours. V 708b

In eschatology, *al-sāʿa* is the Last Hour, which, with the Day of Resurrection
and the Day of Judgement, constitutes one of the 'necessary beliefs' which de-
termine the content of the Muslim faith. V 235b; VIII 656a

♦ sāʿa <u>sh</u>amsiyya → MIZWALA

saʿāda (A) : happiness, bliss; in Islamic philosophy, a central concept to describe
the highest aim of human striving, which can be reached through ethical perfection and increasing knowledge. VIII 657b

sabʿ (A), or *sabʿa* : seven. VIII 662b

♦ al-sabʿ al-ṭiwāl : lit. the seven long ones; a designation for SŪRAS ii-vii and ix.
IX 887b

♦ sabʿiyya : the Seveners, a designation for those <u>sh</u>īʿī sects which recognise a
series of seven IMĀMs. VIII 683b

sabab (A, pl. *asbāb*) : lit. rope, coming to designate anything which binds or con-
nects; hence also 'bond, alliance; a means of arriving at, or achieving, something; way of access'. VIII 666b

In philosophy, ~ is used as a synonym of *ʿilla* 'cause, reason'. The ~ is also
called *mabdaʾ*, 'principle'; it is 'that which a thing needs, whether in its
quiddity or in its existence'. III 1129b; VIII 666b

In medicine, ~ denoted the efficient cause, exclusively that which has an effect
within the human body, whether it produces illness or restores or preserves
health. VIII 667a

In law, ~ is the designation given by the law maker for an injunction (ḤUKM). The ~ may not be the actual cause but merely serves as a mark (*ʿalāma*) to indicate that a certain *ḥukm* should apply. VIII 667a

In prosody, one of two pairs of metrical components distinguished by al-Khalīl, consisting of two consonants each. One is called *sabab khafīf* (when the first consonant is 'moving', i.e. has a short vowel, and the second is 'quiescent') and the other *sabab thaḳīl* (when both consonants are 'moving'). I 670b; a third type was introduced into Persian prosody, the *sabab-i mutawassiṭ*, consisting of an overlong syllable (e.g. *yār*). VIII 667b

In grammar, ~ is used by Sībawayhi to denote a 'semantic link' between words that bring about a change in the expected case ending. In addition to the direct ~ , he recognized an indirect link which he calls *iltibās*, 'involvement'. VIII 668a

♦ sabab khafīf → SABAB

♦ sabab thaḳīl → SABAB

♦ sabab-i mutawassiṭ → SABAB

sabad (A) : smooth, as e.g. in describing goats' hair. S 317a

sabʿānī (A), or *misabbaʿ*, *nuʿmānī*, *baghdādī* : in folk-verse, a composition with the rhyme scheme *a a a z z z a*, which is an elaboration of the monorhyme quatrain. VI 868a

sābāṭ (Ind.P) : in Indian siegecraft, a word used to express two walls, the foundations of which were laid at a distance of about one musket-shot (from the fort). They were protected by planks, fastened together by raw hides and made strong, and thus formed something like a lane which was then carried to the wall of the fort during an assault. III 482a

ṣabbāgh (A) : a dyer, a skilled artisan in the mediaeval Near East. IV 1161a; VIII 671b

sabbāk (A) : a melter, one of the craftsmen employed as staff in the mint who carried out the actual coining operation. II 118a

sabbāla → SABĪL

ṣabīb (A) : liquid colour or tincture, also applied to the object which it colours. V 699b

sābiḳ (A) : the name for the first horse in a horse-race, according to the order of finishing. II 953a

In Druze hierarchy, the right wing, the fourth of the five cosmic ranks in the organisation. II 632a

♦ al-sābiḳūn, or *al-sābiḳūn al-awwalūn* : in early Islam, the circle of early Muslims consisting of those who accepted Islam before the Prophet entered the house of al-Arḳam b. Abi 'l-Arḳam; in Qur'ānic exegesis, those Muslims who prayed in both directions, viz. Jerusalem and Mecca, who emigrated with Muḥammad to Medina, and who took part in the battle of Badr and in the treaty of al-Ḥudaybiya. VIII 828a

sabīl (A, pl. *subul*; T *sebīl*) : lit. way, road, path.

In the Qur᾽ān, ~ is also used figuratively in e.g. the expressions *sabīl Allāh*, the idea of fighting in the way of God, and *ibn al-sabīl* 'son of the road', later taken as 'traveller, wayfarer', and therefore as a fit object of charity or compassion. VIII 679a

In architecture, ~ designates water-houses which provide water for free public use; less common is also *sabbāla* 'public fountain, drinking basin'. The term ~ is also used to designate other charitable objects, such as *ḥawḍ al-sabīl*, i.e. a drinking trough for the animals, or *maktab al-sabīl* which is a charitable elementary school for boys. VIII 679b

For ~ in Turkey, → ČEṢHME

ṣabir (A) : aloes or some other bitter vegetable substance. III 404a

ṣabiyy (A) : a youth, boy, or male child; one that has not yet been weaned, so called from the time of his birth. The fem. counterpart is *ṣabiyya*. VIII 821b

In law, a minor (also *ṣaghīr*), who has the capacity to conclude purely beneficial transactions and to accept donations and charitable gifts. An intelligent (*ṣabiyy yaʿḳilu*), discriminating (MUMAYYIZ) minor, moreover, can adopt Islam, enter into a contract of manumission by *mukātaba*, if he is a slave, and carry out a procuration. VIII 826a; and → ṬIFL

sabʿiyya → SABʿ

sabḳ (A), or *sibāḳ* : the sport of horse-racing. II 953a

sabk-i hindī (P) : 'the Indian style'; the third term of a classification of Persian literature into three stylistic periods, the other two being *sabk-i khurāsānī* (also called *sabk-i turkistānī*) and *sabk-i ʿirāḳī*, referring respectively to the eastern and the western parts of mediaeval Persia. VIII 683b

sabkha (A, pl. *sibākh*; N.Afr. *sebkha*) : in geography, salt marshes or lagoons and the salt flats left by the evaporation of the water from such areas. VIII 685a; S 328a

sabla (A) : a loose gown worn by women in Egypt, synonymous with THAWB. V 741b

sabr (A, pl. *subūr*) : an advance party of a raiding group of Bedouin. II 1055b

ṣabr (A) : patience, endurance; resignation; the cardinal virtue in mysticism. VIII 686b

In botany, ~ denotes the aloe, a species of the *Liliaceae*. Three varieties of the aloe are generally mentioned: *suḳuṭrī*, *ʿarabī* (*ḥaḍramī*) and *simindjānī* (→ SUḲUṬRĪ). VIII 687b

♦ ṣabra : a very hard stone. VIII 688b

sabt (A) : the sabbath, and thus Saturday (*yawm al-~* , technically, Friday evening to Saturday evening); it is also suggested to mean 'a week', that is, from ~ to ~ , as well as a more general sense of a long period of time. VIII 689a

sabuʿ al-baḥr (A) : 'beast of the sea', the sea wolf (*Anarhichas lupus*). VIII 1021a

ṣābūn (A, < Gk) : soap, a mixture of fat or tallow and vegetable ashes, used to dye the hair red, and brought on the market in solid or liquid form. In Spain, ~ also indicates the lye obtained by leaving the ashes to soak in water. VIII 693a

sābūrḳān → ḤADĪD

saʿd wa-naḥs (A) : lit. the fortunate and the unfortunate; in astrology, terms used to describe the stars, based on the influence exerted by the planets and the signs of the Zodiac on earthly events. VIII 705a; *saʿd*, followed by a noun, is given to some stars and constellations. VIII 705b

♦ **al-saʿdānⁱ** (A) : lit. the two lucky (planets); in astrology, the two beneficent planets Jupiter and Venus, contrasting with Saturn and Mars, *al-naḥsānⁱ* 'the two unlucky, maleficent (planets)'. VIII 716b

sadā (A) : the warp of a fabric; the weft is called *luḥma*. S 341a

ṣadā (A) : a term with many meanings, including those of thirst, voice, echo, and screech-owl in the sense of *hāma* (or *hām*, the male owl), which denotes a bird charged with taking shape in the skull of someone who has been murdered, to return to the tomb of the dead man until vengeance was exacted. VIII 706b

ṣadaf (A, s. *ṣadafa*) : in zoology, two classes of molluscs: mussels (*Lamellibranchiata*) and snails (*Gastropoda*), both including the mother-of-pearl. VIII 707a

♦ ṣadaf al-durr, or *al-ṣadaf al-luʾluʾī* : the pearl mussel. VIII 707a

♦ ṣadaf al-firfīr, or *ṣadaf furfūra* : the snail family of the Purpura. VIII 707a

♦ ṣadaf ḳīrūkis : the trumpet-snail (*Tritonium nodiferum* L). VIII 707a

♦ ṣadafkārī ʿaṣā → DEYNEK

ṣadāḳ → MAHR

ṣadaḳa (A) : voluntary alms, a charitable donation which does not require offer and acceptance and which is moreover always irrevocable; obligatory alms are also frequently termed ~ but are commonly known as ZAKĀT. III 350a; V 424b; VIII 495a; VIII 708b

In law, ~ is also used to refer to the tax on livestock, as well as to expiatory penalties. VIII 711b

ṣadāret ḳāʾim-maḳāmi̊ → ḲĀʾIM-MAḲĀM

sadd al-dharāʾiʿ (A) : lit. closing off the means that can lead to evil; in law, a mechanism devised by Mālikī jurists to resolve loopholes in the law, probably the only source of Islamic law to be presented in a negative form. VIII 718a

sadhāb (A) : in botany, the rue plant. II 1071b

ṣadīgh (A) : 'an epithet applied to a child, in the stage extending to his completion of seven days, because his temple becomes firm only to this period' (Lane). VIII 821b

ṣādiḥa → ḲAYNA

ṣadīḳī (Ind.P), correctly *ṣiddīḳī* : in numismatics, a gold coin of the value of two pagodas, weighing 106 grains (= 6.87 g), named thus by Tīpū Sultan of Mysore. VIII 726b

sādin (A) : in early Arabia, the guardian of a shrine. VIII 728a

ṣādirāt (P, < A, s. *ṣādir*) : one of the unfixed taxes in Persia, comprising levies made to meet special expenditure such as that occasioned by a military expedition, the construction or repair of a royal building, or some special festivity, or simply to make good a deficit in the revenue. According to the nature of the occasion, the whole country or a district or section of the community only was subjected to the levy. II 152a; an administrative term covering additional cesses assessed in the same way as the basic tax, i.e. on the produce or ploughland. IV 1042a

sadīs → ʿATŪD

sādj (A) : in botany, the teak tree, *Tectona grandis* L., of the family of the *Verbenaceae*. VIII 732b

sadjʿ (A) : in pre-Islamic times, the rhythmic, rhymed utterance of the soothsayer, which does not have a fixed metre or proper rhyme and is thus distinct from both poetry and prose. V 420a; VIII 732b; in literature of the Islamic period, rhymed prose, and the basis of the *stylus ornatus*, a characteristic feature of the later INSHĀʾ literature, but also of various other genres. III 1242b; VIII 734a; along with *fāṣila*, *ḳarīna* and *sadjʿa*, ~ also refers to its rhyme, as opposed to the rhyme of verse, *ḳāfiya*. VIII 737b

♦ sadjʿa → SADJʿ

sadjda (A) : bowing down. VIII 740a

♦ sadjdat al-tilāwa : a technical term referring to the 14 Qurʾānic passages which require a ritual of bowing to be formed at the end of their recitation. VIII 740a

sadjdja, or *sādjdja* → ṢANDJ

sadjdjāda (A) : a prayer carpet. VIII 740b; S 136a

In mysticism, ~ may refer to the mystical path initiated by a founding saint, hence a synonym of *ṭarīḳa*, *silsila* and *khilāfa*. VIII 743b; and → BAYT AL-SADJDJĀDA; NAḲĪB AL-SADJDJĀDA; SHAYKH AL-SADJDJĀDA

sādjisī (A) : a strain of sheep in the time of al-Djāḥiẓ, which was very large and had wool of a pure white. S 318a

sadl → ḲABḌ

ṣadr (A, pl. *ṣudūr*) : lit. chest, breast, bosom, of all animals or of humans only. When used for only the breast of humans, ~ is contrasted with e.g. the *kirkira* of the camel-stallion, the *labān* of the horse, the *zawr* of the lion, the *djuʾdjuʾ* of the bird, etc. VIII 746b

In a figurative sense, ~ means any ‘first, front, or upper part’ of a thing. VIII 747b

In prosody, the first foot of a verse, as opposed to *ʿadjuz*, the last foot; often also loosely applied to the entire first hemistich. VIII 747b; another meaning of ~ in prosody occurs in the context of MUʿĀḲABA, to describe the case of e.g. in the RAMAL metre, the foot *fāʿilātun* having its first cord *fā-* shortened, thus *faʿilātun*, when the last cord *-tun* of the preceding foot is not shortened. VIII 747b

In architecture, the niche in the centre of the ĪWĀN’s back wall. IX 176a

In epistolography, ~ refers to the introductory formulae of letters and prefaces in books (the latter also *taṣdīr*); exordium, proem. VIII 748

In music, the chest of a stringed instrument. VIII 347b

In a personal sense, an eminent or superior person or *primus inter pares*, whence its use for a chief, president or minister; in the academic sense, ~ is mostly applied to a professor in ADAB and mostly in the derived forms *muṣaddar* and *mutaṣaddir*. The title was especially used in the Persian world for a high religious dignitary whose function was concerned essentially with the administration of religious affairs. VIII 748a; IX 738b; and → ṢADR-I AʿẒAM

In Mug̲h̲al India, the ~ was a provincial level officer in charge of land-grants. VIII 751a

♦ ṣadr al-ṣudūr : the more exalted title of *ṣadr*, borne by the Būrhānī *ṣadr*s of Transoxania in Ḳarak̲h̲ānid and Sald̲j̲ūḳ times. VIII 748b; in Mug̲h̲al India, a central minister, who controlled land-grants and cash-grants, and recommended appointments of *ḳāḍī*s 'judges' and *muftī*s 'interpreters of law and customs'. The local *ṣadr*s were his subordinates. VIII 751a

♦ **ṣadr-i aʿẓam** (T), commonly *ṣadr aʿẓam* : 'the greatest of the high dignitaries', the grand vizier, a title which, in the Ottoman empire, was used synonymously with *wezīr-i aʿẓam* from the mid-10th/16th century. In the 19th century, there were some unsuccessful attempts to convert ~ to *bas̲h̲wekīl* 'chief minister'. VIII 751b ff.

ṣadūḥ → ḲAYNA

ṣadūḳ (A) : 'truthful'; in the science of Tradition, a quality of a reliable transmitter of Tradition, although not as authoritative as T̲H̲IḲA or MUTḲIN. II 462a; VIII 983a

ṣafā (A) : lit. hard, smooth stone, whence also 'tract of stony ground'. VIII 756a

safah, safāha → ḤILM

safan (A) : in zoology, the sephen skate, whose Arabic term is found again in the Latinised nomenclature to specify a sub-species limited to a particular region (*Raia sephen*). VIII 1021b

safar (A) : journey, travel. VIII 764b

ṣafar (A) : name of the second month of the Islamic year, also called ~ *al-k̲h̲ayr* or ~ *al-muẓaffar* because of its being considered to be unlucky. VIII 764b

safarna, safarnāya → ISFIRNĪ

ṣaff (A, pl. *ṣufūf*, B *ṣoff*) : lit. rank, row or line, company of men standing in a rank, row or line.

In religious practice, ~ is used for the lines of worshippers assembled in the mosque or elsewhere for the prescribed worship. VIII 793b; a long rug with a row of MIḤRĀB decorations side by side, which may be used for communal family prayers. VIII 741b

In military terminology, the rank in an army formation. VIII 794a

In certain parts of North Africa, chiefly Algeria, southern Tunisia and Libya, ~ denotes a league, alliance, faction or party, a diffuse system of two (or more)

mutually opposing or rivalling leagues dividing villages or desert towns, clans and families, or comprising whole tribes, whose league members had a strict obligation of mutual assistance. In Morocco, the term *leff* is used with the same meaning throughout. VIII 794a

♦ ṣaffa (A) : a small embroidered bonnet trimmed with coins, worn by women in the Arab East. V 741b

♦ **al-ṣāffāt** (< *ṣaffa* 'to be lined up in a row') : title of SŪRA xxxvii and used three times in text, where generally understood to mean '(angels) standing in ranks'; in sūras xxiv and lxvii, however, ~ is glossed as 'outspread wings' of birds. VIII 798a

saffāḥ (A) : bloodthirsty; generous. Al-Saffāḥ was the surname of the first ʿAbbāsid caliph. I 103a

ṣaffāḳatān → ṢANDJ

ṣafī (A, pl. *ṣafāyā*) : in early Islam, special items consisting of immoveable property selected from booty by the leader. VIII 798a

♦ ṣafiyya (A, pl. *ṣafāyā*) : any special object of the booty which attracted the leader of a foray, and which he had the right to reserve for himself. The term appears as ṢAWĀFĪ in respect to state domains. II 869b; and → ʿANZ

♦ **ṣawāfī** (A, s. *ṣafī*) : in early Islam, crown lands in general, the private estates of the caliph being known as *ḍiyāʿ al-khāṣṣa*, *ḍiyāʿ al-sulṭān* and *ḍiyāʿ al-khulafāʾ*. IV 972b; the land which the IMĀM selects from the conquered territories for the treasury with the consent of those who had a share in the booty. VIII 798b

ṣafīḥa (A) : plate. IX 251b

♦ ṣafīḥa zarḳālliyya : in astronomy, an astrolabic plate serving the latitude of the equator, developed by two Andalusian astronomers in the 5th/11th century, Ibn al-Zarḳāllu and ʿAlī b. Khalaf. It differs from the *ṣafīḥa shakkāziyya* by its set of markings. IX 251b

safīna (A, pl. *sufun*, *safāʾin*, *safīn*) : ship; and → RAMATH

In codicology, a specific kind of shape in use for notebooks. Its architecture is that of an oblong-shaped book, but it is used in a vertical position, the sewing of the leaves being in the top edge, very much as present-day noteblocks. VIII 150a

In astronomy, ~ represents Argus, one of the eastern constellations made up of 45 stars, the brightest of which is *suhayl* or Canopus. The term *safīnat nūḥ* denotes the Great Bear. VIII 811b

♦ safīnat nūḥ → SAFĪNA

safīr (A, pl. *sufarāʾ*, T *sefīr*) : ambassador, messenger.

In Twelver shīʿism, ~ refers to the four deputies of the twelfth IMĀM during the Lesser Occultation (260-329/874-941). The office they held was called *sifāra*. Synonyms of ~ are BĀB and NĀʾIB or *nāʾib khāṣṣ*. VIII 811b ff.

In diplomacy, ~ , initially meaning envoy as well as mediator and conciliator, becomes ambassador or diplomatic agent, the post or embassy being *sifāra*. VIII 812b ff.; and → ELČI

♦ safīr fawḳa 'l-ʿāda : in diplomacy, ambassador extraordinary. VIII 813a

♦ safīr mufawwaḍ : in diplomacy, ambassador plenipotentiary. VIII 813a; the Ottoman term was *orta elči* or simply *sefīr*. II 694a; and → ELČI

♦ safīra : ambassadress, or an ambassador's wife. VIII 813a

ṣafiyya → ʿANZ; ṢAFĪ

ṣafḳa (A) : lit. striking hands together.

In law, the ratification of a commercial contract; ~ , unlike *bayʿ*, contains the meaning of a bargain that is achieved swiftly and profitably. VIII 818a; the *negotium*. I 318b

ṣafrāʾ (A) : yellow; in mediaeval texts, yellow bile, one of the four cardinal humours, the others being black bile, phlegm and blood. S 188b

safsāri (N.Afr) : a large outer wrap for women, worn in Tunisia and Libya. V 746b

safūf (A) : in medicine, a medicinal powder. IX 805a

ṣaghāʾir → KABĀʾIR

ṣaghāna → DJAGHĀNA

ṣāghir nūn → NŪN

ṣaghīr (A) : infant, child; one who has not attained to puberty (opp. *kabīr*). VIII 821b

In law, a minor, as opposed to BĀLIGH. Fifteen was generally regarded as the age that divided between majority and minority for males and females alike. I 993a; VIII 821b; and → ṢABIYY

ṣaḥāb → ṢUḤBA

ṣaḥāba (A, s. *ṣaḥābī*, or ṢĀḤIB), or AṢḤĀB : the Companions of the Prophet, dating from the first conversions (at Mecca in 610 and Medina in June 621) until the death of Anas b. Mālik (91/710 or 93/712). In earlier times the term was restricted to those who had been close to the Prophet. Later, it also included those who had met him during his lifetime, or who had seen him even if only for quite a short time. After the Qurʾān, the Companions were the sources of authentic religious doctrine. Shīʿism in general holds a different attitude towards the Companions, because with their approval the first three caliphs took away the rights of ʿAlī and his family. IV 149a; VIII 827b

ṣaḥābī → ṢAḤĀBA

ṣaḥāfī → ṢIḤĀFA

saḥara (A) : agents of fallen angels. IX 569b

saḥarī (A) : in the mediaeval Near East, a beggar who begins to ply his 'trade' before the dawn. VII 494b

ṣāḥib (A, pl. AṢḤĀB, ṢAḤĀBA) : 'companion'; the counsellor of a ruler; in compounds, partner, match (sometimes 'adversary'), someone (or something) endowed with s.th. or characterised by s.th. (syn. *dhū*), adherent of a specific concept, owner, possessor, lord, chief. VIII 830a; and → AṢḤĀB

In literature, the poet's, soothsayer's, or orator's alter ego among the DJINN, from whom he receives (some of) his inspiration (syn. *shayṭān*, *raʾī*, and *tābiʿ*). VIII 830a; IX 407a

In mysticism, the 'adept', as opposed to the *maṣḥūb* 'master', their relationship being called *ṣuḥba*. VIII 830a

♦ ṣāḥib al-ashghāl : an important official in charge of finance under the Almohads, of whom there seemed to be only one at any given time. He was always mentioned among the high officers of the state. The Ḥafṣids took over the title of ~ , and presumably his office, from the Almohads; later, this official is referred to as *munaffidh*. II 145b

♦ **ṣāḥib al-bāb** : 'high chamberlain', a title borne in Fātimid Egypt by a man of the sword counted among the first rank of AMĪRs (*al-umarāʾ al-muṭawwaḳūn* '*amīr*s bearing a collar'). The ~ ranked next after the vizier. VIII 831b

♦ ṣāḥib ḥadīth → ṢĀḤIB SUNNA

♦ ṣāḥib al-inzāl : in Muslim Spain, the functionary at court who had the responsibility of arranging accommodation for the sovereign's guests and for itinerant poets in the precincts of the palace. IX 232b

♦ ṣāḥib al-khabar : the title of one of a ruler's officers in provincial capitals whose duty it was to report to his master all new happenings, the arrival of strangers etc. This post was often given to the director of the postal service. IV 895b

♦ **ṣāḥib ḳirān** : 'Lord of the (auspicious) conjunction', a title first assumed by Tīmūr, and after his death occasionally applied to lesser sovereigns, but officially assumed by the Mughal emperor Shāh Djahān, who styled himself *ṣāḥib ḳirān-i thānī* 'the second Lord of the conjunction'. VIII 833a

In numismatics, the name of a Persian coin of 1000 dīnārs, the tenth part of a TŪMĀN; it has since been corrupted into *ḳirān* or *ḳrān*. VIII 833b; a coin standard introduced in 1241/1825 in Persia. IX 203b

♦ ṣāḥib al-layl : 'worker by night', in mediaeval Islam, the nocturnal housebreaker who got in either by boring or by scaling walls, *mutasalliḳ*. V 769a

♦ **ṣāḥib al-madīna** : in Muslim Spain, an administrative official. The duties entrusted to the holders of this title were diverse, and could involve policing and public order, justice, the levying of taxes and even leading armies, all of which leads one to think that there were no strictly determined duties but rather a nexus of functions varying in extent according to the confidence placed in the holder. VIII 833b

♦ ṣāḥib al-naẓar fi 'l-maẓālim : an official in early Islam appointed to consider complaints about injustices of the government officials, including the AMĪRs. I 439a

♦ ṣāḥib al-rikāb → RIKĀBDĀR

♦ ṣāḥib al-shārib → SĀḲĪ

♦ ṣāḥib sunna (A) : an individual from among the AHL AL-SUNNA, a MUḤAD-

DIT̲H̲ well-known for his travelling in search of Traditions containing SUNNAS all over the eastern Islamic world. The appellative *ṣāḥib ḥadīt̲h̲* is not a synonym for ~ , as the latter frequently had his handling of Traditions frowned upon and the former was known for his support of one or more BIDʿAS ‘innovations’. IX 880a f.

♦ ṣāḥib al-yad : in law, the person in possession of the object in dispute, thus the defendant. II 171a

♦ ṣāḥib-dīwān : under the Īlk̲h̲āns, the chief financial administrator, on a par with the vizier. VIII 831a

♦ ṣāḥib-i dīwān-i ʿarḍ → ʿARĪḌ

ṣaḥīfa (A, pl. *ṣuḥuf*) : lit. a flat object, a plaque, a leaf, whence, a surface or material on which one can write, applied especially to fragments of the Qurʾān or *ḥadīt̲h̲* ‘Tradition’ or any other document of a solemn nature; the written texts themselves. VIII 834b; according to Ibn Manẓūr, a ~ can be opened out, fixed on a wall or attached to something, differing from a *ruḳʿa*, which is necessarily sealed. VIII 835a; and → MUṢḤAF; RISĀLA

ṣaḥīḥ (A) : lit. sound, healthy.

In the science of Tradition, a sound Tradition, i.e. one supported by a chain of transmitters going back to the Prophet in an uninterrupted manner. Each pair of two transmitters in that chain must both be considered ʿADL ‘upright’ or ‘honest’ to the point that their testimonies are admissible in a court of law, and ḌĀBIṬ ‘painstakingly accurate’, and they should be known to have met each other. A whole collection of such Traditions is also termed ~ . III 25b; VIII 835b

In law, a valid act, i.e. an act carried out in conformity with the prescriptions of the law, and which must in principle produce all its effects. II 389b; VIII 836a; IX 324b

In grammar, ~ refers to the ‘sound’ letters, loosely the consonants of Arabic, defined by default as being neither ‘weak’ letters (→ ḤARF ʿILLA) nor vowels; in later grammar, ~ may also denote a ‘correct’ utterance. VIII 836b

sāḥil (A) : in geography, ‘edge, border zone’; in English, the Sahel, the region to the south of the Sahara (→ ṢAḤRĀʾ) characterised by periodic drought. VIII 836b

saḥḳ → SIḤĀḲ

sahm (A) : arrow; for definition, → NABL

In geometry, the versed sine (*al-d̲j̲ayb al-maʿkūs*) of the arc *a b*, if one erects a perpendicular *c b* in the middle of a chord of an arc, which reaches to the arc; the sine (*al-d̲j̲ayb al-mustawī*) which corresponds to our sine is *a c*. VIII 841b

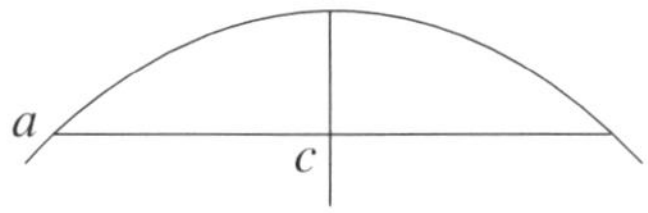

In law, ~ (pl. *ashum*) is found in the context of inheritance where it denotes the fixed share of an heir, and in the context of partnership and profit-sharing, where as a term used in modern share companies, ~ is defined as a partial ownership of a large capital. The holder is called *musāhim*. VIII 842a; and → ESHĀM

♦ sahm al-g̲h̲ayb : in astrology, the arrow, the hitting of the secret of the future. VIII 842a

♦ sahm al-ṣadārat → RASM AL-ṢADĀRAT

ṣaḥn (A) : lit. plate; a flat, stony terrain. IX 763b

In music, a cup-shape instrument, made up of a bronze cup, *ṭusayt*, which was struck against another of its kind, favoured in martial music. IX 10a

ṣaḥrāʾ (A) : fem. of *aṣḥar* 'fawn, tawny coloured'; in geography, an ensemble of stony terrain, steppelands and sands; desert. In English, the Sahara, the desert in the northern part of Africa. VIII 845b

sahrīd̲j̲ (A), or *fasḳiyya* : a reservoir of water. I 24a

saḥūr (A) : the last part of the night when, during the month of Ramaḍān, it is still permitted to eat and drink. V 372b; meal taken after midnight during the fast. IX 94b

ṣaʿīdī → RIDFA

ṣāʾifa (A, pl. *ṣawāʾif*; < *ṣayf* 'summer') : summer raid or military expedition. The term is used in the contexts of Arabo-Byzantine warfare and Muslim-Christian warfare in Spain. I 82b; VIII 869b

ṣāʾig̲h̲ (A, pl. *ṣāg̲h̲a*, *ṣawwāg̲h̲ūn*) : a goldsmith, a skilled craftsman in the mediaeval Near East. VIII 871a

saʿīr (A) : one of various words used in the Qurʾān for hell fire, occurring 16 times. Other terms used are *d̲j̲ahannam* and *saḳar*; unlike them, ~ seems to be a native Arabic formation with the meaning '[place of] fiercely kindled flame'. VIII 872a

sāʾis (A) : under the Mamlūks, a stage groom in the postal service. Other personnel were couriers, *barīdī*, and 'outriders', *sawwāḳ*. I 1045a

sāḳ (A) : lit. leg or thigh; the foot of a compass (syn. *rid̲j̲l*).

In mathematics, the perpendicular of a right-angled triangle with horizontal base, or the equal sides of an isosceles triangle (*ḍilʿ* is also used for any side of any triangle). VIII 872a

In astronomy, ~ may refer to a star that is in a leg of a constellation figure representing a person or an animal, e.g. ~ *al-asad* or *sāḳā 'l-asad* (dual) for either or both of α Bootis and α Virginis. VIII 872a

♦ sāk al-asad → SĀḲ

♦ sāk al-d̲j̲arāda : lit. the locust's leg, in astronomy, the name given to a variety of vertical sundial in which the horizontal gnomon is moved along a groove at the top of the rectangular sundial according to the season (since the shadow-lengths at the hours depend on the solar longitude). VIII 872b

ṣaḳāliba (A, s. *ṣaḳlabī*, *ṣiḳlabī*) : the Slavs and other fair-haired, ruddy-complexioned peoples of northern Europe; ethnic groups of central or eastern Europe;

white slaves of European origin; Germanic tribes. I 490b; IV 1088b; V 1120b; VIII 872b; its singular was often used in the mediaeval period in the sense of ‘eunuch’. I 33a

saḳanḳūr (A) : a Nile creature, said to be the result of a cross between a crocodile and a fish, but which seems to be in reality a kind of skunk. VIII 42b

saḳar (A) : one of the terms in the Qur’ān for ‘hell’ or, more precisely, one of the gates of hell, or else one of the ‘stages’. VIII 881a; and → SAʿĪR

saḳaṭ (A, pl. *asḳāṭ*) : lit. refuse; a term used by Abu ’l-Faḍl D̲jaʿfar al-Dimas̲h̲ḳī (6th/12th century) for spice. S 42b

♦ saḳaṭī : pedlar. IX 57a

sakbīnad̲j : sagapenum, the yellow translucent resin from *Ferula Scowitziana* which causes irritation of the skin and whose smell resembles that of asafoetida. VIII 1042b

sak̲h̲īf → SUK̲H̲F

sak̲h̲la (A, pl. *sak̲h̲l*, *sik̲h̲āl*, *suk̲h̲lān*), and *bahma* (pl. *baham*, *bihām*) : names for newborn lambs and kids, called thus indiscriminately. In ancient terminology, the distinction between lamb and kid only appeared clearly at the age of weaning (*fiṭām*), around four or five months. Until then, the young lamb-kid is called *bad̲h̲ad̲j*, *farīr*, *furār* or *furfur*. After weaning, the kid becomes a *d̲jafr* and the lamb *k̲h̲arūf*, and when the sex is determined, before it is one year old, *d̲jady* and *ʿuṭʿuṭ* for the he-kid, *ʿanāḳ* for the she-kid, *ḥamal* and *immar* for the he-lamb and *rik̲h̲l* and *immara* for the she-lamb. S 319a

sāḳī (A) : cup-bearer, the person charged with pouring wine, to be distinguished from the chief butler or sommelier (*s̲h̲arābī* or *ṣāḥib al-s̲h̲arāb*). Synonyms or quasi-synonyms that are attested are *mudīr*, *k̲h̲ādim*, and the paraphrase *d̲h̲ū zud̲jād̲jāt* ‘the one who holds the glasses’. VIII 883b

In Saudi Arabia, a term used for an underground aqueduct with surface apertures to facilitate cleaning of the channel in the district al-Aflād̲j, in southern Nad̲jd, which itself was named after the term for the same aqueduct, FALAD̲J (pl. *aflād̲j*), still used in Oman. I 233a

♦ sāḳī-nāma (P) : in Persian poetry, a genre in the MUTAḲĀRIB metre wherein the speaker calls to the SĀḲĪ for wine and complains of the instability of the world, the fickleness of destiny, and the inconstancy of his beloved. VIII 885b

saḳīfa (A) : a covered communal place appropriate for conversation and discussion, any type of covered forum or public courtyard; an approximate syn. is ṢUFFA, which seems rather to be applied to the space covered with palm foliage which constituted the primitive mosque. VIII 887b; and → RIWĀḲ; S̲H̲ARAʿA

In historical texts, ~ is applied virtually exclusively to the prolonged and acerbic negotiations which preceded the nomination of Abū Bakr as successor to the Prophet. The expression *saḳīfat Banī Sāʿida*, usually shortened to *al-~* or *yawm al-~* , is invariably applied to this specific historical episode. VIII 887b

saḳīm → ḌAʿĪF

sākin (A) : quiescent.

In grammar, ~ denotes a letter not followed by FATḤA, KASRA or ḌAMMA. III 172a

In archery, ~ denotes a way of loosing an arrow. The archer draws slowly, holding the draw in order to verify that the position of the shot is good, and then looses calmly. IV 800b

sakīna (A) : in the Qurʾān, ~ denotes God's presence, a presence shown in the divine aid vouchsafed to the Prophet and the believers in battle, giving them the victory. VIII 888b

sāḳiya (A) : a complex hydraulic machine with over two hundred component parts, still in use today. It consists essentially of a large vertical wheel erected over the water supply on a horizontal axle. This wheel carries a chain-of-pots or a bucket chain. On the other end of its axle is a gear-wheel that engages a horizontal gear-wheel to which the driving bar is attached. The animal is harnessed to the free end of this bar, and as it walks in a circular path, the gears and the wheel carrying the chain-of-pots rotate. The pots dip in succession into the water and when they reach the top, they empty into a channel. V 861a

ṣakk (A) : in classical Muslim administration, an inventory required for every issue of pay showing the names of the payees, with numbers and amounts, and bearing the signed authority to pay of the sultan. The ~ was also required for the hire of muleteers and camel-drivers. II 79a

In finance, a mandate for payment. III 283b; a medium by which funds were remitted from place to place. III 382b

saḳḳāʾ (A) : lit. water-carrier, a term denoting manual workers who carried water in a leather-bottle (*ḳirba*) or jar (KŪZ) on their shoulders or on a mule. VIII 892a

ṣaḳḳār → BAYYĀZ

ṣaḳr (A) : in zoology, the falcon. I 541b

sākw (A) : a woollen or velvet coat worn by women in the Arab East. V 741b

saḳy (A) : irrigated land, distinct from dry land, BAʿL, which was reserved for the cultivation of cereals. I 491b

sāl-nāme (T) : in Ottoman Turkish administration, official yearbooks issued by the Ottoman central government, by provincial authorities and a number of civil (ministries) and military (army, fleet) institutions, appearing between 1263/1847 and the end of the empire (1918); semi-official and non-governmental annuals. I 75a; I 975a; VIII 898a

salab (A) : spoils of the war, such as clothes, weapons and, occasionally, the mount of an adversary killed in battle. II 1005b

salaf (A) : the 'pious ancients', the main witnesses of early Islam. I 416b; IV 142a; VIII 900a,b

For ~ in law, → ḲARḌ; SALAM

♦ **al-salaf wa 'l-k͟halaf** (A) : lit. the predecessors and the successors, names given to the first three generations and to the following generations of the Muslim community respectively. VIII 900a

salam (A), or *salaf*: in law, a forward sale, one of two contracts (the other is ṢARF) which become invalid if the material transfer does not take place at the time of the agreement. In this contract, the price is to be paid at the time of the contract. IV 326a; payment at later date. VIII 493a; ~ has as its fundamental principle prepayment by a purchaser, *al-musallim*, for an object of sale, *al-musallam fīhi*, to be delivered to him by the vendor, *al-musallam ilayhi*, on a date at the end of a specified period. In such a transaction, the price agreed upon at the contracting parties' meeting for delivery of the merchandise is termed *ra's al-māl*. VIII 914b

salām (A) : safety, salvation; peace (in the sense of quietness); salutation, greeting; a formula of salutation or benediction (containing the word ~). VIII 915b; and → IFTITĀḤ

In Islamic prayer, ~ denotes a *ṣalawāt* (s. ṢALĀT) litany, pronounced from the minarets every Friday about half an hour before the beginning of the midday service before the call to prayer, *adhān*. This part of the liturgy is repeated inside the mosque before the beginning of the regular ceremonies by several people with good voices standing on a DIKKA. The same name is given to the benedictions on the Prophet which are sung during the month of Ramaḍān about half an hour after midnight from the minarets. VIII 917b

In Urdu prosody, a short poem on the theme of the Karbalā' martyrs, normally containing a word such as *salām*, *salāmī*, *mudjrā* or *mudjrā'ī* in the first few verses. VI 610b

In numismatics, ~ (sometimes abbreviated to *s*) on coins means 'of full weight, complete'. VIII 918a

salāmūra (A), or *sanamūra* : the pickling or maceration of fish with spices in brine. VIII 1023a

sālār (P) : commander; essentially a military term, as e.g. in ISPAHSĀLĀR 'supreme army commander', ~ by itself was also often used for the commander of a particular group, such as the Muslim fighters of the faith centred on Lahore in the Ghaznawid period. VIII 924a

♦ ākhur-sālār (P) : 'head of the stables', a term found as far west as Mamlūk Egypt and Syria. VIII 924b; and → AMĪR ĀKHŪR

salāriyye (T), or *salārli̊k* : one of the local taxes in the Ottoman empire which was added to the 'USHR to raise it from one-tenth to one-eighth. II 146b; VIII 203b; VIII 486b

salārli̊k → SALĀRIYYE

ṣalāṣil (A, s. *ṣalṣal*) : in music, term applied to all high-sounding clashed metal instruments. IX 10a

ṣalāt (A) : the ritual prayer, one of the five pillars of Islam. Every Muslim who has attained his majority is bound to observe the five daily prayers (→ 'AṢR, FADJR, 'ISHĀ', MAGHRIB, ẒUHR). In some circles, a sixth prayer is performed (→ ḌUḤĀ). IV 771b; V 74a ff.; V 424b; VII 27a; VIII 925a

♦ ṣalāt 'alā 'l-mayyit, or *ṣalāt al-djanāza* (or *djināza*) : the prayer over a dead person. VIII 931b

♦ ṣalāt al-ʿaẓīmiyya : in the Sanūsiyya brotherhood, a prayer for the Prophet inherited from Aḥmad b. Idrīs, which takes its title from the repetition of *Allāh al-ʿAẓīm*. IX 24b

♦ ṣalāt al-djanāza (or *djināza*) → ṢALĀT ʿALĀ ʾL-MAYYIT

♦ ṣalāt al-djumʿa → YAWM AL-DJUMʿA

♦ ṣalāt al-ghāʾib → GHĀʾIB

♦ ṣalāt al-ḥādja : in Atčeh, the *ṣalāt*s during the night of the middle of Shaʿbān. IX 154a

♦ ṣalāt al-ʿid : the festival of public prayer of the whole community, common to both of the two canonical festivals (→ ʿĪD). It has preserved older forms of the *ṣalāt* than the daily or even the Friday *ṣalāt*. It should be celebrated in the open air, which is still often done, though now mosques are preferred. The time for its performance is between sunset and the moment when the sun has reached its zenith. III 1007a; VIII 930b

♦ ṣalāt al-istisḳāʾ → ISTISḲĀʾ

♦ **ṣalāt al-khawf** : lit. the prayer of fear, an alternative ritual prayer in the context of warfare. When a Muslim army is close to the enemy, and it fears an attack, one group will perform the ritual prayer while the other stands guard, then the roles are reversed. This prayer, with its special measures and regulations, is called ~ . VIII 934a

♦ ṣalāt al-kusūf → KUSŪF

♦ ṣalāt al-nāfila → NĀFILA

♦ ṣalāt al-sahw : 'prayer of negligence', to be added immediately after the regular prayer by someone who has inadvertently omitted or misplaced one of its elements. The ~ consists of performing two prostrations with their TAKBĪR, then sitting for the TASHAHHUD and the final salutation. VIII 928a

♦ ṣalāt al-witr : a prayer performed between the evening prayer and the dawn prayer (preferably towards the end of the night). *Witr* signifies 'uneven' and denotes a special RAKʿA which is performed in isolation or which is added to one or more pairs of *rakʿa*s. VIII 930a

ṣalb (A) : crucifixion, a ḤADD punishment of death. In Abū Ḥanīfa and Mālik, ~ consists in the criminal being tied alive to a cross or a tree and his body ripped up with a spear so that he dies; this is the more original form. According to al-Shāfiʿī and Ibn Ḥanbal, the criminal is first killed with a sword and then his corpse is ignominiously exposed on a tree or cross. IV 770b; VIII 935a; in later Persian and Turkish usage, ~ meant 'hanging'. VIII 935b

salghun (T) : an Ottoman emergency levy, collected by the state in kind, cash or services rendered. VIII 486b

ṣalīb (A, pl. *ṣulub*, *ṣulbān*) : a cross, and, particularly, the object of Christian veneration. The term is used for cross-shaped marks, e.g. brands on camels and designs woven into cloth, and in legal contexts for the instrument of execution. VIII 980a sālig͟h → ʿATŪD

ṣāliḥ (A) : righteous, virtuous, incorrupt. VIII 982b; a Qurʾānic epithet applied to prophets, who are considered to be 'men of goodness'. VIII 498a; and → MURĀBIṬ

In the science of Tradition, ~ indicates a transmitter who, although otherwise praised for his upright conduct, is known to have brought into circulation one or more Traditions spuriously ascribed to the Prophet. The contents of such Traditions, as well as their underlying meaning, characterise their recognised inventor as ~ rather than as *waḍḍaʿ* 'forger' or *kad͟hd͟hāb* 'liar'. Although ~ Traditions can theoretically be found among those labelled ṢAḤĪḤ, the majority fall under the categories of *ḥasan* 'fair' or *ḍaʿīf* 'weak'. VIII 982b; ~ is used by Abū Dāʾūd for Traditions about which he has made no remark, some being sounder than others. III 25b

sālik → MAD͟JD͟HŪB; NĀFID͟H; SULŪK

salīk͟ha → DĀRṢĪNĪ

salīl (A) : a child or male offspring; a child, specifically at the time of his birth and (from then) until its weaning. VIII 821b

sālim (A) : intact, sound, i.e. free of damage or blemish, thus 'well' as opposed to 'ill'.

In numismatics, ~ means unclipped coins of full weight, or a sum of money free from charges and deductions. VIII 990a

In grammar, ~ is used to denote a) a 'sound' root, i.e. one in which none of the radicals is a 'weak' letter (*ḥarf ʿilla*), nor a hamza, nor a geminate; b) a word with a 'sound' ending, no matter whether the preceding radicals are weak or not; and c) the 'sound' plural as opposed to the broken plural. VIII 990a

In prosody, ~ denotes a regular foot, which has not undergone any of the changes called ZIḤĀFĀT or ʿILAL, or a line of poetry consisting of such feet. VIII 990a

salīt (A) : in popular Arabic usage, ~ means 'oil', in Yemen, 'sesame oil'. VIII 1000b

sāliyāne (T, < P *sāl* 'year'), or *sālyāne* : in Ottoman administration, the yearly income allotted to some categories of provincial rulers and governors (16th-19th centuries). VIII 994a

sallār (A) : under the Sald͟jūḳs, a military governor, with S͟HIḤNA. I 434a

salsabīl (A) : in the Qurʾān, the name of a fountain in Paradise. VIII 999a; and → S͟HĀDIRWĀN; UḤD͟JIYYA

ṣalṣāl (A) : dry clay. I 177b

salṭana (A) : sovereignty, ruling power. VIII 1000b

salūḳī (A) : in zoology, the name given to a member of the gazehound family, so-called because it pursues its quarry by sight and not by scent. The ~ has often been mistaken for the greyhound by travellers to the Middle East. VIII 1001b

salwā (A, pl. *salāwā*) : in zoology, both the quail (*Coturnix coturnix*, of the order of Galliformae, family of Phasianidae), also called *sumānā* (pl. *sumānayāt*); and the corncrake or landrail (*Crex crex*, *Crex pratensis*, of the Rallidae family), whose mode of life is quite similar to that of the quail. In North Africa, the corncrake is known as the 'quails' mule', *ba<u>gh</u>l al-sammān*, and the 'slow, lazy one', *abu 'l-ra<u>kh</u>wa*, because of its clumsy flight. VIII 1006a

ṣalwala → IFTITĀḤ

samʿ (A) : scriptural or Traditional authority; according to the Muʿtazila, reflection, *fikr*, must precede recourse to ~ . II 891b

♦ samʿī : authoritarian. I 410a

samāʾ (A) : lit. the upper part of anything, the sky, the heavens; for the ancient Arabs, ~ , in the most common meaning of 'heaven', was not primarily associated with the stars, but it was first the location for the 'high-flying clouds'. VIII 1014a

samāʿ (A) : 'hearing'; song, musical performance.

In lexicology and grammar, ~ signifies 'that which is founded on authority', as opposed to *ḳiyāsī* 'founded on reason'. VIII 1018a

In mysticism, the 'spiritual oratorio' which often accompanies the <u>DH</u>IKR session. II 224a; the hearing of music, the concert, and in its particular sense, the ṣūfī tradition of spiritual concert, in a more or less ritualised form. VIII 1018a

In education, ~ (pl. *samāʿāt*) means [certificate of] hearing, audition; authorisation; licence. VIII 1019b

♦ samaʿ-<u>kh</u>āna : a place for religious music-making and dancing. VIII 240b; VIII 415b

ṣama<u>gh</u> → ṢAM<u>GH</u>

samak (A, pl. *asmāk*, *sumūk*, *simāk*) : fish, whether of fresh water or of the sea, often replaced by one of its two synonyms ḤŪT and *nūn* (< Akk). VIII 1020b

♦ samak ʿankabūt : in zoology, the spider crab (*Maia squinado*). IX 40a

♦ samakat al-Iskandar : lit. the fish of Alexander [the Great], in zoology, the hammer-head shark (*Sphyrna zygaena*). VIII 1021a

samandal (A, < Gk) : in zoology, the salamander, which many early Arabic authors identified as a bird. VIII 1023b

samar (A, pl. *asmār*) : a conversation, an evening gossip; stories told at an evening gathering (especially with Ibn al-Nadīm) or stories in general; tales of the supernatural; reports. III 369b

ṣam<u>gh</u> (A, pl. *ṣumū<u>gh</u>*), or *ṣama<u>gh</u>* : gum resins, the desiccated latexes of several plants and the mixtures of natural resins (*rātīna<u>dj</u>*) with gum-like substances; ~ is usually used alone for ~ *ʿarabī*, gum arabic, so called because it was exported from Arab ports and spread by the Arabs. VIII 1042b

samīḳān (A, s. *samīḳ*) : two yokelets, a form of the yoke consisting of two pieces of wood, each encircling the neck of the ox like a collar and joining under the animal's dewlap, attached to each other by means of a rope. VII 22b

samīn → DASIM

ṣāmit (A) : among several extremist <u>sh</u>īʿī groups, the designation of a messenger of God who does not reveal a new Law, as opposed to *al*-NĀṬIḲ, a speaking prophet. VIII 1047a

samm → SUMM

sāmm (A), or *al-sāmma* : a term for 'death', derived from *samm* 'poison' (→ SUMM). IX 872a

sammād → KANNĀS

ṣammān (A) : in geography, hard stony ground by the side of sands. VIII 1048a

samn (A) : butter, made from cows', goats' and ewes' milk, heated over the fire to extract its impurities, and hence called clarified butter (as distinct from *zubd* which is butter made from churned milk). VIII 1048b; S 318b

samt (A, pl. *sumūt*) : in astronomy, azimuth or direction, usually applied to the direction of a celestial object measured on the horizon, determined by the arc of the horizon between the east- or west-points and the foot of the vertical arc through the celestial object. The complementary arc measured from the meridian was called *inḥirāf*, *munḥarifa* being applied to a vertical sundial inclined at a specific angle to the meridian. VIII 1054a

♦ samt al-ra'shat : lit. direction of the head; in astronomy, a term used to denote the point of the celestial sphere directly above the observer. VIII 1054a

samūm (A, > Eng *simoom*) : a hot wind of the desert accompanied by whirlwinds of dust and sand, and set in motion by moving depressions which form within the trade winds or calm zones of the high, subtropical depressions. This wind is especially characteristic of the Sahara, in Egypt, in Arabia and in Mesopotamia. VIII 1056a; ~ is hardly used in North Africa, where the hot wind is called, after its direction of origin, and according to the various regions, *ḳeblī* or *sharḳī*. VIII 1056b

ṣanʿa → GHINĀʾ

♦ ṣanʿat-i ḳaṭʿ → ḲAṬʿ

sanad → ISNĀD; SILSILA

sanadjāt, or *ṣanadjāt* (< P *sang*; s. *sandja* or *ṣandja*) : the weights of a balance, steelyard; weights of a clock. IX 3a; counterweights or pellets discharged from the mouths of falcons in water-clocks. IX 3b

ṣanam (A) : image, representation; idol. ~ progressively replaced NUṢUB; from being the rough stone making up the *nuṣub*, the idol became 'a carved stone'. IX 5b; IX 282a

sanamūra → SALĀMŪRA

ṣanawbar : pine nut, pine-cone. V 536a; IX 8b

ṣandal (A) : in botany, sandalwood. IX 9a

In the Maghrib, ~ indicates thyme (*nammām*) and the wild cultivated mint. IX 9b

ṣandj, or *ṣindj* (A) : in music, the generic term for any kind of cymbal. Other terms for the cymbal are *zīl* (< T *zill*), *kās*, *kāsa* or *ka's*, *sadjdja* or *sādjdja*, *fuḳaysha* (in Syria), *nuwayḳsa* (in Morocco), *ṣaffāḳatān*, and *musāfiḳ(a)*. IX 9b ff.; as *ṣandj* *ṣīnī* (Chinese ~), this musical instrument with 'open strings' and played on with beating rods was described by Ibn Sīnā and Ibn Zayla. It later became known as the SANṬŪR, and is clearly the dulcimer. VII 191a

sandjaḳ (T) : a flag, standard; ensign, cornet. I 4b; IX 11b

In Ottoman administration, ~ was a political region, a district of the feudal cavalry, and an administrative unit. I 468b; II 723b; IX 13a; and → LIWĀʾ

♦ sandjaḳdār : 'royal standard-bearer', distinguished in Mamlūk times from the ordinary *ʿalamdār*. IX 12b

♦ **sandjaḳ-i sherīf**, *liwāʾ-i sherīf*, or *ʿalem-i nebewī* (T) : the sacred standard of the Prophet, kept in the palace of Topkapı at Istanbul. IX 13b

ṣandūḳ → ḲABR

ṣanf : in geography, an island; a kingdom of the mainland, bordering on the sea; or a sea, apparently referring in travel accounts to Čampā or Champa, situated between Cambodia and the delta of the Song Coi in Vietnam. IX 17a

sang-i mūṣā (Ind.P) : black onyx. VIII 269a

ṣāniʿ → ADJĪR

sāniḥ (A) : a term applied to a wild animal or bird which passes from left to right before a traveller or hunter; it is generally interpreted as a good omen. I 1048a; 'that which travels from right to left', one of the technical terms designating the directions of a bird's flight, or an animal's steps, which play an important part in the application of divination known as FAʾL, ṬĪRA and ZADJR. II 760a; IV 290b

sāniya (A) : in Muslim Spain, a type of pumping machine to irrigate land, along with the NĀʿŪRA. I 492a

saniyya (A) : in the Ottoman empire, lands which were the private freehold of the sultan, administered by a well-organised establishment called the *dāʾira saniyya*. After the revolution of 1908, ~ lands were ceded to the state and were transferred to the newly-formed department of *al-amlāk al-mudawwara*. S 179a

sanṭūr (A, < Ar), or *sinṭīr* : the dulcimer, a stringed musical instrument of similar structure to the psaltery, ḲĀNŪN, but with two of its sides oblique instead of one. The strings, which are mounted dichordally in Egypt, are of metal and are beaten with sticks instead of plectra as in the *ḳānūn*. In the time of Ibn Sīnā, it was called *ṣandj ṣīnī*. VII 191a; IX 19b

♦ sanṭūr turkī : a dulcimer which is very popular in present-day Turkey. It has 160 strings, grouped in fives, giving 32 notes, and a two octave chromatic scale. VII 191b

♦ sanṭūr fransiz : a dulcimer which is very popular in present-day Turkey. It is mounted with 105 strings, grouped in fives, which are placed on the sound-chest in the Occidental way. VII 191b

sarāb (A) : mirage, specifically the illusion of water seen at midday which appears to be on the ground, as opposed to *āl*, which is seen early and late in the day and makes things appear to float in mid-air and quiver. IX 27a

saraḳusṭiyya (A) : a type of fur produced in Saraḳusṭa, in Muslim Spain. IX 37a

sarāparda (P) : lit. palace curtain, term applied to the great tent carried round by the sultans of the Saldjūḳs. IX 39b; and → ĀFRĀG

sarāpāy (P) : in Persian literature, a genre of poetry devoted to the description of an ideal human body 'from top to toe', fashionable in the 10th-11th/16th-17th centuries. VI 834b

sarār → MUNSALAKH

saraṭān (A, pl. *sarāṭīn*) : in zoology, crustaceans (*ḳishriyyāt*) in general and, more specifically, those which are collected for human consumption (*maḥāra*). IX 40a

In astronomy, *al-~* is the term for Cancer, one of the twelve zodiacal constellations. VII 83a; IX 40b

♦ saraṭān al-baḥr : in zoology, the lobster (*Homarus vulgaris*), the crab (*Carcinus*). IX 40a, where many synonyms are found

♦ saraṭān nahrī : in zoology, the crayfish, river lobster. IX 40a

♦ saraṭān nāsik : in zoology, the hermit crab, soldier crab, also known as *ḳaṭā*. IX 40a

sarāy (P) : dwelling, habitation, house, palace; compounded with another substantive ~ indicates a particular kind of building, as in KĀRWĀN SARĀY. IX 44a

sarb (A) : in zoology, the grey gilthead, whose Arabic term is found again in the Latinised nomenclature to specify a sub-species limited to a particular region (*Chrysophrys sarba*). VIII 1021a

ṣard → SARDSĪR

sardāb (P, pl. *sarādīb*; A *sirdāb*) : lit. cool water; an underground recess in a dwelling, motivated by the fierce sun and hot summer of ʿIrāḳ and Persia. II 114a; IX 49b; any kind of underground room or passage. IX 49b

sardār (P, A *sirdār*, T *serdār*) : lit. holding or possessing the head; supreme military commander, whose post or office is called *sardāriyyat*. ~ *bahādur* was a title of honour in British India, given to Indian commissioned officers. IX 50b; in the Ottoman army, *serdār-i ekrem* was the term for the commander-in-chief. IX 14a

♦ sardāriyyat → SARDĀR

sardsīr (P, A *ṣard*) : lit. cold region; a geographical term used to denote cool, temperate highland regions. It also serves as a synonym to the Turkish ḲÎSHLAḲ, i.e. the winter pasture grounds of nomads. In Arabic, ~ or *ṣard* is particularly used for the mountainous Zagros hinterland of Fārs and Kirmān. V 183a

sardj (A, pl. *surūdj*) : horse saddle. IX 51a

♦ sarīdja : mule or camel saddle. IX 51a

ṣarf (A) : in law, the contract of exchange. This is one of two contracts which become invalid if the material transfer does not take place at the time of the agreement, the other being SALAM. IV 326a

In early Arabic grammar, full declination, said of a noun; also, as used by al-Farrāʾ in particular, the divergence or non-identity between two constituents of the sentence. In later grammer ~ came to indicate the science of'morphology'. IX 53a,b; and → NAḤW

sarhang (P) : in medieval Persian (para)military, a rank of officer or commander. In modern Persian, the rank of colonel. IX 54a

sarīʿ (A) : in prosody, the name of the ninth Arabic metre. I 670a; IX 54b

sārīfūn → SHĪḤ

sāriḳ → LIṢṢ

ṣarı̊ḳ (T) : a headband, used to wind around a ḲAVUḲ. IV 806a

sariḳa (A) : theft, for which the Qurʾān prescribes cutting off the right hand. Islamic legal theory distinguishes between two types: *al-sariḳa al-ṣughrā* 'theft' and *al-sariḳa al-kubrā* 'highway robbery or brigandage'. V 768a; IX 62b

sārindā : in music, an Indian open chest viol with three strings. VIII 348b

sarīr (A), and *takht* : a throne-like seat, not used at mealtimes, however. In the case of ~ , two people could sit on it, hence it was quite a long seat; *takht* could mean any of the following: board, seat, throne, sofa, bed, calculating tablet, chest or box. S 99a,b

sarkār → FAWDJDĀR; MAḤALL

♦ **sarkār āḳā** (P) : 'lord and chief', a term used for a number of heterodox religious leaders within the broad shīʿī tradition. IX 63b

ṣarmātiyya (A) : shoemakers. IX 168b

sarrākh → HINDIBĀʾ

sārt (T, < San) : merchant; all sedentary Muslims, irrespective of language or ethnicity; later, ~ came to mean the Persian-speaking sedentary population, in contrast to *türk*, which was used for the Turkic-speaking nomadic or semi-nomadic population; even later, among the Uzbeks in the 19th century, ~ was chiefly used for Turkic-speaking or bilingual town-dwellers, while *tādjīk*, earlier synonymous, was reserved for Persian-speakers only. IX 66b ff.

sarw (A) : in botany, a cypress. IX 70a

sāsānī (A, P, < A *banū sāsān*) : beggar, trickster; pertaining to magic or sleight-of-hand. IX 70a

satr (A) : among the Ismāʿīliyya, ~ denotes the periods of absence of an IMĀM. II 1026b

Among the Druze, ~ refers to the period of absence of al-Ḥākim and Ḥamza. II 1026b

saʾuri, or *tuzghü* : under the Īlkhāns, an *ad hoc* impost laid by governors and officials in position of power on the population under their control. VIII 312b

ṣawāb → KHAṬĀʾ

sawād (A) : rural district, environs of town. VIII 636a; IX 87a; 'black land', the oldest Arabic name for the alluvial land on the Euphrates and Tigris, now Iraq. IX 87a

ṣawāfī → ṢAFĪ

sawār → SUWĀR

sawgand-nāma (P) : in literature, an oath-poem. IX 116b

sawīḳ (A) : in pre-Islamic times, a kind of dried barley meal to which was added water, butter or fat from the tails of sheep. II 1059a; IX 93b; also, a fermented beverage with a basis of barley and honey. II 1060a

ṣawlad̲j̲ān → KURA

sawm (A) : in law, the bargaining involving both vendor and purchaser that occurs before a sale. ~ differs from BAYʿ in that the former is no more than an offer to enter into the latter after the manifest approval of the vendor. IX 93b

ṣawm (A), or *ṣiyām* : fasting, one of the five pillars of Islam. V 424b; IX 94a

♦ ṣawm al-taṭawwuʿ : in religious law, voluntary or supererogatory fasting. IX 95a

ṣawmaʿa (A) : the minaret, other terms for the minaret being MANĀRA and *miʾd̲h̲ana*. Originally, ~ means the cell in which a person (usually a monk) secludes himself, with the particular gloss that the cell has a slender pointed apex; later, ~ came to designate the entire structure of which the cell was a small part. VI 362b

In North Africa, ~ is the standard term for minaret, and is also used more generally to mean 'a higher place' and 'a high building'. VI 362b

sawsan → SŪSAN

ṣawt (A) : in grammar, the resonance (emitted from the chest), which the Arab grammarians contrast with *nafas*, the expiratory breath. III 597a; sound or speech sound. IX 96a

♦ **ṣawtiyya** (A) : in grammar, the modern phonetical description of Arabic. IX 95b

sawwāk → SĀʾIS

saʿy (A) : during the pilgrimage, the ritual of traversing seven times (four times going and three times returning) the distance between al-Ṣafā and al-Marwa. III 35a; IX 97b

ṣayd (A) : the pursuit and capture of wild animals; wild game. IX 98b

ṣaydana (A), or *ṣaydala* : in the eastern Muslim world, pharmacology, in the meaning of pharmacognosy; the druggist's actual store of drugs; the handbook of drugs, the pharmacopeia. The druggist is called *al-ṣaydanālī* or *al-ṣaydanānī*, and is practically synonymous with ʿAṬṬĀR. In the West, the corresponding terms are *[ʿilm] al-adwiya al-mufrada* or *al-murakkaba*, or *[ʿilm] al-ʿuṭūr/ʿaṭṭār*. IX 100a

♦ ṣaydanānī, or *ṣaydanālī* → ṢAYDANA

sayd̲j̲ān (A) : in zoology, the sidjan scarus, whose Arabic term is found again in the Latinised nomenclature to specify a sub-species limited to a particular region (*Scarus siganus*). VIII 1021b

ṣayf → ṢĀʾIFA

sayfī (A) : the 'sword-member', one of two classes of the ordinary members of the AK̲H̲Ī organisation, YIGIT, who probably were the active members. The other class was made up of *ḳawlī*s 'word-members'. I 323a

ṣayḥa (Yem) : a declaimer of tribal poetry. IX 234b

saykarān (A, < Syr shakhrōnā), or *sīkrān*, *shūkrān* : in botany, henbane (*hyoscyamus*) to the early physicians of western Islam. Later Arab botanists used ~ for another henbane (*hyoscyamus muticus*) which drives the taker mad, and also for the hemlock. I 1014b

sayl → NAHR

sayr (A) : in mysticism, a visionary voyage, a degree of the mystical journey. IX 863a

ṣayr (A) : small fish, preserved by salting and smoking. VIII 1023a

sayyāra → KAWKAB

sayyiʾa → DHANB

sayyid (A, pl. *asyād, sāda, sādāt*) : originally chief, e.g. of an Arabian tribe; later, in Islamic times, a title of honour for descendants of the Prophet. IX 115a; IX 333a; master; the equivalent of Mr or Esquire. I 24b; II 687b; IX 332a ff; and → ASHRĀF; MAWLĀY; MURĀBIṬ

♦ sayyid al-shuhadāʾ : appellation of the Prophet's paternal uncle, Ḥamza b. ʿAbd al-Muṭṭalib. IX 204b

♦ sayyid al-tumūr → ṢUFRĪ

♦ sayyida : the title of Madam, in contemporary Arabic usage. IX 332b

♦ sayyidī, or *sīdī* : originally the term used by a slave to address his/her master, came to be applied to persons regarded as holy, especially mystical masters or ṣūfīs in general. IX 332b f.

sāz (T), or *bağlama* : in music, the Turkish lute; used in Persian for a musical instrument in general, stringed instruments, wind instruments, and the musical band itself. IX 120a; a stringed instrument, which frequently accompanied Turkish folk religious poetry, NEFES. VIII 2b; for names in our time corresponding to the different lute sizes, IX 120a

In Balūčistān, ~ also means the tuning of instruments. IX 120a

♦ sāz-i kāsāt (P) : lit. musical bowls, earthenware bowls, the notes of which were determined by the amount of water with which each was filled. IX 11b

♦ sāz-i alwāḥ-i fūlād (P) : 'instrument of slabs of steel', a glockenspiel, comprising 35 slabs, each giving a particular note. IX 11b

sebkha → SABKHA

sefīr → SAFĪR

segāh → SHASHMAḲOM

sekbān (T) : under the Ottomans, a formation of auxiliaries, abolished in 1131/1718, whose members later enlisted in newly-raised formations. II 1121a; III 317b

sekkīn (Mor) : a sword with an almost straight blade, carried by the horsemen making up the *djīsh* (→ DJAYSH). II 511a

selāmlİḳ (T), or *selāmlİḳ dāʾiresi* : under the Ottomans, the outer, more public rooms of a traditionally-arranged house, used e.g. for the reception of guests and non-family members. IX 123a; the men's part of a house. IX 540b

♦ selāmlıḳ ālāyı : the Ottoman sultan's ceremonial procession from the palace to the mosque for Friday worship. IX 123a

semer (T) : a kind of padded saddle, worn on the back of a street-porter in Istanbul, *ḥammāl*, on which the weight of the burden rests. III 139a

sêqut : a land-leasing system in Kurdish Iran, in which the landowner supplies soil and water and receives two-thirds of the harvest. V 473b

serambi : in Indonesia, the front veranda of a mosque, often the place of the religious court; by extension, Islamic judge. VIII 294a

serʿasker (T) : under the Ottomans, an army commander; after the destruction of the Janissaries in 1241/1826, ~ denoted a commanding officer who combined the functions of commander-in-chief and minister of war, inheriting also the responsibility for public security, police, firefighting etc. in the capital. I 838a; II 513a; III 552b

serbest (T) : an Ottoman term connoting the absence of limitations or restrictions. III 589b

♦ serbest tīmār : under the Ottomans, a fief in which all the revenues go to the timariot, as against an ordinary *tīmār* in which certain revenues are reserved for the imperial exchequer. III 589b

serčeshme (T) : under the Ottomans, the title for the leader of all irregular militia, LEWENDS. VIII 185a

serdār → SARDĀR

sergüdhesht-nāme (T) : in Turkish literature, a genre of the tale of adventure, where the poet tells the story of an affair with one beautiful person or stories of four people. IX 213a

setre (T) : a military garment covering the knee and fastened at the front, worn in Turkey up to the 13th/19th century. V 752a; VIII 371a

sêykbar : a land-leasing system in Kurdish Iran, in which the landowner supplies the land, the water, the seed and the beasts of labour, and takes a portion of the harvest. V 473b

shāʾ al-ḍaʾn (A) , and *shiyāh al-ḍaʾn, ḍāʾina* : sheep. S 316b

shab-niwīs (Ind.P) : in the Dihlī sultanate, the secretarial officer on night duty in the palace. IV 759a

shaʿb (A, pl. *shuʿūb*) : in the Sabaean social organisation of pre-Islamic southwest Arabia, a social unit consisting of a number of clans, one of which occupied a dominating position. IV 746a; IV 819a; IX 150b

In geography, ~ (pl. *shiʿbān*) is the coral reef, in particular those off the Arabian coast southwards to the Red Sea. The term ~ is not used for the reef on the Arabian side of the Persian Gulf, where e.g. FASHT is used. I 535a

In politics, ~ evolved from 'a people' to 'the people', i.e. the ruled, later to signify the common people, the deprived lower classes, those who were previously outside the circle of power (also often simply called *djamāhīr* 'masses'). IX 151a ff.

shabāb (A) : young manhood, one of the terms designating a specific period within childhood. VIII 821b; this period extends from puberty to the end of the thirties, or from 15 to 32 years of age. IX 383a

♦ shabābiyya, or *shabība* : with *shabāb*, youth and the beginnings of adulthood, as well as the vigour of this age. IX 383a

shabāblikiyya (A, < Ar ?) : a variety of outer garment, ʿABĀʾ, made in Ḥasbaya and worn in Syria and Palestine. V 741b

shaʿbadha (A), or *shaʿwadha* : in divination, prestidigitation, sleight of hand, hence *mushaʿbidh* (*mushaʿwidh*) 'magician, trickster'. IX 152b

shabala (A) : a technical term of childhood, said of someone who has become a youth or young man. VIII 822a

shaʿbān (A) : name of the eighth month of the Islamic lunar year, called *shab-i barāt* in Indian Islam. IX 154a

♦ shaʿbāna (Mor) : in Morocco, a festival resembling a carnival celebrated on the last day of SHAʿBĀN. IX 154b

shabb → ḲILY

shabība → SHABĀBIYYA

shabrūsh → NUḤĀM

shabūb (A) : in the terminology of horse-riding, a horse that rears. II 954a

shadd (A), or *shadd al-wasṭ* 'binding up the waist' : the act of girding with an initiatic belt or girdle; in certain mystical orders, the belt or girdle itself. The origin of the act of girding is attributed to the *kustī*, the sacred girdle of the Zoroastrians, the girding of which was a rite of passage into manhood. The novice girded with the ~ was known as *mashdūd* or, more fully, *mashdūd al-wasṭ*. IX 167a

♦ shadd al-walad : in guild terminology, the ceremony whereby the apprentice entered into his profession. IX 168b

♦ shadda (A), or *tashdīd* : in orthography, the special sign for marking the doubling of a consonant. IV 1120a

shadh (T) : a rank given to senior members of the princely family below the Ḳaghan. III 1060b

shādhdh (A) : in the science of Tradition, a Tradition from a single authority which differs from what others report. If it differs from what people of greater authority transmit, or if its transmitter is not of sufficient reliability to have his unsupported Traditions accepted, it is rejected. III 25b; VII 576a; irregular. IX 371a

shadīda (A) : 'energetic'; in grammar, a division equivalent in modern phonetics to 'occlusive', designating the letters *hamza, ḳ, dj, ṭ, t, d, b*. III 599a

shādirwān (A, < P) : originally, a precious curtain or drapery suspended on tents of sovereigns and leaders and from balconies of palaces; in architecture, a wall fountain surmounted by a decorative niche, usually made of painted and gilded wood with MUḲARNAS, and connected to a sloping marble panel, *salsabīl*, which led the water from the wall down into a stone or marble basin. The function of the ~ , which faced the SABĪL window, was not only decorative but it served also to air the water coming from the cistern. VIII 680a; IX 175a

shadjara (A) : in botany, a tree; and → RIDFA

♦ shadjarat al-ḥubb → IKLĪL AL-MALIK

♦ shadjarat al-ṣanam → SIRĀDJ AL-ḲUṬRUB

shadjawī (A) : in the mediaeval Near East, a beggar who pretends to have been imprisoned and loaded with chains for fifty years. VII 494b

shadjriyya (A) : in grammar, a term used by al-Khalīl possibly denoting lateral, for use in phonetics, but its meaning remains obscure. III 598a

shādūf (A) : the contrivance used for raising water, still in use in certain eastern countries. It is a simple machine consisting of a wooden beam pivoted on a raised fulcrum. At one end of the beam is a bucket, at the other end a counterweight. The bucket is dipped into the water, then the beam is rotated by means of the counterweight and the contents of the bucket are emptied into a cistern or supply channel. IV 629a; V 861a

shafāʿa (A) : in eschatology, the intercession or mediation by certain persons, and notably Muḥammad, for others on the Last Day. He who makes the intercession is called both *shāfiʿ* and *shafīʿ*. I 334b; IX 177b

In law, intercession for a debtor. IX 177b

Also, the laying of a petition before a king. IX 177b

shafaḳ (A) : the red colour of the sky after sunset. I 733b; the evening twilight, the time at which the MAGHRIB prayer should be performed. V 709a; VIII 928b; morning or evening twilight, the periods between daybreak and sunrise and between sunset and nightfall. IX 179b

♦ al-shafaḳ al-aḥmar : 'the red dawn', which follows upon the 'true dawn' (→ AL-FADJR AL-KĀDHIB). IX 179b

shāgird → MURĪD

shāh (P) : king; in set phrases ~ means 'pre-eminent, principal'. IX 190b f.

In chess, the chesspiece king. A game was won by ~ *māt* 'checkmate'. IX 366b

In the Indian subcontinent, ~ is appended to the names of persons claiming descent from the Prophet and has today become a surname. IX 191a

♦ **shāhanshāh** (P) : king of kings. IX 190b

♦ **shāhī** (P) : lit. 'royal, kingly', in numismatics, a Ṣafawid principal coin, valued at 50 dīnārs. VIII 790a; IX 203a

♦ shāhī safīd : the 'white *shāhī*', term used to distinguish the silver coin from the copper or 'black' *shāhī*. IX 203b

♦ shāhmurk (A, < P *shāhmurgh* 'kingbird') : in zoology, one of the arabicised forms for the Sultan-fowl, whose splendid plumage earned him the title of 'king' of the birds. S 20a

♦ shāhzāde (P, T **shehzāde**) : prince, one of the titles used for the male children born to a reigning Ottoman sultan, gradually superseding the earlier term ČELEBI. IX 414a

shahāda (A) : the Islamic confession of faith, one of the five pillars of Islam. I 332b; IX 201a

In law, testimony, witnessing. I 28b; IX 201a

In Urdu poetry, the *shahādat* is the part of the elegy, MARTHIYA, where the death of the martyr is described, either al-Ḥusayn or some member of his family. VI 611b

♦ shahādat al-lafīf : in law, the testimony of a group of at least twelve men, who need not be ʿADL, a practice which came into existence during the 16th and 17th centuries in North Africa. IX 208a

♦ al-shahāda bi ʾl-tasāmuʿ : in law, testimony on the strength of public knowledge, i.e. without having witnessed the event or the legal act that is at the basis of it. IX 208a

♦ al-shahāda ʿalā ʾl-shahāda : in law, the testimony of a witness which is transmitted by two other witnesses. IX 208a

shāhbandar (P) : lit. 'harbour, port master', a term for a customs officer, collector of taxes; in Turkish usage, a consul and, formerly, a merchant's syndic. I 1013a; IX 193b

In Indonesia, ~ denotes the harbour master, appointed by the local ruler or sultan and chosen from among the foreign traders who had settled in the port. In big harbours, more than one ~ were sometimes active. He supervised the merchandise, took care of the transport and storage, inspected the markets and guaranteed the security of the ships and the well-being of their crew, passengers and tradesmen. Tolls were fixed on his estimate of the value of the goods carried by the ship. VI 209b; IX 194b; S 199b

shāhdānadj (P) : hemp; in modern-day Persian, the hemp seed. III 267a; IX 202a

shāhī → ČAY; MUḤAMMADĪ

shāhid (A, pl. **shawāhid**) : witness, one who gives testimony, *shahāda,* which in Islamic law is the paramount medium of legal evidence, alongside *iḳrār* 'acknowledgement' and *yamīn* 'oath'. IX 207a; and → SHĀHID ʿADL

In literary theory, a probative quotation, most often testimony in verse, which serves to establish a rule in the 'literary sciences'. IX 370b; proof text. IX 459a

♦ shāhid ʿadl, or, briefly, *shāhid* or *ʿadl* : in law, a professional witness whose ʿADĀLA has been established by the court, first appearing in Egypt at the beginning of the 8th century AD. IX 208a

shahīd (A, pl. *shuhadāʾ*) : witness; martyr, of which there are two types: *shuhadāʾ al-maʿraka* 'battlefield martyrs', who have special burial rites, and *shuhadāʾ al-ākhira* 'martyrs in the next world only'. IX 203b ff.

♦ shuhadāʾ al-dunyā : 'martyrs in this world only', martyrs accorded the burial rights of the battlefield martyrs, *shuhadāʾ al-maʿraka*, but not the rewards in the next world, because they went into battle without the right intention. IX 206b

♦ shuhadāʾ al-ghurba : 'martyrs who died far from home', those who leave their homes, e.g. in order to preserve their faith in times of persecution, and die in a foreign land. IX 206a

♦ shuhadāʾ al-ḥubb : 'martyrs of love', according to a prophetic Tradition, those who love, remain chaste, conceal their secret and die. IX 206a

shāhīn : a musical instrument which would appear to have been a small three-holed recorder such as was common with pipe and tabor players in mediaeval Western Europe. It was played with the fingers of one hand, the other hand being used for beating the drum. VII 209b; and → ČAKİR

shaḥna-i mandī → MANDĪ

shāhnāmedji → SHEHNĀMEDJI

shahr (P, T *shehir*) : town; kingdom. IX 212a

♦ **shahrangīz** (P), and *shahrāshūb* 'upsetting the town' : in Persian literature, a genre of short poetical witticisms or love poems on young artisans, usually quatrains but also occurring as ḲAṢĪDAS, fashionable in the 10th-11th/16th-17th centuries. IV 59a; VI 834a; VIII 776b; IX 212a

♦ shahr-āshob (U, < P *shahrāshūb*) : in Urdu literature, a socially-motivated poem, whose main purpose is the portrayal of a city in disarray, by naming a series of professions and describing the state of affairs governing the individuals associated with each of them. IX 213b

♦ shahrāshūb → SHAHRANGĪZ

♦ **shehir emāneti** (T) : in the Ottoman empire, the term for two successive institutions, filled by the *shehir emīni*. The first involved the construction, repair, provisioning and payment of salaries of the personnel of the imperial palaces, and the functionary was in rank one of the four great civilian dignitaries of the outside administration of the palace. This institution died out to appear again in the latter half of the 19th century whereby the functionary, who was more of a town prefect, had duties as that of cleansing and keeping tidy the city and touring the markets and bazaars. IX 413a

♦ **shehir ketkhüdasi̊** (T) : in the Ottoman empire, an official whose primary function was to collect the specified taxation from a town or its quarters. IX 414a

shahristān (P) : lit. place of kingship; province, provincial capital, (large) town; in modern Iran, a sub-provincial administrative district. I 2b; IX 220a

shāhrukhī → TANGA-YI NUḲRA

shāʿir (A) : poet. IX 225a; in northern Egypt, ~ has come to mean Gypsy poets who perform on the Egyptian two-string spike-fiddle, *rabāb*. IX 235b; and → KHAṬĪB

♦ shāʿir al-balāṭ : poet laureate. IX 229b

♦ syair (Mal, Ind, < A *shāʿir*) : an extended verse form, which may run to hundreds of stanzas, each of which consists of four lines with the same end rhyme. The composer of ~ is called a *penyair*. IX 244a

♦ shāʿira (A, pl. *shaʿāʾir*) : term denoting the *budna* (→ SINĀM), extended in the plural to all the rites of the pilgrimage. IX 424b

shaʿīr (A) : in botany, barley. IX 225a

♦ māʾ shaʿīr : lit. barley water; the name for ‘barley beer’, of which a special variety was drunk in mediaeval Islam during the nights of the month of Ramaḍān. VI 721b

♦ shaʿīra : in music, the cylinder inserted into the head of a reed-pipe which lowered the pitch when required. Later, this device was called *ṭawḳ* or *faṣl*. VII 207a

shaḳāʾ → SHAḲĀWA

shaḳāʾiḳ → SHAḲĪḲAT AL-NUʿMĀN

shaḳāwa (A), or *shaḳwa*, *shaḳāʾ* : misfortune, misery, used both in the meaning of a situation in this world and in the hereafter. IX 246b

In astrology, the concept of ~ is described by the term *naḥs* (→ SAʿD WA-NAḤS). IX 247a

shākhiṣ → MIḲYĀS

shakhṣ (A) : lit. bodily form, shape; in philosophy, an individual, a person. I 409b; IX 247b f.; and → MIḲYĀS

In modern law, ~ is found in the compounds *shakhṣ ṭabīʿī* ‘natural person’ and *shakhṣ iʿtibārī* ‘assumed person’, coined under the influence of western legal systems. IX 247b

♦ shakhṣiyya : legal personality, a concept that does not exist in Islamic law, at least historically, and is subsumed by AHLIYYA. IX 248a

shakhshīkha : in music, the general term for the rattle. IX 11b

shakhtūr (Ir) : a wooden raft, used on the Euphrates since it is not navigable by steamers. I 461a

shaḳīḳa (A) : a full sister, in the law of inheritance, as opposed to a half-sister on the father’s side, *ukht li ’l-ab*. I 320a

♦ **shaḳīḳat al-nuʿmān** (A, P *lāla*, Ber *ṭīkūk*, SpA *ḥababawar*), or *shaḳāʾiḳ al-nuʿmān*, *shaḳir* : in botany, the anemone. Both *shaḳāʾiḳ* and *nuʿmān* can be used separately as synonyms. IX 248b

shākima → ḤAKMA

shaḳir → SHAḲĪḲAT AL-NUʿMĀN

shākiriyya (A, < P *čākir*) : a term denoting private militias fighting under the patronage of princes from the ruling dynasty, or commanders belonging to the class of military nobility, during Umayyad and ʿAbbāsid rule. IX 249b

shakk (A) : perplexity, uncertainty, doubt. There is some suggestion that ~ refers to the objective fact of uncertainty and another word, *rayb*, to the state of perplexity consequent to that fact. IX 250a

In mineralogy, arsenic. IX 872b

♦ shakka → ITHTHAGHARA

shāḳḳ → ʿAṢĀ

shakkāziyya (A) : in astronomy, the term for the markings, consisting of two families of orthogonal circles, of a universal stereographic projection which underlies a family of astronomical instruments serving all terrestrial latitudes. IX 251b shakshāk (N.Afr) : in North Africa, a round tambourine with both snares and jingling implements, called in other parts *ṭabīla*. II 621b

shaḳshīr → ČAḲSHĪR

shakwa (A) : a goatskin container, in which fresh milk is churned by swinging on posts. S 318b

shaḳwa → SHAḲĀWA

shalabī → ČELEBĪ

shalba (A) : in zoology, a silurus of the Nile and the Niger, whose Arabic term is found again in the Latinised nomenclature to specify a sub-species limited to a particular region (*Schilbe mystus*). VIII 1021b

shalīl → KABŪSH

shālish → DJĀLISH

shāma (A, pl. *shāmāt*) : naevus, skin blemish, mole. Originally ~ denoted the coloured marks on a horse's body, but is now, with *khāl* (pl. *khīlān*), applied to all marks of a colour different from the main body, including accidental marks, abcesses or freckles caused by an illness and presaging death. IX 281a

shamʿa (A) : candle. IX 281b

♦ shamʿadān : candelabrum, candlestick. IX 282a

♦ shamʿī, or **shammāʿ** : candlemaker. IX 288a

shaman (P) : idolator, an unspecified type of non-Muslim religious person (syn. *but-parast*). IX 282a

shambar (A) : a large veil common to the Hebron area and southern Palestine. V 741b

shamla (A), or *shimāl* : a bag, perhaps made of hedgehog skin, which is used to enclose the maternal mammaries of small livestock in order to wean their young. Another method, also used, is applying a gag (*faṭṭāma*) to the muzzle of the young. S 319a

shams (A) : the sun. IX 291a

♦ **shamsa**, or *shamsiyya* : a jewel used by the ʿAbbāsid and Fāṭimid caliphs as one of the insignia of kingship; not a sunshade but a kind of suspended crown, made out of gold and silver, studded with pearls and precious stones, and hoisted up by the aid of a chain. IX 298b; and → MIẒALLA

♦ shamsī : an alcoholic drink made of honey and dry raisins, of which the mediaeval Egyptians were very fond. VII 907b

♦ shamsiyya → SHAMSA

shamṭāʾ → SHAYB

shamūs (A) : in the terminology of horse-riding, a horse that is difficult to mount. II 954a

shānī → SHĪNĪ

shanīn (A) : a drink make of whey or milk diluted with water. II 1061a

shaʿr (A) : hair, pelt. IX 311b; the wool of goats. IX 764b; the hair of camels and dromedaries is usually called ~ and occasionally WABAR. IX 312a shara'a (A) : verb relating to watering animals at a permanent water-hole, implying lapping at or drinking water; to drive (or lead) animals to water; as noun (pl. *ashruʿ*) ~ means a projecting, covered area, syn. SAḲĪFA. IX 326a

sharābī → SĀḲĪ

sharaf (A) : elevation, nobility, pre-eminence, in the physical and moral sense (cf. *madjd* 'illustriousness on account of birth', *ḥasab* 'individual quality, merit', and *karam* 'illustriousness acquired by oneself'). IX 313b

♦ sharaf al-nisba : the descendants of al-Ḥasan and al-Ḥusayn, one of a class of noble blood, *sharaf*, that existed in Egyptian terminology of the 9th/15th century. IX 332a

sharak (A, pl. *ashrāk*) : a noose, used in hunting small-sized birds by placing them in line on a taut cord. IX 98b

sharḥ (A, pl. *shurūḥ*) : a commentary on a text. I 593a; IX 317a

♦ al-sharḥ al-mazdjī : in literature, a method of interweaving the text with its commentary in such a way that the two together form a smooth and coherent whole. IX 209b

shārī → SHIRĀʾ

shāriʿ (A, pl. *shawāriʿ*) : clearly-defined way, main road, highway; situated on a main road, at the side of a road. ~ was generally the term for a main arterial road, lesser roads in the vocabulary of urban patterning being *sikka*, *ḥāra*, *darb*, *ʿaṭfa* and *zuḳāḳ*, in Cairo, and *nahdj* and *zanḳa*, in Tunis. IX 320b; law-giver, characteristically Muḥammad in his function as model and exemplar of the law, but in a rare extension of meaning, sometimes transferred to the jurists. IX 322a f.

sharīʿa (A, pl. *sharāʾiʿ*) : a prophetic religion in its totality; within Muslim discourse, the rules and regulations governing the lives of Muslims. IX 321a; Islamic jurisprudence. VIII 249b; the area around a water-hole, or the point of entry to it, the place at which the animals drink; the seashore, with special reference to animals which come there. IX 326a

In the Qurʾān, where it appears once, and in Tradition literature, ~ designates a way or path, divinely appointed. Its cognate *shirʿa* and synonym *minhādj* are also used once. IX 321a

sharīdj → FILḲ

sharīf (A, pl. *ashrāf*, **shurafāʾ**, N.Afr *shorfā*) : 'noble', 'exalted', 'eminent', among the pre-Islamic Arab tribes a free man who could claim a distinguished rank because of his descent from illustrious ancestors. In Islamic times, ~ was especially applied to the descendant of Muḥammad's family, AHL AL-BAYT, and with time to the ʿAlids alone. VII 926b; IX 329b ff.; and → ḌAʿĪF

In North Africa, a person who traces his origin to the Prophet's family through ʿAlī and Fāṭima. I 371b

sharika (A), or *shirka* : in law, partnership. VII 671b; IX 348a

♦ sharikat al-ʿaḳd : in law, a contractual partnership. VII 671b

♦ sharikat amwāl : in law, partnership of capital, contracted when two partners put their capital in one project and agree on certain conditions for administration, profit and loss. IX 348b

♦ sharikat ʿinān → ʿINĀN

♦ sharikat al-milk : in law, a proprietary partnership. VII 671b

♦ sharikat al-ṣanāʾiʿ : in law, partnership in crafts or trades. IX 348b

♦ sharikat wudjūh : in law, partnership of personal credit, contracted when two well-known persons ask others to sell to them goods without payment on the basis of their reputation, and then sell the goods for cash. IX 348b

shaʿriyya (A) : a black face veil of goat's wool or horse hair, worn by women in the Arab East. V 741b

sharkh (A) : in the terminology of childhood, 'a youth or young man; the offspring of a man' (Lane). VIII 821b

sharḳi (T) : lit. oriental, eastern; in Turkish music, a certain form of classical Turkish song. IX 353b

In Turkish literature, a genre of Turkish strophic poem composed on literary lines with the aim of being set to music. IX 353b; a type of folk-poetry of Anatolia. I 677b

sharrāliya → HINDIBĀʾ

sharṭ (A, pl. *shurūṭ*, *sharāʾiṭ*) : lit. condition; in law, condition, term, stipulation. IX 358b; and → KHIYĀR AL-SHARṬ

In logic, hypothesis, condition. IX 359b; and → ḲIYĀS ḤAMLĪ

In grammar, ~ denotes the protasis of a conditional sentence, the apodisis being variously referred to as *djawāb*, *djazāʾ* or *mudjāzāt*. IX 360a

In its plural form, *shurūṭ* refers in law to a wide variety of prescribed model documents used in transactions. IX 359a; and → MUWATHTHIḲ

In medicine, scarification. II 481b

shāsh (A) : the winding cloth of a turban in Syria and Palestine. V 741b; and → LITHĀM

♦ shāsha (A) : in Oman and the United Arab Emirates, the local open boat made from palm fibres. VII 53b

shashmaḳom (Tadzhik, < P *shash*, A *maḳām*) : the modal and formal concept of art music played in the urban centres of Uzbekistan. The six *maḳom* cycles are called *buzruk* (< *buzurg*), *rost* (< *rāst*), *navo* (< *nawā*), *dugokh* (< *dogāh*), *segosh* (< *segāh*) and *iroḳ* (< *ʿirāḳ*), based on four of the former twelve main modes and two former 'derived' modes. IX 360b f.

shaṣna (A) : a mole or barrier built in the water for protection. I 180b

shatar (A) : in medicine, an infection of the eyelid. IX 9b

shaṭawī (A) : textile goods from Shaṭā, in Egypt, highly praised by travellers. IX 361a

shatfa (A) : a horizontal strip on an emblem or insignia, RANK, introduced onto the shield in the early 14th century. VIII 431b

shaṭḥ (A, pl. *shaṭaḥāt*), or *shaṭḥiyya* : in mysticism, ecstatic expression, commonly used for mystical sayings that are frequently outrageous in character. I 60b; IX 361b

shāṭir (A, pl. *shuṭṭār*) : 'artful (ones)', the name given to groups of young men who were considered elements of disorder in mediaeval Baghdad. II 961b; and → KHALĪʿ

shaṭr (A) : in prosody, a single hemistich, of 15 or less syllables. VIII 583a

shaṭrandj (P, < San) : the game of chess. The chesspieces were called: *shāh* 'king', *firzān* (*firz*) 'queen', lit. adviser, *fīl* 'bishop', lit. elephant, *baydaḳ* 'pawn', lit. footman, *rukhkh* 'rook', *faras* 'horse'. IX 366a f.

♦ shaṭrandjiyya : a meat pie containing bones with no meat on them. IX 367a

shaṭṭ (A) : originally, one side of a camel's hump; eventually ~ came to mean a stream's bank, and occasionally it was extended to mean a plot of land, close to the bank of a stream. In modern-day Iraq, ~ can describe a stream, as also in ~ *al-ʿarab*, the tidal estuary formed by the united stream of the Tigris and the Euphrates. IX 368a

In geography, ~ is used in the high plains of North Africa and the northern Sahara for the saline pasturages surrounding a salt flat, *sabkha*, often confused with the latter. IX 368a

shaṭwa (A) : a Bethlehem married woman's hat. V 741b

shāʾūsh → ČĀʾŪSH

shaʿwadha → SHAʿBADHA

♦ shaʿwadhī (A) : express courier. IX 152b

shawāhid → SHĀHID

shawdar (A, P *čādur*), or *shawdhar* : a black, enveloping outer wrap for women worn in the Arab East. V 741b

shāwī (A, pl. **shāwiya**) : sheep-breeder or herder. In Syria and the Arabian peninsula, *shāwiya* is the urban term, *ḥukra* being the desert term, for tribes specialising in herding flocks. IX 374b ff.

♦ shāwiya → SHĀWĪ

shawḳ (A) : desire, longing, yearning, craving, much used as a technical term in Islamic religious thought and mysticism. IX 376b

shawka (A) : in botany, *al-shawka al-bayḍāʾ* is the whitethorn, the white acanthus, mostly rendered with *bādhāward*, which is actually the Arabic acanthus, *al-shawka al-ʿarabiyya*. Synonyms or other types of the thistle are *ṭūb(a)* (< L *tubus*), *ibrat al-rāʿī*, *ibrat al-rāhib*, *ayfd* and *tāfrūt* (both Berber). IX 496b

shawna → SHĪNĪ

shāy → ČAY

shayʾ (A) : a thing, entity (L *res*). IX 380b

In the Qurʾān, ~ assumed the meaning of 'belongings' or 'property'. II 361a

In mathematics, ~ is another word for absolute number, especially to denote the unknown quantity in linear problems (syn. *ḍilʿ*). It also serves as a general expression for auxiliary quantities and often takes the place of *al-djidhr*, the root.

II 361a ff.; and → MĀL

♦ shayʾiyya : 'thingness' of e.g. the non-being, *maʿdūm*, a philosophical concept. IX 381a

shayb (A) : lit. white hair; old age, senescence (syn. *aghtham* 'grey which is white rather than black'); in poetry, ~ is frequently found in the expression *al-shayb wa 'l-shabāb* 'old age and youth'. Although not restricted to males, the term *shamṭāʾ* is cited by lexicographers for feminine old age. IX 313a; IX 383a

shaykh (A, pl. *shuyūkh*, *mashāyikh*) : lit. an elder, someone whose age appears advanced and whose hair has gone white, used for a man over fifty years old. ~ carries the idea of authority and prestige and is thus applied to the chief of any human group: family, tribe, guild, etc., as well as to the head of a religious establishment and to any Muslim scholar of a certain level of attainment. IV 335a; VI 725b; VIII 207a; IX 115b; IX 397a; when used with a complement, the term designated the master of various fields. V 1131a; and → MASHYAKHA; MURSHID

In mysticism, the ~ is the spiritual master, the novice's 'educator', ~ *al-tarbiya*. IX 397b

One of three grades of the AKHĪ organisation, which seems to have played practically no active role, but probably refers to the leader of a dervish settlement, to which the members of the organization felt themselves attached. I 323a

In Ḥaḍramawt, ~ denotes class distinction, not a tribal chief; the *mashāyikh* are those noble families with the right to the hereditary title of ~ . S 339a

In Muslim India, ~ is one of the four divisions among the ASHRĀF, Muslims of foreign ancestry; the ~ is said to be descended from the early Muslims of Mecca and Medina. III 411a; IX 397b

♦ shaykh al-baḥr : in zoology, the seal. Other designations are *ʿīdj al-baḥr*, *fuḳma*, *fuḳḳama*, and *bū mnīr*. VIII 1022b

♦ **shaykh al-balad** : the mayor of a town, or an employee looking after the good management of the town. IX 397b; in 18th-century Ottoman Egypt, the title given to the most powerful BEY in Cairo, superseding the titles *amīr miṣr*, *kabīr al-ḳawm*, and *kabīr al-balad*. IX 398b

♦ shaykh al-ḥadjdj → MUṬAWWIF

♦ **shaykh al-islām** : an honorific title applied essentially to religious dignitaries in the Islamic world up to the early 20th century. Under the Ottomans, ~ was given to the individual in the Ottoman empire in whom the right to issue an opinion on a point of law, FATWĀ, was vested exclusively. The office of the ~ was abolished in 1924 and was replaced by a department for religious affairs, attached to the Prime Minister. I 837b; II 867a; III 552b; III 1152a; IX 399b f.

♦ shaykh al-sadjdjāda, or *walī 'l-sadjdjāda* : 'the prayer-rug sitter', a term normally applied to leaders of ṣūfī communities or heads of holy lineages who fell heir to the spiritual authority and blessing of a revered saintly founder. VIII 743b; IX 398a

♦ shaykh al-shuyūkh : during Ayyūbid and Mamlūk rule, the holder of the office of controlling the practice of ṣūfism, whose role was more political than spiritual. The Ottomans later introduced the *shaykh al-ṭuruḳ* 'head of the mystical paths' with the same function. IX 397b

♦ shaykh al-yahūdī, or *abū marīna* : in zoology, the monk seal. VIII 1022b

♦ shaykha : a woman in whom is recognised the quality of a spiritual master, above all vis-à-vis other women. IX 398a; commune. I 863a

shayṭān (A, pl. *shayāṭīn*) : evil spirit, demon, devil, either human or DJINN. IX 406b ff.; and → RADJĪM; ṢĀḤIB

shayyād (A) : a speaker, or one who recited or sang stories or poems in a loud voice, term used in Persian and Turkish between the 7th/13th and 10th/16th centuries, and replaced in the following century by e.g. the Persian *ḳiṣṣakhān*. Its etymology is unclear, Arabic lexicographers equating it with Persian *shayd* 'deceit' which brought about its equation with 'liar' or 'trickster'. Later 19th-century European writers added the meaning 'dervish'. IX 409b f.

shehīlī (Alg) : the sirocco, which brings temperatures of 104° F and higher several times a year. I 366a

shehir emāneti, ~ emīni, ~ ketkhüdasi → SHAHR

shehnāmedji (T), or **shāhnāmedji** : in Ottoman literature, the term for a writer of literary-historical works in a style inspired by the *Shāh-nāma* of Firdawsī. IX 211b

shehrī → ḲASSĀM

shehu (Hau, < A SHAYKH) : once the coveted title of a great scholar and teacher, ~ is nowadays commonly used as a personal name. In the phrase *shehu malami* (→ MALAM), it is used as an epithet for a distinguished exponent of the Islamic sciences. VI 223a

shehzāde → SHĀHZĀDE

shenlik (T) : an Ottoman term for public festivities which marked special occasions, involving the participation of the entire populace. IX 416b

sherbet (T, < A *sharba*) : a sweet, cold drink, made of various fruit juices. Another fruit-based drink, possibly of alcoholic content, was *khō shāb*. VI 864b; IX 417a

shewādān (P) : cellars in houses in Shushtar, in which the inhabitants shelter in the excessive heat of summer; syn. SARDĀB. IX 512b

shiʿār (A) : a term with various significations: the rallying signal for war or for a travel expedition, war cry, standard, mark indicating the place of standing of soldiers in battle or pilgrims in the pilgrimage; a syn. of *idmāʾ* 'to draw blood'; the distinctive clothing, etc. which the DHIMMĪs were required to wear in ʿAbbāsid and later times. IX 424a

shiʿb (A) : a ravine. IX 425a

shibiththth (A, pop. *shibitt*, *shabath*, B *aslīlī*) : in botany, dill. IX 431b

shibr (A) : 'span', that is, the span of the hand from the thumb to the little finger, a pre-modern basic measure of length. VII 137b shibriḳ → DIRṢ

shighār (A) : the exchange of a girl for a wife by her brother or father without any money being spent. This type of union is also applied to married women, whereby a man repudiates his wife and exchanges her for another man's. Although forbidden in Islam, marriage by exchange is nonetheless practised even to the present day. VI 475b

shīḥ (A, < Ar *sīḥā*) : in botany, the plant species Artemisia (*Compositae*), as well as the specific *Artemisia iudaica L.* Other specific types of ~ are *sārīfūn* (probably *A. maritima*), *ṭarkhūn* (*A. dracunculus* 'tarragon'), *ḳayṣūm* (*A. abrotanum* 'southernwood'), *birindjāsaf* (*A. vulgaris* 'mugwort'), and AFSANTĪN or *abū shinthiyā* 'wormwood'. IX 434b

shihāb (A, pl. *shuhub*) : in astronomy, a shooting star. A synonym, of Persian origin, was *nayzak* (pl. *nayāzik*). VIII 103a

shiḥna (A) : a body of armed men, sufficing for the guarding and control of a town or district on the part of the sultan; used by Abu 'l-Faḍl Bayhaḳī in the sense of the commander of such an armed body. IX 437a; under the Saldjūḳs and their successors, a military commander installed at the head of each city, who exercised military, political, and administrative functions; ~ was later superseded by the term DĀRŪGHA. VIII 402b; IX 15a; IX 437a

♦ shiḥnagī : the office of a SHIḤNA. IX 437b

shiḥra (A) : a narrow tract of land. IX 439a

shihrī → HADJĪN

shikārī (P, < *shikār* 'game, prey; the chase, hunting') : a native hunter or stalker, who accompanied European hunters and sportsmen, term current in Muslim India, passing into Urdu and Hindi. IX 439b; *shikargāh* is the game reserve. IX 638a

shikasta (P), *shikasta nastaʿlīḳ*, or *khaṭṭ-i shikasta* : a script which came into existence at the beginning of the 11th/17th century under the Ṣafawids, as a result of writing NASTAʿLĪḲ rapidly and of the calligraphers being under the influence of SHIKASTA TAʿLĪḲ. ~ was used mostly in writing letters and sometimes for official correspondence. Nowadays it is sometimes used in writing poetry in an artistic fashion. IV 1124b; a highly cursive style developed from TAʿLĪḲ and NASTAʿLĪḲ, and now mostly in use in Iran, where it has become a means of expression of the new Islamic Iranian identity. VIII 151b

♦ shikasta taʿlīḳ (P), or *taʿlīḳ* : 'broken' TAʿLĪḲ, the result of writing *taʿlīḳ* rapidly. The letters are written in a more intricate style. It started to appear in the 8th/14th century but declined in use when NASTAʿLĪḲ started to spread in the 10th/16th century. IV 1124a

shīkha (Mor, pl. *shīkhāt*) : a free female singer in Morocco, who participates, in a company of *shīkhāt*, in family feasts or solemn ceremonies. IV 823b

shiḳḳ : in Muslim India, a word sometimes used to denote a province in the 9th/15th century. II 273a

♦ shiḳḳdār : in Muslim India, the functionary in charge of the general administration and civil affairs during the Dihlī sultanate. Later, he was replaced by the FAWDJDĀR under the Mughals. II 273a; II 868a; and → ḲĀNUNGO

shimāl → SHAMLA

shīnī (A) : the average mediaeval Muslim warship. It was a two-banked galley, with a special officer in charge of each bank. The ~ carried a crew of about 140 to 180 oarsmen. VII 44b; IX 444a; other transcriptions are *shawna*, *shīniyya*, *shānī* (pl. *shawānī*). VIII 810a

shinḳāb → SHUNḲUB

shintiyān (Egy) : in Egypt, 'drawers' for women. IX 677b

shipship (T) : an Ottoman Turkish shoe, mule, without heels, but with the end slightly raised and a supple sole. V 752b

shiʿr (A) : poetry. IX 448b; injurious poetry, *hidjāʾ*, especially for the archaic and Umayyad periods. IX 449a; collections of poetry, also called *khabar*. IX 318a; in Urdu, alongside the general meaning of poetry (syn. *shāʿirī*), ~ also means a verse or couplet. IX 469b

♦ al-shiʿr al-ḥurr : free verse. IX 464a; S 34b

♦ al-shiʿr al-mursal : blank verse. VIII 909a; IX 464a; S 34b

shiʿrā (A) : in astronomy, Sirius, the brightest fixed star in the sky; the dual *al-shiʿrayān* designated both Sirius and Procyon. IX 471b, where also can be found the specifying adjectives, which were sometimes used on their own

shirʿa (A) : a fine string, as stretched on a bow, or a lute. IX 326a; and → SHARĪʿA

shirāʾ (A) : buying and selling, a term used in both early Islamic theology, especially associated with the Khāridjites, who were known as *shārī* (pl. *shurāt*), and in (commercial) law, where it had the predominant meaning of buying rather than selling. IX 470a

shirāʿ (A) : in seafaring, the sail of a ship, stretched above it to catch the wind; the neck of a camel. IX 326a

shīradj → DUHN AL-ḤALL

shirāḥa (A) : in agriculture, palm-protection. VI 832a

shirk (A) : polytheism, the giving of partners to God. I 333a; III 1059b; IX 484b; the idolatry of self and of creaturely things. I 70a; and → IKHLĀṢ

♦ shirka → SHARIKA

shīshak → KAMĀNDJA

shīsham (Sin) : in botany, Indian rosewood. IX 638a

shitr → MIẒALLA

shiyāh al-ḍaʾn → SHĀʾ AL-ḌAʾN

shiyāh al-maʿz → MĀʿIZA

shölen → TOY

shorfā → SHARĪF

shūʿ → BĀN

shuʿāʿ (A) : used in the literature of scholastic theology for both the light rays emanating, for example, from the sun, and the visual rays (i.e. rays emanating from the eye). VI 376a

shubha (A, pl. *shubah, shubuhāt*) : lit. resemblance; in theology and philosophy, ~ is a false or specious argument which 'resembles' a valid one; a counter-argument in later scholastic theology. IX 492b
In penal law, semblance, an illicit act which nevertheless 'resembles' a licit one, one of the grounds for avoidance of the fixed penalties. II 831b; III 20b; IX 492b
♦ shubhat al-ʿaḳd : in penal law, a case where the act has been done as the result of a contract which observed merely the conditions of formation. II 832a; IX 493a
♦ shubhat al-fāʿil : in Shāfiʿī law, a case of SHUBHA, as when another woman is substituted for the bride on the wedding night. IX 493a
♦ shubhat al-ṭarīḳ, or *shubhat al-djiha* : in Shāfiʿī law, a case of SHUBHA, applied in cases where the schools of law disagree. IX 493a
♦ shubha fi 'l-fiʿl, or *shubhat ishtibāh, shubhat mushābaha* : in penal law, a case where the action with which the accused is charged resembles an action which is normally permissable. II 832a; IX 492b
♦ shubha fi 'l-maḥall, or *shubhat mulk, shubha ḥukmiyya* : in penal law, a case where the illegality founded upon a proof text may appear dubious because of the existence of another, ambiguous text. II 832a; IX 492b

shudjāʿ → FARD

shufʿa (A) : in law, the right of pre-emption, the right of the co-owner to buy out his partner's share which is for sale. I 172b; III 513a; V 878b; IX 494b

shuhadāʾ → SHAHĪD

shuhra → MAʿRIFA

shukāʿā (A), or *shukāʿ* : in botany, the thistle. IX 496b

shuḳḳa (A, pl. *shiḳāḳ*) : on the Arabian peninsula, an area of gravel and limestone. VIII 575b; and → FALĪDJA

shukkub → SHUNḲUB

shukr (A) : thankfulness, gratitude; achnowledgment; praise. When used on the part of God, ~ means recompense, reward. IX 496b

shūkrān → SAYKARĀN

shūnīz → KAMMŪN

shunḳub (A, pl. *shanāḳib*), or *shukkub, shinḳāb* : in zoology, the common snipe (*Capella gallinago gallinago*), known in the Maghrib and Egypt as *kannis, dadjādjat al-māʾ* and *bikāsīn* (< Fr *bécassine*) and in Iraq as *djuhlūl*, the same term as for the sandpiper (*Tringa*); also, with *shunḳub al-baḥr*, the trumpet fish (*Centriscus*). IX 504b
♦ shunḳub kabīr : the great or solitary snipe (*Capella major* or *media*). IX 504b
♦ shunḳub muzawwaḳ, or *shunḳub khawlī* (Egy) : the painted snipe (*Rostratula benghalensis*). IX 504b
♦ shunḳub ṣaghīr : the Jack snipe (*Limnocryptes minimus*). IX 504b

shūrā (A) : the council; consultative assembly; consultation. I 110a; V 1084a; IX

504b; from the early 19th century, ~ was applied to every type of Western governmental body, including elective and representative parliaments. IX 506a

♦ shūrā-yi dewlet (T) : in the Ottoman empire, a council of justice composed of Muslims and Christians, set up in 1868 under ʿAbd al-ʿAzīz. This was a court of review in administrative cases; it also had certain consultative functions, and was supposed to prepare the drafts of new laws. I 56b; II 641b

shurafāʾ (A, Mor *shorfā*, s. *sharīf*) → SHARĪF

shurāʿiyya (A) : a long-necked camel. IX 326a

shurb (A) : drinking, drink; salted water, drunk e.g. at the ceremony of girding the initiatic belt among the *fityān* (→ FATĀ). IX 167a

shurshur → ABŪ BARĀḲISH

shurṭa (A, pl. *shuraṭ*, pop. pl. *shurṭiyya*) : a special corps, which came into being in early Islam and which was more closely linked to the caliph or governor than the army. This corps was basically concerned less with war than with the maintenance of internal order and, little by little, became a kind of police force. An individual in such a corps is a *shurṭī*. II 505a; IV 373b; VIII 402b; IX 510a

♦ shurṭa ṣughrā : in Muslim Spain, one of three categories of the *shurṭa*, whose jurisdiction, according to Ibn Khaldūn, was applied to the ʿĀMMA, as opposed to the *shurṭa ʿulyā*, whose jurisdiction concerned the misdemeanours of people belonging to the KHĀṢṢA. The third category, *shurṭa wusṭā*, is not mentioned by Ibn Khaldūn. IX 510b

♦ shurṭa ʿulyā → SHURṬA ṢUGHRĀ

♦ shurṭa wusṭā → SHURṬA ṢUGHRĀ

shurūṭ → ʿAHDNĀME; SHARṬ

♦ shurūṭī → MUWATHTHIḲ

shuṭfa (A) : a badge; under the Mamlūks a green badge that the male SHARĪF had to wear fastened to his turban to distinguish him from others. IX 334a

shuturbān → DEVEDJI̊

shuʿūbiyya (A, < *shuʿūb*, s. SHAʿB) : a movement in early Islam which denied any privileged position of the Arabs. IX 513b

shuʿūr (A) : in philosophy, the notion of consciousness or apperception. I 112b

shuwayḥī (A), or *shuwayḥiyya* : a woman's belt, usually woven of goat's hair and quite ornate, worn mainly in southern Palestine. V 741b

shuyūʿiyya (A) : communism (syn. *ibāḥiyya*). IX 517a

sibāḥī → SIPĀHĪ

sibāḳ → SABḲ

ṣiʾbān → ḲAML

ṣiddīḳ (A) : 'eminently veracious', 'believing', in Qurʾānic usage, applied to the prophets Abraham and Idrīs, and to Mary and Joseph. As an epithet, *al-ṣiddīḳ* is applied to the first caliph Abū Bakr. IX 534b

♦ ṣiddīḳī → ṢADĪḲĪ

sīdī → MAWLĀY; SAYYIDĪ

sidjdjīl (A, < Akk) : one of the mysterious words of the Qur'ān, together with SIDJDJĪN, denoting a hard, flint-like stone. IX 538a

sidjdjīn (A) : one of the mysterious words of the Qur'ān, still interpreted in various ways as either the seventh and lowest earth, a rock or well in hell, the home of Iblīs, hell fire, something painful, hard, durable or eternal (influenced by its resemblance to SIDJDJĪL), or the name of the record in which all human acts are set down. IX 538a

sidjill (A, < Ar, < L *sigillum*; pl. *sidjillāt*) : lit. seal, in early Arabic referring to a document, or to a scroll on which documents are written. II 302b; IX 538b; also, the judicial verdict prepared by a judge. II 79a; IX 538b; during the Mamlūk period, the judicial court registers kept by official witnesses. IX 538b

In classical Muslim administration, ~ is the letter given to an envoy or messenger, authorising him, on arrival, to recover the expenses of his journey from any ʿĀMIL. II 79a; IX 538b

In notarial usage, ~ referred to an official record of a case, based on and including the *maḥḍar* 'the minutes of the case or transaction conducted before a judge' and the judge's decision or verdict. IX 539a

In Ottoman administrative usage, ~ was a general term used for 'register'. IX 539a

sidjn (A), and *ḥabs* : prison. IX 547a

ṣidḳ (A) : 'truthfulness, sincerity', a term in mysticism, where it is defined as the complete agreement of one's inner convictions and outward acts. IX 548b

sidr (A, n. of unity *sidra*) : in botany, the jujube, a shrub or tree of the various Rhammaceae belonging to the genus *Ziziphus*, called *ʿilb* in the south of Arabia. I 540b; IX 549a

♦ **sidrat al-muntahā** : 'the lote tree on the boundary', a Qur'ānic phrase describing where Muḥammad met Gabriel for the second time. IX 550a

ṣidriyya (A) : a sleeveless vest worn by both sexes in the Arab East. V 741b

ṣifa (A, pl. *ṣifāt*) : attribute, lit. description; in its plural form, *ṣifāt*, used in theology in particular for the divine attributes. I 333b; I 411a; IX 551b; S 344b

In grammar, ~ (syn. NAʿT) denotes any general or descriptive predicate term, a qualifying adjective. IV 182a; IX 551a; S 344a

sifāra → SAFĪR

ṣifr (A) : 'empty'; in mathematics, the small circle indicating the absence of number, i.e. the zero. III 1139b; IX 556b

ṣīgha (A) : lit. form. I 318b

In Persia, a designation for a second temporary marriage, MUTʿA, with the same man after the expiry of the first, in order to evade the period of abstention, ʿIDDA, which in such a case is considered to be unnecessary. The woman in such an arrangement is also called ~ . VII 759a

sïghnaḳ (T) : place of refuge. IX 557b

ṣiḥāfa (A), or *ṣaḥāfa* : the written press, profession of the journalist, *ṣaḥāfī*. IX 558a

siḥāḳ (A), or *saḥḳ*, *tasāḥuḳ* : lesbianism. Lesbians are called *sāḥiḳāt*, *saḥḥāḳāt* or *musāḥiḳāt*. II 551a; IX 565b

siḥr (A) : lawful, 'white magic', also called *al-ukhdha* 'charm, incantation', and sorcery, 'black magic'. I 1084b; IV 770a; V 100b; IX 567b

siḳāya (A) : the institution of providing water for the pilgrims in Mecca. I 9a; I 80a; VI 144b; the name of the building, close to Zamzam, where the distribution took place. VII 840a

In Fās, the popular term for public fountain. VIII 680b

sikbādj (A, < P *sik* 'vinegar' and *bādj* 'type [of meat]') : a vinegar- and flour-based meat stew or broth cooked with vegetables, fruit, spices and date-juice, originally from the Sāsānid court and later popular under the ʿAbbāsids. IX 576a

sikka (A) : lit. an iron ploughshare; an iron stamp or die used for stamping coins. From this latter meaning, ~ came to denote the result of the stamping, i.e. the legends on the coins, and then the whole operation of minting coins; coinage. I 117b; IX 591b; a post 'stage', also called *ribāṭ* in Persia, of which there were no less than 930 in the ʿAbbāsid empire. I 1044b; VIII 500a; a ploughshare, also called *sinn*, *sinna*, *naʿl*. VII 22a; and → SHĀRIʿ

♦ **sikkat al-ḥadīd** (A, P *rāh-i āhan*, T *demiryolu*) : lit. iron line; the railway. IX 600b

sikke-zen (T), or *sikke-kün* : in Ottoman times, the worker who, under strict supervision, prepared the steel moulds in the mints. II 119a

ṣiḳlabī → ṢAḲĀLIBA

sīkrān → SAYKARĀN

ṣīkūk → BARBŪSHA

ṣila (A) : lit. connection, what is connected; also, a gift, reward, remuneration (syn. *djāʾiza*). IX 607b; and → WAṢL

In grammar 'adjunct' (syn. *ḥashw*, *zāʾid*, *faḍl*, *laghw*), a syntactical term which denotes the clause which complements such word classes termed *mawṣūl*, e.g. the relative pronouns *alladhī*, *man*, *mā*, *ayy-* and the subordinative *an*, *anna*. IX 603a

In literature, ~ denotes the continuation, the complement of a work (for syn., IX 603b). In certain cases, e.g. historiography, a ~ can be both a kind of summary or partial rewriting, with additions of the original work, and a continuation of the latter. IX 603b f.; and → FĀʾIT

silāḥdār (P, A *amīr silāḥ*) : lit. armsbearer, a military-administrative title and function gong back to the days of the Great Saldjūḳs. Chief of the army's arsenal where the armour and weapons were stored, the ~ was one of the most trusted personnel in the sultan's palace, directly responsible to the sultan. Among the Mamlūks, the ~ was one of the nine most important office holders. IX 609b

♦ silāḥdārlar → DÖRT BÖLÜK

♦ silāḥdāriyya (A) : under the Mamlūks, a royal unit with a number of horsemen ranging from 110 to 120, commanded by a SILĀḤDĀR. IX 610a

siʿlāt (A, pl. *saʿālī*) : the female of the G͟HŪL, a fabulous being, although the sources do not all agree on the distinction. II 1078b

silb (A) : in mediaeval agriculture, a term for the piece of wood whose end joins on to the ploughshare, clearly the same pole or beam called *waydj̲* and *hays* in Yemen or in Oman. VII 22a

silḳ (A) : beets, one of the Prophet's preferred vegetables. II 1058a

sillawr (A) : in zoology, the sheat fish. VIII 1021a

silsal → ḲARḲAL

silsila (A) : lit. chain, in particular the chain of saints of a mystical order leading back to the historic founder. II 164b; IX 611a; the chain of initiation and transmission of mystical knowledge also known as *sanad*. IV 950b

sīm (A, var. *sīn*) : argot; *lug͟hat al-~* is a secret vocabulary or argot employed by criminals, beggars, gypsies and other groups for communication among themselves. It is still found in the contemporary Arabic world, notably the ~ *al-ṣāg͟ha* 'argot of gold- and silversmiths', based largely on Hebrew and recorded so far in Cairo and Damascus. IX 611b

sīmā (A), or *sīmāʾ* : a mark of recognition of the believer, either physical or moral; the distinctive mark of Muslims in relation to other peoples. IX 613a

ṣimāda (A) : a bonnet-like hat trimmed with coins most common to women of Ramallah; a man's headcloth in Iraq; a cloth used for covering the head underneath the turban in the Ḥidj̲āz. V 741b; VII 920a

simāṭ (A) : a low oblong table. S 99a

♦ al-simāṭ al-K͟halīlī, or *ʿadas al-K͟halīl* : in mediaeval times, a practice peculiar to Hebron of distributing a daily meal to everybody in town, supposed to honour Abraham's generosity and hospitality. It was at its height during the Mamlūk period. IV 957a

simindj̲ānī → SUḲUṬRĪ

sīmiyāʾ (A, < Gk) : a name for certain genres of magic, a.o. hypnotism and letter magic (also *sīmīyya*), mastered in particular by Aḥmad al-Būnī (d. 622/1225). VIII 430a; IX 612a

simsār → DALLĀL

simsim (A) : in botany, sesame (syn. *dj̲uldj̲ulān*). IX 614a

simṭ (A, pl. *sumūṭ*) : a necklace of pearls; an entire poem. IX 449a; the term for the common-rhyme lines in a MUWAS͟HS͟HAḤ poem. VII 809b

sīmurg͟h (P) : a mythical giant bird of Persian epic tradition. IX 615a

ṣināʿa (A, pl. *ṣināʿāt*) : the occupation of and production by artisans; craft, industry; the action of shipbuilding. IX 625a; in prosody, titivation. IX 455a

sinād (A) : in music, one of three kinds of song, which, according to Ibn al-Kalbī, had a slow refrain but was full of notes. II 1073b

In prosody, a violation of rules applying to vowels and consonants that precede the rhyme letter, *rawī*, namely, the *sinād al-tawdjīh*, the changing of the vowel immediately preceding the quiescent *rawī*; the *sinād al-ishbāʿ*, the changing of the vowel of the DAKHĪL; the *sinād al-ḥadhw*, the changing of the vowel immediately preceding the RIDF; the *sinād al-ridf*, the rhyming of a line that has a *ridf* with one that has not; and the *sinād al-taʾsīs*, the rhyming of a line that has TAʾSĪS with one that has not. IV 412b

For ~ in zoology, → KARKADDAN

sinām (A) : a knife-cut on the two sides of the back, which marked a victim, *budna*, intended to be slaughtered in sacrifice at the time of the pilgrimage. IX 424b

sindhind (A calque 'Sind and Hind', < San *siddhānta* 'perfected') : a term applied to a class of Sanskrit astronomical texts. IX 640b

ṣindj → ṢANDJ

ṣinf (A, pl. *aṣnāf*, *ṣunūf*) : lit. sort, kind; a group of something; various crafts and trades, profession (syn. *ḥirfa*, *kār*); (erroneously) guild. II 967a; IX 626b; IX 644a

ṣīnī (A, P *čīnī*) : a generic term for Chinese ceramics including porcelain. IX 647a

sinn, sinna → SIKKA

sinnawr (A, pl. *sanānīr*), or *sunnār*, *sunār* : in zoology, the cat (syn. *hirr*, *ḳiṭṭ*), both wild and domestic. Of the latter, ~ *miṣrī* 'Egyptian cat' (*Felis maniculata*) and ~ *shīrāzī* 'Persian cat' (*Felis angorensis*) are typical. IX 651b, where are listed many synonyms

In military science, a battering-ram (syn. *kabsh*). III 469b

♦ sinnawr al-zabād → ZABĀD

sīp (P) : mother of pearl. VIII 269a

sipāh (P), or *sipah* : army.

♦ **sipāhī** (P, > Eng *sepoy*, Fr *spahi*) : soldier; in the Ottoman empire, a *tīmār* (→ SERBEST) holder. VIII 203b; cavalryman. IX 656a

In North Africa, a *sbāʾiḥiyya* (s. *sibāḥī*) denoted a corps of mounted gendarmerie. In the 19th and early 20th centuries, it was used for troopers of the corps of locally-raised cavalry organised by the French army there. IX 657a

♦ sipāhī oghlanlarï → DÖRT BÖLÜK

♦ sipahsālār → ISPAHSĀLĀR

sīra (A, pl. *siyar*) : way of going, way of acting, conduct; memorable action, record of such an action; in its pl. form, ~ is also used for 'rules of war and of dealings with non-Muslims'. IX 660b

As a Qurʾānic term, ~ is found with the meaning 'state' or 'appearance'. III 369b

In literature, ~ is used for biography, especially that of the Prophet, and for the genre of romantic biographies of famous characters of antiquity or of the Islamic era. III 369b; V 1161b; IX 660b

♦ **sīra shaʿbiyya** (A) : modern designation for a genre of lengthy Arabic heroic narratives called in western languages either popular epics or popular romances. IX 664a

ṣirāʿ → ṢURʿA

sirādj (A, < P *čirāgh*) : lamp, beacon (syn. *miṣbāḥ*, ḲINDĪL). IX 665a
♦ **sirādj al-ḳuṭrub** (A, < Syr) : lit. the werewolf's lamp; in botany, the name for the mandrake, the plant species of *Mandragora officinarum* L, and more specifically for its forked root (syn. *mandrāghūras*, *yabrūḥ*, *shadjarat al-ṣanam*, *luffāḥ*). IX 667a

sirāḥ (A) : the sweat lost by horses covered by blankets in a thinning-down process for horse-racing. II 953a

ṣirāṭ (A, < ult. L *strata*) : 'way'; in the Qurʾān, ~ is almost always introduced by the verb *hadā* 'to guide' or the verbal noun *hudā* 'guidance', and qualified by *mustaḳīm* 'right'. IX 670b
As a proper name, al-Ṣirāṭ is the bridge which dominates hell. IX 670b

sirbāl (A) : a tunic. VIII 883b; a garment in general. IX 676b

sirdāb → SARDĀB

sirī → ṢUFRĪ

sırık → ḤAMMĀL

sirwāl (A, P *shalwar*; pl. *sarāwīl*) : trousers. IX 676a

sisāmuwīdā (A, < Gk) : in botany, sesame-like plants, considered as classes of a wild sesame. IX 615a

sitāʾish → MADĪḤ

sitāra (A) : in Muslim Spain, an orchestra formed by female singing slaves, named after the curtain which separated in theory the caliph from the singers and musicians. IV 823b; and → ḤIDJĀB

sitr (A) : veil, a curtain behind which the Fāṭimid caliph was concealed at the opening of the audience session. IX 685a; the name given to the curtain by which Muḥammad concealed his women from the gaze of the world. IX 902b; and → ḤIDJĀB

siwāk (A, pl. *suwuk*), and **miswāk** : toothbrush; tooth-pick; the act of cleansing the teeth. The instrument consists of a piece of smooth wood, the end of which is incised so as to make it similar to a brush to some extent. VII 187a

siyāḳat (T, A *siyāḳa*), or *siyāḳ* : in ʿAbbāsid financial administration, 'accounting practice', 'revenue bookkeeping practice'. IX 692b
In calligraphy, a script considered to have been used from the Umayyad period onwards, which has no artistic appearance and was used in financial registers and suchlike. II 332b; IV 1124a; IX 692b; a curious stenographic-like Arabic script in which diacritics are not used. VIII 151b

ṣiyām → ṢAWM

siyar (A) : in jurisprudence, the area concerned with the rules of war and of dealings of non-Muslims, apostates and rebels. V 1162b; VIII 495b; and → SĪRA

siyāsa (A) : statecraft, management of affairs of state; from mid-19th century onwards, politics and political policy. IX 693b; punishment, extending as far as capital punishment; the violence the ruler has to use to preserve his authority, specifically punishment beyond the ḤADD penalties. IX 694a

♦ siyāsa s͟harʿiyya : the concept of 'juridical policy', methodically taken up by Ibn ʿAḳīl, Ibn Taymiyya and Ibn Ḳayyim al-D̲j̲awziyya, or 'governance in accordance with the s͟harīʿa', a sunnī doctrine calling for harmonisation between FIḲH and SIYĀSA. In modern times, a recognition of authority in the state to take legal acts as needed for the public good when the s͟harīʿa has no text, NAṢṢ, on the matter, provided the s͟harīʿa is not infringed thereby. I 276b; IX 694b f.

♦ siyāsat-gāh (P) : place of torture and execution. IX 694a

♦ siyāset (T) : (corporal) punishment in Ottoman penal law. II 518b

ṣoff → LEFF; ṢAFF

ṣofta (T) : under the Ottomans, a student of the theological, legal or other sciences (var. *sūk͟hte*). VIII 221b; IX 702b

sökmen → ALP

ṣolaḳ (T 'left-handed') : in the Ottoman military organisation, the name of part of the sultan's bodyguard, comprising four infantry companies of the Janissaries, originally archers. IX 712a

sonḳor (T), or *sunḳur* : one of many words denoting birds of prey, specifically the gerfalcon (*falco gyrfalco*). IX 730a

soyūrg͟hāl (Mon, P, or *suyūrg͟hāl*) : favour, reward granted by the ruler to someone, sometimes of a hereditary nature; in the course of time, ~ came to mean various grants formerly known as IḲṬĀʿ. IX 731b; in Persia, in post-Tīmūrid times, designation for a grant of immunity, often hereditary, from the payment of taxation, frequently, though not by any means always, granted to members of the religious classes. III 1089b; IV 1043b

sowar (Anglo-Eng, < P **suwār**) : in the Indian Army of British India, the designation for troopers in cavalry regiments. IX 909b

stribant : in India, a custom whereby the sons of each wife are regarded as one group and each group is awarded an equal share in the inheritance. Another custom called *chundawand*, similar in effect, entitles the group to its allotted portion until the extinction of its last member. I 172a

ṣu bas͟hi̊ (T) : in Turkish tribal usage, 'commander of the army, troops'; in the Ottoman empire, a common military and police title. IX 736b

ṣuʾāb → ḲAML

suʿāt (A) : 'runners' in the postal service, first appearing during the Buwayhid dynasty. I 1044b

ṣūba (< ? A *ṣawb* 'patch, track') : in the Mug͟hal empire from Akbar onwards, the term for 'province', which was divided into *sarkār*s and PARGANAS. VIII 271a; IX 738a

♦ **ṣūbadār** : in the Mug͟hal empire, the governor of a province, ṢŪBA, also known as *sipāhsālār* (→ ISPAHSĀLĀR), *nāẓim* and *ṣāḥib ṣūba*. IX 738b

ṣubba → ḲAṬĪʿ

subḥa (A, P *tasbīḥ*, T *tesbīḥ*, modT *tespih*) : rosary, consisting of three groups of beads made of wood, bone, mother of pearl, etc. and used by nearly all classes of Muslims except the Wahhābīs. IX 741b; in classical Tradition, ~ is used in the sense of supererogatory ṢALĀT. IX 742b

subḥān (A) : a Qurʾānic term, recorded solely in the form of an exclamative and annexed to *allāh* or some substitute, e.g. *rabb*, and translated most commonly 'Glory be to God'. IX 742b

sūbiyya (Egy) : an Egyptian spiced beverage, made with either wheat or rice, in either an intoxicating or a legal, non-alcoholic, version. VIII 653a

sūdānī → KŪFĪ

ṣudayra (A) : a short, sleeveless vest, worn by men in Egypt. V 741b

sudda (A) : threshold. IX 762a

ṣudgh (A, P *zulf*) : love locks of hair, one of a number of female hairstyles in pre- and early Islam, along with *ṭurra* 'fore locks' and *limma* 'shoulder locks'. IX 313a

sudjdja (A) : horses; the name of an idol in pre-Islamic Arabia, as are *badjdja* 'blood drawn from an incision of a camel's vein' and *djabha* 'forehead; a lunar mansion, the moon; horses; humiliation; the leading men of a tribe; the persons responsible for levying money for a ransom or debt'. IX 763a

ṣūf (A) : the wool of sheep (syn. *labad*). IX 764b; S 317a

♦ ṣūfa (A) : a woollen tampon. IX 249a

sufahāʾ → AHL AL-FAḌL

ṣuffa (A), or *ẓulla* : in architecture, a colonnade, and according to Lane, a long, covered portico or vestibule, which formed part of the mosque at Medina. I 266a; I 610a; and → SAḲĪFA

ṣūfiyāna (P) : in the Mughal empire, the days of abstinence from eating meat, introduced by Akbar. IX 766b

ṣufr (A) : yellow; in mineralogy, brass. VIII 111b; IX 766a

♦ ṣufrī : a variety of date, in particular from the al-Aflādj district in southern Nadjd, called by al-Hamdānī *sayyid al-tumūr*, although present-day inhabitants regard the *sirī* variety as the *sayyid*. I 233b

sufra (A), and *naṭʿ* : a table (syn. KHULWĀN and *māʾida*), whereby ~ is a skin stretched out on the ground and serving, not only among the early Bedouin, but also in circles of sedentary Arabic civilisation, various functions in the home and in the country. In dialect, ~ is an ordinary table and *sufradjī* is a waiter in a restaurant or cafe. S 99b

♦ sufradjī → SUFRA

suftadja (A, < P *sufta* 'pierced') : in finance, a negotiable instrument in the form of a written bill of credit similar to the modern drawing of a cheque; like ṢAKK, a medium through which funds were remitted. II 382b; VIII 493a; IX 769b

suhayl → SAFĪNA

ṣuḥba (A.), or *ṣaḥāb* : in Yemen, an alliance among the Arab tribes of the desert based on a kind of fraternal relationship. It is an agreement, both defensive and offensive, by which two tribes undertake to take up arms on one another's behalf and henceforth may go to live on the territories of the other and also take advantage of its pastures. Excluded from this treaty are the fornicator and the thief. VI 491a; and → ṢĀḤIB

suḥla (A) : the weanling hare. S 84b

ṣuḥuf → DAFTAR; DJARĪDA; MUṢḤAF

suḥūr → IMSĀKIYYA

sūḳ (A, < Ar; pl. *aswāḳ*) : market, in the sense of both the commercial exchange of goods or services and the place in which this exchange is normally conducted. IX 786b

♦ čahār sūḳ (P) : 'cruciform market'; in architecture, a type of bazaar with four streets for merchants and artisans, or four sides. V 665b; IX 796b

suḵhaymānī → UMMA

suḵhf (A) : lack of substance; indecency, obscenity (more properly, *fuḥsh*); in literature, a genre of poetry of which the basis is sexuality and scatology, although MUDJŪN was preferred among early mediaeval literati. The adjectival form is *saḵhīf*, meaning either shallow-witted or obscene. IV 780b; IX 804a; S 16b

sūḵhte → ṢOFTA

sukkar (A, < P) : the sap crushed from the sugar-cane, solid sugar. Some common types of sugar are *ṭabarzad* 'sugar set hard in moulds', *nabāt* 'sugar, also produced from other substances such as rose syrup or violet syrup, set on palm sticks placed in the recipient where it was being prepared', *fānīd* 'sugar made in elongated moulds produced by adding the oil of sweet almonds or finely-ground white flour to the process of decoction', and *sulaymānī* 'sugar made from hardened "red sugar" broken into pieces and further cooked'. IX 804b

sukkayt (A) : 'silenced by shame at finishing last', the name for the tenth horse in a horse-race, according to the order of finishing. II 953a

suknā (A) : lit. abode; a Qur'ānic term referring to a woman's right upon her husband to provide shelter for her; also her right to stay in the matrimonial house during her waiting period following divorce or death. IX 805a

sukr (A) : in mysticism, 'intoxication', especially in the vocabulary of al-Ḥallādj. III 102b

suku : in Malaysia, matrilineal descent groups. VIII 483b

sukūn → ḤARAKA

sukūt (A) : lit. silence; in law, an individual's action of not actively expressing an opinion when involved in an action or contract that requires acceptance or rejection, which 'answer' is clarified by circumstance. IX 806b; IX 845b

suḳūṭ (A.), or *suḳūṭ al-kusūf* : falling, the ἔμπτωσις of Ptolemy; in astronomy, the phase from the beginning of an eclipse to the beginning of totality. V 536b

suḳuṭrī (A, < *suḳuṭra*) : one of a variety of the aloe, considered to be the best and probably corresponding with the *Aloe Parryi* Baker, the *Aloe Socotrina*, which thrives in great quantities on the island of Socotra. The other frequently mentioned varieties are *'arabī (ḥaḍramī)* and *simindjānī*. VIII 687b

sulaḥfā (A, pl. *salāḥif*), or *sulaḥfāʾ*, *sulaḥfiyya* : in zoology, the tortoise or turtle in general, terrestrial as well as aquatic. The male is also called *g͟haylam*, the female also *ṭuwama*. IX 811a, where dialectal names are also found

In astronomy, *al-sulaḥfā^h* is one of several names for the nineteenth boreal constellation of the Lyre situated between Hercules and the Swan. IX 811a

sulaṭān (A) : in Muslim Spain, a designation for Alfonso VII of Castile after he had come to the throne as a child. IX 849a

sulaymānī → KĀG͟HAD; SUKKAR

ṣulb (A) : in geography, hard, stony ground. VIII 1048a

ṣulḥ (A) : truce, armistice; peace and reconciliation. II 131a; IX 845a

♦ ṣulḥ al-ibrāʾ : in S͟hāfiʿī law, a peace settlement by virtue of which the claimed object would be a HIBA 'donation', as opposed to a *ṣulḥ al-muʿāwaḍa*, when the object is replaced by another. IX 845b

♦ ṣulḥ ʿalā inkār → INKĀR

♦ **ṣulḥ-i kull** (Ind.P) : universal toleration, a policy of the Mug͟hal emperor Akbar. I 317a; IX 846a

sullam (A) : a bilingual Coptic-Arabic vocabulary. IX 848b

sulṭān (A, < Syr; pl. *salāṭīn*) : holder of power, authority; sultan. VIII 1000b; IX 849a

In the S͟hībānid realm, ~ denoted an individual eligible to succeed to the k͟hānate. The sovereign had the title *k͟hān*. IX 429b

♦ sulṭān Ibrāhīm : lit. the sultan Abraham; in zoology, the red mullet (*Mullus barbatus*). VIII 1021a

♦ **sulṭān al-ṭalaba** (A, pop. *al-ṭolba*) : a traditional Moroccan spring festival, celebrated annually in the second half of April, primarily at Fās. A central feature of the feast was the election of a mock sultan. IX 857b

♦ sulṭānī : in numismatics, the first Ottoman gold coin, which, when it was introduced in 882 AH, adopted the weight standard of the Venetian ducat, *ca.* 3.52 g. VIII 228b

♦ sulṭānli̊ḳ (T) : in the Ottoman empire, a fief for which one has received investiture. IX 727b

suluk : in Javanese literature, a poetical genre of short mystical poems. VIII 294a

sulūk (A) : in political theory, conduct or comportment of leaders. IX 861b

In mysticism, ~ is the Islamic version of the archetypal motif of the 'journey' which mystics of different religious traditions have used to describe the various steps to realise union with the divine; the progress which the mystic makes on the *via mystica*; also 'spiritual correctness', the 'travelling-manners' which the mystic must possess to traverse the stations of the Way. The ṣūfī wayfarer is called a *sālik*. IX 862a

ṣuʿlūk (A, pl. *ṣaʿālīk*) : in pre- and early Islam, the knight-errant of the desert, brigand of the highways; brigand-poet. II 963b; VIII 496b; IX 863b; S 122a

sulūḳī (A, pl. *sulūḳiyya*) : the greyhound, used in hawking and falconry. I 1152b sumānā → SALWĀ

sumaniyya (A, < Skr) : the Buddhists. IX 869a

sumayrī (A, pl. *sumayriyyāt*) : a type of ship mentioned as a troop-carrying craft in the historical accounts of the Zandj rebellion in the later 3rd/9th century, and used in 315/927 in order to prevent the Carmathians from crossing the Euphrates. VIII 811a

summ (A, P *zahr*; pl. *sumūm*), or *samm* : poison, venom. IX 872a

sūmūlak : a pudding-like food made of sprouted wheat, which Özbegs distribute to family and friends during the celebration of the New Year. VIII 234b

sunan → SUNNA

sunār → SINNAWR

sunbula (A) : 'the ear of the corn'; in astronomy, *al-~* is the term for Virgo, one of the twelve zodiacal constellations. Some philologists explain ~ to be Coma Berenices. The constellation is also known as *al-ʿadhrāʾ*, while ~ stands for the star α Virginis. VII 83b

sunna (A, pl. **sunan**) : habit, hereditary norm of conduct, custom; a normative custom of the Prophet or of the early community; orthodoxy. I 175b; II 888b; III 23b; IV 147b ff.; IX 878a

In its plural form, *sunan* refers to several important collections of Traditions and legal pronouncements, becoming the generic book title of such works. IX 874a

♦ sunna muʾakkida → NĀFILA

sunnār → SINNAWR

sūr (A, pl. *aswār*, *sīrān*) : the wall of a town or other enclosed urban or built-up space. IX 881b

sūra (A, < Syr *ṣūrṭā*, *sūrthā*; pl. *suwar*) : a Qurʾānic term, ~ refers to a unit of revelation. The Qurʾān gives no indication as to how long these units of revelation were. They were most likely only parts of the present sūras, of which there are 114 of widely varying length and form, divided into a number of verses. V 402a; V 409b ff.; IX 885b

ṣūra (A) : image, form, shape; face, countenance. IX 889a; and → KAWKABA

♦ **ṣūrat al-arḍ** : lit. the form or shape of the earth; title for two early Islamic geographical works covering the world as it was then known. IX 893b

♦ ṣūrat al-rāmī : in astronomy, the constellation of Sagittarius. VIII 842a

ṣurʿa (A), or *ṣirāʿ* : 'wrestling', with the basic idea of hurling one's opponent to the ground. In mediaeval times, it may have been a popular sport; in 251/865 citizens hired *muṣāriʿūn* (s. *muṣāriʿ*) to defend their houses against the violence of the Turkish soldiery. VIII 239a

surādiḳ (A) : among the pre-Islamic Bedouin, a cloth tent of quite large dimensions. IV 1147a

surau : in Sumatra, a centre for religious studies; a religious school. VIII 237b; VIII 296b suray<u>dj</u>iyya → MASʾALA

sur<u>gh</u>ūs (A) : in zoology, the common sargo. VIII 1021a

sürgün (T) : under the Ottomans, the compulsory re-settlement of people from various parts of the empire. IV 225a; IV 238a; IX 655a

sur<u>kh</u> → RATTĪ

sur<u>kh</u>āb → NUḤĀM

sur<u>kh</u>a<u>dj</u>a (P) : in medicine, measles. IX 474b

ṣurra (A, T *ṣurre*) : lit. bag, purse; a sealed purse containing coins. IX 894a Under the Mamlūks, a purse of money distributed as a gift by the ruler. IX 894a Under the Ottomans, payment made by pilgrim caravans on the way to the Holy Cities, in return for the right to enter alien territory and for protection while staying there. I 483b; IV 1133b; VIII 489b; IX 894a

♦ ṣurrat al-ḥaramayn : the sum once sent by Islamic countries such as Egypt and Tunisia for distribution to the poor of Mecca and Medina during the pilgrimage. IV 1133b

surriyya (A) : a concubine. I 28a

sūs (A, P *mahak*, *ma<u>th</u>ak*) : in botany, licorice, both the root and the decoction from the root (syn. *ʿūd al-sūs*, *<u>sh</u>a<u>dj</u>arat al-furs*). IX 897b

sūsan (P, < Mid.P), or more often *sawsan* : in botany, the iris or lily (*Iris florentina* L., or *Lilium sp.*). The blue iris was called *sūsan asmān<u>dj</u>ūnī*; other colours were white and yellow. IX 902b

sutra (A) : initially, a veil or screen, covering, protection, shelter; in Islamic prayer, a technical term for any object placed by the worshipper some distance before him, in front of which no person should pass while the prayer is being performed. VIII 928a; IX 902b

suwār (P, Ind.P *sawār*) : horseman; in Muslim India, a rank in the Mu<u>gh</u>al military indicating the number of troopers (*tābīnān*) and horses the *manṣabdār* (→ MANṢAB) was ordered to maintain. VI 422b; IX 909a

♦ bārgīr-suwār : a category of horsemen in the Mu<u>gh</u>al army, who neither owned horses nor were enrolled as troopers of the *manṣabdār*s (→ MANṢAB), the *ṭābīnān*. However, as they were fit for cavalry service, in times of emergency they were provided with horses and went into action. They were not, however, part of the regular cavalry. V 686b

suyūr<u>gh</u>āl → SOYŪR<u>GH</u>ĀL

suyūrsāt (P) : purveyance; one of the unfixed taxes in Persia, consisting of levies made for the keep and expenses of military forces, government officials, and foreign envoys passing through the country, and like the ṢĀDIRĀT bore heavily upon the peasantry. II 152a; IV 1043a

sūz-u gudāz (P) : in Persian literature, a genre of short poems devoted to the description of painful experiences, fashionable in the 10th-11th/16th-17th centuries. VI 834b

syair → <u>SH</u>ĀʿIR

T

taʿaddī (A) : lit. transgression; in law, tort or negligence. II 105a
taʿāḳul (A) : in law, joint liability by the ʿĀḲILA. I 338a
taʿāruḍ (A) : in law, conflicting possibilities. IX 324b
ṭabaḳa (A, pl. *ṭibāḳ*) : in architecture, the most common type of living-unit in a Cairene RABʿ, a kind of duplex with a vestibule, a recess for water jars, a latrine and a main room consisting of a slightly raised ĪWĀN and a DŪRḲĀʿA. An inner staircase led up to a mezzanine, *mustaraḳa*, used for sleeping. Each unit had its own enclosed private roof. A ~ may also be a triplex with an additional room above the mezzanine. VIII 344a; in Mamlūk times, tiered accommodation. IX 792b; and → ṬABAḲĀT

♦ ṭabaḳāt (A, s. *ṭabaḳa*) : in literature, a genre of biographical works arranged according to generation, *ṭabaḳa*; ultimately applied to those which follow alphabetical order. VI 109b

tabakkala → TAḤASHSHADA
tabardār → BALṬADJÎ
ṭabarzad → SUKKAR
tābiʿ (A, pl. TĀBIʿŪN) : follower; and → ITBĀʿ; ṢĀḤIB

♦ tābiʿūn : the Followers of the Prophet's Companions. A large number of these were contemporaries of the Companions, ṢAḤĀBA; some might even have been alive during the Prophet's lifetime but without satisfying the conditions which would have permitted them to be classed among the *ṣaḥāba*. The last of the ~ died around 180/796. IV 149a; VIII 900a

♦ atbāʿ al-tābiʿūn : the Successors of the TĀBIʿŪN. There are no sufficiently precise criteria enabling us to define exactly this group of men. They are essentially the most eminent disciples of the great *tābiʿūn*. The middle of the 3rd/9th century can be taken as their *terminus ad quem*. IV 149a; VIII 900a

ṭabīʿiyyāt : the science of physics. VIII 105b
ṭabīla → SHAKSHĀK
ṭābīnān → (BĀRGĪR-)SUWĀR
ṭabl (A), or *dawul* : a rather large wooden double-headed drum held slantwise by a strap and beaten with two sticks of uneven dimensions and shape. It was the basic percussion instrument of the Ottoman ensemble, MEHTER. VI 1007b

♦ ṭabla → DJARAS

tabriʾa (A) : an Ibāḍī penal sanction (*tebriya*), viz. 'an indemnity paid by the parents of the murderer to those of the victim for continuing to live within the tribe'; a term used for all sorts of declaratory or constitutive acts which absolve from responsibility. I 1026b
ṭābūn (A), or *ṭābūna* : originally, the cavity in which a fire was made to shelter it from the wind; an oven. II 1059a; a small jar-shaped oven used for baking

bread. In Jordan it consists of a small construction in which is placed a sort of cooking-pot, surrounded by embers to cook the dough in the interior. V 42b

tabur → RADĪF

tābūt (A) : coffin. I 200a; 'water-screw', a kind of hydraulic machine for irrigating the fields, in use in Egypt from the times of the Ptolemys until the present. It consists of a wooden cylinder (about 6-9 feet in length) hooped with iron. While the spiral pipe is fixed between the inside wall of the ~ and an iron axis, its upper extremity is bent into a crank and its lower end turns on a stake set under the water. One or two peasants crouch at the water's edge, endlessly turning the crank handle. The water rises from bend to bend in the spiral pipe until it flows out at the mouth of the canal. V 864a

ṭābya (A) : in architecture, 'cobwork', a technique by which earth with which chalk and crushed baked earth or broken stones are often mixed is rammed between two boards, kept parallel by beams. The wall is plastered over, often in such a way as to simulate joints of heavy bond-work beneath. When this plaster falls, the regularly spaced holes left by the beams become visible. Cobwork was general in the Muslim West in the 5th/11th and 6th/12th centuries. I 1226b

tabyīt (A) : in religious law, each day of fasting. IX 94b

taḍabbaba (A), also *taḥallama*, *ig̲h̲tāla* : in the terminology of childhood, a verb which expresses the stage when a child becomes fat. VIII 822a

tadāwul (A) : a mode of transmission. IX 455b

tadbīr (A) : in law, a grant of enfranchisement which takes effect upon the master's death. The S̲h̲āfiʿī school also applies it to an enfranchisement to take effect from a date after the master's death. A slave freed thus is *mudabbar*. I 30a

tad̲h̲kira (A, pl. *tad̲h̲ākīr*) : memorandum. I 80a

In the science of diplomatic, orders laid down for the higher officials, ambassadors, and commanders of fortresses, chiefly concerned with income and expenditure. I 304a

In Persian literature, a 'memorial' of the poets, a genre characterised by a combination of biography and anthology. VII 529b

In older Turkish literature, a genre of works treating the lives of holy men and great ṣūfīs. V 193a

tad̲h̲yīl (A) : in prosody, a deviation in the metre because of the addition of a quiescent consonant to the *watid mad̲j̲mūʿ* (→ AWTĀD), thus *mustafʿilun* becomes *mustafʿilān*. I 672a

taḍʿīf (A) : in mathematics, the term for duplation. III 1139b

taʿdīl (A) : in law, the attestation of the ʿADĀLA of a witness; the procedure for substantiating the *ʿadāla* is also known as ~ , or TAZKIYA. I 209b

In the science of Tradition, the testing and verification procedure traditionally required at the outset of all transmitters. VIII 900b

In astronomy, equation, as in *taʿdīl al-s̲h̲ams* 'the solar equation' and *taʿdīl al-zamān* (or *taʿdīl al-ayyām bi-layālīhā*) 'the equation of time'. IX 292a ff.

tādj → ʿARAḲIYYA
tadjaʿfara (A) : to convert to Imāmism. IX 116b
tadjānus (A) : in rhetoric, paronomasia. VIII 614b
tādjīk → SĀRT
tādjir → ḤAWĀNTĪ
taʿdjīra (Tun) : a large embroidered shawl, worn by women in Tunisia. V 746b
tadjnīs (A) : in prosody, paronomasia. IX 462b
♦ tadjnīs ishtiḳāḳ : ‘figura etymologica’, in prosody, the accumulation of a number of forms from the same verbal root in the same line of a poem. VIII 577b
tadjwīd (A) : the orthoepic rules of Qurʾān reading, concerning pausal location and division of verses. IX 365b
tadlīs (A) : ‘concealing defects’, a term used in the science of Tradition; the defect may consist in pretending to have heard a Tradition from a contemporary when that is not so (*tadlīs al-isnād*), or in calling one’s authority by an unfamiliar ISM, KUNYA or NISBA (*tadlīs al-shuyūkh*), or in omitting a weak transmitter who comes between two sound ones (*tadlīs al-taswiya*). III 26a; VIII 421a
taḍmīn (A) : in prosody, ‘enjambement’, a defect of the rhyme, occurring when one line runs into another in such a way that the end of the line only makes complete sense when we add the beginning of the next. IV 413a
In Persian prosody, ‘quotation’, a rhetorical figure where a poem by another author is taken as the basis and inserted in one's own poem to obtain humorous effects. III 355a
In rhetoric, implication. VIII 614b
tafarrudj (A, T *teferrüdj*) : in Ottoman guilds, a ceremony, wherein the master awarded his pupil with an apron, once he was qualified in his craft. IX 646a
tafāwut-i ʿamal (P) : under the Ḳādjārs, a sum levied by the provincial governors in addition to the regular tax assessment, for the expenses of the administration; it was abolished by the newly convened National Assembly in 1907. II 152b
tafih → MALĪKH
tafkhīm (A) : in grammar, velarisation. A letter that is velarised is called *mufakhkham*. VIII 343a; IX 96a
tāfrūt → SHAWKA
tafsīr (A) : exegetic interpretation; commentary on the Qurʾān. I 410a; IV 147a; VII 361a; IX 320a
tafwīḍ (A) : a theological doctrine, according to which God had entrusted the care of the worldly creation to the IMĀMS. I 304b; the principle of ‘leaving it to God’ to elucidate through scripture. I 411a
In the science of diplomatic, ~ was the grade of appointment applied to supreme ḲĀḌĪS, used in Mamlūk times only. II 303a
tafwīḳ (A) : in archery, nocking. This consists of bracing the arrow’s nock on the binding of the bow-string. There must be no play there, so that when the archer

draws back the arrow, together with the bow-string, he accompanies the latter in its rearwards path to the chosen anchorage-point. IV 800b

taghazzul (T) : in Turkish prosody, the section of the ḲAṢĪDA which embraces subjects more often found in a GHAZAL, such as love or wine. IV 715b

taghbīr (A) : cantillation (of the Qurʾān). II 1073b

taḥallama → TAḌABBABA

tahammul (A) : in law, the 'acceptance of responsibility'. I 339a

taḥammus → ḤUMS

taḥannuth (A, < Heb) : a form of religious devotion, in which Muḥammad is said to have been engaged one month each year in a cave on Ḥirāʾ. III 166a; III 462a

ṭahār (A) : the name in Mecca for the rite of circumcision. V 20b

ṭahāra (A) : ritual purity, a necessary condition for the valid performance of prayer. III 647a

♦ ṭahāra ḥaḳīḳiyya : 'real' ritual purity, attained by the elimination of any blemish from the body, the clothing and the place. VIII 929a

♦ ṭahāra ḥukmiyya : 'prescribed' ritual purity, attained by WUḌŪʾ or by GHUSL. VIII 929a

taḥashshada (A) : a term used by al-Hamdānī in the 4th/10th century for members of the tribal group of Bakīl transferring their allegiance to the tribal group of Ḥāshid. The opposite was *tabakkala*. III 259b

taḥaykt → ḤĀʾIK

taḥayyur (A) : 'ravishment', the name given by the mystical order ʿĪsāwā to the ecstatic dancing practiced as a form of invoking God. It is also called *ḥayra* or *idjdhāb*. IV 95a; and → RABBĀNĪ

taḥdjīr (A) : 'delimitation'; in law, the defining of the limits of MAWĀT land by e.g. setting stones along the length of each boundary in order to fix the extreme limits of the area to be brought into use. III 1054a

ṭāhir → NADJIS

♦ ṭāhirī → KĀGHAD

ṭahmal (A) : in zoology, a silurus, whose Arabic term is found again in the Latinised nomenclature to specify a sub-species limited to a particular region (*Pimelopterus tahmel*). VIII 1021b

taḥrīr (A) : land census; survey. VIII 291a; VIII 419a; revision of a text, even 'edition', ~ refers to the elements of a text or commentary which have been chosen for comment, clarification or correction. IX 320a

♦ taḥrīrī : 'epistolary'; in calligraphy, a name given to a more simple form of the SHIKASTA *nastaʿlīḳ* script and used for writing letters and taking notes. IV 1124b

ṭāḥūna (A) : in Muslim Spain, a horse-driven mill. I 492a

taḥwīf → ḤAWFĪ

taḥwīl (A) : in Ottoman administration, the annual renewal of the diplomas of the governors of provinces, of the brevets of the MOLLĀs or judges in towns of the first class (~), and of the brevets of the timariots or holders of military fiefs. This task was carried out by an office in the chancellery. VIII 482a

tahyast (Touareg) : a simple camel saddle, with a pommel in the form of a rectangular batten, used by the Touareg of the Sahara. III 667a

ṭāʾif → RAHĪSH

♦ ṭāʾifa (A), or *ṭāyfā* : a tribe, tribal section. IX 221b; IX 245b

♦ ṭāʾifat al-ruʾasā : a guild of corsair captains which, for three centuries, furnished the Algerian treasury with the greater part of its resources. I 368a

ṭāʾir → DADJĀDJA

ṭāḳ : arcade. IX 409a

taḳaddum (A) : in philosophy, the absolute anteriority of God. IX 382a

takārir → FALLĀTA

takārna → FALLĀTA

takayda (Tun) : a pointed woman's bonnet in Tunisia. V 746b

taḳbīl → ḲABĀLA

takbīr (A) : the saying of the formula *allāhu akbar*.

♦ takbīr al-iḥrām : the TAKBĪR with which the ritual prayer begins, and which puts the worshipper into a temporary state of special relationship with God. III 1053a; VIII 929a

taḳdīr (A) : predestination. VIII 125b

takfīr (A) : the act of identifying someone as a KĀFIR 'unbeliever' or, when born a Muslim, 'apostate'. IX 118a

takhalluṣ (A) : in onomastics, the pen-name adopted by a poet or writer. IV 181a
In Persian prosody, the section of the ḲAṢĪDA, also called *gurīzgāh* and *makhlaṣ*, where the poet turns from the prologue to the panegyric. IV 57b

♦ ḥusn al-takhalluṣ : 'good transition', an artifice used in poetry to effect a formal fusion of heterogeneous motifs. IX 452a

takhmīs (A) : in prosody, a five-line MUSAMMAṬ, i.e. a *mukhammas*, which is used to expand, to 'gloss', an existing poem. VII 661a; the addition of three hemistichs after each pair of hemistichs of the original poem. IX 243b

takhṣīṣ (A) : the principle in which a particular prescription is preferred to a general prescription. IV 256a

takht (P) : in the Tīmūrid period, a pavilion with a view. IX 46a; and → SARĪR

taḳiyya (A) : the precautionary dissimulation of one's faith, characteristic of shīʿism. I 1099a; IX 422b

ṭāḳiyya (A) : the common skull cap worn, in the Arab East, by both sexes alone or under the head dress. V 741b; and → ʿATABA

taḳlīd (A) : 'imitation'; in theology, imitation of the Prophet, of his Companions and their pious successors. I 1039a; III 1173b
In law, the unquestioning acceptance of the doctrines of established schools and authorities. A person bound to practise ~ is called *muḳallid*. II 890a; III 1026b; IX 324b

In the science of diplomatic, ~ was a grade of appointment for high officials such as WAZĪRS and ḲĀḌĪS, although under the Mamlūks it was restricted to very special high officials such as the confidential secretary, *kātib al-sirr*. II 303a

taklīf (A) : in theology, the doctrine of individual responsibility. I 272a

In Ottoman administration, *teklīf* (pl. *tekālīf*) was used synonymously with RESM 'taxes and dues introduced by the state'. VIII 486a

♦ tekālīf-i s̲h̲āḳḳa : 'onerous exactions', in Ottoman administration, exactions taken illegally by local authorities. VIII 486b

takmīl (A) : lit. completion; among the *fityān* (→ FATĀ), full initiation, symbolised by the putting on of ritual trousers (*sirwāl*, P *s̲h̲alwar*). IX 167a

♦ takmila (A) : the continuation of an original work, expressing the idea of completion, becoming the latter's perfection. Works bearing this title are fairly late. IX 604a

taḳrīr (A) : remarks on a text. IX 320a

In the science of diplomatic, the documents (diplomatic notes) presented to the Ottoman government by members of the foreign diplomatic corps. II 314a

In Ottoman administration, reports, e.g. those presented to the sultan by the grand vizier acting as representative of the government. VIII 481b

taḳsīm (A) : in music, a solo melodic modal improvisation entrusted to an instrumentalist. VI 97a

taḳsīra (A) : a short-sleeved jacket worn by both sexes in Syria and Palestine. V 742a

takwīn (A) : 'production'; in Ibn Sīnā, the production, with an intermediary, of corruptible beings. III 664b

tāl (H) : in Indian music, a cyclic time-measure punctuated by a stress pattern which is marked on a pair of drums. III 454a

ṭalā (A) : in the terminology of childhood, 'the youngling of any kind; an infant until a month old or more' (Lane). VIII 821b

ṭalaʿa → ITH̲TH̲AG̲H̲ARA

ṭalāḳ (A) : in law, repudiation of the wife by the husband, by way of a simple unilateral declaration. I 27b; II 836b; III 949b; IV 689a; and → TAʿLIḲ-ṬALĀḲ

♦ ṭalāḳ al-tafwīḍ : in law, the right of the wife to divorce the husband. I 172b

tālār (P) : in architecture, a flat-roofed portico. I 616a; (*ṭālār*) a colonnaded verandah associated with private dwellings, where it usually provided an open and sheltered vista toward an enclosed garden, pool, or courtyard that served as the physical centre of domestic space. VIII 789a

talāʾum (A) : in rhetoric, euphony. VIII 614b

talawwun → ḤIRBĀʾ

talbīna (A) : a dish similar to *ḥarīra*, a gruel made from flour cooked with milk, but eaten at funeral meals by pre-Islamic Arabs. II 1059a; VII 908b

tald̲j̲iʾa (A), or **ild̲j̲āʾ** : lit. putting under protection; in the first three or four centuries of Islam, the practice of the 'commending' by an inferior to a superior of a possession of which the former remains the legal owner but for which, by virtue of a tacit agreement, the latter is to be responsible vis-à-vis the administrative authority and more particularly the tax authorities. III 394a; III 1113a

In law, a fictitious sale resorted to by a person who wishes to protect his possessions from possible confiscation. III 394a; III 1113a

talfīḳ (A) : in law, a patchwork approach to the juristic tradition. IX 325b

ṭalḥ (A) : in botany, a variety of acacia (*Acacia seyal*). I 168b

ṭalī (A, pl. *ṭulyān*) : a young lamb. I 541a

tālī (A) : lit. follower; in Druze hierarchy, the Left Wing, the fifth of the five cosmic ranks in the organisation. II 632a

In horse-racing, the name for the sixth horse in a horse-race, according to the order of finishing. II 953a

In logic and arithmetic, the portion following the MUḲADDAM, i.e. the second of two numbers in a proportion. VII 492a

ṭālib (A) : in Mālikī law, the plaintiff in a lawsuit. The defendant is called *maṭlūb*. II 171a; and → ARU; AYḲASH

taʿlīḳ (A) : 'suspension, hanging together'; in calligraphy, a script which is said to have got its name from its letters being connected to each other. According to Persian scholars, ~ is a compound of TAWḲĪʿ, RIḲĀʿ and NASKH scripts. It was used for writing books and letters, and in the DĪWĀNs for official correspondence. It gave place to SHIKASTA TAʿLĪḲ. IV 1124a; there are two variants, Persian ~ and Ottoman ~ . VIII 151b

♦ taʿlīḳ-ṭalāḳ (J) : a Javanese legal institution by which the husband declares to his wife's guardian and the witnesses, immediately after contracting his marriage, that, if he leaves his wife for a certain time without providing for her and without sending her tidings, if he severely illtreats her or commits another unseemly act, then his wife is free to complain before the Muslim authority concerned. If there is evidence of her husband's failing in these respects, the authority states that a ṬALĀḲ has taken place. I 174a; VIII 433a

ṭāliḳa (T, < Sl *taliga*) : a carriage, widely used in the 19th century and still in use in Turkey, with no door, but a footboard, surmounted by a small platform. I 558a

ṭāliḳūn : a copper alloy, which equals μεταλλικόν, and is probably identical with 'Chinese iron' (*khār čīnī, ḥadīd ṣīnī*). Hot ~ dipped in water is said to drive flies off and to prevent eyelashes from growing again after they have been depilated with a pair of tweezers. VIII 111b

talmīḥ (A) : in rhetoric, allusion, which consists of alluding to famous passages in the Qurʾān or Traditions, or in profane literature. A related figure is IḲTIBĀS. III 1091b

talthīma (A) : a woman's veil. V 769b

♦ talthīmat al-bayāḍ : under the Fāṭimids, the distinctive dress of the chief ḲĀDĪs, who wore it along with the turban and ṬAYLASĀN. V 769b talwīn → TAMKĪN

ṭʿām → KUSKUSŪ

ṭamaʿ (A) : in classical Muslim administration, an issue of pay. II 79a

tamattuʿ (A) : 'enjoyment'; one of three methods of performing the pilgrimage, viz. by accomplishing the ʿUMRA at the same time as the pilgrimage, resuming secular life and dedicating oneself once again to the pilgrimage. III 53b

tamәlḥaft → MILḤAFA

tamg̲h̲a (P) : in the Ottoman empire, ~ refers to market dues, the tax levied on all kinds of goods bought and sold in cities, on woven stuffs and slaughtered animals, and normally referred to as *tamg̲h̲a-i siyāh* 'black *tamg̲h̲a*'. I 861b; II 147a; also *ṭamg̲h̲ā* or *tamg̲h̲ā*, a Mongolian tax on trade and urban crafts, possibly originally a poll-tax on urban dwellers and merchants. IV 31a; IV 1050a; and → BĀD̲J̲-I TAMG̲H̲A

tamhīd → TAS̲H̲BĪB

taʿmiya (A) : cryptography. VII 257b

In rhetoric, mystification. VIII 427a

ṭaʿmiyya (Egy) : the national food of Egypt, Egyptian beans, *fūl mudammas* 'Jew's marrow' or *mulūk̲h̲iyya*. II 1065a

tamkīn (A) : 'strengthening, stability'; in mysticism, the spiritual act of endurance and stability, contrasted, according to al-Hud̲j̲wīrī, with *talwīn* which indicates a change, an alternating transition from one state to another. III 84b

tamlīṭ → ID̲J̲ĀZA

tamma (Mon), or *tanma* : in the Mongolian army, contingents selected from the total available Mongol power. Their purpose was to maintain and extend Mongol rule, and they were initially stationed on the steppe-sedentary borders. Some ~ units later formed the bases of the permanent armies of the subsidiary k̲h̲ānates into which the Mongol empire was divided. VII 233a

tamr (A) : dried dates. A basic, and sometimes the only food for Arabs in early times, dates were eaten also fresh (*ruṭab*) or when they were beginning to ripen (*busr*); a special variety called *ʿad̲j̲wa* were considered to be a sovereign remedy against poisons and sorcery. II 1058a

♦ tamr ḥinnāʾ : in Cairo, the mignonette plant. III 461a

tamt̲h̲īl (A) : in rhetoric, the assimilation of one thing to another, e.g. *naḳī al-t̲h̲awb* 'clean of clothing' meaning 'exempt from moral vice'. IV 249a ff.; V 117a; a simile. II 825b

♦ tamt̲h̲īliyya s̲h̲āʿirī (U) : in Urdu poetry, 'gnomic verse', in which the thought expressed in the first hemistich of a verse is followed by an illustrative metaphor or simile in the second. IX 90b

ṭamūḥ (A) : in the terminology of horse-riding, a horse that is regarded as impossible to ride. II 954a

tamyīz (A) : the faculty of 'discernment'; in the terminology of childhood, the faculty which enables the child to grasp ideas and thus to distinguish between

good and evil. VIII 822b
In the context of the Almohad movement, the methodical and stringent elimination of real or suspected dissidents, which took place in 523 or 524/1128-9. III 959b

tamzak (Touareg) : among the Touareg, a camel's saddle, more luxurious than the TARIK. III 667a

ṭanāb → ASHL

tanāsub → MUNĀSABA

tanāsukh (A), or *nāsūkhiyya* : in theology, the doctrine of reincarnation, metempsychosis. I 178b; II 136b; IV 45a; VIII 146a; VIII 147b; and → RADJʿA

tanawwuṭ nassādj (A) : in zoology, the weaver-bird. S 19b

tandjīr (A) : a vessel in which sweetmeats were commonly made, used in the mediaeval kitchen. A special type of MUSTAWḲAD 'fire-place' was recommended for the preparation of sweetmeats, which required long cooking over low heat with much stirring, for the shape and position of this *mustawḳad* made it easier to hold the pan and control the heat. VI 808a

tanga : in numismatics, a coin of the Dihlī Sultanate, weighing 10.76 g. IX 203a
♦ tanga-yi nuḳra : in numismatics, a coin introduced by Tīmūr in 792/1390, weighing 5.38 g. It was later reduced to that of the MITHḲĀL, 4.72 g, and became known as the *shāhrukhī*. IX 203a

ṭanīb (A) : in North Africa, a man who, to safeguard his rights, to escape from justice or to save his life, leaves the clan of his birth, alone or with his family, and goes to establish himself in a different tribe which promises to assist him. The term is linked with *ṭunub* 'tent-cord', the suppliant being obliged, originally, to touch at least a cord of the tent of the one to whom he appeals. S 78b

tanka : in numismatics, an Indian coin. Originally of silver, the ~ became a copper denomination under the Dihlī sultan Shīr Shāh. VIII 618a

tanma → TAMMA

tannūr (A, < Ar) : a domestic baking oven of Mesopotamian origin. Cylindrical and bee-hive shaped, it gave the appearance of a large, inverted pot, from which it probably evolved. II 1059a; V 42b; VI 807b; also, the large stove-shaped candelabra made in Egypt, frequently found in mosques, and made of gold, silver or copper. VI 665b; any place from which water pours forth. VIII 437b

ṭanṭūr (A), or *ṭarṭūr* : a high conical cap resembling a mitre, worn by ṣūfīs in the Arab East. V 742a
In Algeria, a high brimless hat which was part of the uniform of the Turkish military élite. V 745b
Among the Druze, a high pointed woman's headdress of wood, horn, or metal, once very common. V 742a

tanwīn (A) : in grammar, nunation. VIII 121a

tanzīh (A) : 'withdrawal'; in theology, denying God any resemblance to anything. I 410b

tanzīl (A) : a revelation to be proclaimed publicly to mankind. I 1099a
Among the Ismāʿīliyya, the outward revelation, represented by the Prophet, as opposed to the TAʾWĪL 'inner truth', represented by the IMĀM. II 631a
ṭapu resmi (T) : in the Ottoman empire, an occasional (BĀD-I HAWĀ) tax paid on entering into possession of a ČIFTLIK. II 147a
ṭār (A) : in music, a round tambourine with jingling plates fixed in openings in the shell or body of the instrument. II 621a
ṭaradiyya (A) : in literature, the genre of the cynegetic poem. I 1154b
ṭaraf (A, pl. AṬRĀF) : province. I 924b
In the science of Tradition, the ~ is the gist, or most salient feature, of a Tradition. VII 706b; and → AṬRĀF
♦ ṭarafdār (Ind.P) : under the Bahmanīs, the governor of a province originally responsible for both the civil and military administration of the province, and under whom the commanders of the forts were placed. During the century that followed the establishment of the dynasty, the power of the ~ was greatly curtailed. I 924b
♦ ṭarafān (A), or *dhu 'l-ṭarafayn* : in prosody, in the context of MUʿĀḲABA, to describe the case e.g. in the RAMAL metre, of both the first and the last cord of the foot *fāʿilātun* being shortened, thus *faʿilatu*, when the preceding and following cords are not shortened. VIII 747b
taraffuḍ (A) : the harbouring of moderate (?) Rāfiḍī ideas. IX 492a
tarāna (P) : in Indian music, a song composed of meaningless syllables. III 453a; a term of pre-Islamic origin which denoted songs intended for feasting and wine. VIII 579b; and → RUBĀʿĪ
tarannum (A) : in singing, the lengthening of the final vowel in the ḲĀFIYA MUṬLAḲA. IV 413b
tarassul (A) : 'correspondence'; in calligraphy, the name given by the DĪWĀN secretaries to a plainer form of the SHIKASTA TAʿLĪḲ. IV 1124a
ṭarastudj → BARASŪDJ
taraza (N.Afr), or *tarazala, tarazal* : a wide-brimmed straw hat for both sexes, worn in Morocco and Algeria. V 746b
tarazal, tarazala → TARAZA
tarbīʿ (A) : in astrology, the quartile aspect. IV 259b
In prosody, the addition of two hemistichs after each pair of hemistichs of the original poem. IX 243b
tarbiya → MAʿĀRIF; SHAYKH
ṭarbūsh (N.Afr) : hats of various types for men, worn in North Africa. V 746b
tarḍiya (A) : the eulogy *raḍiya 'llāhu ʿanhu*, which it is a duty to pronounce when one mentions the name of a Companion of the Prophet. VIII 828b
tardjahār (A) : a bowl with a graduated orifice in its underside that submerges in a given period, an ancient device for measuring time. S 373a
tardjama (A, pl. *tarādjim*) : in literature, a term in titles introducing a biography;

ʿilm al-tarādjim is a branch of historical research, sometimes confused by the Twelver shīʿīs with *ʿilm al-ridjāl* (→ RIDJĀL). III 1151a; VI 349b

In the science of diplomatic, the designation of the sender in the address, ʿUNWĀN, which developed from the simple *akhūhu* or *waladuhu* to *al-mamlūk al-Nāṣirī*, etc. II 302a

♦ ʿilm al-tarādjim → TARDJAMA

tardjīʿ (A) : in music, the refrain of a song. II 1073b

In Persian literature, a refrain poem, also called *tardjīʿ-band*, a variation of the ḲAṢĪDA written in a single metre composed of parts which each have their own rhyme and are separated by a distich (*tardjīʿ band*) that often serves as a refrain, *wāsiṭa*. I 677b; IV 715a

♦ tardjīʿ-band → TARDJĪʿ

tardjīḥ (A) : in law, the exercise of preference. IX 324b

tarfīl (A) : in prosody, a deviation in the metre consisting of the addition of a moving and a quiescent consonant, a *sabab khafīf* (→ SABAB); thus *mutafāʿilun* becomes *mutafāʿilātun*. I 672a

ṭarḥ (A), and *ilḳāʾ* : in alchemy, an inert or molten substance. III 1087b

♦ ṭarḥa : a large, dark head veil that hangs all the way down the back, worn by women in Egypt. V 742a

taʾrīdj (A) : in classical Muslim administration, an addition register, showing those categories which need to be seen globally, arranged for easy addition, with totals. Receipts for payments made are also registered in the ~ . II 78b

taʿrīf (A) : in literature, a term for biography, appearing in the title of lives of saints, possibly for reasons of discretion, in a period where MANĀḲIB seems to be confined to the hagiographical sphere. This term seems to be particularly common in Morocco. VI 349b; and → ĀLA; MADĪḤ

tarik (Toareg) : among the Touareg, a camel's saddle with a pommel in the form of a cross. VI 667a

ṭarīḳa (A, pl. *ṭuruḳ*) : path; method of instruction, initiation and religious exercise; also, a religious brotherhood which forms the organised expression of religious life in Islam. II 164a

♦ ṭarīḳa khiṭābiyya : 'way of eloquence'; a form employed in Qurʾānic preachings. II 447a

taʾrīkh (A) : history; dating.

In the science of diplomatic, ~ 'dating' is one of the parts of a Turkish document; it is marked by means of an Arabic formula, e.g. *taḥrīr*^{an} *fī* and is followed by the decade of the month, the name of the month, and the year. II 307a; II 315a

In Turkish, a chronogram, consisting of a a group of letters whose numerical equivalents, added together, provide the date of a past or future event, known in Arabic as RAMZ. III 468a

♦ taʾrīkh-i Ilāhī (P **'Ilāhī Era'**) : the 'divine era', introduced by the Mughal emperor Akbar in 992/1584. The first year of this solar year was the year of Akbar's accession, 963/1555-6. S 410b

ṭarḳ (A), also *ḍarb* : lithomancy. The technicalities of this cleromantic rite are unknown to us, but it is supposed to have consisted of casting pebbles (*ḥaṣā*) on the sand and of interpreting the patterns they made, or the signs which are given by the way they fell on top of each other. Instead of pebbles, grain or nuts could be used. From the marks made by the pebbles on the ground, lines were traced in the sand, and from this there has been a gradual development which ultimately results in making *ṭarḳ bi 'l-ḥaṣā* the synonym of *khaṭṭ bi 'l-raml*, i.e. geomancy (→ KHAṬṬ). IV 1128b

tarkhāniyyāt (A) : in the science of diplomatic, concessions granting aged officials exemption from taxes, and possibly also a fixed salary, in the classical period. II 303b

ṭarkhashḳūḳ (A) : in botany, *taraxacum*, the dandelion used in popular medicine because of its bitter substance. S 370b; and → ʿALATH

tarkhīm (A) : in grammar, phonetic reduction. IX 528a

ṭarkhūn → SHĪḤ

tarkīb-band (P) : in Persian literature, a refrain poem like the TARDJĪʿ, but called a ~ if the refrain differs in each instance where it occurs. I 677b; VII 662a; and → MUSADDAS

tarma (A) : a gallery, or wide room, giving on to the courtyard of a house through three bays. II 114a

ṭarrāḥī (A) : in art, designing; in the context of pictures, the production of the underdrawing. VIII 451b

tarsīm (A) : in Mamlūk times, perhaps predominantly, the detaining of a person in one place or putting him under guard. IX 547a

tartīb → ḲĀNŪN

♦ bi 'l-tartīb : lit. step by step; in music, slow motion. IX 101a

tartīl → NASHĪD

ṭarṭūr → ṬANṬŪR

taṣābī (A) : in the expression ~ *'l-shaykh*, a collection of motifs given in poetic dialogues warning the old man not to cavort like a young man. IX 385b

tasāḥuḳ → SIḤĀḲ

tasallum → ḲABḌ

tasbīḥ → SUBḤA

taṣdīr → ṢADR

tasdīs (A) : in astrology, the sextile aspect. IV 259b

tasekkurt (B) : the partridge. IX 536b

tasfīr (A) : the art of bookbinding. VIII 150b

tashahhud (A) : the Islamic affirmation of faith. VIII 929b

tashāhir → KABŪSH

tashbīb (A) : in literature, ~ is frequently used as a simple synonym for GHAZAL and NASĪB. II 1028a; IV 714b; in Urdu literature, ~ is the prelude of the ḲAṢĪDA, also, but less frequently, called *tamhīd*. V 958b

In rhetoric, ~ is synonymous with *ibtidāʾ* 'introduction, prologue', in its widest sense. III 1006a

ta<u>sh</u>bīh (A) : in theology, the comparing of God to the created; anthropomorphism. I 410b; III 160a

In rhetoric, a simile. IV 249b; VIII 614b

For ~ in grammar, → ĀLA

ta<u>sh</u>dīd → <u>SH</u>ADDA

taṣḥīf (A) : in rhetoric, paronomasia based on modifications of the graphic representations of two words and not on sound. II 825b; in prosody, forgery. IX 455b

ta<u>sh</u>lama (T) : in Turkish folk poetry, a satirical genre, which has social injustices as one of its main targets. III 358a

ta<u>sh</u>rīf → <u>KH</u>ILʿA

ta<u>sh</u>t-dār (P) : the 'keeper of the washing vessels'; a palace officer under the <u>Gh</u>aznavids and the Sal<u>dj</u>ūḳs. II 1082a

ta<u>sh</u>ṭīr (A) : in prosody, the intercalation of two hemistichs between the first two of an existing poem. IX 243b; IX 462b

taʾsīs (A) : in prosody, an *alif* of prolongation placed before the rhyme letter, *rawī*, and separated from it by a consonant which may be changed at will. IV 412a

taṣliya → IFTITĀḤ

tasmiya → BASMALA

taṣrīʿ (A) : in prosody, internal rhyme, a shortening or lengthening of the last foot of a rhyme appearing at the end of the first hemistich, in order to make it conform to the pattern of the last foot of the second hemistich. II 825b; IV 413b

taṣrīf (A) : in rhetoric, the transformation of a root (into various *awzān*). VIII 614b; and → NAḤW

taṣrīḥ (A) : in mysticism, an unequivocal declaration of one's feelings and intentions, seen as the opposite of *ramz* (→ I<u>SH</u>ĀRA). VIII 428b

ṭassū<u>dj</u> : in Sāsānid and early Islamic ʿIrāḳ, a sub-province, subdivision of a KŪRA 'province'. The ~ was in turn divided into RUSTĀḲS 'district'. I 3a; VIII 636a

taṭabbub (A) : medical practice. IX 8a

taṭawwuʿ → ṢAWM

ta<u>th</u>lī<u>th</u> (A) : in astrology, the trine aspect. IV 259b; VII 794b

ta<u>th</u>wīb (A) : repetition; the term for the formula *al-ṣalāt <u>kh</u>ayr min al-nawm*, pronounced twice in the morning prayer. I 188a

taʿṭīl (A) : 'stripping'; in theology, ~ is applied to the denial of attributes, that is, the assertion that God does not possess attributes of power, knowledge, speech etc. which are distinct from His essence. I 334a; I 411a; III 953b

taṭwīʿ (Tun) : the diploma of secondary education from the Zaytūna of Tunis. IX 160b

ṭāʿūn (A) : in medicine, the plague. VIII 783a; IX 477a

ṭāʾūs (A) : in zoology, the peacock. I 177b
ṭawāf (A) : the circumambulation of the Kaʿba during the pilgrimage. III 35a
♦ ṭawāf al-ifāḍa : the circumambulation of the Kaʿba on 10 Dhu ʾl-Ḥidjdja, after the sacrifice. III 35b; VII 169b
tawakkul (A) : in mysticism, trust in God to such an extent that one does not support oneself; submission to the divine will. VIII 596a; VIII 691b
tawallud (A) : 'engendered act'; according to the Muʿtazilite Bishr b. al-Muʿtamir, ~ is an act prompted by a cause which is itself the effect of another cause. Thus, in the act of opening a door with a key, there is first a voluntary act, then the movement of the hand which turns the key, and lastly that of the key which turns the tongue of the lock. This last movement is an engendered act for it does not emanate directly from a voluntary decision. I 413b; I 1243b
tawʾamān → DJAWZĀʾ
ṭawāshī (A) : in the Ayyūbid army under Ṣalāḥ al-Dīn, fully-equipped cavalrymen. I 797b; II 507a; VIII 468a; a eunuch. I 33a; IV 1088a
ṭawāsīn (A) : a name for the SŪRAs that begin with the letters *ṭā-sīn*: XXVI-XXVIII. IX 887b
tawātur (A) : in law, a form of testimony which consists of the affirmation of a fact by a number of persons so large (a minimum of twenty-five is generally accepted) as logically to exclude any possibility of fraud or lying. The ~ is superior to all other modes of proof with the exception of confession. II 171b
ṭawb (A) : unbaked brick. I 1226b
tawbīr (A) : an instinctive attempt by a hare to blur its tracks by placing its body weight on the back foot only. The back foot has a pad which is covered with hair and thus prevents the toes and claws from marking the ground. S 85a
tawdjīh (A) : in prosody, the vowel before the quiescent rhyme letter; according to others, also before the vowelled rhyme letter. IV 412a
ṭawf (A) : a raft of early ʿAbbāsid Mesopotamia, similar to the KELEK. VIII 810b
tawḥīd (A) : a kind of dates. I 126b; and → DAWR AL-KASHF; MUWAḤḤIDŪN; NĀṬIḲ
taʾwīl (A) : interpretation of the Qurʾān. IV 147a; and → TANZĪL
ṭawīl (A) : lit. long; in prosody, the name of the first Arabic metre. The ~ forms, with the metres *basīṭ* and *madīd*, the group of metres whose hemistichs consist of 24 consonants each. I 670a
In numismatics, the name of a coin in Ḥasā, on the Arabian peninsula, which is only an inch long and of very base silver, if not copper, without any trace of inscription. V 684a; and → ḲALANSUWA
ṭawḳ → ḤADJRA; SHAʿĪRA
tawḳīʿ (A, T *tewḳiʿ*) : in calligraphy, a variety of the THULUTH script, with its letters somewhat more compressed and rounded. This script was used in Persia for the final page, sc. that with the colophon showing the date and place of copying and the scribe's name, of elongated format Qurʾāns. IV 1123b; for Turkish diplomatic practice, a specific technique for writing more formal and solemn docu-

ments. The script used was the DĪWĀNĪ, also known as *tewḳiʿ* in its various forms. II 315b; VIII 151b

In the science of diplomatic, ~ seems originally to have been the ruler's signature, which was appended in the chancellery. Later on, ~ was also used for letters of appointment, quite generally to begin with, but later only for the lesser officials. II 303a; into the 10/16th century, ~ in the *corroboratio* refers to the seal; not until the 11th/17th century was ~ replaced by the (long overdue) expression MUHR. II 311b; and → IMḌĀ; IṬLĀḲĀT

♦ tawḳīʿ ʿalā ʾl-ḳiṣaṣ : in the science of diplomatic, the decision of petitions in open court, said to have been the custom even in Sāsānid times. II 303b

tawrāt (A) : the Pentateuch. IX 321b

tawrīḳ (A) : in art, arabesque, mostly of the sort restricted to foliage. The term is preserved in Spanish *ataurique*, commonly used by Spanish authors to designate the genuine arabesque. I 498b; I 560b

tawriya (A) : in rhetoric, mispointing information for secrecy. VIII 427a; in prosody, double-meaning. IX 460b

tawt͟hīḳ → MIḲRAN

ṭāwūs (P 'peacock') : a pandore viol from India, with the ESRĀR one of the two best-known examples. The ~ is practically identical with the *esrār*, but is adorned with the figure of a peacock at the bottom of the body of the instrument. VIII 348b

ṭawwāf (A) : the ceremonial circumambulation of the Kaʿba during the pilgrimage. I 610b

tawwaziyya (A) : textiles from the mediaeval city of Tawwad͟j (Tawwaz) in southern Persia. IX 310b

tāy → ČAY

tayammum (A) : ritual purification with sand, soil, or dust, allowed when water is unavailable. II 1104a; VI 709b; VIII 926b

tayd͟ji̊ d͟jemāʿati̊ (T) : in the Ottoman empire, a special category of MÜSELLEM which enjoyed exemption from taxes in exchange for breeding horses for the royal stables. IX 855a

ṭaylasān (P) : a headshawl worn over the turban, worn in mediaeval Islam particularly by religious scholars and notables in the northern and eastern parts of Iran and even by the common folk in Fārs. V 747b

ṭayr (A) : in mysticism, spiritual flight, one of the degrees of the mystical journey. IX 863a

♦ ṭayr al-māʾ : in zoology, the wild water-fowl. I 1152b

tays → ʿATŪD; TAYYĀS

ṭayy (A) : in prosody, a deviation in the metre due to the suppression of the fourth consonant of a foot. I 672a

ṭayyār → BAYYĀZ

♦ ṭayyāra (A) : 'flyer', a name describing a kind of skiff used in mediaeval

Mesopotamia. VIII 811a; and → BĀD-I HAWĀ

tayyās (A), or *tays* : a goat-herd. S 317a

ṭayyibāt : 'jocose poems', a genre in Persian literature, defined by classical Persian literary critics according to its contents rather than to its form. III 355

tazakkara → MUSTAKRISH

taʿzīr (A, pl. *taʿāzir*) : in law, discretionary punishment by the ḲĀḌĪ in the form of corporal chastisement, generally the bastinado. I 29b; II 519a

taʿziya (A) : in literature, a letter of condolence addressed to the parents of the deceased, becoming frequent from the 2nd/8th century onwards. When it is in verse, it is virtually indistinguishable from the MARTHIYA. VI 605a

In Persian literature, the passion play, the occurrence of which is not documented before the late 12th/18th century. IV 50b

tazkiya (A) : in law, the procedure for substantiating the ʿADĀLA of witnesses, also called *taʿdīl*. I 209b

♦ al-tazkiya al-ʿalāniyya : the second stage of the procedure known as TAZKIYA, in which the persons who received a sealed envelope in the first stage (→ AL-TAZKIYYA AL-SIRRIYYA) appear at the public hearing to confirm their former attestation. I 209b

♦ al-tazkiya al-sirriyya : the first stage of the procedure known as TAZKIYA, in which the judge proceeds to a secret investigation, by sending a question in a sealed envelope to qualified persons. I 209b

tebriya → TABRIʾA

teferrüdj → TAFARRUDJ

tegulmust → LITHĀM

tekke → KHĀNḲĀH

teklīf → TAKLĪF

telkhīṣ (T, < A) : in Ottoman administration, memoirs, e.g. those presented to the sultan by the grand vizier acting as representative of the government. The officer to whom they were given was called the *telkhīṣdji*. VIII 481b ff.

♦ telkhīṣdji → TELKHĪṢ

temenggung → BENDAHARA

temidelt → AGADIR

temlīk-nāme (T) : in the Ottoman empire, a special diploma issued by the sultans, recognising proprietary rights on waste land as well as on running water and springs within the area delimited by the document. V 878b

tennūre (T) : in Ottoman Turkey, a long dervish's robe without sleeves. V 752a; IX 168a

teraḳḳī (T) : 'advancement', a bonus granted to cavalrymen in the Ottoman empire. IX 656a

terlik (T) : in Ottoman Turkey, the most popular shoes, worn by men and women, without heels or quarters slightly raised at the end, in leather or material and often decorated. V 752b

tesbīḥ → SUBḤA

teslīm tashı̊ (T) : 'stone of submission', the name given to a small, twelve-fluted disc worn on a cord, sometimes with smaller stones strung along the cord, around the neck, and given to the young Bektāshī dervish at the end of his novitiate. VIII 244b

təstmal (N.Afr) : a fringed head scarf for women worn in Libya. V 746b

tewḳiʿ → TAWḲĪʿ; ṬUGHRA

♦ tewḳīʿī → NISHĀNDJı̊

thabat → FAHRASA

thābit (A) : having the characteristic of 'positive', as e.g. the non-entity in Muʿtazilī thought. I 178b

thaḳāfa → RUMḤ

thaḳalayn → ḤADĪTH AL-THAḲALAYN

thākur (H) : an honorary title, used to address the Hindus of the Lohaṇa caste. VIII 307a

thaldj (A) : snow.

♦ thaldjiyyāt : in poetry, snow poems. IX 8b

thanāyā (A) : in anatomy, the incisors. VIII 695b

thanī (A) : the name for a foal between two and three years old. II 785a; and → ʿATŪD

thaʾr (A) : punitive raids of retaliation, one of the Bedouin's warlike activities. II 1055a

tharīd (A) : a dish consisting of bread crumbled into a broth of meat and vegetables, associated with the tribal tradition of the Ḳuraysh and said to be among the favourite dishes of the Prophet. II 1059a

thawāb (A) : in theology, recompense, especially with reference to the next world, usually only in a good sense. II 518a; and → ʿIWAḌ

thawābit → AL-KAWĀKIB AL-THĀBITA

thawb (A, pl. *thiyāb*, *athwāb* 'clothes') : in early Islam, a general word for garment and fabric. V 733b; in modern times, a basic tunic worn by both sexes throughout the Middle East; a woman's dress. V 742a

thawr (A, < Gk) : in astronomy, *al-~* is the term for Taurus, one of the twelve zodiacal constellations. VII 83a

thaytal → BAḲAR

thayyib (A) : a girl over the age of puberty who is no longer virgin, being either widowed or repudiated. III 17a

thiḳa (A) : 'trustworthy'; in the science of Tradition, the highest quality of a reliable transmitter of Tradition. I 104b; II 462a; VIII 900b; VIII 983a

thiḳāf → RUMḤ

thiyāb → ḲUMĀSH

thughūr (A, s. *thaghr*) : lit. gaps, the forward strongholds in the frontier zone which extended between the Byzantine empire and the empire of the caliphs in the north and north-east of Syria. I 761a; II 503a; VIII 603a; VIII 869b; and → ʿAWĀṢIM

In naval science, strategic ports. S 120a

thulth → NIṢF

thulūl (A) : a wart. S 350a

thuluth (A) : lit. one-third; in calligraphy, a script which is generally said to have derived its name from being based on the principle of a third of each letter being sloping. It was and is still used for every kind of frame and for book titles in all Muslim countries. IV 1123b; VIII 151b

thumn (A) : a measure used in Muslim Spain for weighing olive oil. A ~ contained 2 1/4 Spanish raṭls (503.68 g), i.e. 1.12 kg. VI 121a

thunāʾiyyāt → MUTHANNAYĀT

thurayyā → NADJM

ṭīb → AFĀWĪH

tibāra (H) : a Hindī term also applied to Muslim buildings in India, for a hall with three adjacent bays or doors. V 1214b

tifā(wa) → TUFFA

tīfāf → HINDIBĀʾ

ṭifl (A) : child; according to Lane, 'a child until he discriminates...after which he is called *ṣabiyy*' or 'a child from the time of his birth...until he attains to puberty'. VIII 821b

tiftik (T) : the silky hair of the white long-haired goats in central Anatolia. I 511a

tīghbend (T) : among the Bektāshīs, a girdle fashioned from ram's wool, the girding on of which is the second element in their ceremony of initiation, *iḳrār*. IX 168a; and → ELIFI NEMED

tikka → FŪṬA

ṭīkūk → SHAḲĪḲAT AL-NUʿMĀN

tillīs (A) : a measure of capacity which was used in Egypt in the caliphal period for measuring grain. VI 119a

tīm (P) : term used by Nāṣir-i Khusraw for caravanserai, still used in its diminutive form *tīmča* in parts of the Iranian world. IX 796a

tīmār → SERBEST

tīmča → TĪM

timrād (A, pl. *tamārid*) : narrow pierced pigeon hole in the loft (*ḳurmūṣ*, < Gk) of a pigeon. When placed at the foot of the loft, it forced the pigeon to climb up a ladder inside its nesting-place, which strengthened its muscles, thus becoming an indoor pigeon as distinct from an outside one which returned to the loft through pigeon-holes at the top. III 109b

ṭimṭim → NAḲAD

tīn akhḍar → NĪL

ṭinfisa (A) : a kind of carpet with a pile. S 136a

tinnīn (A) : in folklore, an enormous serpent. III 335a; and → DJAWZAHAR

♦ dhanab (al-tinnīn) → DHANAB

♦ raʾs (al-tinnīn) → RAʾS

tira (P) : a subdivision of a tribe; among the Kurdish, ~ can be best described as a political group, not to be confused with the *hoz*, a group of the same lineage. The ~ is subdivided into many *khel*, each *khel* composed of twenty to thirty tents or households united by economic links as well as by family links. V 472a; among the Shāhsewan in Persia, a tribal section, formed by two or three winter camps of 10-15 households. IX 224a

ṭīra (A) : originally, the observation and interpretation of the spontaneous flight, cries and perching activities of certain birds, used in divination; evil presentiments aroused by the contents of a phrase or a song are generally also grouped under this head. A whole literature, essentially of poetry and proverbs, created to dissuade man from following the ideas inspired in him by ~ , and to which all men are subject, is derived from the term. II 758b ff.; IV 290b

ṭirāz (A) : textiles. I 24a; silken fabrics and brocades designed for ceremonial robes. I 501a; embroidery, especially embroidered bands with writing in them; an elaborately embroidered robe, such as might be worn by a ruler or his entourage. ~ garments were bestowed as tokens of royal favour and were among the standard gifts brought by diplomatic embassies to other rulers as part of foreign policy. III 219a; V 736b; S 341b

In the science of diplomatic, ~ was the term for the introductory protocol in diplomatic documents, with considerable variety in the wording. The purpose seems to have been to endow the document with a certain authenticity. From the 4th/10th century, the ~ was omitted altogether. It is also called *iftitāḥ*. II 301b

tīrkash (P) : in archery, a quiver made of horse-hair, used by archers from the province of Gīlān. IV 799b

ṭirs (A) : parchment from which the original text had been washed off and which then was written on again. II 540b; VIII 408a

tiryāḳ (A) : in medicine, a remedy which could be used as a prophylactic against poison. IX 873a; and → AFYŪN

ṭiʿs (A, pl. *ṭuʿūs*) : in the Arabian peninsula, a dune bare of vegatation. A larger dune is called *naḳāʾ*. II 537a

tōlā : a Mughal measurement of weight equalling 185.5 g. II 121a

ton : 'group', in Mali, *ton jon* 'group of slaves' being the basic social institution of the Bambara empire of Segu, making up the army and a good part of the bureaucracy. IX 121b

toy (T) : a public feast given by the ruler, a practice that was apparently introduced into the Islamic world by the Saldjūḳs from the custom among the pastoral nomads of Eurasia. The institution was also known as *shölen* or *ash*. VI 809b

tozluḳ (T) : breeches worn by men as an outer garment in Ottoman Turkey. V 752b

trīmūlīn (A) : in zoology, the arenicol, a small beach worm (*Arenicola marina*), often used as bait in fishing. VIII 1022a

ṭūb (A) : in the Muslin West, a lump of earth or an unfired brick, whence Sp.

adobe. In Egypt, ~ is used as a synonym of *ā<u>dj</u>urr* 'fired brick'. V 585b; and → <u>SH</u>AWKA

tubbān (A) : very short drawers, made of hair, worn under trousers by Umayyad soldiers. IX 677a

tu<u>dh</u>rī (A) : in music, a trill. II 1073b

tufah → TUFFA

tufangčī (T) : in the Ṣafawid and Ottoman military, a musketeer. I 8a; I 1068a; VIII 786a; IX 477a

tuffa (A), or *tufah, tifā, tifāwa* : in zoology, the Jungle Cat (*Felis chaus*), trained to hunt game. II 739b

ṭu<u>gh</u>ra (T, A *ṭu<u>gh</u>rā*) : in the science of Turkish diplomatic, the device or the sign of the sultan, also called *ni<u>sh</u>ān-i humāyūn, tewḳīʿ* and *ʿalāmet*, and of different design for each sultan. It contains the name of the sultan and all his titles and other distinctions with the formula *muẓaffar dāʾima*, encased in an ornamental design, always with the same motifs and shape. II 314b; IV 1104b; V 232b; VIII 62a

In Ottoman administration, chancellor. VIII 62a

♦ ṭu<u>gh</u>ra-ke<u>sh</u> (T) : in Ottoman administration, a clerk especially assigned to drawing and painting the ṬU<u>GH</u>RA. II 314b

ṭuḥayḥī (A) : on the Arabian peninsula, a small, fierce-looking lizard. I 541b

tuku (J) : the remnant of a bride-price in Java. I 174a

ṭulb (A) : under the Mamlūks, a Royal unit. IX 610a

ṭulma (A) : 'flat bread'; in ancient Arabia, a kind of pancake cooked on a heated stone. V 41b

tūmān (P) : in numismatics, the unit of account which formed the basis of the Persian currency system during the period of Ṣafawid rule; its value was fixed at the currently-established weight of 10,000 silver dīnārs. The weight of the ~ was customarily expressed as a fixed number of MI<u>TH</u>ḲĀLs or *nu<u>kh</u>ūd*s of refined silver which could then be converted into coin with the value of 10,000 dīnārs. One *mi<u>th</u>ḳāl*, weighing approximately 4.60 g, was equal to 24 *nu<u>kh</u>ūd*s which each weighed about 0.192 g. VIII 790a

tumāntōḳ : in Muslim India, a standard appearing in Mu<u>gh</u>al court ceremony, resembling the common ʿALAM but with its shaft adorned with Tibetan yak-tails. VI 533b

ṭūmār (A, < Gk) : a sixth of a papyrus roll, the smallest piece used in the trade. IV 742a; V 173b

ṭunbūr (A) : in music, a lute with a long neck. V 234a

tunḳus (A) : in zoology, the tench. VIII 1021a

ṭunub → ṬANĪB

tūp-<u>kh</u>āna (P) : in the Ṣafawid military, artillery. VIII 786a; artillery park. IX 476b

turʿa (A) : a canal of a river, distinguised from minor branches and the main stream. VIII 38a

turba (A, T *türbe*), or *kümbed* : a tomb surmounted by a dome, ~ is the classical word which was driven out of use by ḲUBBA, until it was again popularised by the Turks. V 289a; VI 652b; VIII 964b

türk → SĀRT

türkü (T) : a type of folk-poetry of Anatolia. I 677b; VIII 2b

ṭurra (A) : *al-~ al-sukayniyya* 'Sukayna-style curls', a particular hair-style made famous by Sukayna bt. al-Ḥusayn, a granddaughter of ʿAlī b. Abī Ṭālib. IX 803a; and → ṢUDGH

turs (A) : shield. IX 891a

ṭuruḳ → SHAYKH AL-SHUYŪKH; ṬARĪḲA

turundjān → NUḤĀM

ṭusayt → ṢAḤN

ṭusūt (A) : in music, the general term for harmonica, played with sticks, *ḳuḍbān*. An author of the 9th/15th century refers to the harmonica as the *kīzān* 'cups' and *khawābiʾ* 'jars'. IX 11b

tutin (P) : a cigar-shaped raft of reeds, found among the population of hunters in Sīstān, on which they travel to fish and hunt waterfowl. IX 682b

tutḳavul → RĀHDĀR

ṭuwama → SULAḤFĀ

tuyugh (T), or *tuyuğ* : in Turkish literature, a type of quatrain, similar to the RUBĀʿĪ. I 677b

tuyūl : in mediaeval Persia, temporary grants in return for services. They frequently carried with them the right to collect (as well as to receive) the taxes, and rights of jurisdiction. III 1089b; IV 1043 ff.; IX 733a

tuzghü → SAʾURI

U

ubna → LŪṬĪ

ʿūd (A) : in music, the lute, whose player is an *ʿūdī*. I 66b

ʿudār (A) : part of the ancient Arabs' repertoire of fabulous animals, the ~ was a male whose habit was to make men submit to assaults, which proved mortal if worms developed in the anus of the victim. II 1078b

ʿudhr (A) : in law, a plea. I 319b

ʿudiya (A) : 'having a single tent-pole'; among the Tiyāha in the Arabian peninsula, a tent whose ridge-pole rests on a row of three poles. The Sbāʿ call it a *gotba*. IV 1148a

udj (T) : frontier. II 1044b; under the Ottomans, a military post. VIII 608b

ʿudjma → ʿADJAM

udm (A), or *idām* : a condiment, eaten with bread by pre-Islamic Arabs. II 1058a

ʿudūl → ʿADL

ufk (A) : falsehood. IX 567b
ufʿuwān → AFʿĀ
uḥbūla → ḤIBĀLA
ʿuhda (A) : in Egypt under Muḥammad ʿAlī, an estate consisting of bankrupt villages whose taxes were collected by their new landholders rather than by members of the government. II 149a
uḥdjiyya (A, pl. *aḥādjīn*) : 'riddle, conundrum', one of three kinds of literary plays upon words, the others being LUGHZ and MUʿAMMĀ. The term denotes a simple guessing game, e.g. 'guess what I have in my hand', but can also mean a type of enigma fairly close to the *lughz*. Thus for *salsabīl* 'wine' : 'What is the alternative sense meant by the person setting forth a riddle when he says: ask (= *sal*) the way (=*sabīl*)?'. V 807a
ʿuhūd → ʿAHD; ʿAHDNĀME
ʿuḳāb (A) : the Prophet's flag, according to the traditional literature. I 349a; the black banner used in the battles against Ḳuraysh. IX 14a; and → NŪSHĀDIR
In zoology, the eagle. I 1152b
ʿuḳda → DJAWZAHAR
ukhdha → SIḤR
uḳḥuwān (A) : in botany, the chrysanthemum; ~ is also used to render the παρθένιον of Dioscorides, by which we should probably understand the medical *Matricaria chamomilla*, still in use today. S 114b
uḳiyānūs → ḲĀMŪS
ʿuḳḳāl → ʿĀḲIL; DJĀHIL
ukla (A) : an itch. IX 435a
uḳṣūṣa → ḲIṢṢA
ūlaḳ : an Özbeg sport in which men on horseback battle to carry the carcass of a cow to a goal, played at the celebration of weddings and circumcisions. VIII 234b
ʿulamāʾ (s. *ʿālim*) → FAḲĪH
ulee (Oromo) : a long, forked stick, carried by pilgrims to the tomb of Shaykh Ḥusayn, having a practical use but being above all a sign of their status as pilgrims. IX 399a
ulu beg (T) : 'senior lord'; in Saldjūḳ and early Ottoman administration, the designation for the father of the ruling family in his capacity as ruler of the state. It was he who concluded treaties, struck coins and was apparently commemorated in the Friday public prayer. VIII 192b
ulus → ĪL
ʿuluww → ISNĀD ʿĀLĪ
ʿumda (A, pl. *ʿumad*) : in 19th-century Egypt, the term for veteran masters in the guilds. S 409b
umdūḥa → MADĪḤ
umm (A) : mother.
In astronomy, the inner surface, usually depressed, on the front of the astrolabe,

enclosed by the outer rim, ḤAD̲J̲RA. I 723a

♦ umm ḥubayn → ḤIRBĀʾ

♦ umm ḳarn : in zoology, the trigger fish (*Balistes*). VIII 1021a; and → KAR-
KADDAN

♦ umm sālim : in zoology, the bifasciated lark. I 541b

♦ umm al-s̲h̲abābīṭ : in zoology, the barbel (*Barbus sharpeyi*). VIII 1021a

♦ umm t̲h̲alāt̲h̲: in zoology, the nickname given to the female sandgrouse, because she lays two or three eggs. IV 744a

♦ umm walad : the title given to a concubine who has a child by her master. I 28a

♦ umm zubayba → K̲H̲ARŪF AL-BAḤR

umma (A) : as a Qurʾānic term, ~ denotes the nation of the Prophet, the Community. II 411a

In geography, term in the Arabian peninsula for the Tihāma fogs, also called
sukhaymānī. IX 39b

ʿumra (A) : the Little Pilgrimage, in contrast to the ḤADJDJ, the Great Pilgrimage.
It consists of walking seven times around the Kaʿba, praying two *rakʿas*, a se-
quence of actions performed in the ṢALĀT, facing the *makām Ibrāhīm* and the
Kaʿba, and finally traversing seven times the distance between Ṣafā and
Marwa. III 31b; III 35a

ʿumrā (A) : as defined by the Ḥanafī, S̲h̲āfiʿī and Ḥanbalī schools of law, a gift
with full ownership but as a life interest, the donee undertaking to restore the
property on his death, at the latest. In the Mālikī school, ~ is a gift of the
usufruct and as such valid; it thus becomes very hard to distinguish it from
ʿāriyya 'loan for use'. III 351a

ūniḳs (A, < Gk) : in zoology, a kind of water-snail, valued because of its aroma.
VIII 707a

ʿunnāb (A) : in botany, the jujube tree (*Ziziphus jujuba*). IX 549b

ʿunwān (A) : direction or address.

In the science of diplomacy, the ~ is part of the introduction of documents. Al-
Ḳalḳas̲h̲andī collected fifteen different forms of the ~ . II 302a

ʿurafāʾ → ʿARĪF

ʿurāt (A) : the 'naked', name for turbulent social elements who grouped themselves around the caliph and barred the path of the besiegers of Bag̲h̲dād in 196/
812 until their resistance was overcome. I 437b

urd̲j̲ūza → RAD̲J̲AZ

urdu (U, < T ORDU), and *zabān-i urdu* : in South Asia, the term used to designate
the mixed Hindustani-Persian-Turkish language of the court and the army; now
the Urdu language of a large proportion of the Muslims in the subcontinent.
VIII 174b

ʿurf (A, P) : administrative regulations on matters of penal law, obligations and
contracts, issued by Muslim rulers, called ḲĀNŪN in Turkey. I 170a; and →
ʿĀDA; AʿRĀF; ʿARĪF

urfī (A) : in zoology, the braize orphe, whose Arabic term is found again in the Latinised nomenclature to specify a sub-species limited to a particular region (*Pagrus orphus*). VIII 1021b

ʿurfuṭ (A) : in botany, the name of a thorny shrub which exudes an evil-smelling resin. III 587a

ūriyā (Syr) : teacher. IX 490a

urka (A), or *ḳattal* : in zoology, the orc or grampus, one of the marine mammals or cetaceans. VIII 1022b

ʿurs (A) : in the Indo-Pakistan subcontinent, a feast held in honour of a saint. VI 896b; among the dervishes, a celebration to commemorate a dead saint. VIII 416a; in South Africa, festival commemorating death anniversaries of ṣūfī saints. IX 731a

ʿurwa (A), or *ḥabs* : part of the suspensory apparatus of the astrolabe, ~ is the handle, which is affixed to the point of the KURSĪ so that it can be turned to either side in the plane of the latter. I 723a

usbūr (A) : in zoology, the sparid fish. VIII 1021a

ʿuṣfur → ḲURṬUM

ʿus̲h̲b → ʿAS̲H̲S̲H̲ĀB

us̲h̲nān (A) : a perfumed (powdered, pasty?) mixture for washing and scenting the clothes and hands, used in mediaeval times. VIII 653a

ʿus̲h̲r (A, T *ʿös̲h̲er*) : in the Ottoman empire, the main land tax for Muslims, a tithe of the produce. VII 507b

us̲h̲turbān (P) : the Persian equivalent of the Arabic *d̲j̲ummāl* 'camel-driver', 'owner and hirer of camels', 'a dealer in camels'. S 241b

üsküf (T) : in the Ottoman empire, a high KÜLĀH 'cap' worn by the Janissaries. Its rear part fell in the form of a covering on the back, a ribbon ornamenting it at the base where a metal case for the officer's spoon or plume was also fixed. V 751b

usra → CĀʾILA

usrub → RAṢĀṢ

usṭā → AD̲J̲ĪR

ustād̲h̲ (A) : teacher; eunuch. I 33a

usṭūl (A) : in the Arab navy, the term for a fleet. S 120a

usṭūra (A, pl. *asāṭīr*) : legend, myth. III 369a

♦ **asāṭīr al-awwalīn** (A) : a Qurʾānic phrase meaning 'stories of the ancients', suggesting a set expression that had been long in use. Its meaning hardly in doubt, most of the discussion has concerned its derivation, for *asāṭīr* was a plural without singular. Nowadays the term has been reinstated in the singular form *usṭura*. III 369a; S 90b

uṣūl → AṢL

♦ uṣūliyya → AK̲H̲BĀRIYYA

utrud̲j̲d̲j̲a (A) : the citron, thought to be found in the Qurʾān under the name of *mitk*, *matk*. II 1058b

ʿuṭʿuṭ → SAKHLA
üzengi ḳurčisi → RIKĀBDĀR
uzuk, or *ūzuk* : in Muslim India, a royal seal (a 'privy' seal), kept often either by one of the royal ladies or by a trusted official. II 806a; a small round seal for decrees relating to titles, high appointments, DJĀGIRs and the sanction of large sums. VII 473b

V

vār : in Muslim Pandjābī literature, an historical ballad. VIII 256b

W

wā-sūkht (P) : in Persian poetry, a genre in which the theme was the lover's turning away from the beloved. VIII 776a; and → WĀSŌKH
wabāʾ (A, P *wabā*) : in medicine, cholera. VIII 783a; pestilence. IX 477a
wabar (A) : camel's hair. IX 764b
♦ ahl al-wabar : 'the people of the camel skin', a designation for nomads, as opposed to *ahl al-madar*, i.e. the sedentaries. V 585a
waʿd (A) : in eschatology, part of the dogma of *waʿd wa-*WAʿĪD, promises and threats in the life beyond, one of the five fundamental principles dear to the Muʿtazilīs. III 465a; IX 341b
waʿda (A) : a communal meal. IX 20b
wadaad (Somali) : in Somali society, a man of religion, who also mediates in disputes between lineages. This term is used in contrast to *waranle* 'warrior', the other class of Somali men. IX 723a
waḍaḥ → DJUDHĀM
waḍḍaʿ → ṢĀLIḤ
wadhārī : an expensive cloth of cotton woven on cotton made in the Transoxianan village of Wadhār, which was made into a light resistant type of yellow overcoat, very popular in winter. VIII 1030b; S 176b
wādī (A, pl. *widyān*) : a watercourse filled only at certain times of the year; stream channel. I 538a; VII 909b
waḍīʿ → ḌAʿĪF
wadjh (A, pl. *wudjūh*) : face; variant. I 155a
wādjib (A) : in theology, a synonym of FARḌ 'a religious duty or obligation', the

omission of which will be punished and the performance of which will be rewarded. The Ḥanafī school, however, makes a distinction between these two terms, applying *farḍ* to those religious duties which are explicitly mentioned as such in the Qurʾān and the SUNNA, or based on consensus, and ~ to those the obligatory character of which has been deduced by reasoning. II 790a

wafḍa (A) : originally, a shepherd's leather bag; in archery, a quiver made from skin entirely, with no wood in its construction. IV 800a

wāfir (A) : in prosody, the name of the fourth Arabic metre. I 670a

wafḳ (A, pl. *awfāḳ*) : in sorcery, a square, in the field of which certain figures are so arranged that the addition of horizontal, vertical and diagonal lines gives in every case the same total (e.g. 15 or 34). II 370a

waḥda (A) : oneness.

♦ waḥdat al-shuhūd : 'the oneness of witness', a main line of mysticism, of which al-Ḥallādj was the exponent. I 416a; III 102a; monotheism. I 297b

♦ waḥdat al-wudjūd : 'the oneness of existence', a main line of mysticism which came to dominate from Ibn al-ʿArabī onwards. I 416b; III 102b; pantheism. I 297b

waḥf (A) : a womanʿs exuberant hair. IX 313a

wāḥid (A), or *fard*, *mufrad* : in grammar, the singular. II 406b

wahm (A) : estimative faculty; imagination. I 112a; III 509b; 'whim'. VIII 953a

♦ wahmiyyāt : the science of *fantasmagorica*. VIII 105b

waḥshī (A) : the part of the point of the nib of a reed-pen to the right of the incision. IV 471b; and → GHARĪB

♦ waḥshiyya : bestiality. II 551a

waḥy → ILHĀM

waʿīd (A) : the Khāridjite and Muʿtazilī doctrine of unconditional punishment of the unrepentant sinner in the hereafter. VII 607a; IX 341b; and → WAʿD

waḳaʿa (A), or *awḳaʿa* : in grammar, the nearest thing to 'transitive'. IX 528a

wakāla (A) : in mediaeval Islam, a meeting-place in cities for commercial agents. IX 788b

waḳf (A, pl. *awḳāf*), or *ḥubūs* : in law, a domain constituted into a pious endowment. I 661a; VIII 512b; and → ḲAṬʿ

wāḳifiyya (A) : in theology, term for the 'Abstentionists'. I 275a

wakīl (A, pl. *wukalāʾ*) : agent; in the context of the pilgrimage, the ~ is especially used to designate an agent of the *muṭawwifūn* (→ MUṬAWWIF). His task is to meet pilgrims arriving in Djudda, help them choose a *muṭawwif*, be responsible for them in Djudda until they depart for Mecca and again when they return to Djudda. Like the *muṭawwifūn*, the *wukalāʾ* are organised in a special guild. VI 170b

In law, the representative of a party. I 319b

In hydraulics, ~ is known in Oman and the United Arab Emirates to be the name for the official in charge of the upkeep of the *falad̲j̲*, a mining installation for extracting water from the depths of the earth. IV 532a

♦ wakīl-i dār : under the Sald̲j̲ūḳs, the intendant, an influential official of the sultan's court entourage. VIII 954a

♦ wakīl-i nafs-i nafīs-i humāyūn : in Ṣafawid Persia, an office created by S̲h̲āh Ismāʿīl, whose functionary was to be the *alter ego* of the s̲h̲āh, superior in rank both to the WAZĪR, the head of the bureaucracy, and the AMĪR AL-UMARĀʾ, the commander in chief of the ḲİZİLBĀS̲H̲ forces. VIII 768b

wakīr (A) : a flock of more than two hundred sheep or goats. When several ~ are joined together with their dogs and carrier donkeys, the large entity ensuing, sometimes numbering several thousand head, is called a *firḳ* or *mug̲h̲nam*. S 319b

waḳḳād (A, Tun *sak̲h̲k̲h̲ān*) : the 'stoker' of the furnace of a **ḥammām** 'steam bath'. III 140a

waḳs (A) : in prosody, a deviation in the metre because of the loss of both the second consonant of a foot and its vowel. I 672a

waʿl (A) : in zoology, the ibex, on the Arabian peninsula also called *badan*. I 541b; IX 98b

walāʾ (A) : proximity.

In law, contractual clientage (syn. *muwālāt*), a solution in early Islam to the problem of affiliating non-tribesman to a tribal society; though most such tribesmen were clearly converts, conversion was not necessary for the legal validity of the tie. The persons linked to one another by ~ were known as MAWLĀ. In pre-Islamic poetry, ~ usually denoted an egalitarian relationship of mutual help, but in later literature, it more commonly designates an unequal relationship of assistance, *mawlā* being a master, manumitter, benefactor or patron on the one hand, and a freedman, protégé or client on the other. I 30b; III 388b; VI 874b ff.

♦ walāʾ al-muwālāt : in Ḥanafī law, an institution between free men. I 30b

walad → AWLĀD

wālī (A) : local ruler. IX 6b; and → AṢḤĀB AL-ARBĀʿ

♦ wālī al-ʿahd : under the Umayyads, the title granted to the heir presumptive, in the sense of beneficiary of a contract (ʿAHD) concluded between him and his community. IV 938b

♦ wāli 'l-ḥarb (A) : the name for the governor of a province, who was still essentially the general of an army of occupation, in the first generations following the Arab conquest. I 184a

walī (A) : in law, a guardian for matrimonial purposes. I 27b; VIII 27a; curator of the *maḥd̲j̲ūr* 'a person who is restricted of the capacity to dispose'. III 50a

In mysticism, a saint, friend of God. I 137b; VIII 742b; and → MURĀBIṬ; WILĀYA

♦ walī mud̲j̲bir : ‘*walī* with power of coercion’, the father or grandfather who has the right to marry his daughter or granddaughter against her will, so long as she is a virgin. VIII 27b

♦ walī ’l-dam : in law, the next of kin who has the right to demand retaliation. IX 547b

♦ walī ’l-sad̲j̲d̲j̲āda → S̲H̲AYK̲H̲ AL-SAD̲J̲D̲J̲ĀDA

wālide (T) : in the Ottoman empire, mother of the reigning sultan. IX 709a

walīma (A) : a wedding dinner-party. III 210a

wangala : in Mauritania, the custom of slaughtering and sharing, each day, a sheep within a given group. VI 313a

waraʿ (A) : in mysticism, the ‘spirit of scruple’, advocated in so-called ‘sober’ ṣūfism. IX 812b

waraḳ (A) : one of the terms for parchment, later to be reserved for paper. VIII 407b; with *waraḳa*, the leaf of a tree or of a manuscript. VIII 835a; and → D̲J̲ILD

♦ warak al-bardī → BARDĪ

ward̲j̲iyya (A), and *wariyya*, *huwayriyya* : in Kuwayt, the local open boat made from palm fibres. VII 53b

wariyya → WARD̲J̲IYYA

wasaṭ al-s̲h̲ams (A) : in astronomy, the mean solar longitude. IX 292b

wasé kuala : in Aceh in Indonesia, a tax demanded by the *shahbandar* ‘harbour master’ for disembarking or loading certain goods, for preserving the water supply for departing ships, and for help for those stranded. S 200b

waṣf → NAʿT

was̲h̲aḳ (A), or *kiṭṭ-namir* : in zoology, the Serval or Tiger-Cat (*Leptailurus serval*). II 739b

waṣī (A0 : in law, the executor of a will. I 28b

waṣīf (A) : in the terminology of childhood, ‘[a boy] who has become of full stature and fit for service’ (Lane). VIII 822a; a male slave; negro. I 24b

wāsima → NĪL

wāsiṭa (A) : mediator. IX 779b; under the Fāṭimids, a minister who was given neither the title nor the office of vizier but only the duty of acting as intermediary between the caliph and his officials and subjects. II 857b; and → TARD̲J̲Īʿ

waṣiyya (A, pl. *waṣāyā*) : in law, a bequest, testament. I 137b; IX 115b; IX 781b In the science of diplomatic, that part of the text of a (state) document in which the duties of the nominee are specified in detail. II 302a

wasḳ (A) : a measure of capacity which was used in the Ḥid̲j̲āz in the days of Muḥammad, equal to 60 MUDDs. The ~ did not spread to other countries. VI 118a

waṣl (A), or *ṣila* : in prosody, a letter of prolongation following the *rawī* ‘rhyme letter’. It can also consist of a vowelless *hāʾ* followed by a short vowel or a *hāʾ* followed by a letter of prolongation and preceded by a short vowel. IV 412a

wasma → NĪL

♦ wasma-d̲j̲ūs̲h̲ : in mediaeval times, a word used in K̲h̲urāsān to designate a special object for grinding KUḤL 'eye cosmetic' and pouring it into narrow-necked vessels. V 357a

wāsōk̲h̲ (U) : a genre of Urdu love poetry, more passionate than the G̲H̲AZAL. IX 378a; and → WĀ-SŪK̲H̲T

wasūṭ (A) : among the pre-Islamic Bedouin, a tent made of hair, generally said to be smaller than the MIẒALLA, but larger than the BAYT or the K̲H̲IBĀʾ, but sometimes described as the smallest tent. IV 1147a

waswās (A) : satanic whispering in the heart, inciting evil. III 1119b

waṭʾ → BĀH

watad → AWTĀD; ḲUṬB

waṭan (A) : fatherland, motherland. I 64a; IV 785b; in early usage, the locality from which a person came. IV 785b

In mediaeval mysticism, used in the sense of 'the heavenly kingdom'. IV 785b

wat̲h̲īḳa (A) : document. IX 733a

watid → AWTĀD

wayd̲j̲ → SILB

waza̲g̲h̲ (A) : a kind of lizard, the killing of which, preferably with one blow, is prescribed by SUNNA. IV 768a

waẓīfa → MUWAẒẒAF

wazīr (A, T *wezīr*) : vizier; head of the bureaucracy. VIII 768b

♦ wazīr al-tafwīḍ : 'vizier with delegated powers'; a term employed by al-Māwardī for the minister under the Fāṭimids who was entrusted with full powers. II 857b

♦ wazīr al-tanfīd̲h̲ : a designation by al-Māwardī for the ministers under the Fāṭimids who, notwithstanding their power and influence over the caliphs, were considered as agents for the execution of the sovereign's will. II 857b

♦ wezīr-i aʿẓam → ṢADR-I AʿẒAM

wazn (A, pl. AWZĀN) : in eschatology, the 'weighing' of deeds on the Last Day, with good deeds being heavy and bad deeds light. III 465a

wēs̲h̲ (Pash) : in Afghanistan, the ancient custom of periodical redistribution of land. I 217a

wezīr → WAZĪR

wid̲j̲āʾ (A) : a form of castration consisting of binding the cord supporting the testicles and making them gush out. IV 1088a

wilāya (A) : in law, the power of a WALĪ to represent his ward. III 50b; guardianship over a child, involving guardianship over property (*wilāyat al-māl*) and over the person (*wilāyat al-nafs*). To these should be added the father's duty to marry his child off when the latter comes of age (*wilāyat al-tazwīd̲j̲*). VIII 824a

In mysticism, sainthood. VIII 742a

Among the K̲h̲arid̲j̲ites, the dogmatic duty of solidarity and assistance to the Muslim. I 1027b

♦ wilāyat al-māl → WILĀYA
♦ wilāyat al-nafs → WILĀYA
♦ wilāyat al-tazwīdj → WILĀYA
wilāyet → EYĀLET
wird → ḤIZB
wisāda (A) : in mediaeval times, a large cushion often used for supporting the back; a pillow. V 1158b
wiṣāl → ITTIṢĀL
wisām (A) : in Morocco, a term applied to each of the nine orders, decorations, that were regulated in a document (*ẓahīr*) of 14 December 1966. VIII 61b
wishāḥ (A) : according to Lane, an ornament worn by women (consisting of) two series of pearls and jewels strung or put together in regular order, which two series are disposed contrariwise, one of them being turned over the other. VII 809b
witr → ṢALĀT AL-WITR
wudjāḳ → ODJAḲ
wudjūd → MUṬLAḲ
wuḍūʾ (A) : the simple ablution, which is sufficient for cleansing after a minor ritual impurity, ḤADATH. III 19b; VIII 764b; VIII 929a
wuḳā (A), and *wuḳāya, awḳā* : a variety of women's bonnets, usually decorated with coins, worn in Syria and Palestine. V 742a
wuḳūʿ-gūʾī (P), or *zabān-i wuḳūʿ* : in Persian poetry, a new style, developed in the 16th century, of introducing in the GHAZAL references to actual experiences of love and incidents occurring in the relationship of lovers and their beloved. The ~ in turn generated a number of subsidiary genres. VIII 776a
wuḳūf (A) : 'halt'; in the context of the pilgrimage, the ~ is the ceremony on 9 Dhu 'l-Ḥidjdja, in the plain of ʿArafat in front of the *Djabal al-raḥma*, a small rocky eminence. The ceremony begins at noon with the joint recital of the prayers of ẒUHR and of ʿAṢR brought forward, and lasts until sunset. III 35b
wushshaḳ (A) : ammoniac, the product of the ammoniac gum tree. VIII 1042b

X

xagaa → GU'
xeer (Somali) : Somali customary law, which exists alongside the SHARĪʿA. IX 713b; IX 723b

Y

yabrūḥ → SIRĀDJ AL-ḲUṬRUB
yad (A) : lit. hand; the very large bead on a rosary that serves as a kind of handle. IX 741b; and → ʿAMAL; ḤISĀB; MILK; MUSALSAL AL-YAD
yaʿḍid → ʿALATH
yāfiʿ (A) : in the terminology of childhood, 'a boy grown up...grown tall' (Lane). VIII 822a
yaḥmūr → BAḲAR
yakhsha (Pah) : a pearl. IX 659a
yaḳḳāsh → AYḲASH
yaḳṭīn (A) : a plant mentioned in the Qurʾān, probably a kind of *Cucurbitacea*. VI 651a; VI 901a; VII 831a
yalı̊ (T) : in Ottoman times, a palace built on the edge of the water. V 642a
yam (Mon) : the effective network of communications established by the Mongols to control the vast extent of their empire. It was designed to facilitate the travels of envoys going to and from the Mongol courts; for the transportation of goods; for the speedy transmission of royal orders; and to provide a framework whereby the Mongol rulers could receive intelligence. VII 234a
yamaḳ (T) : 'adjunct'; in the Ottoman army, an assistant to an auxiliary soldier, ESHKINDJI. II 714b; IX 543a; in Serbia, a self-appointed local Janissary leader outside the regular Ottoman hierarchy. IX 671a
yamīn (A) : oath; and → ḲASAM

♦ yamīn al-ghamūs : in law, an oath to perform a deed that one knows to have been already performed. Expiation is not required, except in the Shāfiʿī school. IV 688b

♦ yamīn al-munkir : in law, an oath taken by a debtor who refuses to recognise his debt or his obligation, used by a petitioner as a method of proof. In former times many Muslims preferred to avoid pronouncing the oath, even though they did not admit to being debtors. III 1236b

♦ yamīnu ṣabr^{in} : an oath imposed by the public authorities and therefore taken unwillingly. VIII 685b

♦ laghw al-yamīn : in law, an oath taken by mistake (through a slip of the tongue) or in a thoughtless manner, which does not require expiation. IV 688b

yarbūʿ (A) : in zoology, the jerboa in general, also the gerbil and jird. S 287b, where many technical terms relating to these animals can be found
yarıcılık (T) : a land-leasing system in Turkey, in which the peasant uses his own tools, plough and livestock and gives half of the harvest to the landowner. V 473a
yarlı̊k (T) : under the Mongols, a decree. IX 43a
yasaḳ-ḳulu (T) : under the Ottomans, a special agent who was authorised to in-

spect any person for bullion or old AḲČE; Ottoman law required that all bullion produced in the country or imported from abroad be brought directly to the mints to be coined, and upon the issue of a new *aḳče*, those possessing the old were to bring it to the mint. II 118b

yasaḳčí (T) : under the Ottomans, Janissaries whose function it was to protect foreign embassies and consulates and to escort diplomats leaving their residences, whether officially or unofficially. IV 808b

yasaḳnāme → ḲĀNŪNNĀME

yasar (A, pl. *aysār*) : a player of MAYSIR; those who presided over the division of the parts were called *al-yāsirūn*. VI 924a

yattūʿ (A) : in botany, wolfs' milk, of the class of Euphorbia, a gum resin. VIII 1042b; IX 872b

yawa (T), or *ḳačḳun* : one of the occasional (BĀD-I HAWĀ) taxes paid in the Ottoman empire while recovering runaway cattle or slaves. II 147a

yawm (A, pl. *ayyām*) : day.

♦ yawm al-aḍāḥī : lit. day of the morning sacrifices; a name for 10 Dhu 'l-Ḥidjdja which can be traced back to the pre-Islamic pilgrimage. III 32b

♦ yawm al-ʿarūba → YAWM AL-DJUMʿA

♦ yawm al-dīn → ḲIYĀMA

♦ yawm al-**djumʿa** : Friday, which in modern times most Muslim states have made an official day of rest. The term is clearly pre-Islamic, when it was known as *yawm al-ʿarūba* or *yawm ʿarūba*, and designated the market day which was held in al-Madīna on Friday. It is the weekly day of communal worship in Islam, when the *ṣalāt al-djumʿa* 'Friday prayer', is performed at the time of the midday prayer, which it replaces. II 592b; VIII 930a

♦ yawm al-ḥisāb : a Qurʾānic expression for the Day of Judgement, synonymous with *yawm al-dīn*. III 465a

♦ yawm al-ḳiyāma → ḲIYĀMA

♦ yawm al-naḥr : 'the day of sacrifice'; the 10th of the month of Dhu 'l-Ḥidjdja. III 36a

♦ yawm al-tarwiya : the name given to the first day of the pilgrimage, possibly because of the rite of drinking a fermented beverage on the occasion. II 1060a; the 'day of watering', the 8th of Dhu 'l-Ḥidjdja. Arabic authors explain this as the day on which the pilgrims water their animals and provide themselves with water for the following days, but some Western scholars see in this name traces of an ancient rain rite. III 35b

♦ **ayyām al-ʿadjūz** : lit. the days of the old woman; an old expression used in the Islamic countries bordering on or near to the Mediterranean to denote certain days of recurrent bad weather usually towards the end of winter. The duration of this period varies from one to ten days; more frequently it lasts one, five or seven days. This yearly cycle varies from country to country, involving the last four (or three) days of February and the first three (or four) days of March of the Julian calendar. I 792b

♦ **ayyām al-ʿarab** : lit. days of the Arabs; a name given in Arabian legend to the combats which the Arabian tribes fought among themselves in the pre-Islamic and also early Islamic era. I 793a

♦ al-ayyām al-bulḳ → AL-LAYĀLĪ AL-BULḲ

♦ ayyām al-tashrīḳ : 11-13 Dhu 'l-Ḥidjdja, days of eating and drinking after the pilgrimage. III 32a

yay → KEMĀN

yaya (T) : in the Ottoman military, a special corps consisting of *reʿāyā* (→ RAʿIYYA) soldiers. VIII 404b; infantry. IX 13a

♦ yayabashi̊ (T) : chief infantryman, commander of the infantry or cavalry unit, BÖLÜK, in the Janissary ODJAḲS. I 1256a

yaylaḳ (T, < *yay* 'spring', later 'summer') : summer quarters, the upland pastures favoured by the nomads of Central Asia for fattening their herds after the harsh steppe or plateau winters. Its Persian synonym is GARMSĪR. V 182b

♦ yaylaḳ resmi (T), or *otlaḳ resmi, resm-i čerāghah* : under the Ottomans, the pasturage dues charged usually at the rate of one sheep or its money equivalent for each flock of sheep of 300 which crossed into another district. It was paid to the person who held the land. I 146b

yaym → AYM

yelek (T, A) : a woman's long coat, tightly fitting, worn in the Arab East; a long vest worn by both sexes in Iraq. V 742a; in Turkey, a waistcoat without sleeves formerly worn as an outer garment. V 752a

yigit (T) : one of three grades in the AKHĪ organization, designating the ordinary unmarried member of the organisation. I 322b

yodjana (San 'league') : a Hindu unit of distance equalling four *goruta* 'cow-roar', the length at which a cow's lowing can be heard, or KROŚA 'earshot'. VII 138b

yük (T) : an Ottoman weight, being the two bales slung across a beast of burden, the equivalent of ca. 154 kg. III 212b; IV 678b

yurt : the domed, felt-covered tent of Turkmen nomads; originally 'homeland, encampment or camping place', and in Orkhon and early Turkish, 'an abandoned campsite'. IV 1150b; VIII 233b

yürük (T) : nomad. IX 674a

yūz → FAHD

yüzbashi̊ → ḲOL AGHASI̊

Z

zabād (A), or *sinnawr al-zabād* : in zoology, the civet cat (*Viverra civetta*). IX
   653b

zabān-i urdu → URDU

zabān-i wuḳūʿ → WUḲŪʿ-GŪʾĪ

zabardjad : in mineralogy, the chrysolith. II 93b

zabbāl (A, Tun *g̲h̲abbār*) : 'superintendent of the supply of dung-fuel for the furnace' of a ḥammām 'steam bath'. III 140a; and → KANNĀS

zabīb (A), or *zbīb* : a non-alcoholic drink made from dried grapes. VI 723b

zabit → ḌĀBIṬ

zabr (A) : the act of pruning, practised in Andalusia on the grapevine to increase
   the vine's productivity with an iron pruning knife, *mind̲j̲al*. IV 659b

zabtiyye → ḌABṬIYYA

zaʿbūt (A) : a woollen garment. IX 765a

zabzab (A) : in zoology, the badger. II 739b

zāde → OG̲H̲UL

zād̲j̲ (A) : in metallurgy, vitriol. VIII 111b

zad̲j̲al (A) : a poetic genre in Muslim Spain, written only in the Arabic dialect of
   Spain. Its most frequent rhyme scheme is *aa bbb a ccc a*, that is, the rhyme
   scheme of a MUSAMMAṬ with introductory lines. III 849b; V 1207a; VII 661b

zad̲j̲d̲j̲āl (Leb) : in Lebanese colloquial poetry, a composer of ZAD̲J̲AL vernacular
   poetry. When contrasted to a *ḳawwāl* 'a performer or "speaker" of *zad̲j̲al*' or
   S̲H̲ĀʿIR, ~ implies a lack of ability to spontaneously or extemporaneously compose. IX 234b

zad̲j̲l (A), or *zid̲j̲āl* : the sport of pigeon-flying, popular from the 2nd-7th/8th-13th
   centuries. The homing pigeon, *zād̲j̲il* (pl. *zawād̲j̲il*), received the closest attention from its owner. III 109a,b

zad̲j̲r (A) : often used as the equivalent of ṬĪRA, ~ originally consisted of the deliberate instigation of the flight and cries of birds, but has now come to stand for
   evil omen or divination in general. I 659b; II 758b; IV 290b

zaʿfarān (A) : in botany, saffron. III 461a

zag̲h̲ārī (A) : a hunting dog. IV 745a

zaḥḥāfa → MĀLAḴ

zāhid (A, pl. *zuhhād*) : an ascetic, pious person who has given up all worldly
   goods. V 1124b; VIII 498a

ẓāhir → BĀṬIN

   ♦ ẓāhira (A) : the heat that reigns during the ẒUHR, 'midday prayer'. Other
   terms used are *hād̲j̲ira*, *ḳāʾila*, *g̲h̲āʾira*. V 709b

zahr (A) : flower.

   In prosody, in particular associated with the folk MAWWĀL, ~ is the expansion of the rhymes into polysyllabic paronomasias, achieved by deliberate distortion of the normal pronunciation. A *mawwāl* devoid of ~ is described as *abyaḍ* ‘white’; if so ornamented, it is either *aḥmar* ‘red’ or *akhḍar* ‘green’. VI 868a ff.

zāʾid → ṢILA

zaʿīm (A) : designation for a tribal chief. IX 115b

zāʾiradja al-ʿālam (A) : a circular divinatory table. VIII 691a

zakāt (A) : obligatory alms, one of the five pillars of Islam. IV 1151b; V 424b; VIII 708b; VIII 925b; the tax levied on both landed and moveable property. I 1144a; the prescribed tithe on agricultural produce. I 968b; II 142b; in Muslim India under the Dihlī sultanate, a category of taxes, payable only by the Muslims. II 154a; and → ṢADAḲA

♦ zakāt al-dawlaba : under the Mamlūks, a tax which was payable by Muslim shopkeepers on their merchandise, abolished by Ḳalāwūn who realised that it tended to impoverish the merchants. IV 485b

♦ zakāt al-fiṭr : ‘alms at the breaking of the fast’. I 27a

zakūrī (A) : in mediaeval ʿIrāḳ, bread collected as alms and intended for prisoners and beggars. VII 494a

zālikha → AṬŪM

ẓalīm (A, pl. *ẓulmān, ẓilmān, aẓlima*) : ‘oppressed’; in zoology, the male ostrich. VII 828a

zallādj (A) : a term used for a Nile boat. VIII 42b

zallīdj (A) : in Morocco, faience mosaic decoration, found e.g. in Fās on the public water fountains. II 748a; VIII 682a

zamāzima → ZAMZAMĪ

zamīn-būs (P) : in Čishtī mystical practice, the practice of prostration before the SHAYKH. IX 786a

zamīndār : lit. master of the land; under the Mughals, a class of land-owners, also comprising the various tributary chiefs and autonomous Rādjas, who were called thus by the Mughal chancery. VII 322a

zammāra (A) : ‘joined’; the name in the mediaeval period for a double reed-pipe. Since the 18th century, it was known in the East as ZUMMĀRA, a vulgarisation of ~ . VII 208a; in southern Tunisia, the name for the GHAYṬA, a reed-pipe of cylindrical bore or an oboe of conical bore. II 1027b

zamzamī (A, pl. *zamāzima*) : part of the pilgrimage service industry, the function of the ~ in Mecca is to distribute the sacred water of Zamzam to those who desire it, whether in the mosque precincts or at home. VI 171a

zanāna → ḤARĪM

zandaḳa → ZINDĪḲ

zāniya (pl. *zawānī*) → BAGHIYY

zanḳa → SHĀRIʿ

zār (A, Somali *saar*) : exorcism, a popular rite in Africa. I 35b; in Somali society, a cult, in which a person is regarded as having been made ill by the presence of a spirit within them. It is generally practised among women and among more disenfranchised groups of people on the margins of society. IX 723b

zar-i maḥbūb : in numismatics, a three-quarter's weight Ottoman gold coin, 2.64 g, introduced in the last years of Aḥmed III's reign (1115-43/1703-30). VIII 229b

zaradkāshiyya (A) : under the Mamlūks, the AMĪRS of the arsenal, whose duty was to guard the arsenal. IX 610a

zarbiyya (A, pl. *zarābī*), or *zirbiyya*, *zurbiyya* : a carpet decorated with multicoloured bands. S 136a

ẓarf (A) : courtesy, elegance. I 175b

In grammar, a temporal adjunct. IX 53b; space/time qualifer. IX 527b; locative. IX 551a

zarrāḳ, zarrāḳa → NAFFĀṬ

zawāl (A) : 'midday', marked for the astronomers by the sun crossing the meridian, and for the simple faithful by the displacement of the shade which moves from the west to the east. V 709b

zāwiya (A) : a religious foundation of a quasi-monastic type. In Mamlūk Cairo, the ~ was generally a small construction housing a SHAYKH, with room for students to group informally around him; in the Near East, ~ denoted small rooms of a mosque shut off by wooden lattices, sometimes also called MAḲṢŪRA. In 6th/12th-century Baghdad, a ~ was a place where an ascetic lived in solitude and by the 8th/14th century, it had come to be used also in the sense of RIBĀṬ, a '*coenobium*'. In Morocco, the ~ is the chapel which contains the tomb of a saint and the buildings attached to it, an oratory and guest-house. Some *zāwiyas* are centres of mysticism and they are always centres of religious instruction. IV 380a; IV 433a; V 1129b; V 1201b; VI 662a; VIII 503b; S 223b; and → KHĀNḲĀH

zawr → ṢADR

zawrā' (A) : in archery, probably a bow with a strong bend made from *nasham* wood (*Chadara velutina*). It was also called *ḳaws munḥaniya*. IV 798a

zawraḳ (A, pl. *zawāriḳ*, < ? P) : in mediaeval Mesopotamia, a skiff or dinghy used for local traffic; larger, sea-going *zawraḳs* are recorded in the Mediterranean. VIII 811a

zaww (A, < ? P *zūd*) : in mediaeval Mesopotamia, a swift type of vessel, often mentioned as used by caliphs and great men of state, which could be a luxuriously-appointed gondola. VIII 811a

zaytūn (A) : in botany, the olive tree. IX 435a

ziba'rā → KARKADDAN

zibbūn (A) : in Libya, a man's jacket with long sleeves. V 746b

zīdj (A, < P originally, 'thread(s) in weaving') : astronomical tables. I 139b; III 1136a; comprehensive astronomical handbook containing both theoretical chapters and relevant tables. VIII 101b

zidjāl → ZADJL
ziḥāfāt (A, s. *ziḥāf*) : 'relaxations'; in prosody, one of two groups of metrical deviations (the other being ʿILAL), ~ are the smaller deviations which occur only in the ḤASHW parts of the line in which the characteristic rhythm runs strongly. As accidental deviations, ~ have no regular or definite place; they just appear occasionally in the feet. I 671b; ~ , usually elisions, are characteristic of the SABAB. VIII 667b
ẓihār (A, < *ẓahr* 'back') : in law, an oath, which may be translated very vaguely as 'incestuous comparison'. Presumably the husband says to his wife: 'You are for me like my mother's back', *ka-ẓahri ummī*, or any other comparison of a part of the body of his wife with that of a woman he could not marry without committing incest. IV 688a; a vow of continence. VIII 28a
zikrāna : a special hut which is not orientated towards the ḲIBLA, in which the DHIKR is recited six times daily by the Dhikrī sect in Baluchistan. S 222b
zīl → ṢANDJ
ẓill (A) : the central theme or aim of a SŪRA (syn. *miḥwar*). IX 887b; and → FAYʾ
zillī māsha → DJAGHĀNA
zīna → DJALSA
zināʾ (A) : unlawful fornication, punishable by penal law if the partners are not married to each other or united by the bond of ownership. I 29b; I 910b; III 20b
zindāna (A) : a song form among women in western Algeria. IX 234a
zindīḳ (A) : anyone who, professing to be a Muslim, is really an unbeliever or anyone who belongs to no religion. He is then accused of *zandaḳa* 'heresy, unbelief'. IV 771b; VI 421b
zindjār : in mineralogy, verdigris. VIII 111b; IX 872b
ziʿnufiyyāt al-aḳdam (A) : in zoology, the class of pinnipeds, which include the seal, the walrus, and the sea lion. VIII 1022b
zīr al-baḥr : in zoology, the squill-fish (*Scyllarus latus*) and the mantis-shrimp (*Squilla mantis*), also called *istākūzā al-raml*. IX 40a
zīr-i zamīn (P) : lit. subterranean; a chamber under the ground in southern Persia where people would spend the hottest time of the day. IX 49b
ziyāda (A) : in architecture, a term used to designate the broad open enclosure on three of the four sides of a mosque, which illusionistically increases its scale. I 620b; VI 679b
In mathematics, ~ is the term used for addition. III 1139b
♦ ziyādāt al-thiḳāt : in the science of Tradition, additions by authorities in ISNĀD or MATN which are not found in other transmissions. III 26a
zolota (T) : in numismatics, a large-sized silver coin, 18.5-19.7 g, introduced under Süleymān II on the European pattern. A half-~ , 8.65-9.85 g, was also struck. VIII 229a
zorṭalbī (U) : in India, a tribute exacted by force due from the feudatory states, a relic of Muslim supremacy. II 597b

zubānayān (A) : lit. the two pincers; in astronomy, the two stars known as the Two Pincers in the constellation of Cancer. IX 40b

zubb al-ḳiṭṭ (A) : 'cat's penis', in botany, the variety *Astralagus cahiricus* of the genus Milk vetch. IX 653b

zubd → SAMN

ẓufr al-ḳiṭṭ → RIDJL AL-ḲIṬṬ

zuhdiyyāt (A) : in literature, 'ascetic' poems, poems denouncing the vanities of the world. IX 4b; IX 453b

ẓuhr (A) : noon, midday.

♦ ṣalāt al-ẓuhr : the midday prayer which is to be performed from the time when the sun begins to decline till the time when shadows are of equal length with the objects by which they are cast, apart from their shadows at noon. VII 27b; VIII 928b

zuḳāḳ → SHĀRIʿ

zukaym :

♦ zukaym al-Ḥabasha : in the mediaeval Near East, a fraudulent warrior engaged in DJIHĀD 'holy war'. VII 495a

♦ zukaym al-marḥūma : in the mediaeval Near East, a band of blind men led by an *isṭīl*, a beggar who pretends to be blind. VII 495a

♦ zukaym al-mughālaṭa : in the mediaeval Near East, a beggar who feigns inability to speak. VII 494b

zulf → ṢUDGH

ẓulla (A) : in pre-Islamic Arabia, a simple shelter in the form of a sort of canopy. IV 1146a; and → ṢUFFA

zullāmī (A) : in the Muslim West, the vulgarisation of *zunāmī*, a reed-pipe invented about the beginning of the 3rd/9th century at the ʿAbbāsid court by a musician named Zunām. The word *zunāmī* was accorded little recognition in the East, but in Spain (Sp. *xelami*) and North Africa, as ~ , it became the most important reed-pipe. VII 207a

zummāra (A, < *zammāra*) : a vulgarisation of ZAMMĀRA, but since the 18th century, the name for a double-reed pipe in the East. It has cylindrical tubes and is played with single beating reeds. It is to be found with a varying number of finger-holes and is named accordingly. In the MAGHRIB, it is called *maḳrūn* and *maḳrūna*. Another type of double reed-pipe, which has only one pipe pierced with finger holes, while the other serves as a drone, is also called ~ when the two pipes are of the same length. When the drone pipe is longer than the chanter pipe, it is known as ARGHŪL. VII 208a

zunāmī → ZULLĀMĪ

zunbūr (A) : in zoology, the hornet. IX 873a

zunnār (A) : a belt, usually made of folded scarf, worn by both men and women in Syria and Palestine. V 742a; a distinctive girdle DHIMMĪs were required to wear in the mediaeval period. IX 167a zurdānī (N.Afr) : in zoology, the Striped rat, or 'Barbarian rat' (*Arvicanthus barbarus*). S 286a

zūrkhāna (P), or *zūr-khāna* : a special gymnasium in Iran, where in the cities specially clothed men in need of exercise practise with Indian clubs and dumbbells to the beat of drums and recitations from the *Shāhnāma*. IV 8b; VIII 239a

zurna (T) : a double-reed shawm with seven holes (6 in front and 1 behind), the basic melody instrument of the Ottoman *mehter* 'ensemble'. VI 1007b; oboe. VIII 178b

♦ ḳaba zurna : a large instrument used by the official Ottoman palace *mehter* 'ensemble' in the capital. It had a range of over two octaves and could produce all the notes needed for pre-19th century Ottoman music. VI 1007